PLANT BASED
COOKBOOK FOR BEGINNERS

Discover The Benefits Of Eating A Plant-Based Diet. 800 Quick & Easy, Healthy Recipes, Including A Delicious 21-Day Meal Plan To Reset & Energize Your Body

AMANDA KALE

Amanda Kale

Copyright ©2021 by Amanda Kale. All rights reserved.

No part of this book may be reproduced in any form or by any mechanical means, including information storage and retrieval systems without permission in writing from the publisher/author, except by a reviewer who may quote passages in a review.

Book is for informational and educational purposes only. Author/publisher will not be held responsible for any damages, monetary loss or reparations that could arise from use of any information contained within the book.

All images, logos, quotes, and trademarks included in this book are subject to use according to trademark and copyright laws of the United States.

Reading of this book constitutes consent agreement to the above requirements.

All rights reserved by **AMANDA KALE**

Amanda Kale

Table Of Contents

INTRODUCTION	14
CHAPTER 1: WHAT IS THE PLANT-BASED DIET	**16**
CHAPTER 2: PLANT-BASED DIET AS A HOLISTIC APPROACH TO BODY WELLNESS	**18**
CHAPTER 3: HOW YOUR WHOLE LIFESTYLE WILL IMPROVE WITH A PLANT-BASED DIET	**20**
Mind Benefits	20
How You Will Feel Lighter, Cleaner, and Healthier Throughout the Day	20
Eating Vegan is Easier Than You Think!	20
CHAPTER 4: HOW SUSTAINABLE THE PLANT-BASED DIET IS FOR OUR LAND	**22**
More Environmentally Sustainable	22
Feel in Harmony with Our Planet	22
CHAPTER 5: HEALTH BENEFITS	**24**
Benefits Overview	24
Myths to Debunk	24
What About Nutrients	25
How You Can Get All the Nutrients Your Body Needs When Following a Plant-Based Diet	25
CHAPTER 6: HOW YOU CAN LOSE WEIGHT. FOCUS	**26**
CHAPTER 7: BOOST THE POSITIVE EFFECTS OF PLANT-BASED DIET	**28**
Whole Foods	28
Why Some People Keep Their Meals SOS-Free	28
CHAPTER 8: HOW TO START AND STICK TO THE PLANT-BASED DIET	**30**
Set Up Your Mindset	30
Advice on Breaking the Old Habits	30
Tips and Tricks To start	30
Practical Advice For Beginners	31
Tips to Improve Your Transition to the Plant-Based Diet	31
CHAPTER 9: WHAT TO EAT AND WHAT TO AVOID	**34**
Suggested to Eat	34
Foods to Avoid	36
CHAPTER 10: SHOPPING LIST WITH THE BEST SUBSTITUTE	**38**
Oils, Fats, and Spreads Substitutes	38
Fruits, Berries, Vegetables, and Nuts	38
Milk/Dairy Substitutes	38
Meat Substitutes	38
Other	38
Shopping on a Budget	39
CHAPTER 11: 21-DAYS MEAL PLAN	**40**
CHAPTER 12: BASICS	**42**
1. Mango Achar From India	42
2. Tartar Sauce	42
3. Cheese Sauce	42
4. Scotch Bonnet Pepper Sauce	42
5. Sambal Sauce	42
6. Louisiana Hot Sauce	43
7. Harissa Sauce	43
8. Piri Sauce	43
9. Barbeque Sauce	43
10. Roasted Veggies In Lemon Sauce	44
11. Hemp Falafel With Tahini Sauce	44
12. Red Applesauce and Beet	44
13. Tomatillo Green Sauce	44
14. Cranberry and Orange Sauce	44
15. Thick Mushroom Sauce	45
16. Thai Peanut Sauce	45
17. Tofu Island Dressing	45
18. Quick Ketchup	45
19. Date Purée	45
20. Vegan Tzatziki	45
21. Nut Milk	46
22. Cashew Mayonnaise	46
23. Tofu Sour Cream	46
24. Tofu Ranch Dressing	46
25. Almond Parmesan Crumbles	46
26. Tofu Feta	47
27. Cashew Cream Cheese	47
28. Macadamia Mozzarella	47
29. Pastry Dough	47
30. Pizza Dough	48
31. Seitan	48
32. Cauliflower Popcorn	48
33. Cinnamon Apple Chips with Dip	49
34. Crunchy Asparagus Spears	49
35. Homemade Trail Mix	49
36. Nut Butter Maple Dip	49
37. Oven Baked Sesame Fries	50
38. Pumpkin Orange Spice Hummus	50
39. Quick English Muffin Mexican Pizzas	50
40. Quinoa Trail Mix Cups	50
CHAPTER 13: BREAKFAST	**52**
41. Max Power Smoothie	52
42. Chai Chia Smoothie	52
43. Tropi-Kale Breeze	52
44. Hydration Station	52
45. Mango Madness	52
46. Chocolate PB Smoothie	53

47.	Pink Panther Smoothie	53
48.	Banana Nut Smoothie	53
49.	Overnight Oats On the Go	53
50.	Oatmeal Breakfast Cookies	54
51.	Sunshine Muffins	54
52.	Applesauce Crumble Muffins	54
53.	Baked Banana French Toast with Raspberry Syrup	55
54.	Cinnamon Apple Toast	55
55.	Muesli and Berries Bowl	55
56.	Chocolate Quinoa Breakfast Bowl	56
57.	Fruit Salad with Zesty Citrus Couscous	56
58.	Fruity Granola	56
59.	Chickpea Scramble	56
60.	Roasted Veg with Creamy Avocado Dip	57
61.	Spinach Artichoke Quiche	57
62.	Pumpkin Muffins	57
63.	Tomato and Asparagus Quiche	58
64.	Simple Vegan Breakfast Hash	58
65.	Chickpeas On Toast	58
66.	Blueberry Muffins	59
67.	Ultimate Breakfast Sandwich	59
68.	Waffles with Fruits	59
69.	Scrambled Tofu Breakfast Burrito	59
70.	Pancake	60
71.	Honey Buckwheat Coconut Porridge	60
72.	Tempeh and Potato	60
73.	Breakfast French Toast	60
74.	Dairy-Free Pumpkin Pancakes	61
75.	Protein Blueberry Bars	61
76.	Chickpea Scramble Breakfast Basin	61
77.	Quinoa, Oats, Hazelnut and Blueberry Salad	61
78.	Chia Flaxseed Waffles	62
79.	Flax Almond Muffins	62
80.	Whole Wheat Pizza with Summer Produce	62
81.	Chives Avocado Mix	62
82.	Zucchini Pan	62
83.	Chili Spinach and Zucchini Pan	63
84.	Basil Tomato and Cabbage Bowls	63
85.	Spinach and Zucchini Hash	63
86.	Tomato and Zucchini Fritters	63
87.	Peppers Casserole	63
88.	Eggplant and Broccoli Casserole	64
89.	Creamy Avocado and Nuts Bowls	64
90.	Avocado and Watermelon Salad	64
91.	Chia and Coconut Pudding	64
92.	Tomato and Cucumber Salad	64
93.	Walnuts and Olives Bowls	64
94.	Kale and Broccoli Pan	65
95.	Spinach and Berries Salad	65
96.	Cauliflower Hash	65
97.	Spinach and Green Beans Casserole	65
98.	Spiced Zucchini and Eggplant Bowls	65

CHAPTER 14: SALADS 66

99.	Black Bean Lentil Salad	66
100.	Cabbage Salad with Seitan	66
101.	Chickpeas Avocado Salad	66
102.	Cold Peanut Noodle Salad	66
103.	Butternut Squash Black Rice Bean Salad	67
104.	Arugula Beans Salad	67
105.	Spring Salad	67
106.	Tomato Lentil Salad	67
107.	White Bean & Tomato Salad	68
108.	Avocado & White Bean Salad	68
109.	Brussels Sprouts Salad	68
110.	Wedge Salad	68
111.	Chef Salad	69
112.	Radish Avocado Salad	69
113.	Mint Coriander Nutty Salad	69
114.	Mix Grain Salad	69
115.	Quinoa and Chickpea Salad	70
116.	Rice and Tofu Salad	70
117.	Kidney Bean and Pomegranate Salad	70
118.	Corn and Bean Salad	70
119.	Cherry Tomato Couscous Salad	70
120.	Spicy Watermelon Tomato Salad	71
121.	Health is Wealth Salad: Dash of Chickpea and Tomato	71
122.	Eggplant Salad	71
123.	Tricolore Salad	71
124.	Potato Salad	71
125.	Cauliflower & Apple Salad	72
126.	Corn & Black Bean Salad	72
127.	Spinach & Orange Salad	72
128.	Red Pepper & Broccoli Salad	72
129.	Lentil Potato Salad	72
130.	Black Bean & Corn Salad with Avocado	72
131.	Summer Chickpea Salad	73
132.	Edamame Salad	73
133.	Fruity Kale Salad	73
134.	Olive & Fennel Salad	73
135.	Avocado & Radish Salad	73
136.	Zucchini & Lemon Salad	74
137.	Watercress & Blood Orange Salad	74
138.	Parsley Salad	74

CHAPTER 15: SOUPS 76

139.	Classic Vegetable Soup	76
140.	Cream of Miso Mushroom Stew	76
141.	Chickpea Noodle Soup	76
142.	Tangy Tomato Soup	76
143.	Yellow Potato Soup	77
144.	Greens And Grains Soup	77
145.	Herby Split Pea Soup	77
146.	Moroccan Eggplant Stew	77
147.	Minestrone in Minutes	78
148.	Three-Bean Chili	78
149.	White Chili	78

#	Recipe	Page
150.	Hot-And-Sour Tofu Soup	79
151.	Spicy Refried Bean Stew	79
152.	Sweet Potato Stew	79
153.	Oyster (Mushroom) Stew	79
154.	New England Corn Chowder	80
155.	Mushroom And Quinoa "Gumbo"	80
156.	Asparagus & Green Peas Soup	80
157.	Black Beans Stew	81
158.	Sniffle Soup	81
159.	Butternut Squash Soup	81
160.	Lemon & Strawberry Soup	81
161.	Tomato Soup with Kale & White Beans	82
162.	Bursting Black Bean Soup	82
163.	Yummy Lentil Rice Soup	82
164.	Tangy Corn Chowder	82
165.	Healthy Cabbage Soup	83
166.	Chunky Potato Soup	83
167.	Yogurt Soup with Rice	83
168.	Zucchini Soup	83
169.	Hearty Vegetarian Lasagna Soup	83
170.	Chunky Black Lentil Veggie Soup	84
171.	Lovely Parsnip & Split Pea Soup	84
172.	Incredible Tomato Basil Soup	84
173.	Spicy Cajun Boiled Peanuts	84
174.	Comfort Soup	85
175.	Tangy Chickpea Soup with a Hint of Lemon	85
176.	Lentil Soup the Vegan Way	85
177.	Quinoa Soup with a Dash of Kale	86
178.	Amazing Chickpea and Noodle Soup	86

CHAPTER 16: RICE & GRAINS 88

#	Recipe	Page
179.	Classic Garlicky Rice	88
180.	Brown Rice with Vegetables and Tofu	88
181.	Basic Amaranth Porridge	88
182.	Country Cornbread with Spinach	88
183.	Rice Pudding with Currants	89
184.	Millet Porridge with Sultanas	89
185.	Quinoa Porridge with Dried Figs	89
186.	Bread Pudding with Raisins	89
187.	Bulgur Wheat Salad	89
188.	Rye Porridge with Blueberry Topping	90
189.	Coconut Sorghum Porridge	90
190.	Dad's Aromatic Rice	90
191.	Everyday Savory Grits	90
192.	Greek-Style Barley Salad	90
193.	Easy Sweet Maize Meal Porridge	90
194.	Mom's Millet Muffins	91
195.	Ginger Brown Rice	91
196.	Sweet Oatmeal "Grits"	91
197.	Freekeh Bowl with Dried Figs	91
198.	Cornmeal Porridge with Maple Syrup	91
199.	Garlic and White Bean Soup	92
200.	Coconut Curry Lentils	92
201.	Tomato, Kale, and White Bean Skillet	92
202.	Chard Wraps With Millet	92
203.	Quinoa Meatballs	93
204.	Rice Stuffed Jalapeños	93
205.	Pineapple Fried Rice	93
206.	Lentil and Wild Rice Soup	93
207.	Black Bean Meatball Salad	94
208.	Bulgur Pancakes with a Twist	94
209.	Chocolate Rye Porridge	94
210.	Authentic African Mielie-Meal	94
211.	Teff Porridge with Dried Figs	95
212.	Decadent Bread Pudding with Apricots	95
213.	Chipotle Cilantro Rice	95
214.	Oat Porridge with Almonds	95
215.	Aromatic Millet Bowl	95
216.	Harissa Bulgur Bowl	96
217.	Coconut Quinoa Pudding	96
218.	Cremini Mushroom Risotto	96

CHAPTER 17: PASTA AND NOODLES 98

#	Recipe	Page
219.	Cannellini Pesto Spaghetti	98
220.	Spicy Eggplant Penne	98
221.	Creamed Kimchi Pasta	98
222.	Roasted Ragu with Whole Wheat Linguine	98
223.	Penne with Swiss Chard and Olives	99
224.	Indonesia Green Noodle Salad	99
225.	Noodles with Red Lentil Curry	99
226.	Tomato and Black Bean Rotini	99
227.	Lemony Broccoli Penne	100
228.	Singapore Rice Noodles	100
229.	Ponzu Pea Rice Noodle Salad	100
230.	Thai Tofu Noodles	100
231.	Sesame Soba Noodles with Vegetables	101
232.	Lemon Bow Tie Pasta	101
233.	Shiitake and Bean Sprout Ramen	102
234.	Spinach Rotelle Provençale	102
235.	Sumptuous Shiitake Udon Noodles	102
236.	Tomato and Artichoke Rigatoni	103
237.	Tomato Spaghetti	103
238.	Noodle Salad with Spinach	103
239.	Garlic & White Wine Pasta	103
240.	Eggplant Vegan Pasta	104
241.	Tomato Pesto Pasta	104
242.	Alfredo with Peas	104
243.	Eggplant Parmesan Pasta	104
244.	Green Chili Mac 'N' Cheese	105
245.	Color Pasta	105
246.	Caramelized Onion Mac 'N' Cheese	105
247.	Cheesy Garlic Pasta with Ciabatta	105
248.	Tomato Red Lentil Pasta	106
249.	Pasta with Sun-Dried Tomato Sauce	106
250.	Zesty Green Pea and Jalapeño Pesto Pasta	106
251.	Lemony Pasta with Broccoli and Chickpeas	107
252.	Penne with Indian-Style Tomato Sauce and Mushrooms	107
253.	Teriyaki Mushrooms and Cashews with Rice Noodles	107

- 254. Linguine With Pea-Basil Pesto 107
- 255. Greek-Inspired Macaroni and Cheese .. 108
- 256. Spicy Mac and Ricotta Cheese with Spinach 108
- 257. Spinach Pesto Pasta 108
- 258. Lasagna Noodles in a Creamy Mushroom Sauce 109

CHAPTER 18: VEGETABLES & SIDE DISHES 110

- 259. Steamed Cauliflower 110
- 260. Cajun Sweet Potatoes 110
- 261. Smoky Coleslaw 110
- 262. Mediterranean Hummus Pizza 110
- 263. Baked Brussels Sprouts 111
- 264. Basic Baked Potatoes 111
- 265. Miso Spaghetti Squash 111
- 266. Garlic and Herb Noodles 111
- 267. Thai Roasted Broccoli 111
- 268. Coconut Curry Noodle 111
- 269. Collard Green Pasta 112
- 270. Jalapeno Rice Noodles 112
- 271. Rainbow Soba Noodles 112
- 272. Spicy Pad Thai Pasta 113
- 273. Linguine with Wine Sauce 113
- 274. Cheesy Macaroni with Broccoli 113
- 275. Soba Noodles with Tofu 114
- 276. Plant-Based Keto Lo Mein 114
- 277. Steamed Tomatoes 114
- 278. Baked Tofu 114
- 279. Potato Carrot Salad 114
- 280. High Protein Salad 115
- 281. Vegan Wrap with Apples and Spicy Hummus 115
- 282. Rice and Veggie Bowl 115
- 283. Cucumber Tomato Chopped Salad 115
- 284. Zucchini Pasta Salad 116
- 285. Egg Avocado Salad 116
- 286. Arugula Salad 116
- 287. Sautéed Cabbage 116
- 288. Avocado Mint Soup 116
- 289. Cucumber Edamame Salad 116
- 290. Garden Salad Wraps 117
- 291. Marinated Mushroom Wraps 117
- 292. Green Beans Gremolata 117
- 293. Minted Peas 118
- 294. Sweet and Spicy Brussels Sprout Hash .. 118
- 295. Glazed Curried Carrots 118
- 296. Carrot-Pineapple Casserole 118
- 297. Vegetable Medley 118

CHAPTER 19: LEGUMES 120

- 298. Sweet Potato Chili with Quinoa 120
- 299. Spicy Sweet Potato Enchiladas 120
- 300. Raw Nut Cheese 120
- 301. Artichoke White Bean Sandwich Spread 121
- 302. Lentil Sandwich Spread 121
- 303. Rice and Bean Burritos 121
- 304. Quinoa Avocado Salad 121
- 305. Green Beans with vegan Bacon 122
- 306. Chickpea Avocado Sandwich 122
- 307. Spicy Chickpeas 122
- 308. Beans & Greens Bowl 122
- 309. Black Beans & Brown Rice 122
- 310. Yucatan Bean & Pumpkin Seed Appetizer 122
- 311. Butter Bean Hummus 123
- 312. Greek-Style Gigante Beans 123
- 313. Brown Rice & Red Beans & Coconut Milk 123
- 314. Black-Eyed Peas with Herns 123
- 315. Curry Lentil Soup 123
- 316. Mexican Lentil Soup 123
- 317. Tex-Mex Tofu & Beans 124
- 318. Black Bean Burgers 124
- 319. Hearty Black Lentil Curry 124
- 320. Flavorful Refried Beans 125
- 321. Smoky Red Beans and Rice 125
- 322. Spicy Black-Eyed Peas 125
- 323. Bean and Carrot Spirals 125
- 324. Peppered Pinto Beans 126
- 325. Pesto and White Bean Pasta 126
- 326. Lentil Tacos 126
- 327. Red Lentil and Chickpea Bowl 126
- 328. Bean and Rice Burritos 126
- 329. Spicy Nut-Butter Noodles 127
- 330. Lentil and Turnip Soup 127
- 331. Tomato and Chickpea Curry 127
- 332. Lentil Stroganoff 127
- 333. Kung Pao Lentils 127
- 334. Lentil Brown Rice Soup 128
- 335. Peanut and Lentil Soup 128
- 336. Lentil with Spinach 129
- 337. Beans And Lentils Soup 129

CHAPTER 20: STUFFED AND BAKED VEGETABLES 130

- 338. Instant Savory Gigante Beans 130
- 339. Instant Turmeric Risotto 130
- 340. Nettle Soup with Rice 130
- 341. Okra with Grated Tomatoes (Slow Cooker) 130
- 342. Oven-baked Smoked Lentil 'Burgers' 131
- 343. Powerful Spinach and Mustard Leaves Puree 131
- 344. Quinoa and Rice Stuffed Peppers (Oven-Baked) 131
- 345. Silk Tofu Penne with Spinach 131
- 346. Slow-Cooked Butter Beans, Okra and Potatoes Stew 132
- 347. Soya Minced Stuffed Eggplants 132
- 348. Triple Beans and Corn Salad 132

349. Vegan Raw Pistachio Flaxseed 'Burgers' 132
350. Vegan Red Bean 'Fricassee' 133
351. Baked Cheesy Eggplant with Marinara 133
352. Creamy Spinach Quiche 133
353. Stuffed Mushrooms 134
354. Winter Vegetarian Frittata 134
355. Cheddar, Squash, And Zucchini Casserole 134
356. Fresh Tomato Basil Tart 134
357. Quinoa Stuffed Bell Peppers 134
358. Stuffed Peppers 135
359. Roasted Vegetable Hummus Plate 135
360. . Stuffed Tomatoes with Bread Crumbs and Cheese 135
361. Stuffed Baked Potato 135
362. Oil-Free Rainbow Roasted Vegetables . 135
363. Kofta-Style Chickpea "Meatball" Pitas 135
364. Spanish Paella 136
365. Veggie And Chickpea Fajitas 136
366. Acorn Squash, Sweet Potatoes, And Apples 136
367. Stuffed Roasted Sweet Potatoes 137
368. Cheesy Hash Browns Egg Bake 137
369. Breakfast Taquitos Casserole 137
370. Potato Gratin 138
371. Swiss Chard And Orzo Gratin 138
372. Baked Cheesy Broccoli With Quinoa 138
373. Mexican Casserole 139
374. Curried Cauliflower Tetrazzini 139
375. Baked Eggplant Parmesan 139

CHAPTER 21: STEWS & CHILIES 142

376. Spanish Chickpea and Sweet Potato Stew 142
377. Pomegranate and Walnut Stew 142
378. Fennel and Chickpeas Provençal 142
379. African Peanut Lentil Soup 143
380. White Bean Stew 143
381. Vegetarian Gumbo 143
382. Black Bean and Quinoa Stew 144
383. Root Vegetable Stew 144
384. Bean and Mushroom Chili 144
385. Five-Bean Chili 144
386. Mushroom & Wild Rice Stew 145
387. Ethiopian Cabbage, Carrot, and Potato Stew 145
388. Balsamic Lentil Stew 145
389. Winter Stew 146
390. Vegan "Beef" Stew 146
391. Egyptian Stew 146
392. Moroccan Stew 146
393. Peas And Carrot Stew 147
394. Mediterranean Vegan Stew 147
395. African Pineapple Peanut Stew 147
396. Cauliflower Stew 147
397. Mushroom Stew 148
398. Tofu And Veggies Stew 148
399. Bell Pepper And Spinach Stew 148
400. Potato And Chickpeas Stew 148
401. Squash And Beans Stew 149
402. Hearty Vegetable Stew 149
403. Barley Lentil Stew 149
404. Fruits Stew 149
405. Quinoa And Black Bean Chili 150
406. Mushroom, Lentil, And Barley Stew 150
407. Sweet Potato, Kale And Peanut Stew ... 150
408. Vegetarian Irish Stew 150
409. White Bean And Cabbage Stew 151
410. Spinach And Cannellini Bean Stew 151
411. Cabbage Stew 151
412. Kimchi Stew 152
413. Spicy Bean Stew 152
414. Eggplant, Onion And Tomato Stew 152
415. Brussel Sprouts Stew 152

CHAPTER 22: STIR-FRIED, GRILLED AND ROASTED VEGETABLES 154

416. Roasted Corn 154
417. Plantain Chips 154
418. Roasted Garlic 154
419. Maple Roasted Brussels sprouts 154
420. Roasted Butternut Squash with Mushrooms and Cranberries 154
421. Roasted Green Beans 155
422. Shishito Peppers 155
423. Baby Bok Choy 155
424. Popcorn Tofu 155
425. Roasted Vegetable Kebabs 156
426. Greek Grilled Eggplant Steaks 156
427. Grilled Broccoli 156
428. Roasted Garlic Grilled Vegetables 156
429. Stir-fry Vegetables 156
430. One-Skillet Veggie Hash 156
431. Veggie Hash 156
432. Grilled Vegetables 157
433. Mixed Vegetable Platter 157
434. Grilled Chopped Veggies 157
435. Garlic Grilled Vegetables 157
436. Broccoli and Tomatoes Air Fried Stew 158
437. Broccoli Mix 158
438. Brussels Sprouts and Tomatoes Mix ... 158
439. Chinese Bowls 158
440. Chinese Cauliflower Rice 158
441. Chinese Long Beans Mix 159
442. Cool Tofu Mix 159
443. Coriander Endives 159
444. Garlic Eggplants 159
445. Hot Cabbage Mix 159
446. Indian Potatoes 160
447. Leeks Medley 160
448. Mediterranean Chickpeas 160
449. Mexican Peppers Mix 160
450. Paprika Broccoli 160

451.	Pumpkin Tasty Seeds	161
452.	Red Potatoes and Green Beans	161
453.	Rice and Veggies	161
454.	White Mushrooms Mix	161
455.	Yam Mix	161

CHAPTER 23: SAUCE, CONDIMENTS & DRESSING 162

456.	White Beans Dip	162
457.	Edamame Hummus	162
458.	Beans Mayonnaise	162
459.	Cashew Cream	162
460.	Lemon Tahini	162
461.	Avocado Dill Dressing	163
462.	Cilantro Chili Dressing	163
463.	Spinach and Avocado Dressing	163
464.	Maple Dijon Dressing	163
465.	Orange Mango Dressing	163
466.	Cashew Mustard Dressing	163
467.	Vinegary Maple Syrup Dressing	163
468.	Garlic Cilantro Dressing	164
469.	Cranberry Dressing	164
470.	Thai Peanut Dressing	164
471.	Herb Avocado Salad Dressing	164
472.	Cesar Style Dressing	164
473.	Vegan Thousand Island	165
474.	Strawberry Peach Vinaigrette	165
475.	Raspberry Vinaigrette	165
476.	Creamy Tahini Dressing	165
477.	Peanut Sauce	165
478.	Cilantro-Lime Dressing	165
479.	Caesar Dressing	166
480.	Coconut Curry Sauce	166
481.	Herbed Croutons	166
482.	Spinach Pesto	166
483.	Refried Beans	166
484.	Simple Barbecue Sauce	167
485.	Garlic Butter	167
486.	Parm Sprinkle	167
487.	Sour Cream	167
488.	Simple Syrup	167
489.	Chocolate Icing	168
490.	Vanilla Icing	168
491.	General Tso Sauce	168
492.	Cashew Cheese Sauce	168
493.	Ranch Dressing	168
494.	Minty Lime Dressing	168

CHAPTER 24: WRAPS AND SPREADS 170

495.	Buffalo Chickpea Wraps	170
496.	Coconut Veggie Wraps	170
497.	Spicy Hummus and Apple Wrap	170
498.	Sun-Dried Tomato Spread	170
499.	Sweet Potato Sandwich Spread	171
500.	Seitan Shawarma	171
501.	Chipotle Seitan Taquitos	171
502.	Mediterranean Chickpea Wraps	171
503.	Barbecue Chickpea Burgers with Slaw	172
504.	Hummus and Quinoa Wrap	172
505.	Mediterranean Veggie Wrap	172
506.	Quick Lentil Wrap	172
507.	Thai Vegetable and Tofu Wrap	173
508.	Plant-Based Buffalo Wrap	173
509.	Colorful Veggie Wrap	173
510.	BBQ Chickpea Wrap	173
511.	Chickpea and Mango Wraps	174
512.	Tofu and Pineapple in Lettuce	174
513.	Quinoa and Black Bean Lettuce Wraps	174
514.	Maple Bagel Spread	174
515.	Peanut and Ginger Tofu Wrap	175
516.	Quick-Fix Veggie Wrap	175
517.	Delicious Collard Wraps	175
518.	Falafel Wrap	175
519.	Curried Mango Chickpea Wrap	176
520.	Paprika Olives Spread	176
521.	Korean Barbecue Tempeh Wraps	176
522.	Black Bean Wrap with Hummus	177
523.	Sprout Wraps	177
524.	Collard Wraps	177
525.	Lite Tuna Melt Wrap	177
526.	Curry Wraps	178
527.	Leeks Spread	178
528.	Eggplant Spread	178
529.	Vegan Mediterranean Wraps	178
530.	Jackfruit Wrap	178

CHAPTER 25: SNACKS & APPETIZERS 180

531.	Nori Snack Rolls	180
532.	Risotto Bites	180
533.	Garden Patch Sandwiches On Multigrain Bread	180
534.	Black Sesame Wonton Chips	180
535.	Tamari Toasted Almonds	181
536.	Avocado And Tempeh Bacon Wraps	181
537.	Tempeh-Pimiento Cheeze Ball	181
538.	Peppers and Hummus	181
539.	Savory Roasted Chickpeas	181
540.	Savory Seed Crackers	182
541.	Tomato and Basil Bruschetta	182
542.	Refried Bean And Salsa Quesadillas	182
543.	Jicama And Guacamole	182
544.	Tempeh Tantrum Burgers	183
545.	Sesame-Wonton Crisps	183
546.	Macadamia-Cashew Patties	183
547.	Lemon Coconut Cilantro Rolls	183
548.	Seeded Crackers	184
549.	Banana Bites	184
550.	Sweet Potato Toast	184
551.	Hummus Toast	184
552.	Tacos	185
553.	Kale Chips	185
554.	Spicy Roasted Chickpeas	185
555.	Nuts Trail Mix	185
556.	Crispy Cauliflower	185

557.	Spinach Mushroom Pockets 186
558.	Breaded Tofu 186
559.	Raisin Protein Balls 186
560.	Cheese Cucumber Bites 186
561.	Hummus without Oil 186
562.	Tempting Quinoa Tabbouleh 187
563.	Quick Peanut Butter Bars 187
564.	Hummus Made with Sweet Potato 187
565.	Crisp Balls Made with Peanut Butter 187
566.	Healthy Protein Bars 188
567.	Tofu Saag 188
568.	Mango Sticky Rice 188
569.	Oatmeal Sponge Cookies 188

CHAPTER 26: DESSERTS 190

570.	Zesty Orange-Cranberry Energy Bites 190
571.	Chocolate and Walnut Farfalle 190
572.	Almond-Date Energy Bites 190
573.	Pumpkin Pie Cups (Pressure Cooker) 190
574.	Granola-Stuffed Baked Apples 191
575.	Better Pecan Bars 191
576.	Chocolate-Almond Bars 191
577.	Coconut and Almond Truffles 191
578.	Pecan and Date-Stuffed Roasted Pears 192
579.	Lime-Macerated Mangos 192
580.	Fudgy Brownies (Pressure Cooker) 192
581.	Chocolate-Banana Fudge 192
582.	Chocolate–Almond Butter Truffles 193
583.	Chocolate Macaroons 193
584.	Chocolate Pudding 193
585.	Avocado Pudding 193
586.	Almond Butter Brownies 193
587.	Raspberry Chia Pudding 193
588.	Chocolate Fudge 194
589.	Quick Chocó Brownie 194
590.	Cinnamon Coconut Chips 194
591.	Peach Cobbler 194
592.	Chocolate Brownies 194
593.	The Keto Lovers "Magical" Grain-Free Granola 194
594.	Keto Ice Cream 194
595.	Apple Mix 195
596.	Almond Butter Fudge 195
597.	The Vegan Pumpkin Spicy Fat Bombs 195
598.	Orange Cake 195
599.	Chia Raspberry Pudding 195
600.	Pumpkin Cake 195
601.	Banana Bread 196
602.	Apple Crisp 196
603.	Secret Ingredient Chocolate Brownies 196
604.	Chocolate Chip Pecan Cookies 197
605.	No-Bake Chocolate Coconut Energy Balls 197
606.	Blueberry Hand Pies 197
607.	Date Squares 198

Plant based cookbook for beginners

608.	Homemade Chocolates with Coconut and Raisins 198
609.	Easy Mocha Fudge 198
610.	Key Lime Pie 198
611.	Chocolate Mint Grasshopper Pie 199
612.	Peanut Butter Energy Bars 199
613.	Black Bean Brownie Pops 199
614.	Lemon Cashew Tart 199
615.	Peppermint Oreos 200
616.	Snickers Pie 200
617.	Double Chocolate Orange Cheesecake 200
618.	Coconut Ice Cream Cheesecake 201
619.	Matcha Coconut Cream Pie 201
620.	Chocolate Peanut Butter Cake 201
621.	Chocolate Raspberry Brownies 202
622.	Brownie Batter 202
623.	Strawberry Mousse 202
624.	Blueberry Mousse 202
625.	Black Bean Balls 203
626.	Chia Soy Pudding 203
627.	Blueberry Ice Cream 203
628.	Chickpea Choco Slices 203
629.	Chocolate Orange Mousse 203

CHAPTER 27: 30 MIN RECIPES 204

630.	Strawberry Shake 204
631.	Chocolatey Banana Shake 204
632.	Fruity Tofu Smoothie 204
633.	Green Fruity Smoothie 204
634.	Protein Latte 204
635.	Chocolatey Bean Mousse 204
636.	Tofu & Strawberry Mousse 205
637.	Tofu & Chia Seed Pudding 205
638.	Banana Brownies 205
639.	Cherry Smoothie with Oat Milk 205
640.	Chocolate Mousse with Almonds 205
641.	Banana and Orange Mousse 205
642.	Golden Milk Smoothie 206
643.	Zucchini Blueberry Smoothie 206
644.	Avocado Banana Green Smoothie 206
645.	Gingery Mango Smoothie 206
646.	Green Spirulina Smoothie 206
647.	Ginger Kale Smoothie 206
648.	Mushroom Scramble 207
649.	Apple-Lemon Bowl 207
650.	Portabella Eggs Florentine 207
651.	Quinoa And Nectarine Slaw 207
652.	Zucchini Fritters 208
653.	Loaded Sweet Potato Nacho Fries 208
654.	Smashed Chickpea Avocado Toasts 208
655.	Broccoli And White Beans On Toast 209
656.	Asparagus, Leek, And Ricotta Flatbreads 209
657.	Middle Eastern Cauliflower Steaks 209
658.	Warm Sweet Potato Noodle Salad 210

659.	Chopped Kale Salad With Apples And Pumpkin Seeds	210
660.	Fresh And Hearty Quinoa Salad	210
661.	Summer Tomato And Burrata Panzanella Salad	210
662.	Lebanese Lentil Salad	211
663.	Chickpea Niçoise Salad	211
664.	Grilled Mediterranean Salad With Quinoa	211
665.	Tortilla Soup	212
666.	Cheesy Broccoli Soup	212
667.	Butternut Squash Soup With Apple Cider	212
668.	Black Bean And Quinoa Wrap	213
669.	Spicy Chickpea Gyros	213

CHAPTER 28: EASIEST RECIPES 214

670.	Blueberry And Banana Smoothie	214
671.	Lemon And Rosemary Iced Tea	214
672.	Lavender And Mint Ice Tea	214
673.	Thai Iced Tea	214
674.	Healthy Coffee Smoothie	214
675.	Berry And Strawberry Smoothie	214
676.	Mint Flavored Pear Smoothie	214
677.	Epic Pineapple Juice	215
678.	Chilled Watermelon Smoothie	215
679.	The Mocha Shake	215
680.	Cinnamon Chiller	215
681.	Sensational Strawberry Medley	215
682.	Alkaline Strawberry Smoothie	215
683.	Awesome Orange Smoothie	215
684.	Pineapple And Coconut Milk Smoothie	216
685.	Sweet Potato And Almond Smoothie	216
686.	The Sunshine Offering	216
687.	Strawberry And Rhubarb Smoothie	216
688.	Vanilla Hemp Drink	216
689.	Minty Cherry Smoothie	216
690.	Hot Pink Smoothie	216
691.	Maca Caramel Frap	217
692.	Peanut Butter Vanilla Green Shake	217
693.	Green Colada	217
694.	Chocolate Oat Smoothie	217
695.	Peach Crumble Shake	217
696.	Wild Ginger Green Smoothie	217
697.	Berry Beet Velvet Smoothie	218
698.	Spiced Strawberry Smoothie	218
699.	Banana Bread Shake With Walnut Milk	218
700.	Double Chocolate Hazelnut Espresso Shake	218
701.	Strawberry, Banana, And Coconut Shake	218
702.	Tropical Vibes Green Smoothie	219
703.	Peanut Butter And Mocha Smoothie	219
704.	Tahini Shake with Cinnamon and Lime	219
705.	Fig Oatmeal Bake	219
706.	Vegan Breakfast Sandwich	219
707.	Vegan Fried Egg	220
708.	Sweet Crepes	220
709.	Tofu Scramble	220

CHAPTER 29: WHOLE FOOD RECIPES 222

710.	Spicy Curry Lentil Burgers	222
711.	Loaded Pizza With Black Beans	222
712.	Thai Pad Bowl	222
713.	Sushi Bowl	222
714.	Sweet Potato Patties	223
715.	Summer Vietnamese Rolls	223
716.	Sesame Stir Fry	223
717.	Lime-Mint Creamy Spaghetti Squash	223
718.	Pesto And Sun-Dried Tomato Quinoa	224
719.	White Bean And Olive Pasta	224
720.	Buckwheat And Spaghetti Meatballs	224
721.	Black-Eyed Pea Burritos	225
722.	Chickpea Curry	225
723.	Sweet Potato Shephard's Pie	225
724.	Stovetop Maple Beans	226
725.	Cabbage Roll Stew	226
726.	Walnut, Coconut, And Oat Granola	226
727.	Ritzy Fava Bean Ratatouille	226
728.	Peppers And Black Peans With Brown Rice	227
729.	Black-Eyed Pea, Beet, And Carrot Stew	227
730.	Koshari	227
731.	Roasted Cauliflower With Navy Bean Purée And Quinoa Risotto	228
732.	Butternut Squash With Quinoa And Almonds	228
733.	Harissa Lentils With Riced Cauliflower	228
734.	Lemony Farro And Pine Nut Chard Rolls with Marinara Sauce	229
735.	Easy Rice Blend With Almond, Parsley, And Cranberries	229
736.	Crispy Buckwheat	230
737.	Simple Maple Navy Bean Bake	230
738.	Nasi Goreng	230
739.	.Chickpea And Black Bean Stew With Pearl Parley	231
740.	Mexican Rice Bowl With Pinto Beans	231
741.	Bibibmbap	231
742.	Lentil, Bulgur, And Mushroom Burgers	232
743.	Easy Chickpea Salad Sandwiches	232
744.	Falafel With Tahini-Milk Sauce	232
745.	Brown Rice with Spiced Vegetables	233
746.	Spiced Tomato Brown Rice	233
747.	Noodle And Rice Pilaf	233
748.	Easy Millet Loaf	233
749.	Spaghetti With Spinach, Tomatoes, And Beans	234

CHAPTER 30: TASTY RECIPES 236

750.	Zucchini Zoodles Soup	236
751.	Broccoli Slaw Wrap	236
752.	Avocado Salad Sandwiches	236

753.	Rainbow Taco Boats	236
754.	Tofu Egg Salad	237
755.	Delicious Chana Masala	237
756.	Easy Gazpacho Soup	237
757.	Greek Quinoa Salad	237
758.	Roasted Butternut Squash Salad	238
759.	Pasta Salad with Yogurt Dressing	238
760.	Vegan Cauliflower Steaks	238
761.	Tomato Cucumber Salad	238
762.	Healthy Apple Chickpea Salad	238
763.	Sweet Potato Chickpea Bowl	239
764.	Skinny Pasta Primavera	239
765.	Grilled Vegetable Sandwich	239
766.	Vegetarian Pancit Bihon	240
767.	Easy Vegetable Lasagna	240
768.	Curry Lentil Soup with Butternut Squash	240
769.	Glazed Avocado	241
770.	Mango and Leeks Meatballs	241
771.	Spicy Carrots and Olives	241
772.	Harissa Mushrooms	241
773.	Leeks and Artichokes Mix	241
774.	Coconut Avocado	242
775.	Avocado Cream	242
776.	Tamarind Avocado Bowls	242
777.	Onion and Tomato Bowls	242
778.	Avocado and Leeks Mix	242
779.	Lemon Lentils and Carrots	243
780.	Cabbage Bowls	243
781.	Pomegranate and Pears Salad	243
782.	Bulgur and Tomato Mix	243
783.	Beans Mix	243
784.	Smoked Green Beans	244
785.	Lentil and Sunflower Seeds Salad	244
786.	Chives Chickpeas Mix	244
787.	Balsamic Olives Salad	244
788.	Chickpeas and Spinach Mix	244
789.	Brussels Sprout Skewers	245
790.	Thai Peanut Butter Cauliflower Wings	245
791.	Potato Salad	245
792.	Carrot Patties	245
793.	Eggplant and Potatoes in Tomato Sauce	246
794.	Grilled Mushrooms with Garlic Sauce	246
795.	Sesame Tofu and Veggies Noodles	246
796.	Bombay Potatoes and Peas	247
797.	BBQ Tofu Pizza	247
798.	Quinoa Tacos	248
799.	Teriyaki Noodle Stir-Fry	248
800.	Garlicky Tofu	248
801.	Mac and Cheese	249
802.	Peanut Butter and Pumpkin Soup	249
803.	Sweet Korean Lentils	249
804.	Pasta Puttanesca	249
805.	Walnut Meat Tacos	249
806.	Couscous with Olives	250
807.	Black Bean and Corn Salad	250
808.	Chickpea Salad Sandwich	250

CONCLUSION **252**

RECIPE INDEX **254**

Amanda Kale

Introduction

While the word "plant-based" sounds a bit new, the concept has been around for nearly 10,000 years. In fact, the Chinese started cultivating grains before they domesticated animals over 5000 years ago, and that was the way they sustained their population for centuries. The modern concept, the one that we all know today, was born in much more recent times. It was 1980 and Dr. Campbell was studying the potential effects of a plant-based diet, low in fat and high in fiber, to minimize cancer development. This is the origin of the "plant-based diet" term, chosen to identify this eating pattern without being linked to any ethical or moral purpose. You might be wondering what a plant-based diet is? The idea is simple: you mainly eat plants or things that come from plants, like seeds and grains. That said, it is a fact that some people sometimes allow in their plant-based diet small portions of animal products, although it's recommended to avoid it. You may be wondering what the difference is with veganism. The plant-based diet is different from veganism in the sense that vegans exclude all animal products from their diet without exception. That's a big difference! Veganism is a lifestyle that excludes meat and animal by-products (such as eggs, milk, honey) from their diet. It's more like a "religion" where people don't eat those products for ethical reasons. Some vegans don't even use or buy animal by-products such as wool, leather, silk, or pearls for the same principle. When you follow a plant-based diet, most of what you eat comes from plants, but it does not mean that you can never eat animal products such as eggs, meat, fish, or honey, although it is highly recommended to avoid them. In principle, a plant-based diet has no particular ethical purpose, although more and more people are coming to this diet because of the awareness that it is more sustainable for our planet. By helping themselves they help the planet, what could be better? What about whole food. This is another important aspect, which often creates confusion among people. Whole food is a product that you eat when it is still almost in its natural state. This means that it has not been processed or manipulated and that elements such as sugar, flavorings, salt, or other super refined ingredients have not been added. If you want to maximize the effects of the plant-based diet, you could use only whole food products. This means eliminating or minimizing as much as possible all refined and highly processed products. Many people have wondered why they should choose a plant-based diet over a regular diet. Here are some of the main reasons:

1. It's healthier! All of the following benefits are associated with a plant-based diet: Lower cholesterol, Diabetes risk reduced, weight loss, Protects against heart disease and cancer, and more.

2. It doesn't impede on your freedom! As said before, if you want to include small quantities of animal products, you will be able to do so.

3. It's economical., you will find yourself eating a lot more but at less cost, because it usually incorporates a variety of plant products.

4. It is good for the environment. A plant-based diet is good for our planet because it reduces greenhouse gas emissions and the need to feed animals and thus influences climate change in the environment.

5. Improve your longevity! Several studies show that people who follow a plant-based diet live much longer than those who do not and tend to have lower rates of heart disease, diabetes, and obesity compared to meat eaters or those who take cholesterol medication (other than vegetarians).

"This cookbook is a godsend. It contains the recipes that I have been looking for all these years...I'm going to try and incorporate some of the recipes into my daily life." - Jessica Parker, Amazon Customer Review "This is a wonderful book full of great tasting, healthy recipes. I have tried many of them already now and they have been DELICIOUS! Thanks so much for sharing your wonderful work." - Dana H. Nathan, Amazon Customer Review Plant-based diets aren't for everyone, but if you are someone who loves to eat healthy and feel bright and full of energy, this cookbook is perfect for you!

Amanda Kale

CHAPTER 1:
What Is The Plant-Based Diet

A plant-based diet is a plant-centered nutrition program focused on foods coming from plant sources. This includes all fruit, vegetables, grains (such as rice, corn, wheat), legumes (such as beans, lentils, peas, and much more), nuts, and seeds. This type of diet excludes or minimizes as much as possible the consumption of animal products such as meat, seafood, or dairy and excludes highly or ultra-processed and refined products such as sugar, many types of flour, and industrial flavorings. There are some foods labeled as "plant-based" that could be misleading because they have been highly processed. Think about refined white flour or some of the vegetable fat out there in the market, they are plant-based as well as refined products, so definitely not ideal for healthy eating. In fact, a refined product is a portion of food without its original nutrients and fibers, which have been removed by an intrusive process. Often those nutrients are added back at the end of the process through unnatural ingredients that are unhealthy and not as well absorbed in our body as the original ones.

A plant-based diet does not have to be difficult or complicated. It is, however, important to ensure that you are getting the proper nutrients and vitamins, and the plants already have all that a human body needs, you just have to make sure to combine a wide range of vegetables, seeds, grains, and fruits when you are planning your meals. This will allow you to get all the nutrients you need!

Plant-based diets are a popular part of today's lifestyle and health. If you want to learn more about the benefits of a plant-based diet, consider the following:

1. Metabolic Advantage (Auckland, New Zealand): this is an online weight loss support program that offers various products and consulting services for the purpose of promoting healthy eating habits. Services include coaching, nutrition packages, coaches, and intermittent fasting plans available through the website.

2. Plant-Based Diet (New York): The Plant-Based Diet is a registered non-profit food education organization dedicated to promoting safe, sustainable diets through public health campaigns and workshops exploring plant-based nutrition from every possible viewpoint. The Plant-Based Diet also offers free resources on its website for both beginners and experienced plant-based diet advocates.

3. The Plant-Based Journey (London): This is a free six-month online course aimed at those who are interested in learning more about the health benefits of a plant-based diet. It is hosted by Dr. Melanie Brown, a Scientific Advisor to The Vegan Society, and has been designed to help you explore how this way of life can work for you. You will have the chance to learn from other people's experiences and get support throughout your journey!

4. Meatless Monday (Washington, D.C.): Meatless Monday is a non-profit organization whose mission is to help reduce global warming, hunger, and poverty by encouraging people to eat more plant-based foods. Their slogan is "One day of the week, cut out the meat."

5. The China Study (California): This is an online resource that provides free access to The China Study, a breakthrough book by Dr. T. Colin Campbell and his son Dr. Thomas M. Campbell II, which describes the relationship between nutrition and heart disease, diabetes, and cancer with detailed information on diet and lifestyle changes proven to prevent and reverse these diseases. 6. McDougall Program (California): This is a free online 12-week program that provides you with the tools to succeed at changing your health. It offers an e-mail support group (for participants who have completed the program) and resources to help and guide you on this journey towards wellness.

CHAPTER 2:
Plant-Based Diet As A Holistic Approach To Body Wellness

What you eat has a lot to do with your well-being. It's no secret that diet, exercise, and sleep are the three pillars of an optimum lifestyle. Yet most people think that once those pillars are in place, it's all set, the rest is really just icing on the cake. In fact, no single aspect of our lives can have as much influence on our mental and physical health as what we choose to put into our bodies. The wrong kind of food creates inflammation (leading to pain), depletes nutrients (leading to fatigue), and destroys cells (leading to cancer). Diet is the basis for maintaining health, but scientists have begun to study the impact of diet on our mood until recently. Research is showing time and again that eating certain foods can profoundly affect people's happiness levels and other mental states. For instance, eating omega-3 fatty acids — found in plants such as walnuts — is shown to increase feelings of contentment, while chromium, found in whole grains like oats or cereal grains like wheat, helps reduce depression.

Although the effect of diet on mental state seems obvious, we all know that switching to a Plant-Based diet can have a huge impact on our friends and family, the scientific community is still debating why some people find it easier to adopt such a lifestyle than others. One thing is certain: your mood may be inextricably linked with what you put into your body. Let's go through some nutrients and how they can affect our body wellness

- **Vitamins and Minerals**

The most common vitamin deficiency is D. Every cell in the human body needs D to maintain metabolism, nerve impulse, immune function, and bone health. The human body cannot produce its own supply of vitamin D from sunlight (unlike most other animals, including many humans living in the Northern hemisphere, who get a significant amount of vitamin D from sun exposure).

A group of Finnish women who were given 50,000 international units (I.U.) of vitamin D over six months experienced a significant decrease in depressive symptoms. The women had less trouble sleeping and fewer overall symptoms of depression. Omega-3 fatty acids also play an important role in your mood. Apparently, your most basic physical feelings are affected by the proteins found in certain foods such as fish or nuts. Omega-3 fatty acids are beneficial because they create chemicals that reduce inflammation in our brains, which can lead to improved cognitive functioning and enhanced moods.

The fact that your body is literally made of what you eat is emphasized by another study that found the foods you eat influence how quickly your brain processes information. The foods with the highest omega-3 content, including walnuts, salmon and olive oil, can positively impact the health of your entire nervous system. For example, in a study involving walnuts, those who ate a daily serving of seven (56 grams) showed better ability to focus than people who didn't. Everyone in the study had high I.Q.s and no signs of cognitive impairment.

Further evidence that "you are what you eat" comes from research on vitamin E deficiency. Those suffering from this deficiency may become apathetic or have trouble concentrating. While a deficiency of this vitamin is rare in developed countries, many women of childbearing age do not get enough due to fad diets and poor eating habits.

- **Fiber**

There are two types of fiber: soluble and insoluble. Soluble fiber dissolves easily in water. This is important because SAM-e prevents depression and tensions caused by stress by keeping the chemicals that cause anxiety balanced within your brain's neurons.

In contrast, insoluble fiber can be found in foods such as whole grains and vegetables. It does not dissolve easily in water, but it absorbs water instead of absorbing energy from the foods consumed. This allows solids to stay together and creates a wall within the intestines that prevents the entry of bacteria, a necessary condition for harmful intestinal bacteria to flourish. Foods high in insoluble fiber include carrots, celery, yams and garlic.

- **Superfoods**

There are certain plants that have been given nicknames due to their supposed health benefits: turmeric, for instance, helps prevent inflammation; blueberries contain more than 60 antioxidants; and so on. Some people use these plants, or some of their extracts, in healing rituals. However, it is questionable whether our current Western diet — which relies heavily on processed foods that are fortified with tons of chemicals and artificially identified "healthy" ingredients — can provide the same kind of healing effects as the traditional cuisine of many cultures that have been eating for thousands of years.

For example, until the 17th century, Europeans did not know that saffron (Crocus sativus) was an effective treatment for depression because they discovered it by accident. In fact, a researcher explains that there were no studies on its effects on mental health until more than two centuries after it was first used for medicinal purposes.

CHAPTER 3:
How Your Whole Lifestyle Will Improve With A Plant-Based Diet

The benefits of eating a plant-based diet are endless, and that leads me to believe that it is not only an ethical choice, but also a sustainable one as well. Food choices ultimately depend on what people are willing to accept at an individual level. That is why I have been practicing a plant-based diet for over twenty years with complete joy and satisfaction. I do this because it just feels right for my body as well as my mind too.

Mind Benefits

1. Neuroprotection: A study found that a Plant-based diet helped protect the brain against inflammation, oxidative stress and cell death in mice models for Alzheimer's disease.
2. The foods found in a plant-based diet are generally easy to digest. Our body's digestive system doesn't have to work as hard to process these foods. This means our digestive system has more energy and can perform better overall, creating less waste that can harm us.
3. Plant-based diets have been linked to anti-aging effects on the brain.
4. Better mood – A plant-based diet has been shown to make people calmer, happier, and less stressed.
5. Better concentration – It's easier to pay attention and focus if you get enough protein from plants instead of meat.
6. Reduced risk of depression – A diet based on plants has been linked with lower rates of depression in multiple studies and there is evidence that suggests this is because it reduces the risk for anxiety disorders like panic attacks.
7. Better memory – A Plant-based diet is more effective at improving short-term memory than a meat-based diet.
8. Reduced stress – Studies show that plant-based diets can lower cortisol levels, the "stress hormone".

How You Will Feel Lighter, Cleaner, and Healthier Throughout the Day

It is a known fact that plant-based foods are some of the best diet choices you can make, but there are so many different ways to achieve this. This plant-based diet cookbook for beginners will help you find a healthy and easy plant-based lifestyle with tons of delicious recipes. You'll feel lighter, cleaner, and healthier throughout the day.

A plant-based diet is very easy to follow. It is actually quite simple. You can easily make changes to your diet daily, weekly, or monthly, which will help your motivation and allow you to try out new recipes without feeling overwhelmed by all the rules and regulations you have to follow.

A plant-based diet can also be easily followed by people with different aims depending on their personal health goals and nutritional needs. Eating healthy is easier than ever with the help of this book. You can also travel with your plant-based foods, so no matter where you are going or how long your trip is, you can be sure that your meals will be full of vitamins and nutrients with little to no prep time needed. Some foods are easily made into snacks for an on-the-go lifestyle. This is a great way to get the most out of your plant-based diet and the recipes in this book.

Eating Vegan is Easier Than You Think!

A plant-based diet may seem very difficult to follow; however, eating vegan is easier than you think when you get started and this book will help you find a way to maintain your new healthy eating habits.

The main thing to remember with plant-based foods is to focus on eating foods that you can grow yourself or find in the grocery store. Find recipe magazines, blogs and get ideas from friends. Once you start eating healthier and start experimenting on your own, you will find limitless options to continue with your new eating style and not get bored about it.

You won't feel like you're missing out on any of your favorite types of foods when you switch to a plant-based diet. You can also enjoy plant-based versions of all your favorite desserts. You won't have to give up the delicious foods you love. You just have to adjust them slightly to make them plant-based.

Plant-based meals can be very filling and are easier to digest than meals containing meat, which also helps with weight loss. Not only is plant-based eating lower in saturated fat, but it is also high in fiber, protein, and vitamins, all of which help with weight loss.

Amanda Kale

There are so many different recipes for plant-based meals that you will never get bored with it! This book gives you tons of healthy vegan meals for breakfast, lunch, dinner, snacks, and even dessert. You will feel lighter, cleaner, and healthier throughout the day with each of these delicious recipes.

CHAPTER 4:
How Sustainable The Plant-Based Diet Is For Our Land

Our environmental footprint is a serious problem—but that's something we can change. If you're ready to make more conscious choices about what you eat, read on! Many healthy Plant-based recipes will help to decrease your carbon footprint while making your meals healthier and more delicious.

More Environmentally Sustainable

The large amount of land needed for livestock farming contributes directly to deforestation. This means the loss of habitat for wild animals, a decline in oxygen levels, and even an increase in greenhouse gases! Every hour, approximately 100 acres are bulldozed to make room for beef farming. To feed livestock, the U.S. uses more than half of its grain production (63 million tons) and 30 percent of its fossil fuels approximately. We could lower up to 75% of the current amount of land used for agriculture if all humans changed to a plant-based diet.

Water Consumption

There is no other activity that consumes more fresh water in the U.S. than agricultural production, including food for direct human consumption and livestock feeding.

Gas Emission

In addition, animal agriculture is responsible for 18 percent of greenhouse gas emissions. It's no wonder that the United Nations has stated that "Livestock is one of the most significant contributors to today's most serious environmental problems".

Animal Cruelty

In addition, by relying on plants, animal pain can be avoided. Factory farming causes many animals to suffer immensely, including confinement indoors or enclosure in cages. They are exploited and denied a free life, only to become food for humans.

Water Contamination

Industrial farms also produce a large amount of waste that pollutes water sources and causes a reduction in biodiversity due to the loss of natural habitat.

Costs

Plant-based diets can be more affordable than ones based on animal products. This is because plant-based foods are also cheap and easy to produce.

The intelligent production of vegetables requires less effort in terms of machinery, water, and land than the production of animal products. A plant-based diet uses less water because plants do not need to be fed as much as animals. In addition, a plant-based diet uses less land than an omnivorous diet.

It takes much less space to grow just vegetables than it does to grow animals in a minimally decent space. I don't even want to consider intensive animal husbandry as an option for growing them. In addition, animals also need to be fed, so the space used to produce the food for them must also be taken into account.

Distribution

Moreover, due to their low cost, the production of plant-based foods is widespread and they are available in almost all local markets. Consuming locally produced products also has a benefit related to the reduction of transportation energy consumption and pollution.

Feel in Harmony with Our Planet

When you eat a plant-based diet, you are committing to live in harmony with the planet. Some people may choose to ignore the fact that human activities are the main origin of our planet´s current struggles, but when you decide to change to a plant-based diet, you are taking responsibility for your actions and you choose to be part of the solution for some of these big problems that the Earth is facing.

The plant-based diet has positive aspects also from an ethical point of view that are mostly similar to those of a vegan diet. Indeed, a plant-based diet does not exclude at all the option of eating animal products sometimes, but this is irrelevant if we think about what a daily diet based on meat entails, as discussed in the previous points.

But perhaps the most important decision you will make when plant-based dieting is choosing health over disease is choosing harmony with the rest of the world, and feeling good about yourself for making it happen.

Amanda Kale

CHAPTER 5:
Health Benefits

Benefits Overview

There are so many benefits to be gained by making the switch to a plant-based diet. Without a doubt you will notice a significant improvement in your health overall. The list below of health benefits should be enough to convince you not only to try it but also to stick with it for the long haul.

1. Weight Loss – It isn't hard to lose weight when you start eating more vegetables. Veggies are low in calories, so you can eat more without gaining extra pounds. Research shows that people who eat a lot of vegetables tend to have a lower body mass index (BMI), and in turn, they have lower rates of obesity.

Also, the body's metabolism and hormonal system are different when you eat plant foods, changing the way it handles your weight and metabolism.

2. Healthier Heart – Eating a plant-based diet can help reduce the risk of heart disease. This diet is naturally lower in calories and saturated fat, which supports heart health. Plant-based diets also tend to have more fiber and provide plenty of potassium without the excess fat found in high-protein diets centered on red meat, which can reduce the risk of heart disease and stroke by lowering blood pressure or helping to control cholesterol levels.

3. Reduces inflammation – Research shows that plant-based diets have a positive impact on the immune system, helping to reduce body inflammation. Lower inflammation has been associated with a lesser risk of developing health problems such as heart disease, cancer, and chronic inflammatory disease.

4. Lowers Diabetes Risk – The chances of developing diabetes are up to 70% lower in people with a plant-based diet compared to meat-eaters. And that's not all. For people who have already developed diabetes, a plant-based diet can help maintain normal blood sugar levels because it is higher in fiber and antioxidants.

5. Lower Cancer Risk – Research also shows that following a plant-based diet reduces the risk of developing cancer by at least 15 % due to a strengthened immune system compared to non-vegetarians.

Plant-based diets rich in fiber have also been shown to reduce the risk of colon cancer significantly. Diets like the Mediterranean diet, which is based on a lot of fruits and vegetables, have been shown to reduce the risk of colon cancer by as much as 40%. This is because fiber helps to eliminate waste more quickly from your body. If a Mediterranean diet can achieve that result, imagine where a diet based only on plants can take you.

Plant-based diets also have more phytochemicals than Western diets. These phytochemicals work together with fiber to help prevent colon cancer.

6. Reduces cholesterol – The plant-based diet can help lower your cholesterol levels and potentially reverse heart disease. Traditional American diets are loaded with saturated fats, which can lead to cholesterol problems and an increased risk of heart disease. Eating more vegetables like kale, spinach, Brussels sprouts and broccoli has been shown to reduce cholesterol levels by as much as 40%.

In addition, a plant-based diet is rich in healthy fats like those found in nuts, avocados or olives, which are lower in saturated fats than animal foods (meat, cheese, etc.).

They also contain omega-3 fatty acids, which can help with the body's inflammatory response and potentially reduce heart disease risks. The good saturated fat found in some plant-based foods (such as coconut oil) can even increase HDL or "good" cholesterol levels compared to meat consumption.

7. Immune System Health – Plant-based foods are full of antioxidants that can help boost your immune system and fight off disease and infection. This is especially true if you are eating lots of fruits and vegetables, since the soil in which they grow were rich in nutrients. Fruits and vegetables naturally have more vitamins C, E, A, and beta-carotene than meat does, so eating these products instead can also benefit your immune system. 8. Healthier Brain – As mentioned previously, a plant-based diet rich in fruit and vegetables is packed with antioxidants, which are the best allies for our cells as they protect them from damage. This will help reduce the risk of developing cognitive impairment and dementia.

Myths to Debunk

There are various myths out there about the deficiency of certain nutrients and micro-nutrients when you are on a plant-based diet. We often hear about low protein, vitamin D or calcium intake. Unfortunately, these are myths supported by the food industry. Here are some considerations about that:

Calcium. Plants absorb calcium from the earth, so we simply take it as a consequence of eating them. It's as simple as that. The same happens when we eat dairy products that come from animals. These contain calcium because the same herbivorous animals get calcium from the plants they eat. So the "news" is that calcium, like all other minerals, comes from the earth. There are many plant-based products and grains rich in calcium, such as broccoli, cabbage, kidney beans, chia seeds, amaranth, oatmeal.

Vitamin B-12 is the only micronutrient that you can't get enough from a plant-based diet, even if you eat a high diversity plant source products. There are many supplements that can solve this small inconvenience and are easily accessible out there in the market. Many types of meat are also deficient in this protein, so many carnivorous people should take vitamin B-12 supplements anyway.

Proteins. A very common concern when talking about a plant-based diet is the lack of protein. The answer is simple: make sure you plan your diet with a sufficient variety of vegetables, grains and seeds that contain protein. This way you will cover your daily protein needs. There are many plant foods that contain a high level of protein, such as seitan, lentils, chickpeas, beans, peas, oats, nuts and many more.

Zinc. This is available from a variety of plant-based foods such as spinach, asparagus, mushrooms, and broccoli. The amount of this mineral inside the vegetables is dependent on the soil where they have been growing, so here again, eating a large variety of vegetables will guarantee enough zinc intake.

What About Nutrients

All of the nutrients and micro-nutrients from the previous paragraph are important to our body, and except for what has been said in chapter 1, you can get all of them following the plant-based diet.

Protein is a building block for your body and aids in muscle growth and repair. A deficiency in protein can cause anemia, fatigue, hair loss, or poor growth in children. When looking for additional protein sources, look at foods like beans, peas and lentils for vegetarian sources of protein. Calcium is necessary for healthy bone structure and development. Iron is necessary for oxygen transport in body tissues and improves cognitive function. Zinc is a mineral that aids in immune system response, wound healing, bone growth and normal carbohydrate metabolism.

There are many other nutrients that you can receive from a plant-based diet. Vitamin A is important for healthy immune system function and vision, Vitamin B1 (thiamine) to promote energy metabolism in cells, Vitamin B2 (riboflavin) to aid in the production of energy, niacin (B3), folic acid, pantothenic acid (B5), vitamin C which aids the absorption of iron and some other vitamins including vitamin D which aids bone health. You may know that vitamin B12 is needed for the production of red blood cells that transport oxygen to different parts of the body, and you're probably also aware that a lack of this vitamin is associated with poor brain function.

How You Can Get All the Nutrients Your Body Needs When Following a Plant-Based Diet

If you're looking to start a plant-based diet, you might be wondering how you'll get all the nutrients your body needs. Healthy, balanced plant-based diets can be chock full of vitamins and minerals — they just require a little more planning than your standard fare. Here are three tips to make sure you're well-fed on this type of diet:

1. Be sure to eat plenty of high-quality fruits and vegetables that offer vitamins A, C, K, and B6, as well as potassium and magnesium.
2. Make sure beans or grains are in every meal for protein as well as fiber — the combo aids digestion and boosts heart health, respectively.
3. Protein-rich plant foods like tofu, tempeh, and nuts are also great choices, but it's important to be aware of the number of calories they provide.

CHAPTER 6:
How You Can Lose Weight. Focus

When you follow a restricted-calorie diet, you may find that it is really frustrating to measure out all of your portions all of the time, add up the calories, or go with some of the low-calorie products that sound like a good idea but are not going to help you out in the taste department. And many of these lower-calorie diets are going to leave you feeling hungry. And this is where the plant-based diet is able to step in and give us some help.

Plant foods are going to have a much higher water content, which helps us get fuller and feel fuller for much longer. Some examples of how these plant foods are going to have a higher content of water in them will include the following:

1. Green vegetables will have at least 90 percent of their makeup be of water.
2. Root vegetables and potatoes will be made up of 70 percent or higher with water.
3. Fresh fruits are going to have about 80 percent or more water in them.
4. Cooked grains, depending on the kind that you are using, are going to have 70 percent or more of their content in water.

We can then take some of these values and compare them with some of the processed foods that we are likely to eat on a regular diet if we were not working with the diet based on plants. Some examples of these foods and the amount of water content they will retain will be:

1. Vegetable oils and other fats that are used for cooking will have no water in them.
2. Corn flakes are going to come in with just 3 percent water.
3. Saltine crackers are going to have around 2 percent water in them.
4. A bagel is going to come in with 37 percent of its mass consisting of water.
5. And potato chips will come in with the least amount with only 2 percent water.

As you can see, plant foods are going to be a lot more filling. Meals that are based on the foods that are plants are a lot more filling to us because of the higher water content, and they are going to be lower in calories as well. They will make sure that you are able to fill up on the foods that you want and get all of the nutrients that you need without going over. And this is going to be a big deal when you are trying your best to lose weight and feel good about yourself. Think about it this way. When you are hungry, which do you think will fill you up better? A whole apple or a whole bag of chips or a whole candy bar? The apple will probably fill you up just fine while only being about 100 calories or so, depending on the size of the apple. On the other hand, the two other options could be 250+ calories each, and depending on the size, they could be twice as much. And you will probably be really hungry with these shortly after. This is why it is best to go with things like the foods found in the plant-based diet. It is sometimes hard to give up some of your old favorites, but when you are able to eat a lot of good and nutritious foods along the way, you will find that it is a lot easier to accomplish Now, you need to make sure that you are eating the right foods along the way and that you are not jumping in and eating foods that you should not. There are a lot of processed and packaged foods out there that claim to be plant-based, but they are filled with a lot of bad stuff that your body doesn't need and can make you sick in the process as well. There are countless studies out there that show how healthy this diet is, and many of them showed not only how this diet can help us to lose a lot of weight quickly, but also how much more weight is possible to lose with this diet plan compared to some of the traditional diets out there. This is good news for those who would like to jump in on this plan and see some amazing results in the process.

With this in mind, there are a lot of other reasons why you will be able to lose weight and improve your overall health when you go on a diet that reduces the animal products and other bad and processed foods that you want to consume in a traditional diet and switch them over to some plant-based alternatives instead. Some of these include:

1. This diet can give you more energy. These plant-based diets are going to be full of lots of healthy nutrients that are good for you and so healthy overall. And this is going to ensure that you have lots of the energy that you need to keep on going all day long.
2. You will feel fuller for longer and much faster than before. As we mentioned before, the foods that are found on this diet plan are filling and so good for you. Both of these are good tricks to follow in order to make losing weight something fun and easy in the long run.
3. There are fewer calories. Even though most of these diets are not going to require that you count your calories and worry about that as much, you will find that you will naturally eat fewer calories. You will feel full and not have to worry

about hunger as often as before, but you will also enjoy that this diet is naturally lower in calories compared to some of the other options.

4. You get lots of nutrition. Think of how many nutrients are actually found in some of the other meals that you eat daily. You may be surprised at the nutrient value is going to be lower than you would think. When we work with the plant-based diet, it gets a lot easier to lose weight and keep it off for the long term, because we are still feeding our body the nutrients that it needs to stay happy and healthy overall. This helps us to still have the energy that we need to get through the day and all of the obligations that we need to do, without feeling like we are tired and worn down in the process.

5. It can be easier to work with. In the beginning, it is easy to assume that this diet is going to be too hard, and you will not be able to find some of the healthy meals that you need here.

6. None of the big insulin spikes: In some of the traditional diets that you may have tried in the past, it is easier to feel a lot of insulin spikes up and down. You will eat unhealthy foods that give you that boost you need for a few hours, but then you come crashing right back down and need to find another way to get the energy back up again. The plant-based diet can take some of these away, which helps to limit how often you get these crashes and can make you feel so much better in no time.

When you are able to combine all of these, you will find that it is a lot easier to get in better health and lose the weight that you want in no time.

CHAPTER 7:
Boost The Positive Effects Of Plant-Based Diet

Whole Foods

We still have an enormous amount of research to do on how our bodies process food in general, but we already know a few things about what makes whole-food diets special. As mentioned in the introduction, whole food is a food that is eaten when it is still in the same state as in nature or very close to it. This means that this product has not been manipulated and its nutritional characteristics have not been altered. In fact, whole food doesn't contain added sugar, salt, flavorings, or other added substances. So a whole food product is an unprocessed or refined food that keeps all its natural nutritional substances. Sometimes you may be misled by the labeling of products that are shown to be plant-based. If you remember what we said in chapter 1, it is not necessarily true that a plant-based product is also a whole food, just think of white sugar. It is certainly a product coming from plants, but what we buy at the supermarket has undergone a refining process causing the alteration of its natural state and its nutritional characteristics. First off, whole foods are superior sources of nutrients. Whole foods contain lots of antioxidants and nutrients that must be digested first before they can be absorbed by your body. On the other hand, micronutrients are those things like vitamins and minerals that can't be digested by your body and must instead be absorbed. When you take a whole food product, most of the nutrition will come from the foods' intact nutrients. Not only are whole foods more nutritious than their modified counterparts, but they also contain critical compounds that protect our bodies from stress and disease. For example, antioxidants are compounds that fight free radicals in our bodies; when we eat refined oils and processed meat (like cheese and bacon), these compounds become depleted. Whole foods like avocados (one of my favorite sources of healthy fats) work to increase levels of antioxidants in your body. And while we're on the topic of fats, we can't forget about the benefit whole foods have to good health. Vegetable oils like those found in coconut oil are an excellent source of plant fat, which is unlike animal fat (like butter or lard). These types of fats are high in saturated fats (which your body can't turn into energy at all), but they still play an essential role in keeping your blood pressure and body temperature steady. But eating whole food is more than just a matter of human physiology. We also know that it's possible for animals such as monkeys, rats and even dogs to live long and healthy lives on a whole food diet. As with humans, the increased longevity of these animals is often linked to lower cancer rates and higher levels of antioxidants. However, many experts believe that the positive effects of whole foods are due to a synergistic effect of all the nutrients, rather than just one specific compound.

Why Some People Keep Their Meals SOS-Free

If you are committed to a plant-based lifestyle, you may want to consider adopting an SOS-free diet for exponential benefits, including greater success in your weight management struggles. In addition to avoiding all animal products, the SOS-free diet is based on achieving a significant reduction in these three elements: oils, salt and sugar. One of the main reasons for avoiding these ingredients is the fact that they are highly addictive, which means we are likely to end up eating far more than we need. The best part about going SOS free is that it can be done in stages. You don't have to do everything at once and you don't need to go full SOS-free overnight! Start by taking on one new change: cut out one of the three Ss from your meals for several days or weeks. Then add another change in addition to the elimination. Before long, you'll be SOS-free in no time! As a general rule, all processed foods should be avoided as they are likely to contain high quantities of salt, oil, or sugar, if not all of them.

Salt

Cutting out the salt from your diet is one of the hardest SOS-free habits to break. We've become so accustomed to salt that we rarely even taste it and don't realize how much we're consuming. Luckily, there are plenty of low-sodium alternatives out there these days; many are even available in regular grocery stores. Check the sodium content on the food label before you buy. If necessary, look for lower-sodium versions at specialty stores or online. Some popular choices that should be avoided are:

- Fast foods: burgers, fries, pizza…
- Salty snacks: salted nuts, crackers, chips…
- Frozen and prepared meals
- Salted canned products: vegetables, pasta, beans…
- Salty soups: canned and packed soups…
- Baked goods high in sodium: crackers, bagels, rolls…

- Sauces: soy sauce, soy, bragg liquid aminos, ketchup, mustard sauce, salad dressings…
- Pickled vegetables: olives, pickles…
- Some drinks: vegetable juice…
- Seasonings: any type of salt.

As a general rule, most processed foods are likely to have high salt content, so please read the label and avoid products that contain more than 200mg of sodium per serving.

Oil

Limit your intake of all oils, not just the ones that come from plants. Even if they are labeled "extra-virgin," olive oil, canola oil, and other oils can be high in polyunsaturated fats. Although polyunsaturated fats are generally considered healthy and are important for human nutrition, many studies have linked them to heart disease when consumed in high quantities. Try making your own salad dressings, hot sauces, mayo substitutes, and baked goods to avoid overindulging in unhealthy fats like hydrogenated vegetable oils. If you're using a store-bought dressing or sauce, look on the label for several keywords: get rid of any product whose ingredients include "hydrogenated" or "partially hydrogenated." These forms of trans fat are some of the worst fats you can consume. Here are some tips to reduce your oil intake:

- Serve oily meals on paper plates to minimize exposure to grease while eating.
- Control your intake of nuts and seeds, which are both high in fat and contain the omega-6 fatty acid linoleic acid (L.A., the type of omega-6 found in most vegetable oils).
- Reduce your intake of saturated fat. Eat plenty of raw fruits and vegetables such as carrots, apples, citrus fruit, bell peppers, celery and leafy greens instead.

Sugar

High sugar consumption is one of the biggest health problems in our society. Its addictive characteristics are contributing to the obesity crisis in all age groups. Some foods such as fruits have naturally occurring sugars, which come with all other health benefits like vitamins, fiber, water, etc. So their consumption should not be avoided. However, added sugars are the big enemy to avoid. These sugars can unbalance your blood sugar levels what can lead to heart disease, diabetes, and obesity. And added sugars are present on at least 70% of processed food available in the market. Even food that you may not imagine like sauces, white breads, yogurts, snacks…Therefore, in addition to avoiding added sugar on the meals that you prepare at home, you should check the labels of any product you buy. Just be aware that added sugar can come under many different names. Here are some of the most common that you can check for:

- Brown sugar
- Corn syrup
- Fruit juice concentrates
- High-fructose corn syrup
- Honey
- Invert sugar
- Malt sugar
- Molasses
- Raw sugar
- Sugar
- Syrup

CHAPTER 8:
How to Start and Stick to the Plant-Based Diet

Set Up Your Mindset

In order to get started on the right foot, you'll need to get into the right headspace for the changes you are incorporating into your life. Having the right mindset for change and for your health will go a long way to help you to be effective and successful at this. It is amazing just trying to imagine the amount of power your mental state and thoughts can have on your life and your decisions. How do we assure that your mind is working on your side? By guiding your opinions and perceptions. And by trying consciously to maintain a positive attitude. Just an overall willingness to do what it will take. You must find, and hold, the strength to commit to new habits, replacing old ones. You are committing to tread into territory that is mysterious to you. You need to be open to fail a little and try something new. The plant-based diet can have a lot of different connotations. Sometimes having a strong misconception can be a roadblock if you let it color your beliefs and choices. Try to keep an open mind going into this change. Many people have the perception that, for example, plant-based food is tasteless. Or that this type of eating has to be difficult. You may agree or think that it is impossible to get the proper nutrients on a plant-based diet. Many people also believe that eating this way must be super expensive. You will find your own path and beliefs as you learn to experiment more. I will give you all of the tools that I can, but you have to be willing to explore and experiment to find your path. There are many ways to go about change, and what you choose will be based on a variety of things. Some people prefer to transition very slowly to make the adjustment not such a shock, and also to pay more attention to the process over the long term. Others like to completely change their life over a month, week, or even overnight. Some people have a lot of fears revolving around change, and some people may have a sense of urgency around the subject, because of a certain upcoming event with a specific date.

Advice on Breaking the Old Habits

Breaking your old habits is going to be the hardest thing, but you have to retrain your brain. For a sweet tooth, there are many things you can try; for instance, look at the recipe in this book for a butterscotch tart or the trail mix bars. Make yourself a satisfying sweet smoothie or have a handful of berries. A teaspoon of organic honey is also quite satisfying to stop the sweet tooth. But if you really must have a sweet, wine, etc., then look for plant-based-friendly alternatives. Once again, train yourself to reach for a healthier alternative to the food you are craving.

Tips and Tricks To start

Getting started with a new diet can be difficult because you are changing some of your habits and may not be fully aware of exactly what to do at first. What follows is an overview of what eating plant-based involves and will help you get started with the diet by making it simple and clear what you are supposed to do:

1. Eat more vegetables - This is how you build your plate on a Plant-based diet. Be sure to eat as many vegetables as possible while avoiding starchy carbs like potatoes, corn, and wheat products like breads, pastas, or rice.
2. Eat more fruits - Having fruit as part of your diet is necessary to keep up a healthy lifestyle. A good tip is to stick with natural fruits like bananas, apples, oranges, and peaches. Avoid having too much fruit in one day and limit it to just 1 or 2 pieces of fruit at the most during the day. It is also wise to snack on nuts and seeds for a quick source of energy, along with the additional vitamins they offer.
3. Have lots of beans - Natural sources of protein are found in beans. Soybeans should not be a staple in one's diet since they are very high in sodium content; however, a small percentage can be consumed safely for strengthening bones and keeping healthy blood pressure levels at bay. Be sure to eat lots of beans. There are many ways to cook them for variety.
4. Eat more nuts - Nuts and seeds are wonderful sources of protein and calcium. Be sure to include nuts and seeds in your daily diet as a source of energy, vitamins, and minerals. Limit the quantity you consume since consuming more than the recommended amount is not healthy.
5. Eat more whole grains - Whole grains are a good source of fiber and can be a great alternative to sugar, fats, or other carbohydrates. Try eating whole grain cereals or oatmeal for breakfast, replacing the traditional breakfast cereal that is not good for you.
6. Drink lots of water - Water is a must to keep up a healthy lifestyle. A human being should take in half their body weight in ounces of water each day. Sweating from exercise or hot weather will dehydrate you, and that is why it is important to drink plenty of water. One glass of water can help you stay away from unhealthy drinks like soda.

7. Have a healthy breakfast - A healthy breakfast contains fruit, whole grains, and protein. This will provide you with energy throughout the day without having to rely on sugary snacks to stay alert. Snacking increases hunger and may make you crave more unhealthy food later in the day.
8. Limit your sugar intake - Sugar should not be a part of your diet at all if possible. If it is not possible to eliminate sugar completely, try to limit it as much as possible by using artificial sweeteners and finding healthier options like fruit juice or dried fruits instead of candy bars or cookies.

Practical Advice For Beginners

When you start a new diet, you might find yourself a little bit unprepared because maybe cooking has never been your greatest passion, and now you would need some practical advice on how to best deal with your new diet.

Best Basic Ingredients for Easy Start

With a little planning, a plant-based diet can be fairly simple and healthy. To show you that cooking on a tight budget is possible with just a few ingredients, here are some of our favorite recipes. If you would like help in planning your diet, you can read the article in the ABA Journal Magazine. Another resource is Vegetarian Options: A Guide to the New Choices.
1. Artichokes: Artichokes can be used in a variety of dishes and go well with other foods such as lentils, legumes and beans, tofu and tempeh, and grains such as quinoa or millet. Cut six artichokes in half so that they sit flat on one of the cut ends. Fill each artichoke with 1/2 cup pot pie filling (A Recipe for Crock-Pot Pies).
2. Cabbage: Cabbage is a great base for stewing or in stir-fries and casseroles. The head should be cut into pieces and then shredded or chopped.
3. Carrots: Carrots are crunchy and sweet, so they make a delicious side dish, whether steamed, roasted, or baked.
4. Corn: There are several ways to cook corn on the cob. If you have a pressure cooker, you may want to try the recipe for Pressure Cooker Corn on the Cob. It is very fast, and it also has some nutritional benefits. If you do not have a pressure cooker or prefer not to use one, you can boil or steam fresh corn on the cob and then serve with your favorite butter.
5. Green Beans: Boil fresh green beans until they are tender; toss them with vegetable oil and seasonings such as thyme and basil. These green beans are delicious when eaten hot or cold.
   5a. Canned beans - this is one of those items that I would say you should always have on hand in your pantry. Just make sure they don't have added salt, sugar or preservatives (look for BPA-free cans).
6. Pasta: Whole wheat pasta is a great base for lots of different dishes. I'd recommend having a few boxes in your pantry because you'll find all sorts of ways to use it - even just tossing it with olive oil and some salt & pepper will make it taste good!

Tips to Improve Your Transition to the Plant-Based Diet

The first real advice may seem trivial, but here it is: focus on plant-based foods, not non-plant-based foods. This is especially true for soy and other protein sources. If it's not possible to find plant-based, soy, or other alternative protein sources (such as tofu, tempeh, seitan, or a nut product like nuts and seeds), then focus on those items that are most frequently found in a varied plant-based diet. That is until you've found your best places to buy the right plant-based products. When you find them and get used to going there all the time, everything will be much more automatic and easy. Finding the right grocery stores will make your life extremely easier. Look for foods that have more of a taste profile that will help you transition easier. For example, if you're just starting out with the idea of going dairy-free, then switch to white rice or quinoa, or couscous for your main carbohydrates. There's a lower chance that you will miss the butter or cheese on your pasta or in your rice when you're not used to them. You'll come to appreciate the change of taste and texture once you've started to learn how to cook. A wide variety of plant-based meals. If going meat-free is what's holding you back, start by trying some meat substitutes. Several products substitute meat in cooking. These include textured vegetable protein and even soya. If you would like a nutritionally dense protein source, try adding nuts and seeds into your diet instead of relying on the grain products listed above. Just as you would approach any other skill, take the time to learn new ways of doing things. It's tempting to try to learn how to cook plant-based meals from a plant-based diet cookbook. However, if you're just cutting out all meat and sticking with grains and vegetables, then you'll likely find yourself missing a variety of foods that you once ate regularly. You'll want to include recipes that help bring in some old favorites in more plant-based forms.

Best Cooking Methods Against Others

Slow cooker: A slow cooker, or crock pot, is a nice kitchen appliance. It'll heat your food to a simmering temperature over time, allowing the flavors of meat and vegetables to mix without burning or sticking to the bottom of the pot. The main disadvantage of the slow cooker is that food usually does not consume calories, so if you want to lose weight, it may not be the best choice. Otherwise, it's a great tool to use for long-term cooking! Boiling: Boiling is another great way to cook food. The big difference between boiling and slow cooking is that during boiling food tends to cook in one step. With slow cooking, all the water will evaporate first, then the meat and veggies get cooked together later.

The main advantage of boiling is that your food cooks faster and better ensures that most of the water has evaporated before you start adding more ingredients. The main disadvantage is that the food flavors don't mix as well, so it's not a great choice for long-term cooking.

Best Cookware To Use

Microwave ovens can sometimes produce a chemical called diacetyl. This chemical may be harmful if your food is exposed to it for too long. It is best to cook plant-based meals quickly in order to avoid exposure to this chemical. If you're still concerned about how your foods are cooked, you might want to look into ceramic cookware. These cookwares are not only of high quality, but they do not produce any additional chemicals while cooking ingredients, and they are also the best for storage.

The next essential thing to consider is your cookware's material. There are many different materials that you can choose from, with ceramic cookware being one of the most popular choices. Foods usually don't stick well in these types of cookware's and they are also easy to clean.

On the other hand, we have cast iron pots and pans, which are another great option for those who follow a plant-based diet. In addition to being durable, they tend to heat up easily and evenly, making them perfect for sautéing your ingredients. Cast iron pots and pans can also be used for a long time, unlike their ceramic or glass counterparts, which break easily if dropped.

You will also find that there are other cookware's made from materials like stainless steel and aluminum. These two materials are great for preparing plant-based meals because they don't require you to add oil to keep your ingredients from sticking. These are also easy to clean and none of them have the potential to melt or warp while cooking. That said, each type of cookware has its own advantages and disadvantages, and you should consider their advantages and disadvantages before deciding which cookware is best for you. Surface non-stick cookware tends to leach harmful chemicals into the food if used for too long, but it also makes cooking easier.

The Ideal Plant-Based Kitchen

To complement your plant-based diet you are going to need a few basic tools for your kitchen as well.

Blender – a lot of the food needs to be puréed or turned into a smoothie. A blender with at least three-speed settings is the best option.

Food processor – a good food processor with a paddle extension, as well as other blending accessories, is a good choice. It should have at least three-speed settings as well as a pulse mode. If you can, get a food processor that has a blender jug - two appliances in one!

Salad bowls – you should have at least two different size salad bowls and some smaller serving dishes to serve the salad into.

Mixing bowls – large, medium, and small mixing bowls are essential for every kitchen, especially when you are making your own homemade sauces.

Whisk – a good normal-sized whisk is needed in every kitchen. They are magic utensils that can fluff egg substitutes to a peak and get the lumps out of any gravy or sauce.

Skillets – large and medium-sized non-stick skillets are best; make sure they have lids.

Saucepans – at least three different sized saucepans, from small to large, with lids.

Cheese grater – a cheese grater or two with normal grating and fine grating sides.

Vegetable peeler – a good sharp potato peeler or two is a must for any kitchen.

Julienne peeler – a julienne peeler is handy to have when working with fresh vegetables or soups.

Wooden spoon – no kitchen is complete without a handy wooden spoon. A few different sizes are an even better option for the kitchen. Better yet, get a bamboo spoon, as it's more sustainable than wood, typically.

Sharp cutting knives – a block of cutting knives with smooth and serrated edges of all shapes and sizes is always needed.

Chopping boards – you need a few shapes and sizes of chopping boards for the cutting of different foods. Look for a bamboo version.

Baking pans and sheets – you will need a few different-sized baking sheets, bread pans, pie dishes, cake tins, and roasting dishes.

Airtight resealable containers – you will need to invest in a few different shapes and sizes of airtight resealable containers that can be used in the fridge and freezer as well as the cupboard. Try getting a few bottles as well to store sauces and trail mix in.

- Serving utensils
- Sieve
- Colander

Amanda Kale

CHAPTER 9:
What To Eat And What To Avoid

Suggested to Eat
Fruits

Fresh or frozen fruits are a main component of a plant-based diet. There are plenty of options, but some provide a more powerful nutritional punch. When shopping for fruit, go to your local farmer's market first. These will often yield the highest nutritional value. At the grocery store, look for organic fruits as these should not be treated with harsh and dangerous chemicals. You want to have a variety of fruits on hand, but you also want to know which fruits are seasonal so you can be sure to have a nice mixture all year round. Below you can find a list of fruits that can usually be found throughout the year, as well as the best fruits to look for according to the season.

Easily found all year:

- Apples
- Bananas
- Lemon
- Papaya
- Coconut
- Spring fruits
- Apricots
- Mango
- Strawberries
- Honeydew
- Pineapple
- Summer fruits
- Blackberries
- Blueberries
- Raspberries
- Peaches
- Plums
- Nectarines
- Watermelon
- Cantaloupe
- Fall fruits
- Grapes
- Guava
- Kiwis
- Cranberries
- Pears
- Pomegranate
- Figs
- Passion fruit
- Winter fruits
- Grapefruit
- Navel oranges
- Passion fruit

Vegetables

Most vegetables you can find throughout the year, but some peak during different seasons. The season they are harvested in may have different flavors, such as carrots. Carrots can be found all year round, but you will find that they are sweetest in the colder winter months. Just as with your fruits, you want to buy vegetables locally or at least organic at the grocery store. While there are many vegetables listed, this is not a full or complete list. All vegetables should be included in the plant-based diet. One last thing to keep in mind is that many vegetables which peak in one season are often plentiful in the following season as well.

- Carrots
- Bell peppers (red, green, yellow, and orange)
- Kale
- Celery
- Cremini, shiitake, portobello, and button mushrooms
- Onions
- Scallions
- Shallots
- Spinach
- Arugula
- Lettuce
- Spring Veggies
- Leeks
- Radish
- Asparagus
- Rhubarb
- Green Beans
- Summer veggies
- Cucumber
- Zucchini
- Green beans
- Eggplant
- Okra
- Fall veggies
- Broccoli
- Fennel
- Pumpkin
- Butternut squash
- Swiss chard
- Brussels sprouts
- Acorn squash
- Yams
- Sweet Potatoes
- Corn
- Winter veggies
- Bok Choy
- Broccoli rabe
- Cabbage
- Turnips

Whole Grains
The grains you include in your plant-based diet should be 100% whole grains. When shopping for bread products and pasta, you can find a variety of whole-grain options.
Whole-grain tends to be the most popular and easiest to find in grocery stores. Always check the labels before you buy, be sure it states 100% whole wheat or that the grain it is claiming to be is at the top of the ingredient list.

- Whole grain barley
- Millet
- Quinoa
- Steel-cut oats
- Brown rice
- Bulgar
- Red rice
- Black rice
- Wild rice
- Buckwheat
- Sorghum
- Amaranth
- Corn

Healthy Fats
There are good and bad fats, but many people often want to avoid eating when they hear the word "fat". Healthy fats form in several plant-based sources that can provide you with high doses of vitamins, fiber, calcium, omega-3 fatty acids, and more. Some of the most beneficial plant-based fats include:

- Avocado
- Nuts
- Seeds
- Banana

Legumes
Legumes refer to the wide selection of beans. While dried beans are ideal, canned beans can help cut back on cooking time and add convenience. When using canned beans, you want to look at the salt content and purchase those that have the least added salt. It is also important to rinse the canned beans to remove excess salt and impurities before cooking with them. Beans are a versatile ingredient and often used as a source of protein for plant-based diets. You will often find recipes that use beans as a substitute for meat products such as burgers, meatloaf, and meatballs. Legumes include:

- Black beans
- Black-eyed peas
- Kidney beans
- Navy beans
- Soybeans
- Chickpeas
- Lentils
- Lima beans
- Pinto beans
- Peas
- Green beans
- Adzuki beans

Seeds and Nuts
Nuts and seeds are healthy fats that can be added to several recipes for extra crunch and flavor. Many nuts and provide you with omega-3 fatty acids, fiber and are a good source of fiber. Nuts also have a high versatility. They can be made into nut butters or even pureed into cheese or cream sauce.

- Walnuts
- Almonds
- Pumpkin seeds
- Brazilian nuts
- Cashews
- Chia seeds
- Flax seeds

Plant-Based Milks
When it comes to dairy substitutes, there is quite a selection to choose from. When choosing plant-based milk, ensure it is non-GMO or organic and unsweetened. Read the label and avoid using sugar-containing products such as sucrose, carrageenan, and glyphosate. Plant-based milks are also just as easy to make at home.
The process is fairly simple and just requires soaking, draining, blending, and straining. Some plant-based milk options include:

- Almond milk
- Cashew milk
- Soy milk
- Oat milk - Coconut milk

Plant-Based Proteins
There are several ways you can get a significant amount of protein into your diet, even when you eliminate or reduce the consumption of animal meat. These plant-based protein sources are some of the best alternatives for anyone switching to a plant-based diet.

- Tofu (silken, soft, and firm)
- Tempeh
- Soybeans

- Chickpeas
- Lentils
- Legumes

Spices and Herbs

Spices and herbs are a great way to add flavor and keep your plant-based meals interesting and unique. These can be found in the whole form and ground up for use, dried or fresh. Some spices and herbs to consider stocking up on include:

- Nutritional yeast
- Turmeric
- Cumin
- Oregano
- Basil
- Rosemary
- Thyme
- Paprika
- Tarragon
- Peppercorn
- Red pepper flake
- Bay leaf

Condiments

There are plenty of sauces and spreads you can include in or with your plant-based meals for a boost in flavor. As with any other products from the stores, check the labels and carefully read over the ingredients list. Some of the condiments on this list can include animal product ingredients like anchovy or casein.

- Amino acids
- Soy sauce
- Worcestershire sauce
- Salsa
- Mustard (dijon, honey, and other varieties)
- Vinegar (balsamic, apple cider, red wine)
- Relish
- Tahini

We will explore in-depth the reasons why you should cut these foods out of your diet and how you can spot unhealthy ingredients, such as added sugars and artificial sweeteners on food labels.

Foods to Avoid

There are five main food categories you will slowly want to wean out of your diet to reap the full benefits of a plant-based diet.

The following categories offer little value to your health and also harm the environment.

Refined Grains

Refined grains make up a majority of most people's diets. These tend to mainly include:

- White bread
- White flour
- White pasta
- White rice

They are referred to as 'refined' because they go through a stripping process where the fiber and most nutrients are taken out of their natural forms to increase their shelf life. This leaves you with a food product that lacks nutrients yet is loaded with calories.

These types of grains have been shown to increase the risk of heart disease, diabetes, and obesity.

Added Sugar

Sugar is frequently hidden in all types of food. Many food labels list some sugar sources to make it seem as though the product doesn't include as much sugar as it actually does. Since labels list ingredients from greatest to least, in quantity, you will often discover two or three sugar sources such as:

- Fructose
- Glucose
- Sucrose
- Cane sugar
- Beet sugar
- Corn syrup
- Sorghum syrup

Even though you may not see sugar clearly labeled, as is the case with many products claiming to be healthy for you, these hidden sugars can add up when combined. Added sugars can affect your health in several ways, from tooth decay to an increased risk of heart disease. Since there are no health benefits to consuming added sugar, the plant-based diet excludes these items and can help you reduce your sugar cravings by supplying you with natural sugars found in many fruits. Foods you should start to eliminate from your diet include:

- Sodas
- Fruit juices
- Table sugar
- Sugar cereals
- Candies
- Pastries
- Cakes
- Cookies

Artificial Sweeteners

Artificial sweeteners are believed to be a healthier alternative to processed sugar, but that is up for debate. This is why many individuals switch from regular sodas to diet sodas. Artificial sweeteners can trick the brain into thinking that the body is consuming sugar, which triggers the glycemic response, spiking up insulin and glucose levels. When this occurs too frequently without glucose actually being produced, which is the case when you consume artificial sweeteners, your body can develop insulin resistance which can result in developing type 2 Diabetes. Aside from this major health concern, artificial sweeteners can also increase your risk of high blood pressure, obesity, heart disease, and stroke, among others.

A plant-based diet excludes all types of artificial sweeteners such as:

- Splenda
- Sweet 'N' Low
- Equal
- NutraSweet
- Advantame

On food labels, these types of artificial sweeteners can be listed under the names of:

- Aspartame
- Acesulfame potassium
- Saccharin
- Sucralose
- Neotame

Packaged Foods

Packaged foods are often loaded with sugars, unhealthy fats, artificial ingredients, and refined carbohydrates. These ingredients on their own have serious negative health effects and when combined can cause a great deal of damage from prolonged consumption. Many packaged foods are created to increase cravings which leads to overconsumption. In addition, most have little to no nutritional value or fiber. These products can be digested quickly in the body because of their lack of fiber content, and only minimal energy is needed to process them. This is why you will often feel hungrier shortly after eating packaged foods. There is nothing about packaged foods that aligns with a plant-based diet and therefore should be avoided. Packaged foods include:

- Chips
- Frozen meals
- Crackers
- Breakfast bars
- Snack foods
- Instant meals or microwaveable meals.

Processed Foods

Processed foods include several items that have been stripped of the natural nutrients they should have.

This is the case with many vegetable oils and refined flours. Although most oils are derived from vegetable sources, it is the directions used to extract these oils that make them unhealthy. The extraction directions tend to remove the nutrients from the oil, so all that is left is fat, which contains a significant number of calories with few nutritional benefits. Plant-based oils such as coconut oil, extra virgin olive oil, or sunflower oil are said to be healthier choices for cooking. While they may provide some benefits, it doesn't mean you should include them in your diet every day.

CHAPTER 10:
Shopping List with the Best Substitute

Here are a few cupboard essentials you will need to start with:

Oils, Fats, and Spreads Substitutes
- Organic coconut oil
- Tahini
- Organic unsweetened applesauce
- Egg white substitute
- Coconut butter (or another nut butter)
- PAM vegan cooking spray

Fruits, Berries, Vegetables, and Nuts
- Frozen mixed berries (or buy them individually or fresh)
- Fresh or frozen blueberries
- Fresh or frozen strawberries
- Fresh or frozen pomegranate seeds
- Chia seeds
- Sunflower seeds
- Flax seeds
- Pumpkin seeds
- Nuts (if you can eat them, must raw and unsalted)
- Fresh fruit of your choice, such as peaches, plums, watermelon, kiwi, mangoes, oranges, lemons, and limes
- Mixed vegetables of your choices fresh or organically frozen
- Potatoes (yellow, purple, or red - avoid Russets for high sugar content)
- Sweet potatoes
- Tomatoes
- Cherry tomatoes
- White onions
- Red onions
- Spring onions
- Scallops
- Carrots
- Avocados
- Celery
- Mixed salad leaves
- Baby spinach
- Cabbage or Choi
- Aubergine/eggplant
- Coconut
- Jackfruit
- Fresh chilies
- Mushrooms
- Basil
- Thyme
- Dill
- Mint
- Rocket
- Garlic

Milk/Dairy Substitutes
- Plant-based "milk" such as coconut milk, almond milk, hemp milk, rice milk, soy milk, etc. Make sure it is organic and non-sweetened
- Plant-based cream, non-sweetened and low fat
- Plant-based yogurt, non-sweetened and low fat

Meat Substitutes
- Tofu
- Tempeh
- Mock meats (limit these, as they can be highly processed and high in sodium and sugars)

Other
- Coconut sugar
- Organic brown sugar
- Chickpeas (unsalted)
- Full mineral salt, like Himalayan Pink
- Ground black pepper
- Chili powder
- Turmeric powder
- Mixed herbs
- Italian seasoning
- Cajun spice
- Curry powder
- Cayenne pepper
- Ground cinnamon
- Ground ginger
- Garlic powder
- Organic low sodium vegetable broth

- Organic balsamic vinegar
- Organic white grape vinegar

Shopping on a Budget

The plant-based diet is a lot cheaper than when you are eating meat and other animal projects. But buying organic and looking for certain products can become costly when you are on a budget.

Buy your fresh produce from fresh produce markets, and don't go for big name brands that cost a fortune. There are lesser name brands that are just as good. Try buying from local farmers and smaller mom-and-pop type stores.

Don't try to buy everything all at once; set a budget and buy certain things two to three at a time when it comes to canned goods, condiments, sauces, and frozen goods. Make fresh produce your priority and those processed/packaged goods your second priority.

CHAPTER 11:
21-Days Meal Plan

Week 1

	Monday	Tuesday	Wednesday	Thursday	Friday	Saturday	Sunday
Breakfast	Max Power Smoothie	Chai Chia Smoothie	Tropi-Kale Breeze	Hydration Station	Mango Madness	Chocolate P.B. Smoothie	Pink Panther Smoothie
Lunch	Black Bean Lentil Salad	Cabbage Salad with Seitan	Chickpeas Avocado Salad	Cold Peanut Noodle Salad	Butternut Squash Black Rice Bean Salad	Arugula Beans Salad	Spring Salad
Dinner	Cannellini Pesto Spaghetti	Spicy Eggplant Penne	Creamed Kimchi Pasta	Roasted Ragu with Whole Wheat Linguine	Penne with Swiss Chard and Olives	Indonesia Green Noodle Salad	Noodles with Red Lentil Curry
Dessert	Zesty orange-cranberry energy bites	Chocolate and walnut farfalle	Almond-date energy bites	Pumpkin Pie Cups (Pressure Cooker)	Granola-stuffed baked apples	Better pecan bars	Chocolate-almond bars

Amanda Kale

Week 2

	Monday	Tuesday	Wednesday	Thursday	Friday	Saturday	Sunday
Breakfast	Banana Nut Smoothie	Overnight Oats On the Go	Oatmeal Breakfast Cookies	Sunshine Muffins	Applesauce Crumble Muffins	Baked Banana French Toast with Raspberry Syrup	Cinnamon Apple Toast
Lunch	Tomato Lentil Salad	White Bean & Tomato Salad	Avocado & White Bean Salad	Brussels Sprouts Salad	Wedge Salad	Chef Salad	Radish Avocado Salad
Dinner	Tomato and Black Bean Rotini	Lemony Broccoli Penne	Singapore Rice Noodles	Ponzu Pea Rice Noodle Salad	Thai Tofu Noodles	Sesame Soba Noodles with Vegetables	Lemon Bow Tie Pasta
Dessert	Coconut and almond truffles	Pecan and date-stuffed roasted pears	Lime-macerated mangos	Fudgy brownies (pressure cooker)	Chocolate-banana fudge	Chocolate–almond butter truffles	Chocolate macaroons

Week 3

	Monday	Tuesday	Wednesday	Thursday	Friday	Saturday	Sunday
Breakfast	Muesli and Berries Bowl	Chocolate Quinoa Breakfast Bowl	Fruit Salad with Zesty Citrus Couscous	Fruity Granola	Chickpea Scramble	Roasted Veg with Creamy Avocado Dip	Spinach Artichoke Quiche
Lunch	Mix Grain Salad	Quinoa and Chickpea Salad	Rice and Tofu Salad	Kidney Bean and Pomegranate Salad	Corn and Bean Salad	Cherry Tomato Couscous Salad	Spicy Watermelon Tomato Salad
Dinner	Shiitake and Bean Sprout Ramen	Spinach Rotelle Provençale	Sumptuous Shiitake Udon Noodles	Tomato and Artichoke Rigatoni	Tomato Spaghetti	Noodle Salad with Spinach	Garlic & White Wine Pasta
Dessert	Chocolate pudding	Avocado pudding	Almond butter brownies	Raspberry chia pudding	Chocolate fudge	Quick chocó brownie	Cinnamon Coconut Chips

CHAPTER 12:
Basics

1. Mango Achar From India
Preparation time: 5 minutes
Cooking time: 8 minutes
Servings: 5
Ingredients:
- 5-6 small or medium-sized raw mangoes
- 1 to 2 tbsp. split mustard seeds
- 1.5 tbsp. split fenugreek seeds
- 1.5 tbsp. nigella seeds
- 2 tbsp. fennel seed whole or coarsely ground
- 1.5 to 2 tbsp. red chili powder
- 1 or 1.5 tbsp. turmeric
- Salt, as needed
- Mustard oil, as needed

Directions:
Wash and dry the mangoes, and then proceed to cut them while discarding the seeds. Add all the spice mixtures to the mango pieces and mix to coat evenly. Now allow this mixture to remain in an air-tight jar for about 4 days and pour in some oil to the brim as a preservative. Store this same bottle in a cool place and dry place before you dig into it!
Per serving: Calories: 60Kcal; Fat: 3.22g; Carbs: 6.85g; Fiber: 3.5g; Protein: 2.84g

2. Tartar Sauce
Preparation time: 3 minutes
Cooking time: 3 minutes
Servings: 4
Ingredients:
- 2 egg yolks
- 250ml groundnut oil
- 250ml olive oil
- 1 tsp. Dijon mustard
- juice of ½ a lemon
- 1 tbsp. chopped tarragon
- 1 tbsp. chopped gherkins
- 2 tbsp. chopped parsley
- 1 tbsp. rinsed capers

Directions:
Start by preparing a mayonnaise of the 2 egg yolks, Dijon mustard, salt, and pepper. Slowly pour in the groundnut oil and olive oil in a steady stream and whisk. Pour in the lemon juice followed by tarragon, gherkins, capers, and parsley. Check for adequate seasoning at this point. Chill and serve.
Per serving: Calories: 114Kcal; Fat: 6.72g; Carbs: 1.24g; Fiber: 0.2g; Protein: 11.68g

3. Cheese Sauce
Preparation time: 5 minutes
Cooking time: 5 minutes **Servings:** 4-6
Ingredients:
- 1 cup Monterey jack cheese or 1 cup asadero cheese or 1 cup Chihuahua cheese, shredded fine
- 1/4 cup cream or half-and-half
- 2 tablespoons onions, chopped fine
- 4 ounces green chilies
- 1/2 teaspoon salt
- 2 teaspoons cumin powder
- 1 tablespoon fresh cilantro, chopped fine (optional)
- 1 Serrano pepper, chopped fine (optional)

Directions:
Place all the ingredients in a double boiler and heat it over a medium flame. Since it is on a slow flame, you will need to stir it only occasionally
Per serving: Calories: 96Kcal; Fat: 6.72g; Carbs: 1.24g; Fiber: 0.2g; Protein: 5.96g

4. Scotch Bonnet Pepper Sauce
Preparation time: 6 minutes
Cooking time: 6 minutes **Servings:** 4
Ingredients:
- Scotch Bonnet Hot Peppers (about 4-6 cups chopped)
- 6 cloves garlic
- 1/2 cup chopped cilantro
- 1 teaspoon sea salt
- 1 cup white vinegar

Directions:
Wash and trim the peppers and roughly chop them up. If you wish for the sauce to be fiery, leave the seeds in, otherwise, de-seed the peppers before using. Roughly chop up the garlic and cilantro as well. If using a mill to make the sauce, then adjust the settings accordingly. This is a traditional method to make the sauce. Add the garlic and cilantro slowly as you run the mill. If not, put all the ingredients in a food processor and pulse it roughly.
Per serving: Calories: 24Kcal; Fat: 0.06g; Carbs: 3.18g; Fiber: 0.3g; Protein: 0.55g

5. Sambal Sauce
Preparation time: 10 minutes
Cooking time: 10 minutes **Servings:** 8
Ingredients:
- 2 pounds dried red or fresh jalapeños, stemmed and chopped very roughly
- 10 fresh Thai chilies, or 1 tablespoon red pepper flakes

- 1 cup minced garlic
- 1/4 cup canola oil
- 2 cups rice wine vinegar
- 1 teaspoon sugar
- 2 teaspoons salt

Directions:
Take a medium pan and mix in the jalapenos, garlic, oil, and Thai chilies and cook on low heat until the ingredients are mixed in thoroughly. Once the mixture is reduced in half, slowly add the vinegar and cook it again on a slow flame. Now take it off the heat and add the salt and sugar, then cool to room temperature. Move this mixture to a food processor, and pulse to an accepted texture. Store in the fridge in a jar till further use.
Per serving: Calories: 578Kcal; Fat: 27.95g; Carbs: 86.16g; Fiber: 11.1g; Protein: 3.19g

6. Louisiana Hot Sauce
Preparation time: 8 minutes
Cooking time: 5 minutes **Servings:** 8
Ingredients:
- 1-1/4 lb. fresh red chilies, such as cayenne, Tabasco, or Serrano
- 1 tsp. finely chopped fresh basil
- 4 medium garlic cloves, halved and peeled
- Kosher salt and freshly ground black pepper
- 1/4 tsp. ground celery seeds
- 1 cup white vinegar
- 1 tsp. finely chopped fresh oregano

Directions:
Place the chilies on a pan in an oven and broil for about five minutes on each side before flipping them over. Bring them out and let them cool down to room temperature. Now skin the chilies and place them along with the seeds in a food processor. Add to this the oregano, basil, garlic, celery seeds, salt, and pepper and run the food processor. Pour the vinegar in a steady stream through the tube and process until the consistency is a smooth mixture. Your sauce is ready to be served and stored in bottles.
Per serving: Calories: 93Kcal; Fat: 5.23g; Carbs: 10.01g; Fiber: 2g; Protein: 1.98g

7. Harissa Sauce
Preparation time: 9 minutes
Cooking time: 7 minutes
Servings: 7
Ingredients:
- 4 ounces dried chilies of your choice (cayenne, ancho, chili de arbor or guajillo)
- 3 to 4 garlic cloves, peeled
- 1 teaspoon cumin seeds
- 1 teaspoon coriander seeds
- 1 teaspoon caraway seeds
- 2 tablespoons extra virgin olive oil, plus more for storing
- 1 teaspoon kosher salt, or to taste

Directions:
To start with, you need to soften the chilies by immersing them in hot water for about 30 minutes. Meanwhile, roast the caraway, cumin, and coriander seeds in a dry pan on low heat until they let out an aromatic fragrance. Then grind them into a dry powder. Drain the soaked chilies, de-seed and de-stem them and make a paste of it along with garlic, salt, the roasted spices in a food processor, allowing a steady drizzle of olive oil into the jar.
Once you achieve your desired texture, turn off the processor and adjust the seasoning accordingly Serve immediately or store in a jar with additional olive oil.
Per serving: Calories: 93Kcal; Fat: 5.23g; Carbs: 10.01g; Fiber: 2g; Protein: 1.98g

8. Piri Sauce
Preparation time: 6 minutes
Cooking time: 4 minutes **Servings:** 4
Ingredients:
- 4 to 8 fresh hot chilies, depending on the heat
- Juice of 1 lemon
- 2 garlic cloves, minced
- 1/2 to 1 cup extra-virgin olive oil, depending on how thin you want it
- Pinch of salt

Directions:
Roughly chop up the peppers by discarding the stems, and place them in the food processor along with garlic, salt, lemon juice, and oil, and puree till your desired consistency. Your sauce is now ready to be served and also stored in an air-tight jar for at least a week in the fridge.
Per serving: Calories: 110Kcal; Fat: 11.64g; Carbs: 1.32g; Fiber: 0.1g; Protein: 0.24g

9. Barbeque Sauce
Preparation time: 5 minutes
Cooking time: 5 minutes **Servings:** 8
Ingredients:
- 2 cups chopped onions
- 1 cup ketchup
- 1 cup Worcestershire sauce
- 1 cup strong black coffee
- 1/2 cup cider vinegar
- 1/2 cup brown sugar
- 1/4 cup hot chili peppers, minced
- 6 cloves garlic, minced
- 3 tablespoons chili powder
- 2 teaspoons salt

Directions:
Place all of the above ingredients in a blender simmer for about half an hour. After a while, it will release a great flavor. Turn off the heat and let it cool down, after which you can puree it with the mixer.
Per serving: Calories: 138Kcal; Fat: 0.55g; Carbs: 33.75g; Fiber: 1.7g; Protein: 1.3g

10. Roasted Veggies In Lemon Sauce

Preparation time: 15 minutes
Cooking time: 20 minutes **Servings:** 5
Ingredients:

- 2 cloves garlic, sliced
- 1 ½ cups broccoli florets
- 1 ½ cups cauliflower florets
- 1 tablespoon olive oil - Salt to taste
- 1 teaspoon dried oregano, crushed
- ¾ cup zucchini, diced
- ¾ cup red bell pepper, diced
- 2 teaspoons lemon zest

Directions:
Preheat your oven to 425 degrees F. In a baking pan, add the garlic, broccoli, and cauliflower. Toss in oil and season with salt and oregano. Roast in the oven for 10 minutes.
Add the zucchini and bell pepper to the pan.
Stir well. Roast for another 10 minutes.
Sprinkle lemon zest on top before serving.
Transfer to a food container and reheat before serving.
Per serving: Calories: 52Kcal; Fat: 3g; Carbs: 5g; Fiber: 2g; Protein: 2g

11. Hemp Falafel With Tahini Sauce

Preparation time: 10 minutes
Cooking time: 10 minutes **Servings:** 6
Ingredients:

- 80g raw hemp hearts
- 4g chopped cilantro
- 4g chopped basil
- 2 cloves garlic, minced
- 2g ground cumin seeds
- 3g chili powder
- 14g flax meal + 30ml filtered water
- Sea salt and pepper, to taste
- Avocado or coconut oil, to fry

Sauce:

- 115g tahini
- 60ml fresh lime juice
- 115ml filtered water
- 30ml extra-virgin olive oil
- Sea salt, to taste
- A good pinch ground cumin seeds

Directions:
Mix flax with filtered water in a small bowl.
Place aside for 10 minutes. In the meantime, combine raw hemp hearts, cilantro, basil, garlic, cumin, chili, and seasonings in a food processor.
Process until it just comes together. Add the flax seeds mixture and process until finely blended and uniform. Heat approximately 2 tablespoons of avocado oil in a skillet. Shape 1 tablespoon mixture into balls and fry for 3-4 minutes or until deep golden brown. Remove from the skillet and place on a plate lined with paper towels. Make the sauce; combine all ingredients in a food blender. Blend until smooth and creamy. Serve falafel with fresh lettuce salad and tahini sauce.
Per serving: Calories: 347Kcal; Fat: 29.9g; Carbs: 7.2g; Fiber: 4.3g; Protein: 13.8g;

12. Red Applesauce and Beet

Preparation time: 5 minutes
Cooking time: 10 minutes **Servings:** 6
Ingredient

- 2 cups unpeeled apple, diced or grated
- 1 cup boneless cherries or mixed berries
- 1 cup unpeeled grated beets
- 1 tablespoon date paste
- ½ teaspoon cinnamon
- 2 tablespoons of water

Directions:
Place all the ingredients in a saucepan. Take to a boil and cook until apples and beets have softened for 10-15 minutes. Crush with a potato masher or process in a food processor for a smoother consistency. Serve alone or use it to decorate Halloween treats.
Per serving: Calories: 247Kcal; Fat: 26.3g; Carbs: 7g; Fiber: 3g; Protein: 13.8g

13. Tomatillo Green Sauce

Preparation time: 5 minutes
Cooking time: 10 minutes **Servings:** 6
Ingredients:

- 8 small tomatillos (approximately 1 pound or 453 grams)
- ½ white onion, cut in half
- 1½ teaspoon ground garlic (approximately 3 small teeth)
- 1 jalapeño, cut in half, and seeded
- 1/3 cup full of chopped cilantro
- 1 can (4 ounces or 113 grams) of chopped soft green chiles

Optional Additions

- ½ tablespoon ground cumin
- Salt and pepper to taste
- Jalapeño Seeds (to add spicily)

Directions:
Preheat the grill. Cover a large baking sheet with foil.
Prepare the tomatillos: remove their lanterns, wash them, and cut them in half. Place the tomatillos and onion upside down on the prepared baking sheet. Add the garlic and jalapeño to the tray. Roast for five to seven minutes or until everything is uniformly charred. In a blender or food processor, mix the charred ingredients, cilantro, and chills until the sauce is smooth.
Per serving: Calories: 223Kcal; Fat: 25g; Carbs: 8g; Fiber: 6g; Protein: 14g

14. Cranberry and Orange Sauce

Preparation time: 15 minutes
Cooking time: 5 minutes **Servings:** 4
Ingredients:

- Zest and juice of an orange
- ½ cup maple syrup
- 1 bag (12 oz - 340 g) of fresh red cranberries
- 1 teaspoon cinnamon

Directions:
In a small saucepan, add all the ingredients and let them boil. Reduce the temperature and simmer for 15 minutes or until the blueberries burst and the sauce begins to thicken. Transfer it to a bowl and refrigerate until it cools down, at least for an hour.
Per serving: Calories: 240Kcal; Fat: 15g; Carbs: 4g Fiber: 10g Protein: 18g

15. Thick Mushroom Sauce
Preparation time: 15 minutes
Cooking time: 5 minutes **Servings:** 4
Ingredients:
- 1 12 oz. (340 g) package of tender white or Portobello mushrooms
- 1 to 2 tablespoons low sodium soy sauce (use one without wheat if you are gluten sensitive)
- 2 tablespoons whole-grain wheat flour (use gluten-free flour if you are gluten sensitive) - 1 to 2 cups of vegetable stock
- Salt or black pepper, to taste (optional)

Directions:
Clean and cut the mushrooms, then skip them in water until they are soft (about 5 minutes). Mix the flour with 1/4 cup of broth until it is lump-free (you can shake it in a small plastic container with a tight-fitting lid). Add the remaining broth to the mushrooms, soy sauce, and about half of the flour mixture. Let the thick sauce simmer for 3 to 5 minutes, stirring regularly. If the sauce is not thick enough for your taste, add the remaining flour mixture and continue heating and stirring until it thickens. Serve hot (and as soon as possible).
Per serving: Calories: 200Kcal; Fat: 10g; Carbs: 7g; Fiber: 15g; Protein: 20g

16. Thai Peanut Sauce
Preparation time: 10 minutes
Cooking time: 0 minutes **Servings:** 6
Ingredients:
- 2 tbsp. soy sauce
- 1 tbsp. rice vinegar
- 1 tsp minced garlic
- 3 tbsp. peanut butter
- ¼ cup almond milk
- 1 tsp Thai chili paste

Directions:
Start by mixing in all the ingredients in a bowl until smooth. Heat this mixture for 30 seconds in the microwave. Serve.
Per serving: Calories: 12Kcal; Fat: 0.7g; Carbs: 1.5g; Fiber: 0.4g; Protein: 0.3g

17. Tofu Island Dressing
Preparation time: 10 minutes
Cooking time: 0 minutes **Servings:** 12
Ingredients:
- 1 (12 oz) package extra-firm silken tofu
- 4 dates, pitted - 1 garlic clove, minced
- ¼ cup red wine vinegar
- ¼ cup tomato purée
- 1 tsp prepared horseradish
- ½ tsp tamari - ½ tsp mustard powder
- ½ tsp paprika

Directions:
Start by adding dates and tofu to a blender until smooth. Toss in the rest of the ingredients and blend until pureed. Serve.
Per serving: Calories: 12Kcal; Fat: 0.1g; Carbs: 1.2g; Fiber: 0.2g; Protein: 0.1 g

18. Quick Ketchup
Preparation time: 10 minutes
Cooking time: 0 minutes **Servings:** 8
Ingredients:
- 1 (6 oz) can tomato paste
- ¼ cup filtered water - 3 tbsp apple cider vinegar
- 1 tbsp balsamic vinegar
- 1 tbsp pure maple syrup
- 1 tsp onion powder
- ½ tsp garlic powder - ½ tsp sea salt
- 1/8 tsp ground allspice

Directions:
Start mixing all the sauce ingredients in a mason jar. Cover the sauce and refrigerate. Serve when needed.
Per serving: Calories: 19Kcal; Fat: 1.1g; Carbs: 2.1g; Fiber: 0.3g; Protein: 0.9g

19. Date Purée
Preparation time: 10 minutes
Cooking time: 0 minutes **Servings:** 8
Ingredients:
- 2 cups Medjool dates, pitted
- 2 cups of water

Directions:
Add water and pitted dates to a food processor. Blend this date mixture until smooth. Refrigerate. Serve.
Per serving: Calories: 13Kcal; Fat: 1.3g; Carbs: 1.8g; Fiber: 0.1g; Protein: 0.2 g

20. Vegan Tzatziki
Preparation time: 10 minutes
Cooking time: 0 minutes **Servings:** 6
Ingredients:
- 1 English cucumber, grated
- 1 cup non-dairy yogurt
- 2 cloves roasted garlic - ½ lemon, juiced
- 1 tbsp dill, chopped
- Kosher salt and black pepper, to taste

Directions:
Start by throwing all the ingredients into a glass bowl. Mix well, then refrigerate.
Serve.
Per serving: Calories: 22Kcal; Fat: 1.5g; Carbs: 6.3g; Fiber: 0.7g; Protein: 0.6g

21. Nut Milk

Preparation time: 5 minutes, Plus Soaking Time
Cooking time: 0 minutes
Servings: 4
Ingredients:

- 1 cup raw nuts, such as almonds, cashews, or macadamias, soaked in water, drained, and rinsed
- 4 cups filtered water - ¼ teaspoon salt
- 1 teaspoon vanilla extract (optional)
- 1 to 2 tablespoons agave nectar or maple syrup (optional)

Directions:
In a blender, combine the soaked nuts, water, salt, vanilla (if using), and agave (if using). Blend on high speed until the nuts are broken down into a very fine meal and the water is white and opaque. This might take 2 to 3 minutes. Line a fine-mesh strainer with 2 layers of cheesecloth and place it over a large bowl. Pour the nut milk through the strainer. Gather the ends of the cheesecloth and twist them closed. Using your hands, squeeze the pulp in the cheesecloth, extracting as much milk as possible. Refrigerate the nut milk in a sealed container for up to 4 days. First-Timer tip: Don't throw away that leftover pulp! Add it to foods like smoothies and oatmeal or fold it into Apple Cinnamon Granola before baking. Not sure what to do with it yet? Freeze the leftover pulp until you're ready to use it.
Per serving (1 cup): Calories: 40Kcal; Fat: 3g; Carbs: 2g; Fiber: 0g; Protein: 1g

22. Cashew Mayonnaise

Preparation time: 5 minutes, Plus Soaking Time
Cooking time: 0 minutes
Servings: 1
Ingredients:

- ¾ cup raw cashews, soaked in water, drained, and rinsed
- 1/3 cup filtered water, plus more as needed
- 2 tablespoons freshly squeezed lemon juice
- 1 tablespoon apple cider vinegar
- 1 teaspoon Dijon mustard
- ½ teaspoon garlic powder - ½ teaspoon salt

Directions:
In a blender, combine the soaked cashews, water, lemon juice, vinegar, Dijon, garlic powder, and salt.
Blend on high speed until smooth and creamy. If the mayo is too thick, add more water, 1 tablespoon at a time, until it reaches your desired consistency. Refrigerate the mayonnaise in an airtight container for up to 1 week. Substitution tip: Use soaked blanched almonds or raw macadamia nuts instead of cashews. If you're allergic to nuts, substitute 1 cup silken tofu for the cashews.
Per serving (1 tablespoon): Calories: 34Kcal; Fat: 3g; Carbs: 2g; Fiber: 0g; Protein: 1g

23. Tofu Sour Cream

Preparation time: 5 minutes
Cooking time: 0 minutes Servings: 1 ½ cup
Ingredients:

- 1 (12-ounce) package silken tofu
- 2 tablespoons freshly squeezed lime juice
- 1 tablespoon apple cider vinegar
- ½ teaspoon salt

Directions:
In a blender, combine the tofu, lime juice, vinegar, and salt. Blend until smooth and creamy.
Refrigerate the sour cream in an airtight container for up to 1 week. First-Timer tip: When buying silken tofu, look for the type in the shelf-stable carton (it doesn't need to be refrigerated). Substitution tip: Use soaked raw nuts in the place of tofu if you like. Try ¾ cup cashews, almonds, or macadamias. See the soaking instructions here.
Per serving (2 tablespoons): Calories: 19Kcal; Fat: 1g; Carbs: 1g; Fiber: 0g; Protein: 2g

24. Tofu Ranch Dressing

Preparation time: 5 minutes
Cooking time: 0 minutes Servings: 1 cup
Ingredients:

- 1 cup silken tofu
- 1 tablespoon freshly squeezed lemon juice
- 1 tablespoon apple cider vinegar
- 1 garlic clove, minced
- 2 teaspoons chopped fresh parsley
- ½ teaspoon dried dill
- ½ teaspoon onion powder
- ½ teaspoon garlic powder
- ½ teaspoon salt

Directions:
In a blender, combine the tofu, lemon juice, vinegar, garlic, parsley, dill, onion powder, garlic powder, and salt. Blend until smooth and creamy.
Refrigerate in an airtight container for up to 1 week.
Substitution tip: If you'd prefer cashew ranch, use ¾ cup-soaked cashews and ¼ cup water instead of silken tofu. See the soaking instructions here.
Fun fact: Ranch dressing was developed by California dude ranch owner Steve Henson. The ranch's customers enjoyed it so much he began selling it for them to take home. The dressing became so popular he eventually opened a factory to manufacture it.
Per serving (2 tablespoons): Calories: 23Kcal; Fat: 1g; Carbs: 1g; Fiber: 0g; Protein: 2g

25. Almond Parmesan Crumbles

Preparation time: 5 minutes
Cooking time: 0 minutes Servings: 1
Ingredients:

- ½ cup raw almonds - ½ cup nutritional yeast
- ½ teaspoon dried mustard
- ½ teaspoon garlic powder - ½ teaspoon salt

Directions:
In a spice grinder or small food processor, pulse the almonds until they're finely ground. Add the nutritional yeast, dried mustard, garlic powder, and salt. Pulse to incorporate. Refrigerate in an airtight container for up to 1 month. First-Timer tip: If you have almond flour on hand, skip the food processor and make this recipe the lazy way. Just toss ½ cup

almond flour in a jar with the nutritional yeast and spices, make sure the lid is on tightly and shake well.
Per serving (2 tablespoons): Calories: 100Kcal; Fat: 4g; Carbs: 9g; Fiber: 5g; Protein: 10g

26. Tofu Feta
Preparation time: 10 minutes, Plus Marinating Time **Cooking time:** 0 minutes **Servings:** 2 cups
Ingredients:
- 1 (14-ounce) package extra-firm tofu, drained and pressed
- ¼ cup freshly squeezed lemon juice
- ¼ cup apple cider vinegar
- 2 tablespoons nutritional yeast
- 1 teaspoon dried oregano
- ½ teaspoon garlic powder - ½ teaspoon salt

Directions:
Crumble the tofu into large chunks and place it into a shallow dish. In a small bowl, whisk the lemon juice, vinegar, nutritional yeast, oregano, garlic powder, and salt to combine. Pour the mixture over the tofu and gently toss to combine. Refrigerate the tofu for 2 to 4 hours to soak up the marinade. First-Timer tip: The longer the tofu sits in the marinade, the stronger the flavor will be. Refrigerate any leftover tofu in the marinade, covered, for 3 to 5 days.
Per serving (2 tablespoons): Calories: 36Kcal; Fat: 2g; Carbs: 1g; Fiber: 1g; Protein: 4g

27. Cashew Cream Cheese
Preparation time: 15 minutes, Plus Soaking And Chilling Time **Cooking time:** 0 minutes **Servings:** ½ cup
Ingredients:
- 1 cup raw cashews, soaked in water, drained and rinsed
- 3 to 4 tablespoons filtered water, plus more as needed
- 1 tablespoon nutritional yeast
- 1 tablespoon freshly squeezed lemon juice
- 1 tablespoon apple cider vinegar
- ½ teaspoon salt

Directions:
In a food processor or blender, combine the soaked cashews, water, nutritional yeast, lemon juice, vinegar, and salt. Process until smooth and creamy. You may need to stop occasionally to scrape down the sides. If the mixture is too thick, add more filtered water, 1 teaspoon at a time, until the consistency is right. Refrigerate the cream cheese in an airtight container for 1 to 2 hours before serving to firm it up.
Keep refrigerated in an airtight container for up to 1 week.
Variation tip: For scallion cream cheese, stir in ¼ cup sliced scallion. For herbed cream cheese, stir in 1 garlic clove, minced, 2 tablespoons chopped fresh dill, 2 tablespoons chopped fresh chives, and 2 tablespoons chopped fresh parsley. For vegetable cream cheese, stir in ¼ cup finely chopped carrot, ¼ cup finely chopped red bell pepper, 2 tablespoons sliced scallion, and 2 tablespoons chopped fresh parsley.
Per serving (2 tablespoons): Calories: 64Kcal; Fat: 5g; Carbs: 4g; Fiber: 1g; Protein: 3g

28. Macadamia Mozzarella
Preparation time: 10 minutes, Plus Soaking And Cooling Time **Cooking time:** 10 minutes
Servings: 1
Ingredients:
- ½ cup unsalted macadamia nuts, soaked in water, drained and rinsed
- ½ cup filtered water
- ¼ cup tapioca starch
- 2 tablespoons nutritional yeast
- 1 tablespoon freshly squeezed lemon juice
- 1 teaspoon white miso
- ½ teaspoon garlic powder
- ½ teaspoon salt

Directions:
In a blender, combine the soaked macadamias, water, tapioca starch, nutritional yeast, lemon juice, miso, garlic powder, and salt. Blend until smooth and creamy. Transfer the mixture to a medium saucepan and place it over medium heat. Cook for about 10 minutes, whisking constantly until the mixture is stretchy and begins to form into a ball. It may get lumpy before it smooths out—keep whisking if it does. Transfer the mixture to a container and cool in the refrigerator for 1 to 2 hours before using.
Keep refrigerated in an airtight container for 2 to 3 days. Substitution tip: Swap the macadamias for soaked blanched almonds or raw cashews if you like. See the soaking instructions here.
Per serving (¼ cup): Calories: 184Kcal; Fat: 13g; Carbs: 15g; Fiber: 4g; Protein: 5g

29. Pastry Dough
Preparation time: 15 minutes, Plus Chilling Time **Cooking time:** 45 minutes (For A Finished Pie)
Servings: 1 Piecrust (About 12 Ounces)
Ingredients:
- 1½ cups all-purpose flour
- ½ teaspoon salt
- ¼ cup ice-cold olive oil, plus more for the pie pan
- 2 tablespoons maple syrup
- 2 to 4 tablespoons ice water

Directions:
In a large bowl, mix the flour and salt. Drizzle the olive oil into the bowl and use a rubber spatula or wooden spoon to stir it into the flour. Mix until the flour resembles pebbles.
Drizzle the maple syrup and 2 tablespoons of ice water into the bowl and mix lightly until the mixture forms a dough. You may need to use your hands to knead the mixture a little until it becomes a stiff dough. If the mixture seems too dry, add more ice water, 1 tablespoon at a time. Form the dough into a ball, wrap it in plastic wrap, and refrigerate it for 2 hours. To make a pie, preheat the oven to 375°F. Lightly coat a 9-inch pie pan with olive oil. Place the dough on a piece of parchment paper and cover it with another piece of parchment. Using a rolling pin, roll out the dough from the center until it's about ¼ inch thick. Carefully transfer the dough to the prepared pie pan. Trim any dough hanging over the edge of the pan and crimp the dough edges using a fork or

your fingers. Fill with your favorite fillings. Bake for 30 to 40 minutes, or until the crust is golden brown and the filling is heated through.

To blind bake, your crust (that is, to bake it without a filling), place a piece of parchment paper inside the crust and fill it with pie weights or dried beans, then bake it for 15 minutes. Remove the crust from the oven and remove the parchment paper and pie weights. Prick the bottom of the crust a few times with a fork, then return it to the oven for another 15 to 20 minutes, or until it's golden brown. First-Timer tip: Place your oil in the freezer about 30 minutes before you're going to make the recipe so that it thickens.

Per serving (1/8 crust): Calories: 169Kcal; Fat: 7g; Carbs: 23g; Fiber: 1g; Protein: 3g

30. Pizza Dough

Preparation time: 15 minutes, Plus Resting Time
Cooking time: 12 minutes (For A Finished Pizza)
Servings: 1 (16-Inch) Pizza Crust
Ingredients:
- 1 cup warm water
- 1 (0.25-ounce) package active dry yeast
- 1 teaspoon sugar
- 2½ cups all-purpose flour, plus more as needed
- 2 tablespoons olive oil
- 1 teaspoon salt

Directions:
In a medium bowl, whisk the water, yeast, and sugar. Let the mixture stand until the yeast dissolves, about 5 minutes.

Add the flour, olive oil, and salt to the mixture and mix until a dough forms. Cover the bowl with a clean kitchen towel and let sit in a draft-free area for about 1 hour or until the dough doubles in size.

To make a pizza, preheat the oven to 450°F. Lightly flour a 16-inch pizza pan and your work surface.

With a rolling pin, roll the dough on the prepared surface until it's 15 to 16 inches in diameter. Transfer it to your prepared pizza pan. If you don't have a rolling pin, use your hands to carefully stretch the dough right on the pizza pan.

Cover the dough with your favorite toppings. Bake for 10 to 12 minutes, or until the crust turns golden brown and the toppings are hot. First-Timer tip: Once the dough has doubled in size, you can refrigerate it in an airtight container for up to 2 weeks or freeze for up to 3 months. Before making your pizza, bring the dough to room temperature on the countertop.

Per serving (1/8 pizza): Calories: 194Kcal; Fat: 4g; Carbs: 34g; Fiber: 1g; Protein: 5g

31. Seitan

Preparation time: 15 minutes, Plus Kneading And Resting Time **Cooking time:** 40 minutes
Servings: 1
Ingredients:
- Vegetable oil, for preparing the baking dish
- 1¼ cups vital wheat gluten
- 2 tablespoons nutritional yeast
- 1 tablespoon garlic powder
- 1 tablespoon onion powder
- 1 cup vegetable stock, plus more as needed
- 2 tablespoons low-sodium soy sauce or tamari
- 1 tablespoon tomato paste

Directions:
Preheat the oven to 350°F. Lightly coat a small baking dish with vegetable oil, or line it with parchment paper. Set aside.

In a large bowl, combine the vital wheat gluten, nutritional yeast, garlic powder, and onion powder.

Add the vegetable stock, soy sauce, and tomato paste. Mix until a dough forms. If the mixture seems too dry, add more vegetable stock, 1 tablespoon at a time. Knead the dough for 3 to 5 minutes, or until it becomes elastic. Cover the dough and let it sit for about 15 minutes, then knead it again for a few more minutes. The longer you knead the dough, the chewier it will be. Flatten the dough until it's about 1 inch thick and place it in the prepared baking dish.

Bake for 20 minutes, flip the seitan and bake for 20 minutes more. It should be firm and meaty in texture. If it seems too soft, bake for a few more minutes.

Slice or chop the cooked seitan and use it in your favorite recipe.

Refrigerate in an airtight container for up to 6 days, or freeze for up to 6 months.

First-Timer tip: Simmered seitan has a softer texture. If you'd prefer to simmer it, separate the dough into 3 or 4 smaller pieces and gently stretch and flatten each piece. Place the pieces in a large pot with enough vegetable stock to cover them (about 4 cups) and bring the mixture to a boil over medium-high heat. As soon as the liquid begins to boil, reduce the heat to low and simmer for 40 minutes. Remove the pot from the heat and cool the seitan in the stock. Once the seitan has cooled, remove it from the stock and use it in your favorite recipe.

FLEXITARIAN TIP: You can vary the taste of your seitan by adding different seasonings to the stock. Try using poultry seasoning for a chicken-style seitan, seaweed for a seafood-flavored seitan, or a vegan Worcestershire sauce for beefy seitan. You can also include aromatics, such as chopped onion or garlic, to infuse extra flavor.

Per serving (2 ounces): Calories: 116Kcal; Fat: 1g; Carbs: 9g; Fiber: 1g; Protein: 20g

32. Cauliflower Popcorn

Preparation time: 1 day and 1 hour
Cooking time: 1 day **Servings:** 2
Ingredients:
- ¼ cup sun-dried tomatoes
- ¾ cup dates
- 2 heads cauliflower
- ½ cup water
- 2 tablespoons raw tahini
- 1 tablespoon apple cider vinegar
- 2 teaspoons onion powder
- 2 teaspoons garlic powder
- 1 teaspoon ground cayenne pepper
- 2 tablespoons nutritional yeast (optional)

Directions:
Cover the sun-dried tomatoes in warm water and let them soak for an hour. If the dates are not soft and fresh, soak

them in warm water for an hour in another bowl. Cut the cauliflower into very small, bite-sized pieces, then set aside.
Put the drained tomatoes and dates in a blender along with the water, tahini, apple cider vinegar, onion powder, garlic powder, cayenne pepper, nutritional yeast and turmeric. Blend into a thick, smooth consistency.
Pour this mixture into the bowl, on top of the cauliflower and mix so that all the pieces are coated.
Place the cauliflower in the dehydrator and spread it out to make a single layer. Sprinkle with a little sea salt and set for 115 degrees Fahrenheit for 12 to 24 hours or until it becomes exactly as crunchy as you like it. I let mine go for 15 to 16 hours, but the time will vary based on your taste preference as well as the ambient humidity.
Store in an airtight container until serving.
Per serving: Calories: 393Kcal; Fat: 9.49g; Carbs: 72.33g; Fiber: 14.1g; Protein: 15.46g

33. Cinnamon Apple Chips with Dip
Preparation time: 3 hours and 30 minutes
Cooking time: 3 hours Servings: 2
Ingredients:
- 1 cup raw cashews
- 2 apples, thinly sliced
- 1 lemon
- 1½ cups water, divided
- Cinnamon plus more to dust the chips
- Another medium cored apple quartered
- 1 tablespoon honey or agave
- 1 teaspoon cinnamon
- ¼ teaspoon sea salt

Directions:
Place the cashews in a bowl of warm water, deep enough to cover them, and let them soak overnight.
Preheat the oven to 200 degrees Fahrenheit. Line two baking sheets with parchment paper.
Juice the lemon into a large glass bowl and add two cups of water. Place the sliced apples in the water as you cut them and when done, swish them around and drain.
Spread the apple slices across the baking sheet in a single layer and sprinkle with a little cinnamon. Bake for 90 minutes.
Remove the slices from the oven and flip each of them over. Put them back in the oven and bake for another 90 minutes or until they are crisp. Remember, they will get crisper as they cool.
While the apple slices are cooking, drain the cashews and put them in a blender, along with the quartered apple, the honey, a teaspoon of cinnamon, and a half cup of the remaining water. Process until thick and creamy. I like to refrigerate my dip for about an hour to chill before serving alongside the room temperature apple slices.
Per serving: Calories: 962Kcal; Fat: 68.42g; Carbs: 87.84g; Fiber: 11.2g; Protein: 16.39g

34. Crunchy Asparagus Spears
Preparation time: 25 minutes
Cooking time: 25 minutes Servings: 4
Ingredients:
- 1 bunch asparagus spears (about 12 spears)
- ¼ cup nutritional yeast
- 2 tablespoons hemp seeds
- 1 teaspoon garlic powder
- ¼ teaspoon paprika (or more if you like paprika)
- 1/8 teaspoon ground pepper
- ¼ cup whole-wheat breadcrumbs
- Juice of ½ lemon

Directions:
Preheat the oven to 350 degrees Fahrenheit. Line a baking sheet with parchment paper.
Wash the asparagus, snapping off the white part at the bottom. Save it for making vegetable stock. Mix the nutritional yeast, hemp seed, garlic powder, paprika, pepper, and breadcrumbs. Place asparagus spears on the baking sheets, giving them a little room in between, and sprinkle with the mixture in the bowl. Bake for up to 25 minutes until crispy. Serve with lemon juice if desired.
Per serving: Calories: 73Kcal; Fat: 2.49g; Carbs: 7.69g; Fiber: 2g; Protein: 5.87g

35. Homemade Trail Mix
Preparation time: 20 minutes
Cooking time: 20 minutes
Servings: 2
Ingredients:
- ½ cup uncooked old-fashioned oatmeal
- ½ cup chopped dates
- 2 cups whole-grain cereal
- ¼ cup raisins
- ¼ cup almonds
- ¼ cup walnuts

Directions:
Mix all the ingredients in a large bowl. Place in an airtight container until ready to use.
Per serving: Calories: 382Kcal; Fat: 8.37g; Carbs: 75.47g; Fiber: 10g; Protein: 8.97g

36. Nut Butter Maple Dip
Preparation time: 1 hour
Cooking time: 1 hour Servings: 2
Ingredients:
- 1/2 tablespoon ground flaxseed
- 1 teaspoon ground cinnamon
- 1/2 tablespoon maple syrup
- 2 tablespoons cashew milk
- ¾ cups crunchy, unsweetened peanut butter

Directions:
In a bowl, combine the flaxseed, cinnamon, maple syrup, cashew milk, and peanut butter. Use a fork to mix everything in. I stir it like I'm scrambling eggs.
The mixture should be creamy. If it's too runny, add a little more peanut butter; if it's too thick, add a little more cashew milk. Refrigerate covered for about an hour, and serve. **Per serving:** Calories: 599Kcal; Fat: 38.14g; Carbs: 44.38g; Fiber: 7g; Protein: 29g

37. Oven Baked Sesame Fries

Preparation time: 30 minutes
Cooking time: 30 minutes **Servings:** 4
Ingredients:
- 1-pound Yukon Gold potatoes, skins on and cut into wedges
- 2 tablespoons sesame seeds
- 1 tablespoon potato starch
- 1 tablespoon sesame oil
- Salt to taste - Black pepper to taste

Directions:
Preheat the oven to 425 degrees Fahrenheit and cover a baking sheet or two with parchment paper. Cut the potatoes and place them in a large bowl. Add the sesame seeds, potato starch, sesame oil, salt, and pepper. Toss with your hands and make sure all the wedges are coated. Add more sesame seeds or oil if needed. Spread the potato wedges on the baking sheets with some room between each wedge.
Bake for 15 minutes, flip the wedges over and then return them to the oven for 10 to 15 more minutes until they look golden and crispy.
Per serving: Calories: 218Kcal; Fat: 6.06g; Carbs: 37.46g; Fiber: 5.2g; Protein: 5.2g

38. Pumpkin Orange Spice Hummus

Preparation time: 30 minutes
Cooking time: 30 minutes **Servings:** 3
Ingredients:
- 1 cup canned, unsweetened pumpkin puree
- 1 16-ounce can garbanzo beans, rinsed and drained
- 1 tablespoon apple cider vinegar
- 1 tablespoon maple syrup - ¼ cup tahini
- 1 tablespoon fresh orange juice
- ½ teaspoon orange zest and additional zest for garnish
- 1/8 teaspoon ground cinnamon
- 1/8 teaspoon ground ginger
- 1/8 teaspoon ground nutmeg - 1/4 teaspoon salt

Directions:
Pour the pumpkin puree and garbanzo beans into a food processor and pulse to break up. Add the vinegar, syrup, tahini, orange juice and orange zest pulse a few times.
Add the cinnamon, ginger, nutmeg and salt and process until smooth and creamy. Serve in a bowl sprinkled with more orange zest with wheat crackers alongside.
Per serving: Calories: 387Kcal; Fat: 15.08g; Carbs: 53.4g; Fiber: 12.5g; Protein: 14.26g

39. Quick English Muffin Mexican Pizzas

Preparation time: 30 minutes
Cooking time: 15 minutes **Servings:** 2
Ingredients:
- 2 whole-wheat English muffins separated
- 1/3 cup tomato salsa
- 1/4 cup refried beans
- 1 small jalapeno, seeded and sliced
- 1/4 cup onion, sliced
- 2 tablespoons diced plum or cherry tomato
- 1/3 cup vegan cheese shreds (pepper jack is really tasty!)

Directions:
Preheat the oven to 400 degrees Fahrenheit and cover a baking sheet with foil. The foil makes the crust crispier.
Separate the English muffin and spread on some salsa and refried beans.
Place some of the jalapenos and onions on top and sprinkle the cheese on top.
Place on the baking sheet and bake for 10 to 15 minutes or until brown. You can turn on the broiler for a minute or two to melt the cheese.
Per serving: Calories: 284Kcal; Fat: 8.35g; Carbs: 43.56g; Fiber: 7g; Protein: 12.31g

40. Quinoa Trail Mix Cups

Preparation time: 30 minutes
Cooking time: 30 minutes
Servings: 16
Ingredients:
- 2 tablespoons ground flaxseed
- 1/3 cup unsweetened soy milk
- 1 cup old-fashioned rolled oats
- 1 cup cooked and cooled quinoa
- ¼ cup brown sugar
- 1 teaspoon ground cinnamon
- ¼ teaspoon salt
- ¼ cup pumpkin or sunflower seeds
- ¼ cup shredded coconut
- ½ cup almonds
- ½ cup raisins or dried cherries/cranberries

Directions:
Whisk the flaxseed and milk together in a small bowl and set aside for 10 minutes so the seed can absorb the milk. Preheat the oven to 350 degrees Fahrenheit and coat a muffin tin with coconut oil.
In a large bowl, mix the oats, quinoa, brown sugar, cinnamon, salt, pumpkin seeds, coconut, almonds and raisins.
Stir in the flaxseed and milk mixture and combine thoroughly. Place two heaping teaspoons of the trail mix mixture in each muffin cup. When done, wet your fingers and press down on each muffin cup to compact the trail mix.
Bake for 12 minutes.
Cool completely before removing, and each little cup will fall out. Store in an airtight container.
Per serving: Calories: 69Kcal; Fat: 2.44g; Carbs: 12.15g; Fiber: 1.9g; Protein: 2.34g

Amanda Kale

CHAPTER 13:
Breakfast

41. Max Power Smoothie
Preparation time: 5 minutes **Cooking time:** 0 minutes
Servings: 3-4 cups
Ingredients:
- 1 banana
- ¼ cup rolled oats, or 1 scoop plant Protein: powder
- 1 tablespoon flaxseed or chia seeds
- 1 cup raspberries or other berries
- 1 cup chopped mango (frozen or fresh)
- ½ cup non-dairy milk (optional)
- 1 cup water

Bonus Boosters (Optional)
- 2 tablespoons fresh parsley, or basil, chopped - 1 cup chopped fresh kale, spinach, collards, or other green
- 1 carrot, peeled
- 1 tablespoon grated fresh ginger

Directions:
Purée everything in a blender until smooth, adding more water (or non-dairy milk) if needed. Add none, some, or all of the bonus boosters, as desired. Purée until blended. Make ahead: Buy extra bananas so that when they ripen, you can peel them and put them in the freezer. Frozen bananas make for max creaminess in your smoothie.
Per serving (3 to 4 cups): Calories: 550Kcal; Fat: 9g; Carbs: 116g; Fiber: 29g; Protein: 13g

42. Chai Chia Smoothie
Preparation time: 5 minutes
Cooking time: 0 minutes
Servings: 3 cups
Ingredients:
- 1 banana- ½ cup coconut milk
- 1 cup water - 1 cup alfalfa sprouts (optional)
- 1 to 2 soft Medjool dates, pitted
- 1 tablespoon chia seeds, or ground flax or hemp hearts
- ¼ teaspoon ground cinnamon
- Pinch ground cardamom
- 1 tablespoon grated fresh ginger or ¼ teaspoon ground ginger

Directions:
Purée everything in a blender until smooth, adding more water (or coconut milk) if needed.
Did you know? Although dates are super sweet, they don't cause a large blood sugar spike. They're great to boost sweetness while also boosting your intake of Fiber: and potassium.
Per serving (3 cups): Calories: 477Kcal; Fat: 29g; Carbs: 57g; Fiber: 14g; Protein: 8g

43. Tropi-Kale Breeze
Preparation time: 5 minutes
Cooking time: 0 minutes **Servings:** 3-4 cups
Ingredients:
- 1 cup chopped pineapple (frozen or fresh)
- 1 cup chopped mango (frozen or fresh)
- ½ to 1 cup chopped kale
- ½ avocado
- ½ cup coconut milk
- 1 cup water or coconut water
- 1 teaspoon matcha green tea powder (optional)

Directions:
Purée everything in a blender until smooth, adding more water (or coconut milk) if needed.
Did you know? Matcha green tea powder contains catechins, which minimize inflammation and maximize Fat-burning potential.
Per serving (3 to 4 cups): Calories: 566Kcal; Fat: 36g; Carbs: 66g; Fiber: 12g; Protein: 8g

44. Hydration Station
Preparation time: 5 minutes
Cooking time: 0 minutes **Servings:** 3-4 cups
Ingredients:
- 1 banana
- 1 orange, peeled and sectioned, or 1 cup pure orange juice
- 1 cup strawberries (frozen or fresh)
- 1 cup chopped cucumber
- ½ cup coconut water
- 1 cup water
- ½ cup ice

Bonus Boosters (Optional)
- 1 cup chopped spinach
- ¼ cup fresh mint, chopped

Directions:
Purée everything in a blender until smooth, adding more water if needed. Add bonus boosters, as desired. Purée until blended. Make ahead: Pour your smoothie in an insulated travel mug or thermos to keep it chilled if you're on the go.
Per serving (3 to 4 cups): Calories: 320Kcal; Fat: 3g; Carbs: 76g; Fiber: 13g; Protein: 6g

45. Mango Madness
Preparation time: 5 minutes
Cooking time: 0 minutes **Servings:** 3-4 cups
Ingredients:
- 1 banana
- 1 cup chopped mango (frozen or fresh)

- 1 cup chopped peach (frozen or fresh)
- 1 cup strawberries
- 1 carrot, peeled and chopped (optional)
- 1 cup water

Directions:
Purée everything in a blender until smooth, adding more water if needed. Options: If you can't find frozen peaches and fresh ones aren't in season, just use extra mango or strawberries, or try cantaloupe.

Per serving (3 to 4 cups): Calories: 376Kcal; Fat: 2g; Carbs: 95g; Fiber: 14g; Protein: 5g

46. Chocolate PB Smoothie

Preparation time: 5 minutes
Cooking time: 0 minutes
Servings: 3-4 cups
Ingredients:
- 1 banana
- ¼ cup rolled oats, or 1 scoop plant Protein: powder
- 1 tablespoon flaxseed or chia seeds
- 1 tablespoon unsweetened cocoa powder
- 1 tablespoon peanut butter, or almond or sunflower seed butter - 1 tablespoon maple syrup (optional)
- 1 cup alfalfa sprouts or spinach, chopped (optional)
- ½ cup non-dairy milk (optional)
- 1 cup water

Bonus Boosters (Optional)
- 1 teaspoon maca powder
- 1 teaspoon cocoa nibs

Directions:
Purée everything in a blender until smooth, adding more water (or non-dairy milk) if needed. Add bonus boosters, as desired. Purée until blended. Did you know? Flavonols found in cocoa appear to help protect our blood vessel linings, and postmenopausal women seem to reap the most cardiovascular benefits from consuming cocoa.

Per serving (3 to 4 cups): Calories: 474Kcal; Fat: 16g; Carbs: 79g; Fiber: 18g; Protein: 13g

47. Pink Panther Smoothie

Preparation time: 5 minutes
Cooking time: 0 minutes
Servings: 3 cups
Ingredients:
- 1 cup strawberries
- 1 cup chopped melon (any kind)
- 1 cup cranberries or raspberries
- 1 tablespoon chia seeds
- ½ cup coconut milk, or other non-dairy milk
- 1 cup water

Bonus Boosters (Optional)
- 1 teaspoon goji berries
- 2 tablespoons fresh mint, chopped

Directions:
Purée everything in a blender until smooth, adding more water (or coconut milk) if needed. Add bonus boosters, as desired. Purée until blended. Options: If you don't have (or don't like) coconut, try using sunflower seeds for an immune boost of zinc and selenium.

Per serving (3 cups): Calories: 459Kcal; Fat: 30g; Carbs: 52g; Fiber: 19g; Protein: 8g

48. Banana Nut Smoothie

Preparation time: 5 minutes **Cooking time:** 0 minutes
Servings: 2 to 3 cups
Ingredients:
- 1 banana - 1 tablespoon almond butter or sunflower seed butter
- ¼ teaspoon ground cinnamon
- Pinch ground nutmeg
- 1 to 2 tablespoons dates or maple syrup
- 1 tablespoon ground flaxseed, or chia, or hemp hearts
- ½ cup non-dairy milk (optional)
- 1 cup water

Directions:
Purée everything in a blender until smooth, adding more water (or non-dairy milk) if needed. Options: You could make this a pumpkin spice smoothie by adding 1 cup cooked pumpkin and a pinch of allspice.

Per serving (2 to 3 cups): Calories: 343Kcal; Fat: 14g; Carbs: 55g; Fiber: 8g; Protein: 6g

49. Overnight Oats On the Go

Preparation time: 5 minutes
Cooking time: 5 minutes
Servings: 1
Ingredients:
Basic Overnight Oats
- ½ cup rolled oats, or quinoa flakes for gluten-free
- 1 tablespoon ground flaxseed, or chia seeds, or hemp hearts
- 1 tablespoon maple syrup or coconut sugar (optional)
- ¼ teaspoon ground cinnamon (optional)

Topping Options
- 1 apple, chopped, and 1 tablespoon walnuts
- 2 tablespoons dried cranberries and 1 tablespoon pumpkin seeds
- 1 pear, chopped, and 1 tablespoon cashews
- 1 cup sliced grapes and 1 tablespoon sunflower seeds
- 1 banana, sliced, and 1 tablespoon peanut butter
- 2 tablespoons raisins and 1 tablespoon hazelnuts
- 1 cup berries and 1 tablespoon unsweetened coconut flakes

Directions:
Mix the oats, flax, maple syrup, and cinnamon (if using) in a bowl or to-go container (a travel mug or short thermos works beautifully). Pour enough cool water over the oats to submerge them, and stir to combine. Leave to soak for a minimum of half an hour or overnight. Add your choice of toppings. Quick morning option: Boil about ½ cup water and pour over the oats. Let them soak about 5 minutes before eating. Did you know? Cinnamon has been shown to help control blood sugar levels, improve insulin response, and

reduce triglycerides, LDL (bad) cholesterol, and total cholesterol.
Per serving (Basic): Calories: 244; Fat: 6g; Carbs: 30g; Fiber: 6g; Protein: 7g **Per serving (Apple and Walnut version):** Calories: 401Kcal; Fat: 15g; Carbs: 63g; Fiber: 10g; Protein: 10g

50. Oatmeal Breakfast Cookies
Preparation time: 15 minutes **Cooking time:** 12 minutes
Servings: 5 big cookies
Ingredients:
- 1 tablespoon ground flaxseed
- 2 tablespoons almond butter or sunflower seed butter
- 2 tablespoons maple syrup
- 1 banana, mashed
- 1 teaspoon ground cinnamon
- ¼ teaspoon ground nutmeg (optional)
- Pinch sea salt
- ½ cup rolled oats
- ¼ cup raisins, or dark chocolate chips

Directions:
Preheat the oven to 350°F. Line a large baking sheet with parchment paper. Mix the ground flax with just enough water to cover it in a small dish, and leave it to sit. In a large bowl, mix the almond butter and maple syrup until creamy, then add the banana. Add the flax-water mixture. Sift the cinnamon, nutmeg, and salt into a separate medium bowl, then stir into the wet mixture. Add the oats and raisins, and fold in.
From 3 to 4 tablespoons of batter into a ball and press lightly to flatten onto the baking sheet. Repeat, spacing the cookies 2 to 3 inches apart. Bake for 12 minutes, or until golden brown. Store the cookies in an airtight container in the fridge, or freeze them for later. Make ahead: The quantity here is for one person, so you don't have too many cookies lying around to tempt you. But they're great to double for a full batch of snacks.
Per serving (1 cookie): Calories: 192Kcal; Fat: 6g; Carbs: 34g; Fiber: 4g; Protein: 4g

51. Sunshine Muffins
Preparation time: 15 minutes **Cooking time:** 30 minutes
Servings: 6 muffins
Ingredients:
- 1 teaspoon coconut oil for greasing muffin tins (optional)
- 2 tablespoons almond butter or sunflower seed butter
- ¼ cup non-dairy milk
- 1 orange, peeled
- 1 carrot, coarsely chopped
- 2 tablespoons chopped dried apricots, or other dried fruit
- 3 tablespoons molasses
- 2 tablespoons ground flaxseed
- 1 teaspoon apple cider vinegar
- 1 teaspoon pure vanilla extract
- 1/2 teaspoon ground cinnamon
- 1/2 teaspoon ground ginger (optional)
- 1/4 teaspoon ground nutmeg (optional)
- ¼ teaspoon allspice (optional)
- ¾ cup rolled oats or whole-grain flour
- 1 teaspoon baking powder
- ½ teaspoon baking soda

Mix-Ins (Optional)
- ½ cup rolled oats
- 2 tablespoons raisins or other chopped dried fruit
- 2 tablespoons sunflower seeds

Directions:
Preheat the oven to 350°F. Prepare a 6-cup muffin tin by rubbing the insides of the cups with coconut oil or using silicone or paper muffin cups. Purée the nut butter, milk, orange, carrot, apricots, molasses, flaxseed, vinegar, vanilla, cinnamon, ginger, nutmeg, and allspice in a food processor or blender until somewhat smooth. Grind the oats in a clean coffee grinder until they're the consistency of flour (or use whole-grain flour). In a large bowl, mix the oats with the baking powder and baking soda. Mix the wet ingredients into the dry ingredients until just combined. Fold in the mix-ins (if using). Spoon about ¼ cup batter into each muffin cup and bake for 30 minutes, or until a toothpick inserted into the center comes out clean. The orange creates a very moist base, so the muffins may take longer than 30 minutes, depending on how heavy your muffin tin is.
Leftovers: Store the muffins in the fridge or freezer, because they are so moist. If you plan to keep them frozen, you can easily double the batch for a full dozen.
Per serving (1 muffin): Calories: 287Kcal; Fat: 12g; Carbs: 41g; Fiber: 6g; Protein: 8g

52. Applesauce Crumble Muffins
Preparation time: 15 minutes
Cooking time: 15 to 20 minutes
Servings: 12 muffins
Ingredients:
- 1 teaspoon coconut oil for greasing muffin tins (optional)
- 2 tablespoons nut butter or seed butter
- 1½ cups unsweetened applesauce
- 1/3 cup coconut sugar
- ½ cup non-dairy milk
- 2 tablespoons ground flaxseed
- 1 teaspoon apple cider vinegar
- 1 teaspoon pure vanilla extract
- 2 cups whole-grain flour
- 1 teaspoon baking soda
- ½ teaspoon baking powder
- 1 teaspoon ground cinnamon
- Pinch sea salt
- ½ cup walnuts, chopped

Toppings (Optional)
- ¼ cup walnuts
- ¼ cup coconut sugar
- ½ teaspoon ground cinnamon

Directions:
Preheat the oven to 350°F. Prepare two 6-cup muffin tins by rubbing the insides of the cups with coconut oil or using silicone or paper muffin cups. In a large bowl, mix the nut butter, applesauce, coconut sugar, milk, flaxseed, vinegar, and vanilla until thoroughly combined, or purée in a food processor or blender. In another large bowl, sift together the flour, baking soda, baking powder, cinnamon, salt, and chopped walnuts. Mix the dry ingredients into the wet ingredients until just combined.

Spoon about ¼ cup batter into each muffin cup and sprinkle with the topping of your choice (if using). Bake for 15 to 20 minutes, or until a toothpick inserted into the center comes out clean. The applesauce creates a very moist base, so the muffins may take longer, depending on how heavy your muffin tins are.

Options: To make this nut-free, swap the walnuts for sunflower seeds and use sunflower seed butter.

Per serving (1 muffin): Calories: 287Kcal; Fat: 12g; Carbs: 41g; Fiber: 6g; Protein: 8g

53. Baked Banana French Toast with Raspberry Syrup

Preparation time: 10 minutes **Cooking time:** 30 minutes
Servings: 8 slices
For The French Toast
- 1 banana - 1 cup coconut milk
- 1 teaspoon pure vanilla extract
- ¼ teaspoon ground nutmeg
- ½ teaspoon ground cinnamon
- 1½ teaspoons arrowroot powder or flour
- Pinch sea salt - 8 slices whole-grain bread

For The Raspberry Syrup
- 1 cup fresh or frozen raspberries or other berries
- 2 tablespoons water, or pure fruit juice
- 1 to 2 tablespoons maple syrup or coconut sugar (optional)

Directions:
To Make The French Toast
Preheat the oven to 350°F.
In a shallow bowl, purée or mash the banana well. Mix in coconut milk, vanilla, nutmeg, cinnamon, arrowroot, and salt. Dip the slices of bread in the banana mixture, and then lay them out in a 13-by-9-inch baking dish. They should cover the bottom of the dish and can overlap a bit but shouldn't be stacked on top of each other. Pour any leftover banana mixture over the bread, and put the dish in the oven. Bake about 30 minutes, or until the tops are lightly browned. Serve topped with raspberry syrup.

To Make The Raspberry Syrup
Heat the raspberries in a small pot with the water and maple syrup (if using) on medium heat. Leave to simmer, stirring occasionally and breaking up the berries, until the liquid has reduced for 15 to 20 minutes. Leftovers: Leftover raspberry syrup makes a great topping for simple oatmeal as a quick and delicious breakfast or as a drizzle on top of whole-grain toast smeared with natural peanut butter.

Per serving (1 slice with syrup): Calories: 166Kcal; Fat: 7g; Carbs: 23g; Fiber: 4g; Protein: 5g

54. Cinnamon Apple Toast

Preparation time: 5 minutes
Cooking time: 10 to 20 minutes Servings: 2 slices
Ingredients:
- 1 to 2 teaspoons coconut oil
- ½ teaspoon ground cinnamon
- 1 tablespoon maple syrup or coconut sugar
- 1 apple, cored and thinly sliced
- 2 slices whole-grain bread

Directions:
In a large bowl, mix the coconut oil, cinnamon, and maple syrup. Add the apple slices and toss with your hands to coat them. To panfry the toast, place the apple slices in a medium skillet on medium-high and cook for about 5 minutes, or until slightly soft, then transfer to a plate. Cook the bread in the same skillet for 2 to 3 minutes on each side. Top the toast with the apples. Alternately, you can bake the toast. Use your hands to rub each slice of bread with some of the coconut oil mixture on both sides. Lay them on a small baking sheet, top with the coated apples, and put in the oven or toaster oven at 350°F for 15 to 20 minutes, or until the apples have softened.

Options: For a more everyday version, toast the bread, spread with nut butter, top with apple slices, and sprinkle with a pinch of cinnamon and coconut sugar.

Per serving (1 slice): Calories: 187Kcal; Fat: 8g; Carbs: 27g; Fiber: 4g; Protein: 4g

55. Muesli and Berries Bowl

Preparation time: 10 minutes Cooking time: 0 minutes
Servings: 5 cups
Ingredients:
For The Muesli
- 1 cup rolled oats
- 1 cup spelt flakes, or quinoa flakes, or more rolled oats
- 2 cups puffed cereal
- ¼ cup sunflower seeds
- ¼ cup almonds
- ¼ cup raisins
- ¼ cup dried cranberries
- ¼ cup chopped dried figs
- ¼ cup unsweetened shredded coconut
- ¼ cup non-dairy chocolate chips
- 1 to 3 teaspoons ground cinnamon

For The Bowl
- ½ cup non-dairy milk, or unsweetened applesauce
- ¾ cup muesli
- ½ cup berries

Directions:
Put the muesli ingredients in a container or bag and shake. Combine the muesli and bowl ingredients in a bowl or to-go container. Substitutions: Try chopped Brazil nuts, peanuts, dried cranberries, dried blueberries, dried mango, or whatever inspires you. Ginger and cardamom are interesting flavors if you want to branch out on spices.

Per serving (1 bowl): Calories: 441Kcal; Fat: 20g; Carbs: 63g; Fiber: 13g; Protein: 10g

56. Chocolate Quinoa Breakfast Bowl

Preparation time: 5 minutes
Cooking time: 30 minutes **Servings:** 2
Ingredients:

- 1 cup quinoa
- 1 teaspoon ground cinnamon
- 1 cup non-dairy milk
- 1 cup water
- 1 large banana
- 2 to 3 tablespoons unsweetened cocoa powder or carob
- 1 to 2 tablespoons almond butter or other nut or seed butter
- 1 tablespoon ground flaxseed, or chia or hemp seeds
- 2 tablespoons walnuts
- ¼ cup raspberries

Directions:
Put the quinoa, cinnamon, milk, and water in a medium pot. Bring to a boil over high heat, then turn down low and simmer, covered, for 25 to 30 minutes. While the quinoa is simmering, purée or mash the banana in a medium bowl and stir in the cocoa powder, almond butter, and flaxseed. To serve, spoon 1 cup cooked quinoa into a bowl, top with half the pudding and half the walnuts and raspberries. Make ahead: This is a great way to use leftover quinoa or plan ahead and make extra quinoa for dinner, so you can whip this together on a weekday morning as quickly as you would a smoothie.
Per serving (1 bowl): Calories: 392Kcal; Fat: 19g; Carbs: 49g; Fiber: 10g; Protein: 12g

57. Fruit Salad with Zesty Citrus Couscous

Preparation time: 5 minutes
Cooking time: 5 minutes
Servings: 1
Ingredients:

- 1 orange, zested, and juiced
- ¼ cup whole-wheat couscous, or corn couscous
- 1 cup assorted berries (strawberries, blackberries, blueberries)
- ½ cup cubed or balled melon (cantaloupe or honeydew)
- 1 tablespoon maple syrup or coconut sugar (optional)
- 1 tablespoon fresh mint, minced (optional)
- 1 tablespoon unsweetened coconut flakes

Directions:
Put the orange juice in a small pot, add half the zest, and bring to a boil. Put the dry couscous in a small bowl and pour the boiling orange juice over it. If there isn't enough juice to fully submerge the couscous, add just enough boiling water to do so. Cover the bowl with a plate or seal with wrap, and let steep for 5 minutes. In a medium bowl, toss the berries and melon with the maple syrup (if using) and the rest of the zest. You can either keep the fruit cool or heat it lightly in the small pot you used for the orange juice. When the couscous is soft, remove the cover and fluff it with a fork. Top with fruit, fresh mint, and coconut. Options: This would also be fantastic with cooked quinoa instead of couscous. Just leave it to marinate with the orange juice while you prepare the fruit.
Per serving: Calories: 496Kcal; Fat: 10g; Carbs: 97g; Fiber: 14g; Protein: 11g

58. Fruity Granola

Preparation time: 15 minutes
Cooking time: 45 minutes **Servings:** 5 cups
Ingredients:

- 2 cups rolled oats
- ¾ cup whole-grain flour
- 1 tablespoon ground cinnamon
- 1 teaspoon ground ginger (optional)
- ½ cup sunflower seeds, or walnuts, chopped
- ½ cup almonds, chopped
- ½ cup pumpkin seeds
- ½ cup unsweetened shredded coconut
- 1¼ cups pure fruit juice (cranberry, apple, or something similar)
- ½ cup raisins, or dried cranberries
- ½ cup goji berries (optional)

Directions:
Preheat the oven to 350°F.
Mix the oats, flour, cinnamon, ginger, sunflower seeds, almonds, pumpkin seeds, and coconut in a large bowl. Sprinkle the juice over the mixture, and stir until it's just moistened. You might need a bit more or a bit less liquid, depending on how much your oats and flour absorb. Spread the granola on a large baking sheet (the more spread out it is, the better), and put it in the oven. After about 15 minutes, use a spatula to turn the granola so that the middle gets dried out. Let the granola bake until it's as crunchy as you want it, about 30 minutes more.
Take the granola out of the oven and stir in the raisins and goji berries (if using).
6. Store leftovers in an airtight container for up to 2 weeks.
Leftovers: Serve with non-dairy milk and fresh fruit, use as a topper for morning porridge or a smoothie bowl to add a bit of crunch, or make a granola parfait by layering with non-dairy yogurt or puréed banana.
Per serving (½ cup): Calories: 398Kcal; Fat: 25g; Carbs: 39g; Fiber: 8g; Protein: 11g

59. Chickpea Scramble

Preparation time: 5 minutes
Cooking time: 15 minutes **Servings:** 1
Ingredients:

- 1 teaspoon olive oil, or 1 tablespoon vegetable broth or water
- ½ cup mushrooms, sliced - Pinch sea salt
- ½ cup chopped zucchini
- ½ cup chickpeas (cooked or canned)
- 1 teaspoon smoked paprika or regular paprika - 1 teaspoon turmeric
- 1 tablespoon nutritional yeast (optional)
- Freshly ground black pepper
- ½ cup cherry tomatoes, chopped

- ¼ cup fresh parsley, chopped

Directions:
Heat a large skillet to medium-high. Once the skillet is hot, add the olive oil and mushrooms, along with the sea salt to help them soften, and sauté, stirring occasionally 7 to 8 minutes. Add the zucchini to the skillet. If you're using canned chickpeas, rinse and drain them. Mash the chickpeas with a potato masher, fork, or fingers. Add them to the skillet and cook until they are heated through. Sprinkle the paprika, turmeric, and nutritional yeast over the chickpeas, and stir to combine. Toss in the black pepper, cherry tomatoes, and fresh parsley at the end, just to warm, reserving a small bit of parsley to use as garnish. Did You Know? Nutritional yeast is a yellow flaky seasoning with a savory and salty flavor. Most regular grocery stores carry it these days. Vegans often use it to add a cheesy or deeply savory taste to foods like popcorn.
Per serving: Calories: 265Kcal; Fat: 8g; Carbs: 37g; Fiber: 12g; Protein: 16g

60. Roasted Veg with Creamy Avocado Dip

Preparation time: 10 minutes
Cooking time: 30 minutes **Servings:** 2
Ingredients:
For The Avocado Dip
- 1 avocado
- 1 tablespoon apple cider vinegar
- ¼ to ½ cup water
- 2 tablespoons nutritional yeast
- 1 teaspoon dried dill or 1 tablespoon fresh dill - Pinch sea salt

For The Roasted Veg
- 1 small sweet potato, peeled and cubed
- 2 small beets, peeled and cubed
- 2 small carrots, peeled and cubed
- 1 teaspoon sea salt
- 1 teaspoon dried oregano
- ¼ teaspoon cayenne pepper
- Pinch freshly ground black pepper

Directions:
To Make the Avocado Dip
In a blender, purée the avocado with the other dip ingredients, using just enough water to get a smooth, creamy texture. Alternately, you can mash the avocado thoroughly in a large bowl, then stir in the rest of the dip ingredients.
To Make the Roasted Veg
Preheat the oven to 350°F. Put the sweet potato, beets, and carrots in a large pot with a small amount of water, and bring to a boil over high heat. Boil for 15 minutes until they're just barely soft, then drain. Sprinkle the salt, oregano, cayenne, and pepper over them and stir gently to combine. (Use more or less cayenne depending on your taste.)Spread the vegetables on a large baking sheet and roast them in the oven for 10 to 15 minutes until they've browned around the edges. Serve the veg with the avocado dip on the side.Make ahead: Make the roasted veg in large batches so that you have them on hand through the week to add to salads, bowls, and wraps.
Per serving: Calories: 335Kcal; Fat: 12g; Carbs: 51g; Fiber: 16g; Protein: 11g

61. Spinach Artichoke Quiche

Preparation time: 10 minutes
Cooking time: 55 minutes **Servings:** 4
Ingredients:
- 14 oz. tofu, soft
- 14 oz. of artichokes, chopped
- 2 cups spinach
- ½ of a large onion, peeled, chopped
- 1 lemon, juiced
- 1 teaspoon minced garlic
- ¼ teaspoon salt
- ¼ teaspoon ground black pepper
- 1 teaspoon dried basil
- ½ teaspoon turmeric
- 1 tablespoon coconut oil
- 1 teaspoon Dijon mustard
- ½ cup nutritional yeast
- 2 large tortillas, cut into half

Directions:
Switch on the oven, then set it to 350°f and let it preheat. Take a pie plate, grease it with oil, place tortilla to cover the bottom and sides of the plate, and bake for 10 to 15 minutes until baked. Meanwhile, take a large pan, place it over medium heat, add oil, and when hot, add onion and fry for 5 minutes. Then add garlic, cook for 1 minute until fragrant, stir in spinach and cook for 4 minutes until the spinach has wilted, set aside when done. Place tofu in a food processor, add all the spices, yeast, and lemon juice, and pulse for 2 minutes until smooth. Then add cooked onion mixture and artichokes, blend for 15 to 25 times until combined, and then pour the mixture over crust into the pie plate.
Bake quiche for 45 minutes until done, then cut it into wedges and serve.
Per serving: Calories: 105Kcal; Fat: 4.7g; Carbs: 25g; Fiber: 0.7g; Protein: 9.3g

62. Pumpkin Muffins

Preparation time: 15 minutes
Cooking time: 30 minutes **Servings:** 9
Ingredients:
- 2 tablespoons mashed ripe banana
- 2 flax eggs
- 1 teaspoon vanilla extract, unsweetened
- ¼ cup maple syrup
- ¼ cup olive oil
- 2/3 cup coconut sugar
- 3/4 cup pumpkin puree
- 1 ¼ teaspoon pumpkin pie spice
- ¼ teaspoon sea salt
- ½ teaspoon ground cinnamon
- 2 teaspoons baking soda
- ½ cup water
- ½ cup almond meal
- 1 cup gluten-free flour blend
- 3/4 cup rolled oats

For the Crumble
- 2 tablespoons chopped pecans
- 3 ½ tablespoons gluten-free flour blend
- 3 tablespoons coconut sugar
- 1/8 teaspoon cinnamon
- 1/8 teaspoon pumpkin pie spice
- 1 ¼ tablespoon coconut oil

Directions:
Switch on the oven, then set it to 350°f and let it preheat. Meanwhile, prepare the muffin batter and for this, place the first seven ingredients in a bowl and whisk until combined. Then whisk in the next five ingredients until mixed and gradually beat in remaining ingredients until incorporated and smooth batter comes together. Prepare crumble, and for this, place all of its ingredients in a bowl and stir until combined. Distribute the batter evenly between ten muffin tins lined with muffin liners, top with prepared crumble, and then bake for 30 minutes until muffins are set and the tops are golden brown. When done, let muffins cool for 5 minutes, then take them out to cool completely and serve.

Per serving: Calories: 329Kcal; Fat: 12.7g; Carbs: 52.6g; Protein: 4.6g; Fiber: 5g

63. Tomato and Asparagus Quiche

Preparation time: 40 minutes
Cooking time: 35 minutes
Servings: 12
Ingredients:
For the Dough:
- 2 cups whole wheat flour
- ½ teaspoon salt
- 3/4 cup vegan margarine
- 1/3 cup water

For the Filling:
14 oz. silken tofu
- 6 cherry tomatoes, halved
- 2 green onions, cut into rings
- 10 sun-dried tomatoes in oil, chopped
- 7 oz. green asparagus, diced
- 1 ½ tablespoons herbs de Provence
- 1 tablespoon cornstarch
- 1 teaspoon turmeric - 3 tablespoons olive oil

Directions:
Switch on the oven, then set it to 350°f and let it preheat. Prepare the dough and for this, take a bowl, place all the ingredients for it, beat until incorporated, then knead for 5 minutes until smooth, and refrigerate the dough for 30 minutes. Meanwhile, take a skillet pan, place it over medium heat, add 1 tablespoon oil and when hot, add green onion and cook for 2 minutes. Set aside until required. Place a pot half full with salty water over medium heat, bring it to boil, then add asparagus and boil for 3 minutes until tender. Drain and set aside until required. Take a medium bowl, add tofu along with herbs de Provence, starch, turmeric, and oil, whisk until smooth and then fold in tomatoes, green onion, and asparagus until mixed. Divide the prepared dough into twelve sections, take a muffin tray, line twelve cups with baking cups, and then press a dough ball at the bottom of each cup and all the way

Plant based cookbook for beginners

up. Fill the cups with prepared tofu mixture, top with tomatoes, and bake for 35 minutes until cooked. Serve straight away.

Per serving: Calories: 206Kcal; Fat: 14g; Carbs: 16g; Protein: 4g; Fiber: 2g

64. Simple Vegan Breakfast Hash

Preparation time: 10 minutes
Cooking time: 25 minutes
Servings: 4
Ingredients:
For The Potatoes:
- 1 large sweet potato, peeled, diced
- 3 medium potatoes, peeled, diced
- 1 tablespoon onion powder - 2 teaspoons sea salt
- 1 tablespoon garlic powder
- 1 teaspoon ground black pepper
- 1 teaspoon dried thyme
- ¼ cup olive oil

For The Skillet Mixture:
- 1 medium onion, peeled, diced
- 5 cloves of garlic, peeled, minced
- ¼ teaspoon of sea salt
- ¼ teaspoon ground black pepper
- 1 teaspoon olive oil

Directions:
Switch on the oven, then set it to 450°f and let it preheat. Meanwhile, take a casserole dish, add all the ingredients for the potatoes, toss until coated, and then cook for 20 minutes until crispy, stirring halfway. Then take a skillet pan, place it over medium heat, add oil, and when hot, add onion and garlic, season with salt and black pepper, and cook for 5 minutes until browned. When potatoes have roasted, add garlic and cooked onion mixture, stir until combined, and serve.

Per serving: Calories: 212Kcal; Fat: 10g; Carbs: 28g; Protein: 3g; Fiber: 4g

65. Chickpeas On Toast

Preparation time: 5 minutes
Cooking time: 15 minutes
Servings: 6
Ingredients:
- 14-oz cooked chickpeas
- 1 cup baby spinach
- ½ cup chopped white onion
- 1 cup crushed tomatoes
- ½ teaspoon minced garlic
- ¼ teaspoon ground black pepper
- ½ teaspoon brown sugar
- 1 teaspoon smoked paprika powder
- 1/3 teaspoon sea salt
- 1 tablespoon olive oil
- 6 slices of gluten-free bread, toasted

Directions:
Take a frying pan, place it over medium heat, add oil, and when hot, add onion and cook for 2 minutes. Then stir in garlic, cook for 30 seconds until fragrant, stir in paprika and

continue cooking for 10 seconds. Add tomatoes, stir, bring the mixture to simmer, season with black pepper, sugar, and salt, and then stir in chickpeas. Stir in spinach, cook for 2 minutes until leaves have wilted, then remove the pan from heat and taste to adjust seasoning. Serve cooked chickpeas on toasted bread.

Per serving: Calories: 305Kcal; Fat: 7.6g; Carbs: 45g; Fiber: 8g; Protein: 13g

66. Blueberry Muffins

Preparation time: 5 minutes
Cooking time: 15 minutes **Servings:** 12
Ingredients:

- 2 cups fresh blueberries
- 2 cups all-purpose flour
- 2 ½ teaspoons baking powder
- ½ teaspoon salt
- ¼ teaspoon baking soda
- ½ cup and 2 tablespoon sugar
- Zest of 1 lemon
- 1 teaspoon apple cider vinegar
- ¼ cup and 2 tablespoons canola oil
- 1 cup of soy milk
- 1 teaspoon vanilla extract, unsweetened

Directions:
Switch on the oven, then set it to 450°f and let it preheat. Meanwhile, take a small bowl, add vinegar and milk, whisk until combined, and let it stand to curdle. Take a large bowl, add flour, salt, baking powder, and soda, and stir until mixed. Whisk in sugar, lemon zest, oil, and vanilla into soy milk mixture, then gradually whisk in flour mixture until incorporated and fold in berries until combined. Take a twelve cups muffin tray, grease them with oil, distribute the prepared batter in them and bake for 25 minutes until done and the tops are browned. Let muffins cool for 5 minutes, then cool them completely and serve.

Per serving: Calories: 160Kcal; Fat: 5g; Carbs: 25g; Fiber: 2g; Protein: 2g

67. Ultimate Breakfast Sandwich

Preparation time: 40 minutes
Cooking time: 10 minutes **Servings:** 4
Ingredients:
For the Tofu:

- 12 ounces tofu, extra-firm, pressed, drain
- ½ teaspoon garlic powder
- 1 teaspoon liquid smoke
- 2 tablespoons nutritional yeast
- 1 teaspoon Sirach sauce
- 2 tablespoons soy sauce
- 2 tablespoons olive oil
- 2 tablespoons water
- For the Vegan Breakfast Sandwich:
- 1 large tomato, sliced
- 4 English muffins, halved, toasted
- 1 avocado, mashed

Directions:
Prepare tofu, and for this, cut tofu into 4 slices and set aside. Stir together the remaining ingredients of tofu, pour the mixture into a bag, add tofu pieces, toss until coated, and marinate for 30 minutes. Take a skillet pan, place it over medium-high heat, add tofu slices along with the marinade and cook for 5 minutes per side.
Prepare sandwich and for this, spread mashed avocado on the inner of the muffin, top with a slice of tofu, layer with a tomato slice, and then serve.

Per serving: Calories: 277Kcal; Fat: 9.1g; Carbs: 33.1g; Fiber: 3.6g; Protein: 16.1g

68. Waffles with Fruits

Preparation time: 10 minutes
Cooking time: 20 minutes **Servings:** 4
Ingredients:

- 1 ¼ cups all-purpose flour
- 2 teaspoons baking powder
- 3 tablespoons sugar
- ¼ teaspoon salt
- 2 teaspoons vanilla extract, unsweetened
- 2 tablespoons coconut oil
- 1 ¼ cup soy milk
- Sliced fruits for topping
- Vegan whipping cream for topping

Directions:
Switch on the waffle maker and let it preheat. Meanwhile, place flour in a bowl, stir in salt, baking powder, and sugar, and whisk in remaining ingredients, except for topping, until incorporated.
Ladle the batter into the waffle maker and cook until firm and brown.
When done, top waffles with fruits and whipped cream and serve.

Per serving: Calories: 277Kcal; Fat: 8.3g; Carbs: 42.5g; Fiber: 1.5g; Protein: 6.2g

69. Scrambled Tofu Breakfast Burrito

Preparation time: 15 minutes
Cooking time: 20 minutes **Servings:** 4
Ingredients:

- 4 large tortillas
- 1 medium avocado, chopped
- Cilantro as needed
- Salsa as needed

For the Tofu:
12-ounce tofu, extra-firm, pressed

- ¼ cup minced parsley
- 1 ½ teaspoons minced garlic
- 1 teaspoon nutritional yeast
- ¼ teaspoon sea salt
- ½ teaspoon red chili powder
- ½ teaspoon cumin
- 1 teaspoon olive oil
- 1 tablespoon hummus

For the Vegetables:

- 5 baby potatoes, chopped

- 1 medium red bell pepper, sliced
- 2 cups chopped kale
- ½ teaspoon ground cumin
- 1/8 teaspoon sea salt
- ½ teaspoon red chili powder
- 1 teaspoon oil

Directions:
Switch on the oven, then set it to 400°f and let it preheat. Take a baking sheet, add potato and bell pepper, drizzle with oil, season with all the spices, toss until coated, and bake for 15 minutes until tender and nicely browned. Then add kale to the potatoes, cook for 5 minutes, and set aside until required. In the meantime, take a skillet pan, place it over medium heat, add oil and when hot, add tofu, crumble it well and cook for 10 minutes until lightly browned. In the meantime, take a small bowl, add hummus and remaining ingredients for the tofu and stir until combined. Add hummus mixture into tofu, stir and cook for 3 minutes, set aside until required.

Assemble the burritos and for this, distribute roasted vegetables on the tortilla, top with tofu, avocado, and cilantro, and salsa, roll and then serve.

Per serving: Calories: 441Kcal; Fat: 19.6g; Carbs: 53.5g; Fiber: 8g; Protein: 16.5g

70. Pancake

Preparation time: 10 minutes **Cooking time:** 18 minutes
Servings: 4
Ingredients:
Dry Ingredients:
- 1 cup buckwheat flour
- 1/8 teaspoon salt
- ½ teaspoon gluten-free baking powder
- ½ teaspoon baking soda

Wet Ingredients:
- 1 tablespoon almond butter
- 2 tablespoons maple syrup
- 1 tablespoon lime juice
- 1 cup coconut milk, unsweetened

Directions:
Take a medium bowl, add all the dry ingredients and stir until mixed. Take another bowl, place all the wet ingredients, whisk until combined, and then gradually whisk in dry ingredients mixture until smooth and incorporated. Take a frying pan, place it over medium heat, add 2 teaspoons oil and when hot, drop in batter and cook for 3 minutes per side until cooked and lightly browned.

Serve pancakes and fruits and maple syrup.

Per serving: Calories: 148Kcal; Fat: 8.2g; Carbs: 15g; Fiber: 1.7g; Protein: 4.6g

71. Honey Buckwheat Coconut Porridge

Preparation time: 20 minutes **Cooking time:** 15 minutes
Servings: 2
Ingredients:
- ¼ cup buckwheat, toasted, ground
- 1 tablespoon coconut, shredded
- 2 tablespoons pecans, chopped
- ½ cup + 2 tablespoons coconut milk

Plant based cookbook for beginners

- 1 tablespoon raw honey
- ¾ teaspoon vanilla
- ¾ cup of water
- 2 tablespoons currants
- 1 drizzle coconut syrup

Directions:
In a small pot, boil the coconut milk, honey, vanilla, and water. Stir in the ground buckwheat, then reduce the heat to low. Cook for 10 minutes, covered. Add extra liquid during the cooking if needed.

Transfer to a bowl and serve with shredded coconut, pecans, currants, and a drizzle of coconut syrup.

Per serving: Calories: 268Kcal; Fat: 19.86g; Carbs: 22.33g; Fiber: 4.1g; Protein: 3.64g

72. Tempeh and Potato

Preparation time: 30 minutes **Cooking time:** 20 minutes
Servings: 4
Ingredients:
- 1 package (8 oz) tempeh, finely diced
- 4 red potatoes
- 6 leaves lacinato kale, stemmed, chopped
- 2 tablespoons olive oil
- 1 medium onion, chopped
- 1 medium green bell pepper, diced
- 1 teaspoon smoked paprika
- 1 teaspoon seasoning, salt-free
- Ground pepper, salt, to taste

Directions:
Microwave the potatoes until done, but still firm. Finely chop them when cool. Preheat oil in a skillet over medium heat. Sauté onions until translucent. Add tempeh, potatoes and bell pepper, and sauté, stirring constantly over medium-high heat until golden brown. Stir in the kale and seasoning, then cook, stirring constantly until the mixture is a bit browned. Occasionally add water to prevent sticking if necessary. Sprinkle with pepper and salt to taste. Serve hot.

Per serving: Calories: 342Kcal; Fat: 7.41g; Carbs: 64.1g; Fiber: 7.4g; Protein: 7.84g

73. Breakfast French Toast

Preparation time:
Cooking time: 6 minutes **Servings:** 1
Ingredients:
- 2 slices bread, gluten-free
- 2 teaspoons cinnamon
- 2 tablespoons flaxseed, ground
- 6 oz. soy milk
- 2 teaspoons vanilla extract
- 1 scoop vegan Protein: powder

Directions:
Mix cinnamon, flaxseed, soy milk, vanilla extract, and Protein: powder in a deep baking dish. Deep the bread slices into the mixture to coat. Preheat a non-stick frying pan over medium heat and toast the bread for 3 minutes per side. Enjoy!

Per serving: Calories: 506Kcal; Fat: 15.99g; Carbs: 52.99g; Fiber: 12.5g; Protein: 35.24g

74. Dairy-Free Pumpkin Pancakes

Preparation time: 10 minutes
Cooking time: 10 minutes **Servings:** 12
Ingredients:
- 1-cup all-purpose flour - 2 teaspoons baking powder
- ½ cup pumpkin puree
- 1 egg - 3 tablespoons chia seeds
- 3 tablespoons coconut oil, melted, slightly cooled
- 1 cup almond milk
- 2 teaspoons vanilla extract
- 1 tablespoon white vinegar
- 1 tablespoon maple syrup
- 1 teaspoon pumpkin pie spice
- ½ teaspoon kosher salt

Directions:
Combine almond milk and vinegar in a bowl. Let rest for 5 minutes. Mix flour, baking powder, baking soda, chia seeds, pumpkin pie spice, and salt in a separate bowl. Whisk eggs into the almond milk, then stir in pumpkin puree, coconut oil, vanilla, and maple syrup. Pour the wet ingredients into the dry ingredients and mix until blended. Add in more almond milk if the batter is thick. Place a non-stick frying pan over medium heat. Scoop out 1/3 of the batter and pour it into the pan. Cook for 1 minute, then flip to the other side and cook until golden brown. Do this with the remaining batter and serve.
Per serving: Calories: 124Kcal; Fat: 6.99g; Carbs: 12.34g; Fiber: 0.7g; Protein: 3.43g

75. Protein Blueberry Bars

Preparation time: 1 hour
Cooking time: 5 minutes **Servings:** 16
Ingredients:
- ½ cup dried blueberries
- 1 ½ cups rolled oats
- ¾ cup whole almonds
- 1/3 cup ground flaxseed
- 1/3 cup walnuts
- ¼ cup sunflower seeds
- ½ cup pistachios
- 1/3 cup pepitas
- ¼ cup apple sauce
- 1/3 cup maple syrup
- 1 cup almond butter

Directions:
In a bowl, mix rolled oats, blueberries, almonds, flaxseed, walnuts, sunflower seeds, pistachios, and pepitas together. Stir in apple sauce and maple syrup. Mix in almond butter, then pour the batter into a baking sheet lined with parchment paper (paper should be big enough to cover and hang over the baking sheet edges). Firmly press down the batter using your palms, then spread evenly. Refrigerate for 1 hour. Remove from the freezer afterward and lift the batter from the pan by lifting from the paper. Place on a working surface and gently remove the paper. Cut the dough into 16 bars and serve.
Per serving: Calories: 221Kcal; Fat: 15.96g; Carbs: 18.26g; Fiber: 5g; Protein: 7.77g

76. Chickpea Scramble Breakfast Basin

Preparation time:
Cooking time: 10 minutes **Servings:** 2
Ingredients:
For chickpea scramble:
- 1 can (15 oz.) chickpeas
- A drizzle of olive oil
- ¼ white onion, diced
- 2 garlic cloves, minced
- ½ teaspoon turmeric
- ½ teaspoon pepper
- ½ teaspoon salt

For breakfast basin:
- 1 avocado, wedged
- Greens, combined
- Handful parsley, minced
- Handful cilantro, minced

Directions:
For chickpea scramble:
Scoop out the chickpeas and a little bit of its water into a bowl. Slightly mash the chickpeas using a fork, intentionally omitting some. Stir in turmeric, pepper, and salt until adequately combined.
Sauté onions in olive oil until soft, then add garlic and cook for 1 minute. Stir in the chickpeas and sauté for 5 minutes.
For breakfast basin and serving:
Get 2 breakfast basins. Layer the bottom of the basins with the combined greens. Top with chickpea scramble, parsley, and cilantro. Enjoy with avocado wedges.
Per serving: Calories: 348Kcal; Fat: 18.3g; Carbs: 39.63g; Fiber: 15.2g; Protein: 11.42g

77. Quinoa, Oats, Hazelnut and Blueberry Salad

Preparation time: 10 minutes
Cooking time: 35 minutes **Servings:** 8
Ingredients:
- 1 cup golden quinoa, dry
- 1 cup oats, cut into pieces
- 2 cups blueberries
- 2 cups hazelnuts, roughly chopped, toasted
- ½ cup dry millet
- 2 large lemons, zested, juiced
- 3 tablespoons olive oil, divided
- ½ cup maple syrup
- 1 cup Greek yogurt
- 1 (1-inch) piece fresh ginger, peeled, cut
- ¼ teaspoon nutmeg

Directions:
Combine quinoa, oats, and millet in a large bowl. Rinse, drain and set aside.
Add one tablespoon olive oil into a saucepan and place over medium-high heat. Cook the rinsed grains in it for 3 minutes. Add 4 ½ cups of water and salt. Add the zest of 1 lemon and ginger.

When the mixture boils, cover the pot and cook in reduced heat for 20 minutes. Remove from heat. Let rest for 5 minutes. Uncover and fluff with a fork. Discard the ginger and layer the grains on a large baking sheet. Let cool for 30 minutes.

Transfer the grains into a large bowl and mix in the remaining lemon zest.

Combine the juice of both lemons with the remaining olive oil in a separate bowl. Stir in the yogurt, maple syrup, and nutmeg. Pour the mixture into the grains and stir. Mix in the blueberries and hazelnuts. Refrigerate overnight, then serve.

Per serving: Calories: 522Kcal, Fat: 28.49g; Carbs: 64.34g; Fiber: 8.7g; Protein: 11.93g

78. Chia Flaxseed Waffles

Preparation time: 15 minutes
Cooking time: 10 minutes **Servings:** 8
Ingredients:

- 2 cups ground golden flaxseed
- 2 tsp cinnamon - 10 tsp ground chia seed
- 15 tbsp warm water
- 1/3 cup coconut oil, melted
- 1/2 cup water
- 1 tbsp baking powder
- 1 tsp sea salt

Directions:
Preheat the waffle iron. In a small bowl, mix ground chia seed and warm water. In a large bowl, mix ground flaxseed, sea salt, and baking powder. Set aside. Add melted coconut oil, chia seed mixture, and water into the blender and blend for 30 seconds. Transfer coconut oil mixture into the flaxseed mixture and mix well. Add cinnamon and stir well. Scoop waffle mixture into the hot waffle iron and cook on each side for 3-5 minutes. Serve and enjoy.

Per serving: Calories: 240Kcal; Fat: 20.6g; Carbs: 12.9g; Protein: 7g

79. Flax Almond Muffins

Preparation time: 10 minutes
Cooking time: 35 minutes **Servings:** 6
Ingredients:

- 1 tsp cinnamon
- 2 tbsp coconut flour
- 20 drops liquid stevia
- 1/4 cup water - 1/4 tsp vanilla extract
- 1/4 tsp baking soda
- 1/2 tsp baking powder
- 1/4 cup almond flour
- 1/2 cup ground flax
- 2 tbsp ground chia

Directions:
Preheat the oven to 350 F/ 176 C. Spray muffin tray with cooking spray and set aside. In a small bowl, add 6 tablespoons of water and ground chia. Mix well and set aside. In a mixing bowl, add ground flax, baking soda, baking powder, cinnamon, coconut flour, and almond flour and mix well. Add chia seed mixture, vanilla, water, and liquid stevia and stir well to combine. Pour mixture into the prepared muffin tray and bake in preheated oven for 35 minutes. Serve and enjoy. **Per serving:** Calories: 92Kcal; Fat: 6.3g; Carbs: 6.9g; Protein: 3.7g

80. Whole Wheat Pizza with Summer Produce

Preparation time: 15 minutes
Cooking time: 15 minutes **Servings:** 2
Ingredients:

- 1-pound whole wheat pizza dough
- 4 ounces goat cheese
- 2/3 cup blueberries
- 2 ears corn, husked
- 2 yellow squash, sliced
- 2 tbsp olive oil

Directions:
Preheat the oven to 450°f. Roll the dough out to make a pizza crust. Crumble the cheese on the crust. Spread remaining ingredients, then drizzle with olive oil. Bake for about 15 minutes. Serve.
Per serving: Calories: 470; Carbs: 66g; Fat: 18g; Protein: 17g

81. Chives Avocado Mix

Preparation time: 5 minutes **Cooking time:** 0 minutes
Servings: 4
Ingredients:
2 avocados, peeled, pitted, and roughly cubed

- 1 tomato, cubed
- 1 cucumber, sliced
- 1 celery stalk, chopped
- 2 tablespoons avocado oil
- 1 tablespoon lime juice
- Salt and black pepper to the taste
- 2 scallions, chopped
- ½ teaspoon cayenne pepper
- 1 tablespoon chives, chopped

Directions:
In a bowl, combine the avocados with the tomato, cucumber, and the other ingredients, toss, divide between plates and serve for breakfast. **Per serving:** Calories: 232Kcal; Fat: 20.7g; Carbs: 13.2g; Fiber: 8g; Protein: 2.9g

82. Zucchini Pan

Preparation time: 5 minutes
Cooking time: 15 minutes
Servings: 4
Ingredients:

- 2 shallots, chopped
- 1 tablespoon olive oil
- 3 zucchinis, roughly cubed
- 2 garlic cloves, minced
- 2 sun-dried tomatoes, chopped
- 1 tablespoon capers, drained
- Salt and black pepper to the taste
- 1 tablespoon dill, chopped

Directions:
Heat a pan with the oil over medium heat, add the shallots, garlic, and tomatoes and sauté for 5 minutes.
Add the zucchinis and the other ingredients, toss, cook over medium heat for 10 minutes more, divide between plates and serve. **Per serving:** Calories: 73gKcal; Fat: 4g; Carbs: 9.2g; Fiber: 2.6g; Protein: 2.8g

83. Chili Spinach and Zucchini Pan
Preparation time: 5 minutes
Cooking time: 15 minutes
Servings: 4
Ingredients:
1-pound baby spinach
- 1 tablespoon olive oil
- 2 zucchinis, sliced
- 1 tomato, cubed
- 2 shallots, chopped
- 1 tablespoon lime juice
- 2 garlic cloves, minced
- 2 teaspoons red chili flakes
- 1 teaspoon chili powder
- Salt and black pepper to the taste

Directions:
Heat a pan with the oil over medium heat, add the shallots, garlic, chili powder, and chili flakes, stir and sauté for 5 minutes.
Add the spinach, zucchinis and the other ingredients, toss, cook over medium heat for 10 minutes more, divide into bowls and serve for breakfast.
Per serving: Calories: 85gKcal; Fat: 4.3g; Carbs: 10.6g; Fiber: 4.1g; Protein: 4.9g

84. Basil Tomato and Cabbage Bowls
Preparation time: 5 minutes
Cooking time: 0 minutes **Servings:** 4
Ingredients:
- 1-pound cherry tomatoes, halved
- 1 cup red cabbage, shredded
- 2 tablespoons balsamic vinegar
- 2 shallots, chopped
- 1 tablespoon avocado oil
- Salt and black pepper to the taste
- 1 tablespoon basil, chopped

Directions:
In a bowl, combine the cabbage with the tomatoes and the other ingredients, toss and serve for breakfast.
Per serving: Calories: 35Kcal; Fat: 0.7g; Carbs: 6.6g; Fiber: 2g; Protein: 1.4g

85. Spinach and Zucchini Hash
Preparation time: 5 minutes
Cooking time: 15 minutes
Servings: 4
Ingredients:
- 2 zucchinis, cubed
- 2 cups baby spinach
- A pinch of salt and black pepper
- 1 tablespoon olive oil
- 1 teaspoon chili powder
- 1 teaspoon rosemary, dried
- ½ cup coconut cream
- 1 tablespoon chives, chopped

Directions:
Heat a pan with the oil over medium heat, add the zucchinis and the chili powder, stir and cook for 5 minutes. Add the rest of the ingredients, toss, cook the mix for 10 minutes more, divide between plates and serve for breakfast.
Per serving: Calories: 121Kcal; Fat: 11.1g; Fiber: 2.5g; Carbs: 6.1g; Protein: 2.4g

86. Tomato and Zucchini Fritters
Preparation time: 5 minutes
Cooking time: 10 minutes
Servings: 4
Ingredients:
- 1-pound zucchinis, grated
- 2 tomatoes, cubed
- 2 garlic cloves, minced
- Salt and black pepper to the taste
- 1 tablespoon coconut flour
- 1 tablespoon flaxseed mixed with 2 tablespoons water
- 1 tablespoon dill, chopped
- 2 tablespoons olive oil

Directions:
In a bowl, mix the zucchinis with the tomatoes and the other ingredients, except for the oil, stir well, shape medium fritters out of this mix, and flatten them.
Heat a pan with the oil over medium heat, add the fritters, cook them for 5 minutes on each side, divide between plates and serve for breakfast.
Per serving: Calories: 111Kcal; Fat: 8.2g; Carbs: 9g; Fiber: 3.4g; Protein: 2.8g

87. Peppers Casserole
Preparation time: 10 minutes
Cooking time: 25 minutes
Servings: 4
Ingredients:
- 1-pound mixed bell peppers, cut into strips
- Salt and black pepper to the taste
- 4 scallions, chopped
- ½ teaspoon cumin, ground
- ½ teaspoon oregano, dried
- ½ teaspoon basil, dried
- 2 garlic cloves, minced
- 1 tablespoon avocado oil
- 2 tomatoes, cubed
- 1 cup cashew cheese, grated
- 2 tablespoons parsley, chopped

Directions:
Heat a pan with the oil over medium heat, add the scallions and the garlic and sauté for 5 minutes.

Add the rest of the ingredients, except for the cheese, stir and cook for 5 minutes more.
Sprinkle the cashew cheese on top and bake everything at 380 degrees F for 15 minutes.
Divide the mix between plates and serve for breakfast.
Per serving: Calories: 85Kcal; Fat: 3.6g; Carbs: 11.8g; Fiber: 3.9g; Protein: 3.3g

88. Eggplant and Broccoli Casserole
Preparation time: 10 minutes
Cooking time: 35 minutes
Servings: 4
Ingredients:
- 1-pound eggplants, roughly cubed
- 1 cup broccoli florets
- 1 cup cashew cheese, shredded
- ¼ cup almond milk
- 2 scallions, chopped
- 1 tablespoon olive oil
- 2 tablespoons flaxseed mixed with 2 tablespoons water
- 1 tablespoon cilantro, chopped
- Salt and black pepper to the taste

Directions:
In a roasting pan, combine the eggplants with the broccoli and the other ingredients, except for the cashew cheese and the almond milk, and toss.
In a bowl, combine the milk with the cashew cheese, stir, pour over the eggplant mix, spread, introduce the pan in the oven and bake at 380 degrees F for 35 minutes.
Cool the casserole down, slice, and serve.
Per serving: Calories: 161Kcal; Fat: 11.4g; Carbs: 12.8g; Fiber: 6.6g; Protein: 4.2g

89. Creamy Avocado and Nuts Bowls
Preparation time: 5 minutes
Cooking time: 0 minutes
Servings: 4
Ingredients:
- 1 tablespoon walnuts, chopped
- 1 tablespoon pine nuts, toasted
- 2 avocados, peeled, pitted, and roughly cubed
- 1 tablespoon lime juice
- 1 tablespoon avocado oil
- Salt and black pepper to the taste
- ¼ cup coconut cream

Directions:
In a bowl, combine the avocados with the nuts and the other ingredients, toss, divide into smaller bowls and serve for breakfast.
Per serving: Calories: 273Kcal; Fat: 26.3g; Carbs: 11.1g; Fiber: 7.5g; Protein: 3.1g

90. Avocado and Watermelon Salad
Preparation time: 5 minutes
Cooking time: 0 minutes **Servings:** 4
Ingredients:
- 2 cups watermelon, peeled and roughly cubed
- 2 avocados, peeled, pitted, and roughly cubed
- 1 tablespoon lime juice
- 1 tablespoon avocado oil
- ¼ cup almonds, chopped

Directions:
In a bowl, combine the watermelon with the avocados and the other ingredients, toss and serve for breakfast.
Per serving: Calories: 270Kcal; Fat: 23.1g; Carbs: 16.7g; Fiber: 3g; Protein: 3.7g

91. Chia and Coconut Pudding
Preparation time: 10 minutes
Cooking time: 0 minutes.
Servings: 4
Ingredients:
- ¼ cup walnuts, chopped
- 2 cups coconut milk - ¼ cup coconut flakes
- 3 tablespoons chia seeds
- 1 tablespoon stevia
- 1 teaspoon almond extract

Directions:
In a bowl, combine the milk with the coconut flakes and the other ingredients, toss, leave aside for 10 minutes and serve for breakfast.
Per serving: Calories: 414Kcal; Fat: 39.2g; Carbs: 14.3g; Fiber: 8.5g; Protein: 7.1g

92. Tomato and Cucumber Salad
Preparation time: 5 minutes
Cooking time: 0 minutes
Servings: 4
Ingredients:
- 2 cups cherry tomatoes, halved
- 2 cucumbers, sliced
- 1 tablespoon lime juice
- A pinch of salt and black pepper
- 1 tablespoon olive oil
- ½ cup kalamata olives, pitted and halved
- 1 tablespoon chives, chopped

Directions:
In a bowl, combine the tomatoes with the cucumbers and the other ingredients, toss, and serve for breakfast.
Per serving: Calories: 91Kcal; Fat: 5.7g; Carbs: 11g; Fiber: 2.5g; Protein: 2g

93. Walnuts and Olives Bowls
Preparation time: 5 minutes
Cooking time: 0 minutes **Servings:** 4
Ingredients:
- 1 cup walnuts, roughly chopped
- 1 cup black olives, pitted and halved
- 1 cup green olives, pitted and halved
- 1 tablespoon lime juice
- 1 teaspoon chili powder

- 1 teaspoon rosemary, dried
- 1 teaspoon cumin, ground
- 2 spring onions, chopped
- 1 tablespoon cilantro, chopped
- A pinch of salt and black pepper
- 2 tablespoons avocado oil

Directions:
In a bowl, mix olives with the walnuts and the other ingredients, toss, divide into smaller bowls and serve for breakfast.
Per serving: Calories: 260 Kcal; Fat: 24g; Carbs: X8.5g; Fiber: 4.5g; Protein: 8.4 g

94. Kale and Broccoli Pan
Preparation time: 5 minutes
Cooking time: 12 minutes **Servings:** 4
Ingredients:
- 1 cup broccoli florets - 2 shallots, chopped
- 1 tablespoon olive oil
- 1 teaspoon sweet paprika
- 1 teaspoon turmeric powder
- 1 cup kale, torn
- Salt and black pepper to the taste
- ¼ cup cashew cheese, grated
- 2 tablespoons chives, chopped

Directions:
Heat a pan with the oil over medium heat, add the shallots and sauté for 2 minutes. Add the broccoli, kale and the other ingredients, toss, cook for 10 minutes more, divide between plates and serve.
Per serving: Calories: 63Kcal; Fat: 4.4g; Carbs: 5.3g; Fiber: 1.3g; Protein: 1.8g

95. Spinach and Berries Salad
Preparation time: 5 minutes
Cooking time: 0 minutes **Servings:** 4
Ingredients:
- 1 cup baby spinach - 1 cup blackberries
- 1 cup blueberries - 1 tablespoon avocado oil
- 1 tablespoon balsamic vinegar
- 1 tablespoon parsley, chopped
- ½ cup pine nuts, chopped
- Salt and black pepper to the taste

Directions:
In a salad bowl, combine the spinach with the berries and the other ingredients, toss and serve for breakfast.
Per serving: Calories: 158Kcal; Fat: 12.4g; Carbs: 11.5g; Fiber: 3.8g; Protein: 3.4g

96. Cauliflower Hash
Preparation time: 10 minutes **Cooking time:** 15 minutes
Servings: 4
Ingredients:
- 2 cups cauliflower florets, roughly chopped
- ½ teaspoon basil, dried
- 1 teaspoon sage, dried
- 2 spring onions, chopped

- 1 tablespoon avocado oil
- ½ cup coconut cream
- ½ teaspoon sweet paprika
- Salt and black pepper to the taste
- 1 tablespoon cilantro, chopped

Directions:
Heat a pan with the oil over medium heat, add the onions and sauté for 5 minutes. Add the cauliflower and the other ingredients, toss, cook everything for 10 minutes more, divide between plates, and serve for breakfast.
Per serving: Calories: 90Kcal; Fat: 7.77g; Carbs: 5.3g; Fiber: 2.4g; Protein: 1.9g

97. Spinach and Green Beans Casserole
Preparation time: 10 minutes **Cooking time:** 40 minutes
Servings: 4
Ingredients:
- 1-pound green beans, trimmed and halved
- 4 scallions, chopped -1 cup baby spinach
- 1 tablespoon coconut oil, melted
- 2 tablespoons flaxseed mixed with 3 tablespoons water - ½ cup cashew cheese, grated
- Salt and black pepper to the taste
- ½ teaspoon thyme, chopped

Directions:
Heat a pan with the oil over medium heat, add the scallions and sauté for 5 minutes. Add the green beans and the other ingredients, except for the cheese, stir and cook for 5 minutes more. Sprinkle the cheese on top and bake the mix at 390 degrees F for 30 minutes. Divide the mix between plates and serve. **Per serving:** Calories: 273Kcal; Fat: 13.7g; Carbs: 2.2g; Fiber: 0.2g; Protein: 1.5g

98. Spiced Zucchini and Eggplant Bowls
Preparation time: 10 minutes
Cooking time: 15 minutes **Servings:** 4
Ingredients:
- 1 tablespoon olive oil
- 4 scallions, chopped
- 2 zucchinis, cubed - 1 eggplant, cubed
- 1 tablespoon cilantro, chopped
- 1 teaspoon rosemary, dried
- 1 teaspoon allspice, ground
- 1 teaspoon nutmeg, ground
- ¼ cup coconut cream
- Salt and black pepper to the taste
- 1 tablespoon chives, chopped

Directions:
Heat a pan with the oil over medium heat, add the scallions, allspice, and the nutmeg and sauté for 5 minutes. Add the zucchini, eggplant, and the other ingredients, toss, cook over medium heat for 10 minutes, divide into bowls and serve for breakfast.
Per serving: Calories: 242Kcal; Fat: 6.4g; Carbs: 10g; Fiber: 2g; Protein: 2g

CHAPTER 14:
Salads

99. Black Bean Lentil Salad
Preparation time: 10 minutes
Cooking time: 20 minutes **Servings:** 5
Ingredients:
- 1 Red Bell Pepper, diced
- 2/3 cup Cilantro
- 1 cup Green Lentils
- 2 Roma Tomatoes, diced
- ½ of 1 Red Onion, small & diced
- 15 oz. Black Beans

For dressing:
- ½ tsp. Oregano
- Juice of 1 Lime
- 1/8 tsp. Salt
- 2 tbsp. Olive Oil
- 1 tsp. Cumin
- 1 tsp. Dijon Mustard
- 2 Garlic cloves

Directions:
To begin with, cook the lentils in a large pan over medium heat, following the manufacturer's instructions. Tip: The lentils should be cooked to firm but not mushy. In the meantime, mix all the ingredients needed to make the dressing in a small bowl until combined well. After that, combine the beans with bell pepper, red onion, cilantro, and red onion. Spoon on the dressing. Toss well and serve immediately. Tip: If desired, you can add your choice of seasoning like cayenne pepper, etc.
Per serving: Calories: 285Kcal; Fat: 6g; Carbs: 41g; Protein: 15g

100. Cabbage Salad with Seitan
Preparation time: 5 minutes
Cooking time: 55 minutes **Servings:** 4
Ingredients:
For the dressing:
- 1/3 cup Mango Chutney
- 1/3 cup Peanut Butter, natural & creamy

For the salad:
- 1 Cucumber, small & cut into half thin moons
- 1 tbsp. Olive Oil
- 3 Green Onions, sliced thinly
- 18 oz. Seitan, sliced into strips
- 6 cups Red Cabbage, shredded
- 3 Garlic Cloves, minced
- ¾ tsp. Curry Powder, mild

Directions:
First, to make the dressing, you need to combine the chutney, 1/3 cup water, and peanut butter in a high-speed blender. Blend the mixture until it becomes smooth. Set the dressing aside. After that, take a large skillet and heat it over medium heat. Stir in one tablespoon of olive oil and then the seitan. Add salt if needed and sauté the seitan for 5 to 7 minutes or until it becomes brown. Next, spoon in the garlic and the remaining olive oil. Cook for a further 30 seconds and then add the curry powder. Sauté for 2 minutes and remove from the heat. Finally, add the cabbage and cucumber along with the dressing in a large mixing bowl. Top it with the seitan and green onions.
Serve immediately. Tip: If preferred, you can add carrots as well.
Per serving: Calories: 330Kcal; Fat: 19g; Carbs: 32g; Protein: 15g

101. Chickpeas Avocado Salad
Preparation time: 10 minutes
Cooking time: 20 minutes **Servings:** 4
Ingredients:
For the salad:
- 1 ½ tbsp. Tahini
- 30 Cherry Tomatoes, sliced
- 4 ½ cups Chickpeas, cooked
- 1 Avocado, medium & diced
- 1 cup Quinoa, dried - ¼ tsp. Salt
- ½ of 1 Red Onion, medium & diced
- 1/3 cup Water - 2 tbsp. Lemon Juice
- Pepper, as needed
- 1 ½ tsp. Dijon Mustard
- ½ cup Cilantro, packed

Directions:
To make this healthy salad, you first need to cook the quinoa by following the instructions given in the packet. Next, take 1/3 rd of the chickpeas and place in a high-speed blender along with the water, lemon juice, pepper, Dijon mustard, and salt. Blend for a minute or until you get a creamy consistency. Now, toss the cooked quinoa, cherry tomatoes, red onion, avocado, and cilantro into a large mixing bowl.
Drizzle the dressing over it and serve immediately. Tip: If preferred, you can add carrots as well.
Per serving: Calories: 604Kcal; Fat: 17g; Carbs: 90g; Protein: 25g

102. Cold Peanut Noodle Salad
Preparation time: 20 minutes
Cooking time: 5 minutes **Servings:** 2
Ingredients:
For the salad:
- 8 oz. Rice Noodles
- ½ tsp. Black Sesame Seeds
- 1 cup Carrots, shredded
- ½ of 1 Red Bell Pepper, sliced thinly

- 1/3 cup Peanuts, chopped
- 2 Scallions, chopped

For the peanut dressing:
- 2 tbsp. Hot Water
- 1/3 cup Peanut Butter, creamy
- 2 Garlic cloves, minced
- 3 tbsp. Sriracha - 1 tbsp. Rice Vinegar

Directions:
First, cook the noodles by following the instructions given on the packet. Drain the excess water and then rinse it under cold water. Keep aside. After that, combine all the ingredients needed to make the dressing in a small bowl until mixed well. Set it aside. Mix the noodles with all the remaining ingredients and dressing. Combine and then place in the refrigerator until you're ready to serve. Tip: If preferred, you can use habanero sauce instead of sriracha.
Per serving: Calories: 604Kcal; Fat: 17g; Carbs: 90g; Protein: 25g

103. Butternut Squash Black Rice Bean Salad

Preparation time: 10 minutes
Cooking time: 25 minutes **Servings:** 8
Ingredients:
For the salad:
- 1 lb. Butternut Squash, chopped
- 2 tbsp. Olive Oil - 2 cups Black Rice, dried
- 10 oz. Mushrooms, sliced
- ¼ cup Cranberries, dried
- 6 oz. Spinach, fresh & chopped
- ¼ cup Pumpkin Seeds
- 15 oz. White Beans, cooked
- Black Pepper, as needed

For the peanut dressing:
- 1 cup Coconut Cream
- ¼ cup Extra Virgin Olive Oil
- 2 tbsp. Curry Paste - ¼ cup Almond Milk
- 1/3 cup Rice Vinegar

Directions:
Preheat the oven to 400°F. After that, put the squash, pepper, and olive oil in a baking pan. Toss them once or twice so that the oil and pepper coat the squash well. Now, roast the squash for 10 to 15 minutes or until cooked. Set it aside. In the meantime, cook the black rice until al dente. Keep it aside. Next, mix all the ingredients needed to make the peanut dressing in another bowl until smooth. Finally, combine the roasted squash, cooked rice, and the remaining ingredients in a large bowl. Spoon the dressing over the ingredients and serve immediately. Tip: If possible, use red curry paste.
Per serving: Calories: 618 Kcal Protein: 22.2g Carbs: 85.1g Fat: 24.1g

104. Arugula Beans Salad

Preparation time: 10 minutes **Cooking time:** 25 minutes **Servings:** 8
Ingredients:
For the salad:
- 15 oz. Lentils, cooked
- 4 tbsp. Capers
- 15 oz. Green Kidney Beans
- 2 handful of Arugula

For the dressing:
- 1 tbsp. Balsamic Vinegar
- 1 tbsp. Caper Brine
- 1 tbsp. Tahini
- 2 tbsp. Hot Sauce
- 2 tbsp. Peanut Butter
- 1 tbsp. Tamari

Directions:
Begin by placing all the ingredients needed to make the dressing in a medium bowl and whisk it well until combined. After that, combine the arugula, capers, kidney beans, and lentils in a large bowl. Pour the dressing over it. Serve and enjoy. Tip: Instead of green beans, you can also use red beans.
Per serving: Calories: 543Kcal; Fat: 36g; Carbs: 85.4g; Protein: 36g

105. Spring Salad

Preparation time: 10 minutes
Cooking time: 10 minutes **Servings:** 1
Ingredients:
- 2 tbsp. Pepitas
- 2 cups Spring Mix Greens
- 1 tbsp. Hemp Hearts
- ½ cup Hummus
- ¼ cup Sun-dried Tomatoes
- 1 Watermelon Radish, sliced thinly
- 2 Carrots, medium & julienned
- 1/3 English Cucumber, cubed

Directions:
First, place all the ingredients in a large mixing bowl and toss them well. Serve immediately.
Tip: If desired, you can use microgreens as well.
Per serving: Calories: 629Kcal; Fat: 33g; Carbs: 63g; Protein: 31g

106. Tomato Lentil Salad

Preparation time: 10 minutes
Cooking time: 30 minutes **Servings:** 6
Ingredients:
- 1 tbsp. Olive Oil, divided
- 2 tbsp. Extra Virgin Olive Oil
- ¼ tsp. Crushed Red Pepper
- 1 cup Green Lentil
- 1 Head of Garlic
- 2 tbsp. Lemon Juice
- 1 ½ cup Grape Tomatoes, halved
- ½ cup Red Pepper, diced
- 1 cup Red Onion, sliced
- Salt and pepper, as needed
- 2 ¾ cup Vegetable Broth
- ½ cup Celery, diced

Directions:
Preheat the oven to 375°F.
Next, slice the top of the garlic head and put it in foil.

Brush half of the olive oil on the garlic and close the foil. Then, place the tomatoes and onion in a single layer on a parchment paper-lined baking sheet.

Spoon the olive oil over the tomato-onion mixture. Sprinkle salt and pepper over it. Now, cook for 28 to 30 minutes or until slightly dried. After that, open the foil and allow the garlic to cool. Take the garlic cloves from the head and keep them in a bowl while breaking the garlic. Meanwhile, bring the broth mixture to a boil and stir in lentils to it. Reduce the heat and simmer for 28 to 30 minutes or until tender.

Drain the lentils and set them aside. Meanwhile, whisk all the ingredients in a small bowl together until combined well. Finally, add the tomatoes, celery, red pepper, tomatoes, and red onion. Spoon the dressing and serve immediately. Tip: Instead of roasted tomatoes, you can also use sun-dried tomatoes.

Per serving: Calories: 194Kcal; Fat: 7g; Carbs: 23g; Protein: 8g

107. White Bean & Tomato Salad
Preparation time: 5 minutes
Cooking time: 5 minutes **Servings:** 4
Ingredients:
For the dressing:
- 3 tbsp freshly squeezed lemon juice
- ¼ cup olive oil
- 1 garlic clove, minced
- ¼ tsp salt - 1/8 tsp black pepper

For the salad:
- 2 (15 oz) cans white beans, drained and rinsed
- 2 cups cherry tomatoes, quartered
- ½ small red onion, sliced
- 1 garlic clove, minced
- ½ cup chopped fresh parsley

Directions:
Mix the dressing's ingredients in a large bowl until well-combined and add the white beans, garlic, tomatoes, onion, and parsley. Coat the salad with the dressing. Serve immediately.

Per serving: Calories: 201Kcal; Fat: 8g; Carbs: 25g; Protein: 9g

108. Avocado & White Bean Salad
Preparation time: 10 minutes
Cooking time: 10 minutes **Servings:** 2 to 4
Ingredients:
- 1 Avocado, chopped
- 1 Roma Tomato, chopped
- 14 oz. White Beans
- ¼ of 1 Sweet Onion, chopped

For the vinaigrette:
- ¼ cup Lemon Juice - 1 ½ tbsp. Olive Oil
- Salt and pepper, to taste
- Fresh Basil, as needed, for garnish
- 1 tsp. Mustard
- ½ tsp. Garlic, finely chopped

Directions:
First, whisk together all the ingredients needed to make the dressing in a small bowl until combined well. Next, toss all the ingredients in a large mixing bowl and set it aside. Pour the vinaigrette over the salad and place it in the refrigerator until you're ready to serve. Serve and enjoy. Tip: You can avoid onion if you desire. **Per serving:** Calories: 452Kcal Protein: 13.3g Carbs: 39.7g Fat: 28.7g

109. Brussels Sprouts Salad
Preparation time: 5 minutes
Cooking time: 15 minutes **Servings:** 3 cups
Ingredients:
- 14 ounces of shredded Brussels sprouts
- 1 ¼ cup of grated parmesan cheese
- 1/3 cup of raw hazelnuts*
- 2 tablespoons of extra virgin olive oil
- 1 ½ teaspoon of ground pepper
- 1 teaspoon of sea salt
- Pinch of crushed red pepper
- Zest of 1 lemon

Directions:
Toast nuts for better taste. Put them on a skillet on medium heat. Toast for 3–5 minutes, stirring frequently. After that, let it cool for a few minutes. Put a large skillet on medium heat. Add olive oil, red pepper with ground pepper, and cook for 30–60 seconds. Add Brussels sprouts into the skillet and cook for about 2 minutes, without stirring, until they start softening. Spread some salt and continue cooking for 2 minutes more until Brussels sprouts start becoming lightly golden-brown. Pour over the cooked Brussels sprouts into a medium bowl. Add parmesan, hazelnuts, and lemon zest. Serve immediately and enjoy! **Per serving:** Calories: 225Kcal; Fat: 6g; Carbs: 39.5g; Protein: 5.5g

110. Wedge Salad
Preparation time: 15 minutes
Cooking time: 0 minutes **Servings:** 4
Ingredients:
- 2 carrots, finely diced
- 2 tablespoons low-sodium soy sauce or tamari
- 2 teaspoons pure maple syrup
- ½ teaspoon smoked paprika
- 2 ripe avocados - ¼ cup cashews
- 2 tablespoons apple cider vinegar
- 1 tablespoon nutritional yeast
- 1 teaspoon spirulina powder (optional)
- 1 small red onion, sliced
- 1 cup cherry or grape tomatoes, halved
- 1 head iceberg lettuce, cut into 4 wedges
- Freshly ground black pepper

Directions:
Place the carrots in a small bowl and let sit for 10 minutes. In a measuring cup, whisk together the soy sauce, maple syrup, and paprika and pour it over the carrots. Set aside. Cut the avocados in half and remove the pits. Dice the flesh of one of the avocado halves in the peel, then gently scoop it out into a small bowl. Set aside. Scoop the flesh from the 3 remaining

avocado halves into a blender. Add the cashews, vinegar, nutritional yeast, and spirulina (if using) and purée until very smooth, creamy, and pourable. Add 1 to 2 tablespoons of water, if necessary, to reach the right consistency. Pour the dressing into a medium bowl. Add the onion, tomatoes, and carrots (along with the liquid in the bowl) to the bowl with the dressing and stir to combine. Gently fold the diced avocado into the dressing. Place a wedge of lettuce on each of the four salad plates. Dress the lettuce by spooning about ½ cup of dressing over each wedge, then repeat until the dressing is used up. Sprinkle a pinch or two of black pepper over each salad and serve.
Per serving: Calories: 289Kcal; Fat: 4g; Carbs: 29g; Protein: 8g

111. Chef Salad
Preparation time: 15 minutes
Cooking time: 15 minutes **Servings:** 4
Ingredients:
- 6 fingerling potatoes, unpeeled, cut in half
- 2 teaspoons smoked paprika, divided
- ½ teaspoon ground turmeric
- ½ teaspoon freshly ground black pepper
- ¼ teaspoon black salt
- 2 cups fresh or drained canned pineapple chunks
- 1 small cucumber, unpeeled, cut into ¼-inch dice - 1 tablespoon rice vinegar
- 6 ounces silken tofu - 1 tablespoon lime juice
- 2 garlic cloves, peeled - 2 teaspoons tomato powder
- 2 heads romaine lettuce, chopped

Directions:
Fill a large saucepan with about 2 inches of water, insert a steamer basket, and bring to a boil over high heat. Reduce the heat to medium-high and place the potatoes in the steamer. Cover and steam for 15 minutes. Transfer the potatoes to a small bowl, sprinkle with 1 teaspoon of paprika, turmeric, pepper, and black salt, and toss until evenly coated. Place in the refrigerator to chill. In a small bowl, combine the pineapple and the remaining 1 teaspoon of paprika until evenly coated. Set aside. In another small bowl, combine the cucumber and vinegar. Set aside. In a food processor or blender, combine the tofu, lime juice, garlic, and tomato powder and purée until thick and creamy. Remove the food processor blade, add the cucumber-vinegar mixture, and stir to combine. Place the lettuce in a large bowl. Pour the tofu dressing over the lettuce and toss until evenly coated. Portion the salad into four large salad bowls. Top each bowl with three pieces of potato and ½ cup of pineapple mixture, then serve.
Per serving: Calories: 219; Fat: 1.g; Protein: 11g; Carbs: 43g

112. Radish Avocado Salad
Preparation time: 10 minutes
Cooking time: 0 minutes **Servings:** 2
Ingredients:
- 6 shredded carrots - 6 ounces diced radishes
- 1 diced avocado - 1/3 cup ponzu

Directions:
Place together all the ingredients in a serving bowl and toss. Enjoy!
Per serving: Calories: 292Kcal; Fat: 18g; Carbs: 29g; Protein: 7g

113. Mint Coriander Nutty Salad
Preparation time: 10 minutes
Cooking time: 0 minutes **Servings:** 2
Ingredients:
- ½ cup Almond whole
- ½ cup Peanuts, roasted
- 2 cups Cabbage, sliced
- 2 Cucumber, diced
- 2 Carrot, diced
- 1 Lime, juiced
- 2 Onion, diced
- 2 Tomato, diced
- ½ Sea salt
- ½ Coriander
- ¼ Mint

Directions:
Place together all the ingredients in a large bowl. Combine them well and serve.
Per serving: Calories: 150Kcal; Fat: 2g; Carbs: 12g; Protein: 5g

114. Mix Grain Salad
Preparation time: 20 minutes
Cooking time: 20 minutes **Servings:** 6
Ingredients:
Dressing
- ¼ cup fresh lime juice
- 2 tablespoons maple syrup
- 1 tablespoon Dijon mustard
- ½ teaspoon ground cumin
- 1 teaspoon garlic powder
- Salt and ground black pepper, to taste
- ½ cup extra-virgin olive oil
- Salad
- 2 cups fresh mango, peeled, pitted, and cubed
- 2 tablespoon fresh lime juice, divided
- 2 avocados, peeled, pitted, and cubed
- Pinch of salt
- 1 cup cooked quinoa
- 2 (14-ounce) cans black beans, rinsed and drained
- 1 (15¼-ounce) can corn, rinsed and drained
- 1 small red onion, chopped
- 1 jalapeño, seeded and chopped finely
- ½ cup fresh cilantro, chopped
- 6 cups romaine lettuce, shredded

Directions:
For the dressing: in a blender, add all the ingredients (except oil) and pulse until well combined. While the motor is running, gradually add the oil and pulse until smooth. For the salad: in a bowl, add the mango and 1 tablespoon of lime juice and toss to coat well. In another bowl, add the avocado, a

pinch of salt, and remaining lime juice and toss to coat well. In a large serving bowl, add the mango, avocado, and remaining salad ingredients and mix. Place the dressing and toss to coat well. Serve immediately.
Per serving: Calories: 631Kcal; Fat: 33g; Carbs: 73g; Protein: 16g

115. Quinoa and Chickpea Salad

Preparation time: 20 minutes
Cooking time: 0 minutes **Servings:** 4
Ingredients:
- 2 cups cooked quinoa
- 1½ cups canned red kidney beans, rinsed and drained - 3 cups fresh baby spinach
- 1/4 cup sun-dried tomatoes, chopped
- ¼ cup fresh dill - ¼ cup fresh parsley
- ½ cup sunflower seeds
- ¼ cup walnuts, chopped
- 3 tablespoons fresh lemon juice
- Salt and ground black pepper, as required

Directions:
In a large bowl, add all the ingredients and toss to coat well. Serve immediately. **Per serving:** Calories: 489Kcal; Fat: 13g; Carbs: 73g; Protein: 23g

116. Rice and Tofu Salad

Preparation time: 15 minutes
Cooking time: 0 minutes **Servings:** 4
Ingredients:
Salad
- 1 (12-ounce) package firm tofu, pressed, drained, and sliced
- 1½ cups cooked brown rice
- 3 large tomatoes, peeled and chopped
- ¼ cup fresh basil leaves

Dressing
- 3 scallions, chopped
- 2 tablespoons black sesame seeds, toasted
- 2 tablespoons low-sodium soy sauce
- ½ teaspoon sesame oil, toasted
- Drop of hot pepper sauce
- 1 tablespoon maple syrup
- ¼ teaspoon red chili powder

Directions:
In a large serving bowl, place all the ingredients and toss to coat well. Serve immediately. **Per serving:** Calories: 393Kcal; Fat: 8.6g; Carbs: 67g; Protein: 15g

117. Kidney Bean and Pomegranate Salad

Preparation time: 15 minutes **Cooking time:** 0 minutes **Servings:** 3
Ingredients:
- 2 cups canned white kidney beans, rinsed and drained
- 1 cup fresh pomegranate seeds
- 1/3 cup scallion (green part), chopped finely
- 2 tablespoons fresh parsley, chopped

- 1 tablespoon fresh lime juice
- Salt and ground black pepper, as required

Directions:
In a large serving bowl, place all the ingredients and toss to coat well. Serve immediately.
Per serving: Calories: 180Kcal; Fat: 0g; Carbs: 35g; Protein: 12g

118. Corn and Bean Salad

Preparation time: 15 minutes
Cooking time: 0 minutes **Servings:** 8
Ingredients:
Salad
- 1 (10-ounce) package frozen corn kernels, thawed
- 3 (15-ounce) cans black beans, rinsed and drained
- 2 large red bell peppers, seeded and chopped
- 1 large red onion, chopped

Dressing
- ¼ cup fresh cilantro, minced
- 1 garlic clove, minced
- 1 tablespoon maple syrup
- ½ cup balsamic vinegar - ½ cup olive oil
- 1 tablespoon fresh lime juice
- 1 tablespoon fresh lemon juice
- ½ teaspoon red pepper flakes, crushed
- Salt and ground black pepper, as required

Directions:
For the salad: add all the ingredients to a large serving bowl and mix well. For the dressing: add all the ingredients to a bowl and beat until well combined. Place the dressing over salad and gently toss to coat well. Serve immediately.
Per serving: Calories: 310Kcal; Fat: 14g; Carbs: 36g; Protein: 10g

119. Cherry Tomato Couscous Salad

Preparation time: 5 minutes
Cooking time: 15 minutes **Servings:** 5
Ingredients:
- 1 cup couscous
- ½ cup small fresh basil leaves
- 2 tablespoons minced shallots
- 8-ounce sliced cherry tomatoes
- 1 tablespoon olive oil
- 3 tablespoons vinegar
- ¾ teaspoon ground black pepper
- ½ teaspoon salt

Directions:
In a saucepan, add water and salt and bring it to a boil. Now toast couscous in a small pan cook it over medium flame.
Cook it for around 7 minutes and move it in a circular motion. Add it immediately in the salty boiling water and cook for an additional 6 minutes and drain and rinse it.
Now take a bowl and mix all the remaining ingredients and cooked couscous. Mix them well and serve them after 15 minutes.
Per serving: Calories: 95Kcal; 2.86Fat: g; Carbs: 15.95g; Protein: 1.91g

120. Spicy Watermelon Tomato Salad

Preparation time: 20 minutes
Cooking time: 0 minutes **Servings:** 8
Ingredients:
- 1 diced yellow tomato
- 2 cups diced seeded watermelon
- ¼ cup vinegar
- 1 cubed red tomato
- 2 teaspoons honey
- ¼ cup olive oil
- 2 tablespoons chili-garlic sauce
- 1 tablespoon chopped lemon basil
- ½ teaspoon salt
- ½ teaspoon black pepper

Directions:
Drain some moisture from watermelon and red and yellow tomatoes by spreading it over the paper towel. Now put all the ingredients, including the drained ingredients.
Mix all the ingredients well and serve it.
Per serving: Calories: 89Kcal; Fat: 7.18g; Carbs: 6.2g; Protein: 0.77g

121. Health is Wealth Salad: Dash of Chickpea and Tomato

Preparation time: 10 minutes
Cooking time: 10 minutes **Servings:** 3-4
Ingredients:
- 1 freshly chopped red pepper
- 2 cups of cooked chickpeas
- 1/3 cup of freshly chopped parsley 5 freshly chopped spring onions 1 cup of rinsed baby spinach leaves ½ a lemon, juiced
- 5 freshly chopped medium tomatoes 1 tablespoon of balsamic vinegar 2 tablespoons of sesame seeds ½ thinly sliced hot pepper
- 2 tablespoons of olive oil
- 2 tablespoons of flax seeds

Directions:
Thoroughly clean and chop all the vegetables. Do not chop the baby spinach. In a big salad bowl, mix the chickpeas, onions, tomatoes, pepper, spinach, and parsley. Toss with the sesame seeds and sprinkle the flax seeds. Drizzle with olive oil, lemon juice, and balsamic vinegar. Give all of the ingredients a thorough mix. Add salt and pepper to taste and serve this summer staple. It is fresh and healthy, and you cannot say no to this delicious salad.
Per serving: Calories: 310Kcal; Fat: 14g; Carbs: 36g; Protein: 10g

122. Eggplant Salad

Preparation time: 15 minutes
Cooking time: 25 minutes **Servings:** 6
Ingredient:
- 2 eggplants
- 1 teaspoon salt
- 1 white onion, diced
- 1 teaspoon Pink salt
- 1 oz fresh cilantro
- 3 tablespoon lemon juice
- 4 tablespoon olive oil
- 1 garlic clove, peeled

Directions:
Cut eggplants into halves. Preheat oven to 365F. Put eggplants in the oven and cook for 25 minutes or until they are tender. Meanwhile, blend diced onion and transfer in the cheesecloth. Pour olive oil and lemon juice into the bowl. Squeeze blended onion in the oil mixture. Add salt. Chop cilantro and grind garlic. Add ingredients to the oily mixture too. Stir it. Remove the eggplants from the oven and chill them a little. Remove the flesh from the eggplants and transfer it to the salad bowl. Add oil mixture and stir gently.
Per serving: Calories: 292Kcal; Fat: 17.32g; Carbs: 26.99g; Protein: 10.51g

123. Tricolore Salad

Preparation time: 10 minutes
Cooking time: 0 minutes **Servings:** 5
Ingredients:
- 1 avocado, peeled
- ½ cup kalamata olives
- 2 tablespoon olive oil
- 1 teaspoon minced garlic
- ¼ teaspoon salt
- 2 tomatoes, chopped
- 1 teaspoon apple cider vinegar
- 6 oz Provolone cheese, chopped

Directions:
Mix up together salt, apple cider vinegar, minced garlic, and olive oil.
Cut kalamata olives into halves.
Slice avocado and place in a salad bowl.
Add olive halves, chopped tomato, and cheese.
Stir gently and sprinkle with olive oil mixture.
Per serving: Calories: 257Kcal; Fat: 21.89g; Carbs: 7.21g; Protein: 10.09g

124. Potato Salad

Preparation time: 10 minutes
Cooking time: 15 minutes **Servings:** 4
Ingredients:
- 8 oz turnip, peeled
- 1 carrot, peeled
- 1 bay leaf
- ¼ teaspoon peppercorns
- 1 teaspoon salt
- ½ teaspoon cayenne pepper
- 1 tablespoon fresh parsley, chopped
- 3 eggs, boiled
- 3 tablespoon sour cream
- 1 tablespoon mustard
- 2 cups water, for vegetables

Directions:
Put turnip and carrot in the saucepan. Add water, peppercorns, bay leaf, and salt. Close the lid and boil vegetables for 15 minutes over high heat. The cooked

vegetables should be tender. Meanwhile, peel eggs and chop them. Put the chopped eggs in the bowl. Sprinkle them with cayenne pepper and chopped parsley. In the separate bowl, stir together mustard and sour cream. When the vegetables are cooked, strain them and transfer them to the salad bowl. Add mustard sauce and stir. **Per serving:** Calories: 140Kcal; Fat: 8.78g; Carbs: 6.04g; Protein: 9.08g

125. Cauliflower & Apple Salad

Preparation time: 25 minutes
Cooking time: 0 minutes **Servings:** 4
Ingredients:
- 3 Cups Cauliflower, Chopped into Florets
- 2 Cups Baby Kale 1 Sweet Apple, Cored & Chopped
- ¼ Cup Basil, Fresh & Chopped
- ¼ Cup Mint, Fresh & Chopped
- ¼ Cup Parsley, Fresh & Chopped
- 1/3 Cup Scallions, Sliced Thin
- 2 Tablespoons Yellow Raisins
- 1 Tablespoon Sun-Dried Tomatoes, Chopped
- ½ Cup Miso Dressing, Optional
- ¼ Cup Roasted Pumpkin Seeds, Optional

Directions:
Combine everything, tossing before serving. Interesting Facts: This vegetable is an extremely high source of vitamin A, vitamin B1, B2, and B3.
Per serving: Calories: 166Kcal; Fat: 7.15g; Carbs: 16.43g; Protein: 11.06g

126. Corn & Black Bean Salad

Preparation time: 10 minutes
Cooking time: 0 minutes **Servings:** 6
Ingredients:
- ¼ Cup Cilantro, Fresh & Chopped
- 1 Can Corn, Drained (10 Ounces)
- 1/8 Cup Red Onion, Chopped
- 1 Can Black Beans, Drained (15 Ounces)
- 1 Tomato, Chopped
- 3 Tablespoons Lemon Juice, Fresh
- 2 Tablespoons Olive Oil
- Sea Salt & Black Pepper to Taste

Directions:
Mix everything, and then refrigerate until cool. Serve cold.
Per serving: Calories: 64Kcal; Fat: 2.95g; Carbs: 10.03g; Protein: 1.08g

127. Spinach & Orange Salad

Preparation time: 15 minutes
Cooking time: 0 minutes
Servings: 6
Ingredients:
- ¼ -1/3 Cup Vegan Dressing
- 3 Oranges, Medium, Peeled, Seeded & Sectioned - ¾ lb. Spinach, Fresh & Torn
- 1 Red Onion, Medium, Sliced & Separated into Rings

Directions:
Toss everything together and serve with dressing.
Per serving: Calories: 33Kcal; Fat: 0.39g; Carbs: 6.52g; Protein: 1.75g

128. Red Pepper & Broccoli Salad

Preparation time: 15 minutes
Cooking time: 0 minutes **Servings:** 2
Ingredients:
- Lettuce Salad Mix
- 1 Head Broccoli, Chopped into Florets
- 1 Red Pepper, Seeded & Chopped

Dressing:
- 3 Tablespoons White Wine Vinegar
- 1 Teaspoon Dijon Mustard
- 1 Clove Garlic, Peeled & Chopped Fine
- ½ Teaspoon Black Pepper
- ½ Teaspoon Sea Salt, Fine
- 2 Tablespoons Olive Oil
- 1 Tablespoon Parsley, Chopped

Directions:
In boiling water, put broccoli, then drain it on a paper towel. Whisk together all dressing ingredients.
Toss ingredients together before serving.
Per serving: Calories: 153 Kcal; Fat: 13.93g; Carbs: 5.95g; Protein: 1.98g

129. Lentil Potato Salad

Preparation time: 35 minutes
Cooking time: 0 minutes
Servings: 2
Ingredients:
- ½ Cup Beluga Lentils - 8 Fingerling Potatoes
- 1 Cup Scallions, Sliced Thin
- ¼ Cup Cherry Tomatoes, Halved
- ¼ Cup Lemon Vinaigrette
- Sea Salt & Black Pepper to Taste

Directions:
Bring two cups of water to simmer in a pot, adding your lentils. Cook for twenty to twenty-five minutes, and then drain. Your lentils should be tender.
Reduce to a simmer, cooking for fifteen minutes, and then drain. Halve your potatoes once they're cool enough to touch. Put your lentils on a serving plate, and then top with scallions, potatoes, and tomatoes. Drizzle with your vinaigrette, and season with salt and pepper.
Per serving: Calories: 1189 Kcal; Fat: 1.65g; Carbs: 270.19g; Protein: 33.02g

130. Black Bean & Corn Salad with Avocado

Preparation time: 20 mins.
Cooking time: 0 mins. **Servings:** 6
Ingredients:
- 1 and 1/2 cups corn kernels, cooked & frozen or canned
- 1/2 cup olive oil

- 1 minced clove garlic
- 1/3 cup lime juice, fresh
- 1 avocado (peeled, pitted & diced)
- 1/8 tsp. cayenne pepper
- 2 cans black beans, (approximately 15 oz.)
- 6 thinly sliced green onions
- 1/2 cup chopped cilantro, fresh
- 2 chopped tomatoes
- 1 chopped red bell pepper
- Chili powder
- 1/2 tsp. salt

Directions:
In a small jar, place the olive oil, lime juice, garlic, cayenne, and salt. Cover with lid; shake until all the ingredients under the jar are mixed well. Toss the green onions, corn, beans, bell pepper, avocado, tomatoes, and cilantro together in a large bowl or plastic container with a cover. Shake the lime dressing for a second time and transfer it over the salad ingredients.
Stir salad to coat the beans and vegetables with the dressing; cover & refrigerate.
To blend the flavors completely, let this sit for a moment. Remove the container from the refrigerator from time to time; turn upside down & back gently a couple of times to reorganize the dressing.
Per serving: Calories: 433Kcal; Fat: 42.31g; Carbs: 270.19g; Protein: 33.02g

131. Summer Chickpea Salad
Preparation time: 15 minutes
Cooking time: 0 minutes **Servings:** 4
Ingredients:
- 1 ½ Cups Cherry Tomatoes, Halved
- 1 Cup English Cucumber, Slices
- 1 Cup Chickpeas, Canned, Unsalted, Drained & Rinsed
- ¼ Cup Red Onion, Slivered
- 2 Tablespoon Olive Oil
- 1 ½ Tablespoon Lemon Juice, Fresh
- 1 ½ Tablespoon Lemon Juice, Fresh
- Sea Salt & Black Pepper to Taste

Directions:
Mix everything, and toss to combine before serving.
Per serving: Calories: 139Kcal; Fat: 7.88g; Carbs: 14.3g; Protein: 4.02g

132. Edamame Salad
Preparation time: 15 minutes
Cooking time: 0 minutes **Servings:** 1
Ingredients:
- ¼ Cup Red Onion, Chopped
- 1 Cup Corn Kernels, Fresh
- 1 Cup Edamame Beans, Shelled & Thawed
- 1 Red Bell Pepper, Chopped
- 2-3 Tablespoons Lime Juice, Fresh
- 5-6 Basil Leaves, Fresh & Sliced
- 5-6 Mint Leaves, Fresh & Sliced
- Sea Salt & Black Pepper to Taste

Directions:
Place everything into a Mason jar, and then seal the jar tightly. Shake well before serving.
Per serving: Calories: 202Kcal; Fat: 3.24g; Carbs: 44.2g; Protein: 7.89g

133. Fruity Kale Salad
Preparation time: 30 minutes
Cooking time: 0 minutes **Servings:** 4
Ingredients:
Salad:
- 10 Ounces Baby Kale
- ½ Cup Pomegranate Arils
- 1 Tablespoon Olive Oil - 1 Apple, Sliced

Dressing:
- 3 Tablespoons Apple Cider Vinegar
- 3 Tablespoons Olive Oil
- 1 Tablespoon Tahini Sauce (Optional)
- Sea Salt & Black Pepper to Taste

Directions:
Wash and dry the kale. If kale is too expensive, you can also use lettuce, arugula, or spinach. Take the stems out and chop them. Combine all of your salad ingredients. Combine all of your dressing ingredients before drizzling it over the salad to serve.
Per serving: Calories: 183Kcal; Fat: 14.04g; Carbs: 15.56g; Protein: 1.01g

134. Olive & Fennel Salad
Preparation time: 5 minutes
Cooking time: 0 minutes **Servings:** 3
Ingredients:
- 6 Tablespoons Olive Oil
- 3 Fennel Bulbs, Trimmed, Cored & Quartered
- 2 Tablespoons Parsley, Fresh & Chopped
- 1 Lemon, Juiced & Zested
- 12 Black Olives
- Sea Salt & Black Pepper to Taste

Directions:
Grease your baking dish, and then place your fennel in it. Make sure the cut side is up. Mix your lemon zest, lemon juice, salt, pepper, and oil, pouring it over your fennel. Sprinkle your olives over it and bake at 400F. Serve with parsley. **Per serving:** Calories: 338Kcal; Fat: 29.08g; Carbs: 20.73g; Protein: 3.47g

135. Avocado & Radish Salad
Preparation time: 10 minutes
Cooking time: 0 minutes **Servings:** 2
Ingredients:
- 1 Avocado, Sliced - 6 Radishes, Sliced
- 2 Tomatoes, Sliced
- 1 Lettuce Head, Leaves Separated
- ½ Red Onion, Peeled & Sliced

Dressing:
- ½ Cup Olive Oil
- ¼ Cup Lime Juice, Fresh
- ¼ Cup Apple Cider Vinegar

- 3 Cloves Garlic, Chopped Fine
- Sea Salt & Black Pepper to Taste

Directions:
Spread your lettuce leaves on a platter, and then layer with your onion, tomatoes, avocado, and radishes. Whisk your dressing ingredients together before drizzling it over your salad. **Per serving:** Calories: 915Kcal; Fat: 70.44g; Carbs: 71.82g; Protein: 12.54g

136. Zucchini & Lemon Salad

Preparation time: 3 Hours 10 minutes
Cooking time: 0 minutes **Servings:** 2
Ingredients:
- 1 Green Zucchini, Sliced into Rounds
- 1 Yellow Squash, Zucchini, Sliced into Rounds
- 1 Clove Garlic, Peeled & Chopped
- 2 Tablespoons Olive Oil
- 2 Tablespoons Basil, Fresh
- 1 Lemon, Juiced & Zested
- ¼ Cup Coconut Milk
- Sea Salt & Black Pepper to Taste

Directions:
Refrigerate all ingredients for three hours before serving. **Per serving:** Calories: 207Kcal; Fat: 20.81g; Carbs: 6.34g; Protein: 1.5g

137. Watercress & Blood Orange Salad

Preparation time: 10 minutes
Cooking time: 0 minutes **Servings:** 4
Ingredients:
- 1 Tablespoon Hazelnuts, Toasted & Chopped
- 2 Blood Oranges (or Navel Oranges)
- 3 Cups watercress, Stems Removed
- 1/8 Teaspoon Sea Salt, Fine
- 1 Tablespoon Lemon Juice, Fresh
- 1 Tablespoon Honey, Raw
- 1 Tablespoon Water
- 2 Tablespoons Chives, Fresh

Directions:
Whisk your oil, honey, lemon juice, chives, salt, and water together. Add in your watercress, tossing until it's coated. Arrange the mixture onto salad plates and top with orange slices. Drizzle with remaining liquid, and sprinkle with hazelnuts. **Per serving:** Calories: 201Kcal; Fat: 17.51g; Carbs: 9.79g; Protein: 4.96g

138. Parsley Salad

Preparation time: 30 minutes
Cooking time: 0 minutes **Servings:** 8
Ingredients:
- 3 Lemons, Juiced
- 150 Grams Flat Leaf Parsley, Chopped Fine
- 1 Cup Boiled Water
- 5 Tablespoons Olive Oil
- Sea Salt & Black Pepper to Taste
- 6 Green Onions, Chopped Fine
- 1 Cup Bulgur
- 4 Tomatoes, Chopped Fine

Directions:
Add your Bulgur to your water, and mix well. Put a towel on top of it to steam it. Keep it to the side, and then chop your spring onions, tomatoes, and parsley. Put them in your salad bowl.
Pour your juice into the mixture, and then add in your olive oil, salt, and pepper.
Put this mixture over your bulgur to serve.
Per serving: Calories: 530Kcal; Fat: 17.81g; Carbs: 82.66g; Protein: 35.35g

Amanda Kale

CHAPTER 15:
Soups

139. Classic Vegetable Soup
Preparation time: 10 minutes
Cooking time: 20 minutes **Servings:** 4 to 6
Ingredients:
- 1 tablespoon red miso paste
- 2 cups diced onion
- 1 cup diced carrots
- 1 cup diced russet potatoes
- 3 garlic cloves, minced
- ½ teaspoon dried basil
- ½ teaspoon dried oregano
- ½ teaspoon dried thyme
- 3 cups Vegetable Broth
- 1 cup chopped frozen or fresh green beans
- 1 cup diced tomato

Directions:
In a large saucepan, bring ¼ cup water to a simmer over medium-high heat. Add the miso and whisk until thick and smooth. Add the onion, carrots, potatoes, garlic, basil, oregano, thyme, and broth, and bring to a boil. Reduce the heat to medium-low, cover, and simmer for 10 minutes.
Add the green beans and tomato and bring them back to a boil. Reduce the heat, cover, and simmer for 5 minutes more, then serve.
ALLERGEN TIP: To make this soy-free, sauté the vegetables with 2 teaspoons Spicy Umami Blend instead of the miso paste.
Per serving (2 cups): Calories: 103Kcal; Fat: 1g; Carbs: 23g; Fiber: 4g; Protein: 4g

140. Cream of Miso Mushroom Stew
Preparation time: 10 minutes
Cooking time: 15 minutes **Servings:** 4 To 6
Ingredients:
- 1 tablespoon low-sodium soy sauce or tamari
- 1 cup julienned green onions
- 2 cups sliced mushrooms (shiitake, oyster, or baby bella)
- 2 cups Miso Cream Sauce
- 2 cups Vegetable Broth
- 1 tablespoon rice vinegar

Directions:
In a large saucepan, heat the soy sauce over medium-high heat. Add the green onions and mushrooms and sauté until tender, 3 to 5 minutes. Add the miso cream sauce and sauté until it begins to thicken, about 3 minutes. Add the broth and bring to a boil. Reduce the heat to low and simmer, stirring occasionally, for 10 minutes. Remove from the heat. Stir in the vinegar and serve.

SWAP IT: I call for green onions because they are easy to find, but negi (Japanese leeks), leeks, or bunching onions are great substitutes.
ALLERGEN TIP: Use gluten-free tamari or coconut aminos and be sure to use a gluten-free miso paste in your Miso Cream Sauce.
Per serving (1½ cups): Calories: 156Kcal; Fat: 7g; Carbs: 13g; Fiber: 2g; Protein: 8g

141. Chickpea Noodle Soup
Preparation time: 10 minutes
Cooking time: 25 minutes **Servings:** 4 to 6
Ingredients:
- 4 ounces dried soba noodles
- 4 cups Vegetable Broth, divided
- 2 cups diced onions
- 1 cup chopped carrots
- 1 cup chopped celery
- 3 garlic cloves, finely diced
- ½ teaspoon dried parsley
- ½ teaspoon dried sage
- ½ teaspoon dried thyme
- ½ teaspoon freshly ground black or white pepper
- 1 (15-ounce) can chickpeas, drained and rinsed
- ¼ cup chopped fresh parsley, for garnish (optional)

Directions:
In a large saucepan, bring 4 cups of water to a boil over high heat. Add the soba noodles and cook, stirring occasionally, until just tender, 4 to 5 minutes. Drain in a colander and rinse well under cold water. Set aside. In the same saucepan, heat ¼ cup of broth over medium-high heat. Add the onions, carrots, celery, garlic, parsley, sage, thyme, and pepper and sauté for 5 minutes, or until the carrots are fork-tender. Add the chickpeas and remaining 3¾ cups of broth and bring to a boil. Reduce the heat to low, cover, and simmer for 15 minutes. Serve garnished with parsley, if desired.
INGREDIENT TIP: I love using soba noodles in Spring Rolls with Pistachio Sauce or as a grain addition to a salad. Make an entire package at once, use what you need for this soup, and store the rest in an airtight container in the refrigerator for up to 5 days.
Per serving (1 cup): Calories: 266Kcal; Fat: 0g; Carbs: 53g; Fiber: 8g; Protein: 12g

142. Tangy Tomato Soup
Preparation time: 5 minutes
Cooking time: 30 minutes **Servings:** 4
Ingredients:
- 1 large sweet onion, coarsely chopped
- 1 (28-ounce) can diced tomatoes
- 1 (28-ounce) can crushed tomatoes

- 1 cup Vegetable Broth
- 2 teaspoons dried tarragon
- 1 Medjool date, pitted and chopped (optional)
- ¼ cup balsamic vinegar

Directions:
In a large saucepan, dry sauté the onion over medium-high heat, stirring frequently, until just beginning to brown, 8 to 10 minutes. Add the diced and crushed tomatoes, broth, and tarragon and bring to a boil. Reduce the heat to medium-low and simmer, stirring frequently, for 20 minutes. Add the date and use an immersion blender to purée the soup directly in the pan until smooth (or transfer the soup to a standing blender and carefully purée it, then return the soup to the pan). Pour in the vinegar, quickly stir, and serve hot.
SWAP IT: No tarragon? No problem! Use ¼ teaspoon ground fennel seed and ¼ teaspoon ground anise seed.
Per serving (2 cups): Calories: 153Kcal; Fat: 0g; Carbs: 35g; Fiber: 9g; Protein: 6g

143. Yellow Potato Soup

Preparation time: 10 minutes
Cooking time: 25 minutes **Servings:** 4
Ingredients:
- 3 cups cubed potatoes (any kind)
- 1 cup diced onion
- 1 cup chopped carrots
- ½ teaspoon chipotle chile powder
- ½ teaspoon ground cinnamon
- ½ teaspoon sea salt, or 1 teaspoon Spicy Umami Blend
- ½ teaspoon ground turmeric
- ¼ teaspoon cayenne pepper
- 2 cups diced Anjou pear
- ½ cup dried yellow split peas
- 4 cups Vegetable Broth
- ½ teaspoon freshly ground black pepper

Directions:
In a large saucepan, combine the potatoes, onion, carrots, chipotle powder, cinnamon, salt, turmeric, and cayenne and dry sauté over medium-high heat for 5 minutes. Add the pear, split peas, and broth and bring to a boil. Reduce the heat to medium-low, cover, and simmer until the split peas are tender, 15 to 20 minutes.
Serve garnished with black pepper.
INGREDIENT TIP: You want a very firm pear for this soup, which is why I specifically call for the Anjou variety. Asian pears are fairly firm and work great, too.
Per serving (2 cups): Calories: 252Kcal; Fat: 0g; Carbs: 55g; Fiber: 13g; Protein: 9g

144. Greens And Grains Soup

Preparation time: 5 minutes
Cooking time: 35 minutes **Servings:** 6
Ingredients:
- 2 cups sliced onions
- 1 cup diced carrots
- 1 cup diced celery
- 1 cup dry farro
- 1 teaspoon dried basil
- 1 teaspoon dried oregano
- ½ teaspoon dried rosemary
- ½ teaspoon dried thyme
- 1 (15-ounce) can diced tomatoes
- 1 (15-ounce) can white kidney beans, drained and rinsed
- 5 ounces arugula
- 3 tablespoons lemon juice

Directions:
In a large saucepan, combine the onions, carrots, and celery and dry sauté over medium-high heat, stirring occasionally until the carrots are softened, about 5 minutes. Add the farro and stir until coated. Add the basil, oregano, rosemary, thyme, and 4 cups water and bring to a boil. Reduce the heat to low, cover, and simmer for 30 minutes. Add the tomatoes and beans, raise the heat to medium-high, and bring back to a boil. Add the arugula and lemon juice and cook, stirring, until the arugula is a deep green and lightly wilted, 1 to 2 minutes more. Remove from the heat and serve.
SWAP IT: Wheat berries or pearled barley can be substituted for the farro and cooked for the same amount of time.
Per serving (2 cups): Calories: 183Kcal; Fat: 0g; Carbs: 38g; Fiber: 9g; Protein: 9g

145. Herby Split Pea Soup

Preparation time: 5 minutes
Cooking time: 30 minutes **Servings:** 4
Ingredients:
- ¼ cup Vegetable Broth
- 2 large carrots, diced
- 2 large celery stalks, diced
- 1 small russet potato, unpeeled, cubed
- 1 cup dried split peas
- 1 tablespoon herbes de Provence
- ½ teaspoon sea salt, or 1½ teaspoons Spicy Umami Blend

Directions:
In a large saucepan, heat the broth over medium-high heat. Add the carrots, celery, and potato and sauté for 5 minutes. Add the split peas, herbes de Provence, and 2 cups of water and bring to a boil. Reduce the heat to medium-low, cover, and cook for 25 minutes. Stir in the salt and serve.
APPLIANCE TIP: Combine all the ingredients in a multicooker like an Instant Pot or a pressure cooker and cook for 15 minutes on high pressure, then use a quick pressure release.
Per serving (1 cup): Calories: 227Kcal; Fat: 0g; Carbs: 43g; Fiber: 15g; Protein: 13g

146. Moroccan Eggplant Stew

Preparation time: 5 minutes
Cooking time: 15 minutes
Servings: 4
Ingredients:
- 2 teaspoons Spicy Umami Blend
- 1 leek, white part only, thinly sliced and rinsed well
- 1 medium eggplant, diced

- 2 cups chopped mushrooms
- 1 tablespoon paprika
- 2 teaspoons ground cumin
- 1 teaspoon ground cinnamon
- 1 (15-ounce) can chickpeas, drained and rinsed
- 1 (15-ounce) can diced tomatoes
- 1 cup Vegetable Broth

Directions:
In a large saucepan, combine the umami blend and 3 tablespoons water and heat over medium-high heat until bubbling. Add the leek, eggplant, mushrooms, paprika, cumin, and cinnamon and sauté, stirring frequently, for 8 to 10 minutes. If the mixture begins to stick, add water 1 teaspoon at a time as needed.
Add the chickpeas, tomatoes, and broth and bring to a boil. Reduce the heat to medium-low, cover, and simmer for 10 minutes. Remove from the heat and serve.
SWAP IT: Instead of canned tomatoes, you can use 2 cups chopped fresh tomatoes and add an extra ½ cup vegetable broth.
Per serving (2 cups): Calories: 200Kcal; Fat: 3g; Carbs: 37g; Fiber: 13g; Protein: 10g

147. Minestrone in Minutes
Preparation time: 5 minutes
Cooking time: 15 minutes **Servings:** 4 to 6
Ingredients:
- 1 cup diced red onion
- ½ cup diced carrot - ½ cup diced celery
- 2 to 3 garlic cloves, minced
- 2 teaspoons dried basil
- 1 (15.5-ounce) can cannellini beans, drained and rinsed
- 1 (15.5-ounce) can red beans, drained and rinsed
- 1 (15-ounce) can no-salt tomato sauce
- 3 cups Vegetable Broth
- 1 cup diced mushrooms
- ½ teaspoon red pepper flakes
- 3 tablespoons lemon juice

Directions:
In a large saucepan, heat ¼ cup water over medium-high heat. Add the onion, carrot, celery, and garlic and cook until the vegetables begin to soften, about 3 minutes. Add the basil, cannellini beans, red beans, tomato sauce, broth, mushrooms, and red pepper flakes, stir well, and bring to a boil. Reduce the heat to medium-low and cook, stirring occasionally, for about 10 minutes. Remove from the heat and serve.
SWAP IT: Skip the mushrooms and use 1 cup of frozen or fresh vegetables. Zucchini, green beans, and peas are all tasty and add a pop of color.
Per serving (1½cups): Calories: 267Kcal; Fat: 0g; Carbs: 50g; Fiber15: g; Protein: 17g

148. Three-Bean Chili
Preparation time: 10 minutes
Cooking time: 25 minutes **Servings:** 6
Ingredients:
- 1 cup diced onion
- 3 teaspoons minced garlic
- 1 teaspoon chipotle chile powder
- 1 teaspoon paprika
- 1 teaspoon chili powder
- 1 teaspoon ground cumin
- ½ teaspoon red pepper flakes
- 1 (14-ounce) can black beans, drained and rinsed
- 1 (14-ounce) can kidney beans, drained and rinsed
- 1 (14-ounce) can pinto beans, drained and rinsed
- 1 (14.5-ounce) can fire-roasted diced tomatoes
- 2 teaspoons tomato paste
- 3 cups Vegetable Broth
- 1 to 2 tablespoons diced jalapeño (optional)
- ½ teaspoon sea salt, or 1 teaspoon Spicy Umami Blend
- ½ teaspoon freshly ground black pepper
- 2 tablespoons lime juice

Directions:
In a large saucepan, heat 2 tablespoons water over medium-high heat. Add the onion and garlic and sauté until the onion is translucent, 5 minutes. Add the chipotle powder, paprika, chili powder, cumin, and red pepper flakes and stir well. Add the black beans, kidney beans, pinto beans, diced tomatoes, tomato paste, broth, jalapeño (if using), salt, and black pepper, and bring to a boil. Reduce the heat to low, cover, and simmer for 15 minutes.
Stir in the lime juice just before serving.
INGREDIENT TIP: Substitute 1½ cups cooked beans for each 14-ounce can.
PAIR IT: Try ladling this chili over some BBQ Baked French Fries and drizzle a little Cheesy Chickpea Sauce on top.
Per serving (2 cups): Calories: 220Kcal; Fat: 2g; Carbs: 40g; Fiber: 6g; Protein: 13g

149. White Chili
Preparation time: 5 minutes
Cooking time: 25 minutes **Servings:** 6
Ingredients:
- 1 large onion, chopped
- 4 garlic cloves, minced
- 2 (4-ounce) cans chopped green chiles
- 1 tablespoon ground cumin
- 1 tablespoon dried oregano
- 2 teaspoons cayenne pepper
- 1 (15-ounce) can cannellini or great northern beans, drained and rinsed
- 1 (15-ounce) can black-eyed peas, drained and rinsed - 4 cups Vegetable Broth
- 1 teaspoon salt, or 1 tablespoon Spicy Umami Blend

Directions:
In a large saucepan, combine the onion, garlic, green chiles, and ¼ cup water and sauté over medium-high heat until the onion is tender, about 5 minutes. Add the cumin, oregano, cayenne, cannellini beans, black-eyed peas, broth, and salt and bring to a boil. Reduce the heat to medium-low, cover, and simmer for 15 minutes. Remove from the heat and serve.

SMART SHOPPING: In love with black-eyed peas? Stock up! Buy several bags of the frozen variety and keep them in your freezer.
Per serving (1 cup): Calories: 138Kcal; Fat: 0g; Carbs: 26g; Fiber: 8g; Protein: 9g

150. Hot-And-Sour Tofu Soup

Preparation time: 5 minutes
Cooking time: 15 minutes **Servings:** 2
Ingredients:

- ¼ cup low-sodium soy sauce
- 2 teaspoons red or yellow miso paste
- 2 teaspoons Red Chili Paste
- 1 teaspoon minced garlic
- 2 teaspoons minced fresh ginger
- 1 cup sliced mushrooms
- 12 ounces silken tofu
- ¼ cup crushed peanuts (optional)
- ¼ cup chopped green onions

Directions:
In a large saucepan, heat the soy sauce over medium-high heat until it just begins to bubble. Add the miso and whisk and mash it with a fork to create a thick slurry. Add the chili paste, garlic, and ginger and cook, stirring frequently, for 3 minutes. Add the mushrooms and 3 cups water and bring to a boil. Reduce the heat to medium-low and add the tofu, crumbling it with your fingers and dropping it into the pan. Cover and simmer for 10 minutes.
Divide the crushed peanuts (if using) and green onions between two large bowls. Ladle half the soup into each bowl and serve.
VEGGIE BOOST: Add 1 cup of your favorite frozen veggies (corn, peas, or green beans are nice options) when you crumble in the tofu.
Per serving (2 cups): Calories: 147Kcal; Fat: 1g; Carbs: g; Fiber: 2g; Protein: 16g

151. Spicy Refried Bean Stew

Preparation time: 5 minutes
Cooking time: 30 minutes **Servings:** 6
Ingredients:

- 1¼ cups Vegetable Broth, divided
- 1 small onion, halved and thinly sliced
- 1 small jalapeño, seeded and finely diced
- 2 garlic cloves, minced
- ½ to 1 teaspoon chili powder
- ½ teaspoon chipotle or ancho chile powder
- 1 teaspoon Spicy Umami Blend
- 1 (15-ounce) can pinto beans, drained and rinsed
- 1 (15-ounce) can vegetarian refried beans
- 1 (14.5-ounce) can no-salt-added diced tomatoes

Directions:
In a large saucepan, heat ¼ cup of broth over medium-high heat. Add the onion, jalapeño, garlic, chili powder, chipotle powder, and umami blend and cook, stirring occasionally, until the onion is tender, about 5 minutes.
Add the pinto beans, refried beans, tomatoes, 1 cup water, and remaining 1 cup of broth, stir well, and bring to a boil. Reduce the heat to low, cover, and simmer for 20 minutes. Remove from the heat and serve.
PROTEIN BOOST: For a "meaty" chili, swap the canned pinto beans for ½ cup TVP (textured vegetable Protein:) or 6 ounces extra-firm tofu, crumbled.
INGREDIENT TIP: Use refried pinto or black beans. You can also use 1½ cups cooked pinto beans instead of canned if you have purchased them frozen or in bulk.
Per serving (1½ cups): Calories: 150Kcal; Fat: 1g; Carbs: 27g; Fiber: 8g; Protein: 9g

152. Sweet Potato Stew

Preparation time: 10 minutes
Cooking time: 40 minutes **Servings:** 6
Ingredients:

- ¼ cup balsamic vinegar
- 1 large sweet potato, cut into bite-size pieces
- 1 cup diced onion - ½ cup chopped carrot
- ½ cup chopped celery
- 2 teaspoons dried thyme
- 1 teaspoon dried oregano
- 1-pound Brussels sprouts, halved and thinly sliced
- 1 (15-ounce) can black beans, drained and rinsed
- 3 cups Vegetable Broth - 1 bay leaf
- 1 teaspoon Spicy Umami Blend
- ½ teaspoon freshly ground black pepper

Directions:
In a large saucepan, heat the vinegar over medium-high heat. Add the sweet potato, onion, carrot, celery, thyme, and oregano and sauté until the sweet potato brightens in color and the onion is tender, about 5 minutes.
Add the Brussels sprouts, black beans, broth, bay leaf, umami blend, and pepper, stir well, and bring to a boil.
Reduce the heat to medium-low and simmer, stirring occasionally, until the sweet potatoes are tender, about 30 minutes. Remove from the heat, discard the bay leaf, and serve.
APPLIANCE TIP: To make this in a multicooker, use the Sauté function for step 1.
Add the rest of the ingredients to the pot and cook on low pressure for 8 minutes, then use a natural pressure release.
INGREDIENT TIP: Use 1½ cups cooked black beans instead of canned.
Per serving (2 cups): Calories: 134Kcal; Fat: 1g; Carbs: 27g; Fiber: 8g; Protein: 7g

153. Oyster (Mushroom) Stew

Preparation time: 10 minutes
Cooking time: 25 minutes **Servings:** 2
Ingredients:

- ¾ cup unsweetened plant-based milk, divided, plus more if needed
- 1-pound oyster mushrooms, trimmed and cut into thick slices
- 1 small yellow or sweet onion, diced
- 3 garlic cloves, minced - 2 teaspoons dried sage
- 1 (15-ounce) can cannellini or great northern beans, drained and rinsed

- ¼ cup Miso Cream Sauce
- 1 tablespoon low-sodium soy sauce
- 2 cups Vegetable Broth, divided
- 2 teaspoons Red Chili Paste

Directions:
In a large saucepan, heat ½ cup of plant-based milk over medium-high heat. Add the mushrooms, onion, garlic, and sage and cook until the mushrooms begin to brown, 5 to 8 minutes. Meanwhile, in a blender, combine the beans, miso cream sauce, and remaining ¼ cup of milk and purée until smooth and easy to pour. Add more milk a little at a time, if needed, to reach the desired consistency. Transfer the bean purée to the saucepan and stir well. Add 1 cup of broth and bring to a boil, stirring frequently. Add the remaining 1 cup of broth and stir well. Reduce the heat to medium-low, cover, and simmer for 10 minutes. Stir in the chili paste just before serving.
CHANGE IT UP: You can turn this into a cream of mushroom soup easily. Reserve about ½ cup of browned mushrooms. Use an immersion blender to purée the stew directly in the pot (or transfer it to a standing blender), then stir in the reserved browned mushrooms and serve.
ALLERGEN TIP: To make a gluten-free version, be sure to use a nut or seed milk and replace the soy sauce with tamari that is labeled "gluten-free" or coconut aminos.
Per serving (2 cups): Calories: 323Kcal; Fat: 1g; Carbs: 54g; Fiber: 16g; Protein: 23g

154. New England Corn Chowder
Preparation time: 5 minutes
Cooking time: 20 minutes **Servings:** 6
Ingredients:
- 1-pound fingerling potatoes, unpeeled, cut in half
- 3 tablespoons aquafaba (see Tip)
- 1¾ cups fresh, canned, or frozen corn kernels (14 ounces) - 1 teaspoon chili powder
- 1 small sweet onion, diced
- 2 cups Vegetable Broth
- 2 cups unsweetened plant-based milk, divided
- 1 teaspoon dried thyme - 1 teaspoon dried basil
- ½ teaspoon freshly ground black pepper
- ½ teaspoon paprika

Directions:
Place the potatoes in a large saucepan, cover with water, and bring to a boil over medium-high heat. Reduce the heat to medium and simmer until the potatoes are tender, 10 to 15 minutes. While the potatoes are cooking, in a large saucepan, heat the aquafaba over medium-high heat. Add the corn and chili powder and cook until the corn begins to brown, about 10 minutes. Drain the potatoes and roughly mash them with a potato masher, leaving some chunks. Set aside. Add the onion, vegetable broth, 1 cup of plant-based milk, thyme, basil, and pepper to the pan with the corn and bring to a boil.
Add the mashed potatoes and remaining 1 cup of milk, stir to combine, and return to a boil. Reduce the heat to low and simmer for 5 minutes, then serve.

MAKE IT FASTER: Opt for fire-roasted frozen corn, omit the aquafaba and chili powder, and skip step 2.
Per serving (1½ cups): Calories: 187Kcal; Fat: 2g; Carbs: 38g; Fiber: 5g; Protein: 7g

155. Mushroom And Quinoa "Gumbo"
Preparation time: 15 To 30 minutes
Cooking time: 30 minutes
Servings: 6
Ingredients:
- 2 cups chopped portobello mushrooms
- ¼ cup balsamic vinegar
- 1 cup chopped onion
- 1 cup chopped green bell pepper
- 1 cup chopped celery
- 1 tablespoon filé powder
- 1 tablespoon tomato powder, or 2 teaspoons tomato paste
- 1 teaspoon dried basil
- 1 teaspoon cayenne pepper
- 1 teaspoon dried thyme
- 3 cups Vegetable Broth, divided
- ½ cup dry quinoa, rinsed and drained
- 4 cups chopped mustard greens

Directions:
In a large skillet, combine the mushrooms and vinegar. Set aside to marinate for 15 to 30 minutes.
Place the skillet over medium-high heat and cook the mushrooms for 3 minutes. Add the onion, bell pepper, and celery and cook for 3 minutes more. Add the filé, stir to coat the vegetables, and cook, stirring frequently for 5 minutes more.
Add the tomato powder, basil, cayenne, thyme, 2 cups of broth, and the quinoa and bring to a boil.
Reduce the heat to medium-low, cover, and cook until the quinoa is tender, about 15 minutes.
Raise the heat to medium-high, add the mustard greens and remaining 1 cup of broth, stir to combine, and bring the mixture back to a boil.
Reduce the heat to low, cover, and simmer for 5 minutes more. Remove from the heat and serve.
INGREDIENT TIP: Filé powder is a fantastic salt-free spice that you can use in all kinds of recipes, stews, soup, and sauces. It thickens and creates a slightly sweet contrast in savory dishes.
SWAP IT: Use arugula or spinach instead of mustard greens.
Per serving (2 cups): Calories: 97; Saturated Fat: 0g; Fat: 1g; Protein: 4g; Total Carbs: 18g; Fiber: 4g; Sodium: 29mg

156. Asparagus & Green Peas Soup
Preparation time: 15 minutes
Cooking time: 25 minutes **Servings:** 4
Ingredients:
- 12 ounces fresh asparagus, trimmed
- 4 tablespoons avocado oil, divided
- 2 cups fresh peas, shelled
- 4 garlic cloves, minced
- 1 medium shallot, sliced thinly

- Salt and ground black pepper, to taste
- 1½ cups vegetable broth
- 2 cups unsweetened soy milk
- 2 tablespoons nutritional yeast
- 1 tablespoon fresh lemon juice

Directions:
Preheat your oven to 400°F.
Place the asparagus spears, 2 tablespoons of oil, salt, and black pepper onto a baking sheet, and toss to coat well. Then, arrange the asparagus spears in a single layer. Roast for about 15 minutes. Remove the baking sheet from the oven and set it aside. Heat the remaining oil over medium heat and sauté the shallot, garlic, salt, and black pepper for about 2–3 minutes.
Add peas, broth, and almond milk and bring to a boil. Remove the pan of soup from heat and set it aside to cool slightly. Transfer the soup into a blender along with asparagus in 2 batches and pulse until smooth. Return the soup to the pan and over medium heat and bring to a gentle simmer. Add nutritional yeast and whisk until well combined. Cook for about 3–4 minutes or until heated completely. Stir in lemon juice, salt, and black pepper, and remove from heat. Serve hot.
Per serving: Calories: 228Kcal; Fat: 16.67g; Carbs: 15.18g; Protein: 6.45g

157. Black Beans Stew
Preparation time: 10 minutes
Cooking time: 30 minutes **Servings:** 4
Ingredients:
- 1 tablespoon olive oil
- 2 small onions, chopped
- 5 garlic cloves, chopped finely
- 1 teaspoon of dried oregano
- 1 teaspoon ground cumin
- ½ teaspoon ground ginger
- Salt and ground black pepper, to taste
- 1 (14-ounce) can diced tomatoes
- 2 (13½-ounce) cans black beans, rinsed and drained
- ½ cup vegetable broth

Directions:
Heat the olive oil in a pan over medium heat and cook the onion for about 5–7 minutes, stirring frequently. Add garlic, oregano, spices, salt, and black pepper, and cook for about 1 minute. Add the tomatoes and cook for about 1–2 minutes. Add in the beans and broth and bring to a boil. Now, adjust the heat to medium-low and simmer, covered for about 15 minutes. Serve hot. **Per serving:** Calories: 247Kcal; Fat: 5.5g; Carbs: 39.4g; Fiber: 13.5g; Protein: 13g

158. Sniffle Soup
Preparation time: 5 minutes
Cooking time: 33 minutes **Servings:** 6
Ingredients:
- 1½ tbsp plus 4 cups water, divided
- 1½ cups onion, diced
- 1 cup carrot, diced
- 1 cup celery, diced
- 3 large cloves garlic, minced
- 1 tsp paprika
- 1 tsp mild curry powder
- ½ tsp sea salt
- ¼ tsp dried thyme
- ¼ tsp ground black pepper
- 2 cups dried red lentils
- 3 cups vegetable stock
- 1½ tbsp apple cider vinegar

Directions:
Heat a large pot over medium heat. Add all ingredients to the pot and stir occasionally. Cook for 8 minutes. Increase heat and bring it to a boil.
Once it is boiled, let it simmer for 25 minutes. Serve and enjoy.
Per serving: Calories: 293Kcal; Fat: 1g; Carbs: 53.2g; Fiber: 23.1g; Protein: 18.5g

159. Butternut Squash Soup
Preparation time: 15 minutes
Cooking time: 25 minutes **Servings:** 6
Ingredients:
- 2 tbsp. olive oil
- 1 cup onion, chopped
- 1 cup cilantro
- 1 ginger, sliced thinly
- 2 cups pears, chopped
- ½ tsp. ground coriander
- Salt to taste
- 2 ½ lb. butternut squash, cubed
- 1 tsp. lime zest
- 26 oz. coconut milk
- 1 tbsp. lime juice
- ½ cup plain yogurt

Directions:
Pour the oil into a pan over medium heat. Add the onion, cilantro, ginger, pears, coriander, and salt. Stir and cook for 5 minutes. Transfer to a pressure cooker. Stir in the squash and lime zest. Pour in the coconut milk. Cook on high for 20 minutes. Release pressure naturally. Stir in the lime juice. Transfer to a blender. Pulse until smooth.
Reheat and stir in yogurt before serving.
Per serving: Calories: 274Kcal; Fat: 14g; Carbs: 36g; Fiber: 6g; Protein: 5g

160. Lemon & Strawberry Soup
Preparation time: 4 hours and 10 minutes
Cooking time: 0 minutes **Servings:** 4
Ingredients:
- 1 cup buttermilk
- 3 cups strawberries, sliced
- 1 tsp. lemon thyme
- 2 tsp. lemon zest
- 2 tbsp. honey

Directions:
Blend the buttermilk and strawberries in your food processor. Transfer this mixture to a bowl. Add the thyme and lemon zest. Chill in the refrigerator for 4 hours. Strain the soup and stir in the honey. Serve in bowls. **Per serving:** Calories: 92Kcal; Fat: 1g; Carbs: 20g; Fiber: 2g; Protein: 3g

161. Tomato Soup with Kale & White Beans

Preparation time: 5 minutes
Cooking time: 7 minutes **Servings:** 4
Ingredients:

- 28 oz. tomato soup - 1 tbsp. olive oil
- 3 cups kale, chopped
- 14 oz. cannellini beans, rinsed and drained
- 1 tsp. garlic, crushed and minced
- ¼ cup Parmesan cheese, grated

Directions:
Pour the soup into a pan over medium heat.
Add the oil and cook the kale for 2 minutes.
Stir in the beans and garlic. Simmer for 5 minutes.
Sprinkle with Parmesan cheese before serving.
Per serving: Calories: 200Kcal; Fat: 6g; Carbs: 29g; Fiber: 6g; Protein: 9g

162. Bursting Black Bean Soup

Preparation time: 2 hours and 10 minutes
Cooking time: 6 hours **Servings:** 6
Ingredients:

- 1 pound of black beans, uncooked
- 1/4 cup of lentils, uncooked
- 1 medium-sized carrot, peeled and chopped
- 2 medium-sized green bell peppers, cored and chopped
- 1 stalk of celery, chopped
- 28 ounce of diced tomatoes
- 2 jalapeno pepper, seeded and minced
- 1 large red onion, peeled and chopped
- 3 teaspoons of minced garlic
- 1 tablespoon of salt
- 1/2 teaspoon ground black pepper
- 2 tablespoons of red chili powder
- 2 teaspoons of ground cumin
- 1/2 teaspoon of dried oregano
- 3 tablespoons of apple cider vinegar
- 1/2 cup of brown rice, uncooked
- 3 quarts of water, divided

Directions:
Place a large pot over medium-high heat, add the beans, pour in 1 1/2 quarts of water and boil it.
Let it boil for 10 minutes, then remove the pot from the heat, let it stand for 1 hour, and then cover the pot. Drain the beans and add them to a 6-quarts slow cooker. Pour in the remaining 1 1/2 quarts of water and cover it with the lid. Plug in the slow cooker and let it cook for 3 hours at the high setting or until it gets soft. When the beans are done, add the remaining ingredients, except for the rice, and continue cooking for 3 hours on the low heat setting. When it is 30 minutes left to finish, add the rice to the slow cooker and let it cook. When done, using an immersion blender, process half of the soup and then serve.
Per serving: Calories: 116Kcal; Fat: 1.5g; Carbs: 19g; Fiber: 4g; Protein: 5.6g

163. Yummy Lentil Rice Soup

Preparation time: 15 minutes
Cooking time: 4 hours **Servings:** 6
Ingredients:

- 2 cups of brown rice, uncooked
- 2 cups of lentils, uncooked
- 1/2 cup of chopped celery
- 1 cup of chopped carrots
- 1 cup of sliced mushrooms
- 1/2 of a medium-sized white onion, peeled and chopped - 1 teaspoon of minced garlic
- 1 tablespoon of salt
- 1/2 teaspoon of ground black pepper
- 1 cup of vegetable broth
- 8 cups of water

Directions:
Using a 6-quarts slow cooker, place all the ingredients, except for the mushrooms, and stir until it mixes properly. Cover with lid, plug in the slow cooker, and let it cook for 3 to 4 hours at the high setting or until it is cooked thoroughly. Pour in the mushrooms, stir and continue cooking for 1 hour at the low heat setting or until it is done.
Serve right away.
Per serving: Calories: 226Kcal; Fat: 2g; Carbs: 41g; Fiber: 12g; Protein: 13g

164. Tangy Corn Chowder

Preparation time: 15 minutes
Cooking time: 5 hours **Servings:** 6
Ingredients:

- 24 ounce of cooked kernel corn
- 3 medium-sized potatoes, peeled and diced
- 2 red chile peppers, minced
- 1 large white onion, peeled and diced
- 1 teaspoon of minced garlic
- 2 teaspoons of salt
- 1/2 teaspoon of ground black pepper
- 1 tablespoon of red chili powder
- 1 tablespoon of dried parsley
- 1/4 cup of vegan margarine
- 14 fluid ounce of soy milk
- 1 lime, juiced
- 24 fluid ounce of vegetable broth

Directions:
Using a 6-quarts slow cooker place all the ingredients, except for the soy milk, margarine, and lime juice.
Stir properly and cover it with the lid. Then plug in the slow cooker and let it cook for 3 to 4 hours at the high setting or until it is cooked thoroughly. When done, process the mixture with an immersion blender or until it gets smooth. Pour in the milk, margarine and stir properly. Continue cooking the soup for 1 hour at the low heat setting. Drizzle it with lime juice and serve.
Per serving: Calories: 237Kcal; Carbs:18g; Protein: 7.4g; Fat: 15g; Fiber: 2.2g

165. Healthy Cabbage Soup

Preparation time: 15 minutes
Cooking time: 4 hours **Servings:** 6
Ingredients:
- 5 cups of shredded cabbage
- 3 medium-sized carrots, peeled and chopped
- 3 1/2 cups of diced tomatoes
- 1 medium-sized white onion, chopped
- 2 teaspoons of minced garlic
- 1 teaspoon of salt
- 1 teaspoon of dried oregano
- 1 tablespoon of dried parsley
- 1 1/2 cups of tomato sauce
- 5 cups of vegetable broth

Directions:
Using a 6-quarts slow cooker, place all the ingredients and stir properly. Cover it with the lid, plug in the slow cooker, and let it cook for 4 hours at the high heat setting or until the vegetables are tender. Serve right away.
Per serving: Calories: 150Kcal; Fat: 5g; Carbs: 4g; Fiber: 2g; Protein: 20g

166. Chunky Potato Soup

Preparation time: 10 minutes
Cooking time: 6 hours **Servings:** 6
Ingredients:
- 1 medium-sized carrot, grated
- 6 medium-sized potatoes, peeled and diced
- 2 stalks of celery, diced
- 1 medium-sized white onion, peeled and diced
- 2 teaspoons of minced garlic
- 1 1/2 teaspoons of salt
- 1 teaspoon of ground black pepper
- 1 1/2 teaspoons of dried sage
- 1 teaspoon of dried thyme
- 2 tablespoons of olive oil
- 2 bay leaves
- 8 1/2 cups of vegetable water

Directions:
Using a 6-quarts slow cooker, place all the ingredients and stir properly. Cover it with the lid, plug in the slow cooker, and let it cook for 6 hours at the high heat setting or until the potatoes are tender.
Serve right away.
Per serving: Calories: 200Kcal; Fat: 8g; Carbs: 26g; Fiber: 2g; Protein: 6g

167. Yogurt Soup with Rice

Preparation time: 15 minutes
Cooking time: 48 minutes **Servings:** 6
Ingredients:
- ½ cup brown rice, rinsed and drained
- 1 egg
- 4 cups yogurt
- 3 tbsp. rice flour
- 3 cups water
- ½ cup mint, chopped
- ½ cup cilantro, chopped
- ½ cup dill, chopped
- ½ cup parsley, chopped
- 2 cups arugula
- Salt to taste

Directions:
Combine the rice, egg, yogurt, and flour in a pot.
Put it over medium heat and cook for 1 minute, stirring frequently. Pour in the water and increase heat to boil. Reduce heat and simmer for 45 minutes.
Add the arugula, herbs, and salt. Cook for 2 minutes.
Add more water to adjust consistency.
Per serving: Calories: 186Kcal; Fat: 7g; Carbs: 24g; Fiber: 2g; Protein: 9g

168. Zucchini Soup

Preparation time: 5 minutes
Cooking time: 15 minutes **Servings:** 4
Ingredients:
- 3 cups vegetable broth
- 1 tbsp. tarragon, chopped
- 3 zucchinis, sliced
- 3 oz. cheddar cheese
- Salt and pepper to taste

Directions:
Pour the broth into a pot. Stir in the tarragon and zucchini. Bring to a boil and then simmer for 10 minutes. Transfer to a blender and blend until smooth. Put it back on the stove and stir in cheese.
Season with salt and pepper.
Per serving: Calories: 110Kcal; Fat: 5g; Carbs: 7g; Fiber: 2g; Protein: 10g

169. Hearty Vegetarian Lasagna Soup

Preparation time: 20 minutes
Cooking time: 7 hours **Servings:** 10
Ingredients:
12 ounces of lasagna noodles
- 4 cups of spinach leaves
- 2 cups of brown mushrooms, sliced
- 2 medium-sized zucchinis, stemmed and sliced
- 28 ounce of crushed tomatoes
- 1 medium-sized white onion, peeled and diced
- 2 teaspoon of minced garlic
- 1 tablespoon of dried basil
- 2 bay leaves
- 2 teaspoons of salt
- 1/8 teaspoon of red pepper flakes
- 2 teaspoons of ground black pepper
- 2 teaspoons of dried oregano
- 15-ounce of tomato sauce
- 6 cups of vegetable broth

Directions:
Grease a 6-quarts slow cooker and place all the ingredients in it except for the lasagna and spinach. Cover the top, plug in the slow cooker; adjust the cooking time to 7 hours and let it cook on the low heat setting or until it is properly done. In the

meantime, cook the lasagna noodles in boiling water for 7 to 10 minutes or until it gets soft. Then drain and set it aside until the slow cooker is done cooking.

When it is done, add the lasagna noodles into the soup along with the spinach and continue cooking for 10 to 15 minutes or until the spinach leaves wilts.

Using a ladle, serving it in a bowl.

Per serving: Calories: 188Kcal; Fat: 9g; Carbs: 13g; Fiber: 0.5g; Protein: 18g

170. Chunky Black Lentil Veggie Soup

Preparation time: 35 minutes
Cooking time: 4 hours
Servings: 8
Ingredients:
- 1 1/2 cups of black lentils, uncooked
- 2 small turnips, peeled and diced
- 10 medium-sized carrots, peeled and diced
- 1 medium-sized green bell pepper, cored and diced
- 3 cups of diced tomatoes
- 1 medium-sized white onion, peeled and diced
- 2 tablespoons of minced ginger
- 1 teaspoon of minced garlic
- 1 teaspoon of salt
- 1/2 teaspoon of ground coriander
- 1/2 teaspoon of ground cumin
- 3 tablespoons of unsalted butter
- 32 fluid ounce of vegetable broth
- 32 fluid ounce of water

Directions:
Using a medium-sized microwave, cover the bowl, place the lentils, and pour in the water. Microwave lentils for 10 minutes or until softened, stirring after 5 minutes. Drain lentils and add to a 6-quarts slow cooker along with remaining ingredients and stir until just mix. Cover with top, plug in slow cooker; adjust cooking time to 6 hours and let cook on low heat setting or until carrots are tender. Serve straight away.

Per serving: Calories: 90Kcal; Fat: 2g; Carbs: 15g; Fiber: 3g; Protein: 3g

171. Lovely Parsnip & Split Pea Soup

Preparation time: 10 minutes
Cooking time: 5 hours **Servings:** 8
Ingredients:
- 1 tablespoon of olive oil
- 2 large parsnips, peeled and chopped
- 2 large carrots, peeled and chopped
- 1 medium-sized white onion, peeled and diced
- 1 1/2 teaspoon of minced garlic
- 2 1/4 cups of dried green split peas, rinsed
- 1 teaspoon of salt
- 1/2 teaspoon of ground black pepper
- 1 teaspoon of dried thyme
- 2 bay leaves
- 6 cups of vegetable broth
- 1 teaspoon of liquid smoke

Directions:
Place a medium-sized non-stick skillet pan over an average pressure of heat, add the oil and let it heat.

Add the parsnip, carrot, onion, garlic, and let it cook for 5 minutes or until it is heated. Transfer this mixture into a 6-quarts slow cooker and add the remaining ingredients. Stir until mixed properly and cover the top. Plug in the slow cooker; adjust the cooking time to 5 hours and let it cook on the high heat setting or until the peas and vegetables get soft.

When done, remove the bay leaf from the soup and blend it with a submersion blender or until the soup reaches your desired state. Add the seasoning and serve.

Per serving: Calories: 199Kcal; Fat: 5g; Carbs: 21g; Fiber: 8g; Protein: 18g

172. Incredible Tomato Basil Soup

Preparation time: 1 hour and 10 minutes **Cooking time:** 5 hours
Servings: 6
Ingredients:
- 1 cup of chopped celery
- 1 cup of chopped carrots
- 74 ounce of whole tomatoes, canned
- 2 cups of chopped white onion
- 2 teaspoons of minced garlic
- 1 tablespoon of salt
- 1/2 teaspoon of ground white pepper
- 1/4 cup of basil leaves and more for garnishing
- 1 bay leaf
- 32 fluid ounce of vegetable broth
- 1/2 cup of grated Parmesan cheese

Directions:
Using 8 quarts or larger slow cooker, place all the ingredients. Stir until it is mixed properly and cover the top. Plug in the slow cooker; adjust the cooking time to 5 hours and let it cook on the high heat setting or until the vegetables are tender. Blend the soup with a submersion blender or until the soup reaches your desired state. Garnish it with cheese, basil leaves, and serve.

Per serving: Calories: 210Kcal; Fat: 10g; Carbs: 11g; Fiber: 3g; Protein: 12g

173. Spicy Cajun Boiled Peanuts

Preparation time: 5 minutes
Cooking time: 8 hours **Servings:** 15
Ingredients:
- 5 pounds of peanuts, raw and in shells
- 6-ounce of dry crab boil
- 4-ounce of jalapeno peppers, sliced
- 2-ounce of vegetable broth

Directions:
Take a 6-quarts slow cooker, place the ingredients in it and cover it with water. Stir properly and cover the top. Plug in the slow cooker; adjust the cooking time to 8 hours and let it cook on the low heat setting or until the peanuts are soft and floats on top of the cooking liquid. Drain the nuts and serve right away.

Per serving: Calories: 309Kcal; Fat: 26g; Carbs: 5g; Fiber: 0g; Protein: 0g

174. Comfort Soup
Preparation time: 5 minutes
Cooking time: 35 minutes **Servings:** 5-6
Ingredients:
- ½ cups of freshly diced onion
- 1 teaspoon of paprika
- ½ tablespoon of water
- 3 ½ cups of water
- 1 cup of freshly diced carrots
- 3 freshly minced large cloves of garlic
- 1 cup of freshly diced celery
- 1 teaspoon of mild curry powder
- 2 cups of dried red lentils
- ½ teaspoon of sea salt
- Freshly ground black pepper to taste
- ¼ teaspoon of dried thyme
- 3 cups of vegetable stock
- 1 – 1 ½ teaspoon of lemon juice/apple cider vinegar
- 2 teaspoons of freshly chopped rosemary

Directions:
Put a large pot on the stove over medium heat. Add 1 ½ teaspoon of water along with celery, onion, carrot, paprika, garlic, curry powder, sea salt, black pepper, and thyme. After all the herbs and spices are inside the pot, cover them and cook for about 7-8 minutes, stirring occasionally so that the spices do not burn. Rinse the lentils and add them to 3 ½ cups of water. Stir into the stock. Cover the pot and allow everything to simmer for 12-15 minutes. Add the rosemary and simmer for another 10 minutes. You will know that your soup is ready when the lentils are fully softened. Add the vinegar and some more water if you want a thinner liquid. Serve the soup with your favorite bread. If you do not have fresh rosemary, you can also add dried rosemary. In that case, add it with the rest of the herbs and spices at the beginning. You can use ½ to 1 teaspoon of dried rosemary.
Per serving: Calories: 180Kcal; Fat: 5g; Carbs: 23g; Protein: 7.6g

175. Tangy Chickpea Soup with a Hint of Lemon
Preparation time: 10 minutes
Cooking time: 30 minutes **Servings:** 6
Ingredients:
- 2 cups of freshly diced onion
- 3 freshly minced large garlic cloves
- ½ cup of freshly diced celery
- ¾ teaspoon of sea salt
- Freshly ground black pepper to taste
- 1 teaspoon of mustard seeds
- ½ teaspoon of dried oregano
- 1 teaspoon of cumin seeds
- ½ teaspoon of paprika
- 1 ½ teaspoon of dried thyme
- 3 ½ cups of cooked chickpeas
- 1 cup of dried red lentils
- 3 cups of vegetable stock
- 2 dried bay leaves
- 2 cups of freshly chopped tomatoes or zucchini
- 2 cups of water
- ¼ to 1/3 cup of fresh lemon juice

Directions:
Put a large pot on the stove on medium heat.
Add onion, water, salt, celery, garlic, pepper, cumin, and mustard seeds along with thyme, oregano, and paprika. Stir everything to combine well. Cover the pot and cook for about 7 minutes, stirring occasionally. Rinse the lentils. Add the lentils along with 2 ½ cups of chickpeas, zucchini/tomatoes, stock, bay leaves, and water. Stir everything to combine well. Increase the heat to bring to a boil.
Once the ingredients start to boil, cover the pot, Reduce the heat, and simmer for 20-25 minutes.
You will know that the soup is ready when the lentils are tender. After removing the bay leaves, add the lemon juice. Once the ingredients have cooled down, use a hand blender to puree the ingredients, but keep a somewhat coarse texture instead of having a smooth puree. Add the remaining chickpeas. Taste the soup and adjust the salt, pepper, and lemon juice to taste. Enjoy this amazing soup with your favorite bread.
Per serving: Calories: 290Kcal; Fat: 2.8g; Carbs: 31.1g; Protein: 7.1g

176. Lentil Soup the Vegan Way
Preparation time: 5 minutes
Cooking time: 20 minutes **Servings:** 4
Ingredients:
- 2 tablespoons of water
- 4 stalks of thinly sliced celery
- 2 cloves of freshly minced garlic
- 4 thinly sliced large carrots
- Sea salt
- 2 freshly diced small shallots
- Pepper
- 3 cups of red/yellow baby potatoes
- 2 cups of chopped sturdy greens
- 4 cups of vegetable broth
- 1 cup of uncooked brown or green lentils
- Fresh rosemary/thyme

Directions:
Put a large pot over medium heat. Once the pot is hot enough, add the shallots, garlic, celery, and carrots to water. Season the veggies with a little bit of pepper and salt. Sauté the veggies for 5 minutes until they are tender. You will know that the veggies are ready when they have turned golden brown. Be careful with the garlic, because it can easily burn. Add the potatoes and some more seasoning. Cook for 2 minutes. Mix the vegetable broth with the rosemary. Now Increase the heat to medium-high. Allow the veggies to be on a rolling simmer. Add the lentils and give everything a thorough stir. Once it starts to simmer again, decrease the heat and simmer for about 20 minutes without a cover. You will know that the veggies are ready when both the lentils and potatoes are soft Add the greens. Cook for 4 minutes until they wilt. You can adjust the flavor with seasonings. Enjoy this with rice or flatbread.

The leftovers are equally tasty, so store them well to enjoy on a day when you are not in the mood to cook.
Per serving: Calories: 260Kcal; Fat: 8.3g; Carbs: 52.7g; Protein: 8.4g

177. Quinoa Soup with a Dash of Kale
Preparation time: 15 minutes
Cooking time: 45 minutes **Servings:** 4-6
Ingredients:
- 3 carrots freshly peeled and chopped
- 3 tablespoons of extra virgin olive oil
- 6 freshly minced or pressed garlic cloves
- 2 freshly chopped celery stalks
- 1 freshly chopped medium-sized white or yellow onion
- 1-2 cups of seasonal veggies: butternut squash, yellow squash, zucchini, sweet potato, bell pepper
- ½ teaspoon of dried thyme
- 1 cup of rinsed quinoa
- 1 can of diced tomatoes
- 2 cups of water
- 2 bay leaves
- 4 cups of vegetable broth
- 1 teaspoon of salt
- Freshly ground black pepper to taste
- 1 cup of freshly chopped kale or collard greens
- Red pepper flakes
- 1-2 teaspoons of lemon juice
- 1 can of rinsed and dried great northern beans or chickpeas
- Freshly grated parmesan cheese

Directions:
On medium heat, warm the olive oil in a soup pot. Once the oil starts to shimmer, start adding the carrot, onion, celery, and seasonal veggies, along with salt. Cook everything until the onion softens. You will know that the veggies have become tender when the onions become translucent. This will take about 6-8 minutes. Add the thyme and garlic to the veggies. After cooking for about 1 minute, it will turn fragrant. Add the diced tomatoes and cook everything for a few more minutes. Add the quinoa, water, and broth. Add the bay leaves along with 1 teaspoon of salt and red pepper flakes. Increase the heat and bring everything to a boil. Cover the pot partially and Reduce the heat so that the ingredients continue to simmer. Simmer for about 25 minutes.

Uncover the pot, and add the greens and beans. Simmer for another 5 minutes. Let the greens soften a bit. Remove the pot from the heat, and remove the bay leaves. Add 1 teaspoon of lemon juice. Taste the soup and add salt and pepper to taste. Divide the warm, hearty soup equally in bowls and top with parmesan cheese. Dig in and enjoy a bowl full of happiness.
Per serving: Calories: 290Kcal; Fat: 7.8g; Carbs: 28.4g; Protein: 4.7g

178. Amazing Chickpea and Noodle Soup
Preparation time: 10 minutes
Cooking time: 20 minutes
Servings: 4
Ingredients:
- 1 freshly diced celery stalk
- ¼ cup of poultry seasoning
- 1 cup of freshly diced onion
- 3 cloves of freshly crushed garlic
- 2 cups of cooked chickpeas
- 4 cups of vegetable broth
- Freshly chopped cilantro
- 2 freshly cubed medium-size potatoes
- 2 freshly sliced carrots
- ½ teaspoon of dried thyme
- Pepper
- 2 cups of water
- 6 ounces of gluten-free spaghetti
- 1 tablespoon of garlic powder
- 2 teaspoons of sea salt
- 1 1/3 cup of nutritional yeast
- 3 tablespoons of onion powder
- 1 teaspoon of oregano
- ½ teaspoon of turmeric
- 1 ½ tablespoon of dried basil

Directions:
Put a pot on medium heat and sauté the onion. It will soften within 3 minutes. Add celery, potato, and carrots and sauté for another 3 minutes Add the poultry seasoning to the garlic, thyme, water, and vegetable broth. Simmer the mix on medium-high heat. Cook the veggies for about 20 minutes until they soften. Add the cooked pasta and chickpeas.

Add salt and pepper to taste. Put the fresh cilantro on top and enjoy the fresh soup!
Per serving: Calories: 290Kcal; Fat: 8.3g; Carbs: 52.7g; Protein: 8.4g

Amanda Kale

CHAPTER 16:
Rice & Grains

179. Classic Garlicky Rice
Preparation time: 4 minutes
Cooking time: 16 minutes
Servings: 4
Ingredients:
- 4 tablespoons olive oil
- 4 cloves garlic, chopped
- 1 ½ cups white rice
- 2 ½ cups vegetable broth

Directions:
In a saucepan, heat the olive oil over a moderately high flame. Add in the garlic and sauté for about 1 minute or until aromatic.Add in the rice and broth. Bring to a boil; immediately turn the heat to a gentle simmer.Cook for about 15 minutes or until all the liquid has been absorbed. Fluff the rice with a fork, season with salt and pepper, and serve hot!
Per serving: Calories: 422Kcal; Fat: 15.1g; Carbs: 61.1g; Protein: 9.3g

180. Brown Rice with Vegetables and Tofu
Preparation time: 12 minutes
Cooking time: 33 minutes **Servings:** 4
Ingredients:
- 4 teaspoons sesame seeds
- 2 spring garlic stalks, minced
- 1 cup spring onions, chopped
- 1 carrot, trimmed and sliced
- 1 celery rib, sliced
- 1/4 cup dry white wine
- 10 ounces tofu, cubed
- 1 ½ cups long-grain brown rice, rinsed thoroughly
- 2 tablespoons soy sauce
- 2 tablespoons tahini
- 1 tablespoon lemon juice

Directions:
In a wok or large saucepan, heat 2 teaspoons of the sesame oil over medium-high heat. Now, cook the garlic, onion, carrot, and celery for about 3 minutes, stirring periodically to ensure even cooking.Add the wine to deglaze the pan and push the vegetables to one side of the wok. Add in the remaining sesame oil and fry the tofu for 8 minutes, stirring occasionally. Bring 2 ½ cups of water to a boil over medium-high heat. Bring to a simmer and cook the rice for about 30 minutes or until it is tender; fluff the rice and stir it with the soy sauce and tahini. Stir the vegetables and tofu into the hot rice; add a few drizzles of the fresh lemon juice and serve warm. Bon appétit!
Per serving: Calories: 410Kcal; Fat: 13.2g; Carbs: 60g; Protein: 14.3g

181. Basic Amaranth Porridge
Preparation time: 30 minutes
Cooking time: 5 minutes **Servings:** 4
Ingredients:
- 3 cups water - 1 cup amaranth
- 1/2 cup coconut milk
- 4 tablespoons agave syrup
- A pinch of kosher salt
- A pinch of grated nutmeg

Directions:
Bring the water to a boil over medium-high heat; add in the amaranth and turn the heat to a simmer.
Let it cook for about 30 minutes, stirring periodically to prevent the amaranth from sticking to the bottom of the pan.Stir in the remaining ingredients and continue to cook for 1 to 2 minutes more until cooked through. Bon appétit!
Per serving: Calories: 261Kcal; Fat: 4.4g; Carbs: 49g; Protein: 7.3g

182. Country Cornbread with Spinach
Preparation time: 25 minutes
Cooking time: 25 minutes **Servings:** 8
Ingredients:
- 1 tablespoon flaxseed meal
- 1 cup all-purpose flour
- 1 cup yellow cornmeal
- 1/2 teaspoon baking soda
- 1/2 teaspoon baking powder
- 1 teaspoon kosher salt
- 1 teaspoon brown sugar
- A pinch of grated nutmeg
- 1 ¼ cups oat milk, unsweetened
- 1 teaspoon white vinegar
- 1/2 cup olive oil
- 2 cups spinach, torn into pieces

Directions:
Start by preheating your oven to 420 degrees F. Now, spritz a baking pan with a nonstick cooking spray.
To make the flax eggs, mix flaxseed meal with 3 tablespoons of water. Stir and let it sit for about 15 minutes. In a mixing bowl, thoroughly combine the flour, cornmeal, baking soda, baking powder, salt, sugar, and grated nutmeg.Gradually add in the flax egg, oat milk, vinegar, and olive oil, whisking constantly to avoid lumps. Afterward, fold in the spinach. Scrape the batter into the prepared baking pan. Bake your cornbread for about 25 minutes or until a tester inserted in the middle comes out dry and clean. Let it stand for about 10 minutes before slicing and serving. Bon appétit!
Per serving: Calories: 282Kcal; Fat: 15.4g; Carbs: 30g; Protein: 4.6g

183. Rice Pudding with Currants

Preparation time: 5 minutes
Cooking time: 40 minutes **Servings:** 4
Ingredients:
- 1 ½ cups water - 1 cup white rice
- 2 ½ cups oat milk, divided
- 1/2 cup white sugar - A pinch of salt
- A pinch of grated nutmeg
- 1 teaspoon ground cinnamon
- 1/2 teaspoon vanilla extract
- 1/2 cup dried currants

Directions:
In a saucepan, bring the water to a boil over medium-high heat. Immediately turn the heat to a simmer, add in the rice and let it cook for about 20 minutes. Add in the milk, sugar, and spices and continue to cook for 20 minutes more, stirring constantly to prevent the rice from sticking to the pan. Top with dried currants and serve at room temperature. Bon appétit!
Per serving: Calories: 423Kcal; Fat: 5.3g; Carbs: 85g; Protein: 8.8g

184. Millet Porridge with Sultanas

Preparation time: 5 minutes
Cooking time: 20 minutes **Servings:** 3
Ingredients:
- 1 cup water - 1 cup coconut milk
- 1 cup millet, rinsed
- 1/4 teaspoon grated nutmeg
- 1/4 teaspoon ground cinnamon
- 1 teaspoon vanilla paste
- 1/4 teaspoon kosher salt
- 2 tablespoons agave syrup
- 4 tablespoons sultana raisins

Directions:
Place the water, milk, millet, nutmeg, cinnamon, vanilla, and salt in a saucepan; bring to a boil. Turn the heat to a simmer and let it cook for about 20 minutes; fluff the millet with a fork and spoon into individual bowls. Serve with agave syrup and sultanas. Bon appétit!
Per serving: Calories: 353Kcal; Fat: 5.5g; Carbs: 65.2g; Protein: 9.8g

185. Quinoa Porridge with Dried Figs

Preparation time: 5 minutes
Cooking time: 20 minutes **Servings:** 3
Ingredients:
- 1 cup white quinoa, rinsed
- 2 cups almond milk
- 4 tablespoons brown sugar - A pinch of salt
- 1/4 teaspoon grated nutmeg
- 1/2 teaspoon ground cinnamon
- 1/2 teaspoon vanilla extract
- 1/2 cup dried figs, chopped

Directions:
Place the quinoa, almond milk, sugar, salt, nutmeg, cinnamon, and vanilla extract in a saucepan. Bring it to a boil over medium-high heat. Turn the heat to a simmer and let it cook for about 20 minutes; fluff with a fork. Divide between three serving bowls and garnish with dried figs. Bon appétit!
Per serving: Calories: 414Kcal; Fat: 9g; Carbs: 71.2g; Protein: 13.8g

186. Bread Pudding with Raisins

Preparation time: 15 minutes
Cooking time: 45 minutes
Servings: 4
Ingredients:
- 4 cups day-old bread, cubed
- 1 cup brown sugar - 4 cups coconut milk
- 1/2 teaspoon vanilla extract
- 1 teaspoon ground cinnamon
- 2 tablespoons rum
- 1/2 cup raisins

Directions:
Start by preheating your oven to 360 degrees F. Lightly oil a casserole dish with a nonstick cooking spray. Place the cubed bread in the prepared casserole dish. In a mixing bowl, thoroughly combine the sugar, milk, vanilla, cinnamon, rum, and raisins. Pour the custard evenly over the bread cubes.
Let it soak for about 15 minutes.
Bake in the preheated oven for about 45 minutes or until the top is golden and set. Bon appétit!
Per serving: Calories: 474Kcal; Fat: 12.2g; Carbs: 72g; Protein: 14.4g

187. Bulgur Wheat Salad

Preparation time: 12 minutes
Cooking time: 13 minutes
Servings: 4
Ingredients:
- 1 cup bulgur wheat
- 1 ½ cups vegetable broth
- 1 teaspoon sea salt
- 1 teaspoon fresh ginger, minced
- 4 tablespoons olive oil
- 1 onion, chopped
- 8 ounces canned garbanzo beans, drained
- 2 large roasted peppers, sliced
- 2 tablespoons fresh parsley, roughly chopped

Directions:
In a deep saucepan, bring the bulgur wheat and vegetable broth to a simmer; let it cook, covered, for 12 to 13 minutes. Let it stand for about 10 minutes and fluff with a fork. Add the remaining ingredients to the cooked bulgur wheat; serve at room temperature or well-chilled. Bon appétit!
Per serving: Calories: 359Kcal; Fat: 15.5g; Carbs: 48.1g; Protein: 10.1g

188. Rye Porridge with Blueberry Topping

Preparation time: 9 minutes
Cooking time: 6 minutes **Servings:** 3
Ingredients:
- 1 cup rye flakes - 1 cup water
- 1 cup coconut milk
- 1 cup fresh blueberries
- 1 tablespoon coconut oil - 6 dates, pitted

Directions:
Add the rye flakes, water, and coconut milk to a deep saucepan; bring to a boil over medium-high. Turn the heat to a simmer and let it cook for 5 to 6 minutes.
In a blender or food processor, puree the blueberries with coconut oil and dates. Ladle into three bowls and garnish with the blueberry topping. Bon appétit!
Per serving: Calories: 359Kcal; Fat: 11g; Carbs: 56.1g; Protein: 12.1g

189. Coconut Sorghum Porridge

Preparation time: 10 minutes
Cooking time: 15 minutes **Servings:** 2
Ingredients:
- 1/2 cup sorghum - 1 cup water
- 1/2 cup coconut milk
- 1/4 teaspoon grated nutmeg
- 1/4 teaspoon ground cloves
- 1/2 teaspoon ground cinnamon
- Kosher salt, to taste
- 2 tablespoons agave syrup
- 2 tablespoons coconut flakes

Directions
Place the sorghum, water, milk, nutmeg, cloves, cinnamon, and kosher salt in a saucepan; simmer gently for about 15 minutes. Spoon the porridge into serving bowls. Top with agave syrup and coconut flakes. Bon appétit!
Per serving: Calories: 289Kcal; Fat: 5.1g; Carbs: 57.8g; Protein: 7.3g

190. Dad's Aromatic Rice

Preparation time: 5 minutes
Cooking time: 15 minutes **Servings:** 4
Ingredients:
- 3 tablespoons olive oil
- 1 teaspoon garlic, minced
- 1 teaspoon dried oregano
- 1 teaspoon dried rosemary
- 1 bay leaf - 1 ½ cups white rice
- 2 ½ cups vegetable broth
- Sea salt and cayenne pepper, to taste

Directions:
In a saucepan, heat the olive oil over a moderately high flame. Add in the garlic, oregano, rosemary, and bay leaf; sauté for about 1 minute or until aromatic.
Add in the rice and broth. Bring to a boil; immediately turn the heat to a gentle simmer. Cook for about 15 minutes or until all the liquid has been absorbed.
Fluff the rice with a fork, season with salt and pepper, and serve immediately. Bon appétit!
Per serving: Calories: 384Kcal; Fat: 11.4g; Carbs: 60.4g; Protein: 8.3g

191. Everyday Savory Grits

Preparation time: 5 minutes
Cooking time: 30 minutes **Servings:** 4
Ingredients:
- 2 tablespoons vegan butter
- 1 sweet onion, chopped
- 1 teaspoon garlic, minced
- 4 cups water
- 1 cup stone-ground grits
- Sea salt and cayenne pepper, to taste

Directions:
In a saucepan, melt the vegan butter over medium-high heat. Once hot, cook the onion for about 3 minutes or until tender. Add in the garlic and continue to sauté for 30 seconds more or until aromatic; reserve. Bring the water to a boil over moderately high heat. Stir in the grits, salt, and pepper. Turn the heat to a simmer, cover, and continue to cook for about 30 minutes or until cooked through. Stir in the sautéed mixture and serve warm. Bon appétit!
Per serving: Calories: 238Kcal; Fat: 6.5g; Carbs: 38.7g; Protein: 3.7g

192. Greek-Style Barley Salad

Preparation time: 5 minutes
Cooking time: 30 minutes **Servings:** 4
Ingredients:
- 1 cup pearl barley
- 2 ¾ cups vegetable broth
- 2 tablespoons apple cider vinegar
- 4 tablespoons extra-virgin olive oil
- 2 bell peppers, seeded and diced
- 1 shallot, chopped
- 2 ounces sun-dried tomatoes in oil, chopped
- 1/2 green olives, pitted and sliced
- 2 tablespoons fresh cilantro, roughly chopped

Directions:
Bring the barley and broth to a boil over medium-high heat; now, turn the heat to a simmer. Continue to simmer for about 30 minutes until all the liquid has absorbed; fluff with a fork. Toss the barley with vinegar, olive oil, peppers, shallots, sun-dried tomatoes, and olives; toss to combine well.
Garnish with fresh cilantro and serve at room temperature or well-chilled. Enjoy!
Per serving: Calories: 378Kcal; Fat: 15.6g; Carbs: 50g; Protein: 10.7g

193. Easy Sweet Maize Meal Porridge

Preparation time: 5 minutes
Cooking time: 10 minutes
Servings: 2
Ingredients:
- 2 cups water - 1/2 cup maize meal
- 1/4 teaspoon ground allspice

- 1/4 teaspoon salt
- 2 tablespoons brown sugar
- 2 tablespoons almond butter

Directions:
In a saucepan, bring the water to a boil; then gradually add in the maize meal and turn the heat to a simmer. Add in the ground allspice and salt. Let it cook for 10 minutes. Add in the brown sugar and almond butter and gently stir to combine. Bon appétit!

Per serving: Calories: 278Kcal; Fat: 12.7g; Carbs: 37.2g; Protein: 3g

194. Mom's Millet Muffins
Preparation time: 10 minutes
Cooking time: 25 minutes **Servings:** 8
Ingredients:
- 2 cup whole-wheat flour
- 1/2 cup millet
- 2 teaspoons baking powder
- 1/2 teaspoon salt
- 1 cup coconut milk
- 1/2 cup coconut oil, melted
- 1/2 cup agave nectar
- 1/2 teaspoon ground cinnamon
- 1/4 teaspoon ground cloves
- A pinch of grated nutmeg
- 1/2 cup dried apricots, chopped

Directions:
Begin by preheating your oven to 400 degrees F. Lightly oil a muffin tin with nonstick oil. In a mixing bowl, mix all dry ingredients. In a separate bowl, mix the wet ingredients. Stir the milk mixture into the flour mixture; mix just until evenly moist and do not overmix your batter. Fold in the apricots and scrape the batter into the prepared muffin cups. Bake the muffins in the preheated oven for about 15 minutes or until a tester inserted in the center of your muffin comes out dry and clean. Let it stand for 10 minutes on a wire rack before unmolding and serving. Enjoy!

Per serving: Calories: 367Kcal; Fat: 15.9g; Carbs: 53.7g; Protein: 6.5g

195. Ginger Brown Rice
Preparation time: 15 minutes
Cooking time: 30 minutes
Servings: 4
Ingredients:
- 1 ½ cups brown rice, rinsed
- 2 tablespoons olive oil
- 1 teaspoon garlic, minced
- 1 (1-inch) piece ginger, peeled and minced
- 1/2 teaspoon cumin seeds
- Sea salt and ground black pepper, to taste

Directions:
Place the brown rice in a saucepan and cover it with cold water by 2 inches. Bring to a boil. Turn the heat to a simmer and continue to cook for about 30 minutes or until tender. In a sauté pan, heat the olive oil over medium-high heat. Once hot, cook the garlic, ginger, and cumin seeds until aromatic. Stir the garlic/ginger mixture into the hot rice; season with salt and pepper and serve immediately. Bon appétit!

Per serving: Calories: 318Kcal; Fat: 8.8g; Carbs: 53.4g; Protein: 5.6g

196. Sweet Oatmeal "Grits"
Preparation time: 5 minutes
Cooking time: 15 minutes
Servings: 4
Ingredients:
- 1 ½ cups steel-cut oats, soaked overnight
- 1 cup almond milk
- 2 cups water
- A pinch of grated nutmeg
- A pinch of ground cloves
- A pinch of sea salt
- 4 tablespoons almonds, slivered
- 6 dates, pitted and chopped
- 6 prunes, chopped

Directions:
In a deep saucepan, bring the steel-cut oats, almond milk, and water to a boil.
Add in the nutmeg, cloves, and salt. Immediately turn the heat to a simmer, cover, and continue to cook for about 15 minutes or until they've softened.
Then, spoon the grits into four serving bowls; top them with the almonds, dates, and prunes.
Bon appétit!

Per serving: Calories: 380Kcal; Fat: 11.1g; Carbs: 59g; Protein: 14.4g

197. Freekeh Bowl with Dried Figs
Preparation time: 15 minutes
Cooking time: 35 minutes **Servings:** 2
Ingredients:
- 1/2 cup freekeh, soaked for 30 minutes, drained
- 1 1/3 cups almond milk
- 1/4 teaspoon sea salt
- 1/4 teaspoon ground cloves
- 1/4 teaspoon ground cinnamon
- 4 tablespoons agave syrup
- 2 ounces dried figs, chopped

Directions
Place the freekeh, milk, sea salt, ground cloves, and cinnamon in a saucepan. Bring to a boil over medium-high heat.
Immediately turn the heat to a simmer for 30 to 35 minutes, stirring occasionally to promote even cooking. Stir in the agave syrup and figs. Ladle the porridge into individual bowls and serve. Bon appétit!

Per serving: Calories: 458Kcal; Fat: 6.8g; Carbs: 90g; Protein: 12.4g

198. Cornmeal Porridge with Maple Syrup
Preparation time: 5 minutes
Cooking time: 15 minutes **Servings:** 4
Ingredients:
- 2 cups water - 2 cups almond milk

- 1 cinnamon stick
- 1 vanilla bean
- 1 cup yellow cornmeal
- 1/2 cup maple syrup

Directions:
In a saucepan, bring the water and almond milk to a boil. Add in the cinnamon stick and vanilla bean.
Gradually add in the cornmeal, stirring continuously; turn the heat to a simmer. Let it simmer for about 15 minutes.
Drizzle the maple syrup over the porridge and serve warm. Enjoy!
Per serving: Calories: 328Kcal; Fat: 4.8g; Carbs: 63.4g; Protein: 6.6g

199. Garlic and White Bean Soup
Preparation time: 1 hour
Cooking time: 10 minutes **Servings:** 4
Ingredients:
- 45 ounces cooked cannellini beans
- 1/4 teaspoon dried thyme
- 2 teaspoons minced garlic
- 1/8 teaspoon crushed red pepper
- 1/2 teaspoon dried rosemary
- 1/8 teaspoon ground black pepper
- 2 tablespoons olive oil
- 4 cups vegetable broth

Directions:
Place one-third of white beans in a food processor, then pour in 2 cups broth and pulse for 2 minutes until smooth. Place a pot over medium heat, add oil and when hot, add garlic and cook for 1 minute until fragrant. Add pureed beans into the pan along with remaining beans, sprinkle with spices and herbs, pour in the broth, stir until combined, and bring the mixture to boil over medium-high heat. Switch heat to medium-low level, simmer the beans for 15 minutes, and then mash them with a fork. Taste the soup to adjust seasoning and then serve.
Per serving: Calories: 222Kcal; Fat: 7g; Carbs: 13g; Fiber: 9.1g; Protein: 11.2g

200. Coconut Curry Lentils
Preparation time: 10 minutes
Cooking time: 40 minutes **Servings:** 4
Ingredients:
- 1 cup brown lentils
- 1 small white onion, peeled, chopped
- 1 teaspoon minced garlic
- 1 teaspoon grated ginger
- 3 cups baby spinach
- 1 tablespoon curry powder
- 2 tablespoons olive oil
- 13 ounces coconut milk, unsweetened
- 2 cups vegetable broth
- 4 cups cooked rice
- 1/4 cup chopped cilantro

Directions:
Place a large pot over medium heat, add oil and when hot, add ginger and garlic and cook for 1 minute until fragrant. Add onion, cook for 5 minutes, stir in curry powder, cook for 1 minute until toasted, add lentils, and pour in broth. Switch heat to medium-high level, bring the mixture to a boil, then switch heat to the low level and simmer for 20 minutes until tender and all the liquid is absorbed. Pour in milk, stir until combined, turn heat to medium level, and simmer for 10 minutes until thickened. Then remove the pot from heat, stir in spinach, let it stand for 5 minutes until its leaves wilts and then top with cilantro.
Serve lentils with rice.
Per serving: Calories: 184Kcal; Fat: 3.7g; Carbs: 30g; Fiber: 10.7g; Protein: 11.3g

201. Tomato, Kale, and White Bean Skillet
Preparation time: 10 minutes
Cooking time: 10 minutes **Servings:** 4
Ingredients:
- 30 ounces cooked cannellini beans
- 7 ounces sun-dried tomatoes, packed in oil, chopped
- 6 ounces kale, chopped
- 1 teaspoon minced garlic
- 1/4 teaspoon ground black pepper
- 1/4 teaspoon salt
- 1/2 tablespoon dried basil
- 1/8 teaspoon red pepper flakes
- 1 tablespoon apple cider vinegar
- 1 tablespoon olive oil
- 2 tablespoons oil from sun-dried tomatoes

Directions:
Prepare the dressing and for this, place basil, black pepper, salt, vinegar, and red pepper flakes in a small bowl, add oil from sun-dried tomatoes and whisk until combined. Take a skillet pan, place it over medium heat, add olive oil and when hot, add garlic and cook for 1 minute until fragrant. Add kale, splash with some water and cook for 3 minutes until kale leaves have wilted. Add tomatoes and beans, stir well and cook for 3 minutes until heated. Remove pan from heat, drizzle with the prepared dressing, toss until mixed and serve.
Per serving: Calories: 264Kcal; Fat: 12g; Carbs: 38g; Fiber: 13g; Protein: 9g

202. Chard Wraps With Millet
Preparation time: 25 minutes
Cooking time: 0 minutes
Servings: 4
Ingredients:
- 1 carrot, cut into ribbons
- 1/2 cup millet, cooked
- 1/2 of a large cucumber, cut into ribbons
- 1/2 cup chickpeas, cooked
- 1 cup sliced cabbage
- 1/3 cup hummus
- Mint leaves as needed for topping
- Hemp seeds as needed for topping
- 1 bunch of Swiss rainbow chard

Directions:
Spread hummus on one side of the chard, place some millet, vegetables, and chickpeas on it, sprinkle with some mint leaves and hemp seeds, and wrap it like a burrito. Serve straight away.
Per serving: Calories: 152Kcal; Fat: 4.5g; Carbs: 25g; Fiber: 2.4g; Protein: 3.5g

203. Quinoa Meatballs
Preparation time: 10 minutes
Cooking time: 35 minutes **Servings:** 4
Ingredients:
- 1 cup quinoa, cooked
- 1 tablespoon flax meal
- 1 cup diced white onion
- 1 ½ teaspoon minced garlic
- 1/2 teaspoon salt
- 1 teaspoon dried oregano
- 1 teaspoon lemon zest
- 1 teaspoon paprika
- 1 teaspoon dried basil
- 3 tablespoons water
- 2 tablespoons olive oil
- 1 cup grated vegan mozzarella cheese
- Marinara sauce as needed for serving

Directions:
Place flax meal in a bowl, stir in water, and set aside until required. Take a large skillet pan, place it over medium heat, add 1 tablespoon oil and when hot, add onion and cook for 2 minutes. Stir in all the spices and herbs, then stir in quinoa until combined and cook for 2 minutes. Transfer quinoa mixture in a bowl, add flax meal mixture, lemon zest, and cheese, stir until well mixed and then shape the mixture into twelve 1 ½ inch balls. Arrange balls on a baking sheet lined with parchment paper, refrigerate the balls for 30 minutes and then bake for 20 minutes at 400 degrees F.
Serve balls with marinara sauce.
Per serving: Calories: 100Kcal; Fat: 100g; Carbs: 100g; Fiber: 100g; Protein: 100g

204. Rice Stuffed Jalapeños
Preparation time: 5 minutes
Cooking time: 15 minutes **Servings:** 6
Ingredients:
- 3 medium-sized potatoes, peeled, cubed, boiled
- 2 large carrots, peeled, chopped, boiled
- 3 tablespoons water
- 1/4 teaspoon onion powder
- 1 teaspoons salt
- 1/2 cup nutritional yeast
- 1/4 teaspoon garlic powder
- 1 lime, juiced - 3 tablespoons water
- Cooked rice as needed
- 3 jalapeños pepper, halved
- 1 red bell pepper, sliced, for garnish
- ½ cup vegetable broth

Directions:
Place boiled vegetables in a food processor, pour in broth, and pulse until smooth. Add garlic powder, onion powder, salt, water, and lime juice, pulse until combined, then add yeast and blend until smooth. Tip the mixture in a bowl, add rice, and stir until incorporated. Cut each jalapeno into half lengthwise, brush them with oil, season them with some salt, stuff them with rice mixture and bake them for 20 minutes at 400 degrees F until done.
Serve straight away.
Per serving: Calories: 148Kcal; Fat: 3.7g; Carbs: 12.2g; Fiber: 2g; Protein: 2g

205. Pineapple Fried Rice
Preparation time: 5 minutes
Cooking time: 12 minutes **Servings:** 2
Ingredients:
- 2 cups brown rice, cooked
- 1/2 cup sunflower seeds, toasted
- 2/3 cup green peas
- 1 teaspoon minced garlic
- 1 large red bell pepper, cored, diced
- 1 tablespoon grated ginger
- 2/3 cup pineapple chunks with juice
- 2 tablespoons coconut oil
- 1 bunch of green onions, sliced
- For the Sauce: 4 tablespoons soy sauce
- 1/2 cup pineapple juice
- 1/2 teaspoon sesame oil - 1/2 a lime, juiced

Directions:
Take a skillet pan, place it over medium-high heat, add oil, and when hot, add red bell pepper, pineapple pieces, and two-third of onion, cook for 5 minutes, then stir in ginger and garlic and cook for 1 minute.
Switch heat to the high level, add rice to the pan, stir until combined, and cook for 5 minutes.
When done, fold in sunflower seeds and peas and set aside until required. Prepare the sauce and for this, place sesame oil in a small bowl, add soy sauce and pineapple juice and whisk until combined. Drizzle sauce over rice, drizzle with lime juice, and serve straight away.
Per serving: Calories: 179Kcal; Fat: 5.5g; Carbs: 30g; Fiber: 2g; Protein: 3.3g

206. Lentil and Wild Rice Soup
Preparation time: 10 minutes
Cooking time: 40 minutes **Servings:** 4
Ingredients:
- 1/2 cup cooked mixed beans
- 12 ounces cooked lentils
- 2 stalks of celery, sliced
- 1 1/2 cup mixed wild rice, cooked
- 1 large sweet potato, peeled, chopped
- 1/2 medium butternut, peeled, chopped
- 4 medium carrots, peeled, sliced
- 1 medium onion, peeled, diced
- 10 cherry tomatoes
- 1/2 red chili, deseeded, diced

- 1 ½ teaspoon minced garlic
- 1/2 teaspoon salt
- 2 teaspoons mixed dried herbs
- 1 teaspoon coconut oil
- 2 cups vegetable broth

Directions:
Take a large pot, place it over medium-high heat, add oil and when it melts, add onion and cook for 5 minutes. Stir in garlic and chili, cook for 3 minutes, then add remaining vegetables, pour in the broth, stir and bring the mixture to a boil. Switch heat to medium-low heat, cook the soup for 20 minutes, then stir in remaining ingredients and continue cooking for 10 minutes until soup has reached to desired thickness. Serve straight away.
Per serving: Calories: 331Kcal; Fat: 2g; Carbs: 54g; Fiber: 12g; Protein: 13g

207. Black Bean Meatball Salad
Preparation time: 10 minutes
Cooking time: 25 minutes **Servings:** 4
Ingredients:
For the Meatballs:
- 1/2 cup quinoa, cooked
- 1 cup cooked black beans
- 3 cloves of garlic, peeled
- 1 small red onion, peeled
- 1 teaspoon ground dried coriander
- 1 teaspoon ground dried cumin
- 1 teaspoon smoked paprika
- For the Salad:
- 1 large sweet potato, peeled, diced
- 1 lemon, juiced
- 1 teaspoon minced garlic
- 1 cup coriander leaves
- 1/3 cup almonds
- 1/3 teaspoon ground black pepper
- ½ teaspoon salt
- 1 1/2 tablespoons olive oil

Directions:
Prepare the meatballs and for this, place beans and puree in a blender, pulse until pureed, and place this mixture in a medium bowl. Add onion and garlic, process until chopped, add to the bean mixture, add all the spices, stir until combined, and shape the mixture into uniform balls. Bake the balls on a greased baking sheet for 25 minutes at 350 degrees F until browned. Meanwhile, spread sweet potatoes on a baking sheet lined with baking paper, drizzle with ½ tablespoon oil, toss until coated, and bake for 20 minutes with the meatballs. Prepare the dressing, and for this, place the remaining ingredients for the salad in a food processor and pulse until smooth. Place roasted sweet potatoes in a bowl, drizzle with the dressing, toss until coated, and then top with meatballs. Serve straight away.
Per serving: Calories: 140Kcal; Fat: 8g; Carbs: 8g; Fiber: 4g; Protein: 10g

Plant based cookbook for beginners

208. Bulgur Pancakes with a Twist
Preparation time: 30 minutes
Cooking time: 20 minutes
Servings: 4
Ingredients:
- 1/2 cup bulgur wheat flour
- 1/2 cup almond flour
- 1 teaspoon baking soda
- 1/2 teaspoon fine sea salt
- 1 cup full-Fat coconut milk
- 1/2 teaspoon ground cinnamon
- 1/4 teaspoon ground cloves
- 4 tablespoons coconut oil
- 1/2 cup maple syrup
- 1 large-sized banana, sliced

Directions:
In a mixing bowl, thoroughly combine the flour, baking soda, salt, coconut milk, cinnamon, and ground cloves; let it stand for 30 minutes to soak well. Heat a small amount of coconut oil in a frying pan.
Fry the pancakes until the surface is golden brown. Garnish with maple syrup and banana. Bon appétit!
Per serving: Calories: 414Kcal; Fat: 21.8g; Carbs: 51.8g; Protein: 6.5g

209. Chocolate Rye Porridge
Preparation time: 4 minutes
Cooking time: 6 minutes **Servings:** 4
Ingredients:
- 2 cups rye flakes
- 2 ½ cups almond milk
- 2 ounces dried prunes, chopped
- 2 ounces dark chocolate chunks

Directions:
Add the rye flakes and almond milk to a deep saucepan; bring to a boil over medium-high. Turn the heat to a simmer and let it cook for 5 to 6 minutes.
Remove from the heat. Fold in the chopped prunes and chocolate chunks, gently stir to combine.
Ladle into serving bowls and serve warm.
Bon appétit!
Per serving: Calories: 460Kcal; Fat: 13.1g; Carbs: 72.2g; Protein: 15g

210. Authentic African Mielie-Meal
Preparation time: 5 minutes
Cooking time: 10 minutes
Servings: 4
Ingredients:
- 3 cups water - 1 cup coconut milk
- 1 cup maize meal
- 1/3 teaspoon kosher salt
- 1/4 teaspoon grated nutmeg
- 1/4 teaspoon ground cloves
- 4 tablespoons maple syrup

Directions:
In a saucepan, bring the water and milk to a boil; then gradually add in the maize meal and turn the heat to a simmer.

Add in the salt, nutmeg, and cloves. Let it cook for 10 minutes. Add in the maple syrup and gently stir to combine. Bon appétit!

Per serving: Calories: 336Kcal; Fat: 15.1g; Carbs: 47.9g; Protein: 4.1g

211. Teff Porridge with Dried Figs

Preparation time: 10 minutes
Cooking time: 20 minutes **Servings:** 4
Ingredients:
- 1 cup whole-grain teff - 1 cup water
- 2 cups coconut milk
- 2 tablespoons coconut oil
- 1/2 teaspoon ground cardamom
- 1/4 teaspoon ground cinnamon
- 4 tablespoons agave syrup
- 7-8 dried figs, chopped

Directions:
Bring the whole-grain teff, water, and coconut milk to a boil. Turn the heat to a simmer and add in the coconut oil, cardamom, and cinnamon. Let it cook for 20 minutes or until the grain has softened and the porridge has thickened. Stir in the agave syrup and stir to combine well. Top each serving bowl with chopped figs and serve warm. Bon appétit!

Per serving: Calories: 356Kcal; Fat: 12.1g; Carbs: 56.5g; Protein: 6.8g

212. Decadent Bread Pudding with Apricots

Preparation time: 15 minutes
Cooking time: 45 minutes **Servings:** 4
Ingredients:
- 4 cups day-old ciabatta bread, cubed
- 4 tablespoons coconut oil, melted
- 2 cups coconut milk - 1/2 cup coconut sugar
- 4 tablespoons applesauce
- 1/4 teaspoon ground cloves
- 1/2 teaspoon ground cinnamon
- 1 teaspoon vanilla extract
- 1/3 cup dried apricots, diced

Directions:
Start by preheating your oven to 360 degrees F. Lightly oil a casserole dish with a nonstick cooking spray. Place the cubed bread in the prepared casserole dish. In a mixing bowl, thoroughly combine the coconut oil, milk, coconut sugar, applesauce, ground cloves, ground cinnamon, and vanilla. Pour the custard evenly over the bread cubes; fold in the apricots. Press with a wide spatula and let it soak for about 15 minutes. Bake in the preheated oven for about 45 minutes or until the top is golden and set. Bon appétit! **Per serving:** Calories: 418Kcal; Fat: 18.8g; Carbs: 56.9g; Protein: 7.3g

213. Chipotle Cilantro Rice

Preparation time: 10 minutes
Cooking time: 18 minutes
Servings: 2
Ingredients:
- 4 tablespoons olive oil
- 1 chipotle pepper, seeded and chopped
- 1 cup jasmine rice
- 1 ½ cups vegetable broth
- 1/4 cup fresh cilantro, chopped
- Sea salt and cayenne pepper, to taste

Directions:
In a saucepan, heat the olive oil over a moderately high flame. Add in the pepper and rice and cook for about 3 minutes or until aromatic.
Pour the vegetable broth into the saucepan and bring to a boil; immediately turn the heat to a gentle simmer. Cook for about 18 minutes or until all the liquid has been absorbed. Fluff the rice with a fork, add in the cilantro, salt, and cayenne pepper; stir to combine well. Bon appétit!

Per serving: Calories: 313Kcal; Fat: 15g; Carbs: 37.1g; Protein: 5.7g

214. Oat Porridge with Almonds

Preparation time: 8 minutes
Cooking time: 12 minutes **Servings:** 2
Ingredients:
- 1 cup water
- 2 cups almond milk, divided
- 1 cup rolled oats
- 2 tablespoons coconut sugar
- 1/2 vanilla essence
- 1/4 teaspoon cardamom
- 1/2 cup almonds, chopped
- 1 banana, sliced

Directions:
In a deep saucepan, bring the water and milk to a rapid boil. Add in the oats, cover the saucepan and turn the heat to medium. Add in the coconut sugar, vanilla, and cardamom. Continue to cook for about 12 minutes, stirring periodically.
Spoon the mixture into serving bowls; top with almonds and banana. Bon appétit!

Per serving: Calories: 533Kcal; Fat: 13.7g; Carbs: 85g; Protein: 21.6g

215. Aromatic Millet Bowl

Preparation time: 10 minutes
Cooking time: 20 minutes **Servings:**
Ingredients:
- 1 cup water
- 1 ½ cups coconut milk
- 1 cup millet, rinsed and drained
- 1/4 teaspoon crystallized ginger
- 1/4 teaspoon ground cinnamon
- A pinch of grated nutmeg
- A pinch of Himalayan salt
- 2 tablespoons maple syrup

Directions:
Place the water, milk, millet, crystallized ginger cinnamon, nutmeg, and salt in a saucepan; bring to a boil. Turn the heat to a simmer and let it cook for about 20 minutes; fluff the millet with a fork and spoon into individual bowls. Serve with maple syrup. Bon appétit!

Per serving: Calories: 363Kcal; Fat: 6.7g; Carbs: 63.5g; Protein: 11.6g

216. Harissa Bulgur Bowl

Preparation time: 12 minutes
Cooking time: 13 minutes **Servings:** 4
Ingredients:
- 1 cup bulgur wheat
- 1 ½ cups vegetable broth
- 2 cups sweet corn kernels, thawed
- 1 cup canned kidney beans, drained
- 1 red onion, thinly sliced
- 1 garlic clove, minced
- Sea salt and ground black pepper, to taste
- 1/4 cup harissa paste
- 1 tablespoon lemon juice
- 1 tablespoon white vinegar
- 1/4 cup extra-virgin olive oil
- 1/4 cup fresh parsley leaves, roughly chopped

Directions:
In a deep saucepan, bring the bulgur wheat and vegetable broth to a simmer; let it cook, covered, for 12 to 13 minutes. Let it stand for 5 to 10 minutes and fluff your bulgur with a fork.
Add the remaining ingredients to the cooked bulgur wheat; serve warm or at room temperature. Bon appétit!
Per serving: Calories: 353Kcal; Fat: 15.5g; Carbs: 48.5g; Protein: 8.4g

217. Coconut Quinoa Pudding

Preparation time: 25 minutes
Cooking time: 20 minutes **Servings:** 3
Ingredients:
- 1 cup water
- 1 cup coconut milk
- 1 cup quinoa
- A pinch of kosher salt
- A pinch of ground allspice
- 1/2 teaspoon cinnamon
- 1/2 teaspoon vanilla extract
- 4 tablespoons agave syrup
- 1/2 cup coconut flakes

Directions:
Place the water, coconut milk, quinoa, salt, ground allspice, cinnamon, and vanilla extract in a saucepan.
Bring it to a boil over medium-high heat. Turn the heat to a simmer and let it cook for about 20 minutes; fluff with a fork and add in the agave syrup.
Divide between three serving bowls and garnish with coconut flakes. Bon appétit!
Per serving: Calories: 391Kcal; Fat: 10.6g; Carbs: 65.2g; Protein: 11.1g

218. Cremini Mushroom Risotto

Preparation time: 5 minutes
Cooking time: 15 minutes **Servings:** 3
Ingredients:
- 3 tablespoons vegan butter
- 1 teaspoon garlic, minced
- 1 teaspoon thyme
- 1-pound Cremini mushrooms, sliced
- 1 1/2 cups white rice
- 2 ½ cups vegetable broth
- 1/4 cup dry sherry wine
- Kosher salt and ground black pepper, to taste
- 3 tablespoons fresh scallions, thinly sliced

Directions:
In a saucepan, melt the vegan butter over a moderately high flame. Cook the garlic and thyme for about 1 minute or until aromatic.
Add in the mushrooms and continue to sauté until they release the liquid or about 3 minutes.
Add in the rice, vegetable broth, and sherry wine. Bring to a boil; immediately turn the heat to a gentle simmer. Cook for about 15 minutes or until all the liquid has been absorbed. Fluff the rice with a fork, season with salt and pepper, and garnish with fresh scallions.
Bon appétit!
Per serving: Calories: 513Kcal; Fat: 12.5g; Carbs: 88g; Protein: 11.7g

CHAPTER 17:
Pasta and Noodles

219. Cannellini Pesto Spaghetti
Preparation time: 5 minutes
Cooking time: 10 minutes
Servings: 4
Ingredients:
- 12 ounces (340 g) whole-grain spaghetti, cooked, drained, and kept warm, ½ cup cooking liquid reserved
- 1 cup pesto
- 2 cups cooked cannellini beans, drained and rinsed

Directions:
Put the cooked spaghetti in a large bowl and add the pesto. Add the reserved cooking liquid and beans and toss well to serve. **Per serving:** Calories: 549Kcal; Fat: 34g; Carbs: 45g; Fiber: 10g; Protein: 18g

220. Spicy Eggplant Penne
Preparation time: 15 minutes
Cooking time: 30 minutes
Servings: 4
Ingredients:
- 1 medium yellow onion, peeled and diced
- 2 medium eggplants (about 1½ pounds / 680 g), stemmed, peeled, quartered, and cut into ½-inch pieces
- 6 cloves garlic, peeled and minced
- 2 teaspoons minced oregano
- 1 teaspoon crushed red pepper flakes, or to taste
- 1 (28-ounce / 794-g) can diced tomatoes
- 2 tablespoons red wine vinegar
- Salt, to taste
- 1-pound (454 g) penne, cooked according to package directions, drained, and kept warm
- ½ cup chopped basil

Directions:
Place the onion in a large saucepan and sauté over medium heat for 10 minutes. Add water 1 to 2 tablespoons at a time to keep the onion from sticking to the pan. Add the eggplant and cook, stirring constantly for 5 minutes, adding water only when the eggplant starts to stick to the pan. Add the garlic, oregano, and crushed red pepper flakes and cook for 30 seconds. Add the tomatoes and red wine vinegar and cook, covered, for 10 minutes. Season with salt.
Remove from the heat, add the pasta, and toss well. Garnish with basil.
Per serving: Calories: 105Kcal; 0.78Fat: g; Carbs: 24.11g; Fiber: 11.2g; Protein: 4.41g

221. Creamed Kimchi Pasta
Preparation time: 5 minutes
Cooking time: 4 to 5 minutes **Servings:** 4 to 6
Ingredients:
- 8 ounces (227 g) dried small pasta
- 2 1/3 cups vegetable stock
- 2 garlic cloves, minced
- ½ red onion, sliced
- ½ to 1 teaspoon salt
- 1¼ cups kimchi, with any larger pieces chopped - ½ cup coconut cream

Directions:
In the Instant Pot, combine the pasta, stock, garlic, red onion, and salt. Set the lid in place. Select the Manual mode and set the cooking time for 1 minute on High Pressure. When the timer goes off, do a quick pressure release. Carefully open the lid.
Select Sauté mode. Stir in the kimchi. Simmer for 3 to 4 minutes. Stir in the coconut cream and serve.
Per serving: Calories: 748Kcal; Fat: 80g; Carbs: 13.17g; Fiber: 2.5g; Protein: 2.39g

222. Roasted Ragu with Whole Wheat Linguine
Preparation time: 15 minutes
Cooking time: 45 minutes
Servings: 8
Ingredients:
- 4 beefsteak tomatoes, halved
- 1 yellow onion, cut into slices and left as rings
- 2 large zucchini, cubed
- 2 large yellow squash, cubed
- 1 small red bell pepper, diced
- 3 garlic cloves, minced
- 1 teaspoon Italian seasoning
- ½ teaspoon freshly ground black pepper
- 1 pound (454 g) whole wheat linguine
- ¼ cup tomato paste
- 1 teaspoon red pepper flakes
- ¼ teaspoon dried oregano
- 1 tablespoon packed minced fresh Italian parsley
- 2 tablespoons fresh basil chiffonade, divided

Directions:
Preheat the oven to 450ºF (235ºC). Line 2 baking sheets with parchment paper.
Place the tomato halves on 1 prepared baking sheet, cut-side up. Place the onion rings on the same baking sheet. Roast on the center rack for 10 minutes.
While the tomatoes roast in a large bowl, toss together the zucchini, squash, bell pepper, garlic, Italian seasoning, and

pepper. Spread the vegetables on the other prepared baking sheet. Place the vegetables on a lower rack (but not the lowest) and bake for 15 minutes. Flip the vegetables. Remove the tomato sheet and set it aside. Move the vegetables to the center rack and roast for 15 minutes more. Bring a large pot of water to a boil over high heat. Cook the pasta according to the package directions to al dente. Reserve ½ cup of the pasta water and drain the pasta. Keep the pasta in the strainer. Return the pasta pot to medium heat. Transfer the roasted tomatoes and onions to the pot and stir in the tomato paste, reserved pasta water, red pepper flakes, and oregano. You can mash the tomatoes and onion using a heavy spoon for a chunky texture or purée using an immersion blender, as you like. Add the pasta, roasted vegetables, parsley, and 1 tablespoon of basil to the pot. Toss to combine and coat. Serve garnished with the remaining 1 tablespoon of basil.
Per serving: Calories: 272Kcal; Fat: 2g; Carbs: 55g; Fiber: 5g; Protein: 11g

223. Penne with Swiss Chard and Olives
Preparation time: 15 minutes
Cooking time: 20 minutes
Servings: 4
Ingredients:
- 4 large shallots, peeled and diced small
- 2 bunches Swiss chard, ribs removed and chopped, leaves chopped
- 4 cloves garlic, peeled and minced
- 2 teaspoons minced thyme
- 1-pound (454 g) whole-grain penne, cooked according to package directions, drained, and kept warm, ½ cup cooking liquid reserved
- Salt and freshly ground black pepper to taste
- ½ cup kalamata olives, pitted and coarsely chopped
- ½ cup dried currants

Directions:
Place the shallots and chard ribs in a large saucepan and sauté over medium heat for 5 minutes. Add water 1 to 2 tablespoons at a time to keep the vegetables from sticking to the pan. Add the garlic and thyme and cook for another minute. Add half of the chard leaves and a few tablespoons of the reserved pasta cooking liquid and cook until the leaves start to wilt, adding more leaves as the chard cooks down, until all the leaves are wilted, about 10 minutes.
Season with salt and pepper and add the olives, currants, and cooked pasta. Toss well before serving.
Per serving: Calories: 279Kcal; Fat: 13.27g; Carbs: 4.07g; Fiber: 1.3g; Protein: 34.29g

224. Indonesia Green Noodle Salad
Preparation time: 10 minutes
Cooking time: 8 minutes
Servings: 4
Ingredients:
- 12 ounces (340 g) brown rice noodles, cooked, drained, and rinsed until cool
- 1 cup snow peas, trimmed and sliced in half on the diagonal
- 2 medium cucumbers, peeled, halved, deseeded, and sliced thinly
- 2 heads baby bok choy, trimmed and thinly sliced
- 4 green onions, green and white parts, trimmed and thinly sliced
- 3 tablespoons sambal oelek
- ½ cup chopped cilantro
- 2 tablespoons soy sauce
- ¼ cup fresh lime juice
- ¼ cup finely chopped mint

Directions:
Combine all the ingredients in a large bowl and toss to coat well.
Serve immediately.
Per serving: Calories: 288Kcal; Fat: 1g; Carbs: 64g; Fiber: 18g; Protein: 12g

225. Noodles with Red Lentil Curry
Preparation time: 10 minutes
Cooking time: 37 minutes **Servings:** 4
Ingredients:
- 3 cups vegetable stock
- 1 cup red lentils, rinsed
- 1 medium red onion, peeled and diced small
- 2 tablespoons plus 2 teaspoons curry powder, or to taste
- 6 cups packed baby spinach
- Zest and juice of 2 lemons
- ½ teaspoon crushed red pepper flakes (optional)
- Salt and freshly ground black pepper, to taste
- 1 pound (454 g) brown rice noodles, cooked according to package directions, drained, and kept warm
- Finely chopped cilantro

Directions:
Bring the vegetable stock to a boil in a medium saucepan over medium-high heat. Add the lentils and cook for 20 to 25 minutes, or until the lentils are tender but not mushy.
Place the onion in a large skillet and stir-fry over medium heat for 7 to 8 minutes or until the onion starts to brown. Add water 1 to 2 tablespoons at a time to keep the onion from sticking to the pan. Stir in the curry powder and spinach and cook until the spinach wilts, about 5 minutes. Add the cooked lentils, lemon zest and juice, and crushed red pepper flakes (if using) and season with salt and pepper.
To serve, divide the noodles among 4 individual plates. Spoon some of the lentil sauce over the noodles and garnish with the cilantro.
Per serving: Calories: 1795Kcal; Fat: 166.6g; Carbs: 72.81g; Fiber: 15g; Protein: 23.06g

226. Tomato and Black Bean Rotini
Preparation time: 5 minutes
Cooking time: 9 to 10 minutes
Servings: 4
Ingredients:
- 1 red onion, diced
- 1 to 2 teaspoons olive oil

- 1 to 2 teaspoons ground chipotle pepper
- 1 (28-ounce / 794-g) can crushed tomatoes
- 8 ounces (227 g) rotini
- 1 cup water
- 1½ cups fresh corn
- 1½ cups cooked black beans
- Salt and freshly ground black pepper to taste

Directions:
Press the Sauté button on the Instant Pot and heat the oil. Add the red onion and cook for 5 to 6 minutes, stirring occasionally, or until the onion is lightly browned. Stir in the chipotle pepper, tomatoes, rotini, and water. Lock the lid. Select the Manual mode and set the cooking time for 4 minutes on High Pressure. Once the timer goes off, perform a natural pressure release for 4 minutes, then release any remaining pressure. Carefully open the lid.
Stir in the corn and black beans. Taste and season with salt and pepper.
Serve immediately.
Per serving: Calories: 410Kcal; Fat: 4.25g; Carbs: 81.76g; Fiber: 13.3g; Protein: 15.49g

227. Lemony Broccoli Penne

Preparation time: 25 minutes
Cooking time: 15 minutes
Servings: 4
Ingredients:
- 1 medium yellow onion, peeled and thinly sliced
- 1-pound (454 g) broccoli rabe, trimmed and cut into 1-inch pieces
- ¼ cup golden raisins
- Zest and juice of 2 lemons
- 4 cloves garlic, peeled and minced
- ½ teaspoon crushed red pepper flakes
- 1-pound (454 g) whole-grain penne, cooked, drained, and kept warm, ¼ cup cooking liquid reserved
- Salt and freshly ground black pepper, to taste (optional)
- ¼ cup pine nuts, toasted
- ½ cup chopped basil

Directions:
Put the onion in a large skillet over medium-high heat and sauté for 10 minutes, or until the onion is lightly browned.
Add the broccoli rabe and cook, stirring frequently, until the rabe is tender, about 5 minutes.
Add the raisins, lemon zest and juice, garlic, crushed red pepper flakes, and the cooked pasta and reserved cooking water. Remove from the heat. Mix well and season with salt (if desired) and pepper. Serve garnished with pine nuts and basil.
Per serving: Calories: 278Kcal; Fat: 7g; Carbs: 49g; Fiber: 9g; Protein: 8g

228. Singapore Rice Noodles

Preparation time: 20 minutes
Cooking time: 10 minutes **Servings:** 2
Ingredients:
- 1 small yellow onion, peeled and cut into ½-inch slices
- 2 medium carrots, peeled and cut into matchsticks
- 1 medium red bell pepper, seeded and cut into ½-inch slices
- 8 ounces (227 g) shiitake mushrooms, stems removed
- ½ cup vegetable stock
- 4 teaspoons low-sodium soy sauce, or to taste
- 1 tablespoon grated ginger
- 2 cloves garlic, peeled and minced
- 1 tablespoon curry powder, or to taste
- 4 ounces (113 g) brown rice noodles, cooked according to the package directions, drained, and kept warm
- Freshly ground black pepper to taste

Directions:
Heat a large skillet over high heat. Add the onion, carrots, red pepper, and mushrooms and stir-fry for 3 to 4 minutes. Add water 1 to 2 tablespoons at a time to keep the vegetables from sticking to the pan. Add the vegetable broth, soy sauce, ginger, garlic, and curry powder and cook for 3 to 4 minutes. Add the cooked noodles, toss well, and season with black pepper.
Per serving: Calories: 649Kcal; Fat: 55.55g; Carbs: 41.42g; Fiber: 7g; Protein: 5.19g

229. Ponzu Pea Rice Noodle Salad

Preparation time: 5 minutes
Cooking time: 10 minutes
Servings: 4
Ingredients:
- 16 cups water
- 1 pound (454 g) brown rice noodles
- ½ pound (227 g) snow peas, trimmed and cut into matchsticks
- 3 medium carrots, peeled and cut into matchsticks
- ½ cup unsweetened Ponzu sauce
- 3 green onions, white and green parts, cut into ¾-inch pieces
- ½ cup coarsely chopped cilantro

Directions:
Bring water to a boil in a large pot, add the rice noodles and cook for 10 minutes or until al dente.
Add the snow peas and carrots during the last minute of cooking. Drain and rinse the mixture until cooled and place them in a large bowl. Add the ponzu sauce, green onions, and cilantro. Toss well before serving.
Per serving: Calories: 179Kcal; Fat: 1g; Carbs: 39g; Fiber: 4g; Protein: 4g

230. Thai Tofu Noodles

Preparation time: 30 minutes
Cooking time: 20 minutes **Servings:** 4
Ingredients:
Sauce:
- 3 tablespoons tamarind paste
- ¾ cup boiling water
- ¼ cup soy sauce
- 2 tablespoons rice vinegar
- 3 tablespoons date sugar (optional)

- 1 tablespoon vegetable oil (optional)
- 1/8 teaspoon cayenne pepper

Noodles:
- 8 ounces (227 g) rice noodles
- 14 ounces (397 g) extra-firm tofu, cut into ¾-inch cubes
- 1/3 cup cornstarch
- ¼ cup vegetable oil, divided (optional)
- 1 shallot, minced
- 3 garlic cloves, minced
- 6 ounces (170 g) bean sprouts
- 4 scallions, sliced thinly
- Salt, to taste (optional)
- ¼ cup minced fresh cilantro
- 2 tablespoons chopped dry-roasted peanuts
- Lime wedges, for garnish

Directions:
For the Sauce
Soak the tamarind paste in boiling water until softened, about 10 minutes. Strain the mixture through a fine-mesh strainer, pressing on solids to extract as much pulp as possible, then discard the solids. Whisk the soy sauce, vinegar, sugar (if desired), oil (if desired), and cayenne into tamarind liquid.

For the Noodles
Cover the noodles with hot water in a large bowl and stir to separate. Let noodles soak until softened, about 20 minutes. Drain noodles.
Meanwhile, spread tofu on a paper towel-lined baking sheet and let drain for 20 minutes. Gently pat dry with paper towels. Toss the drained tofu with cornstarch in a medium bowl, then transfer to a fine-mesh strainer and shake gently to remove excess cornstarch. Heat 3 tablespoons of vegetable oil (if desired) in a skillet over medium-high heat until just smoking. Add tofu and cook, turning constantly, until crisp and browned on all sides, 12 minutes. Transfer the tofu to a paper towel-lined plate to drain. Heat the remaining 1 tablespoon oil (if desired) in the skillet over medium heat until shimmering.
Add shallot and garlic and cook until lightly browned, about 2 minutes. Whisk sauce to recombine. Add noodles and sauce to skillet, increase heat to high, and cook, tossing gently, until noodles are evenly coated, about 1 minute.
Add the browned tofu, bean sprouts, and scallions and cook, tossing gently, until tofu is warmed through and noodles are tender, about 2 minutes.
Season with salt (if desired), sprinkle with cilantro and peanuts, and serve with lime wedges.
Per serving: Calories: 523Kcal; Fat: 25g; Carbs: 62g; Fiber: 3g; Protein: 15g

231. Sesame Soba Noodles with Vegetables

Preparation time: 15 minutes
Cooking time: 8 minutes
Servings: 4
Ingredients:
Sauce:
- 3 tablespoons toasted sesame seeds
- 1½ tablespoons rice vinegar
- ¼ cup soy sauce
- 3 tablespoons peanut butter
- 1 tablespoon grated fresh ginger
- 1 garlic clove, minced
- 1½ tablespoons date sugar (optional)
- ¾ teaspoon unsweetened hot sauce

Noodles and Vegetables:
- 16 cups water
- 12 ounces (340 g) soba noodles
- Salt, to taste (optional)
- 6 ounces (170 g) snow peas, strings removed and halved lengthwise
- 10 radishes, trimmed, halved, and sliced thin
- 1 celery rib, sliced thinly
- 2 tablespoons toasted sesame oil (optional)
- ½ cup fresh cilantro leaves
- 1 tablespoon toasted sesame seeds

Directions:
For the Sauce
Process sesame seeds, vinegar, soy sauce, peanut butter, ginger, garlic, sugar (if desired), and hot sauce in a blender until smooth.

For the Noodles and Vegetables
Bring 16 cups of water to a boil in a large pot. Add noodles and 1 tablespoon salt (if desired) and cook, stirring often, for 8 minutes or until al dente. Drain noodles, rinse with cold water, and drain again. Transfer noodles to a large bowl and toss with snow peas, radishes, celery, the sauce, and oil (if desired) to coat well. Sprinkle with cilantro and sesame seeds and serve.
Per serving: Calories: 512Kcal; Fat: 17g; Carbs: 77g; Fiber: 3g; Protein: 19g

232. Lemon Bow Tie Pasta

Preparation time: 5 minutes **Cooking time:** 11 to 12 minutes **Servings:** 4 to 5
Ingredients:
- 1 Vidalia onion, diced
- 2 garlic cloves, minced
- 1 tablespoon olive oil
- 3½ cups water
- 10 ounces (283 g) bow tie pasta
- Grated zest and juice of 1 lemon
- ¼ cup black olives, pitted and chopped
- Salt and freshly ground black pepper to taste

Directions:
Press the Sauté button on the Instant Pot and heat the oil. Add the onion and garlic to the pot. Cook for 7 to 8 minutes, stirring occasionally, or until the onion is lightly browned. Add the water and pasta.
Set the lid in place. Select the Manual mode and set the cooking time for 4 minutes on High Pressure. When the timer goes off, do a quick pressure release. Carefully open the lid. Stir the pasta and drain any excess water. Stir in the lemon zest and juice and the olives. Season with salt and pepper. Serve immediately.
Per serving: Calories: 127Kcal; Fat: 3.84g; Carbs: 22.29g; Fiber: 3.6g; Protein: 2.19g

233. Shiitake and Bean Sprout Ramen

Preparation time: 20 minutes
Cooking time: 1 hour 15 minutes **Servings:** 4 to 6
Ingredients:

- 4 ounces (113 g) bean sprouts
- 3 tablespoons soy sauce, divided
- 4 teaspoons toasted sesame oil, divided (optional)
- 1 tablespoon rice vinegar
- 1 onion, chopped
- 1 (3-inch) piece ginger, peeled and sliced into ¼-inch thick
- 5 garlic cloves, smashed
- 8 ounces (227 g) shiitake mushrooms, stems removed and reserved, caps sliced thin
- ½ ounce (14 g) kombu
- ¼ cup mirin
- 4 cups vegetable broth
- 20 cups water, divided
- 2 tablespoons red miso
- Salt, to taste (optional)
- 12 ounces (340 g) dried ramen noodles
- 2 scallions, sliced thinly
- 1 tablespoon toasted black sesame seeds

Directions:
Combine the bean sprouts, 1 teaspoon soy sauce, 1 teaspoon sesame oil (if desired), and vinegar in a small bowl; set aside.
Heat the remaining 1 tablespoon sesame oil (if desired) in a large saucepan over medium-high heat until shimmering.
Stir in onion and cook until softened and lightly browned, about 6 minutes. Add ginger and garlic and cook until lightly browned, about 2 minutes. Stir in mushroom stems, kombu, mirin, broth, 4 cups of water, and remaining soy sauce and bring to boil. Reduce heat to low, cover, and simmer for 1 hour. Strain broth through a fine-mesh strainer into a large bowl. Wipe the saucepan clean and return the strained broth to the saucepan.
Whisk miso into the broth and bring to a gentle simmer over medium heat, whisking to dissolve miso completely.
Stir in mushroom caps and cook until warmed through, about 1 minute; season with salt, if desired. Remove from heat and cover to keep warm.
Meanwhile, bring 16 cups water to a boil in a large pot. Add the ramen noodles and 1 tablespoon salt (if desired) and cook, stirring often, until al dente, about 2 minutes. Drain the noodles and divide evenly among serving bowls. Ladle soup over noodles, garnish with bean sprouts, scallions, and sesame seeds. Serve hot.
Per serving: Calories: 237Kcal; Fat: 5g; Carbs: 37g; Fiber: 4g; Protein: 8g

234. Spinach Rotelle Provençale

Preparation time: 8 minutes
Cooking time: 12 minutes **Servings:** 6
Ingredients:

- 2 (15-ounce / 425-g) cans unsweetened stewed tomatoes
- 1 (19-ounce / 539-g) can white beans, drained and rinsed
- 20 cups water
- 1 (10-ounce / 283-g) package spinach rotelle
- ¼ cup chopped fresh parsley

Directions:
Put the beans and tomatoes in a saucepan and heat over medium heat for 8 minutes or until the mixture thickened and has a sauce consistency.
Meanwhile, bring the water to a boil in a large pot. Add the spinach rotelle and cook, uncovered, for 12 minutes.
Drain the rotelle and transfer it into a large bowl. Add the tomato-bean sauce and toss to coat.
Sprinkle with fresh parsley before serving.
Per serving: Calories: 40Kcal; Fat: 1g; Carbs: 8g; Fiber: 4g; Protein: 2g

235. Sumptuous Shiitake Udon Noodles

Preparation time: 20 minutes
Cooking time: 21 minutes
Servings: 4 to 6
Ingredients:

- 1 tablespoon vegetable oil (optional)
- 8 ounces (227 g) shiitake mushrooms, stemmed and sliced thinly
- ½ ounce (14 g) dried shiitake mushrooms, rinsed and minced
- ¼ cup mirin
- 3 tablespoons rice vinegar
- 3 tablespoons soy sauce
- 2 garlic cloves, smashed and peeled
- 1 (1-inch) piece ginger, peeled, halved, and smashed
- 1 teaspoon toasted sesame oil (optional)
- 18 cups water, divided
- 1 teaspoon unsweetened Asian chili-garlic sauce
- 1-pound (454 g) mustard greens, stemmed and chopped into 2-inch pieces
- Salt and ground black pepper, to taste (optional)
- 1 pound (454 g) fresh udon noodles

Directions:
Heat the vegetable oil (if desired) in a Dutch oven over medium-high heat until shimmering. Add the mushrooms and cook, stirring occasionally, until softened and lightly browned, about 5 minutes. Stir in the dried mushrooms, mirin, vinegar, soy sauce, garlic, ginger, sesame oil (if desired), 2 cups of water, and chili-garlic sauce and bring to a simmer. Reduce the heat to medium-low and simmer until liquid has reduced by half, 8 minutes. Turn off the heat, discard the garlic and ginger, cover the pot to keep warm.
Meanwhile, bring 16 cups of water to a boil in a large pot. Add mustard greens and 1 tablespoon salt (if desired) and cook until greens are tender, about 5 minutes.
Add noodles and cook until greens and noodles are tender, about 2 minutes. Reserve 1/3 cup cooking water, drain noodles and greens, and return them to pot.
Add sauce and reserved cooking water, and toss to combine.

Cook over medium-low heat, tossing constantly, until sauce clings to noodles, about 1 minute.

Season with salt (if desired) and pepper, and serve.

Per serving: Calories: 184Kcal; Fat: 3g; Carbs: 32g; Fiber: 3g; Protein: 6g

236. Tomato and Artichoke Rigatoni

Preparation time: 20 minutes
Cooking time: 25 minutes
Servings: 4
Ingredients:

- 5 cloves garlic, peeled and minced
- 2 large tomatoes, diced small
- ½ cup dry white wine
- 2 tablespoons unsweetened tomato paste
- 1 tablespoon oregano
- 1 (15-ounce / 425-g) can artichoke hearts (oil-free), drained and halved
- 1 cup kalamata olives, pitted and halved
- 1-pound (454 g) whole-grain rigatoni, cooked, drained, and kept warm
- Salt and freshly ground black pepper, to taste (optional)
- Chopped parsley for garnish

Directions:
Put the garlic in a skillet and sauté over low heat for 5 minutes. Raise the heat to medium and add the tomatoes, white wine, tomato paste, and oregano and cook for 15 minutes, or until the liquid is reduced by half. Add the artichokes, olives, and cooked rigatoni, mix well, and cook for another 5 minutes. Season with salt (if desired) and pepper. Serve garnished with parsley.

Per serving: Calories: 272Kcal; Fat: 5g; Carbs: 54g; Fiber: 17g; Protein: 8g

237. Tomato Spaghetti

Preparation time: 5 minutes
Cooking time: 10 minutes **Servings:** 4
Ingredients:

- 3 medium tomatoes, chopped
- Zest and juice of 2 lemons
- 1 cup finely chopped basil
- 6 cloves garlic, peeled and minced
- 3 ears corn, kernels removed (about 2 cups)
- 1-pound (454 g) spaghetti, cooked, drained
- Salt and freshly ground black pepper, to taste (optional)

Directions:
Combine the tomatoes, lemon zest and juice, basil, garlic, and corn in a large bowl. Add the cooked spaghetti and toss well. Season with salt (if desired) and pepper. Serve immediately.

Per serving: Calories: 263Kcal; Fat: 2g; Carbs: 57g; Fiber: 8g; Protein: 10g

238. Noodle Salad with Spinach

Preparation time: 15 minutes
Cooking time: 10 minutes **Servings:** 2
Ingredients:

- 8 ounces (227 g) spaghetti
- 1 teaspoon toasted sesame oil (optional)
- **Sauce:**
- 1 garlic clove, finely chopped
- 2 tablespoons sesame oil (optional)
- ¼ cup almond butter
- 3 tablespoons low-sodium soy sauce
- 2 tablespoons mirin
- 2 tablespoons unseasoned rice vinegar
- 1½ tablespoons maple syrup (optional)
- ½ tablespoon fresh lime juice
- 1/8 teaspoon sriracha

Servings:

- 3 cups baby spinach
- 1 cup thinly sliced English cucumber
- ½ red bell pepper, thinly sliced
- 2 scallions, thinly sliced
- 1/3 cup coarsely chopped mint leaves
- ¼ cup coarsely chopped roasted peanuts

Directions:
Bring a large pot of water to a boil over medium-high heat. Add the spaghetti to the pot and cook for 10 minutes, or until al dente, stirring constantly. Drain the spaghetti and rinse in cold water. Transfer to a large bowl and toss with the sesame oil (if desired).

In a blender, combine all the ingredients for the sauce and blend until smooth. Pour the sauce over the spaghetti and stir until well mixed. Set in a refrigerator for 15 minutes.

Add all the ingredients for the serving to the bowl with the spaghetti. Toss to combine well. Serve immediately.

Per serving: Calories: 678Kcal; Fat: 43g; Carbs: 60g; Fiber: 12g; Protein: 21g

239. Garlic & White Wine Pasta

Preparation time: 10 minutes
Cooking time: 20 minutes **Servings:** 4
Ingredients:
Brussels Sprouts

- 16 oz Brussels sprouts, halved
- 1-2 tbsp olive oil
- 1 pinch sea salt
- 1/4 tsp black pepper
- Pasta
- 3 tbsp olive oil
- 4 large cloves garlic, chopped
- 1/3 cup dry white wine
- 4 tbsp arrowroot starch
- 1 3/4 cup almond milk
- 4 tbsp nutritional yeast
- Sea salt and black pepper, to taste
- 1/4 cup vegan parmesan cheese
- 10 oz vegan, gluten-free pasta

For Serving:

- Garlic bread
- Simple green salad

Directions:
Start by preheating the oven to 400 degrees F. Spread the Brussels sprouts on a baking sheet. Add oil, salt, and black

pepper, then give it a toss. Now, boil the pasta in a pot filled with water until al dente, then drain. Now, heat oil in a rimmed skillet over medium heat. Add garlic and sauté for 3 minutes until golden. Stir in white wine and cook for 2 minutes. Whisk in arrowroot and almond milk.

Mix well, then blend with vegan parmesan cheese, salt, and pepper in a food processor.

Heat the almond milk sauce in a skillet over medium heat until it bubbles. 1Bake the Brussels sprouts in the oven for 15 minutes until golden. 1Toss the drained pasta with cheese sauce and Brussels sprouts in a large bowl. Mix well and serve.

Per serving: Calories: 248Kcal; Fat: 15.7g; Carbs: 31.4g; Fiber: 0.4g; Protein: 4.9g

240. Eggplant Vegan Pasta

Preparation time: 10 minutes
Cooking time: 20 minutes **Servings:** 4
Ingredients:

- 12 oz dry pasta
- 1/2 small eggplant, cubed
- 2 cups cremini mushrooms, sliced
- 3 cloves garlic, minced
- 1 1/2 cups vegan marinara sauce
- 2 cups water - 2 tsp sea salt
- 1 tsp ground black pepper
- 3 tbsp olive oil
- Fresh parsley or basil

Directions:
Place the eggplant in a colander and sprinkle salt on top. Let them rest for 30 minutes and rinse thoroughly. Now, place a saucepan over medium-high heat. Add eggplant along with olive oil and 1/3 minced garlic, and ½ teaspoon salt. Stir, cook for 6 minutes until golden brown, then toss in mushrooms.

Sauté for 2 minutes approximately then transfer to a bowl. Cook pasta with water, remaining garlic, and marinara sauce in a saucepan. Add salt and black pepper to pasta to adjust seasoning. After cooking it to a boil, let it simmer for 10 minutes until pasta is al dente. Toss in the eggplant mixture, then garnish as desired. Serve.

Per serving: Calories: 246Kcal; Fat: 14.8g; Carbs: 40.3g; Fiber: 2.4g; Protein:2.4 g

241. Tomato Pesto Pasta

Preparation time: 10 minutes
Cooking time: 10 minutes
Servings: 3
Ingredients:

- 10 oz gluten-free pasta
- 3 oz sun-dried tomatoes
- ¼ cup olive oil
- 1 cup fresh basil
- 4 cloves garlic
- 2 tbsp vegan parmesan cheese

Directions:
Start by boiling the water with salt in a saucepan.
Add pasta and cook until al dente, then drains. Take a blender jug and add basil, garlic, vegan parmesan, olive oil, and tomatoes. Blend well until it forms a puree to form the pesto. Toss the cooked pasta with pesto in a salad bowl. Top with parmesan and olive oil. Mix well and serve.

Per serving: Calories: 338Kcal; Fat: 3.8g; Carbs: 58.3g; Fiber: 2.4g; Protein: 5.4g

242. Alfredo with Peas

Preparation time: 10 minutes
Cooking time: 10 minutes **Servings:** 4
Ingredients:

- 2 tbsp extra virgin olive oil
- 3 cloves garlic, minced
- 4 tbsp all-purpose flour
- ¾ cup 2% milk
- 1 cup vegetable stock
- 1 tbsp pesto
- ¼ tsp salt
- ¼ tsp black pepper
- ½ cup freshly grated vegan parmesan cheese
- 1 cup green peas
- ¾ box whole grain pasta

Directions:
Start by cooking the pasta as per the given instructions on the box, then drain.

Place a saucepan over medium heat, then add garlic along with olive oil. Sauté for 1 minute, then add flour while constantly whisking. After 1 minute, add vegetable stock and milk. Mix well until smooth, then add pesto, black pepper, parmesan cheese, and salt.

Continue cooking until the mixture bubbles. Toss in peas and pasta. Mix well and serve.

Per serving: Calories: 438Kcal; Fat: 1.7g; Carbs: 52.3g; Fiber: 2.3g; Protein: 2.1g

243. Eggplant Parmesan Pasta

Preparation time: 10 minutes
Cooking time: 55 minutes **Servings:** 2
Ingredients:
Eggplant Parmesan

- 1 medium eggplant
- 1/4 cup unbleached all-purpose flour
- 1 cup panko bread crumbs
- 2 tbsp vegan parmesan
- 1 tsp dried oregano
- 1/4 tsp sea salt
- 1/2 cup almond milk
- 1 tsp cornstarch
- Pasta - 8 oz pasta
- 2 cups marinara sauce

Directions:
Start by slicing the eggplant into ½-inch thick rounds.
Place them in a colander and sprinkle salt over the eggplant. Let them rest for 15 minutes, then squeeze the excess water out using a dish towel. Prepare a baking tray by lining it with aluminum foil. Preheat the oven to 400 degrees F. Boil the pasta as per the given instructions on the box. Now, mix almond milk with salt, oregano, vegan parmesan, and cornstarch in a bowl until smooth. Dip the eggplant in the

flour, then in the almond milk mixture, and then breadcrumbs. Place the coated slices in the baking tray. Bake the eggplant for 30 minutes. Meanwhile, warm up 2 tablespoons of oil in a skillet and sear the baked slices in batches until golden on both sides. Warm the marinara in a pan and spread over the cooked pasta. Place the eggplant slices on top. Garnish as desired.
Serve.

Per serving: Calories: 378Kcal; Fat: 13.8g; Carbs: 43.3g; Fiber: 2.4g; Protein: 5.4g

244. Green Chili Mac 'N' Cheese

Preparation time: 10 minutes
Cooking time: 27 minutes **Servings:** 4
Ingredients:
- 10 oz large macaroni shells
- 1/2 medium white onion, diced
- 3-4 cloves garlic, minced
- 1 cup raw cashews
- 1 1/2 cups vegetable broth
- 1 tbsp cornstarch - 1/2 tsp cumin
- 3/4 tsp chili powder
- 2 tbsp nutritional yeast
- 1 4-oz can dice chills
- 1 cup tortilla chips
- Fresh cilantro

Directions:
Finely crush the tortilla chips to get the crumbs.
Spread the crumbs on a baking sheet lined with a parchment sheet.
Season with salt and avocado oil, then toss well to evenly coat. Bake the chips for 10 minutes in an oven at 350 degrees F until golden. Meanwhile, cook the macaroni as per the given instructions on the box and set it aside. Take a medium skillet and place over medium-low heat. Stir in garlic, olive oil, and onion to the skillet. Sauté for 7 minutes, then set it aside.
Transfer this garlic mixture to a blender along with the remaining ingredients, except for the tortilla chips and half of the green chilies. Blend this mixture until smooth, then transfer to a bowl.
1Toss drained pasta with cashew cheese blend.
1Garnish with reserved chilies and tortilla chips.
1Serve.

Per serving: Calories: 304Kcal; Fat: 30.6g; Carbs: 21.4g; Fiber: 0.2g; Protein: 4.6g

245. Color Pasta Errore. Il segnalibro non è definito.

Preparation time: 10 minutes
Cooking time: 10 minutes **Servings:** 1
Ingredients:
- 1 medium carrot
- 1 small-medium zucchini
- 2 oz whole-wheat spaghetti
- 1/3-1/2 cup tomato sauce
- 3 tbsp sundried tomato spread
- Vegan parmesan cheese
- Fresh basil

Directions:
Start by cooking the noodles as per the given instructions on the box until al dente. Pass the zucchini and carrot through a spiralizer to get the noodles. Heat the tomato spread with tomato sauce in a pan. Boil the carrot and zucchini noodle in the pasta water for 4 minutes until al dente. Drain and toss the veggies with cooked pasta noodles and tomato mixture in a bowl.
Garnish as desired.
Serve.

Per serving: Calories: 341Kcal; Fat: 4g; Carbs: 36.4g; Fiber: 1.2g; Protein: 10.3g

246. Caramelized Onion Mac 'N' Cheese

Preparation time: 10 minutes
Cooking time: 12 minutes **Servings:** 4
Ingredients:
Pasta
- 1 small-medium eggplant
- 1 tbsp olive oil
- 1 1/2 yellow onions, sliced
- 10 oz macaroni noodles
- 4 tbsp nutritional yeast
- 1 3/4 cups almond milk
- 2 tsp garlic powder
- 1 tbsp cornstarch - Sea salt

Topping
- 1/4 cup panko bread crumbs
- 1 tbsp olive oil

Directions:
Slice the eggplant into ½ inch thick rounds.
Place them in a colander, then sprinkle salt over the eggplant. Let them sit for 20 minutes until the water is fully drained (squeeze out any excess). Add olive oil along with onions to a skillet placed over medium heat. Stir cook for 12 minutes until caramelized, then transfer to a bowl. Set your oven at high broil mode and place a rack in the top portion. Cook the pasta in water until al dente, then drain. Spread the eggplant on a baking sheet, then broil for 4 minutes. Set them aside covered with a foil for 5 minutes, then peel their skin off. Blend the eggplant slices with garlic powder, salt, cornstarch, yeast, and almond milk in a food processor. 1Once it's smooth, transfer to a bowl. 1Heat the eggplant sauce in a pan for 5 minutes.
1Toss in noodles along with caramelized onions.
1Divide the mixture in the serving bowls and garnish it with bread crumbs.
1Serve.

Per serving: Calories: 248Kcal; Fat: 15.7g; Carbs: 40.4g; Fiber: 0.1g; Protein: 4.9g

247. Cheesy Garlic Pasta with Ciabatta

Preparation time: 10 minutes
Cooking time: 10 minutes **Servings:** 4
Ingredients:
Alfredo Sauce
- 1 tbsp extra virgin olive oil
- 3 cloves garlic, minced

- 1 cup low-Fat milk
- 1/2 cup veggie broth
- 2-4 tbsp flour - 1/4 tsp salt
- 1/4 tsp black pepper
- 1/4 cup grated parmesan cheese
- 1 tbsp pesto
- 1 healthy pinch red pepper flakes
- 10-12 oz pasta, boiled
- Cheesy Garlic Ciabatta Bread
- 1 ciabatta bread roll
- 2 tbsp butter
- 1 tsp garlic powder
- 1 sprinkle mozzarella and parmesan cheese

Directions:
Start by preheating the oven to 400 degrees F.
Place a large saucepan over medium heat, then add garlic and olive oil. Sauté until golden, then add broth and milk. Mix well, then add flour with constant mixing until smooth. Toss in cheese, pesto, red pepper flakes, black pepper, and salt, then mix well. Stir, cook for 5 minutes, then set it aside.
Cook the pasta to a boil until al dente, then drain.
Slice the ciabatta roll in half, then butter them.
Further cut the roll into strips and place them on a baking sheet. Sprinkle mozzarella, garlic powder, and parmesan over the strips. 1Toast them for approximately 5 minutes in the oven. 1Toss the pasta with prepared sauce in a large bowl. 1Garnish with bread strips. Serve.
Per serving: Calories: 301Kcal; Fat: 12.2g; Carbs: 5g; Fiber: 0.9g; Protein: 28.8g

248. Tomato Red Lentil Pasta

Preparation time: 10 minutes
Cooking time: 30 minutes **Servings:** 6
Ingredients:
- ¼ cup extra virgin olive oil
- 1 sweet onion, chopped
- 6 cloves garlic, minced - 1 tbsp dried basil
- 1 tbsp dried oregano
- 2 tsp ground turmeric
- Kosher salt and black pepper, to taste
- 1 28-oz can fire-roasted tomatoes
- ½ cup oil-packed sundried tomatoes, chopped
- 1 tbsp apple cider vinegar
- 1 (8-oz) box red lentil pasta
- 2 large handfuls baby spinach

Directions:
Start by warming up the olive oil in a large pot over medium heat. Add onion and sauté for 10 minutes approximately. Stir in black pepper, salt, turmeric, oregano, basil, and garlic. Sauté for 1 minute, then toss tomatoes along with its juices, sundried tomatoes, and vinegar. Cook for 15 minutes on a simmer, then blend using an immersion blender. Toss spinach into the sauce and mix well to cook for another 5 minutes. Boil the pasta as per the given instructions on the box, then drain. Serve pasta with spinach mixture on top. Garnish as desired. Serve.
Per serving: Calories: 248Kcal; Fat: 2.4g; Carbs: 32.2g; Fiber: 0.7g; Protein: 44.3g

249. Pasta with Sun-Dried Tomato Sauce

Preparation time: 5 minutes
Cooking time: 10 minutes **Servings:** 4
Ingredients:
- 3 cups dried fusilli or rotini pasta
- 1 large tomato, chopped
- 2/3 cup sun-dried tomatoes, chopped
- 2 cloves garlic, coarsely chopped
- ½ cup fresh parsley, coarsely chopped
- ½ cup fresh grated Parmesan cheese
- ¼ cup balsamic vinegar
- 1/3 cup extra-virgin olive oil

Directions:
Bring a large pot of salted water to a boil. Add the pasta and cook according to package instructions. While the pasta is cooking, combine the tomato, sun-dried tomatoes, garlic, parsley, Parmesan cheese, balsamic vinegar, and olive oil in a blender. Blend until smooth. Drain the pasta and transfer it to serving plates. Ladle the sauce over the pasta and serve hot. **Per serving:** Calories: 419; Fat: 22g; Total carbs: 48g; Fiber: 7g; Sugar: 5g; Protein: 14g; Sodium: 324mg

250. Zesty Green Pea and Jalapeño Pesto Pasta

Preparation time: 5 minutes
Cooking time: 10 minutes **Servings:** 4
Ingredients:
- 3 cups dried fusilli or rotini pasta
- 1¼ cups fresh or defrosted frozen green peas, divided - 4 sun-dried tomatoes, chopped
- 1 cup fresh basil leaves, chopped
- ¾ cup fresh mint leaves, chopped
- 1 small onion, chopped
- 2 cloves garlic, coarsely chopped
- 1 jalapeño pepper, seeded and chopped
- 3 tablespoons lemon juice - ¼ teaspoon salt
- ¼ teaspoon freshly ground black pepper
- 3 tablespoons extra-virgin olive oil

Directions:
Bring a large pot of salted water to a boil. Add the pasta and cook according to package instructions.
Two minutes before the pasta is finished cooking, toss in 1 cup of the peas. While the pasta is cooking, combine the remaining ¼ cup of the peas with sun-dried tomatoes, basil, mint, onion, garlic, jalapeño pepper, lemon juice, salt, pepper, and olive oil in a blender. Blend until smooth. Add another tablespoon of olive oil if the mixture is too thick to process. Drain the pasta and peas and toss with the pesto.
Serve hot or warm, or cold as a salad.
Per serving: Calories: 345Kcal; Fat: 13g; Carbs: 52g; Fiber: 10g; Protein: 11g

251. Lemony Pasta with Broccoli and Chickpeas

Preparation time: 5 minutes
Cooking time: 10 minutes **Servings:** 6
Ingredients:
- 3 cups dried fusilli or rotini pasta
- 3 cups broccoli florets
- 1 (14-ounce) can chickpeas, drained and rinsed
- 1/3 cup sun-dried tomatoes, chopped
- 2 tablespoons extra-virgin olive oil
- ½ tablespoon minced garlic
- ½ teaspoon paprika
- 3 tablespoons lemon juice
- 1 teaspoon salt

Directions:
Bring a large pot of salted water to a boil. Add the pasta and cook according to package instructions.
In the last 4 minutes of the pasta cooking time, add the broccoli florets.
Drain the pasta and broccoli and add to a large bowl.
Add the chickpeas, sun-dried tomatoes, olive oil, garlic, paprika, lemon juice, and salt. Stir to combine and serve warm or cold.
SUBSTITUTION TIP: Instead of buying broccoli florets, use the florets and stem from a fresh head of broccoli. The stems are sweet and tender, once peeled, and have the same nutritional value as the crown. You can peel and chop the stem and add to the pasta cooking water, just as with the florets.
Per serving: Calories: 270Kcal; Fat: 7g; Carbs: 43g; Fiber: 9g; Protein: 10g

252. Penne with Indian-Style Tomato Sauce and Mushrooms

Preparation time: 5 minutes
Cooking time: 20 minutes **Servings:** 4
Ingredients:
- 2 tablespoons extra-virgin olive oil
- 1 (8-ounce) package sliced white mushrooms
- 2 tablespoons minced fresh ginger
- 2 tablespoons minced garlic
- ½ tablespoon garam masala
- ¼ teaspoon dried red chili flakes
- 1 (28-ounce) can crushed or diced tomatoes
- ½ teaspoon salt
- 3 cups dried penne pasta

Directions:
In a medium saucepan, heat the olive oil over medium heat. When hot, dd the mushrooms and sauté for 5 minutes. Add the ginger, garlic, garam masala, and red chili flakes, and stir for 3 more minutes. Stir in the tomatoes and salt. Bring to a boil, being careful of splattering. Lower the heat and simmer for 10 minutes. While the sauce is simmering, bring a large pot of salted water to a boil. Add the pasta and cook according to package instructions.
Drain the pasta, return to the pot, and stir in the tomato sauce.
Serve hot.
Per serving: Calories: 326Kcal; Fat: 9g; Carbs: 52g; Fiber: 9g; Protein: 11g

253. Teriyaki Mushrooms and Cashews with Rice Noodles

Preparation time: 5 minutes **Cooking time:** 20 minutes
Servings: 2
Ingredients:
- 2 cups water
- 2½ ounces rice noodles
- 3½ tablespoons sesame oil, divided
- ¼ cup raw cashews, halved or coarsely chopped
- 1 tablespoon brown sugar
- 1 tablespoon tamari or soy sauce
- 1 tablespoon rice vinegar
- ½ teaspoon dried red chili flakes
- 1 green onion, white and green parts, finely sliced
- ½ tablespoon minced garlic
- 1 tablespoon minced fresh ginger
- 1 (8-ounce) package sliced white mushrooms

Directions:
Bring the water to a boil in a medium saucepan. Stir in the rice noodles, cover, and remove from the heat. Let sit for 5 minutes or up to 10 minutes for wider rice noodles. While the noodles are resting, heat 2 tablespoons of the sesame oil in a medium nonstick pan or wok over medium-low heat. When hot, add the cashew pieces and fry, stirring frequently, for 5 to 8 minutes, until golden brown. Remove from the pan using a slotted spoon and set aside. Add 1 tablespoon of the oil to the pan and stir in the brown sugar, tamari or soy sauce, rice vinegar, red chili flakes, green onion, garlic, and ginger. Stir for 1 to 2 minutes to dissolve the sugar. Increase the heat to medium-high and add the mushrooms. Cook, stirring frequently, for 5 minutes until the mushrooms begin to brown.
Stir in the cashew pieces and toss to combine.
Drain the rice noodles, stir in the remaining ½ tablespoon of the sesame oil, and transfer to serving plates. Spoon the mushrooms and cashews over each portion and serve immediately.
INGREDIENT TIP: Rice noodles range in width from very fine (rice vermicelli) to ¼-inch wide. These mushrooms will look attractive with any width of rice noodle, but wider noodles will provide a more "toothsome" experience.
Per serving: Calories: 438Kcal; Fat: 28g; Carbs: 40g; Fiber: 3g; Protein: 9g

254. Linguine With Pea-Basil Pesto

Preparation time: 5 minutes
Cooking time: 10 minutes **Servings:** 4
Ingredients:
- 8 ounces dried linguine
- 1¼ cup fresh or defrosted frozen green peas, divided
- 2 tablespoons extra-virgin olive oil
- 1 small onion, chopped
- 1 tablespoon minced garlic
- 1 jalapeño pepper, seeded and chopped

- ½ cup walnuts, chopped
- ½ cup fresh basil leaves
- ½ teaspoon salt - 2/3 cup water
- Freshly ground black pepper

Directions:
Bring a large pot of salted water to a boil. Add the pasta and cook according to package instructions.
Two minutes before the pasta is finished cooking, toss in ½ cup of the peas.
While the pasta is cooking, heat the olive oil in a nonstick skillet over medium heat. Add the onion, garlic, and jalapeño pepper, and stir for 3 to 4 minutes to soften the onion.
Stir in the remaining ¾ cup of peas and walnuts. Continue to stir for another minute.
Add the basil, salt, and water. Stir for a minute and then remove from the heat.
Transfer the contents of the skillet to a blender and process until smooth, adding more water if the pesto is too thick.
Drain the pasta and peas and rinse quickly with cold water.
Return the pasta to the pot and add the pesto and black pepper. Toss gently and serve hot.
LEFTOVER TIP: Place leftover pasta in a bowl, cover with plastic wrap, and refrigerate for up to 3 days. Drizzle a little olive oil into the pasta and toss again before serving.
Per serving: Calories: 415Kcal; Fat: 19g; Carbs: 50g; Fiber: 10g; Protein: 12g

255. Greek-Inspired Macaroni and Cheese

Preparation time: 10 minutes
Cooking time: 15 minutes **Servings:** 6
Ingredients:
- 1-pound dried macaroni
- 2 cups fresh spinach, chopped
- 2 tablespoons unsalted butter
- 1 onion, finely chopped
- 1 tablespoon minced garlic
- 2 tablespoons all-purpose flour
- 1 (12-ounce) can evaporated milk or 2 cups heavy cream
- 1 cup grated Swiss cheese
- 1 cup feta cheese, crumbled
- 1 cup pitted black or Kalamata olives, sliced or chopped
- Freshly ground black pepper (optional)

Directions:
Bring a large pot of salted water to a boil. Add the macaroni and cook until al dente, according to package instructions.
Add the spinach and cook for another few minutes.
Drain the pasta and spinach and return to the pot.
While the pasta is cooking, melt the butter over medium heat in a medium saucepan. Add the onion and garlic and stir for 5 minutes to soften the onion.
Add the flour to the pan and stir for another 2 minutes.
Whisk in the evaporated milk and bring to a slow boil over medium-high heat. Continue to whisk constantly for 3 to 4 minutes until the mixture is creamy and thickened.
Add the Swiss and feta cheeses and stir for 2 to 3 minutes to melt. Turn the heat off and stir in the olives. Add the cheese mixture to the pasta and spinach and stir to combine. Serve hot or warm, seasoned with freshly ground black pepper, if desired.
LEFTOVER TIP: Refrigerate leftovers in a sealed container for up to 3 days. To reheat, put the macaroni and cheese in a covered oven-safe bowl or casserole dish and stir in a few tablespoons of milk. Reheat in a 350°F oven for 10 to 20 minutes before serving.
Per serving: Calories: 572Kcal; Fat: 22g; Carbs: 70g; Fiber: 4g; Protein: 23g

256. Spicy Mac and Ricotta Cheese with Spinach

Preparation time: 5 minutes
Cooking time: 25 minutes
Servings: 4 to 6
Ingredients:
- 2 cups dried macaroni
- 2 tablespoons extra-virgin olive oil or unsalted butter
- 1 medium shallot or small yellow onion, finely chopped
- 1 (10-ounce) bag fresh spinach, chopped
- 1 large tomato, finely chopped
- 1 or 2 fresh red or green chiles, seeded and minced
- ½ teaspoon turmeric
- 2/3 teaspoon ground coriander
- ½ teaspoon ground cumin
- ¼ teaspoon cayenne pepper
- 1 cup firm ricotta cheese, crumbled or mashed
- 1 to 2 teaspoons salt

Directions:
Bring a large pot of salted water to a boil. Stir in the macaroni and cook until al dente, according to package instructions.
While the pasta is cooking, heat the olive oil in a large saucepan over medium heat. Add the shallot or onion to the pan and sauté for 4 to 5 minutes, or until softened.
Add handfuls of the spinach, stirring frequently, until it begins to wilt. Once all of the spinach has been added, stir in the tomato, chiles, turmeric, coriander, cumin, and cayenne. Simmer for 5 minutes, or until the tomato is softened and most of the liquid has evaporated. Reserve 1 2/3 cups of the pasta cooking liquid and drain the pasta in a strainer. Stir the reserved pasta cooking water into the sauce and bring to a gentle simmer over medium-high heat. Stir in the cooked pasta, ricotta cheese, and salt. Reduce the heat to medium-low and continue to simmer for another 5 minutes, stirring occasionally. Serve immediately.
SUBSTITUTION TIP: If you can't find or don't want to fuss with fresh chiles, use ¼ to ½ teaspoons dried red chili flakes instead.
Per serving: Calories: 313Kcal; Fat: 13g; Carbs: 36g; Fiber: 4g; Protein: 15g

257. Spinach Pesto Pasta

Preparation time: 5 minutes
Cooking time: 10 minutes **Servings:** 4
Ingredients:
- 8 ounces dried linguine or fettuccini

- ¼ cup pine nuts
- 1 (5-ounce) bag fresh spinach leaves
- 2 cloves garlic, chopped
- ¼ cup extra-virgin olive oil
- ¼ cup fresh grated Parmesan cheese
- ½ tablespoon balsamic vinegar or red wine vinegar
- ½ teaspoon salt
- Freshly ground black pepper (optional)

Directions:
Bring a large pot of salted water to a boil. Add the pasta and cook according to package instructions.
While the pasta is cooking, toast the pine nuts in a small dry skillet over medium-low heat for 5 minutes, tossing or stirring frequently.
In a blender or food processor, combine the pine nuts, spinach, and garlic, and process until well chopped.
Pour in the olive oil and process for another half minute until blended.
Transfer the spinach pesto to a medium bowl and stir in the Parmesan cheese, balsamic vinegar, and salt.
Drain the pasta and rinse quickly with cold water.
Return the pasta to the pot and add the pesto. Toss gently and serve hot with freshly ground black pepper, if desired.
SUBSTITUTION TIP: Unsalted pistachios or almonds can be substituted for pine nuts. If they are already roasted, skip the second step.
Per serving: Calories: 398Kcal; Fat: 21g; Carbs: 45g; Fiber: 3g; Protein: 12g

258. Lasagna Noodles in a Creamy Mushroom Sauce

Preparation time: 5 minutes
Cooking time: 25 minutes **Servings:** 4
Ingredients:

- 4 tablespoons unsalted butter
- 2 medium onions, chopped
- 1 (16-ounce) package sliced white mushrooms
- 1 (14-ounce) can coconut milk or cream
- 4 tablespoons lemon juice
- 2 tablespoons fresh parsley, chopped
- 1 tablespoon all-purpose flour
- ½ teaspoon dry mustard powder
- 1 teaspoon salt
- 8 ounces dried lasagna noodles
- Freshly ground black pepper (optional)

Directions:
In a large saucepan or wok, melt the butter over medium heat. Add the onions and cook, stirring often for 5 minutes to soften. Raise the heat to medium-high and add the mushrooms. Cook, stirring often, for 5 minutes until lightly browned but still plump. Reduce the heat to medium-low and stir in the coconut milk or cream, lemon juice, parsley, flour, dry mustard powder, and salt. Simmer without boiling for 15 minutes, stirring occasionally. If the sauce becomes too thick, stir in a little water.
While the sauce is simmering, break the lasagna noodles into 2- to 3-inch pieces.
Bring a large pot of salted water to boil. Add the noodles and cook until al dente, according to package instructions.
Drain the noodles and rinse quickly with cold water. Return the noodles to the pot.
Remove the sauce from the heat and add to the pasta. Toss gently and serve hot, seasoned with freshly ground black pepper, if desired.
INGREDIENT TIPS: Do not substitute coconut milk from a carton for canned coconut milk, as it is much more watery. Avoid oven-ready (or no-boil) lasagna noodles for this recipe.
Per serving: Calories: 550Kcal; Fat: 37g; Carbs: 48g; Fiber: 5g; Protein: 14g

CHAPTER 18:
Vegetables & Side Dishes

259. Steamed Cauliflower
Preparation time: 5 minutes
Cooking time: 10 minutes
Servings: 6
Ingredients:
- 1 large head cauliflower
- 1 cup water
- ½ teaspoon salt
- 1 teaspoon red pepper flakes (optional)

Directions:
Remove any leaves from the cauliflower, and cut them into florets.
In a large saucepan, bring the water to a boil. Place a steamer basket over the water, and add the florets and salt. Cover and steam for 5 to 7 minutes, until tender.
In a large bowl, toss the cauliflower with the red pepper flakes (if using). Transfer the florets to a large airtight container or 6 single-serving containers. Let cool before sealing the lids.
Per serving: Calories: 35Kcal; Fat: 0g; Carbs: 7g; Fiber: 4g; Protein: 3g

260. Cajun Sweet Potatoes
Preparation time: 5 minutes
Cooking time: 30 minutes **Servings:** 4
Ingredients:
- 2 pounds sweet potatoes
- 2 teaspoons extra-virgin olive oil
- ½ teaspoon ground cayenne pepper
- ½ teaspoon smoked paprika
- ½ teaspoon dried oregano
- ½ teaspoon dried thyme
- ½ teaspoon garlic powder
- ½ teaspoon salt (optional)

Directions:
Preheat the oven to 400°F. Line a baking sheet with parchment paper.
Wash the potatoes, pat dry, and cut into ¾-inch cubes. Transfer to a large bowl, and pour the olive oil over the potatoes.
In a small bowl, combine the cayenne, paprika, oregano, thyme, and garlic powder. Sprinkle the spices over the potatoes and combine until the potatoes are well coated. Spread the potatoes on the prepared baking sheet in a single layer. Season with the salt (if using). Roast for 30 minutes, stirring the potatoes after 15 minutes. Divide the potatoes evenly among 4 single-serving containers. Let cool completely before sealing.
Per serving: Calories: 219Kcal; Fat: 3g; Carbs: 46g; Fiber: 7g; Protein: 4g

261. Smoky Coleslaw
Preparation time: 10 minutes
Cooking time: 0 minutes
Servings: 6
Ingredients:
- 1-pound shredded cabbage
- 1/3 cup vegan mayonnaise
- ¼ cup unseasoned rice vinegar
- 3 tablespoons plain vegan yogurt or plain soymilk
- 1 tablespoon vegan sugar
- ½ teaspoon salt
- ¼ teaspoon freshly ground black pepper
- ¼ teaspoon smoked paprika
- ¼ teaspoon chipotle powder

Directions:
Put the shredded cabbage in a large bowl. In a medium bowl, whisk the mayonnaise, vinegar, yogurt, sugar, salt, pepper, paprika, and chipotle powder. Pour over the cabbage and mix with a spoon or spatula and until the cabbage shreds are coated. Divide the coleslaw evenly among 6 single-serving containers. Seal the lids.
Per serving: Calories: 73Kcal; Fat: 4g; Carbs: 8g; Fiber: 2g; Protein: 1g

262. Mediterranean Hummus Pizza
Preparation time: 10 minutes
Cooking time: 30 minutes **Servings:** 2 pizzas
Ingredients:
- ½ zucchini, thinly sliced
- ½ red onion, thinly sliced
- 1 cup cherry tomatoes, halved
- 2 to 4 tablespoons pitted and chopped black olives
- Pinch sea salt
- Drizzle olive oil (optional)
- 2 prebaked pizza crusts
- ½ cup Classic Hummus
- 2 to 4 tablespoons Cheesy Sprinkle

Directions:
Preheat the oven to 400°F. Place the zucchini, onion, cherry tomatoes, and olives in a large bowl, sprinkle them with the sea salt and toss them a bit. Drizzle with a bit of olive oil (if using) to seal in the flavor and keep them from drying out in the oven. Lay the two crusts out on a large baking sheet. Spread half the hummus on each crust, and top with the veggie mixture and some Cheesy Sprinkle. Pop the pizzas in the oven for 20 to 30 minutes or until the veggies are soft. **Per serving:** Calories: 500; Fat: 25g; Carbs: 58g; Fiber: 12g; Protein: 13g

263. Baked Brussels Sprouts

Preparation time: 10 minutes
Cooking time: 40 minutes **Servings:** 4
Ingredients:
- 1-pound Brussels sprouts
- 2 teaspoons extra-virgin olive or canola oil
- 4 teaspoons minced garlic (about 4 cloves)
- 1 teaspoon dried oregano
- ½ teaspoon dried rosemary
- ½ teaspoon salt
- ¼ teaspoon freshly ground black pepper
- 1 tablespoon balsamic vinegar

Directions:
Preheat the oven to 400°F. Line a rimmed baking sheet with parchment paper. Trim and halve the Brussels sprouts. Transfer to a large bowl. Toss with olive oil, garlic, oregano, rosemary, salt, and pepper to coat well.
Transfer to the prepared baking sheet. Bake for 35 to 40 minutes, shaking the pan occasionally to help with even browning until crisp on the outside and tender on the inside. Remove from the oven and transfer to a large bowl. Stir in the balsamic vinegar, coating well. Divide the Brussels sprouts evenly among 4 single-serving containers. Let cool before sealing the lids. **Per serving:** Calories: 77Kcal; Fat: 3g; Carbs: 12g; Fiber: 5g; Protein: 4g

264. Basic Baked Potatoes

Preparation time: 5 minutes
Cooking time: 60 minutes **Servings:** 5
Ingredients:
- 5 medium Russet potatoes or a variety of potatoes, washed and patted dry
- 1 to 2 tablespoons extra-virgin olive oil
- ¼ teaspoon salt
- ¼ teaspoon freshly ground black pepper

Directions:
Preheat the oven to 400°F. Pierce each potato several times with a fork or a knife. Brush the olive oil over the potatoes, then rub each with a pinch of the salt and a pinch of the pepper. Place the potatoes on a baking sheet and bake for 50 to 60 minutes until tender. Place the potatoes on a baking rack and cool completely. Transfer to an airtight container or 5 single-serving containers. Let cool before sealing the lids.
Per serving: Calories: 171Kcal; Fat: 3g; Carbs: 34g; Fiber: 5g; Protein: 4g

265. Miso Spaghetti Squash

Preparation time: 5 minutes
Cooking time: 40 minutes **Servings:** 4
Ingredients:
- 1 (3-pound) spaghetti squash
- 1 tablespoon hot water
- 1 tablespoon unseasoned rice vinegar
- 1 tablespoon white miso

Directions:
Preheat the oven to 400°F. Line a rimmed baking sheet with parchment paper. Halve the squash lengthwise and place, cut-side down, on the prepared baking sheet. Bake for 35 to 40 minutes, until tender. Cool until the squash is easy to handle. With a fork, scrape out the flesh, which will be stringy, like spaghetti. Transfer to a large bowl. In a small bowl, combine the hot water, vinegar, and miso with a whisk or fork. Pour over the squash. Gently toss with tongs to coat the squash. Divide the squash evenly among 4 single-serving containers. Let cool before sealing the lids.
Per serving: Calories: 117Kcal; Fat: 2g; Carbs: 25g; Fiber: 0g; Protein: 3g

266. Garlic and Herb Noodles

Preparation time: 10 minutes **Cooking time:** 2 minutes
Servings: 4 **Ingredients:**
- 1 teaspoon extra-virgin olive oil or 2 tablespoons vegetable broth
- 1 teaspoon minced garlic (about 1 clove)
- 4 medium zucchinis, spiral
- ½ teaspoon dried basil
- ½ teaspoon dried oregano
- ¼ to ½ teaspoon red pepper flakes, to taste
- ¼ teaspoon salt (optional)
- ¼ teaspoon freshly ground black pepper

Directions:
In a large skillet over medium-high heat, heat the olive oil.
Add the garlic, zucchini, basil, oregano, red pepper flakes, salt (if using), and black pepper. Sauté for 1 to 2 minutes, until barely tender. Divide the noodles evenly among 4 storage containers. Let cool before sealing the lids.
Per serving: Calories: 44Kcal; Fat: 2g; Carbs: 7g; Fiber: 2g; Protein: 3g

267. Thai Roasted Broccoli

Preparation time: 5 minutes
Cooking time: 15 minutes
Servings: 4
Ingredients:
- 1 head broccoli, cut into florets
- 2 tablespoons olive oil
- 1 tablespoon soy sauce or gluten-free tamari

Directions:
Preheat the oven to 425°F. Line a baking sheet with parchment paper. In a large bowl, combine the broccoli, oil, and soy sauce. Toss well to combine.
Spread the broccoli on the prepared baking sheet. Roast for 10 minutes. Toss the broccoli with a spatula and roast for an additional 5 minutes, or until the edges of the florets begin to brown.
Per serving: Calories: 44Kcal; Fat: 2g; Carbs: 7g; Fiber: 2g; Protein: 3g

268. Coconut Curry Noodle

Preparation time: 10 minutes
Cooking time: 30 minutes
Servings: 4
Ingredients:
- ½ tablespoon oil
- 3 garlic cloves, minced
- 2 tablespoons lemongrass, minced

- 1 tablespoon fresh ginger, grated
- 2 tablespoons red curry paste
- 1 (14 oz) can coconut milk
- 1 tablespoon brown sugar
- 2 tablespoons soy sauce
- 2 tablespoons fresh lime juice
- 1 tablespoon hot chili paste
- 12 oz linguine
- 2 cups broccoli florets
- 1 cup carrots, shredded
- 1 cup edamame, shelled
- 1 red bell pepper, sliced

Directions:
Fill a suitably-sized pot with salted water and boil it on high heat. Add pasta to the boiling water and cook until it is al dente, then rinse under cold water. Now, place a medium-sized saucepan over medium heat and add oil. Stir in ginger, garlic, and lemongrass, then sauté for 30 seconds.
Add coconut milk, soy sauce, curry paste, brown sugar, chili paste, and lime juice.
Stir this curry mixture for 10 minutes or until it thickens.
Toss in carrots, broccoli, edamame, bell pepper, and cooked pasta.
Mix well, then serve warm.
Per serving: Calories: 44Kcal; Fat: 2g; Carbs: 7g; Fiber: 2g; Protein: 3g

269. Collard Green Pasta

Preparation time: 10 minutes
Cooking time: 20 minutes
Servings: 4
Ingredients:
- 2 tablespoons olive oil
- 4 garlic cloves, minced
- 8 oz whole wheat pasta
- ½ cup panko bread crumbs
- 1 tablespoon nutritional yeast
- 1 teaspoon red pepper flakes
- 1 large bunch collard greens
- 1 large lemon, zest, and juiced

Directions:
Fill a suitable pot with salted water and boil it on high heat. Add pasta to the boiling water and cook until it is al dente, then rinse under cold water. Reserve ½ cup of the cooking liquid from the pasta. Place a non-stick pan over medium heat and add 1 tablespoon olive oil. Stir in half of the garlic, then sauté for 30 seconds. Add breadcrumbs and sauté for approximately 5 minutes.
Toss in red pepper flakes and nutritional yeast, then mix well. Transfer the breadcrumbs mixture to a plate and clean the pan. Add the remaining tablespoon of oil to the nonstick pan. Stir in the garlic clove, salt, black pepper, and chard leaves. Cook for 5 minutes until the leaves are wilted.
Add pasta along with the reserved pasta liquid.
Mix well, then add garlic crumbs, lemon juice, and zest. Toss well, then serve warm.
Per serving: Calories: 45Kcal; Fat: 2.5g; Carbs: 9g; Fiber: 4g; Protein: 4g

270. Jalapeno Rice Noodles

Preparation time: 10 minutes
Cooking time: 25 minutes **Servings:** 4
Ingredients:
- ¼ cup soy sauce
- 1 tablespoon brown sugar
- 2 teaspoons sriracha
- 3 tablespoons lime juice
- 8 oz rice noodles
- 3 teaspoons toasted sesame oil
- 1 package extra-firm tofu, pressed
- 1 onion, sliced
- 2 cups green cabbage, shredded
- 1 small jalapeno, minced
- 1 red bell pepper, sliced
- 1 yellow bell pepper, sliced
- 3 garlic cloves, minced
- 3 scallions, sliced
- 1 cup Thai basil leaves, roughly chopped
- Lime wedges for serving

Directions:
Fill a suitably-sized pot with salted water and boil it on high heat. Add pasta to the boiling water and cook until it is al dente, then rinse under cold water.
Put the lime juice, soy sauce, sriracha, and brown sugar in a bowl, then mix well. Place a large wok over medium heat, then add 1 teaspoon sesame oil.
Toss in tofu and stir for 5 minutes until golden-brown. Transfer the golden-brown tofu to a plate and add 2 teaspoons of oil to the wok. Stir in scallions, garlic, peppers, cabbage, and onion.
Sauté for 2 minutes, then add cooked noodles and prepared sauce. Cook for 2 minutes, then garnish with lime wedges and basil leaves. Serve fresh.
Per serving: Calories: 45Kcal; Fat: 2.5g; Carbs: 9g; Fiber: 4g; Protein: 4g

271. Rainbow Soba Noodles

Preparation time: 10 minutes
Cooking time: 20 minutes
Servings: 4
Ingredients:
- 8 oz tofu, pressed and crumbled
- 1 teaspoon olive oil
- ½ teaspoon red pepper flakes
- 10 oz package buckwheat soba noodles, cooked
- 1 package broccoli slaw
- 2 cups cabbage, shredded
- ¼ cup very red onion, thinly sliced

Peanut Sauce
- ¼ cup peanut butter
- ¾ cup hot water
- 2 tablespoons apple cider vinegar
- 1 tablespoon maple syrup
- 1–2 garlic cloves, minced
- 1 lime, zest, and juice
- Salt and crushed red pepper flakes, to taste

- Cilantro for garnish
- Crushed peanuts for garnish

Directions:
Crumble tofu on a baking sheet and toss in 1 teaspoon oil and 1 teaspoon red pepper flakes.
Bake the tofu for 20 minutes at 400°F in a preheated oven. Meanwhile, whisk peanut butter with hot water, garlic cloves, maple syrup, cider vinegar, lime zest, salt, lime juice, and pepper flakes in a large bowl.
Toss in cooked noodles, broccoli slaw, cabbages, and onion. Mix well, then stir in tofu, cilantro, and peanuts. Enjoy.
Per serving: Calories: 45Kcal; Fat: 2.5g; Carbs: 9g; Fiber: 4g; Protein: 4g

272. Spicy Pad Thai Pasta

Preparation time: 10 minutes
Cooking time: 10 minutes **Servings:** 4
Ingredients:
Spicy Tofu
- 1 lb. extra-firm tofu, sliced
- 1 tablespoon peanut butter
- 3 tablespoons soy sauce
- 2 tablespoons Sriracha
- 2 tablespoons rice vinegar
- 2 teaspoons sesame oil
- 2 teaspoons ginger, grated

Pad Thai
- 8 oz brown rice noodles
- 2 teaspoons coconut oil
- 1 red pepper, sliced
- ½ white onion, sliced
- 2 carrots, sliced
- 1 Thai chili, chopped
- ½ cup peanuts, chopped
- ½ cup cilantro, chopped

Spicy Pad Thai Sauce
- 3 tablespoons soy sauce
- 3 tablespoons fresh lime juice
- 1 tablespoon Sriracha
- 3 tablespoons brown sugar
- 3 tablespoons vegetable broth
- 1 teaspoon garlic-chili paste
- 2 garlic cloves, minced

Directions:
Fill a suitably-sized pot with water and soak rice noodles in it. Press the tofu to squeeze excess liquid out of it. Place a non-stick pan over medium-high heat and add tofu. Sear the tofu for 2-3 minutes per side until brown. Whisk all the ingredients for tofu crumbles in a large bowl. Stir in tofu and mix well.
Separately mix the pad Thai sauce in a bowl and add to the tofu. Place a wok over medium heat and add 1 teaspoon oil. Toss in chili, carrots, onion, and red pepper, then sauté for 3 minutes. Transfer the veggies to the tofu bowl. Add more oil to the same pan and stir in drained noodles, then stir cook for 1 minute. Transfer the noodles to the tofu and toss it all well. Add cilantro and peanuts. Serve fresh.
Per serving: Calories: 45Kcal; Fat: 2.5g; Carbs: 4g; Fiber: 4g; Protein: 4g

273. Linguine with Wine Sauce

Preparation time: 10 minutes
Cooking time: 18 minutes **Servings:** 4
Ingredients:
- 1 tablespoon olive oil
- 5 garlic cloves, minced
- 16 oz shiitake, chopped
- ¼ teaspoon salt
- ¼ teaspoon ground pepper
- 1 pinch red pepper flakes
- ½ cup dry white wine
- 12 oz linguine - 2 teaspoons vegan butter
- ¼ cup Italian parsley, finely chopped

Directions:
Fill a suitably-sized pot with salted water and bring it to a boil on high heat. Add pasta to the boiling water, then cook until it is al dente, then rinse under cold water. Place a non-stick skillet over medium-high heat, then add olive oil. Stir in garlic and sauté for 1 minute. Stir in mushrooms and cook for 10 minutes. Add salt, red pepper flakes, and black pepper for seasoning. Toss in the cooked pasta and mix well.
Garnish with parsley and butter. Enjoy.
Per serving: Calories: 40Kcal; Fat: 2g; Carbs: 7g; Fiber: 4g; Protein: 5g

274. Cheesy Macaroni with Broccoli

Preparation time: 10 minutes
Cooking time: 25 minutes **Servings:** 6
Ingredients:
- 1/3 cup melted coconut oil
- ¼ cup nutritional yeast
- 1 tablespoon tomato paste
- 1 tablespoon dried mustard
- 2 garlic cloves, minced
- 1 ½ teaspoons salt
- ½ teaspoon ground turmeric
- 4 ½ cups almond milk
- 3 cups cauliflower florets, chopped
- 1 cup raw cashews, chopped
- 1 lb. shell pasta - 1 tablespoon white vinegar
- 3 cups broccoli florets

Directions:
Place a suitably-sized saucepan over medium heat and add coconut oil. Stir in mustard, yeast, garlic, salt, tomato paste, and turmeric. Cook for 1 minute, then add almond milk, cashews, and cauliflower florets. Continue cooking for 20 minutes on a simmer.
Transfer the cauliflower mixture to a blender jug, then blend until smooth. Stir in vinegar and blend until creamy. Fill a suitably-sized pot with salted water and bring it to a boil on high heat. Add pasta to the boiling water. Place a steamer basket over the boiling water and add broccoli to the basket. Cook until the pasta is al dente. Drain and rinse the pasta and transfer the broccoli to a bowl. Add the cooked pasta to the cauliflower-cashews sauce. Toss in broccoli florets, salt, and black pepper. Mix well, then serve.
Per serving: Calories: 40Kcal; Fat: 2g; Carbs: 7g; Fiber: 4g; Protein: 5g

275. Soba Noodles with Tofu

Preparation time: 10 minutes
Cooking time: 38 minutes **Servings:** 4
Ingredients:
Marinated Tofu
- 2 tablespoons olive oil
- 8 oz firm tofu, pressed and drained
- ¼ cup cilantro, finely chopped
- ¼ cup mint, finely chopped
- 1-inch fresh ginger, grated
- Soba Noodles
- 8 oz soba noodles
- ¾ cup edamame
- 2 cucumbers, peeled and julienned
- 1 large carrot, peeled and julienned
- 2 tablespoons black sesame seeds
- 2 tablespoons white sesame seeds
- 2 scallions, chopped
- Ginger-Soy Sauce
- 2 tablespoons fresh lime juice
- 2 tablespoons soy sauce
- 1 tablespoon brown sugar
- 1 tablespoon fresh ginger, grated
- 2 tablespoons sesame oil
- ½ tablespoon garlic chili sauce

Directions:
Blend herbs, ginger, salt, black pepper, and olive oil in a blender. Add the spice mixture to the tofu and toss it well to coat. Allow the tofu to marinate for 30 minutes at room temperature. Fill a suitably-sized pot with salted water and bring it to a boil on high heat.
Add pasta to the boiling water, then cook until it is al dente, then rinse under cold water. Place a large wok over medium heat and add marinated tofu. Sauté for 5–8 minutes until golden-brown, then transfer to a large bowl. Add veggies to the same wok and stir until veggies are soft. Transfer the veggies to the tofu and add cooked noodles. Toss well, then serve warm. Enjoy.
Per serving: Calories: 30Kcal; Fat: 3.5g; Carbs: 6g; Fiber: 4g; Protein: 6g

276. Plant-Based Keto Lo Mein

Preparation time: 10 minutes
Cooking time: 10 minutes **Servings:** 2
Ingredients:
- 2 tablespoons carrots, shredded
- 1 package kelp noodles, soaked in water
- 1 cup broccoli, frozen

For the Sauce
- 1 tablespoon sesame oil
- 2 tablespoons tamari
- ½ teaspoon ground ginger
- ¼ teaspoon Sriracha
- ½ teaspoon garlic powder

Directions:
Put the broccoli in a saucepan on medium-low heat and add the sauce ingredients. Cook for about 5 minutes and add the noodles after draining water. Allow to simmer about 10 minutes, occasionally stirring to avoid burning. When the noodles have softened, mix everything well and dish out to serve.
Per serving: Calories: 30Kcal; Fat: 3.5g; Carbs: 6g; Fiber: 4g; Protein: 6g

277. Steamed Tomatoes

Preparation time: 5 minutes
Cooking time: 10 minutes **Servings:** 4
Ingredients:
- 1 cup water - 4 large tomatoes
- 1 tablespoon herbed butter
- 1 cup vegan cheese, shredded

Directions:
Place the steamer trivet in the bottom of a pressure cooker and add water. Scoop out the pulp of the tomatoes and stuff with vegan cheese. Put the stuffed tomatoes on the trivet and secure the lid. Cook at high pressure for about 8 minutes and release the pressure naturally. Heat herbed butter in a skillet over medium heat and add stuffed tomatoes. Sauté for about 2 minutes and dish out to serve hot.
Per serving: Calories: 140Kcal; Fat: 3.7g; Carbs: 9.3g; Fiber: 2.2g; Protein: 7.4g

278. Baked Tofu

Preparation time: 20 minutes
Cooking time: 30 minutes **Servings:** 8
Ingredients:
- 2/3 cup low-sodium soy sauce
- 1 tablespoon garlic, minced
- 1 teaspoon cayenne pepper
- 1 tablespoon olive oil
- 2 tablespoons fresh cilantro leaves, chopped
- 4 tablespoons balsamic vinegar
- 2 (16-ounce) packages extra-firm tofu, drained, pressed and cubed
- 2 teaspoons white sesame seeds, toasted

Directions:
Preheat the oven to 400 degrees f and grease a large baking sheet lightly. Mix soy sauce, vinegar, garlic, and cayenne pepper in a bowl and coat tofu in it. Cover the bowl and refrigerate for at least 3 hours. Place the tofu cubes onto the baking sheet in a single layer and transfer them into the oven. Bake for about 15 minutes on each side and remove from the oven. Dish out in a platter and garnish with sesame seeds and cilantro to serve.
Per serving: Calories: 132Kcal; Fat: 0.9g; Carbs: 4.2g; Fiber: 0.5g; Protein: 12.7g

279. Potato Carrot Salad

Preparation time: 15 minutes
Cooking time: 10 minutes **Servings:** 6
Ingredients:
- Water

- Six potatoes, sliced into cubes
- Three carrots, sliced into cubes
- One tablespoon milk
- One tablespoon Dijon mustard
- ¼ cup mayonnaise
- Pepper to taste
- Two teaspoons fresh thyme, chopped
- One stalk celery, chopped
- Two scallions, chopped

Directions:
Fill your pot with water. Place it over medium-high heat. Boil the potatoes and carrots for 10 to 15 minutes or until tender. Drain and let cool.
In a bowl, mix the milk mustard, mayo, pepper, and thyme. Stir in the potatoes, carrots, and celery.
Coat evenly with the sauce. Cover and refrigerate for 4 hours. Top with the scallions before serving.
Per serving: Calories: 106Kcal; Fat: 5.3g; Carbs: 12.6g; Fiber: 1.8g; Protein: 2g

280. High Protein Salad

Preparation time: 5 minutes
Cooking time: 5 minutes **Servings:** 4
Ingredients:
Salad:
- One 15-oz can green kidney beans
- 4 tbsp capers
- 4 handfuls arugula
- 15-oz can lentils

Dressing:
- 1 tbsp caper brine
- 1 tbsp tamari
- 1 tbsp balsamic vinegar
- 2 tbsp peanut butter
- 2 tbsp hot sauce
- 1 tbsp tahini

Directions:
For the dressing:
In a bowl, stir together all the materials until they come together to form a smooth dressing.
For the salad:
Mix the beans, arugula, capers, and lentils. Top with the dressing and serve.
Per serving: Calories: 205Kcal; Fat: 2g; Carbs: 31g; Fiber: 17g; Protein: 13g

281. Vegan Wrap with Apples and Spicy Hummus

Preparation time: 10 minutes
Cooking time: 0 minutes
Servings: 2
Ingredients:
- One tortilla
- 6-7 tbsp Spicy Hummus (mix it with a few tbsp of salsa)
- Only some leaves of fresh spinach or romaine lettuce
- 1 tsp fresh lemon juice
- 1½ cups broccoli slaw
- ½ apple, sliced thin
- 4 tsp dairy-free plain unsweetened yogurt
- Salt and pepper

Directions:
Mix the yogurt and the lemon juice with the broccoli slaw. Add the salt and a dash of pepper for taste. Mix well and set aside.
Lay the tortilla flat.
Spread the spicy hummus over the tortilla.
Lay the lettuce down on the hummus.
On one half, pile the broccoli slaw on the lettuce.
Place the apple slices on the slaw.
Fold the sides of the tortilla up, starting with the end that has the apple and the slaw. Roll tightly.
Cut it in half and serve.
Per serving: Calories: 205Kcal; Fat: 2g; Carbs: 32g; Fiber: 9g; Protein: 12g

282. Rice and Veggie Bowl

Preparation time: 5 minutes
Cooking time: 15 minutes **Servings:** 6
Ingredients:
- 2 tbsp coconut oil
- 1 tsp ground cumin
- 1 tsp ground turmeric
- 1 tsp chili powder
- One red bell pepper, chopped
- 1 tsp tomato paste
- One bunch of broccoli, cut into bite-sized florets with short stems - 1 tsp salt, to taste
- One large red onion, sliced
- Two garlic cloves, minced
- One head of cauliflower, sliced into bite-sized florets
- 2 cups cooked rice
- Newly ground black pepper to taste

Directions:
Heat the coconut grease over medium-high heat in a large pan Wait until the oil is hot, stir in the turmeric, cumin, chili powder, salt, and tomato paste. Cook the content for 1 minute. Stir repeatedly until the spices are fragrant. Add the garlic and onion. Sauté for 3 minutes or until the onions are softened. Add the broccoli, cauliflower, and bell pepper. Cover the pot. Cook for 3 to 4 minutes and stir occasionally. Add the cooked rice. Stir so it will combine well with the vegetables—Cook for 2 to 3 minutes. Stir until the rice is warmed through. Check the seasoning. And make adjustments to taste if desired. Lower the heat and cook on low for 2 to 3 more minutes so the flavors will meld.
Serve with freshly ground black pepper.
Per serving: Calories: 260Kcal; Fat: 9g; Carbs: 36g; Fiber: 5g; Protein: 9g

283. Cucumber Tomato Chopped Salad

Preparation time: 15 minutes
Cooking time: 0 minutes **Servings:** 6
Ingredients:
- ½ cup light mayonnaise

- One tablespoon lemon juice
- One tablespoon fresh dill, chopped
- One tablespoon chive, chopped
- ½ cup feta cheese, crumbled
- Salt and pepper to taste - One red onion, chopped
- One cucumber, diced - One radish, diced
- Three tomatoes, diced
- Chives, chopped

Directions:
Combine the mayo, lemon juice, fresh dill, chives, feta cheese, salt, and pepper in a bowl. Mix well. Stir in the onion, cucumber, radish, and tomatoes. Coat evenly. Garnish with the chopped chives.
Per serving: Calories: 187Kcal; Fat: 16.7g; Carbs: 6.7g; Fiber: 2g; Protein: 3.3g

284. Zucchini Pasta Salad

Preparation time: 4 minutes
Cooking time: 0 minutes **Servings:** 15
Ingredients:
- Five tablespoons olive oil
- Two teaspoons Dijon mustard
- Three tablespoons red-wine vinegar
- One clove garlic, grated
- Two tablespoons fresh oregano, chopped
- One shallot, chopped
- ¼ teaspoon red pepper flakes
- 16 oz. zucchini noodles
- ¼ cup Kalamata olives pitted
- 3 cups cherry tomatoes, sliced in half
- ¾ cup Parmesan cheese shaved

Directions:
Mix the olive oil, Dijon mustard, red wine vinegar, garlic, and oregano, shallot, and red pepper flakes in a bowl. Stir in the zucchini noodles. Sprinkle on top the olives, tomatoes, and Parmesan cheese.
Per serving: Calories: 299Kcal; Fat: 24.7g; Carbs: 11.6g; Fiber: 2.8g; Protein: 7g

285. Egg Avocado Salad

Preparation time: 10 minutes **Cooking time:** 0 minutes
Servings: 4
Ingredients:
- One avocado
- Six hard-boiled eggs, peeled and chopped
- One tablespoon mayonnaise
- Two tablespoons freshly squeezed lemon juice - ¼ cup celery, chopped
- Two tablespoons chives, chopped
- Salt and pepper to taste

Directions:
Add the avocado to a large bowl. Mash the avocado using a fork. Stir in the egg and mash the eggs.
Add the mayo, lemon juice, celery, chives, salt, and pepper. Chill in the refrigerator. Wait for at least 30 minutes before serving. **Per serving:** Calories: 224Kcal; Fat: 18g; Carbs: 6.1g; Fiber: 3.6g; Protein: 10.6g

286. Arugula Salad

Preparation time: 15 minutes
Cooking time: 0 minutes **Servings:** 4
Ingredients:
- 6 cups fresh arugula leaves
- 2 cups radicchio, chopped
- ¼ cup low-Fat balsamic vinaigrette
- ¼ cup pine nuts, toasted and chopped

Directions:
Arrange the arugula leaves in a serving bowl.
Sprinkle the radicchio on top. Drizzle with the vinaigrette. Sprinkle the pine nuts on top.
Per serving: Calories: 85Kcal; Fat: 6.6g; Carbs: 5.1g; Fiber: 1g; Protein: 2.2g

287. Sautéed Cabbage

Preparation time: 8 minutes
Cooking time: 12 minutes **Servings:** 8
Ingredients:
- ¼ cup butter
- One onion, sliced thinly
- One head cabbage, sliced into wedges
- Salt and pepper to taste

Directions:
Add the butter to a pan over medium-high heat.
Cook the onion for 1 minute, stirring frequently.
Season with salt and pepper. Add the cabbage, then stir it for 12 minutes.
Per serving: Calories: 77Kcal; Fat: 5.9g; Carbs: 6.1g; Fiber: 2.4g; Protein: 1.3g

288. Avocado Mint Soup

Preparation time: 10 minutes
Cooking time: 10 minutes **Servings:** 2
Ingredients:
- One medium avocado, peeled, pitted, and cut into pieces
- 1 cup of coconut milk
- Two romaine lettuce leaves
- 20 fresh mint leaves
- 1 tbsp fresh lime juice
- 1/8 tsp salt

Directions:
Combine all materials into the blender. The soup should be thick, not as a puree. Wait and blend until it is smooth. Pour into the serving bowls and place them in the refrigerator for 10 minutes. Stir well and serve chilled. **Per serving:** Calories: 268Kcal; Fat: 25.6g; Carbs: 10.2g; Protein: 2.7g

289. Cucumber Edamame Salad

Preparation time: 5 minutes
Cooking time: 8 minutes
Servings: 2
Ingredients:
- 3 tbsp. Avocado oil
- 1 cup cucumber, sliced into thin rounds
- ½ cup fresh sugar snap peas cut up or whole

- ½ cup fresh edamame
- ¼ cup radish, sliced
- One large avocado, peeled, pitted, sliced
- One nori sheet, crumbled
- 2 tsp. Roasted sesame seeds
- 1 tsp. Salt

Directions:
Make a medium-sized pot filled halfway with water to a boil over medium-high heat. Add the sugar snaps and cook them for about 2 minutes. Remove the pot from the heat, drain the excess water, transfer the sugar snaps to a medium-sized bowl, and set aside.
Fill the pot with water again, add the teaspoon of salt and bring to a boil over medium-high heat.
Add the edamame to the pot and let them cook for about 6 minutes. Take the pot off the heat, drain the excess water, transfer the soybeans to the bowl with sugar snaps, and cool down for about 5 minutes.
Combine all ingredients, except for the nori crumbs and roasted sesame seeds, in a medium-sized bowl. Delicately stir, using a spoon, until all ingredients are evenly coated in oil. Top the salad along with the nori crumbs and roasted sesame seeds.
Shift the bowl to the fridge and allow the salad to cool for at least 30 minutes.
Serve chilled and enjoy!
Per serving: Calories: 409Kcal; Fat: 38.25g; Carbs: 7.1g; Protein: 7.6g

290. Garden Salad Wraps

Preparation time: 15 minutes
Cooking time: 10 minutes
Servings: 4
Ingredients:
Six tablespoons olive oil
- 1-pound extra-firm tofu, drained, patted dry, and cut into 1/2-inch strips
- One tablespoon soy sauce
- A quarter cup apple cider vinegar
- One teaspoon yellow or spicy brown mustard
- A half teaspoon salt
- A quarter teaspoon freshly ground black pepper
- 3 cups shredded romaine lettuce
- Three ripe Roma tomatoes, finely chopped
- One large carrot, shredded
- One medium English cucumber, peeled and chopped
- 1/3 cup minced red onion
- A quarter cup sliced pitted green olives
- 4 (10-inch) whole-grain flour tortillas or lavash flatbread

Directions:
In a large frypan, heat two tablespoons of the oil over medium heat. Add the tofu. Cook it until golden brown, about 10 minutes. Sprinkle with soy sauce and set aside to cool.
Combine the vinegar, mustard, salt, and pepper with the remaining four tablespoons of oil, stirring to blend well. Set aside.
Mix the lettuce, tomatoes, carrot, cucumber, onion, and olives. Pour on the dressing and flip to coat.
To assemble wraps, place one tortilla on a work surface and spread it with about one-quarter of the salad. Place a few strips of tofu on the tortilla and roll up tightly. Slice in half
Per serving: Calories: 89Kcal; Fat: 8g; Carbs: 3g; Fiber: 2g; Protein: 4g

291. Marinated Mushroom Wraps

Preparation time: 15 minutes
Cooking time: 0 minutes
Servings: 2
Ingredients:
- Three tablespoons soy sauce
- Three tablespoons fresh lemon juice
- 1 1/2 tablespoons toasted sesame oil
- Two portobello mushroom caps cut into 1/4-inch strips
- One ripe Hass avocado pitted and peeled
- 2 cups fresh baby spinach leaves
- One medium red bell pepper cut down into 1/4-inch strips
- One ripe tomato, chopped
- Salt and freshly ground black pepper

Directions:
Combine the soy sauce, two tablespoons of lemon juice, and the oil. Add the portobello strips, toss to combine, and marinate for 1 hour or overnight. Drain the mushrooms and set them aside. Mash the avocado with the remaining one tablespoon of lemon juice. To assemble wraps, place one tortilla on a work surface and spread with some of the mashed avocados. Topmost with a layer of baby spinach leaves. In the lower third of each tortilla, arrange strips of the soaked mushrooms and some bell pepper strips. Sprinkle with the tomato and salt and black pepper to taste. Roll up tightly and cut in half diagonally. Repeat with the remaining ingredients and serve.
Per serving: Calories: 89Kcal; Fat: 8g; Carbs: 3g; Fiber: 2g; Protein: 4g

292. Green Beans Gremolata

Preparation time: 15 minutes
Cooking time: 5 minutes
Servings: 6
Ingredients:
- 1 Pound Fresh Green Beans, Trimmed, Or Frozen Or Canned Green Beans
- 3 Garlic Cloves, Minced
- Zest Of 2 Oranges
- 3 Tablespoons Minced Fresh Parsley
- 2 Tablespoons Pine Nuts
- 3 Tablespoons Olive Oil
- Sea Salt
- Freshly Ground Black Pepper

Directions:
Fill a large pot about half full with water and bring to a boil over high heat. Add the green beans and cook for 2 to 3 minutes. Drain the beans in a colander and rinse with cold

water to stop the cooking. In a small bowl, mix the garlic, orange zest, and parsley. In a large sauté pan over medium-high heat, toast the pine nuts in the dry, hot pan until they are fragrant, 2 to 3 minutes. Remove from the pan and set aside. Heat the olive oil in the same pan until it shimmers. Add the beans and cook, -stirring frequently, until heated through, about 2 minutes. Remove the pan from the heat and add the parsley mixture and pine nuts. Season with salt and pepper. Serve immediately.
Per serving: Calories: 63Kcal; Fat: 6.81g; Carbs: 0.67g; Fiber: 0.1g; Protein: 0.17g

293. Minted Peas

Preparation time: 5 minutes
Cooking time: 5 minutes **Servings:** 4
Ingredients:
- 1 Tablespoon Olive Oil
- 4 Cups Peas, Fresh Or Frozen (Not Canned)
- ½ Teaspoon Sea Salt
- Freshly Ground Black Pepper
- 3 Tablespoons Chopped Fresh Mint

Directions:
In a large sauté pan, heat the olive oil over medium-high heat until hot. Add the peas and cook, about 5 minutes. Remove the pan from heat. Season with pepper and salt, and stir in the mint. Serve hot.
Per serving: Calories: 277Kcal; Fat: 16.4g; Carbs: 0.26g; Fiber: 0.1g; Protein: 30.25g

294. Sweet and Spicy Brussels Sprout Hash

Preparation time: 10 minutes
Cooking time: 15 minutes **Servings:** 4
Ingredients:
- 3 Tablespoons Olive Oil
- 2 Shallots, Thinly Sliced
- 1½ Pounds Brussels Sprouts, Trimmed And Cut Into Thin Slices
- 3 Tablespoons Apple Cider Vinegar
- 1 Tablespoon Pure Maple Syrup
- ½ Teaspoon Sriracha Sauce (Or To Taste) - Sea Salt
- Freshly Ground Black Pepper

Directions:
In a large sauté pan, heat the olive oil over medium-high heat until it shimmers. Add the shallots and Brussels sprouts and cook, stirring frequently, until the -vegetables soften and begin to turn golden brown, about 10 minutes. Stir in the vinegar, using a spoon to scrape any browned bits from the bottom of the pan. Stir in the maple syrup and Sriracha.
Simmer, stirring frequently, until the liquid reduces, 3 to 5 minutes. Season with salt and pepper and serve immediately.
Per serving: Calories: 111Kcal; Fat: 10.17g; Carbs: 5.35g; Fiber: 0.1g; Protein: 0.26g

Plant based cookbook for beginners

295. Glazed Curried Carrots

Preparation time: 5 minutes
Cooking time: 15 minutes **Servings:** 6
Ingredients:
- 1 Pound Carrots, Peeled And Thinly Sliced
- 2 Tablespoons Olive Oil
- 2 Tablespoons Curry Powder
- 2 Tablespoons Pure Maple Syrup
- Juice Of ½ LemonSea Salt
- Freshly Ground Black Pepper

Directions:
Place the carrots in a large pot and cover them with water. Cook on medium-high heat until tender, about 10 minutes. Drain the carrots and return them to the pan over medium-low heat.
Stir in olive oil, curry powder, maple syrup, and lemon juice. Cook, stirring constantly, until the liquid reduces, about 5 minutes. Season with salt and pepper and serve immediately.
Per serving: Calories: 68Kcal; Fat: 4.82g; Carbs: 6.55g; Fiber: 1.4g; Protein: 0.38g

296. Carrot-Pineapple Casserole

Preparation time: 10 minutes
Cooking time: 50 minutes
Servings: 4
Ingredients:
- 3 large carrots
- 1 large pineapple
- 2 tablespoons all-purpose flour
- 1 tablespoon honey
- ½ teaspoon ground cinnamon
- 1 tablespoon olive oil
- 1/2 cup pineapple juice

Directions:
Preheat oven to 350 degrees F.
Peel and slice carrots and pineapples. Bring 1 quart of water to a boil in a medium-sized pot. Boil carrots for 5 minutes or until tender. Drain.
Layer carrots and pineapples in a large casserole dish. Using a fork, mix flour, honey, and cinnamon in a small bowl. Mix in olive oil to make a crumb topping.
Sprinkle flour mixture over carrots and pineapples, then drizzle with juice. Bake for 50 minutes or until pineapples and carrots are tender and the topping is golden brown.
Per serving: Calories: 94Kcal; Fat: 2.9g; Carbs: 17.4g; Fiber: 1.8g; Protein: 0.9g

297. Vegetable Medley

Preparation time: 5 minutes
Cooking time: 12 minutes
Servings: 3
Ingredients:
- 2 carrots, peeled and diced
- 1 small sweet potato, peeled and diced
- 3 pink potatoes, quartered
- 1½ cups butternut squash
- 1 sprig rosemary
- Salt and black pepper, to taste

- 1 tablespoon olive oil - ½ cup water

Directions:
Heat olive oil in a skillet and add rosemary sprig.
Sauté for about 2 minutes and stir in the rest of the ingredients.
Cover the lid and cook for about 10 minutes on medium heat.
Dish out in a bowl and serve hot.
Per serving: Calories: 386Kcal; Fat: 5.2g; Carbs: 79.8g; Fiber: 9.8g; Protein: 8.9g

CHAPTER 19:
Legumes

298. Sweet Potato Chili with Quinoa
Preparation time: 15 minutes
Cooking time: 30 minutes **Servings:** 4
Ingredients:
- onion 1 large, finely chopped
- garlic 2 cloves, crushed - olive oil
- mild chili powder 1 tablespoon(s)
- ground cumin 1 teaspoon(s)
- 3 medium sweet potatoes, peeled and cubed - 1 cup quinoa, and drained
- 1 can of chopped tomatoes
- 2 quarts of vegetable stock
- 1 can of black beans, rinsed and drained
- coriander a small bunch, to serve
- soured cream or yogurt to serve (optional)

Directions:
Take a large pot. Dice the onion. Cook the onion and garlic in 1 tablespoon(s) olive oil until soft. Add the chili powder and cumin, cook for a minute, then add the sweet potato, quinoa, tomatoes, and stock. Let simmer for about 10 minutes, then put in the beans. Half cover the pot with a lid, letting it simmer for maybe 20 to 30 more minutes. The squash and quinoa should be soft enough to poke through with a fork. The liquid should also be noticeably thicker.
Sprinkle over the coriander you've chopped up and serve in bowls with a dollop of soured cream or yogurt if you like.
Per serving: Calories: 388Kcal; Fat: 5.8g; Carbs: 65.3g; Protein: 12.1g

299. Spicy Sweet Potato Enchiladas
Preparation time: 10 minutes
Cooking time: 20 minutes **Servings:** 6
Ingredients:
- 1 large sweet potatoes - 1 red or yellow onion
- 1 red bell pepper - 1 green bell pepper
- 1 teaspoon cumin seeds
- 1 teaspoon dried chili flakes
- 3 tablespoons olive oil
- 1 small bunch of cilantro/coriander
- 4 large tortillas
- 1 ½ cups grated vegan cheese
- sour cream to serve - salad to serve
- Enchilada Sauce
- 1 can chopped tomatoes
- 1 teaspoon smoked paprika
- 1 teaspoon garlic salt (or use half Himalaya salt, half garlic powder)
- 1 teaspoon dried oregano
- 1 teaspoon sugar

Directions:
Heat the oven to 200°C / 400°F /gas mark 6. Chop all of the fresh ingredients, leaving the skins on the potatoes. Finely chop the herbs. Put the potatoes, onion, bell peppers/capsicum, and spices on a non-stick baking tray or a baking sheet lined with wax parchment paper. Add the oil and lots of salt and pepper, and toss well. Cook for half an hour or until the potato is tender enough to pierce with a fork (but not mushy). Meanwhile, blend the sauce ingredients in a blender. Take the veg out of the oven and leave to cool a little. Stir through ½ the coriander. Lay out the tortillas flat and spread out the veggie mixture evenly between them. Roll up the tortillas; you may want to look up a video on the internet for this, as it helps to watch. Place the tortillas cut-side down into an oiled baking dish. Spoon over the sauce and sprinkle over the cheese, using the nut cheese recipe. Put them in the oven and bake for about 20 minutes or until bubbling and golden. Serve with vegan sour cream, the other half of the chopped coriander, and a fresh side salad.
Per serving: Calories: 495Kcal; Fat: 19.4g; Carbs: 60.7g; Protein: 13.9g

300. Raw Nut Cheese
Preparation time: 10 minutes + 12 hours soak time + 12 hours set / rise time
Cooking time: 0 minutes **Servings:** 3
Ingredients:
- 3 2/3 cups raw cashews
- 1 teaspoon of probiotic powder
- 2 tablespoons onion powder
- 1 tablespoon garlic powder
- 4-5 tablespoons nutritional yeast
- salt and pepper to taste

Directions:
Drain the water from the overnight soaked cashews. Put them in a blender with the probiotic powder, blending until smooth. Transfer the mixture into a bowl and cover with plastic wrap or beeswax wrap, being careful to leave a couple of tiny spaces open for air to get in. Leave the bowl at room temperature for 8-12 hours, or until the cheese has risen in size and on quality. Season to taste with onion powder, garlic powder, nutritional yeast, salt, and pepper. It's wonderful on crackers or sprinkled/grated atop any pasta dish to make a vegan, perfectly combined meal.
Per serving: Calories: 890Kcal; Fat: 65g; Carbs: 59.7g; Protein: 36g

301. Artichoke White Bean Sandwich Spread

Preparation time: 10 minutes
Cooking time: 15 minutes **Servings:** 2
Ingredients:

- ½ cup raw cashews, chopped
- Water - 1 clove garlic, cut into half
- 1 tablespoon lemon zest
- 1 teaspoon fresh rosemary, chopped
- ¼ teaspoon salt - ¼ teaspoon pepper
- 6 tablespoons almond, soy or coconut milk
- 1 15.5-ounce can cannellini beans, rinsed and drained well
- 3 to 4 canned artichoke hearts, chopped
- ¼ cup hulled sunflower seeds
- Green onions, chopped, for garnish

Directions:
Soak the raw cashews for 15 minutes in enough water to cover them. Drain and dab with a paper towel to make them as dry as possible. Transfer the cashews to a blender and add the garlic, lemon zest, rosemary, salt, and pepper. Pulse to break everything up and then add the milk, one tablespoon at a time, until the mixture is smooth and creamy. Mash the beans in a bowl with a fork. Add the artichoke hearts and sunflower seeds. Toss to mix. Pour the cashew mixture on top and season with more salt and pepper if desired. Mix the ingredients well and spread on whole-wheat bread, crackers, or a wrap.
Per serving: Calories: 110Kcal; Fat: 4g; Carbs: 14g; Protein: 6g

302. Lentil Sandwich Spread

Preparation time: 15 minutes
Cooking time: 20 minutes **Servings:** 3
Ingredients:

- 1 tablespoon water or oil
- 1 small onion, chopped
- 2 cloves garlic, minced
- 1 cup dry lentils
- 2 cups vegetable stock
- 1 tablespoon apple cider vinegar
- 2 tablespoons tomato paste
- 3 sun-dried tomatoes
- 2 tablespoons maple
- 1 teaspoon dried oregano
- ½ teaspoon ground cumin
- 1 teaspoon coriander
- 1 teaspoon turmeric
- ½ lemon, juiced
- 1 tablespoon fresh parsley, chopped

Directions:
Warm a Dutch oven over medium heat and add the water or oil. Immediately add the onions and sauté for two to three minutes or until softened. Add more water if this starts to stick to the pan. Add the garlic and sauté for one minute. Add the lentils, vegetable stock and vinegar; bring to a boil. Turn down to a simmer and cook for 15 minutes or until the lentils are soft and the liquid is almost completely absorbed. Ladle the lentils into a food processor and add the tomato paste, sun-dried tomatoes and syrup; process until smooth. Add the oregano, cumin, coriander, turmeric and lemon; process until thoroughly mixed. Remove the spread to a bowl and apply it to bread, toast, a wrap, or pita. Sprinkle With toppings as desired.
Per serving: Calories: 360Kcal; Fat: 5.4g; Carbs: 60.7g; Protein: 17.5g

303. Rice and Bean Burritos

Preparation time: 10 minutes
Cooking time: 15 minutes **Servings:** 8
Ingredients:

- 2 16-ounce cans Fat-free refried beans
- 6 tortillas - 2 cups cooked rice
- ½ cup salsa - 1 tablespoon olive oil
- 1 bunch green onions, chopped
- 2 bell peppers, finely chopped
- Guacamole

Directions:
Preheat the oven to 375°F. Dump the refried beans into a saucepan and place over medium heat to warm.
Heat the tortillas and lay them out on a flat surface.
Spoon the beans in a long mound that runs across the tortilla, just a little off from the center.
Spoon some rice and salsa over the beans; add the green pepper and onions to taste, along with any other finely chopped vegetables you like.
Fold over the shortest edge of the plain tortilla and roll it up, folding in the sides as you go.
Place each burrito, seam side down, on a nonstick-sprayed baking sheet.
Brush with olive oil and bake for 15 minutes.
Serve with guacamole.
Per serving: Calories: 290Kcal; Fat: 6g; Carbs: 49g; Protein: 9g

304. Quinoa Avocado Salad

Preparation time: 15 minutes
Cooking time: 4 minutes **Servings:** 4
Ingredients:

- 2 tablespoons balsamic vinegar
- ¼ cup cream
- ¼ cup buttermilk
- 5 tablespoons freshly squeezed lemon juice, divided
- 1 clove garlic, grated
- 2 tablespoons shallot, minced
- Salt and pepper to taste
- 2 tablespoons avocado oil, divided
- 1 1/4 cups quinoa, cooked
- 2 heads endive, sliced
- 2 firm pears, sliced thinly
- 2 avocados, sliced
- ¼ cup fresh dill, chopped

Directions:
Combine the vinegar, cream, milk, 1 tablespoon lemon juice, garlic, shallot, salt, and pepper in a bowl.
Pour 1 tablespoon oil into a pan over medium heat.

Heat the quinoa for 4 minutes. Transfer quinoa to a plate. Toss the endive and pears in a mixture of remaining oil, remaining lemon juice, salt, and pepper. Transfer to a plate. Toss the avocado in the reserved dressing. Add to the plate. Top with the dill and quinoa. **Per serving:** Calories: 431Kcal; Fat: 28.5g; Carbs: 8g; Protein: 4g

305. Green Beans with vegan Bacon
Preparation time: 15 minutes
Cooking time: 20 minutes **Servings:** 8
Ingredients:
- 2 slices of vegan bacon, chopped
- 1 shallot, chopped
- 24 oz. green beans
- Salt and pepper to taste
- ½ teaspoon smoked paprika
- 1 teaspoon lemon juice
- 2 teaspoons vinegar

Directions:
Preheat your oven to 450 degrees F.
Add the vegan bacon to the baking pan and roast for 5 minutes. Stir in the shallot and beans. Season with salt, pepper, and paprika. Roast for 10 minutes. Drizzle with lemon juice and vinegar. Roast for another 2 minutes.
Per serving: Calories: 49Kcal; Fat: 1.2g; Carbs: 55g; Protein: 15g

306. Chickpea Avocado Sandwich
Preparation time: 10 minutes
Cooking time: 5 minutes
Servings: 2
Ingredients:
- Chickpeas – 1 can
- Avocado – 1
- Dill, dried – .25 teaspoon
- Onion powder – .25 teaspoon
- Sea salt – .5 teaspoon
- Celery, chopped – .25 cup
- Green onion, chopped – .25 cup
- Lime juice – 3 tablespoons
- Garlic powder – .5 teaspoon
- Dark pepper, ground – dash
- Tomato, sliced – 1
- Lettuce – 4 leaves
- Bread – 4 slices

Directions:
Drain the canned chickpeas and rinse them under cool water. Place them in a bowl along with the herbs, spices, sea salt, avocado, and lime juice. Using a potato masher or fork, mash the avocado and chickpeas together until you have a thick filling. Try not to mash the chickpeas all the way, as they create texture. Stir the celery and green onion into the filling and prepare your sandwiches. Lay out two slices of bread, top them with the chickpea filling, some lettuce, and sliced tomato. Top them off with the two remaining slices, slice the sandwiches in half, and serve.
Per serving: Calories: 270Kcal; Fat: 15g; Carbs: 5g; Protein: 9g

307. Spicy Chickpeas
Preparation time: 15 minutes
Cooking time: 20 minutes **Servings:** 8
Ingredients:
- 1 Tbsp extra-virgin olive oil
- 1 yellow onion, diced
- 1 tsp curry - ¼ tsp allspice
- 1 can diced tomatoes
- 2 cans chickpeas, rinsed, drained
- Salt, cayenne pepper, to taste

Directions:
Simmer onions in 1 Tbsp oil for 4 minutes.
Add allspice and pepper, cook for 2 minutes.
Stir in tomatoes, and cook for another 2 minutes.
Add chickpeas, and simmer for 10 minutes.
Season with salt, and serve.
Per serving: Calories: 146Kcal; Fat: 3g; Carbs: 25g; Protein: 5g

308. Beans & Greens Bowl
Preparation time: 2 minutes
Cooking time: 2 minutes **Servings:** 1
Ingredients:
- 1½ cups curly kale, washed, chopped
- ½ cup black beans, cooked
- ½ avocado
- 2 Tbsp feta cheese, crumbled

Directions:
Mix the kale and black beans in a microwavable bowl and heat for about 1 ½ minute.
Add the avocado and stir well. Top with feta.
Per serving: Calories: 340Kcal; Fat: 19g; Carbs: 32g; Protein: 13g

309. Black Beans & Brown Rice
Preparation time: 2 minutes
Cooking time: 45 minutes **Servings:** 4
Ingredients:
- 4 cups water
- 2 cups brown rice, uncooked
- 1 can no-salt black beans
- 3 cloves garlic, minced

Directions:
Bring the water and rice to boil, simmer for 40 minutes. In a pan, cook the black beans with their liquid and the garlic for 5 minutes. Toss the rice and beans together, and serve.
Per serving: Calories: 220Kcal; Fat: 1.5g; Carbs: 45g; Protein: 7g

310. Yucatan Bean & Pumpkin Seed Appetizer
Preparation time: 10 minutes
Cooking time: 3 minutes **Servings:** 8
Ingredients:
- ¼ cup pumpkin seeds
- 1 can white beans - 1 tomato, chopped

- 1/3 cup onion, chopped
- 1/3 cup cilantro, chopped
- 4 Tbsp lime juice - Salt, pepper, to taste

Directions:
Toast the pumpkin seeds for 3 minutes to lightly brown. Let cool, and then chop in a food processor.
Mix in the remaining ingredients. Season with salt and pepper, and serve.
Per serving: Calories: 12Kcal; Fat: 2g; Carbs: 12g; Protein: 5g

311. Butter Bean Hummus

Preparation time: 5 minutes
Cooking time: 0 minutes **Servings:** 4
Ingredients:
- 1 can butter beans, drained, rinsed
- 2 garlic cloves, minced
- ½ lemon, juiced - 1 Tbsp olive oil
- 4 sprigs of parsley, minced - Sea salt, to taste

Directions:
Blend all ingredients in a food processor into a creamy mixture. Serve as a dip for bread, crackers, or any type of vegetables.
Per serving: Calories: 150Kcal; Fat: 4g; Carbs: 23g; Protein: 8g

312. Greek-Style Gigante Beans

Preparation time: 8 hours 5 minutes
Cooking time: 10 hours **Servings:** 10
Ingredients:
12 ounces gigante beans
- 1 can tomatoes with juice, chopped
- 2 stalks celery, diced - 1 onion, diced
- 4 garlic cloves, minced - Salt, to taste

Directions:
Soak beans in water for 8 hours. Combine drained beans with the remaining ingredients. Stir and pour water to cover. Cook for 10 hours on low. Season with salt, and serve.
Per serving: Calories: 63Kcal; Fat: 2g; Carbs: 13g; Protein: 4g

313. Brown Rice & Red Beans & Coconut Milk

Preparation time: 10 minutes
Cooking time: 1 hour **Servings:** 6
Ingredients:
- 2 cups brown rice, uncooked
- 4 cups water
- 1 Tbsp olive oil
- 1 onion, diced
- 3 cloves garlic, minced
- 2 cans red beans
- 1 can coconut milk

Directions:
Bring brown rice in water to a boil, then simmer for 30 minutes. Sauté onion in olive oil. Add garlic and cook until golden. Mix the onions and garlic, beans, and coconut milk into the rice. Simmer for 15 minutes.Serve hot.
Per serving: Calories: 280Kcal; Fat: 3g; Carbs: 49g; Protein: 8g

314. Black-Eyed Peas with Herns

Preparation time: 10 minutes
Cooking time: 1 hour **Servings:** 8
Ingredients:
- 2 cans no-sodium black-eyed beans
- ½ cup extra-virgin olive oil
- 1 cup parsley, chopped
- 4 green onions, sliced •2 carrots, grated
- 2 Tbsp tomato paste •2 cups water
- Salt, pepper, to taste

Directions:
Drain the beans, reserve the liquid.
Sauté beans, parsley, onions, and carrots in oil for 3 minutes. Add remaining ingredients, 2 cups reserved beans liquid, and water. Cook for 30 minutes.
Season with salt, pepper, and serve.
Per serving: Calories: 230Kcal; Fat: 15g; Carbs: 23g; Protein: 11g

315. Curry Lentil Soup

Preparation time: 5 minutes
Cooking time: 40 minutes **Servings:** 6
Ingredients:
- 1 cup brown lentils
- 1 medium white onion, peeled, chopped
- 28 ounces diced tomatoes
- 1 ½ teaspoon minced garlic
- 1 inch of ginger, grated
- 3 cups vegetable broth
- 1/2 teaspoon salt
- 2 tablespoons curry powder
- 1 teaspoon cumin
- 1/2 teaspoon cayenne
- 1 tablespoon olive oil
- 1 1/2 cups coconut milk, unsweetened
- ¼ cup chopped cilantro

Directions:
Take a soup pot, place it over medium-high heat, add oil and when hot, add onion, stir in garlic and ginger and cook for 5 minutes until golden brown.
Then add all the ingredients, except for the milk and cilantro, stir until mixed and simmer for 25 minutes until lentils have cooked. When done, stir in milk, cook for 5 minutes until thoroughly heated, and then garnish the soup with cilantro. Serve straight away
Per serving: Calories: 269Kcal; Fat: 15g; Carbs: 26g; Protein: 10g

316. Mexican Lentil Soup

Preparation time: 5 minutes
Cooking time: 45 minutes
Servings: 6
Ingredients:
- 2 cups green lentils
- 1 medium red bell pepper, cored, diced
- 1 medium white onion, peeled, diced
- 2 cups diced tomatoes

- 8 ounces diced green chilies
- 2 celery stalks, diced
- 2 medium carrots, peeled, diced
- 1 ½ teaspoon minced garlic
- 1/2 teaspoon salt
- 1 tablespoon cumin
- 1/4 teaspoon smoked paprika
- 1 teaspoon oregano
- 1/8 teaspoon hot sauce
- 2 tablespoons olive oil
- 8 cups vegetable broth
- ¼ cup cilantro, for garnish
- 1 avocado, peeled, pitted, diced, for garnish

Directions:
Take a large pot over medium heat, add oil, and when hot, add all the vegetables, reserving tomatoes and chilies, and cook for 5 minutes until softened.
Then add garlic, stir in oregano, cumin, and paprika, and continue cooking for 1 minute.
Add lentils, tomatoes, and green chilies, season with salt, pour in the broth, and simmer the soup for 40 minutes until cooked.
When done, ladle soup into bowls, top with avocado and cilantro, and serve straight away
Per serving: Calories: 235Kcal; Fat: 9g; Carbs: 32g; Fiber: 10g; Protein: 9g

317. Tex-Mex Tofu & Beans
Preparation time: 25 minutes
Cooking time: 12 minutes
Servings: 2
Ingredients:
- 1 cup dry black beans
- 1 cup dry brown rice
- 1 14-oz. Package firm tofu, drained
- 2 tbsp. Olive oil
- 1 small purple onion, diced
- 1 medium avocado, pitted, peeled
- 1 garlic clove, minced
- 1 tbsp. Lime juice
- 2 tsp. Cumin
- 2 tsp. Paprika
- 1 tsp. Chili powder
- ¼ tsp salt
- ¼ tsp pepper

Directions:
Cut the tofu into ½-inch cubes.
Heat the olive oil in a large skillet over high heat. Add the diced onions and cook until soft, for about 5 minutes. Add the tofu and cook an additional 2 minutes, flipping the cubes frequently. Meanwhile, cut the avocado into thin slices and set aside. Lower the heat to medium and mix in the garlic, cumin, and cooked black beans. Stir until everything is incorporated thoroughly, and then cook for an additional 5 minutes. Add the remaining spices and lime juice to the mixture in the skillet. Mix thoroughly and remove the skillet from the heat.

Serve the tex-mex tofu and beans with a scoop of rice and garnish with the fresh avocado. Enjoy immediately, or store the rice, avocado, and tofu mixture separately.
Per serving: Calories: 585Kcal; Fat: 23.4g; Carbs: 76g; Fiber: 14.4g; Protein: 23.7g

318. Black Bean Burgers
Preparation time: 10 minutes
Cooking time: 15 minutes **Servings:** 6
Ingredients:
- 1 Onion, diced - ½ cup Corn Nibs
- 2 Cloves Garlic, minced
- ½ teaspoon Oregano, dried
- ½ cup Flour
- 1 Jalapeno Pepper, small
- 2 cups Black Beans, mashed & canned ¼ cup Breadcrumbs (Vegan)
- 2 teaspoons Parsley, minced ¼ teaspoon cumin - 1 tablespoon Olive Oil
- 2 teaspoons Chili Powder
- ½ Red Pepper, diced
- Sea Salt to taste

Directions:
Set your flour on a plate, and then get out your garlic, onion, peppers, and oregano, throwing it in a pan. Cook over medium-high heat, and then cook until the onions are translucent. Place the peppers in and sauté until tender. Cook for two minutes, and then set it to the side. Use a potato masher to mash your black beans, then stir in the vegetables, cumin, breadcrumbs, parsley, salt, and chili powder, and then divide it into six patties.
Coat each side, and then cook until it is fried on each side.
Per serving: Calories: 357Kcal; Fat: 5.1g; Carbs: 61.1g; Protein: 17.9g

319. Hearty Black Lentil Curry
Preparation time: 30 minutes
Cooking time: 6 hours and 15 minutes
Servings: 4
Ingredients:
- 1 cup of black lentils, rinsed and soaked overnight
- 14 ounce of chopped tomatoes
- 2 large white onions, peeled and sliced
- 1 1/2 teaspoon of minced garlic
- 1 teaspoon of grated ginger
- 1 red chili
- 1 teaspoon of salt
- 1/4 teaspoon of red chili powder
- 1 teaspoon of paprika
- 1 teaspoon of ground turmeric
- 2 teaspoons of ground cumin
- 2 teaspoons of ground coriander
- 1/2 cup of chopped coriander
- 4-ounce of vegetarian butter
- 4 fluid of ounce water
- 2 fluid of ounce vegetarian double cream

Directions:
Place a large pan over moderate heat, add butter and let heat until melt.
Add the onion and garlic and ginger and cook for 10 to 15 minutes or until onions are caramelized.
Then stir in salt, red chili powder, paprika, turmeric, cumin, ground coriander, and water. 4. Transfer this mixture to a 6-quarts slow cooker and add tomatoes and red chili.
Drain lentils, add to slow cooker, and stir until just mix.
Plugin slow cooker; adjust cooking time to 6 hours and let cook on low heat setting.
7. When the lentils are done, stir in cream and adjust the seasoning.
8. Serve with boiled rice or whole wheat bread.
Per serving: Calories: 299Kcal; Fat: 27.9g; Carbs: 9.8g; Protein: 5.5g

320. Flavorful Refried Beans
Preparation time: 15 minutes
Cooking time: 8 hours
Servings: 8
Ingredients:
- 3 cups of pinto beans, rinsed
- 1 small jalapeno pepper, seeded and chopped
- 1 medium-sized white onion, peeled and sliced
- 2 tablespoons of minced garlic
- 5 teaspoons of salt
- 2 teaspoons of ground black pepper
- 1/4 teaspoon of ground cumin
- 9 cups of water

Directions:
Using a 6-quarts slow cooker, place all the ingredients and stir until it mixes properly.
Cover the top, plug in the slow cooker, adjust the cooking time to 6 hours, let it cook on the high heat setting, and add more water if the beans get too dry.
When the beans are done, drain them, then reserve the liquid. Mash the beans using a potato masher and pour in the reserved cooking liquid until it reaches your desired mixture. Serve immediately.
Per serving: Calories: 268Kcal; Fat: 1.7g; Carbs: 46.6g; Protein: 16.5g

321. Smoky Red Beans and Rice
Preparation time: 15 minutes
Cooking time: 6 minutes **Servings:** 6
Ingredients:
- 30 ounce of cooked red beans
- 1 cup of brown rice, uncooked
- 1 cup of chopped green pepper
- 1 cup of chopped celery
- 1 cup of chopped white onion
- 1 1/2 teaspoon of minced garlic 1/2 teaspoon of salt
- 1/4 teaspoon of cayenne pepper
- 1 teaspoon of smoked paprika
- 2 teaspoons of dried thyme
- 1 bay leaf
- 2 1/3 cups of vegetable broth

Directions:
Using a 6-quarts slow cooker, place all the ingredients, except for the rice, salt, and cayenne pepper. Stir until it mixes properly, and then cover the top. Plug in the slow cooker, adjust the cooking time to 4 hours, and steam on a low heat setting.
Then pour in and stir the rice, salt, cayenne pepper and continue cooking for an additional 2 hours at a high heat setting. Serve straight away.
Per serving: Calories: 791Kcal; Fat: 86.4g; Carbs: 9.6g; Protein: 3.2g

322. Spicy Black-Eyed Peas
Preparation time: 12 minutes
Cooking time: 8 hours and 8 minutes **Servings:** 8
Ingredients:
- 32-ounce black-eyed peas, uncooked
- 1 cup of chopped orange bell pepper
- 1 cup of chopped celery
- 8-ounce of chipotle peppers, chopped
- 1 cup of chopped carrot
- 1 cup of chopped white onion
- 1 teaspoon of minced garlic 3/4 teaspoon of salt
- 1/2 teaspoon of ground black pepper
- 2 teaspoons of liquid smoke flavoring
- 2 teaspoons of ground cumin
- 1 tablespoon of adobo sauce
- 2 tablespoons of olive oil
- 1 tablespoon of apple cider vinegar
- 4 cups of vegetable broth

Directions:
Place a medium-sized non-stick skillet pan over an average temperature of heat; add the bell peppers, carrot, onion, garlic, oil, and vinegar. Stir until it mixes properly and let it cook for 5 to 8 minutes or until it gets translucent. Transfer this mixture to a 6-quarts slow cooker and add the peas, chipotle pepper, adobo sauce, and vegetable broth. Stir until mixed properly and cover the top. Plug in the slow cooker, adjust the cooking time to 8 hours, and let it cook on the low heat setting or until peas are soft.
Serve right away.
Per serving: Calories: 1071Kcal; Fat: 13.6g; Carbs: 18.5g; Protein: 5.3g

323. Bean and Carrot Spirals
Preparation time: 10 minutes
Cooking time: 40 minutes **Servings:** 24
Ingredients:
- 4 8-inch flour tortillas
- 1 ½ cups of Easy Mean White Bean dip
- 10 ounces spinach leaves
- ½ cup diced carrots - ½ cup diced red peppers

Directions:
Start by preparing the bean dip, seen above. Next, spread out the bean dip on each tortilla, making sure to leave about a ¾ inch white border on the tortillas' surface. Next, place spinach in the center of the tortilla, followed by carrots and red peppers. Roll the tortillas into tight rolls, and cover every roll

with plastic wrap or aluminum foil. Let them chill in the fridge for twenty-four hours. Afterward, remove the wrap from the spirals and remove the very ends of the rolls. Slice the rolls into six individual spiral pieces, and arrange them on a platter for serving. Enjoy! **Per serving:** Calories: 205Kcal; Fat: 4.16g; Carbs: 35.13g; Protein: 6.41g

324. Peppered Pinto Beans

Preparation time: 10 minutes
Cooking time: 15 minutes **Servings:** 6
Ingredients:

- 1 tsp. Chili powder
- 1 tsp. ground cumin
- .5 cup Vegetable
- 2 cans Pinto beans
- 1 Minced jalapeno
- 1 Diced red bell pepper
- 1 tsp. Olive oil

Directions:
Take out a pot and heat the oil. Cook the jalapeno and pepper for a bit before adding in the pepper, salt, cumin, broth, and beans.
Place to a boil and then reduce the heat to cook for a bit. After 10 minutes, let it cool and serve.
Per serving: Calories: 183Kcal; Fat: 2g; Carbs: 32g; Protein: 11g

325. Pesto and White Bean Pasta

Preparation time: 10 minutes
Cooking time: 10 minutes **Servings:** 4
Ingredients:

- .5 cup Chopped black olives
- .25 Diced red onion
- 1 cup Chopped tomato
- .5 cup Spinach pesto
- 1.5 cup Cannellini beans
- 8 oz. Rotini pasta, cooked

Directions:
Bring out a bowl and toss together the pesto, beans, and pasta. Add in the olives, red onion, and tomato, and toss around a bit more before serving.
Per serving: Calories: 544Kcal; Fat: 17g; Carbs: 83g; Protein: 23g

326. Lentil Tacos

Preparation time: 10 minutes;
Cooking time: 12 minutes
Servings: 8
Ingredients:

- 2 cups cooked lentils
- ½ cup chopped green bell pepper
- ½ cup chopped white onion
- ½ cup halved grape tomatoes
- 1 teaspoon minced garlic
- ½ teaspoon garlic powder
- 1 teaspoon red chili powder
- ½ teaspoon smoked paprika
- ½ teaspoon ground cumin
- 8 whole-grain tortillas

Directions:
Take a large skillet pan, place it over medium heat, add oil, and let it heat. Add onion, bell pepper, and garlic, stir until mixed, and then cook for 5 minutes until vegetables begin to soften. Add lentils and tomatoes, stir in all the spices and then continue cooking for 5 minutes until hot. Assemble the tacos and for this, heat the tortillas until warmed and then fill each tortilla with ¼ cup of the cooked lentil mixture. Serve straight away.
Per serving: Calories: 315Kcal; Fat: 7.8g; Carbs: 49.8g; Fiber: 16.2g; Protein: 13g

327. Red Lentil and Chickpea Bowl

Preparation time: 5 minutes
Cooking time: 25 minutes **Servings:** 4
Ingredients:

- Salt (1 teaspoon.)
- Curry powder (.5 teaspoon.)
- Garam masala seasoning (2 teaspoons.)
- Drained chickpeas (15 oz.)
- Diced Roma tomatoes
- Water (1 c.)
- Vegetable broth (2 c.)
- Vegan milk (1 c.)
- Dried red lentils (1.5 c.)
- Diced onion (.5 c.)
- Chopped carrots (1 c.)

Directions:
To start this recipe, take out a pot and start boiling some water and carrots on the stove. After 5 minutes, you can drain these and set them to one side.
As the carrots are boiling, you can heat a bit of oil in a frying pan and cook the onion for a bit. It will take about ten minutes. In a big pan, add in the chickpeas, carrots, milk, water, vegetable broth, lentils, and onion along with the seasonings and spices.
Bring all of this to a boil before reducing the heat and letting it simmer for a bit. After twenty minutes of cooking, you can take it off the heat before serving and enjoying it.
Per serving: Calories: 189Kcal; Fat: 11g; Carbs: 22g; Protein: 16g

328. Bean and Rice Burritos

Preparation time: 10 minutes
Cooking time: 20 minutes
Servings: 6
Ingredients:

- 32 ounces refried beans
- 2 cups cooked rice
- 2 cups chopped spinach
- 1 tablespoon olive oil
- 1/2 cup tomato salsa
- 6 tortillas, whole-grain, warm
- Guacamole as needed for serving

Directions:
Switch on the oven, then set it to 375 degrees F and let it preheat. Take a medium saucepan, place it over medium heat,

add beans, and cook for 3 to 5 minutes until softened, remove the pan from heat. Place one tortilla in a clean working space, spread some of the beans on it into a log, leaving 2-inches of the edge, top beans with spinach, rice, and salsa, and then tightly wrap the tortilla to seal the filling like a burrito. Repeat with the remaining tortillas, place these burritos on a baking sheet, brush them with olive oil and then bake for 15 minutes until golden. Serve burritos with guacamole.

Per serving: Calories: 421Kcal; Fat: 9g; Carbs: 70g; Protein: 15g

329. Spicy Nut-Butter Noodles

Preparation time: 15 minutes
Cooking time: 15 minutes **Servings:** 4
Ingredients:

- 1 package soba noodles - ½ cup vegetable stock
- 1 tablespoon minced fresh ginger
- 2 garlic cloves, minced
- ¼ cup soy sauce
- ¼ cup peanut butter or another nut butter
- 1 teaspoon sriracha or chili paste
- 4 green onions (white and green parts), chopped
- chopped peanuts (optional)

Directions:
Prepare the soba noodles according to package directions. Drain and set aside. In a small saucepan, combine the vegetable stock, ginger, garlic, soy sauce, peanut butter, and Sriracha over medium-high heat, stirring until the peanut butter is melted and the sauce is heated through. Toss the sauce with the hot noodles. Top with chopped green onions and peanuts, if using. Serve immediately.

Per serving: Calories: 401Kcal; Fat: 36.83g; Carbs: 15.61g; Protein: 6.76g

330. Lentil and Turnip Soup

Preparation time: 10 minutes
Cooking time: 25 minutes **Servings:** 4
Ingredients:

- 1 cup red lentils
- 2 medium white onions, peeled, sliced
- 14 ounces turnip, peeled, cubed
- 2 tablespoons lemon juice
- 2 ½ teaspoons salt - 2 bay leaves
- 2 tablespoons lemon zest
- 4 tablespoons olive oil
- 6 cups boiling water

Directions:
Take a large pot, place it over medium heat, add oil, and then let it heat. Add onions, cook for 5 minutes until onions turn tender, and then add turnip pieces along with red lentils and bay leaves.
Pour in the water, stir until mixed, and then boil the soup for 15 minutes until lentils and turnip turn tender. Add salt, lemon juice, and zest into the juice, stir until mixed, and then cook for 3 minutes.
Serve straight away.

Per serving: Calories: 111.7Kcal; Fat: 2g; Carbs: 18.2g; Fiber: 6.4g; Protein: 6.7g

331. Tomato and Chickpea Curry

Preparation time: 5 minutes
Cooking time: 15 minutes
Servings: 4
Ingredients:

- 28 ounces cooked chickpeas
- 2 medium white onions, peeled, sliced
- 4 medium tomatoes, chopped
- 1 teaspoon salt - 4 tablespoons olive oil
- 2 teaspoons curry powder
- 1 tablespoon soy sauce
- 1 teaspoon ground cumin
- 2 bay leaves
- 14 ounces coconut milk, unsweetened

Directions:
Take a large pot, place it over medium-high heat, add oil and then let it heat until hot.
Add onion, stir in salt and then cook for 2 minutes.
Add bay leaves and all the spices, stir until mixed, and then cook for 1 minute. Add chickpeas, cook for another minute, add tomatoes and then continue cooking for 3 minutes.
Add milk, simmer for 5 minutes until thoroughly hot, stir in milk and soy sauce and then cook for 1 minute. Serve straight away.

Per serving: Calories: 177.3Kcal; Fat: 5g; Carbs: 29g; Fiber: 6.2g; Protein: 6g

332. Lentil Stroganoff

Preparation time: 10 minutes
Cooking time: 50 minutes **Servings:** 4;
Ingredients:

- 1 cup brown lentils
- 1 medium white onion, peeled, chopped
- 2 dill pickles - 1 teaspoon salt
- ¼ teaspoon ground nutmeg
- 1 tablespoon paprika
- 1 tablespoon soy sauce
- 5 tablespoons tomato sauce
- 2 tablespoons cashew cream
- 3 cups of water

Directions:
Take a medium pot, place it over medium-high heat, add lentil, and then pour in water. Add onion, stir until mixed, bring the mixture to a boil and then continue boiling the lentils for 40 minutes until lentils turn soft. Add pickles and tomato sauce, stir in salt, paprika, nutmeg, soy sauce, and cashew cream and bring the mixture to a boil. Serve straight away.

Per serving: Calories: 240Kcal; Fat: 100g; Carbs: 33g; Fiber: 4g; Protein: 24.5g

333. Kung Pao Lentils

Preparation time: 10 minutes;
Cooking time: 45 minutes; **Servings:** 3;
Ingredients:
For the Lentils:

- ½ cup brown lentils

- 1 ½ cups water
- ¼ teaspoon salt

For the Sauce:
- 3 tablespoons soy sauce
- 2 tablespoons of rice wine vinegar
- 1 tablespoon rice wine
- 1 teaspoon hoisin sauce
- 1 teaspoon toasted sesame oil
- 2 tablespoons maple syrup
- ¼ teaspoon lime zest
- 2 teaspoons cornstarch
- 3 tablespoons water

For the Vegetables:
- ¾ cup chopped celery
- 3 tablespoons cashews
- 1 medium green bell pepper, cored, chopped
- ½ cup chopped red onion
- 1 medium red bell pepper, cored, chopped
- 1 tablespoon minced garlic
- ½ teaspoon ground black pepper
- 1 teaspoon red pepper flakes
- 1-inch piece of ginger, grated
- 2 tablespoons lemon juice
- 2 teaspoon grapeseed oil

Directions:
Prepare the lentils and for this, take a medium saucepan, place it over medium-high heat, add lentils in it, pour in water, and then stir in salt.
Bring the lentils to boil, cook for 6 minutes, switch heat to medium level, and then continue boiling for 25 minutes until lentils turn tender.
When done, let the lentil rest for 5 minutes, drain excess liquid from the pan, and then set aside until required.
Prepare the sauce and for this, take a medium bowl, place all of its ingredients in it and then stir until combined, set aside until required.
Prepare the vegetables and for this, take a large skillet pan, place it over medium-high heat, add oil and then let it heat until hot.
Add onion, cook for 3 minutes, add cashews and then cook for 1 minute.
Stir in bell peppers, celery, garlic, and ginger, cook for 4 minutes, add lentils, pour in the sauce, and then stir until mixed.
Switch heat to the low level and then cook the lentils for 4 minutes until the sauce has thickened.
Stir in red pepper flakes, black pepper, and lemon juice, and then serve.
Per serving: Calories: 283Kcal; Fat: 9g; Carbs: 37g; Fiber: 12g; Protein: 12g

334. Lentil Brown Rice Soup

Preparation time: 10 minutes
Cooking time: 50 minutes
Servings: 4;
Ingredients:
- ½ cup diced carrots
- ½ cup brown lentils, soaked
- 1 cup broccoli florets
- 1/3 cup brown rice, soaked
- ½ cup diced red bell pepper
- ½ of a medium white onion, peeled, chopped
- 1 cup baby spinach
- 1 ½ cups diced tomatoes
- 1 green chili, chopped
- 1 tablespoon minced garlic
- 1-inch piece of ginger, grated
- ¾ teaspoon salt
- ½ teaspoon turmeric powder
- ¼ teaspoon ground black pepper
- ½ teaspoon cumin seeds
- 1 bay leaf
- ½ teaspoon mustard seeds
- ½ teaspoon paprika
- 1 teaspoon coriander powder
- ½ teaspoon curry powder
- ¼ teaspoon chipotle pepper
- 1 teaspoon lemon juice
- 1 teaspoon olive oil
- 2 teaspoons ketchup
- 4 cups of water

Directions:
Take a large saucepan, place it over medium heat, add oil and then let it heat until hot.
Add mustard and cumin seeds, cook for 1 minute until golden, add onion, ginger, garlic, and bay leaf, and then continue cooking for 5 minutes. Add all the spices, stir until mixed, cook for 1 minute, add tomatoes, and then cook for 5 minutes until mixture turn saucy.
Add all the vegetables, season with salt, add ketchup and then stir until mixed.
Add rice and lentils, pour in the water, stir until mixed, cover the pan with its lid and then cook for 40 minutes until lentils and vegetables have thoroughly cooked.
When done, add spinach into the soup, stir until mixed, and then continue cooking for 5 minutes until spinach leaves wilt. Serve straight away.
Per serving: Calories: 205Kcal; Fat: 2g; Carbs: 37g; Fiber: 10g; Protein: 9.5g

335. Peanut and Lentil Soup

Preparation time: 5 minutes
Cooking time: 35 minutes **Servings:**
Ingredients:
- ½ cup red lentils
- ½ cup diced zucchini
- ½ cup diced sweet potato
- ½ cup diced potato
- ½ cup chopped broccoli florets
- ½ of a medium onion, peeled, chopped
- 2 tomatoes
- ½ cup baby spinach
- 2 tablespoons peanuts
- 4 cloves of garlic, peeled
- 1-inch piece of ginger

- 1 ½ teaspoon ground cumin
- ¾ teaspoon salt
- ¼ teaspoon ground black pepper
- 2 teaspoons ground coriander
- 1 ½ teaspoon Harissa Spice Blend
- 1 tablespoon sambal oelek
- 1 teaspoon lemon juice
- ¼ cup peanut butter
- 1 tablespoon tomato paste
- 1 teaspoon olive oil
- 2 ½ cups vegetable stock
- 2 tablespoons chopped cilantro

Directions:
Take a large saucepan, place it over medium heat, add oil and then let it heat. Add onion, stir until coated in oil, and then cook for 5 minutes.
Place tomatoes in a blender, add garlic, ginger, all the spices, tomato paste, and chili sauce, and then pulse until pureed. Pour the tomato mixture into the onion mixture, stir until mixed, and then cook for 5 minutes. Add half of the nuts, lentils, and all the vegetables, stir in salt, peanut butter, and lemon juice, pour in the stock, cover the pan with its lid and then cook for 20 minutes until vegetables turn tender.
Add spinach, continue cooking for 5 minutes, garnish with cilantro, and then serve.
Per serving: Calories: 411Kcal; Fat: 17g; Carbs: 50g; Fiber: 18g; Protein: 20g

336. Lentil with Spinach

Preparation time: 5 minutes;
Cooking time: 25 minutes; **Servings:** 2;
Ingredients:
- ½ cup red lentils
- 1 cup chopped spinach
- ½ teaspoon mustard seeds
- ½ teaspoon ground turmeric
- 1/3 teaspoon cumin seeds
- 1/3 teaspoon cayenne
- 1/3 teaspoon nigella seeds
- 2/3 teaspoon salt
- 1/8 teaspoon fennel seeds
- 1/8 teaspoon fenugreek seeds
- 1 teaspoon olive oil
- 2 ½ cups water

Directions:
Take a large saucepan, place it over medium heat, add oil and then let it heat until hot. Add all the seeds, stir until coated in oil, and then cook for 1 to 2 minutes until seeds begin to pop. Stir in cayenne pepper and turmeric, stir in lentils and then cook for 1 minute until roasted. Season with salt, pour in the water, and then cook for 20 minutes until lentils have thoroughly cooked; cover the pan partially with its lid. Stir in spinach, simmer for 2 minutes until spinach leaves wilts, and then serve.
Per serving: Calories: 193Kcal; Fat: 3g; Carbs: 28g; Fiber: 14g; Protein: 12g

337. Beans And Lentils Soup

Preparation time: 10 minutes
Cooking time: 48 minutes **Servings:** 4
Ingredients:
- 2 tbsp water
- 1½ cups onion, diced
- 3 cups potatoes, cut into chunks
- ½ cup celery, diced
- 1 cup carrots, diced
- 4 cloves garlic, minced
- 1½ tsp dried rosemary leaves
- 1 tsp dried thyme leaves
- 1½ tsp ground mustard
- 1 tsp sea salt
- ¼ tsp ground black pepper
- 1 cup green lentils, rinsed
- 2 cups vegetable stock
- 5 cups water
- 1 tbsp red miso
- 1½ tbsp blackstrap molasses
- 2 dried bay leaves
- 15-oz white beans

Directions:
Heat a large pot over medium heat. Add all ingredients to it and cook for 8 minutes, stirring occasionally. Increase heat and bring it to a boil. Once it is boiled, let it cook for 40 minutes. Remove bay leaf. Serve and enjoy.
Per serving: Calories: 230Kcal; Fat: 1.8g; Carbs: 40g; Fiber: 10.2g; Protein: 10.5g

CHAPTER 20:
Stuffed and Baked Vegetables

338. Instant Savory Gigante Beans
Preparation time: 10-30 minutes
Cooking time: 55 minutes **Servings:** 6
Ingredients:
- 1 lb Gigante Beans soaked overnight
- 1/2 cup olive oil
- 1 onion sliced
- 2 cloves garlic crushed or minced
- 1 red bell pepper (cut into 1/2-inch pieces)
- 2 carrots, sliced
- 1/2 tsp salt and ground black pepper
- 2 tomatoes peeled, grated
- 1 Tbsp celery (chopped)
- 1 Tbsp tomato paste (or ketchup)
- 3/4 tsp sweet paprika
- 1 tsp oregano
- 1 cup vegetable broth

Directions:
Soak Gigante beans overnight.
Press the SAUTÉ button on your Instant Pot and heat the oil. Sauté onion, garlic, sweet pepper, carrots with a pinch of salt for 3 - 4 minutes; stir occasionally.
Add rinsed Gigante beans into your Instant Pot along with all remaining ingredients and stir well.
Lock lid into place and set on the MANUAL setting for 25 minutes. When the beep sounds, quickly release the pressure by pressing Cancel and twisting the steam handle to the Venting position.
Taste and adjust seasonings to taste. Serve warm or cold. Keep refrigerated.
Per serving: Calories: 502Kcal; Fat: 19.6g; Carbs: 173g; Protein: 18g

339. Instant Turmeric Risotto
Preparation time: 10-30 minutes
Cooking time: 40 minutes
Servings: 4
Ingredients:
- 4 Tbsp olive oil
- 1 cup onion
- 1 tsp minced garlic
- 2 cups long-grain rice
- 3 cups vegetable broth
- 1/2 tsp paprika (smoked)
- 1/2 tsp turmeric
- 1/2 tsp nutmeg
- 2 Tbsp fresh basil leaves chopped
- Salt and ground black pepper to taste

Directions:
Press the SAUTÉ button on your Instant Pot and heat oil. Sauté the onion and garlic with a pinch of salt until softened. Add the rice and all remaining ingredients and stir well. Lock lid into place and set on and select the "RICE" button for 10 minutes.
Press "Cancel" when the timer beeps and carefully flip the Quick Release valve to let the pressure out. Taste and adjust seasonings to taste. Serve.
Per serving: Calories: 560Kcal; Fat: 18.57g; Carbs: 90.5 g; Protein: 7.2g

340. Nettle Soup with Rice
Preparation time: 10-30 minutes
Cooking time: 40 minutes **Servings:** 5
Ingredients:
- 3 Tbsp of olive oil
- 2 onions finely chopped
- 2 cloves garlic finely chopped
- Salt and freshly ground black pepper
- 4 medium potatoes cut into cubes
- 1 cup of rice - 1 Tbsp arrowroot
- 2 cups vegetable broth
- 2 cups of water
- 1 bunch of young nettle leaves packed
- 1/2 cup fresh parsley finely chopped
- 1 tsp cumin

Directions:
Heat olive oil in a large pot. Sauté onion and garlic with a pinch of salt until softened. Add potato, rice, and arrowroot; sauté for 2 to 3 minutes. Pour broth and water, stir well, cover and cook over medium heat for about 20 minutes. Cook over medium heat for about 20 minutes.
Add young nettle leaves, parsley, and cumin; stir and cook for 5 to 7 minutes. Transfer the soup to a blender and blend until combined well. Taste and adjust salt and pepper. Serve hot.
Per serving: Calories: 421Kcal; Fat: 9.8g; Carbs: 78g; Protein: 6.8g

341. Okra with Grated Tomatoes (Slow Cooker)
Preparation time: 10-30 minutes
Cooking time: 3 hours and 10 minutes **Servings:** 4
Ingredients:
- 2 lbs fresh okra cleaned
- 2 onions finely chopped
- 2 cloves garlic finely sliced
- 2 carrots sliced
- 2 ripe tomatoes grated
- 1 cup of water

- 4 Tbsp olive oil
- Salt and ground black pepper
- 1 Tbsp fresh parsley finely chopped

Directions:
Add okra in your Crock-Pot: sprinkle with a pinch of salt and pepper. Add in chopped onion, garlic, carrots, and grated tomatoes; stir well. Pour water and oil, season with salt, pepper, and give a good stir.
Cover and cook on LOW for 2-3 hours or until tender. Open the lid and add fresh parsley; stir. Taste and adjust salt and pepper. Serve hot.
Per serving: Calories: 223.5Kcal; Fat: 14g; Carbs: 5.5g; Protein: 1.7g

342. Oven-baked Smoked Lentil 'Burgers'

Preparation time: 10-30 minutes
Cooking time: 1 hour and 20 minutes **Servings:** 6
Ingredients:

- 1 1/2 cups dried lentils
- 3 cups of water
- Salt and ground black pepper to taste
- 2 Tbsp olive oil
- 1 onion finely diced
- 2 cloves minced garlic
- 1 cup button mushrooms sliced
- 2 Tbsp tomato paste
- 1/2 tsp fresh basil finely chopped
- 1 cup chopped almonds
- 3 tsp balsamic vinegar
- 3 Tbsp coconut aminos
- 1 tsp liquid smoke
- 3/4 cup silken tofu soft
- 3/4 cup corn starch

Directions:
Cook lentils in salted water until tender or for about 30-35 minutes; rinse, drain, and set aside. Heat oil in a frying skillet and sauté onion, garlic, and mushrooms for 4 to 5 minutes; stir occasionally. Stir in the tomato paste, salt, basil, salt, and black pepper; cook for 2 to 3 minutes. Stir in almonds, vinegar, coconut aminos, liquid smoke, and lentils. Remove from heat and stir in blended tofu and corn starch. Keep stirring until all ingredients combined well. Form mixture into patties and refrigerate for an hour. Preheat oven to 350 F.
Line a baking dish with parchment paper and arrange patties on the pan.
Bake for 20 to 25 minutes.
Serve hot with buns, green salad, tomato sauce...etc.
Per serving: Calories: 439Kcal; Fat: 17.48g; Carbs: 36.70g; Protein: 9.8g

343. Powerful Spinach and Mustard Leaves Puree

Preparation time: 10-30 minutes
Cooking time: 50 minutes **Servings:** 4
Ingredients:

- 2 Tbsp almond butter
- 1 onion finely diced
- 2 Tbsp minced garlic
- 1 tsp salt and black pepper (or to taste)
- 1 lb mustard leaves, cleaned, rinsed
- 1 lb frozen spinach thawed
- 1 tsp coriander - 1 tsp ground cumin
- 1/2 cup almond milk

Directions:
Press the SAUTÉ button on your Instant Pot and heat the almond butter. Sauté onion, garlic, and a pinch of salt for 2-3 minutes; stir occasionally. Add spinach and the mustard greens and stir for a minute or two. Season with salt and pepper, coriander, and cumin; give a good stir. Lock lid into place and set on the MANUAL setting for 15 minutes. Use Quick Release - turn the valve from sealing to venting to release the pressure. Transfer mixture to a blender, add almond milk, and blend until smooth.
Taste and adjust seasonings. Serve.
Per serving: Calories: 180.53Kcal; Fat: 82.6g; Carbs: 4.5g; Protein: 3.5g

344. Quinoa and Rice Stuffed Peppers (Oven-Baked)

Preparation time: 10-30 minutes
Cooking time: 35 minutes **Servings:** 8
Ingredients:

- 3/4 cup long-grain rice
- 8 bell peppers (any color)
- 2 Tbsp olive oil
- 1 onion finely diced
- 2 cloves chopped garlic
- 1 can (11 oz) crushed tomatoes
- 1 tsp cumin - 1 tsp coriander
- 4 Tbsp ground walnuts
- 2 cups cooked quinoa
- 4 Tbsp chopped parsley
- Salt and ground black pepper to taste

Directions:
Preheat oven to 400 F/200 C. Boil rice and drain in a colander. Cut the top stem section of the pepper off, remove the remaining pith and seeds, rinse peppers. Heat oil in a large frying skillet, and sauté onion, and garlic until soft. Add tomatoes, cumin, ground almonds, salt, pepper, and coriander; stir well and simmer for 2 minutes, stirring constantly. Remove from the heat and add the rice, quinoa, and parsley; stir well. Taste and adjust salt and pepper.
Fill the peppers with a mixture, and place peppers cut side-up in a baking dish; drizzle with little oil.
Bake for 15 minutes. Serve warm.
Per serving: Calories: 335Kcal; Fat: 9.58g; Carbs: 70g; Protein: 14g

345. Silk Tofu Penne with Spinach

Preparation time: 10-30 minutes
Cooking time: 25 minutes **Servings:** 4
Ingredients:

- 1 lb penne, uncooked
- 12 oz of frozen spinach, thawed

- 1 cup silken tofu mashed
- 1/2 cup soy milk (unsweetened)
- 1/2 cup vegetable broth
- 1 Tbsp white wine vinegar
- 1/2 tsp Italian seasoning
- Salt and ground pepper to taste

Directions:
Cook penne pasta; rinse and drain in a colander. Drain spinach well. Place spinach with all remaining ingredients in a blender and beat until smooth. Pour the spinach mixture over pasta. Taste and adjust the salt and pepper. Store pasta in an airtight container in the refrigerator for 3 to 5 days.
Per serving: Calories: 492Kcal; Fat: 27g; Carbs: 35g; Protein: 13g

346. Slow-Cooked Butter Beans, Okra and Potatoes Stew

Preparation time: 10-30 minutes
Cooking time: 6 hours and 5 minutes
Servings: 6
Ingredients:
- 2 cups frozen butter (lima) beans, thawed
- 1 cup frozen okra, thawed
- 2 large Russet potatoes cut into cubes
- 1 can (6 oz) whole-kernel corn, drained
- 1 large carrot sliced
- 1 green bell pepper finely chopped
- 1 cup green peas
- 1/2 cup chopped celery
- 1 medium onion finely chopped
- 2 cups vegetable broth
- 2 cans (6 oz) tomato sauce
- 1 cup of water
- 1/2 tsp salt and freshly ground black pepper

Directions:
Combine all ingredients in your Slow Cooker; give a good stir. Cover and cook on HIGH for 6 hours.
Taste, adjust seasonings, and serve hot.
Per serving: Calories: 241.7Kcal; Fat: 1.28g; Carbs: 95g; Protein: 26g

347. Soya Minced Stuffed Eggplants

Preparation time: 10-30 minutes
Cooking time: 1 hour
Servings: 4
Ingredients:
- 2 eggplants
- 1/3 cup sesame oil
- 1 onion finely chopped
- 2 garlic cloves minced
- 1 lb soya mince
- Salt and ground black pepper
- 1/3 cup almond milk
- 2 Tbsp fresh parsley, chopped
- 1/3 cup fresh basil chopped
- 1 tsp fennel powder
- 1 cup of water
- 4 Tbsp tomato paste (fresh or canned)

Directions:
Rinse and slice the eggplant in half lengthwise. Submerge sliced eggplant into a container with salted water. Soak soya mince in water for 10 to 15 minutes. Preheat oven to 400 F. Rinse eggplant and dry with a clean towel. Heat oil in a large frying skillet, and sauté onion, and garlic with a pinch of salt until softened.
Add drained soya mince, and cook over medium heat until cooked through. Add all remaining ingredients (except water and tomato paste) and cook for a further 5 minutes; remove from heat. Scoop out the seed part of each eggplant. Spoon in the filling and arrange stuffed eggplants onto the large baking dish.
Dissolve tomato paste into the water and pour evenly over eggplants. Bake for 20 to 25 minutes. Serve warm. **Per serving:** Calories: 287Kcal; Fat: 16.42g; Carbs: 21g; Protein: 3.5g

348. Triple Beans and Corn Salad

Preparation time: 10-30 minutes
Cooking time: 15 minutes **Servings:** 8
Ingredients:
- 1 can (15 oz) kidney beans, drained and rinsed
- 1 can (15 oz) white beans, drained and rinsed
- 1 can (15 oz) black beans, rinsed and drained
- 1 can (11 oz) frozen corn kernels thawed
- 1 green bell pepper, chopped
- 1 red onion, chopped
- 1 clove crushed garlic
- 1 Tbsp salt and ground black pepper to taste
- 1/2 cup olive oil - 3 Tbsp red wine vinegar
- 3 Tbsp lemon juice
- 1/4 cup chopped fresh cilantro
- 1/2 Tbsp ground cumin

Directions:
In a large bowl, combine beans, corn, pepper, onion, and garlic. Season salad with salt and pepper; stir to combine well. In a separate bowl, whisk together olive oil, red wine vinegar, lemon juice, cilantro, and cumin. Pour olive oil dressing over salad, and toss to combine well. Refrigerate for one hour and serve.
Per serving: Calories: 696Kcal; Fat: 155g; Carbs: 85g; Protein: 35g

349. Vegan Raw Pistachio Flaxseed 'Burgers'

Preparation time: 10-30 minutes
Cooking time: 15 minutes **Servings:** 4
Ingredients:
- 1 cup ground flaxseed
- 1 cup pistachio finely sliced
- 2 cups cooked spinach drained
- 2 Tbsp sesame oil
- 4 cloves garlic finely sliced
- 2 Tbsp lemon juice, freshly squeezed

- Sea salt to taste

Directions:
Add all ingredients into a food processor or high-speed blender; process until combined well.
Form mixture into patties. Refrigerate for one hour.
Serve with your favorite vegetable dip.
Per serving: Calories: 273Kcal; Fat: 21.6g; Carbs: 45g; Protein: 18g

350. Vegan Red Bean 'Fricassee'

Preparation time: 10-30 minutes
Cooking time: 40 minutes **Servings:** 4
Ingredients:
- 4 Tbsp olive oil
- 1 onion finely sliced
- 2 cloves garlic finely chopped
- Salt and freshly ground black pepper to taste
- 1 can (15 oz) red beans
- 1 large carrot grated
- 1 1/2 cup vegetable broth
- 1 cup of water
- 1 can (6 oz) tomato paste
- 1 tsp ground paprika
- 1 tsp parsley

Directions:
Heat oil in a large pot and sauté onion and garlic with a pinch of salt until soft. Add red beans together with all remaining ingredients and stir well. In a separate pan, sauté onion and garlic in the olive oil. Reduce heat to medium, and simmer for 25 to 30 minutes.
Taste and adjust salt and pepper if needed. Serve hot.
Per serving: Calories: 318Kcal; Fat: 15.4g; Carbs: 73g; Protein: 22g

351. Baked Cheesy Eggplant with Marinara

Preparation time: 5 minutes
Cooking time: 45 minutes
Servings: 3
Ingredients:
- 1 clove garlic, sliced
- 1 large eggplant
- 1 tablespoon olive oil
- 1/2 pinch salt, or as needed
- 1/4 cup and 2 tablespoons dry bread crumbs
- 1/4 cup and 2 tablespoons ricotta cheese
- 1/4 cup grated Parmesan cheese
- 1/4 cup water, plus more as needed
- 1/4 teaspoon red pepper flakes
- 1-1/2 cups prepared marinara sauce
- 2 tablespoons shredded pepper jack cheese
- freshly ground black pepper to taste

Directions:
Preparing the ingredients. Cut eggplant crosswise into 5 pieces. Peel and chop two pieces into ½-inch cubes. Lightly grease baking pan of Air Fryer with 1 tbsp olive oil for 5 minutes, heat oil at 390°F. Add half eggplant strips and cook for 2 minutes per side. Transfer to a plate. Add 1 ½ tsp olive oil and add garlic. Cook for a minute. Add chopped eggplants. Season with pepper flakes and salt. Cook for 4 minutes. Lower heat to 330°F. and continue cooking eggplants until soft, around 8 minutes more.
Stir in water and marinara sauce. Cook for 7 minutes until heated through. Stirring every now and then. Transfer to a bowl. In a bowl, whisk well pepper, salt, pepper jack cheese, Parmesan cheese, and ricotta. Evenly spread cheeses over eggplant strips and then fold in half. Lay folded eggplant in baking pan. Pour the marinara sauce on top. In a small bowl, whisk well olive oil and bread crumbs. Sprinkle all over the sauce. Air Frying. Lock the air fryer lid. Cook for 15 minutes at 390°F until tops are lightly browned.
Serve and enjoy.
Per serving: Calories: 405Kcal; Fat: 21.4g; Carbs: 25g; Protein: 12.7g

352. Creamy Spinach Quiche

Preparation time: 10 minutes
Cooking time: 20 minutes **Servings:** 4
Ingredients:
- Premade quiche crust, chilled and rolled flat to a 7-inch round
- 6 eggs - ¼ cup of milk
- Pinch of salt and pepper
- 1 clove of garlic, peeled and finely minced
- ½ cup of cooked spinach, drained and coarsely chopped
- ¼ cup of shredded mozzarella cheese
- ¼ cup of shredded cheddar cheese

Directions:
Preparing the ingredients. Preheat the Instant Crisp Air Fryer to 360 degrees. Press the premade crust into a 7-inch pie tin or any appropriately sized glass or ceramic heat-safe dish. Press and trim at the edges if necessary. With a fork, pierce several holes in the dough to allow air circulation and prevent cracking of the crust while cooking. In a mixing bowl, beat the eggs until fluffy and until the yolks and white are evenly combined. Add milk, garlic, spinach, salt and pepper, and half the cheddar and mozzarella cheese to the eggs. Set the rest of the cheese aside for now, and stir the mixture until completely blended. Make sure the spinach is not clumped together but rather spread among the other ingredients. Pour the mixture into the pie crust slowly and carefully to avoid splashing. The mixture should almost fill the crust, but not completely – leaving a ¼ inch of crust at the edges. Air Frying. Lock the air fryer lid. Set the air-fryer timer for 15 minutes. After 15 minutes, the Instant Crisp Air Fryer will shut off, and the quiche will already be firm and the crust begins to brown. Sprinkle the rest of the cheddar and mozzarella cheese on top of the quiche filling. Reset the Instant Crisp Air Fryer at 360 degrees for 5 minutes. After 5 minutes, when the Instant Crisp Air Fryer shuts off, the cheese will have formed an exquisite crust on top and the quiche will be golden brown and perfect. Remove from the Instant Crisp Air Fryer using oven mitts or tongs, and set on a heat-safe surface to cool for a few minutes before cutting.
Per serving: Calories: 285Kcal; Fat: 20.5g; Carbs: 15g; Protein: 8.6g

353. Stuffed Mushrooms
Preparation time: 7 minutes
Cooking time: 8 minutes **Servings:** 12
Ingredients:
- ½ Onion, Diced - ½ Bell Pepper, Diced
- 1 Small Carrot, Diced
- 24 Medium Size Mushrooms (Separate the caps & stalks)
- 1 cup Shredded Cheddar Plus Extra for the Top
- ½ cup Sour Cream

Directions:
Preparing the ingredients. Chop the mushrooms stalks finely and fry them up with the onion, pepper, and carrot at 350 ° for 8 minutes. When the veggies are fairly tender, stir in the sour cream & the cheese. Keep on the heat until the cheese has melted and everything is mixed nicely. Now grab the mushroom caps and heap a plop of filling on each one. Place in the fryer basket and top with a little extra cheese.
Per serving: Calories: 185Kcal; Fat: 20.5g; Carbs: 16g; Protein: 8.6g

354. Winter Vegetarian Frittata
Preparation time: 5 minutes
Cooking time: 30 minutes
Servings: 4
Ingredients:
- 1 leek, peeled and thinly sliced into rings
- 2 cloves garlic, finely minced
- 3 medium-sized carrots, finely chopped
- 2 tablespoons olive oil
- 6 large-sized eggs
- Sea salt and ground black pepper, to taste
- 1/2 teaspoon dried marjoram, finely minced
- 1/2 cup yellow cheese of choice

Directions:
Preparing the ingredients. Sauté the leek, garlic, and carrot in hot olive oil until they are tender and fragrant; reserve. In the meantime, preheat your Air Fryer to 330 degrees F. In a bowl, whisk the eggs along with the salt, ground black pepper, and marjoram. Then, grease the inside of your baking dish with a nonstick cooking spray. Pour the whisked eggs into the baking dish. Stir in the sautéed carrot mixture. Top with the cheese shreds. Air Frying. Place the baking dish in the Instant Crisp Air Fryer cooking basket. Lock the air fryer lid. Cook for about 30 minutes and serve warm.
Per serving: Calories: 230Kcal; Fat: 15.5g; Carbs: 30.6g; Protein: 12.4g

355. Cheddar, Squash, And Zucchini Casserole
Preparation time: 5 minutes
Cooking time: 30 minutes **Servings:** 4
Ingredients:
- 1 egg
- 5 saltine crackers, or as needed, crushed
- 2 tablespoons bread crumbs
- 1/2-pound yellow squash, sliced
- 1/2-pound zucchini, sliced
- 1/2 cup shredded Cheddar cheese
- 1-1/2 teaspoons white sugar
- 1/2 teaspoon salt
- 1/4 onion, diced
- 1/4 cup biscuit baking mix
- 1/4 cup butter

Directions:
Preparing the ingredients. Lightly grease baking pan of Instant Crisp Air Fryer with cooking spray. Add onion, zucchini, and yellow squash. Cover pan with foil and for 15 minutes, cook on 360° F or until tender. Stir in salt, sugar, egg, butter, baking mix, and cheddar cheese. Mix well. Fold in crushed crackers. Top with bread crumbs. Air Frying Lock the air fryer lid. Cook for 15 minutes at 390° F until tops are lightly browned. Serve and enjoy.
Per serving: Calories: 275Kcal; Fat: 21g; Carbs: 7g; Protein: 13g

356. Fresh Tomato Basil Tart
Preparation time: 30 minutes
Cooking time: 55 minutes **Servings:** 8
Ingredients:
- 2/3 cup whole wheat flour
- 1/3 cup flour, all purpose
- ½ cup cold butter
- 5 Tbsp cold water
- 4 tomatoes, sliced
- 3 cups mozzarella cheese, shredded
- Salt, pepper, to taste

Directions:
Mix the flours, butter, and water to form a dough. Refrigerate for 30 minutes. Roll out the dough. Bake in a tart pan at 350°F for 15 minutes. Top with cheese and tomato. Garnish with salt, pepper. Bake for another 30 minutes. Serve warm.
Note: For ovo-lacto vegetarian, lacto vegetarian, pescatarian diets.
Per serving: Calories: 300Kcal; Fat: 23g; Carbs: 14g; Protein: 13g

357. Quinoa Stuffed Bell Peppers
Preparation time: 15 minutes
Cooking time: 10 minutes **Servings:** 4
Ingredients:
- 4 bell peppers, halved, hollowed out
- ½ cup quinoa, cooked
- 1/3 cup sun-dried tomatoes
- 12 black olives, halved
- ½ cup baby spinach
- 2 cloves garlic, minced
- Salt, pepper, to taste

Directions:
Bake the hollowed-out peppers in an oven at 400°F for 10 minutes.
Mix the cooked quinoa with the remaining ingredients.
Stuff peppers. Serve.
Per serving: Calories: 126Kcal; Fat: 5g; Carbs: 19g; Protein: 3g

358. Stuffed Peppers

Preparation time: 15 minutes
Cooking time: 15 minutes
Servings: 6
Ingredients:
- 1 cup Kalamata olives, halved
- 6 oz. goat cheese, crumbled
- ¼ cup basil, chopped
- 2 Tbsp garlic cloves, chopped
- 1 lb sweet peppers, halved, seeded
- Salt, pepper, to taste

Directions:
Preheat oven to 450° F.
Combine all ingredients and stir well. Stuff the peppers with the mixture. Broil peppers for 15 min on a baking sheet.
Note:
For ovo-lacto vegetarian, lacto vegetarian, pescatarian diets.
Per serving: Calories: 130Kcal; Fat: 7g; Carbs: 15g; Protein: 3g

359. Roasted Vegetable Hummus Plate

Preparation time: 15 minutes
Cooking time: 10 minutes **Servings:** 1
Ingredients:
- 4 asparagus spears
- 1 pepper, seeded, cut into strips
- 1 cup mixed salad greens
- ¼ cup hummus

Directions:
Preheat oven to 425°F. Combine asparagus and pepper strips with olive oil and put them on the baking sheet. Roast for about 10 minutes.
Put the salad greens on a serving plate, top with roasted vegetables. Dip vegetables in hummus.
Per serving: Calories: 173Kcal; Fat: 7g; Carbs: 24g; Protein: 9g

360. Stuffed Tomatoes with Bread Crumbs and Cheese

Preparation time: 10 minutes
Cooking time: 20 minutes
Servings: 4
Ingredients:
- 4 medium-large tomatoes - ¾ cup breadcrumbs
- 1 batch vegan cheddar cheese sauce
- ½ tsp onion powder - Salt, pepper, to taste

Directions:
Preheat oven to 350°F. Cut off the top of tomatoes, season with salt and pepper. Combine the remaining ingredients. Spoon the mixture on the top of each tomato. Bake on a baking sheet for 20 minutes. Serve. **Per serving:** Calories: 215Kcal; Fat: 7g; Carbs: 67g; Protein: 7g

361. Stuffed Baked Potato

Preparation time: 20 minutes
Cooking time: 1 hour 15 minutes **Servings:** 2
Ingredients:
- 2 large Russet potatoes
- ½ cup non-dairy milk
- 4 Tbsp oil-free hummus
- 1 cup cooked vegetables, chopped
- ½ tsp hot sauce
- Salt, pepper, to taste

Directions:
Preheat oven to 375°F. Bake the potatoes for 1 hour. Split in half and scoop out the flesh. Mash the potato flesh with the remaining ingredients. Spoon mixture back into the potato shells. Bake for 15 minutes. Serve immediately.
Per serving: Calories: 310Kcal; Fat: 8g; Carbs: 56g; Protein: 9g

362. Oil-Free Rainbow Roasted Vegetables

Preparation time: 5 minutes
Cooking time: 25 minutes **Servings:** 4
Ingredients:
- 3 cups red bell peppers, chopped
- 2 cups carrots, chopped
- 1 2/3 cup zucchini, chopped
- 1 cup broccoli florets
- 1 cup onions, chopped
- 1 Tbsp dried thyme

Directions:
Preheat oven to 400°F. Put the vegetables on the baking sheet, add the thyme. Bake for about 25 minutes. Serve or store the veggies in a sealed container.
Per serving: Calories: 56Kcal; Fat: 8g; Carbs: 56g; Protein: 9g

363. Kofta-Style Chickpea "Meatball" Pitas

Preparation time: 10 minutes
Cooking time: 35 minutes **Servings:** 4
Ingredients:
- 1 tablespoon unsalted butter
- ½ cup finely chopped mushrooms
- 1 (15-ounce) can chickpeas, drained and rinsed
- 2 teaspoons garlic paste or minced garlic
- 1 tablespoon dried oregano
- 1 teaspoon ground allspice
- ½ teaspoon kosher salt
- ¼ teaspoon freshly ground black pepper
- ½ cup panko
- 1 large egg
- 2 pita rounds
- 3 tablespoons Tzatziki, plus more for serving
- Cherry tomatoes, quartered, for serving
- Red onion slices
- Baby spinach for serving

Directions:
Preheat the oven to 350°F. Line a baking sheet with parchment paper. Melt the butter in a large skillet over medium heat. Add the mushrooms and sauté until softened, about 5 minutes. Add the chickpeas, garlic, oregano, allspice, salt, and pepper, and sauté for another 5 minutes. Coarsely mash the

chickpeas with a fork and place everything in a bowl to cool for 5 minutes. Add the panko and egg, and stir with a metal spoon to mix well. Use an ice cream scooper or large spoon to form 8 balls. Place the balls on the prepared baking sheet. Bake for 20 minutes.

Cut the pita rounds in half and carefully open the pockets. Spread the tzatziki in the pockets and place 2 chickpea balls, a few tomatoes, red onion, and spinach leaves inside. Serve with additional tzatziki.

Per serving: Calories: 285Kcal; Fat: 11g; Carbs: 56g; Fiber: 11g; Protein: 16g

364. Spanish Paella

Preparation time: 15 minutes
Cooking time: 40 minutes **Servings:** 6
Ingredients:

- 1 cup short-grain rice, such as Arborio
- 1 teaspoon olive oil
- 1¾ cups vegetable broth
- 1 teaspoon kosher salt
- 1 teaspoon freshly ground black pepper
- ¾ teaspoon smoked paprika
- 4 jarred piquillo or 2 roasted red peppers, cut into thin strips
- 1 (8-ounce) can fire-roasted tomatoes with their juices
- 1 (15-ounce) can chickpeas, drained and rinsed
- 1 cup thinly sliced scallions
- ¼ cup sliced black olives, such as Kalamata
- ¼ cup pine nuts
- ¼ cup chopped fresh parsley or cilantro

Directions:
Arrange an oven rack in the center of the oven and preheat the oven to 350°F. In a small bowl, toss the rice in olive oil and spread it in an even layer on a rimmed baking sheet. Toast in the oven for 5 minutes. Meanwhile, in a medium saucepan over medium heat, bring the broth, salt, pepper, and paprika to a simmer. Add the peppers, tomatoes, and chickpeas to the baking sheet with the toasted rice and stir to combine. Pour the broth over the rice and vegetables. Cover the baking sheet tightly with aluminum foil. Bake for 20 minutes. Uncover the baking sheet and stir the rice. Scatter the scallions, olives, and pine nuts over the rice. Bake, uncovered, for another 15 minutes, or until the rice is tender, with a slightly crispy skin. Transfer the mixture to a serving dish and toss with the parsley.

FLEXITARIAN TIP: Cut a ½-pound cooked Linguiça Portuguese sausage link into ½-inch slices and add them in step 5. Gently press the slices down so that the rice separates around them, allowing the rice to a crisp. **Per serving:** Calories: 300Kcal; Fat: 8g; Carbs: 47g; Fiber: 7g; Protein: 11g

365. Veggie And Chickpea Fajitas

Preparation time: 15 minutes
Cook time: 30 minutes **Servings:** 6
Ingredients:

- 2 bell peppers, any color, sliced into ¼-inch strips- 1 large red onion, sliced into ½-inch wedges
- 2 zucchini, sliced into ½-inch wedges
- 4 ears corn, kernels sliced off the cob (about 4 cups)
- 1 (15-ounce) can chickpeas, drained and rinsed
- 2 tablespoons olive oil
- 1 tablespoon freshly squeezed lime juice
- 2 teaspoons ground cumin
- 2 teaspoons kosher salt, divided
- 1 teaspoon garlic powder
- 1 teaspoon freshly ground black pepper, divided
- 8 (8-inch) flour tortillas

Directions:
Preheat the oven to 450°F. Place one oven rack in the upper third of the oven and another in the lower third. Line two baking sheets with parchment paper.

Place the peppers, onion, zucchini, corn kernels, and chickpeas in a large bowl. Add the olive oil, lime juice, cumin, 1 teaspoon of salt, garlic powder, and ½ teaspoon of pepper, and toss to thoroughly coat the vegetables.

Spread the vegetables in an even layer on the baking sheets. Be careful not to crowd the vegetables too close together, as this promotes steaming instead of roasting. Roast for 20 minutes. Stir the vegetables around a little, sprinkle with the remaining salt and pepper, and roast for another 10 minutes, or until the vegetables are tender and just a little charred on the edges. Wrap the tortillas in aluminum foil. Place on one of the baking sheets for the final 5 minutes of roasting. Divide the filling between the tortillas and serve. Finish as desired with your favorite toppings.

Per serving: Calories: 440Kcal; Fat: 12g; Carbs: 74g; Fiber: 11g; Protein: 15g

366. Acorn Squash, Sweet Potatoes, And Apples

Preparation time: 20 minutes
Cooking time: 20 minutes **Servings:** 4
Ingredients:

- 1 acorn squash, halved, seeded, and cut into ½-inch wedges
- 2 sweet potatoes, sliced crosswise into 1-inch disks
- 2 apples, such as Honeycrisp or Fuji, cored and quartered- 1 red onion, cut into 6 wedges
- ¼ cup Miso Butter
- 2 tablespoons maple syrup
- 1½ teaspoons kosher salt, divided
- 1 cup water
- 1 cup freshly squeezed orange juice
- 1 cup quinoa - Roasted Pumpkin Seeds or store-bought, for serving

Directions:
Preheat the oven to 425°F. Place the squash, sweet potatoes, apples, and onion on a rimmed baking sheet. In a small bowl, whisk together the miso butter, maple syrup, and 1 teaspoon of salt. Drizzle this over the vegetables and apple slices, and toss with your hands to completely coat. Arrange the vegetables and apple slices in a single layer, with as much space between each other as possible. Roast until everything is tender and slightly caramelized, 15 to 18 minutes. Meanwhile, in a saucepan on the stove top, bring the water and orange

juice to a boil with the remaining ½ teaspoon salt. Add the quinoa. Reduce the heat to low, cover, and cook at a low simmer until the quinoa is tender, about 15 minutes. Remove the pan from the heat, and keep it covered for 5 minutes. The quinoa will be very tender, and you will see a little curlicue in each seed when it is done.

Spread the cooked quinoa on a serving plate, and spoon the roasted vegetables and apple slices over it. Top with roasted pumpkin seeds.

FLEXITARIAN TIP: Add 1-pound bone-in split chicken breasts to the baking sheet, and arrange so that the breasts are directly on the pan, not on the squash or potatoes. Lightly oil the chicken and sprinkle with salt and pepper. Bake everything in a preheated 350°F oven for 40 minutes or until the internal temperature of the chicken reaches 165°F. Serve everything over the quinoa, and top with the pumpkin seeds.

Per serving: Calories: 447Kcal; Fat: 9g; Carbs: 85g; Fiber: 12g; Protein: 10g

367. Stuffed Roasted Sweet Potatoes

Preparation time: 20 minutes **Cooking time:** 30 minutes
Servings: 4
Ingredients:

- 4 medium sweet potatoes, halved lengthwise
- 1 red onion, quartered
- 1½ tablespoons olive oil, divided
- ½ teaspoon kosher salt, divided
- ¼ teaspoon freshly ground black pepper
- 1 (15-ounce) can chickpeas, drained, rinsed, and dried - ½ teaspoon smoked paprika
- ½ teaspoon ground cinnamon
- ¼ teaspoon ground cumin
- 2 cups baby spinach
- 1 avocado, peeled and diced
- ½ cup halved cherry tomatoes
- ½ cup Tzatziki

Directions:
Preheat the oven to 400°F. Lightly oil a baking sheet.
Rub the sweet potatoes and onion in 1 tablespoon of olive oil and season with ¼ teaspoon of salt and pepper. Arrange in a single layer on the baking sheet, with the potatoes cut-side down. In a medium bowl, toss the chickpeas in the remaining ½ tablespoon of olive oil and ¼ teaspoon of salt. Place them on the same baking sheet with the sweet potatoes and onion.
Roast for 20 minutes, then flip the potatoes cut-side up and shift the onion and chickpeas around a bit. Roast for another 10 minutes, or until the sweet potatoes are tender when pierced with a fork. Break up the sweet potato flesh with a fork and place it in a medium bowl, and arrange the potato skins on a serving plate. Lightly mash the sweet potato filling with a fork, and add the roasted onion and chickpeas, the paprika, cinnamon, and cumin. Toss together and add the spinach, avocado, and tomatoes. Toss again and scoop into the potato skins.
Drizzle with the tzatziki. Serve any extra sauce on the side.
Per serving: Calories: 482Kcal; Fat: 24g; Carbs: 56g; Fiber: 51g; Protein: 13g

368. Cheesy Hash Browns Egg Bake

Preparation time: 10 minutes
Cooking time: 6 minutes **Servings:** 6
Ingredients:

- ½ tablespoon unsalted butter, at room temperature
- 1 tablespoon olive oil
- 1 medium onion, diced
- 1 medium bell pepper, any color, diced
- 1½ teaspoons kosher salt, divided
- 1 cup baby spinach
- ½ (30-ounce) bag frozen hash brown potatoes
- 10 large eggs
- 1 cup milk
- ¼ cup sour cream
- 1 tablespoon Dijon mustard
- ¼ teaspoon freshly ground black pepper
- 1½ cups shredded sharp Cheddar cheese

Directions:
Preheat the oven to 375°F. Grease a 9-by-13-inch baking dish with butter. Warm the oil in a medium skillet over medium heat. Add the onion, bell pepper, and ½ teaspoon of salt and sauté, stirring occasionally, until the vegetables are soft, about 5 minutes. Add the spinach and toss until wilted, about 1 minute. Transfer the mixture to the baking dish. Add the hash browns, stir to combine, and spread into an even layer on the bottom of the dish.
In a large bowl, whisk together the eggs, milk, sour cream, mustard, remaining 1 teaspoon of salt, and pepper. Fold in the cheese. Pour the mixture over the vegetables. Bake for 45 minutes, or until the top is lightly browned and a knife inserted in the middle comes out clean. Let cool for 5 minutes before slicing.
Per serving: Calories: 356Kcal; Fat: 26g; Carbs: 12g; Fiber: 1g; Protein: 20g

369. Breakfast Taquitos Casserole

Preparation time: 10 minutes
Cooking time: 30 minutes **Servings:** 4
Ingredients:

- 2 tablespoons unsalted butter, divided
- 1½ cups frozen hash browns
- 1 teaspoon kosher salt, divided
- ½ teaspoon freshly ground black pepper, divided
- 6 large eggs, beaten
- 6 (8-inch) flour tortillas
- 1 avocado, halved and sliced lengthwise into thin wedges
- ½ cup salsa verde
- 2/3 cup grated Cheddar cheese

Directions:
Preheat the oven to 400°F.
Melt 1 tablespoon of butter in a medium skillet over medium heat. Add the hash browns, season them with ½ teaspoon of salt and ¼ teaspoon of black pepper, and cook according to the package instructions, about 15 minutes.
While the hash browns are cooking, melt the remaining 1 tablespoon of butter in another medium skillet over medium heat. Add the eggs, season with the remaining ½ teaspoon of

salt and ¼ teaspoon of pepper, and scramble, about 15 minutes. Wrap the tortillas in a paper towel and warm in the microwave for about 20 seconds to make them morepliable.
Lay the tortillas on a flat surface and spoon the hash browns mixture and eggs horizontally across each tortilla, slightly below the center. Place the avocado slices over the eggs. Fold the bottom edge of each tortilla up tightly over the filling, rolling from bottom to top. Place the tortillas seam-side down in a 12-by-12-inch baking dish. Drizzle the salsa over the taquitos and sprinkle with the cheese.
Bake until the cheese has melted, 12 to 15 minutes.
Per serving: Calories: 611Kcal; Fat: 37g; Carbs: 50g; Fiber: 6g; Protein: 22g

370. Potato Gratin

Preparation time: 10 minutes
Cooking time: 35 minutes **Servings:** 6
Ingredients:
- 2 tablespoons unsalted butter, plus more for greasing
- 2 teaspoons garlic paste or minced garlic
- 1½ cups 2% milk
- ¼ cup heavy (whipping) cream
- ¼ cup vegetable broth
- 1 red bell pepper, diced
- ¾ teaspoon kosher salt
- ¼ teaspoon freshly ground black pepper
- 2 cups shredded Gruyère or Swiss cheese, divided
- 2 pounds mixed yellow Yukon Gold potatoes and sweet potatoes
- ¼ cup finely chopped fresh chives

Directions:
Preheat the oven to 375°F and butter a 2-quart baking dish. In a medium pot, combine the butter, garlic, milk, cream, broth, bell pepper, salt, and pepper, and bring to a gentle simmer over medium heat, about 5 minutes. Be careful not to bring it to a boil. Stir in 1 cup of cheese. While the liquid is coming to a simmer, slice the potatoes thinly. I use a handheld mandoline on the thinnest setting, which slices potatoes 1/8 inch thick in about 30 seconds. You can use a chef's knife, too, but it will take longer.
Layer the potatoes in the prepared baking dish and pour the hot milk mixture over them. Sprinkle the remaining 1 cup of cheese on top. Bake for 30 minutes. Allow to rest for 10 minutes before serving.
Serve with a flourish of chives.
Per serving: Calories: 374Kcal; Fat: 20g; Carbs: 32g; Fiber: 2g; Protein: 16g

371. Swiss Chard And Orzo Gratin

Preparation time: 10 minutes
Cooking time: 20 minutes **Servings:** 4
Ingredients:
- ½ tablespoon unsalted butter, at room temperature
- ¾ cup orzo
- 1 (15-ounce) can cannellini or other white beans, drained and rinsed
- 1 tablespoon olive oil
- ½ cup chopped shallot
- ½ teaspoon kosher salt
- 1 teaspoon freshly ground black pepper
- 1 cup heavy (whipping) cream
- 1½ cups vegetable broth
- 2 large bunches Swiss chard, stems removed and leaves coarsely chopped
- ½ cup coarsely chopped jarred roasted red peppers
- ¾ cup grated Parmesan cheese
- 1/3 cup Lemony Breadcrumbs

Directions:
Preheat the oven to 400°F. Grease a 12-by-12-inch baking dish with butter. Bring a medium pot of well-salted water to a boil. Add the orzo and cook for 5 minutes. The pasta won't be done at that time, but it will finish cooking in the oven. Drain the orzo and spread it across the bottom of the baking dish.
Evenly spread the beans over the orzo.
Heat the olive oil in a medium skillet over medium heat. Add the shallot, salt, and pepper, and sauté until the shallot is completely softened, about 4 minutes. Stir in the cream and broth and bring to a boil. Reduce the heat to low and simmer until the liquid is reduced to 2 cups, about 10 minutes. Add the Swiss chard in batches, tossing to coat. Cook until the chard is wilted, about 3 minutes. Pour the chard and sauce into the baking dish. Top with the roasted red peppers, followed by the cheese. Finish with a flurry of breadcrumbs.
Bake for 25 to 30 minutes.
INGREDIENT TIP: Swiss chard is a vitamin and mineral powerhouse, boasting high levels of vitamin K and potassium. Additionally, it's loaded with antioxidants for fighting inflammation and free-radical damage and for promoting eye health.
Per serving: Calories: 544Kcal; Fat: 33g; Carbs: 46g; Fiber: 9g; Protein: 20g

372. Baked Cheesy Broccoli With Quinoa

Preparation time: 15 minutes
Cooking time: 45 minutes **Servings:** 8
Ingredients:
- ½ tablespoon unsalted butter, at room temperature
- 1½ cups bite-size broccoli pieces or frozen broccoli florets
- 2 large eggs
- 1 cup whole or 2% milk
- 1 tablespoon Dijon mustard
- 1 teaspoon kosher salt
- ½ teaspoon freshly ground black pepper
- ½ yellow onion, diced
- 2 teaspoons garlic paste or 5 garlic cloves, minced - 2 cups cooked quinoa
- 1½ cups grated Cheddar cheese
- ½ cup Lemony Breadcrumbs

Directions:
Preheat the oven to 350°F. Grease a 9-by-13-inch baking dish with butter. Fill a medium pot with about 2 inches of water and add a steamer. Bring to a boil and add the broccoli. Steam until just tender, about 10 minutes.

In a large bowl, beat together the eggs, milk, mustard, salt, and pepper. Fold in broccoli, onion, garlic, quinoa, and cheese. Pour everything into the baking dish. Top with the breadcrumbs. Bake for 35 to 40 minutes.
SUBSTITUTION TIP: Swap cauliflower for the broccoli, and add 1½ teaspoons of curry powder.
Per serving: Calories: 243Kcal; Fat: 11g; Carbs: 23g; Fiber: 3g; Protein: 13g

373. Mexican Casserole
Preparation time: 15 minutes
Cooking time: 35 minutes **Servings:** 6
Ingredients:
- Olive oil, for greasing
- 1 cup cooked quinoa (here)
- 1 (15-ounce) can black beans, drained and rinsed
- 1 cup fresh or frozen corn kernels
- 1 cup halved cherry tomatoes
- 2 bell peppers, any color, diced
- 1/3 cup chopped red onion
- 1½ tablespoons freshly squeezed lime juice
- 1½ teaspoons ground cumin
- 2 teaspoons kosher salt
- 2 cups grated Monterey Jack cheese, divided
- 2 tablespoons Roasted Pumpkin Seeds (optional)

Directions:
Preheat the oven to 400°F. Lightly oil a 9-by-11-inch baking dish. Combine the cooked quinoa, black beans, corn, tomatoes, bell peppers, onion, lime juice, cumin, salt, and 1½ cups of cheese in a large bowl.
Spread evenly in the baking dish. Bake for 30 minutes. Spread the remaining ½ cup of cheese over the top of the casserole. Bake for another 5 minutes.
Sprinkle the pumpkin seeds over the top (if using). Serve warm.
Per serving: Calories: 325Kcal; Fat: 14g; Carbs: 33g; Fiber: 8g; Protein: 18g

374. Curried Cauliflower Tetrazzini
Preparation time: 15 minutes
Cooking time: 55 minutes **Servings:** 6
Ingredients:
- 2½ tablespoons unsalted butter, divided
- 1 medium cauliflower, cut into bite-size pieces, or 4 cups frozen florets
- 2 small leeks, white and light greens parts only, diced
- 2 tablespoons olive oil
- 2½ teaspoons curry powder, divided
- 2 teaspoons kosher salt, divided
- 1 teaspoon freshly ground black pepper, divided
- ½ pound spaghetti
- 3 tablespoons all-purpose flour
- 1 cup milk
- ½ cup sour cream or plain Greek yogurt
- 1 tablespoon garlic paste or minced garlic
- 1 cup grated Parmesan cheese, divided
- ½ cup Lemony Breadcrumbs

Directions:
Preheat the oven to 400°F. Grease a 9-by-13-inch baking dish with ½ tablespoon of butter.
Place the cauliflower and leeks in the baking dish and toss with the olive oil, 1½ teaspoons of curry powder, 1 teaspoon of salt, and ½ teaspoon of black pepper. Roast until the cauliflower pieces are tender and begin to brown, about 30 minutes.
While the cauliflower is roasting, bring a large pot of salted water to a boil. Break the spaghetti into thirds so that the noodles are all around 3 inches long. Add to the boiling water and cook according to the package instructions. Drain.
Melt the remaining 2 tablespoons of butter in a medium skillet over medium heat. Once it's bubbling, whisk in the flour until the butter becomes a paste. Cook, stirring constantly, for 1 minute. Gradually whisk the milk into the paste. Add the sour cream, garlic, ½ cup of Parmesan, the remaining 1 teaspoon of salt, ½ teaspoon of black pepper, and 1 teaspoon of curry powder, and whisk to thoroughly mix.
Fold in the cooked spaghetti. Pour this over the roasted vegetables and lightly toss them together. Top with the remaining ½ cup of Parmesan and the breadcrumbs.
Lower the oven temperature to 350°F and bake for 15 minutes or until bubbly.
SUBSTITUTION TIP: Swap out the cauliflower for broccoli or butternut squash.
FLEXITARIAN TIP: Since this dish was made famous with chicken, just replace the cauliflower with 4 cups diced cooked chicken. You can eliminate the curry if you wish, but it goes well with chicken, too.
Per serving: Calories: 425Kcal; Fat: 18g; Carbs: 52g; Fiber: 6g; Protein: 17g

375. Baked Eggplant Parmesan
Preparation time: 20 minutes
Cooking time: 1 hour **Servings:** 8
Ingredients:
- 2 medium eggplants
- 2 large eggs, beaten
- 1/3 cup basil pesto
- 4 cups Italian breadcrumbs
- 1 cup Parmesan cheese
- 6 cups Tomato-Mushroom Ragù or 2 (24-ounce) jars tomato-based pasta sauce
- 2 cups shredded mozzarella cheese, divided

Directions:
Preheat the oven to 375°F. Line a baking sheet with parchment paper.
Slice the eggplants into ½-inch rounds.
In a small bowl, whisk the eggs together with the pesto. In a second small bowl, combine the breadcrumbs and Parmesan cheese.
Dip an eggplant slice into the egg-pesto mixture. Let the excess drip off, then dip it in the breadcrumbs and coat it on both sides. Place the slice on the baking sheet. Repeat for all the eggplant slices, and arrange them on the baking sheet in a single layer.
Bake the eggplant for 20 minutes. Flip the slices over and bake for 20 minutes more.

Increase the oven temperature to 400°F. In a 9-by-13-inch baking dish, spread just enough tomato sauce to cover the bottom. Layer half of the eggplant slices in the bottom of the baking dish. Top them with one-third of the mozzarella, followed by half of the remaining sauce. Repeat with the remaining eggplant, the second third of the cheese, and the remaining sauce. Sprinkle the remaining cheese over the top. Bake for 20 minutes. Let sit for 5 minutes before serving.

INGREDIENT TIP: If you find eggplant too bitter for you, place the slices in a colander and generously salt them. Let them sit for 1 hour. Rinse, pat dry, and begin the recipe with step 3.

Per serving: Calories: 423Kcal; Fat: 14g; Carbs: 57g; Fiber: 10g; Protein: 19g

Amanda Kale

CHAPTER 21:
Stews & Chilies

376. Spanish Chickpea and Sweet Potato Stew
Preparation time: 5 minutes
Cooking time: 35 minutes **Servings:** 4
Ingredients:
- 14 ounces cooked chickpeas
- 1 small sweet potato, peeled, cut into ½-inch cubes - 1 medium red onion, sliced
- 3 ounces baby spinach
- 14 ounces crushed tomatoes
- 2 teaspoons minced garlic - 1 teaspoon salt
- 1 1/2 teaspoons ground cumin
- 2 teaspoons harissa paste
- 2 teaspoons maple syrup
- ½ teaspoon ground black pepper
- 2 teaspoons sugar
- 1 tablespoon olive oil
- 1/2 cup vegetable stock
- 2 tablespoons chopped parsley
- 1-ounce slivered almonds, toasted
- Brown rice, cooked for serving

Directions:
Take a large saucepan, place it over low heat, add oil and when hot, add onion and garlic and cook for 5 minutes. Then add sweet potatoes, season with cumin, stir in the harissa paste and cook for 2 minutes until toasted. Switch heat to medium-low level, add tomatoes and chickpeas, pour in vegetable stock, stir in maple syrup and sugar and simmer for 25 minutes until potatoes have softened, stirring every 10 minutes. Then add spinach, cook for 1 minute until its leaves have wilted, and season with salt and black pepper. When done, distribute cooked rice between bowls, top with stew, garnish with parsley and almonds and serve.
Per serving: Calories: 348Kcal; Fat: 16.5g; Carbs: 41.2g; Fiber: 5.3g; Protein: 7.2g

377. Pomegranate and Walnut Stew
Preparation time: 10 minutes
Cooking time: 55 minutes **Servings:** 6
Ingredients:
- 1 head of cauliflower, cut into florets
- 1 medium white onion, peeled, diced
- 1 1/2 cups California walnuts, toasted
- 1 cup yellow split peas
- 1 1/2 tablespoons honey
- ¼ teaspoon salt
- ½ teaspoon turmeric
- ½ teaspoon cinnamon
- 2 tablespoons olive oil, separated
- 4 cups pomegranate juice
- 2 tablespoons chopped parsley
- 2 tablespoons chopped walnuts for garnishing

Directions:
Take a medium saute pan, place it over medium heat, add walnuts, cook for 5 minutes until toasted and then cool for 5 minutes.
Transfer walnuts to the food processor, pulse for 2 minutes until ground, and set aside until required.
Take a large saute pan, place it over medium heat, add 1 tablespoon oil and when hot, add onion and cook for 5 minutes until softened.
Switch heat to medium-low heat, then add lentils and walnuts, stir in cinnamon, salt, and turmeric, pour in honey and pomegranate, stir until mixed and simmer the mixture for 40 minutes until the sauce has reduced by half and lentils have softened. Meanwhile, place cauliflower florets in a food processor and then pulse for 2 minutes until the mixture resembles rice.
Take a medium to saute pan, place it over medium heat, add remaining oil and when hot, add cauliflower rice, cook for 5 minutes until softened, and then season with salt.
Serve cooked pomegranate and walnut sauce with cooked cauliflower rice and garnish with walnuts and parsley.
Per serving: Calories: 439Kcal; Fat: 25g; Carbs: 67g; Fiber: 3g; Protein: 21g

378. Fennel and Chickpeas Provençal
Preparation time: 10 minutes
Cooking time: 50 minutes **Servings:** 4
Ingredients:
- 15 ounces cooked chickpeas
- 3 fennel bulbs, sliced
- 1 medium onion, peeled, sliced
- 15 ounces diced tomatoes
- 10 black olives, pitted, cured
- 10 Kalamata olives, pitted
- 1 ½ teaspoon minced garlic
- 1 teaspoon salt
- 1/8 teaspoon ground black pepper
- 1 teaspoon Herbes de Provence
- 1/2 teaspoon red pepper flakes
- 2 tablespoons olive oil
- 1/2 cup water
- 2 tablespoons chopped parsley

Directions:
Take a saucepan, place it over medium-high heat, add oil and when hot, add onion, fennel, and garlic and cook for 20 minutes until softened. Then add remaining ingredients, except for olives and chickpeas, bring the mixture to boil, switch heat to medium-low level and simmer for 15 minutes.

Then add remaining ingredients, cook for 10 minutes until hot, garnish stew with parsley and serve.
Per serving: Calories: 395Kcal; Fat: 13g; Carbs: 56g; Fiber: 13g; Protein: 16g

379. African Peanut Lentil Soup
Preparation time: 10 minutes
Cooking time: 25 minutes **Servings:** 3
Ingredients:
- 1/2 cup red lentils
- 1/2 medium white onion, sliced
- 2 medium tomatoes, chopped
- 1/2 cup baby spinach
- 1/2 cup sliced zucchini
- 1/2 cup sliced sweet potatoes
- ½ cup sliced potatoes
- ½ cup broccoli florets
- 2 teaspoons minced garlic
- 1 inch of ginger, grated
- 1 tablespoon tomato paste
- 1/4 teaspoon ground black pepper
- 1 teaspoon salt
- 1 ½ teaspoon ground cumin
- 2 teaspoons ground coriander
- 2 tablespoons peanuts
- 1 teaspoon Harissa Spice Blend
- 1 tablespoon sambal oelek
- 1/4 cup almond butter
- 1 teaspoon olive oil
- 1 teaspoon lemon juice
- 2 ½ cups vegetable stock

Directions:
Take a large saucepan, place it over medium heat, add oil and when hot, add onion and cook for 5 minutes until translucent. Meanwhile, place tomatoes in a blender, add garlic, ginger and sambal oelek along with all the spices and pulse until pureed. Pour this mixture into the onions, cook for 5 minutes, then add remaining ingredients, except for the spinach, peanuts and lemon juice and simmer for 15 minutes.
Taste to adjust the seasoning, stir in spinach, and cook for 5 minutes until cooked.
Ladle soup into bowls, garnish with lime juice and peanuts and serve.
Per serving: Calories: 411Kcal; Fat: 17g; Carbs: 50g; Fiber: 18g; Protein: 20g

380. White Bean Stew
Preparation time: 5 minutes
Cooking time: 10 hours and 10 minutes **Servings:** 10
Ingredients:
- 2 cups chopped spinach
- 28 ounces diced tomatoes
- 2 pounds white beans, dried
- 2 cups chopped chard
- 2 large carrots, peeled, diced
- 2 cups chopped kale
- 3 large celery stalks, diced
- 1 medium white onion, peeled, diced
- 1 ½ teaspoon minced garlic
- 2 tablespoons salt
- 1 teaspoon dried rosemary
- ½ teaspoon Ground black pepper, to taste
- 1 teaspoon dried thyme
- 1 teaspoon dried oregano
- 1 bay leaf - 10 cups water

Directions:
Switch on the slow cooker, add all the ingredients in it, except for kale, chard, and spinach and stir until combined. Shut the cooker with lid and cook for 10 hours at a low heat setting until thoroughly cooked.
When done, stir in kale, chard, and spinach, and cook for 10 minutes until leaves wilt.
Serve straight away.
Per serving: Calories: 109Kcal; Fat: 2.4g; Carbs: 17.8g; Fiber: 6g; Protein: 5.3g

381. Vegetarian Gumbo
Preparation time: 10 minutes
Cooking time: 45 minutes **Servings:** 4
Ingredients:
- 1 1/2 cups diced zucchini
- 16-ounces cooked red beans
- 4 cups sliced okra
- 1 1/2 cups diced green pepper
- 1 1/2 cups chopped white onion
- 1 1/2 cups diced red bell pepper
- 8 cremini mushrooms, quartered
- 1 cup sliced celery
- 3 teaspoons minced garlic
- 1 medium tomato, chopped
- 1 teaspoon red pepper flakes
- 1 teaspoon dried thyme
- 3 tablespoons all-purpose flour
- 1 tablespoon smoked paprika
- 1 teaspoon dried oregano
- 1/4 teaspoon nutmeg - 1 teaspoon soy sauce
- 1 1/2 teaspoons liquid smoke
- 2 tablespoons mustard
- 1 tablespoon apple cider vinegar
- 1 tablespoon Worcestershire sauce, vegetarian
- 1/2 teaspoon hot sauce
- 3 tablespoons olive oil
- 4 cups vegetable stock
- 1/2 cups sliced green onion
- 4 cups cooked jasmine rice

Directions:
Take a Dutch oven, place it over medium heat, add oil and flour and cook for 5 minutes until fragrant.
Switch heat to the medium low level, and continue cooking for 20 minutes until the roux becomes dark brown, whisking constantly. Meanwhile, place the tomato in a food processor, add garlic and onion along with remaining ingredients, except for the stock, zucchini, celery, mushroom, green and red bell

pepper, and pulse for 2 minutes until smooth. Pour the mixture into the pan, return pan over medium-high heat, stir until mixed, and cook for 5 minutes until all the liquid has evaporated. Stir in stock, bring it to simmer, then add remaining vegetables and simmer for 20 minutes until tender. Garnish gumbo with green onions and serve with rice.
Per serving: Calories: 160Kcal; Fat: 7.3g; Carbs: 20g; Fiber: 5.7g; Protein: 7g

382. Black Bean and Quinoa Stew
Preparation time: 10 minutes
Cooking time: 6 hours **Servings:** 6
Ingredients:
- 1-pound black beans, dried, soaked overnight
- 3/4 cup quinoa, uncooked
- 1 medium red bell pepper, cored, chopped
- 1 medium red onion, peeled, diced
- 1 medium green bell pepper, cored, chopped
- 28-ounce diced tomatoes
- 2 dried chipotle peppers
- 1 ½ teaspoon minced garlic
- 2/3 teaspoon sea salt
- 2 teaspoons red chili powder
- 1/3 teaspoon ground black pepper
- 1 teaspoon coriander powder
- 1 dried cinnamon stick
- 1/4 cup cilantro
- 7 cups of water

Directions:
Switch on the slow cooker, add all the ingredients in it, except for salt, and stir until mixed. Shut the cooker with lid and cook for 6 hours at a high heat setting until cooked. When done, stir salt into the stew until mixed, remove cinnamon sticks and serve.
Per serving: Calories: 308Kcal; Fat: 2g; Carbs: 70g; Fiber: 32g; Protein: 23g

383. Root Vegetable Stew
Preparation time: 10 minutes
Cooking time: 8 hours and 10 minutes **Servings:** 6
Ingredients:
- 2 cups chopped kale
- 1 large white onion, peeled, chopped
- 1-pound parsnips, peeled, chopped
- 1-pound potatoes, peeled, chopped
- 2 celery ribs, chopped
- 1-pound butternut squash, peeled, deseeded, chopped
- 1-pound carrots, peeled, chopped
- 3 teaspoons minced garlic
- 1-pound sweet potatoes, peeled, chopped
- 1 bay leaf
- 1 teaspoon ground black pepper
- 1/2 teaspoon sea salt
- 1 tablespoon chopped sage
- 3 cups vegetable broth

Directions:
Switch on the slow cooker, add all the ingredients in it, except for the kale, and stir until mixed. Shut the cooker with lid and cook for 8 hours at a low heat setting until cooked. When done, add kale into the stew, stir until mixed, and cook for 10 minutes until leaves have wilted. Serve straight away.
Per serving: Calories: 120Kcal; Fat: 1g; Carbs: 28g; Fiber: 6g; Protein: 4g

384. Bean and Mushroom Chili
Preparation time: 15 minutes
Cooking time: 38 minutes **Servings:** 6
Ingredients:
- 1 large onion, peeled and chopped
- 1-pound (454 g) button mushrooms, chopped
- 6 cloves garlic, peeled and minced
- 1 tablespoon ground cumin
- 4 teaspoons ground fennel
- 1 tablespoon ancho chile powder
- ½ teaspoon cayenne pepper
- 1 tablespoon unsweetened cocoa powder
- 4 cups cooked pinto beans, drained and rinsed
- 1 (28-ounce / 794-g) can diced tomatoes
- Salt, to taste (optional)

Directions:
Put the mushrooms and onion in a saucepan and sauté over medium heat for 10 minutes. Add the garlic, cumin, fennel, chile powder, cayenne pepper, and cocoa powder and cook for 3 minutes.
Add the beans, tomatoes, and 2 cups of water and simmer, covered, for 25 minutes. Season with salt, if desired. Serve immediately.
Per serving: Calories: 436Kcal; Fat: 2g; Carbs: 97g; Fiber: 23g; Protein: 19g

385. Five-Bean Chili
Preparation time: 10 minutes
Cooking time: 1 hour
Servings: 8
Ingredients:
- 2 (26- to 28-ounce / 737- to 794-g) cans diced tomatoes
- 1 (19-ounce / 539-g) can red kidney beans, drained and rinsed
- 1 (19-ounce / 539-g) can white kidney beans, drained and rinsed
- 1 (19-ounce / 539-g) can chickpeas, drained and rinsed
- 1 (19-ounce / 539-g) can black beans, drained and rinsed
- 1 (19-ounce / 539-g) can pinto beans, drained and rinsed
- 2 1/2 cups fresh mushrooms, sliced
- 1 medium red bell pepper, chopped
- 1 large yellow onion, chopped
- 1 cup corn, canned or frozen
- 1½ tablespoons chili powder
- 1 teaspoon ground cumin

- ½ teaspoon freshly ground black pepper
- ½ teaspoon pink Himalayan salt
- ¼ teaspoon cayenne pepper
- ¼ teaspoon garlic powder

Directions:
Combine all the ingredients in a large pot over medium heat. Cover the pot with a lid and cook, stirring occasionally, for 45 to 60 minutes. Serve as is, or on a bed of brown rice, quinoa, or with a fresh avocado. If you have leftovers or you're doing meal prep, store in reusable containers in the refrigerator for up to 5 days or freeze for up to 2 months.
Per serving: Calories: 756Kcal; Fat: 5g; Carbs: 139g; Fiber: 41g; Protein: 41g

386. Mushroom & Wild Rice Stew

Preparation time: 10 minutes
Cooking time: 50 minutes **Servings:** 6
Ingredients:
- 1 to 2 teaspoons olive oil
- 2 cups chopped mushrooms
- ½ to 1 teaspoon salt
- 1 onion, chopped, or 1 teaspoon onion powder
- 3 or 4 garlic cloves, minced, or ½ teaspoon garlic powder
- 1 tablespoon dried herbs - ¾ cup brown rice
- ¼ cup wild rice or additional brown rice
- 3 cups water
- 3 Vegetable Broth or store-bought broth
- 2 to 4 tablespoons balsamic vinegar (optional) - Freshly ground black pepper
- 1 cup frozen peas, thawed
- 1 cup unsweetened nondairy milk (optional)
- 1 to 2 cups chopped greens, such as spinach, kale, or chard

Directions:
Heat the olive oil in a large soup pot over medium-high heat. Add the mushrooms and a pinch of salt, and sauté for about 4 minutes, until the mushrooms are softened. Add the onion and garlic (if using fresh), and sauté for 1 to 2 minutes more. Stir in the dried herbs (plus the onion powder and/or garlic powder, if using), white or brown rice, wild rice, water, vegetable broth, vinegar (if using), and salt and pepper to taste. Bring to a boil, turn the heat to low, and cover the pot. Simmer the soup for 15 minutes (for white rice) or 45 minutes (for brown rice). Turn off the heat and stir in the peas, milk (if using), and greens. Let the greens wilt before serving.
Leftovers will keep in an airtight container for up to 1 week in the refrigerator or up to 1 month in the freezer.
Per serving (2 cups): Calories: 201Kcal; Fat: 3g; Carbs: 44g; Fiber: 4g; Protein: 6g

387. Ethiopian Cabbage, Carrot, and Potato Stew

Preparation time: 10 minutes
Cooking time: 20 minutes **Servings:** 6
Ingredients:
- 3 russet potatoes, peeled and cut into ½-inch cubes
- 2 tablespoons olive oil
- 6 carrots, peeled, halved lengthwise, and cut into ½-inch slices
- 1 onion, chopped
- 4 garlic cloves, minced
- 1 tablespoon ground turmeric
- 1 teaspoon ground cumin
- 1 teaspoon ground ginger
- 1½ teaspoons sea salt
- 1½ cups low-sodium vegetable broth, divided
- 4 cups shredded or thinly sliced green cabbage

Directions:
Bring a large pot of water to a boil over medium-high heat. Add the potatoes and cook for 10 minutes, or until fork-tender. Drain and set aside. While the potatoes are cooking, heat the oil in a large skillet over medium-high heat. Add the carrots and onion and sauté for 5 minutes. Add the garlic, turmeric, cumin, ginger, and salt and sauté for 1 additional minute, until fragrant. Add the cooked potatoes and 1 cup of broth to the skillet, bring to a boil and reduce to a simmer. Scatter the cabbage on top of the potatoes. Cover and simmer for 3 minutes. Mix the cabbage into the potatoes, add the remaining ½ cup of broth, cover, and simmer for 5 more minutes, or until the cabbage is wilted and tender. Stir the cabbage from time to time while cooking to incorporate it with the other ingredients as it continues to wilt.
Per serving: Calories: 216Kcal; Fat: 5.03g; Carbs: 39.85g; Fiber: 3.6g; Protein: 5.12g

388. Balsamic Lentil Stew

Preparation time: 10 minutes
Cooking time: 30 minutes **Servings:** 5
Ingredients:
- 1 teaspoon olive oil
- 4 carrots, peeled and chopped
- 1 onion, chopped
- 3 garlic cloves, minced
- 2 tablespoons balsamic vinegar
- 4 Vegetable Broth or water
- 1 (28-ounce) can crushed tomatoes
- 1 tablespoon sugar
- 2 cups dried lentils or 2 (15-ounce) cans lentils, drained and rinsed
- 1 teaspoon salt
- Freshly ground black pepper

Directions:
Heat the olive oil in a large soup pot over medium heat. Add the carrots, onion, and garlic and sauté for about 5 minutes, until the vegetables are softened. Pour in the vinegar, and let it sizzle to deglaze the bottom of the pot. Add the vegetable broth, tomatoes, sugar, and lentils. Bring to a boil, then reduce the heat to low. Simmer for about 25 minutes, until the lentils are soft. Add the salt and season to taste with pepper. Leftovers will keep in an airtight container for up to 1 week in the refrigerator or up to 1 month in the freezer.
Per serving (2 cups): Calories: 353Kcal; Fat: 2g; Carbs: 67g; Fiber: 27g; Protein: 22g

389. Winter Stew

Preparation time: 10 minutes
Cooking time: 20 minutes **Servings:** 6
Ingredients:
- ½ cup red lentils
- 1 cup mushrooms, chopped
- 1 yellow onion, chopped
- 2 sweet potatoes, chopped
- 1 carrot, chopped
- ½ cup red kidney beans, canned
- 1 tablespoon tomato paste
- 2 cups of water
- ½ cup almond milk
- 1 teaspoon salt
- ½ teaspoon peppercorns
- 1 teaspoon olive oil

Directions:
Cook mushrooms with onion and olive oil on Saute mode for 10 minutes.
Then add red lentils, sweet potatoes, carrot, red kidney beans, tomato paste, almond milk, water, salt, and peppercorns.
Mix up the ingredients gently.
Close and seal the lid.
Set High-pressure mode and cook the stew for 10 minutes.
Then allow natural pressure release.
Mix up the cooked stew carefully.
Per serving: Calories: 177Kcal; Fat: 5.9g; Carbs: 23.8g; Fiber: 8.6g; Protein: 8.8g

390. Vegan "Beef" Stew

Preparation time: 10 minutes
Cooking time: 45 minutes
Servings: 2
Ingredients:
- ½ yellow onion, chopped roughly
- 1 oz celery stalk, chopped
- ¼ cup carrot, chopped
- 1 garlic clove, diced
- 1 tablespoon tomato sauce
- ¼ cup green peas
- 1 tomato, chopped
- 1 cup vegetable stock
- 1 teaspoon salt
- 1 teaspoon thyme
- 2 Yukon potatoes

Directions:
Chop Yukon potatoes roughly and transfer them to the instant pot. Add celery stalk, yellow onion, carrot, garlic, tomato sauce, green peas, tomato, salt, thyme, and mix up. Then add vegetable stock and close the lid. Set Sauté mode and cook the stew for 45 minutes. When the time is over, check if all the ingredients are cooked and mix up the stew gently.
Per serving: Calories: 100Kcal; Fat: 1.2g; Carbs: 22.4g; Fiber: 4.5g; Protein: 3g

391. Egyptian Stew

Preparation time: 10 minutes
Cooking time: 12 minutes
Servings: 5
Ingredients:
- 1 tablespoon tomato paste
- 1 tablespoon olive oil
- 1 tablespoon red pepper
- 1 teaspoon paprika
- 4 potatoes, peeled, chopped
- 2 cups lentils
- 6 cups of water
- 1 teaspoon salt
- 1 cup fresh dill, chopped
- 3 tablespoons lemon juice

Directions:
Place tomato paste, paprika, potatoes, lentils, water, and salt in the instant pot. Close and seal the lid.
After this, set Manual mode and cook the stew for 12 minutes.
Then use quick pressure release.
Open the lid and add lemon juice. Mix it up.
Transfer the stew to the serving bowls.
Then mix up together red pepper and olive oil.
Pour the mixture over the stew.
Garnish the meal with fresh dill.
Per serving: Calories: 451Kcal; Fat: 4.4g; Carbs: 81.1g; Fiber: 29.5g; Protein: 25.1g

392. Moroccan Stew

Preparation time: 10 minutes
Cooking time: 18 minutes **Servings:** 4
Ingredients:
- 1 cup butternut squash, chopped
- ½ cup chickpeas, canned
- 1 teaspoon turmeric
- 1 teaspoon sage
- 1 teaspoon ground coriander
- 1 teaspoon thyme
- 1 teaspoon harissa
- 1 teaspoon ground ginger
- ¼ teaspoon saffron
- 1 lemon slice
- 1 teaspoon salt
- 1 teaspoon tomato paste
- 2 cups of water

Directions:
In the instant pot, combine water, tomato paste, salt, saffron, ground ginger, harissa, thyme, ground coriander, sage, turmeric, and canned chickpeas.
Add butternut squash and mix the ingredients. Add lemon slice and close the lid. Set Manual mode (high pressure) and cook the stew for 8 minutes. Then allow natural pressure release for 10 minutes more.
Open the lid and chill the stew till room temperature.
Per serving: Calories: 117Kcal; Fat:1.9; Carbs: 21.1g; Fiber: 5.5g; Protein: 5.5g

393. Peas And Carrot Stew

Preparation time: 5 minutes
Cooking time: 15 minutes **Servings:** 5
Ingredients:
- 3 potatoes, peeled, chopped
- 2 carrots, chopped
- 1 cup green peas, frozen
- 2 cups of water
- 1 tablespoon tomato paste
- 1 teaspoon salt
- 1 teaspoon cayenne pepper

Directions:
Place carrots, potatoes, and green peas in the instant pot. Then in the separated bowl, combine tomato paste, water, salt, and cayenne pepper. Whisk the liquid until it gets a light red color, and then pour it into the instant pot. Close and seal the lid. Cook the stew on Manual mode for 10 minutes.
Then allow natural pressure release for 5 minutes.
Per serving: Calories: 125Kcal; Fat: 0.3g; Carbs: 27.5g; Fiber: 5.4g; Protein: 4.1g

394. Mediterranean Vegan Stew

Preparation time: 10 minutes
Cooking time: 35 minutes **Servings:** 4
Ingredients:
- ¼ cup white cabbage, shredded
- 1 potato, chopped
- ½ cup corn kernels
- 1 sweet pepper, chopped
- ½ cup fresh parsley
- 1 cup tomatoes, chopped
- ¼ cup green beans, chopped
- 1 ½ cup water - 1 teaspoon salt
- 1 tablespoon coconut cream
- 1 teaspoon white pepper

Directions:
Place all the ingredients in the instant pot and mix them up. After this, close the lid and ser Saute mode.
Cook the stew for 35 minutes. When the time is over, open the lid and mix the stew well. Check if all the ingredients are cooked and close the lid.
Let the stew rest for 10-15 minutes before serving.
Per serving: Calories: 83Kcal; Fat: 1.4g; Carbs: 16.8g; Fiber: 3.2g; Protein: 2.8g

395. African Pineapple Peanut Stew

Preparation time: 30 mins.
Cooking time: 10 minutes **Servings:** 4
Ingredients:
- 4 cups sliced kale
- 1 cup chopped onion
- 1/2 cup peanut butter
- 1 tbsp. hot pepper sauce or 1 tbsp. Tabasco sauce
- 2 minced garlic cloves
- 1/2 cup chopped cilantro
- 2 cups pineapple, undrained, canned & crushed
- 1 tbsp. vegetable oil

Directions:
In a saucepan (preferably covered), sauté the garlic and onions in the oil until the onions are lightly browned, approximately 10 minutes, stirring often.
Wash the kale till the time the onions are sautéed.
Get rid of the stems. Mound the leaves on a cutting surface & slice crosswise into slices (preferably 1" thick).
Now put the pineapple and juice to the onions & bring to a simmer. Stir the kale in, cover and simmer until just tender, stirring frequently for approximately 5 minutes.
Mix in the hot pepper sauce, peanut butter & simmer for 5 minutes.
Add salt according to your taste.
Per serving: Calories: 382Kcal; Fat: 20.3g; Carbs: 27.6g; Fiber: 5g; Protein: 11.4g

396. Cauliflower Stew

Preparation time: 15 minutes
Cooking time: 50 minutes
Servings: 4
Ingredients:
- 1 fresh green chili, seeded and chopped
- 1 teaspoon ground coriander
- 1¼ cups homemade vegetable broth
- Salt and black pepper, to taste
- 1 teaspoon fresh ginger root, minced
- ½ teaspoon cayenne pepper
- 2 tablespoons lemon juice, freshly squeezed
- 2 tablespoons fresh cilantro, chopped
- 2 tablespoons olive oil
- 3 large garlic cloves, minced
- 1 teaspoon ground cumin
- 2 cups fresh tomatoes, finely chopped
- 1 bay leaf
- 1 medium yellow onion, chopped
- ½ teaspoon dried thyme, crushed
- 1 medium head cauliflower, cut into florets
- 2 tablespoons sugar-free tomato paste

Directions:
Heat olive oil in a large dutch oven over medium heat and add onion.
Sauté for about 4 minutes and add garlic, ginger, green chili, thyme and spices.
Sauté for about 1 minute and stir in the tomatoes.
Cook for about 3 minutes, stirring constantly and add the cauliflower.
Cook for about 2 minutes and stir in the bay leaf, tomato paste and broth.
Increase the heat and bring to a boil.
Reduce the heat to low and allow to simmer, covered for about 40 minutes.
Squeeze in the lemon juice, salt and black pepper and discard the bay leaf.
Garnishing with cilantro and serve hot.
Per serving: Calories: 130Kcal; Fat: 8.5g; Carbs: 10.5g; Fiber: 2.3g; Protein: 5.4g

397. Mushroom Stew

Preparation time: 15 minutes
Cooking time: 17 minutes
Servings: 4
Ingredients:

- ¼ cup fresh cilantro, chopped
- 3 small garlic cloves, minced
- 2 tablespoons fresh lime juice
- ¼ pound fresh shiitake mushrooms, sliced
- ¼ pound fresh portobello mushrooms, sliced
- 1 small yellow onion, chopped
- Salt and black pepper, to taste
- ½ pound fresh button mushrooms, sliced
- ½ cup coconut milk, unsweetened
- ¼ cup homemade vegetable broth
- 2 tablespoons olive oil
- 2 tablespoons fresh lemon juice
- 1 tablespoon fresh parsley, chopped

Directions:
Heat olive oil in a large skillet over medium heat and add garlic and onions. Sauté for about 5 minutes and stir in the mushrooms, salt and black pepper. Cook for about 7 minutes and stir in the broth and coconut milk. Bring to a boil and allow to simmer for about 5 minutes. Whisk in the lemon juice and parsley and dish out to serve hot.
Per serving: Calories: 185Kcal; Fat: 14.6g; Carbs: 8.3g; Fiber: 2.5g; Protein: 4.6g

398. Tofu and Veggies Stew

Preparation time: 15 minutes
Cooking time: 15 minutes **Servings:** 8
Ingredients:

- 1 (16-ounce) jar roasted red peppers, rinsed, drained and chopped
- 1 jalapeño pepper, seeded and chopped
- 2 cups homemade vegetable broth
- 1 medium red bell pepper, seeded and thinly sliced
- 1 medium yellow bell pepper, seeded and thinly sliced
- 1 (16-ounce) package extra-firm tofu, drained, pressed and cubed
- Salt and black pepper, to taste
- 2 cups water
- 1 medium green bell pepper, seeded and thinly sliced
- 1 (10-ounce) package frozen baby spinach, thawed
- ¼ cup fresh basil leaves, chopped

Directions:
Put the garlic sauce, jalapeño pepper and roasted red peppers in a food processor and pulse until smooth.
Add the puree, broth and water in a large pan over medium-high heat and bring to a boil. Stir in the bell peppers and tofu and reduce the heat. Cook for about 5 minutes and add the spinach. Cook for 5 more minutes and season with salt and black pepper. Remove from heat and garnish with basil to serve hot.
Per serving: Calories: 90Kcal; Fat: 4g; Carbs: 7.4g; Fiber: 2g; Protein: 8.5g

399. Bell Pepper and Spinach Stew

Preparation time: 15 minutes
Cooking time: 15 minutes **Servings:** 5
Ingredients:

- 4 cups water
- ½ cup sour cream
- 2 tablespoons garlic, peeled
- 1 jalapeño pepper, seeded and chopped
- 1 (16-ounce) jar roasted red peppers, rinsed, drained and chopped
- 2 cups vegetable broth
- 2 cups water
- 1 medium green bell pepper, seeded and thinly sliced
- 1 medium red bell pepper, seeded and thinly sliced
- 1 (10-ounce) package frozen baby spinach, thawed

Directions:
Put garlic, jalapeño pepper and roasted red peppers in a food processor and pulse until smooth.
Put the puree, broth and water in a large pan over medium-high heat and bring to a boil.
Stir in the bell peppers and tofu and reduce the heat.
Cook for about 5 minutes and add the spinach.
Cook for 5 more minutes and dish out to serve hot.
Per serving: Calories: 119Kcal; Fat: 5.9g; Carbs: 13.18g; Fiber: 3.2g; Protein: 5.8g

400. Potato and Chickpeas Stew

Servings: 6
Preparation time: 15 minutes
Cooking time: 35 minutes **Ingredients:**

- 2 tablespoons olive oil
- 1 teaspoon fresh ginger, minced
- 2 garlic cloves, minced
- 1 teaspoon ground cumin
- 2 large potatoes, scrubbed and cubed
- 2 (15-ounce) cans chickpeas, rinsed and drained
- 2 cups vegetable broth
- ¼ cup fresh cilantro, chopped
- 1 onion, chopped
- 1 tablespoon hot curry powder
- ¼ teaspoon ground turmeric
- 2 (15-ounce) cans diced tomatoes with liquid
- Salt and black pepper, to taste

Directions:
Heat olive oil in a large pan over medium heat and add onions. Sauté for about 4 minutes and add ginger, garlic, curry powder, and spices. Sauté for about 1 minute and stir in the potatoes. Cook for about 5 minutes and stir in the remaining ingredients, except for the cilantro. Reduce the heat to medium-low and cover the lid. Let it simmer for about 25 minutes and dish out in a bowl. Garnish with cilantro and serve hot.
Per serving: Calories: 691Kcal; Fat: 14.2g; Carbs: 113.6g; Fiber: 29.9g; Protein: 32.7g

401. Squash and Beans Stew

Preparation time: 15 minutes
Cooking time: 1 hour 10 minutes **Servings:** 8
Ingredients:
- 2 large white onions, chopped
- 2 tablespoons ground cinnamon
- 8 large tomatoes, seeded and chopped finely
- 4 tablespoons vegetable oil
- 8 garlic cloves, minced
- 2 tablespoons red chili powder
- 2 tablespoons cumin seeds, toasted
- 2 cups canned pinto beans
- 3 cups water
- Salt and black pepper, to taste
- 2 medium acorn squash, peeled and chopped
- 4 tablespoons fresh lemon juice

Directions:
Heat olive oil in a large pan over medium heat and add onions. Sauté for about 4 minutes and add garlic and spices. Sauté for about 1 minute and stir in the tomatoes. Cook for about 3 minutes and add beans, squash, and water. Bring to a boil and reduce the heat to medium-low. Cover the lid and allow it to simmer for about 1 hour. Stir in the lemon juice, salt, and black pepper and dish out in a bowl to serve hot.
Per serving: Calories: 340Kcal; Fat: 8.7g; Carbs: 56.2g; Fiber: 13.9g; Protein: 14g

402. Hearty Vegetable Stew

Preparation time: 30 minutes
Cooking time: 25 minutes
Servings: 6
Ingredients:
- ¼ cup portobello mushrooms, sliced
- 1 teaspoon rosemary, dried
- 2 carrots, chopped
- 2 ribs celery, chopped
- 2 potatoes, chopped
- 2 tomatoes, diced
- 1 teaspoon Italian seasoning
- 1 large onion, chopped
- 1 small onion, minced
- 1 clove garlic, minced
- 1 rib celery, minced
- 1 carrot, minced
- ¼ cup vegetable broth
- ¼ cup button mushrooms, sliced
- ½ cup red wine
- 3 cups low sodium vegetable broth
- ½ teaspoon salt
- ¼ teaspoon black pepper
- ½ cup tomato sauce
- 1 tablespoon balsamic vinegar
- 1 tablespoon cornstarch
- 1 cup peas, frozen

Directions:
Heat ¼ cup vegetable broth in a pot and add minced onion, celery, and carrots. Cook for about 5 minutes on high heat until they soften and then add the large onion to it. Cook for about 4 minutes and stir in the mushrooms. Cook for about 5 minutes until their liquid comes out. Season with Italian seasoning and rosemary. Add the wine to the pot afterward and cook for about 3 minutes. Stir in the tomatoes, tomato sauce, and broth and cook for 3 more minutes. Add the remaining chopped veggies, turn the flame high and boil the contents in the pot.
Add the rest of the seasonings to the pot and bring to a boil. Stir in the peas to the pot and mix well until combined. 1Whisk the cornstarch with some water and add it to the pot. Allow it to simmer for about 4 minutes until it is thickened. Dish out to serve hot and delve into the delicious blend.
Per serving: Calories: 137Kcal; Fat: 0.7g; Carbs: 26.3g; Fiber: 5.1g; Protein: 14.1g

403. Barley Lentil Stew

Preparation time: 5 minutes
Cooking time: 50 minutes **Servings:** 3
Ingredients:
- ½ onion, chopped
- 2 stalks celery, chopped
- 1 carrot, diced
- 1 tablespoon olive oil
- 3 cups vegetable stock
- 2 small red potatoes, skin on, chopped
- ¼ cup dry, uncooked barley
- ¾ cup cooked lentils

Directions:
Place a large pot over medium-high heat and add the oil. Once it is heated, add the vegetables and sauté for three to four minutes, until slightly softened.
Add the vegetable stock and the potatoes and bring the pot to a boil. Reduce the heat to a simmer and add the barley and lentils. Simmer gently for 45 minutes, adding water if needed until the barley is plump and soft.
Serve hot.
Per serving: Calories: 367Kcal; Fat: 5.8g; Carbs: 63.1g; Fiber: 20.8g; Protein: 17.3g

404. Fruits Stew

Preparation time: 10 minutes
Cooking time: 10 minutes **Servings:** 4
Ingredients:
- 1 avocado, peeled, pitted, and sliced
- 1 cup plums, stoned and halved
- 2 cups water - 2 teaspoons vanilla extract
- 1 tablespoon lemon juice
- 2 tablespoons stevia

Directions:
In a pan, combine the avocado with the plums, water, and the other ingredients, bring to a simmer and cook over medium heat for 10 minutes. Divide the mix into bowls and serve cold.
Per serving: Calories: 178Kcal; Fat: 4.4g; Carbs: 3g; Fiber: 2g; Protein: 5g

405. Quinoa and Black Bean Chili

Preparation time: 10 minutes
Cooking time: 32 minutes **Servings:** 10
Ingredients:

- 1 cup quinoa, cooked
- 38 ounces cooked black beans
- 1 medium white onion, peeled, chopped
- 1 cup of frozen corn
- 1 green bell pepper, deseeded, chopped
- 1 zucchini, chopped
- 1 tablespoon minced chipotle peppers in adobo sauce
- 1 red bell pepper, deseeded, chopped
- 1 jalapeno pepper, deseeded, minced
- 28 ounces crushed tomatoes
- 2 teaspoons minced garlic
- 1/3 teaspoon ground black pepper
- ¾ teaspoon salt - 1 teaspoon dried oregano
- 1 tablespoon red chili powder
- 1 tablespoon ground cumin
- 1 tablespoon olive oil
- 1/4 cup chopped cilantro

Directions:
Take a large pot, place it over medium heat, add oil, and when hot, add onion and cook for 5 minutes.
Then stir in garlic, cumin, and chili powder, cook for 1 minute, add remaining ingredients, except for the corn and quinoa, stir well and simmer for 20 minutes at medium-low heat until cooked. Then stir in corn and quinoa, cook for 5 minutes until hot and then top with cilantro. Serve straight away.
Per serving: Calories: 233Kcal; Fat: 3.5g; Carbs: 42g; Fiber: 11.8g; Protein: 11.5g

406. Mushroom, Lentil, and Barley Stew

Preparation time: 10 minutes
Cooking time: 6 hours **Servings:** 8
Ingredients:

- 3/4 cup pearl barley
- 2 cups sliced button mushrooms
- 3/4 cup dry lentils
- 1-ounce dried shiitake mushrooms
- 2 teaspoons minced garlic
- 1/4 cup dried onion flakes
- 2 teaspoons ground black pepper
- 1 teaspoon dried basil - 2 ½ teaspoons salt
- 2 teaspoons dried savory - 3 bay leaves
- 2 quarts vegetable broth

Directions:
Switch on the slow cooker, place all the ingredients in it, and stir until combined. Shut with lid and cook the stew for 6 hours at a high heat setting until cooked.
Serve straight away.
Per serving: Calories: 213Kcal; Fat: 1.2g; Carbs: 44g; Fiber: 9g; Protein: 8.4g

407. Sweet Potato, Kale and Peanut Stew

Preparation time: 10 minutes
Cooking time: 45 minutes **Servings:** 3
Ingredients:

- 1/4 cup red lentils
- 2 medium sweet potatoes, peeled, cubed
- 1 medium white onion, peeled, diced
- 1 cup kale, chopped
- 2 tomatoes, diced
- 1/4 cup chopped green onion
- 1 teaspoon minced garlic
- 1 inch of ginger, grated
- 2 tablespoons toasted peanuts
- ¼ teaspoon ground black pepper
- 1 teaspoon ground cumin
- 1/2 teaspoon turmeric
- 1/8 teaspoon cayenne pepper
- 1 tablespoon peanut butter
- 1 1/2 cups vegetable broth
- 2 teaspoons coconut oil

Directions:
Take a medium pot, place it medium heat, add oil and when it melts, add onions and cook for 5 minutes. Then stir in ginger and garlic, cook for 2 minutes until fragrant, add lentils and potatoes along with all the spices, and stir until mixed. Stir in tomatoes, pour in the broth, bring the mixture to boil, then switch heat to the low level and simmer for 30 minutes until cooked. Then stir in peanut butter until incorporated and then puree by using an immersion blender until half-pureed. Return stew over low heat, stir in kale, cook for 5 minutes until its leaves wilts, and then season with black pepper and salt. Garnish the stew with peanuts and green onions and then serve.
Per serving: Calories: 401Kcal; Fat: 6.7g; Carbs: 77.3g; Fiber: 16g; Protein: 10.8g

408. Vegetarian Irish Stew

Preparation time: 5 minutes
Cooking time: 38 minutes
Servings: 6
Ingredients:

- 1 cup textured vegetable protein, chunks
- ½ cup split red lentils
- 2 medium onions, peeled, sliced
- 1 cup sliced parsnip
- 2 cups sliced mushrooms
- 1 cup diced celery,
- 1/4 cup flour
- 4 cups vegetable stock
- 1 cup rutabaga
- 1 bay leaf
- ½ cup fresh parsley
- 1 teaspoon sugar
- ¼ teaspoon ground black pepper

- 1/4 cup soy sauce
- ¼ teaspoon thyme
- 2 teaspoons marmite
- ¼ teaspoon rosemary
- 2/3 teaspoon salt
- ¼ teaspoon marjoram

Directions:
Take a large soup pot, place it over medium heat, add oil and when it gets hot, add onions and cook for 5 minutes until softened. Then switch heat to the low level, sprinkle with flour, stir well, add remaining ingredients, stir until combined, and simmer for 30 minutes until vegetables have cooked. When done, season the stew with salt and black pepper and then serve.

Per serving: Calories: 117.4Kcal; Fat: 4g; Carbs: 22.8g; Fiber: 7.3g; Protein: 6.5g

409. White Bean and Cabbage Stew

Preparation time: 5 minutes
Cooking time: 8 hours **Servings:** 4
Ingredients:

- 3 cups cooked great northern beans
- 1.5 pounds potatoes, peeled, cut in large dice
- 1 large white onion, peeled, chopped
- ½ head of cabbage, chopped
- 3 ribs celery, chopped
- 4 medium carrots, peeled, sliced
- 14.5 ounces diced tomatoes
- 1/3 cup pearled barley
- 1 teaspoon minced garlic
- ½ teaspoon ground black pepper
- 1 bay leaf
- 1 teaspoon dried thyme
- ½ teaspoon crushed rosemary
- 1 teaspoon salt
- ½ teaspoon caraway seeds
- 1 tablespoon chopped parsley
- 8 cups vegetable broth

Directions:
Switch on the slow cooker, then add all the ingredients, except for the salt, parsley, tomatoes, and beans, and stir until mixed. Shut the slow cooker with a lid, and cook for 7 hours at a low heat setting until cooked. Then stir in remaining ingredients, stir until combined, and continue cooking for 1 hour.
Serve straight away

Per serving: Calories: 150Kcal; Fat: 0.7g; Carbs: 27g; Fiber: 9.4g; Protein: 7g

410. Spinach and Cannellini Bean Stew

Preparation time: 10 minutes
Cooking time: 15 minutes **Servings:** 6
Ingredients:

- 28 ounces cooked cannellini beans
- 24 ounces tomato passata
- 17 ounces spinach chopped
- ¼ teaspoon ground black pepper
- 2/3 teaspoon salt
- 1 ¼ teaspoon curry powder
- 1 cup cashew butter
- ¼ teaspoon cardamom
- 2 tablespoons olive oil
- 1 teaspoon salt
- ¼ cup cashews
- 2 tablespoons chopped basil
- 2 tablespoons chopped parsley

Directions:
Take a large saucepan, place it over medium heat, add 1 tablespoon oil and when hot, add spinach and cook for 3 minutes until fried. Then stir in butter and tomato passata until well mixed, bring the mixture to a near boil, add beans, and season with ¼ teaspoon curry powder, black pepper, and salt. Take a small saucepan, place it over medium heat, add remaining oil, stir in cashew, stir in salt and curry powder and cook for 4 minutes until roasted, set aside until required.
Transfer cooked stew into a bowl, top with roasted cashews, basil, and parsley, and then serve.

Per serving: Calories: 242Kcal; Fat: 10.2g; Carbs: 31g; Fiber: 8.5g; Protein:11g

411. Cabbage Stew

Preparation time: 10 minutes
Cooking time: 50 minutes
Servings: 6
Ingredients:

- 12 ounces cooked Cannellini beans
- 8 ounces smoked tofu, firm, sliced
- 1 medium cabbage, chopped
- 1 large white onion, peeled, julienned
- 2 ½ teaspoon minced garlic
- 1 tablespoon sweet paprika
- 5 tablespoons tomato paste
- 3 teaspoons smoked paprika
- 1/3 teaspoon ground black pepper
- 2 teaspoons dried thyme
- 2/3 teaspoon salt
- ½ tsp ground coriander
- 3 bay leaves
- 4 tablespoons olive oil
- 1 cup vegetable broth

Directions:
Take a large saucepan, place it over medium heat, add 3 tablespoons oil and when hot, add onion and garlic and cook for 3 minutes or until sauté.
Add cabbage, pour in water, simmer for 10 minutes or until softened, then stir in all the spices and continue cooking for 30 minutes.
Add beans and tomato paste, pour in water, stir until mixed and cook for 15 minutes until thoroughly cooked. Take a separate skillet pan, add 1 tablespoon oil and when hot, add tofu slices and cook for 5 minutes until golden brown on both sides.
Serve cooked cabbage stew with fried tofu.

Per serving: Calories: 182Kcal; Fat: 8.3g; Carbs: 27g; Fiber:9.4; Protein: 5.5g

412. Kimchi Stew

Preparation time: 10 minutes
Cooking time: 25 minutes
Servings: 4
Ingredients:
- 1-pound tofu, extra-firm, pressed, cut into 1-inch pieces
- 4 cups napa cabbage kimchi, vegan, chopped
- 1 small white onion, peeled, diced
- 2 cups sliced shiitake mushroom caps
- 1 ½ teaspoon minced garlic
- 2 tablespoons soy sauce
- 2 tablespoons olive oil, divided
- 4 cups vegetable broth
- 2 tablespoons chopped scallions

Directions:
Take a large pot, place it over medium heat, add 1 tablespoon oil and when hot, add tofu pieces in a single layer and cook for 10 minutes until browned on all sides.
When cooked, transfer tofu pieces to a plate, add remaining oil to the pot and when hot, add onion and cook for 5 minutes until soft.
Stir in garlic, cook for 1 minute until fragrant, stir in kimchi, continue cooking for 2 minutes, then add mushrooms and pour in broth.
Switch heat to medium-high level, bring the mixture to a boil, then switch heat to medium-low level, and simmer for 10 minutes until mushrooms are softened.
Stir in tofu, taste to adjust seasoning, and garnish with scallions.
Serve straight away.
Per serving: Calories: 153Kcal; Fat: 8.2g; Carbs: 25g; Fiber: 2.6g; Protein: 8.4g

413. Spicy Bean Stew

Preparation time: 5 minutes
Cooking time: 50 minutes **Servings:** 4
Ingredients:
- 7 ounces cooked black eye beans
- 14 ounces chopped tomatoes
- 2 medium carrots, peeled, diced
- 7 ounces cooked kidney beans
- 1 leek, diced
- ½ a chili, chopped
- 1 teaspoon minced garlic
- 1/3 teaspoon ground black pepper
- 2/3 teaspoon salt
- 1 teaspoon red chili powder
- 1 lemon, juiced
- 3 tablespoons white wine
- 1 tablespoon olive oil
- 1 2/3 cups vegetable stock

Directions:
Take a large saucepan, place it over medium-high heat, add oil and when hot, add leeks and cook for 8 minutes or until softened. Then add carrots, continue cooking for 4 minutes, stir in chili and garlic, pour in the wine, and continue cooking for 2 minutes.
Add tomatoes, stir in lemon juice, pour in the stock and bring the mixture to boil. Switch heat to medium level, simmer for 35 minutes until stew has thickened, then add both beans along with remaining ingredients and cook for 5 minutes until hot. Serve straight away.
Per serving: Calories: 114Kcal; Fat: 1.6g; Carbs: 19g; Fiber: 8.4g; Protein: 6g

414. Eggplant, Onion and Tomato Stew

Preparation time: 5 minutes
Cooking time: 5 minutes **Servings:** 4
Ingredients:
- 3 1/2 cups cubed eggplant
- 1 cup diced white onion
- 2 cups diced tomatoes
- 1 teaspoon ground cumin
- 1/8 teaspoon ground cayenne pepper
- 1 teaspoon salt
- 1 cup tomato sauce
- 1/2 cup water

Directions:
Switch on the instant pot, place all the ingredients in it, stir until mixed, and seal the pot. Press the 'manual' button and cook for 5 minutes at a high-pressure setting until cooked. When done, do quick pressure release, open the instant pot, and stir the stew. Serve straight away.
Per serving: Calories: 88Kcal; Fat: 1g; Carbs: 21g; Fiber: 6g; Protein: 3g

415. Brussel Sprouts Stew

Preparation time: 10 minutes
Cooking time: 55 minutes **Servings:** 4
Ingredients:
- 35 ounces Brussels sprouts
- 5 medium potato, peeled, chopped
- 1 medium onion, peeled, chopped
- 2 carrot, peeled, cubed
- 2 teaspoon smoked paprika
- 1/8 teaspoon ground black pepper
- 1/8 teaspoon salt
- 3 tablespoons caraway seeds
- 1/2 teaspoon red chili powder
- 1 tablespoon nutmeg
- 1 tablespoon olive oil
- 4 ½ cups hot vegetable stock

Directions:
Take a large pot, place it over medium-high heat, add oil, and when hot, add onion and cook for 1 minute.
Then add carrot and potato, cook for 2 minutes, then add Brussel sprouts and cook for 5 minutes.
Stir in all the spices, pour in vegetable stock, bring the mixture to boil, switch heat to medium-low and simmer for 45 minutes until cooked and stew reaches the desired thickness. Serve straight away.
Per serving: Calories: 156Kcal; Fat: 3g; Carbs: 22g; Fiber: 5g; Protein: 12g

CHAPTER 22:
Stir-Fried, Grilled and Roasted Vegetables

416. Roasted Corn
Preparation time: 5 minutes **Cooking time:** 10 minutes
Servings: 4
Ingredients:
- 4 ears of corn, husk removed
- ½ teaspoon ground black pepper
- 1 teaspoon salt - 3 teaspoons olive oil

Directions:
Switch on the air fryer, insert the fryer basket, then shut it with the lid, set the frying temperature to 400 degrees F, and let it preheat for 5 minutes. Meanwhile, remove husk and silk from corn, rinse them well, and pat dry. Then cut the corns to fit into the fryer basket, drizzle with oil, and season with black pepper and salt. Open the preheated fryer, place corns in it, close the lid and cook for 10 minutes until golden brown and cooked, turning halfway. When done, the air fryer will beep and then open the lid and transfer corn to a dish.
Serve straight away.
Per serving: Calories: 175Kcal; Fat: 7.7g; Carbs: 27g; Fiber: 3g; Protein: 4.8g

417. Plantain Chips
Preparation time: 5 minutes
Cooking time: 20 minutes **Servings:** 2
Ingredients:
- 3 green plantains, peeled, sliced
- 1 lime, zested - ½ teaspoon garlic powder
- 1 teaspoon of sea salt
- 1/8 teaspoon red chili powder
- 2 teaspoons olive oil
- 1 cup guacamole, for serving

Directions:
Switch on the air fryer, insert the fryer basket, then shut it with the lid, set the frying temperature 374 degrees F, and let it preheat for 5 minutes. Meanwhile, take a large bowl, add plantain slices in it along with remaining ingredients, except for the guacamole and toss until coated. Open the preheated fryer, place plantain in it, close the lid and cook for 20 minutes until golden brown and cooked, shaking every 5 minutes. When done, the air fryer will beep and then open the lid and transfer plantain chips to a dish. Serve plantain chips with guacamole.
Per serving: Calories: 220Kcal; Fat: 12g; Carbs: 25g; Fiber: 2g; Protein: 1g

418. Roasted Garlic
Preparation time: 10 minutes
Cooking time: 25 minutes **Servings:** 4
Ingredients:
- 1 medium head of garlic
- Olive oil spray

Directions:
Switch on the air fryer, insert the fryer basket, then shut it with the lid, set the frying temperature to 400 degrees F, and let it preheat for 5 minutes. Meanwhile, remove excess peel from the garlic head, and then expose the top of garlic by removing ¼-inch off the top. Spray the garlic head with oil generously and then wrap it with a foil. Open the preheated fryer, place wrapped garlic head in it, close the lid and cook for 25 minutes until done.
When done, the air fryer will beep, then open the lid, transfer garlic to a dish and let it cool for 5 minutes.
Then squeeze the garlic out of its skin and serve with warmed garlic or as desired.
Per serving: Calories: 160Kcal; Fat: 2.5g; Carbs: 27g; Fiber: 3g; Protein: 6g

419. Maple Roasted Brussels sprouts
Preparation time: 5 minutes
Cooking time: 10 minutes **Servings:** 2
Ingredients:
- 2 cups Brussels sprouts, ¼-inch thick sliced
- 1/4 teaspoon sea salt
- 1 tablespoon balsamic vinegar
- 1 tablespoon maple syrup

Directions:
Switch on the air fryer, insert the fryer basket, then shut it with the lid, set the frying temperature to 400 degrees F, and let it preheat for 5 minutes.
Meanwhile, take a large bowl, add Brussel sprouts in it, season with salt, drizzle with vinegar and maple syrup and toss until well coated. Open the preheated fryer, place Brussel sprouts in it, close the lid and cook for 10 minutes until golden brown and cooked, shaking halfway. When done, the air fryer will beep, then open the lid and transfer Brussel sprouts to a dish.
Serve straight away.
Per serving: Calories: 85.3Kcal; Fat: 3.3g; Carbs: 13.1g; Fiber: 2.8g; Protein: 2.8g

420. Roasted Butternut Squash with Mushrooms and Cranberries
Preparation time: 5 minutes **Cooking time:** 30 minutes
Servings: 6
Ingredients:
- 4 cups diced butternut squash
- 1 cup sliced green onions
- 8 ounces button mushrooms, destemmed, quartered
- ¼ cup dried cranberries

For the Sauce:
- 1 tablespoon maple syrup
- 4 cloves of garlic, peeled
- 1 tablespoon soy sauce

- 1 tablespoon balsamic vinegar
- 1 tablespoon olive oil

Directions:
Switch on the air fryer, insert the fryer basket, then shut it with the lid, set the frying temperature to 400 degrees F, and let it preheat for 5 minutes. Meanwhile, prepare the sauce and for this, place all of its ingredients in a food processor and puree for 1 minute until blended. Take a large bowl, place all the vegetables and berries, add sauce and toss until coated. Open the preheated fryer, place vegetables in it, close the lid and cook for 30 minutes until golden brown and cooked, shaking every 10 minutes.

When done, the air fryer will beep, then open the lid, transfer vegetables and berries to a dish and garnish with some more green onions.

Serve straight away.

Per serving: Calories: 128Kcal; Fat: 2.6g; Carbs: 28g; Fiber: 8.6g; Protein: 2.2g

421. Roasted Green Beans

Preparation time: 5 minutes
Cooking time: 10 minutes **Servings:** 2
Ingredients:
- 8 ounces green beans, trimmed
- 1 teaspoon sesame oil
- 1 tablespoon soy sauce

Directions:
Switch on the air fryer, insert the fryer basket, then shut it with the lid, set the frying temperature to 400 degrees F, and let it preheat for 5 minutes. Meanwhile, snap the green beans into half, place them in a large bowl, add oil and soy sauce and toss until well coated. Open the preheated fryer, place green beans in it, spray with olive oil, close the lid and cook for 10 minutes until golden brown and cooked, shaking halfway.

When done, the air fryer will beep and then open the lid and transfer green beans to a dish.

Serve straight away.

Per serving: Calories: 33.2Kcal; Fat: 2.5g; Carbs: 2.7g; Fiber: 1.3g; Protein: 0g

422. Shishito Peppers

Preparation time: 5 minutes
Cooking time: 6 minutes **Servings:** 4
Ingredients:
- 20 Shishito peppers
- 1 teaspoon salt
- Olive oil spray

Directions:
Switch on the air fryer, insert the fryer basket, then shut it with the lid, set the frying temperature 390 degrees F, and let it preheat for 5 minutes. Open the preheated fryer, place peppers in it, spray well with olive oil, close the lid and cook for 6 minutes until cooked and lightly charred, shaking halfway. When done, the air fryer will beep, open the lid, transfer peppers to a dish, and season with salt. Serve straight away.

Per serving: Calories: 21Kcal; Fat: 1g; Carbs: 5g; Fiber: 2g; Protein: 1g

423. Baby Bok Choy

Preparation time: 5 minutes
Cooking time: 6 minutes **Servings:** 4
Ingredients:
- 4 bunches of babies bok choy
- 1 teaspoon garlic powder
- Olive oil spray

Directions:
Switch on the air fryer, insert the fryer basket, then shut it with the lid, set the frying temperature to 350 degrees F, and let it preheat for 5 minutes.

Meanwhile, prepare the bok choy and for this, slice off the bottom, separate the leaves, rinse and drain well. Open the preheated fryer, place bok choy in it, spray generously with olive oil, sprinkle with garlic powder, shake well, close the lid and cook for 6 minutes until golden brown and cooked, shaking halfway. When done, the air fryer will beep, then open the lid and transfer bok choy to a dish.

Serve straight away.

Per serving: Calories: 58Kcal; Fat: 2g; Carbs: 5g; Fiber: 1g; Protein: 1g

424. Popcorn Tofu

Preparation time: 5 minutes
Cooking time: 24 minutes **Servings:** 4
Ingredients:
- 14 ounces tofu, extra-firm, pressed, drained
- 1 ½ cup panko bread crumbs

For the Batter:
- 1 teaspoon onion powder
- 1/2 cup cornmeal
- 1/2 cup chickpea flour
- 1 teaspoon garlic powder
- 1/2 teaspoon ground black pepper
- 1/2 teaspoon salt
- 1 tablespoon Vegetarian Bouillon
- 2 tablespoons nutritional yeast
- 1 tablespoon Dijon mustard
- 3/4 cup almond milk, unsweetened

Directions:
Switch on the air fryer, insert the fryer basket, then shut it with the lid, set the frying temperature to 350 degrees F, and let it preheat for 5 minutes.

Meanwhile, prepare the batter and for this, place all of its ingredients in a large bowl and then whisk until combined until smooth batter comes together. Take a shallow dish and then place bread crumbs in it.

Cut tofu into bite-size pieces, dip into prepared batter and then dredge with bread crumbs until coated on both sides. Open the preheated fryer, place tofu in it in a single layer, spray with olive oil, close the lid and cook for 12 minutes until golden brown and cooked, shaking halfway.

When done, the air fryer will beep, open the lid, transfer popcorns to a dish, and cover with foil to keep them warm.

Cook remaining tofu popcorns in the same manner and then serve.

Per serving: Calories: 261Kcal; Fat: 5.5g; Carbs:37.5; Fiber: 4.8g; Protein: 16g

425. Roasted Vegetable Kebabs

Preparation time: 5 minutes
Cooking time: 15 minutes **Servings:** 8
Ingredients:
- 2 cups zucchini
- 2 cups mushrooms
- 2 cups onions
- 2 cups bell peppers
- 2 Tbsp olive oil
- 1 Tbsp roasted garlic & herb seasoning

Directions:
Cut vegetables into pieces and toss them with seasoning and oil. Thread the vegetables onto skewers. Grill for 15 minutes on medium heat until tender.
Per serving: Calories: 68Kcal; Fat: 4g; Carbs: 8g; Protein: 4g

426. Greek Grilled Eggplant Steaks

Preparation time: 20 minutes
Cooking time: 15 minutes **Servings:** 6
Ingredients:
- 2 eggplants - 8 ounces feta, diced
- 4 Roma tomatoes, diced
- 1 hothouse cucumber, diced
- 1 cup parsley, chopped
- 1 Tbsp olive oil
- Kosher salt, pepper, to taste

Directions:
Slice eggplants into 3 thick steaks. Drizzle with oil, salt, pepper. Grill the eggplant in a pan for 4 minutes per side. Top eggplant steaks with remaining ingredients. Serve.
Note: For ovo-lacto vegetarian, lacto vegetarian, pescatarian diets.
Per serving: Calories: 86Kcal; Fat: 7g; Carbs: 12g; Protein: 83g

427. Grilled Broccoli

Preparation time: 5 minutes
Cooking time: 20 minutes **Servings:** 6
Ingredients:
- 6 cups broccoli spears
- 3 Tbsp lemon juice
- 2 Tbsp olive oil
- ¼ tsp salt
- ¼ tsp pepper
- ¾ cup Parmesan cheese, grated

Directions:
Combine broccoli, lemon juice, oil, salt, pepper. Set aside for 30 minutes. Drain marinade and add cheese to coat broccoli. Grill broccoli for 10 minutes per side. Note: For ovo-lacto vegetarian, lacto vegetarian, pescatarian diets.
Per serving: Calories: 107Kcal; Fat: 8g; Carbs: 5g; Protein: 6g

428. Roasted Garlic Grilled Vegetables

Preparation time: 10 minutes
Cooking time: 15 minutes **Servings:** 8
Ingredients:
- 1 ear of corn, cut into chunks -1 onion, sliced
- 3 bell peppers, cut into chunks
- 1 squash, sliced
- 1 cup mushroom halves - 2 Tbsp oil
- 1 Tbsp roasted garlic & herb seasoning

Directions:
Combine vegetables with oil and seasoning in a large dish. Put vegetables in a grill basket or grill rack.
Grill for 15 minutes over medium heat.
Per serving: Calories: 68Kcal; Fat: 4g; Carbs: 8g; Protein: 4g

429. Stir-fry Vegetables

Preparation time: 15 minutes
Cooking time: 10 minutes **Servings:** 10
Ingredients:
- 1 Tbsp oil - 1 onion, sliced
- 1 cup carrots, sliced
- 2 cups broccoli florets
- 2 cups sugar snap peas
- 1 bell pepper, cut into strips
- 1 Tbsp soy sauce
- 1 tsp garlic powder

Directions:
Combine onion, carrots, and oil. Stir-fry for 2 minutes. Add other vegetables, stir-fry for another 7 minutes. Add soy sauce, garlic powder. Stir fry until blended. Serve hot.**Per serving:** Calories: 50Kcal; Fat: 2g; Carbs: 6g; Protein: 2g

430. One-Skillet Veggie Hash

Preparation time: 10 minutes
Cooking time: 25 minutes **Servings:** 4
Ingredients:
- 3 Tbsp olive oil
- 1 onion, diced
- 1 bell pepper, diced
- 3 cloves garlic, minced
- 1 Tbsp sage leaves, chopped
- 3 medium red potatoes, diced
- 1 15-oz can black beans
- 2 cups Swiss chard, chopped
- 1 Tbsp parsley, chopped
- Salt, pepper, to taste

Directions:
In a skillet, cook onion, garlic, and potato in olive oil for 20 minutes. Add the beans and Swiss chard to the skillet, cook for another 3 minutes. Season with salt, pepper. Top with parsley and serve.
Per serving: Calories: 273Kcal; Fat: 11g; Carbs: 39g; Protein: 9g

431. Veggie Hash

Preparation time: 10 minutes
Cooking time: 40 minutes **Servings:** 4
Ingredients:
- 2 medium red potatoes, diced
- 1 can pinto beans
- 1 cup zucchini, chopped
- 1 cup squash, chopped

- 1 red bell pepper, chopped
- ½ cup mushrooms, sliced
- ½ tsp paprika
- Pepper, to taste

Directions:
Preheat oven to 425°F.
Season potatoes with salt and pepper and bake on a baking sheet for 25 minutes. In a baking dish, combine the remaining ingredients. Put in the oven and bake next to potatoes for 15 minutes. Add potatoes to a baking dish, mix well. **Per serving:** Calories: 245Kcal; Fat: 14g; Carbs: 47g; Protein: 11g

432. Grilled Vegetables

Preparation time: 10 minutes
Cooking time: 10 minutes **Servings:** 6
Ingredients:
- 3 red bell peppers, seeded and halved
- 3 yellow squash, julienned
- 3 zucchinis, sliced into rectangles
- 3 Japanese eggplant, sliced into rectangles
- 1 onion, sliced
- 12 cremini mushrooms
- 1 bunch (1 lb) asparagus, trimmed
- 12 green onions, roots cut off
- 1/4 cup + 2 tbsp olive oil
- Salt and freshly ground black pepper, to taste
- 3 tbsp balsamic vinegar
- 2 garlic cloves, minced
- 1 tsp parsley leaves, chopped
- 1 tsp fresh basil leaves, chopped
- 1/2 tsp fresh rosemary leaves, chopped

Directions:
Start by preparing and preheating the grill over medium heat. Toss all the veggies with spices, herbs, and oil in a large bowl. Grease the grilling grates and spread the veggies on the grill. Use a tong to flip the veggies. Grill all the veggies until they are slightly charred. Serve warm.
Per serving: Calories: 372Kcal; Fat: 11.1g; Carbs: 16.9g; Fiber: 0.2g; Protein: 13.5g

433. Mixed Vegetable Platter

Preparation time: 10 minutes
Cooking time: 10 minutes **Servings:** 6
Ingredients:
- 1/4 cup olive oil
- 2 tbsp maple syrup
- 4 tsp balsamic vinegar
- 1 tsp dried oregano
- 1/2 tsp garlic powder
- 1/8 tsp pepper
- Salt, to taste
- 1 medium red onion, cut into wedges
- 1 lb fresh asparagus, trimmed
- 3 small carrots, cut in half
- 1 large sweet red pepper, cut into strips
- 1 medium yellow summer squash, cut into slices

Directions:
Start by whisking the first 7 ingredients in a bowl.
Add 3 tablespoons of this marinade to a plastic bag.
Toss all the veggies into the plastic bag, then seal it.
Shake the bag well, then marinate for 2 hours. Preheat a grill over medium heat and grease its grilling grates. Grill the marinated veggies for 4 minutes per side until crispy Garnish with remaining marinade.
Serve.
Per serving: Calories: 114Kcal; Fat: 5.7g; Carbs: 31.4g; Fiber: 0.6g; Protein: 4.1g

434. Grilled Chopped Veggies

Preparation time: 10 minutes
Cooking time: 10 minutes **Servings:** 4
Ingredients:
- 1 red pepper, sliced
- 1 orange bell pepper, sliced
- 1 green bell pepper, sliced
- 1 zucchini squash, sliced
- 1 red onion, quartered
- 12 oz baby portobello mushrooms
- 1 pinch salt
- 1 pinch black pepper
- 1 loaf sourdough bread, sliced
- 3 tbsp olive oil
- 4 garlic cloves, minced
- Fresh basil and oregano for garnish

Vinaigrette
- 3 tbsp red wine vinegar
- 1/4 cup fresh basil, chopped
- 2 garlic cloves, minced
- 1 1/2 tbsp maple syrup
- 1 tsp Dijon mustard
- 1/4 tsp salt
- 1/4 tsp black pepper
- 1/4 tsp red pepper flakes
- 1/3 cup olive oil

Directions:
Make basil vinaigrette by whisking together all ingredients, then set aside. Preheat the grill over high heat. Slice the bread into slices and brush them with a mixture of olive oil and garlic. Season the vegetables with salt and black pepper. Grill the veggies on the hot grill for 3 minutes per side, then transfer them to a sheet pan. Grill the bread slices for 2 minutes per side. Chop the cooked veggies and add them to a bowl. Toss in basil vinaigrette and mix well.
Garnish with oregano and basil. Serve with grilled bread.
Per serving: Calories: 249Kcal; Fat: 11.9g; Carbs: 41.8g; Fiber: 1.1g; Protein: 1g

435. Garlic Grilled Vegetables

Preparation time: 10 minutes
Cooking time: 15 minutes **Servings:** 6
Ingredients:
- 1 ear corn, cut into chunks
- 1 medium red onion, wedged

- 1 small green bell pepper, diced
- 1 small red bell pepper, diced
- 1 small yellow bell pepper, diced
- 1 small yellow squash, sliced
- 1 cup mushroom halves
- 2 tbsp oil
- 1 tbsp garlic & herb seasoning

Directions:
Start by tossing the vegetables with seasonings and oil in a bowl. Thread the veggies on skewers.
Prepare and preheat the grill over medium heat.
Grill the skewers for 15 minutes while rotating occasionally. Serve warm.
Per serving: Calories: 213Kcal; Fat: 14g; Carbs: 53g; Fiber: 0.7g; Protein: 12g

436. Broccoli and Tomatoes Air Fried Stew

Preparation time: 18 minutes
Cooking time: 12 minutes **Servings:** 4
Ingredients:

- 2 tsp. coriander seeds
- 1 broccoli head, florets separated
- 1 tbsp. olive oil
- salt and black pepper to taste
- 1 yellow onion, chopped
- 28 ounces canned tomatoes, pureed
- 1 pinch of red pepper, crushed
- 1 garlic clove, minced
- 1 small ginger piece, chopped

Directions:
Heat a pan suitable for your air fryer with oil over medium heat, add the onion, salt, pepper, and chili, stir and cook for 7 minutes. Add ginger, garlic, coriander seeds, tomatoes, and broccoli, mix, place in the air fryer and cook at 360°F for 12 minutes. Divide into bowls and serve.
Per serving: Calories: 103Kcal; Fat: 6.43g; Carbs: 11.47g; Fiber: 4.9g; Protein: 2.38g

437. Broccoli Mix

Preparation time: 12 min
Cooking time: 20 minutes **Servings:** 2
Ingredients:

- 2 cups vegetable broth - 3 cups broccoli
- 1 tbsp. cumin powder
- 1 tbsp. cayenne powder
- 3 green onion - salt to taste

Directions:
Add vegetable broth into the air fryer pot. Combine broccoli, cumin powder, cayenne pepper powder, green onion, and salt. Bake at 300°F for 20 minutes. When it's ready, serve and enjoy!
Per serving: Calories: 192Kcal; Fat: 2g; Carbs: 28.2g; Fiber: 2.75g; Protein: 2.7g

438. Brussels Sprouts and Tomatoes Mix

Preparation time: 15 min
Cooking time: 10 minutes **Servings:** 2
Ingredients:

- salt and black pepper to taste
- 1-pound Brussels sprouts, trimmed
- 6 cherry tomatoes, halved
- 1 tbsp. olive oil
- ¼ cup green onions, chopped

Directions:
Spice the Brussels sprouts with salt and pepper, put them in the air fryer, and bake at 350°F for 10 minutes. Transfer them to a bowl, add salt, pepper, cherry tomatoes, greens onions, and olive oil, mix well and serve. **Per serving:** Calories: 184Kcal; Fat: 7.57g; Carbs: 26.88g; Fiber: 9.6g; Protein: 8.46g

439. Chinese Bowls

Preparation time: 25 min
Cooking time: 15 minutes **Servings:** 4
Ingredients:

- 3 tbsp. maple syrup
- 12 ounces firm tofu, cubed
- ¼ cup coconut aminos
- 2 tbsp. lime juice - 2 tbsp. sesame oil
- 2 cup red quinoa, cooked
- 1-pound fresh Romanesco, roughly chopped
- 1 red bell pepper, chopped
- 3 carrots, chopped
- 8 ounces spinach, torn

Directions:
In a bowl, mix the tofu cubes with oil, maple syrup, coconut aminos, and lime juice, mix, transfer to your air fryer and cook at 370°F for 15 minutes, stirring frequently. Add the romanesco, carrot, spinach, pepper, and quinoa, toss, divide into bowls and serve.
Per serving: Calories: 611Kcal; Fat: 28.93g; Carbs: 42.09g; Fiber: 7.4g; Protein: 48.95g

440. Chinese Cauliflower Rice

Preparation time: 30 minutes
Cooking time: 20 minutes
Servings: 4
Ingredients:

- ½ block firm tofu, cubed
- 4 tbsp. coconut aminos
- 1 cup carrot, chopped
- 1 tsp. turmeric powder
- ½ cup yellow onion, chopped
- 3 cups cauliflower, riced
- 1 tbsp. rice vinegar
- 1½ tsp. sesame oil
- ½ cup peas
- ½ cup broccoli florets, chopped
- 2 garlic cloves, minced
- 1 tbsp. ginger, minced

Directions:
In an enormous bowl, combine 2 tbsp. of tofu with coconut aminos, ½ cup onion, turmeric, and carrot, mix to cover, transfer to the air fryer and cook at 370°F for 10 minutes, stirring halfway through cooking. In a bowl, combine the cabbage with riced cauliflower with the rest of the coconut aminos, the sesame oil, garlic, vinegar, ginger, broccoli, and peas, stir, add the tofu mixture from the fryer, mix and cook everything at 370°F for 10 minutes.
Divide between plates and serve.
Per serving: Calories: 111Kcal; Fat: 5.44g; Carbs: 11.34g; Fiber: 3.7g; Protein: 6.56g

441. Chinese Long Beans Mix

Preparation time: 20 minutes
Cooking time: 10 minutes
Servings: 3
Ingredients:
- 1 tbsp. olive oil
- ½ tsp. coconut aminos
- 1 pinch of salt and black pepper
- 4 long beans, trimmed and sliced
- 4 garlic cloves, minced

Directions:
In a pan suitable for your air fryer, combine the long beans with oil, coconut aminos, salt, pepper, and garlic, mix, place in your air fryer and cook at 350°F for 10 minutes.
Divide between plates and serve.
Per serving: Calories: 52Kcal; Fat: 4.55g; Carbs: 2.77g; Fiber: 0.3g; Protein: 0.56g

442. Cool Tofu Mix

Preparation time: 20 min
Cooking time: 10 minutes
Servings: 4
Ingredients:
- 1 cup kale, torn
- 3 ounces firm tofu, pressed and crumbled
- ½ cup broccoli florets
- ¼ cup cherry tomatoes, halved
- ½ cup mushrooms, halved
- ½ cup carrot, grated
- ¼ tsp. onion powder
- ¼ cup microgreens
- ¼ tsp. garlic powder
- ½ tsp. yellow curry powder
- salt and black pepper to taste
- ¼ tsp. sweet paprika
- vegan cooking spray

Directions:
Heat your air fryer to 380°F, grease the pan with cooking spray, add the tofu, kale, broccoli, mushrooms, tomatoes, carrots, garlic powder, onion powder, curry, paprika, salt, and pepper, mix, cover, and cook 10 minutes.
Divide between plates, add the micro vegetables, mix and serve.
Per serving: Calories: 50Kcal; Fat: 2.13g; Carbs: 4.76g; Fiber: 1.7g; Protein: 4.52g

443. Coriander Endives

Preparation time: 20 minutes
Cooking time: 15 minutes
Servings: 4
Ingredients:
- 1 tbsp. coriander, chopped
- 2 endives, trimmed and halved
- 1 tsp. sweet paprika
- 1 pinch of salt and black pepper
- ½ cup almonds, chopped
- 2 tbsp. olive oil
- 2 tbsp. white vinegar

Directions:
Toss the endive with cilantro and other ingredients in the air fryer's pan, mix, bake at 350°F for 15 minutes, divided into dishes, and serve.
Per serving: Calories: 68Kcal; Fat: 6.92g; Carbs: 1.49g; Fiber: 0.4g; Protein: 0.34g

444. Garlic Eggplants

Preparation time: 20 minutes
Cooking time: 9 minutes **Servings:** 4
Ingredients:
- 2 garlic cloves, minced
- 2 tbsp. olive oil
- 3 eggplants, halved and sliced
- 1 green onion stalk, chopped
- 1 red chili pepper, chopped
- 1 tbsp. ginger, grated
- 1 tbsp. balsamic vinegar
- 1 tbsp. coconut aminos

Directions:
Heat a pan suitable for your air fryer with oil over medium-high heat, add the eggplant slices and cook for 2 minutes. Add the chili, garlic, green onions, ginger, coconut aminos, and vinegar, place it in the air fryer and cook at 320°F for 7 minutes. Divide between plates and serve.
Per serving: Calories: 175Kcal; Fat: 7.57g; Carbs: 26.74g; Fiber: 12.6g; Protein: 4.41g

445. Hot Cabbage Mix

Preparation time: 30 min
Cooking time: 20 minutes **Servings:** 2
Ingredients:
- 1 yellow onion, chopped
- ½ cabbage head, chopped
- salt and black pepper to taste
- 1 dash of Tabasco sauce
- 1 cup coconut cream

Directions:
Place the cabbage in a pan suitable for your air fryer. Add onion, salt, pepper, Tabasco sauce, and coconut cream, mix, put in the air fryer, and cook at 400°F for 20 minutes. Divide between plates and serve.
Per serving: Calories: 506Kcal; Fat: 46.59g; Carbs: 23.97g; Fiber: 6.7g; Protein: 7.25g

446. Indian Potatoes

Preparation time: 10 min
Cooking time: 12 minutes **Servings:** 3
Ingredients:
- 1 tbsp. cumin seeds
- 1 tbsp. coriander seeds
- salt and black pepper to taste
- ½ tsp. red chili powder
- ½ tsp. turmeric powder
- 1 tsp. pomegranate powder
- 2 tbsp. olive oil
- 2 tsp. fenugreek, dried
- 1 tbsp. pickled mango, chopped
- 5 potatoes, boiled, peeled, and cubed

Directions:
Heat a pan suitable for your fryer with oil over medium heat, add the coriander and cumin seeds, stir and cook for 2 minutes. Add salt, pepper, turmeric, chili powder, pomegranate powder, mango, fenugreek, and potatoes, mix, place in an air fryer and cook at 360°F for 10 minutes. Divide among plates and serve hot.
Per serving: Calories: 387Kcal; Fat: 11.34g; Carbs: 69.12g; Fiber: 9.9g; Protein: 7.36g

447. Leeks Medley

Preparation time: 22 minutes
Cooking time: 12 minutes **Servings:** 4
Ingredients:
- 1 tbsp. cumin, ground
- 6 leeks, roughly chopped
- 1 tbsp. mint, chopped
- salt and black pepper to taste1 tsp. garlic, minced
- 1 tbsp. parsley, chopped
- 1 drizzle of olive oil

Directions:
In a pan suitable for your air fryer, mix the leeks with the cumin, mint, parsley, garlic, salt, pepper, and oil, mix, place in your air fryer and cook at 350°F for 12 minutes. Divide the leek mixture between plates and serve.
Per serving: Calories: 174Kcal; Fat: 5.11g; Carbs: 20.68g; Fiber: 2.8g; Protein: 12.57g

448. Mediterranean Chickpeas

Preparation time: 10 minutes
Cooking time: 12 minutes **Servings:** 2
Ingredients:
- 3 shallots, chopped
- vegan cooking spray
- 2 garlic cloves, minced
- ½ tsp. smoked paprika
- ½ tsp. sweet paprika
- 1 tbsp. parsley, chopped
- ½ tsp. cinnamon powder
- 2 tomatoes, chopped
- salt and black pepper to taste
- 2 cup chickpeas, cooked

Directions:
Sprig the air fryer with cooking spray and preheat to 365°F. Add the chives, garlic, sweet and smoked paprika, cinnamon, salt, pepper, tomatoes, parsley, and chickpeas, mix, cover, and cook for 12 minutes. Divide into bowls and serve.
Per serving: Calories: 404.5Kcal; Fat: 6.35g; Carbs: 68.82g; Fiber: 13.8g; Protein: 21.6g

449. Mexican Peppers Mix

Preparation time: 28 minutes
Cooking time: 16 minutes **Servings:** 4
Ingredients:
- ½ cup tomato juice
- 4 bell peppers, cut into medium chunks
- 2 tbsp. jarred jalapenos, chopped
- ¼ cup yellow onion, chopped
- 1 cup tomatoes, chopped
- ¼ cup green peppers, chopped
- 2 cups tomato sauce
- 2 tsp. onion powder
- 1 tsp. cumin, ground
- 1 tsp. chili powder
- ½ tsp. red pepper, crushed
- ½ tsp. garlic powder
- salt and black pepper to taste

Directions:
In a pan suitable for your air fryer, combine the tomato juice, jalapeño, tomatoes, onion, green peppers, salt, pepper, onion powder, red pepper, chili powder, garlic powder, oregano, and cumin, mix well, mix well in your air fryer and cook at 350°F for 6 minutes Add the peppers and cook at 320°F for another 10 minutes. Divide the pepper mixture between plates and serve.
Per serving: Calories: 194Kcal; Fat: 1.5g; Carbs: 37.35g; Fiber: 10.6g; Protein: 5.59g

450. Paprika Broccoli

Preparation time: 30 min
Cooking time: 15 minutes **Servings:** 4
Ingredients:
- juice of ½ lemon
- 1 broccoli head, florets separated
- 1 tbsp. olive oil
- 1 tbsp. sesame seeds
- salt and black pepper to taste
- 2 tsp. paprika
- 3 garlic cloves, minced

Directions:
In a portable bowl, toss the broccoli with the lemon juice, oil, paprika, salt, pepper, and garlic and toss to coat. Transfer in the basket of the air fryer, bake at 360°F for 15 minutes, sprinkle sesame seeds, cook another 5 minutes, divide between the plates and serve.
Per serving: Calories: 55Kcal; Fat: 4.8g; Carbs: 3.08g; Fiber: 0.9g; Protein: 0.96g

451. Pumpkin Tasty Seeds

Preparation time: 16 min
Cooking time: 15 minutes **Servings:** 3
Ingredients:

- 2 tbsp. olive oil
- 1 onion, chopped
- 1 carrot, chopped
- 2 cloves garlic, minced
- 2 tsp. curry powder
- salt to taste - 4 cups vegetable broth
- 2 tbsp. pumpkin seeds
- parsley to garnish

Directions:
Add oil into the air fryer pot. Combine the onion, carrots, garlic, curry powder, vegetable broth, pumpkin seeds, and salt. Bake at 300°F for 15 minutes. When it's ready, garnish with the parsley to serve.
Per serving: Calories: 154Kcal; Fat: 11.7g; Carbs: 11.5g; Fiber: 2.3g; Protein: 2.4g

452. Red Potatoes and Green Beans

Preparation time: 25 minutes
Cooking time: 15 minutes **Servings:** 4
Ingredients:

- 1-pound green beans
- 1-pound red potatoes, cut into wedges
- 2 garlic cloves, minced
- ½ tsp. oregano, dried
- salt and black pepper to taste
- 2 tbsp. olive oil

Directions:
In a pan suitable for your air fryer, mix the potatoes with the green beans, garlic, oil, salt, pepper, and oregano, mix, place in your air fryer and cook at 380°F for 15 minutes. Divide between plates and serve. **Per serving:** Calories: 171Kcal; Fat: 7.47g; Carbs: 24.58g; Fiber: 4.3g; Protein: 3.74g

453. Rice and Veggies

Preparation time: 20 minutes
Cooking time: 10 minutes **Servings:** 4
Ingredients:

- 1 tbsp. olive oil - 2 cups rice, cooked
- salt and black pepper to taste
- 2 carrots, chopped - 10 tbsp. coconut cream
- 4 garlic cloves, minced
- 3 small broccoli florets

Directions:
Warm your air fryer to 350°F, add the oil, garlic, carrots, broccoli, salt, and pepper, and mix. Add the rice and coconut cream, mix, cover, and cook for 10 minutes. Divide the rice and vegetables between plates and serve.
Per serving: Calories: 362Kcal; Fat: 28.79g; Carbs: 36.8g; Fiber: 14.3g; Protein: 9.94g

454. White Mushrooms Mix

Preparation time: 25 minutes
Cooking time: 15 minutes **Servings:** 2
Ingredients:

- 7 ounces snow peas
- salt and black pepper to taste
- 8 ounces white mushrooms, halved
- 1 tsp. olive oil
- 2 tbsp. coconut aminos
- 1 yellow onion, cut into rings

Directions:
In a portable bowl, peas with mushrooms, onion, coconut aminos, oil, salt, and pepper, mix well, transfer to a saucepan suitable for your air fryer, place in the air fryer, and cook at 350°F for 15 minutes.
Divide between plates and serve.
Per serving: Calories: 105Kcal; Fat: 3.06g; Carbs: 16.18g; Fiber: 5.6g; Protein: 5.8g

455. Yam Mix

Preparation time: 18 minutes
Cooking time: 8 minutes **Servings:** 4
Ingredients:

- ½ tsp. cinnamon powder
- 16 ounces canned candied yams, drained
- ¼ tsp. allspice, ground
- 1 tbsp. flax meal mixed with 2 tbsp. water
- ½ cup coconut sugar
- 2 tbsp. coconut cream
- vegan cooking spray
- ½ cup maple syrup

Directions:
In a bowl, combine the sweet potatoes with the cinnamon and all the spices, mash with a fork and mix well.
Grease your air fryer with cooking spray, preheat to 400°F, and drizzle with the sweet potato mixture on the bottom.
Add the sugar, flax flour, coconut cream, and maple syrup, mix gently, cover, and cook for 8 minutes. Divide the sweet potato mixture between plates and serve for breakfast.
Per serving: Calories: 314Kcal; Fat: 2.89g; Carbs: 71.95g; Fiber: 5g; Protein: 2.1g

CHAPTER 23:
Sauce, Condiments & Dressing

456. White Beans Dip
Preparation time: 15 minutes
Cooking time: 0 minutes **Servings:** 6
Ingredients:
- ½ cup olive oil
- 2 tablespoons garlic cloves, chopped
- 2 (15.8-ounce) cans white beans, drained and rinsed
- ¼ cup fresh lemon juice
- 4 tablespoons fresh parsley, chopped and divided
- 1 teaspoon ground cumin
- ½ tablespoon salt
- 1 teaspoon ground white pepper

Directions:
In a small saucepan, place the olive oil and garlic over medium-low heat and cook for about 2 minutes, stirring continuously. Remove the pan of garlic oil from heat and let it cool slightly. Strain the garlic oil, reserving both the oil and garlic in separate bowls. In a food processor, place the beans, garlic, lemon juice, 2 tablespoons of parsley, and cumin, and pulse until smooth. While the motor is running, add the reserved oil and pulse until light and smooth. Transfer the dip into a bowl and stir in salt and white pepper. Serve with the garnishing of remaining parsley.
Per serving: Calories: 263Kcal; Fat: 18.1g; Carbs: 20.2g; Fiber: 5.7g; Protein: 7g

457. Edamame Hummus
Preparation time: 15 minutes
Cooking time: 15 minutes **Servings:** 8
Ingredients:
- 10 ounces frozen edamame pods
- 1 ripe avocado, peeled, pitted, and chopped roughly
- ½ cup fresh cilantro, chopped
- ¼ cup scallion, chopped
- 1 jalapeño pepper - 1 garlic clove, peeled
- 2–3 tablespoons fresh lime juice
- Salt and ground black pepper, to taste
- ¼ cup avocado oil
- 2 tablespoons fresh basil leaves

Directions:
In a small pot of boiling water, cook the edamame pods for 6–8 minutes. Drain the edamame pods and let them cool completely. Remove soybeans from the pods. In a food processor, add edamame and remaining ingredients (except for oil) and pulse until mostly pureed. While the motor is running, add the reserved oil and pulse until light and smooth. Transfer the hummus into a bowl and serve with the garnishing of remaining basil leaves.
Per serving: Calories: 339Kcal; Fat: 33.8g; Carbs: 6.3g; Fiber: 3.1g; Protein: 5.1g

458. Beans Mayonnaise
Preparation time: 10 minutes
Cooking time: 0 minutes **Servings:** 4
Ingredients:
- 1 (15-ounce) can white beans, drained and rinsed
- 2 tablespoons apple cider vinegar
- 1 tablespoon fresh lemon juice
- 2 tablespoons yellow mustard
- ¾ teaspoon salt
- 2 garlic cloves, peeled
- 2 tablespoons aquafaba (liquid from the can of beans)

Directions:
In a food processor, add all ingredients (except for oil) and pulse until mostly pureed. While the motor is running, add the reserved oil and pulse until light and smooth. Transfer the mayonnaise into a container and refrigerate to chill before serving.
Per serving: Calories: 8Kcal; Fat: 1.1g; Carbs: 14.3g; Fiber: 4.1g; Protein: 5.2g

459. Cashew Cream
Preparation time: 10 minutes
Cooking time: 0 minutes **Servings:** 5
Ingredients:
- 1 cup raw, unsalted cashews, soaked for 12 hours, and drained
- ½ cup water
- 1 tablespoon nutritional yeast
- 1 teaspoon fresh lemon juice
- 1/8 teaspoon salt

Directions:
In a food processor, add all ingredients and pulse at high speed until creamy and smooth. Serve immediately. **Per serving:** Calories: 165Kcal; Fat: 2.5g; Carbs: 9.9g; Fiber: 1.3g; Protein: 5.1g

460. Lemon Tahini
Preparation time: 15 minutes
Cooking time: 0 minutes **Servings:** 4
Ingredients:
- ¼ cup fresh lemon juice
- 4 medium garlic cloves, pressed
- ½ cup tahini
- ½ teaspoon fine sea salt
- Pinch of ground cumin
- 6 tablespoons ice water

Directions:
In a medium bowl, combine the lemon juice and garlic and set aside for 10 minutes. Through a fine-mesh sieve, strain the

mixture into another medium bowl, pressing the garlic solids. Discard the garlic solids. In the bowl of lemon juice, add the tahini, salt, and cumin, and whisk until well blended. Slowly, add water, 2 tablespoons at a time, whisking well after each addition.
Per serving: Calories: 187Kcal; Fat: 16.3g; Carbs: 7.7g; Fiber: 2.9g; Protein: 5.4g

461. Avocado Dill Dressing

Preparation time: 20 minutes
Cooking time: 0 minutes **Servings:** 1 cup
Ingredients:

- 2 ounces raw, unsalted cashews (about ½ cup) - ½ cup water
- 3 tablespoons lemon juice
- ½ medium, ripe avocado, chopped
- 1 medium clove garlic
- 2 tablespoons chopped fresh dill
- 2 green onions, white and green parts, chopped

Directions:
Put the cashews, water, lemon juice, avocado, and garlic into a blender. Keep it aside for at least 15 minutes to soften the cashews.
Blend until everything is fully mixed. Fold in the dill and green onions, and blend briefly to retain some texture. Store in an airtight container in the fridge for up to 3 days and stir well before serving.
Per serving: Calories: 312Kcal; Fat: 21g; Carbs: 23g; Protein: 8g

462. Cilantro Chili Dressing

Preparation time: 5 minutes
Cooking time: 0 minutes **Servings:** ¾ cup
Ingredients:

- 1 (4-ounce) can chopped green chilies
- 1 to 2 cloves garlic
- ¼ cup fresh lime juice
- ¼ cup water
- ¼ cup chopped fresh cilantro
- 2 teaspoons maple syrup (optional)
- Freshly ground pepper, to taste

Directions:
Combine all the ingredients in a food processor and pulse until creamy and smooth.
Per serving: Calories: 54Kcal; Fat: 2g; Carbs: 6g; Protein: 2g

463. Spinach and Avocado Dressing

Preparation time: 10 minutes
Cooking time: 0 minutes **Servings:** 1 cup
Ingredients:

- 2 ounces spinach leaves (about 1 cup chopped and packed)
- ¼ medium, ripe avocado
- ¼ cup water, plus more as needed
- 1 small clove garlic
- 1 tablespoon Dijon mustard
- 1 green onion, white and green parts, sliced

Directions:
Blitz all the ingredients in a blender until thoroughly mixed. Add a little more water if a thinner consistency is desired.
Per serving: Calories: 146Kcal; Fat: 1g; Carbs: 1g; Protein: 2g

464. Maple Dijon Dressing

Preparation time: 5 minutes
Cooking time: 0 minutes **Servings:** ½ cup
Ingredients:

- ¼ cup apple cider vinegar
- 2 teaspoons Dijon mustard
- 2 tablespoons maple syrup
- 2 tablespoons low-sodium vegetable broth
- ¼ teaspoon black pepper
- Salt, to taste (optional)

Directions:
Mix the apple cider vinegar, Dijon mustard, maple syrup, vegetable broth, and black pepper in a resealable container until well incorporated. Season with salt, if desired.
Per serving: Calories: 82Kcal; Fat: 0g; Carbs: 19g; Protein: 1g

465. Orange Mango Dressing

Preparation time: 5 minutes
Cooking time: 0 minutes **Servings:** ¾ cup
Ingredients:

- 1 medium mango, peeled and cut into chunks
- 1 clove garlic, crushed
- ½ cup orange juice
- 1 teaspoon soy sauce
- ¼ teaspoon curry powder

Directions:
Place all the ingredients in a blender and blend until creamy and smooth.
Per serving: Calories: 51Kcal; Fat: 1g; Carbs: 11g; Protein: 1g

466. Cashew Mustard Dressing

Preparation time: 20 minutes
Cooking time: 0 minutes **Servings:** 1 cup
Ingredients:

- 2 ounces raw, unsalted cashews (about ½ cup) - ½ cup water - 3 tablespoons lemon juice
- 2 teaspoons apple cider vinegar
- 2 tablespoons Dijon mustard
- 1 medium clove garlic

Directions:
Put all the ingredients in a food processor and keep it aside for at least 15 minutes. Purée until the ingredients are combined into a smooth and creamy mixture. Thin the dressing with a little extra water as needed to achieve your preferred consistency.
Per serving: Calories: 187Kcal; Fat: 13g; Carbs: 11g; Protein: 6g

467. Vinegary Maple Syrup Dressing

Preparation time: 5 minutes
Cooking time: 0 minutes **Servings:** 2/3 cup
Ingredients:

- ¼ cup rice vinegar

- ¼ cup balsamic vinegar
- 2½ tablespoons maple syrup (optional)
- 1½ tablespoons Dijon mustard
- Freshly ground pepper, to taste

Directions:
Combine all the ingredients in a jar. Cover and shake until well blended.
Per serving: Calories: 49Kcal; Fat: 0g; Carbs: 12g; Protein: 0g

468. Garlic Cilantro Dressing
Preparation time: 10 minutes
Cooking time: 0 minutes **Servings:** 1 cup
Ingredients:
- 1/2 cup almonds
- 1/2 cup water
- 1 bunch cilantro
- 1 red chili pepper, chopped
- 2 cloves garlic, crushed
- 2 tablespoons fresh lime juice
- 1 teaspoon lime zest
- Sea salt and ground black pepper
- 5 tablespoons extra-virgin olive oil

Directions:
Place the almonds and water in your blender and mix until creamy and smooth. Add in the cilantro, chili pepper, garlic, lime juice, lime zest, salt, and black pepper; blitz until everything is well combined. Then, gradually add in the olive oil and mix until smooth.
Per serving: Calories: 181Kcal; Fat: 18g; Carbs: 5g; Protein: 3g

469. Cranberry Dressing
Preparation time: 5 minutes
Cooking time: 0 minutes **Servings:** 2 cups
Ingredients:
- ¼ cup rice vinegar
- ¼ cup Dijon mustard
- ¼ cup cranberry sauce
- ¼ cup apple cider vinegar
- ¼ cup walnut oil
- 1 cup vegetable oil
- 1 garlic clove, chopped
- Salt and ground black pepper, as required

Directions:
Put rice vinegar, Dijon mustard, cranberry sauce, apple cider vinegar, garlic, salt, and black pepper in a blender and pulse until smooth. Add walnut oil and vegetable and pulse to form a creamy mixture.
Dish out in a bowl and serve to enjoy.
Per serving: Calories: 220Kcal; Fat: 12g; Carbs: 7g; Protein: 5g

470. Thai Peanut Dressing
Preparation time: 10 minutes
Cooking time: 0 minutes **Servings:** ½ cup
Ingredients:
- 2 tbsp. Water
- ¼ cup Natural Peanut Butter
- Pinch of Cayenne - 2 tbsp. Sesame Oil
- Juice of ½ of 1 Lemon
- 2 tbsp. Soy Sauce - 1 tsp. Maple Syrup
- 1 tbsp. Rice Vinegar
- 2 Garlic cloves, minced
- 2 tsp. Ginger, fresh & grated

Directions:
Mix all the ingredients in a large bowl, excluding the water, with an immersion blender or blend in a high-speed blender. Blend until you get a smooth, thickened sauce. Add water as needed to get the consistency you desire.
Per serving: Calories: 75Kcal; Fat: 1g; Carbs: 15g; Protein: 4g

471. Herb Avocado Salad Dressing
Preparation time: 10 minutes
Cooking time: 0 minutes **Servings:** 2 cups
Ingredients:
- 1 medium-sized avocado, pitted, peeled, and mashed
- 4 tablespoons extra-virgin olive oil
- 4 tablespoons almond milk
- 2 tablespoons cilantro, minced
- 2 tablespoons parsley, minced
- 1 lemon, juiced - 2 garlic cloves, minced
- 1/2 teaspoon mustard seeds
- 1/2 teaspoon red pepper flakes
- Kosher salt and cayenne pepper, to taste

Directions:
Mix all the above ingredients in your food processor or blender. Blend until uniform, smooth and creamy.
Per serving: Calories: 101Kcal; Fat: 9g; Carbs: 4g; Protein: 1g

472. Cesar Style Dressing
Preparation time: 5 minutes
Cooking time: 0 minutes **Servings:** 1 ½ cup
Ingredients:
- 3 tablespoons vegan mayonnaise
- 2 tablespoons vegan Worcestershire sauce
- 1 tablespoon Dijon mustard
- 1 teaspoon red wine vinegar
- 4 teaspoons minced garlic (about 4 cloves)
- ¾ cup extra-virgin olive oil
- ¼ cup nutritional yeast
- ¼ teaspoon salt
- ¼ teaspoon freshly ground black pepper

Directions:
In a blender or food processor, combine mayonnaise, Worcestershire, mustard, vinegar, and garlic. Blend until the ingredients are well combined. You might need to stop and scrape down the sides during this process to ensure all ingredients are mixed well. With the blender running, slowly add the olive oil until the dressing begins to thicken. Continue to add olive oil until desired consistency. Add the nutritional yeast and pulse a few times to incorporate. Season with salt and pepper, and do a final pulse or two.
Per serving: Calories: 127Kcal; Fat: 14g; Carbs: 2g; Protein: 1g

473. Vegan Thousand Island

Preparation time: 10 minutes
Cooking time: 0 minutes **Servings:** 2 cups
Ingredients:
- 1¼ cups vegan mayonnaise
- 2 tablespoons unsweetened almond milk or soymilk, plus more if needed
- 1/4 cup ketchup
- 2 teaspoons vegan Worcestershire sauce
- ¼ teaspoon salt, plus more if needed
- 4 to 6 tablespoons sweet pickle relish, to taste

Directions:
In a blender or food processor, combine the mayonnaise, milk, ketchup, Worcestershire sauce, and ¼ teaspoon salt. Pulse until smooth, about 30 seconds. Add more nut milk if you prefer a smoother consistency. Transfer the dressing to a bowl. Stir in the relish, and add additional salt to taste.
Per serving: Calories: 96Kcal; Fat: 8g; Carbs: 4g; Protein: 2g

474. Strawberry Peach Vinaigrette

Preparation time: 5 minutes
Cooking time: 0 minutes **Servings:** 1 ¼ cup
Ingredients:
- 1 peach, pitted
- 4 strawberries
- ¼ cup water
- 2 tablespoons balsamic vinegar

Directions:
In a blender, combine the peach, strawberries, water, and vinegar. Blend on high for 1 to 2 minutes or until the dressing has a smooth consistency.
Per serving: Calories: 10Kcal; Fat: 0g; Carbs: 2g; Protein: 0g

475. Raspberry Vinaigrette

Preparation time: 5 minutes
Cooking time: 0 minutes **Servings:** 1
Ingredients:
- ½ cup raspberries
- ½ cup olive oil
- ¼ cup balsamic vinegar or white wine vinegar
- 2 to 3 tablespoons sugar, maple syrup, or Simple Syrup - ¼ cup water - Pinch salt

Directions:
In a small blender or food processor, combine the raspberries, olive oil, vinegar, sugar, water, and salt. Purée until smooth. Store in an airtight container in the refrigerator for up to 1 week. Shake before using.
PRO TIP: Add ¼ cup fresh basil leaves for a truly special flavor.
Per serving (2 tablespoons): Calories: 139Kcal; Fat: 14g; Carbs: 10g; Fiber: 1g; Protein: 0g

476. Creamy Tahini Dressing

Preparation time: 5 minutes
Cooking time: 0 minutes
Servings: 1
Ingredients:
- ½ cup tahini
- ¼ cup freshly squeezed lemon juice or apple cider vinegar
- 1 tablespoon olive oil (optional)
- 1 garlic clove, minced, or ½ teaspoon garlic powder (optional)
- 1 tablespoon sugar or maple syrup (optional)
- ¼ cup water, plus more as needed

Directions:
In a small bowl, mix the tahini and lemon juice, stirring until it becomes thick and creamy.
Stir in the olive oil (if using), garlic (if using), sugar (if using), and water. If it's too thick for your liking, add more water, 1 tablespoon at a time, until you get the consistency you desire. Store in an airtight container in the refrigerator for up to 1 week. It will thicken to a spreadable consistency as it sits, so if using it as a dressing, add 2 tablespoons of water and stir well.
Per serving (2 tablespoons): Calories: 111Kcal; Fat: 10g; Carbs: 4g; Fiber: 1g; Protein: 3g

477. Peanut Sauce

Preparation time: 10 minutes
Cooking time: 0 minutes
Servings: 1
Ingredients:
- ½ cup creamy peanut butter
- 3 tablespoons apple cider vinegar or freshly squeezed lime juice
- 2 tablespoons soy sauce
- 1 to 2 teaspoons toasted sesame oil
- 1 tablespoon sugar or maple syrup (optional)
- Pinch red pepper flakes (optional)
- ¼ cup water, plus more as needed

Directions:
In a small bowl, mix the peanut butter, vinegar, and soy sauce, stirring until it becomes light in color and very thick and creamy.
Stir in the sesame oil, sugar (if using), red pepper flakes (if using), and water. Add more water if you like, 1 tablespoon at a time, until you get the consistency you desire. Store in an airtight container in the refrigerator for up to 1 week. It will thicken to a spreadable consistency as it sits, so if you're using it as a dressing, add 2 tablespoons of water and stir until smooth.
SUBSTITUTION TIP: If you use chunky peanut butter, add 1 extra tablespoon to make up for the chunks.
Per serving (2 tablespoons): Calories: 110Kcal; Fat: 9g; Carbs: 5g; Fiber: 1g; Protein: 4.5g

478. Cilantro-Lime Dressing

Preparation time: 10 minutes
Cooking time: 0 minutes **Servings:** 1
Ingredients:
- ¼ cup chopped fresh cilantro
- ¾ cup canned coconut milk
- 1 tablespoon tahini or ¼ cup plain nondairy yogurt
- 3 tablespoons freshly squeezed lime juice
- 1 tablespoon sugar
- Salt

Directions:
In a small blender or food processor, combine the cilantro, coconut milk, tahini, lime juice, and sugar, and season to taste with salt. Blend for about 1 minute until smooth. Taste, and add more salt as needed. Store in an airtight container in the refrigerator for up to 1 week.
PRO TIP: Add some minced jalapeño pepper for a spicy boost—up to one whole pepper, depending on your preferred spice level. Remove the seeds if you like; they're very spicy.
Per serving (2 tablespoons): Calories: 59Kcal; Fat: 6g; Carbs: 2g; Fiber: 0g; Protein: 1g

479. Caesar Dressing
Preparation time: 5 minutes
Cooking time: 0 minutes **Servings:** 1
Ingredients:
- ½ cup plain nondairy yogurt plus ¼ cup tahini, or ¾ cup plain nondairy yogurt, or ½ cup tahini plus ¼ cup water
- 2 tablespoons nutritional yeast
- 2 to 3 tablespoons freshly squeezed lemon juice - 3 or 4 pitted green olives
- 2 teaspoons Dijon mustard
- 1 garlic clove or ½ teaspoon garlic powder - Pinch salt

Directions:
In a small blender, combine the yogurt, tahini, nutritional yeast, lemon juice, olives, mustard, garlic, and salt. Purée until smooth, adding water as needed to thin it to your desired consistency. Store in an airtight container in the refrigerator for up to 1 week. It will thicken to a spreadable consistency as it sits, so if you're using it as a dressing, add 2 tablespoons of water and stir until smooth.
Per serving (2 tablespoons): Calories: 71Kcal; Fat: 5g; Carbs: 5g; Fiber: 2g; Protein: 3g

480. Coconut Curry Sauce
Preparation time: 5 minutes
Cooking time: 0 minutes **Servings:** 1
Ingredients:
- ¾ cup canned coconut milk
- 1 tablespoon curry paste or 1 to 2 teaspoons curry powder
- 1 tablespoon sugar
- 1 tablespoon freshly squeezed lime juice or lemon juice
- Salt

Directions:
In a small bowl, whisk together the coconut milk, curry paste, sugar, and lime juice. Season to taste with salt. Store in an airtight container in the refrigerator for up to 1 week.
A CLOSER LOOK: Curry paste is available in the Asian section of most grocery stores; the red variety is slightly spicier than the green.
Per serving (2 tablespoons): Calories: 56Kcal; Fat: 5g; Carbs: 2g; Fiber: 0g; Protein: 1g

481. Herbed Croutons
Preparation time: 5 minutes
Cooking time: 10 minutes **Servings:** 4
Ingredients:
- 2 tablespoons olive oil or vegan margarine, melted
- 1 teaspoon dried herbs
- Salt
- 1 slice bread, cut into bite-size cubes

Directions:
Preheat the oven or toaster oven to 400°F or heat a small skillet over medium-high heat. In a small bowl, stir together the olive oil and dried herbs, season to taste with salt. Add the bread cubes and toss to coat in the oil. Transfer to a small rimmed baking sheet, toaster oven tray, or skillet. Bake or fry for 10 minutes, turning occasionally, until lightly browned. Store in an airtight container in the refrigerator for up to 5 days.
Per serving: Calories: 77Kcal; Fat: 7g; Carbs: 3g; Fiber: 1g; Protein: 1g

482. Spinach Pesto
Preparation time: 5 minutes
Cooking time: 0 minutes **Servings:** 1
Ingredients:
- ½ cup unsalted raw pumpkin seeds
- 2 cups packed raw spinach
- ¼ cup fresh parsley or fresh basil
- 3 tablespoons olive oil, plus more as needed
- 2 to 4 tablespoons nutritional yeast (optional)
- 1 tablespoon freshly squeezed lemon juice, plus more as needed
- 1 small garlic clove, peeled
- 3 to 4 tablespoons water, plus more as needed (depending on how much nutritional yeast you use)
- Salt

Directions:
In a food processor or small blender, process the pumpkin seeds until they're broken up quite a bit.
Add the spinach, parsley, olive oil, nutritional yeast (if using), lemon juice, garlic, and water, and process until smooth. Season to taste with salt. If necessary, stir in an extra drizzle of olive oil, lemon juice, and/or water to get a creamy texture. Store in an airtight container in the refrigerator for up to 5 days or in the freezer indefinitely.
PREP TIP: If you prefer a softer garlic flavor, when you have the oven on for something else (between 350°F and 400°F), put some garlic cloves in their skins, in a small oven-proof dish and bake for about 10 minutes, until soft. Squeeze them out of their skins to use—they're great spread on bread or mashed into potatoes.
Per serving (2 tablespoons): Calories: 133Kcal; Fat: 12g; Carbs: 4g; Fiber: 1g; Protein: 5g

483. Refried Beans
Preparation time: 10 minutes
Cooking time: 10 minutes **Servings:** 3
Ingredients:
- 1 tablespoon olive oil

- ¼ onion, finely diced, or 1 teaspoon onion powder
- Salt
- 1 garlic clove, minced, or ½ teaspoon garlic powder
- ½ to 1 teaspoon chili powder
- 1 (15-ounce) can pinto beans or black beans, drained and rinsed
- 1 tablespoon freshly squeezed lime juice (optional)
- Freshly ground black pepper

Directions:
Heat the olive oil in a skillet over medium heat. Add the onion and a pinch of salt, and sauté for about 3 minutes, until the onion is soft. Stir in the garlic and chili powder, and sauté for 1 to 2 minutes more.
Stir in the pinto beans, and cook for about 2 minutes to heat them through.
Using a fork or potato masher, mash the beans to your desired consistency. Stir in the lime juice (if using) and season to taste with pepper. Taste, and add more salt and pepper as needed. Store in an airtight container in the refrigerator for up to 1 week.
Per serving (½ cup): Calories: 61Kcal; Fat: 2g; Carbs: 8g; Fiber: 3g; Protein: 3g

484. Simple Barbecue Sauce
Preparation time: 5 minutes
Cooking time: 5 minutes **Servings:** 1
Ingredients:
- 2/3 cup ketchup
- 1/3 cup apple cider vinegar
- ¼ cup packed brown sugar
- 2 tablespoons soy sauce or tamari
- ¼ teaspoon garlic powder (optional, but highly recommended)
- Pinch red pepper flakes, or to taste

Directions:
In a medium saucepan, stir together the ketchup, vinegar, brown sugar, soy sauce, garlic powder (if using), and red pepper flakes. Bring to a simmer over medium-low heat, and cook for about 5 minutes.
Alternatively, stir together the ingredients in a microwave-safe bowl, cover, and heat on high power for 1 minute. Let cool. Store in an airtight container in the refrigerator for up to 1 week. PRO TIP: For a smoky flavor, add 1 to 2 teaspoons smoked paprika and/or a few drops of liquid smoke.
Per serving (2 tablespoons): Calories: 44Kcal; Fat: 0g; Carbs: 10g; Fiber: 0g; Protein: 1g

485. Garlic Butter
Preparation time: 5 minutes
Cooking time: 0 minutes **Servings:** ¼ CUP
Ingredients:
- ¼ cup coconut oil or vegan margarine, softened - 2 teaspoons garlic powder or 4 small garlic cloves, minced
- 4 teaspoons nutritional yeast (optional)
- Large pinch salt

Directions:
In a small bowl, stir together the coconut oil, garlic powder, nutritional yeast (if using), and salt. Store in an airtight container in the refrigerator.
If you used fresh garlic, it will keep for up to 2 weeks. It will keep for a while longer if you used garlic powder. **Per serving (1 tablespoon):** Calories: 134Kcal; Fat: 14g; Carbs: 3g; Fiber: 1g; Protein: 2g

486. Parm Sprinkle
Preparation time: 5 minutes
Cooking time: 0 minutes **Servings:** ½ Cup
Ingredients:
- ½ cup seeds or nuts, such as sunflower, pumpkin, sesame, or hemp seeds, or walnuts, cashews, or almonds
- ¼ cup nutritional yeast
- Pinch salt

Directions:
In a small blender or clean coffee grinder, pulse the seeds or nuts until crumbly. Add the nutritional yeast and salt, and pulse a few more times. Store in an airtight container at room temperature for up to 1 week.
Per serving (2 tablespoons): Calories: 203Kcal; Fat: 15g; Carbs: 11g; Fiber: 6g; Protein: 11g

487. Sour Cream
Preparation time: 5 minutes
Cooking time: 0 minutes
Servings: 1
Ingredients:
- 8 ounces silken tofu, or 1 cup plain nondairy yogurt, or 6 ounces firm tofu plus 2 tablespoons water
- 2 tablespoons freshly squeezed lemon juice
- 1 tablespoon olive oil
- 1 tablespoon apple cider vinegar
- 1 teaspoon onion powder
- 1/2 teaspoon garlic powder
- 1/8 to ¼ teaspoon salt, plus more as needed

Directions:
In a small blender or food processor, combine the tofu, lemon juice, olive oil, vinegar, onion powder, garlic powder, and salt. Purée until smooth and creamy. Taste and add more salt as needed. Store in an airtight container in the refrigerator for up to 1 week.
Per serving (2 tablespoons): Calories: 63Kcal; Fat: 4g; Carbs: 2g; Fiber: 1g; Protein: 5g

488. Simple Syrup
Preparation time: 5 minutes
Cooking time: 5 To 10 minutes **Servings:** 1
Ingredients:
- ¾ cup water
- ¾ cup packed dark brown sugar, granulated sugar, unrefined coconut sugar, or muscovado sugar

Directions:
In a small saucepan, bring the water to a light boil over medium heat. Add the brown sugar, and stir to dissolve. Reduce the heat to low and simmer for a few minutes or

longer if you want a thicker syrup. Alternatively, put the water in a microwave-safe container and heat it on high power for 2 minutes. Stir in the sugar and let sit. Or, boil the water in a kettle and combine it with the sugar in a small heat-proof bowl. Let stand for a few minutes. Store in an airtight container in the refrigerator or at room temperature for up to 2 weeks.
PRO TIP: Look for maple extract in the baking aisle, and add a drop or two to give the syrup a maple flavor.
Per serving (1 tablespoon): Calories: 27Kcal; Fat: 0g; Carbs: 6g; Fiber: 0g; Protein: 0g

489. Chocolate Icing
Preparation time: 5 minutes
Cooking time: 0 minutes **Servings:** 1
Ingredients:
- 1 tablespoon unsweetened cocoa powder
- 1 tablespoon sugar
- 2 teaspoons nondairy milk

Directions:
In a small bowl, stir together the cocoa powder and sugar. Slowly add the milk, 1 teaspoon at a time, stirring to bring the icing together.
SUBSTITUTION TIP: Swap carob powder for the cocoa powder. It doesn't taste like chocolate, but it has a similar vibe and more calcium and natural sweetness than cocoa.
Per serving: Calories: 49Kcal; Fat: 1g; Carbs: 12g; Fiber: 2g; Protein: 1g

490. Vanilla Icing
Preparation time: 5 minutes
Cooking time: 0 minutes **Servings:** ½ cup
Ingredients:
- 1 tablespoon coconut oil or unsalted vegan margarine, softened
- ¾ cup powdered sugar or ½ cup granulated sugar plus ¼ cup cornstarch, plus more as needed
- 1 tablespoon nondairy milk
- ½ teaspoon vanilla extract (optional)

Directions:
In a medium bowl, stir together the coconut oil, powdered sugar, milk, and vanilla (if using) until smooth.
Add more powdered sugar as needed, 1 tablespoon at a time, to get a spreadable consistency.
Per serving (2 tablespoons): Calories: 137Kcal; Fat: 4g; Carbs: 25g; Fiber: 0g; Protein: 0g

491. General Tso Sauce
Preparation time: 5 minutes **Cooking time:** 10 minutes
Servings: 4
Ingredients:
- Rice Vinegar (1/4 C.) - Water (1/2 C.)
- Sriracha Sauce (1 ½ T.)
- Soy Sauce (1/4 C.)
- Corn Starch (1 ½ T.) - Sugar (1/2 C.)

Directions:
1. General Tso Sauce is a classic, and you can now make a healthier version of it! All you must do is take out your saucepan and place all the ingredients in. 2. Once in place, bring everything over medium heat and whisk together for ten minutes or until the sauce begins to get thick. Finally, remove from the heat and enjoy! **Per serving:** Calories: 150Kcal; Fat: 0g; Carbs: 30g; Protein: 2g

492. Cashew Cheese Sauce
Preparation time: 5 minutes **Cooking time:** 0 minutes
Servings: 8
Ingredients:
- Olive Oil (1 T.)
- Water (1/2 C.)
- Raw Cashews (3/4 C.)
- Lemon Juice (1 T.)
- Tamari Sauce (1/2 t.)
- Salt (to Taste)

Directions:
1. As you begin a plant-based diet, you may be thinking you will miss your cheese. Luckily, this cashew cheese is an excellent replacement! 2. All you will have to do is take the rest of the components, place them into a blender, and combine until completely smoothed out. Once you are done, place in the fridge and enjoy! **Per serving:** Calories: 90Kcal; Fat: 10g; Carbs:5; Protein: 5g

493. Ranch Dressing
Preparation time: 10 minutes
Cooking time: 0 minutes **Servings:** 8
Ingredients:
- Water (1 C.)
- Dried Dill (1/2 t.)
- Garlic Powder (1 t.)
- Chives (2 T., Chopped)
- Lemon Juice (3 T.)
- Salt (to Taste)
- Dried Parsley (1 t.)
- Raw Cashews (1 1/3 C.)
- Onion Powder (1 t.)

Directions:
Before you begin this recipe, you will want to soak your cashews for at least one hour. This will make the next step much easier!
Once the cashews are done, place them into your blender along with the garlic, onion, lemon, and water. Go ahead and blend these ingredients on high until the sauce gets creamy.
When this is all set, you can gently stir in the chives, dill, and parsley and then enjoy your vegan dressing!
Per serving: Calories: 140Kcal; Fat: 10g; Carbs: 9g; Protein: 3g

494. Minty Lime Dressing
Preparation time: 10 minutes
Cooking time: 0 minutes **Servings:** 4
Ingredients:
- Olive Oil (6 T.)
- Fresh Chives (1 T.)
- Fresh Mint (1 T.)
- Lime (1)
- Salt (to Taste)

- White Wine Vinegar (2 T.)

Directions:

For a salad dressing that is cool and refreshing, this recipe will certainly hit the spot! You will want to start by getting a small mixing bowl and adding together the fresh herbs with the vinegar, salt, and juice from your lime.

When these are combined well, you will slowly want to add in the olive oil while continuously whisking the ingredients together.

Once all the olive oil is in, season to your liking, and then enjoy over your favorite salad.

Per serving: Calories: 10Kcal; Fat: 0g; Carbs: 2g; Protein: 0g

CHAPTER 24:
Wraps and Spreads

495. Buffalo Chickpea Wraps
Preparation time: 20 minutes
Cooking time: 5 minutes **Servings:** 4
Ingredients:
- ¼ cup plus 2 tablespoons hummus
- 2 tablespoons lemon juice
- 1½ tablespoons maple syrup
- 1 to 2 tablespoons hot water
- 1 head Romaine lettuce, chopped
- 1 15-ounce can chickpeas, drained, rinsed, and patted dry
- 4 tablespoons hot sauce, divided
- 1 tablespoon olive or coconut oil
- ¼ teaspoon garlic powder
- 1 pinch sea salt - 4 wheat tortillas
- ¼ cup cherry tomatoes, diced
- ¼ cup red onion, diced
- ¼ of a ripe avocado, thinly sliced

Directions:
Mix the hummus with lemon juice and maple syrup in a large bowl. Use a whisk and add the hot water, a little at a time, until it is thick but spreadable. Add the Romaine lettuce and toss to coat. Set aside. Pour the prepared chickpeas into another bowl. Add three tablespoons of the hot sauce, olive oil, garlic powder, and salt; toss to coat. Heat a metal skillet (cast iron works the best) over medium heat and add the chickpea mixture. Sauté for three to five minutes and mash gently with a spoon. Once the chickpea mixture is slightly dried out, remove it from the heat and add the rest of the hot sauce. Stir it in well and set aside. Lay the tortillas on a clean, flat surface and spread a quarter cup of the buffalo chickpeas on top. Top with tomatoes, onion, and avocado (optional) and wrap.
Per serving: Calories: 254Kcal; Fat: 6.7g; Carbs: 39.4g; Protein: 9.1g

496. Coconut Veggie Wraps
Preparation time: 5 minutes
Cooking time: 15 minutes **Servings:** 5
Ingredients:
- 1½ cups shredded carrots
- 1 red bell pepper, seeded, thinly sliced
- 2½ cups kale - 1 ripe avocado, thinly sliced
- 1 cup fresh cilantro, chopped
- 5 coconut wraps - 2/3 cups hummus
- 6½ cups green curry paste

Directions:
Slice, chop and shred all the vegetables. Lay a coconut wrap on a clean flat surface and spread two tablespoons of the hummus and one tablespoon of the green curry paste on top of the end closest to you. Place some carrots, bell pepper, kale, and cilantro on the wrap and start rolling it up, starting from the edge closest to you. Roll tightly and fold in the ends. Place the wrap, seam down, on a plate to serve.
Per serving: Calories: 236Kcal; Fat: 14.3g; Carbs: 23.6g; Protein: 5.5g

497. Spicy Hummus and Apple Wrap
Preparation time: 10 minutes
Cooking time: 15 minutes **Servings:** 1
Ingredients:
- 3 to 4 tablespoons hummus
- 2 tablespoons mild salsa
- ½ cup broccoli slaw
- ½ teaspoon fresh lemon juice
- 2 teaspoons plain yogurt
- salt and pepper to taste
- 1 tortilla - Lettuce leaves
- ½ Granny Smith or another tart apple, cored and thinly sliced

Directions:
In a small bowl, mix the hummus with the salsa. Set the bowl aside. In a large bowl, mix the broccoli slaw, lemon juice, and yogurt. Season with salt and pepper.
Lay the tortilla on a flat surface and spread on the hummus mixture. Lay down some lettuce leaves on top of the hummus. On the upper half of the tortilla, place a pile of the broccoli slaw mixture and cover it with the apples. Fold and wrap.
Per serving: Calories: 121Kcal; Fat: 2g; Carbs: 27g; Protein: 4g

498. Sun-Dried Tomato Spread
Preparation time: 20 minutes
Cooking time: 15 minutes **Servings:** 16
Ingredients:
- 1 cup sun-dried tomatoes
- 1 cup raw cashews
- Water for soaking tomatoes and cashews
- ½ cup water - 1 clove garlic, minced
- 1 green onion, chopped
- 5 large basil leaves
- ½ teaspoon lemon juice
- ¼ teaspoon salt
- 1 dash pepper
- Hulled sunflower seeds

Directions:
Soak tomatoes and cashews for 30 minutes in separate bowls, with enough water to cover them. Drain and pat dry. Put the tomatoes and cashews in a food processor and puree them, drizzling the water as it purees to make a smooth, creamy

paste. Add the garlic, onion, basil leaves, lemon juice, salt, and pepper and mix thoroughly. Scrape into a bowl, cover, and refrigerate overnight. Spread on bread or toast and sprinkle with sunflower seeds for a little added crunch.
Per serving: Calories: 60Kcal; Fat: 4.2g; Carbs: 5.6g; Protein: 1.2g

499. Sweet Potato Sandwich Spread
Preparation time: 10 minutes
Cooking time: 15 minutes **Servings:** 4
Ingredients:
- 1 large sweet potato baked, peeled
- 1 teaspoon cumin
- 1 teaspoon chili powder
- 1 teaspoon garlic powder
- Salt and pepper to taste
- 2 slices whole-wheat bread
- 1 to 2 tablespoons pinto beans, drained
- Lettuce

Directions:
Bake and peel the sweet potato and mash it in a bowl. If it is too thick, add a little almond or coconut milk.
Mix in the cumin, chili powder, garlic powder, salt, and pepper. Spread the mixture on a slice of bread and spoon some beans on top.
Top with lettuce leaves and the other slice of bread.
Per serving: Calories: 253Kcal; Fat: 6g; Carbs: 49g; Protein: 8g

500. Seitan Shawarma
Preparation time: 20 minutes
Cooking time: 15 minutes **Servings:** 4
Ingredients:
- 1/4 cup tahini
- 1/4 cup water
- 2 tablespoons freshly squeezed lemon juice
- 1 teaspoon garlic powder
- 2 teaspoons vegetable oil
- 1 small red onion, thinly sliced
- 1-pound Seitan, or store-bought seitan, thinly sliced
- 1/2 teaspoon ground cumin
- 1/2 teaspoon ground turmeric
- 1/2 teaspoon paprika - 1/4 teaspoon salt
- ¼ teaspoon freshly ground black pepper
- 4 pitas, or flatbreads of choice
- 1 large tomato, sliced - 1 cup sliced cucumber
- 2 cups sliced romaine lettuce

Directions:
In a small bowl, whisk the tahini, water, lemon juice, and garlic powder to blend. Set aside. In a large pan over medium-high heat, heat the vegetable oil. Add the red onion and cook for about 5 minutes, stirring frequently, until it begins to soften and brown. Add the seitan, cumin, turmeric, paprika, salt, and pepper. Cook, stirring frequently, for about 10 minutes until the seitan browns and some of the edges get crispy. To assemble the sandwiches, stuff each pita with some of the seitan mixture. Add tomato and cucumber slices and romaine lettuce. Drizzle each with the tahini dressing. Substitution tip: Swap store-bought vegan beef for the seitan, if you prefer. You can also use sliced portobello mushrooms to keep your shawarma veggie-centric.
Per serving: Calories: 354Kcal; Fat: 12g; Carbs: 41g; Protein: 20g

501. Chipotle Seitan Taquitos
Preparation time: 15 minutes
Cooking time: 15 minutes **Servings:** 12
Ingredients:
- ½ cup Cashew Cream Cheese, or store-bought nondairy cream cheese
- 2 canned chipotle peppers in adobo sauce, minced, sauce reserved
- 12 (6-inch) corn tortillas
- 1-pound Seitan, or store-bought seitan, cut into slices

Directions:
Preheat the oven to 400°F. Have a large baking dish or sheet nearby. In a small bowl, stir together the cashew cream cheese, chipotle peppers, and 2 tablespoons of the reserved adobo sauce. Place a tortilla on a clean surface and spread a line (about 2 teaspoons) of the chipotle cream cheese mixture down the middle. Top with a few slices of seitan. Roll up the tortilla as tightly as possible and place it, seam-side down, in the baking dish. Repeat with the remaining tortillas. Bake for 15 minutes or until the tortillas are crisp. Fun fact: Chipotles are not their type of pepper. They're dried, smoked jalapeños. When buying them for this recipe, look for chipotles in adobo sauce, which come in small cans found in the grocery store's Mexican food section. You'll need both the peppers and the sauce.
Per serving: Calories: 193Kcal; Fat: 7g; Carbs: 25g; Protein: 8g

502. Mediterranean Chickpea Wraps
Preparation time: 15 minutes
Cooking time: 0 minutes **Servings:** 4
Ingredients:
- 1/4 cup extra-virgin olive oil
- 2 tablespoons freshly squeezed lemon juice
- 1 teaspoon dried dill
- 1 teaspoon dried oregano
- 1/4 teaspoon salt
- 1 (15-oz.) can chickpeas, drained and rinsed, or 1½ cups cooked chickpeas
- ½ cup Tofu Feta, or store-bought nondairy feta
- 1 cup chopped cucumber
- 1 large tomato, diced -¼ cup diced red onion
- 2 cups fresh baby spinach
- 4 (12-inch) tortillas, or flatbreads of choice

Directions:
In a small bowl, whisk the olive oil, lemon juice, dill, oregano, and salt to combine. In a large bowl, gently toss together the chickpeas, feta, cucumber, tomato, and red onion. Add the dressing and toss to combine.
Assemble the wraps by placing ½ cup of spinach on each tortilla and topping it with ¼ of the chickpea mixture. Roll up the wrap, tucking in the sides as you go. Substitution tip: If you'd like to keep your wraps gluten-free and you can't find

gluten-free flatbread, use collard greens. You'll need 4 large collard leaves. Cut off the stem from each and shave off the thick part of the stem that's left in the center with a sharp knife. Assemble the wrap the way you would a tortilla, by filling it with the spinach and chickpea mixture and rolling the leaf, tucking in the sides as you go.
Per serving: Calories: 623Kcal; Fat: 25g; Carbs: 80g; Protein: 20g

503. Barbecue Chickpea Burgers with Slaw
Preparation time: 15 minutes
Cooking time: 25 minutes **Servings:** 4
Ingredients:
- 1 cup rolled oats
- 1 (15-oz.) can chickpeas, drained and rinsed, or 1½ cup cooked chickpeas
- ½ cup Barbecue Sauce, or store-bought vegan barbecue sauce, divided
- 1 garlic clove, minced - ½ teaspoon salt
- ½ teaspoon freshly ground black pepper
- 2 cups shredded cabbage
- 2 carrots, grated or shredded
- ¼ cup Cashew Mayonnaise, or store-bought nondairy mayonnaise
- 4 burger buns of choice

Directions:
Preheat the oven to 400°F. Line a large baking sheet with parchment paper. In a food processor, pulse the rolled oats until they resemble a coarse meal. Add the chickpeas, ¼ cup of barbecue sauce, garlic, salt, and pepper. Pulse until the chickpeas are mashed and everything is well combined. It's okay if there are a few whole chickpeas. Form the mixture into 4 patties and place them on the prepared baking sheet. Bake the burgers for 20 to 25 minutes, flipping them at the halfway point. They should be golden brown and firm. While the burgers bake, make the slaw. In a large bowl, stir together the cabbage, carrots, and mayonnaise. Serve each burger on a bun topped with 1 tablespoon of the remaining barbecue sauce and 1/4 cup of slaw. First-Timer tip: If you don't have a food processor, mash your chickpeas well using a potato masher or large fork. Rolled oats won't mash well by hand, so use oat flour or all-purpose flour instead. Combine the mashed chickpeas, flour, barbecue sauce, garlic, salt, and pepper in a large bowl before shaping into patties.
Per serving: Calories: 433Kcal; Fat: 10g; Carbs: 73g; Protein: 13g

504. Hummus and Quinoa Wrap
Preparation time: 10 minutes
Cooking time: 10 minutes **Servings:** 4
Ingredients:
- Lettuce Leaves
- Cooked Quinoa (1 cup)
- Cabbage (½ cup)
- Sprouts (½ cup)
- Avocado (1 cup, Sliced)
- Hummus (1 cup)

Directions:
For this recipe, the lettuce leaves are going to act as your wrap! When you are all set, spread the wrap out and place the hummus and avocado into each leaf.
Once this is set, layer your quinoa and cabbage on top before wrapping the leaf up and eating!
Per serving: Calories: 280Kcal; Fat: 10g; Carbs: 40g; Protein: 10g

505. Mediterranean Veggie Wrap
Preparation time: 15 minutes
Cooking time: 0 minutes **Servings:** 4
Ingredients:
- Whole-grain Tortillas
- Chickpeas (3 cups)
- Onion (1/4 cup, Diced)
- Tomato (1, Diced)
- Salt (to Taste)
- Kalamata Olives (4 tablespoons)
- Garlic Clove (1, Minced)
- Lettuce (2 cups)
- Lemon Juice (2 tablespoons)
- Cucumber (1, Grated)
- Fresh Dill (2 tablespoons)
- Plant-based Yogurt (7 Oz.)
- Green Pepper (1/4 cup, Diced)
- Pepper (to Taste)

Directions:
Before you begin preparing this wrap, you will want to take half of your cucumber and grate it into a mixing bowl. After this step is complete, lightly sprinkle the cucumber with salt to help get some of the excess water out. As this process happens, you can now take your chickpeas and mash them down well with a fork. With that, all set, take out a dish and combine the cucumber, yogurt, citrus juice, garlic, and dill altogether. Once this is done, season with pepper and salt to your liking.
When you are ready, lay out your wraps and layer your smashed chickpeas, lettuce, and mixed vegetables. For some extra flavor, try adding some tzatziki sauce over the top before rolling up.
Per serving: Calories: 400Kcal; Fat: 5g; Carbs: 30g; Protein: 15g

506. Quick Lentil Wrap
Preparation time: 10 minutes
Cooking time: 30 minutes **Servings:** 4
Ingredients:
- Whole-grain Wraps
- Garlic Clove (1, Minced)
- Olive Oil (2 tablespoons)
- Onion (1, Diced)
- Cilantro (1/3 cup, Cilantro)
- Lentils (2 cups)
- Tomato Paste (1/3 cup)

Directions:
Begin this recipe by taking out a skillet and place two cups of water and lentils in. You will want to get everything to a boil before turning the temperature down and simmer for ten minutes or until the lentils are soft. Once the lentils are cooked through, add in the tomato paste, garlic, and onion. Go ahead and cook all of these ingredients together for another five minutes before turning off heat and seasoning to your liking. Finally, lay out your wraps, spread the mixture in the center, and then roll the wrap up for lunch.

Per serving: Calories: 400Kcal; Fat: 5g; Carbs: 50g; Protein: 20g

507. Thai Vegetable and Tofu Wrap

Preparation time: 5 minutes
Cooking time: 30 minutes
Servings: 1
Ingredients:

- Extra-firm Tofu (1 cup, Diced)
- Peanut Sauce (1/4 cup)
- Olive Oil (1 teaspoon)
- Cucumber (1/3 cup, Diced)
- Carrot (1/3 cup, Shredded)
- Cilantro (1/4 cup)
- Garlic Cloves (1, Minced)
- Whole-wheat Wrap

Directions:
Tofu is an excellent Protein: to have on hand because it is so versatile! To begin this recipe, you will want to take a skillet and place it over medium heat.

As it warms, add in your olive oil and begin cooking the tofu for around five minutes. After five minutes, combine the garlic and cook for an additional minute. At this point, all of the liquid from the tofu should be gone. Next, eliminate the skillet from the cooker and add in the peanut sauce. Be sure to stir very well to help coat the tofu pieces evenly! When you are set to make your wraps, spread the tofu into your wrap, top with the diced and shredded vegetables, and roll everything up together nice and tight before serving.

For extra flavor, feel free to add some fresh cilantro to your wrap!

Per serving: Calories: 270Kcal; Fat: 15g; Carbs: 12g; Protein: 20g

508. Plant-Based Buffalo Wrap

Preparation time: 5 minutes
Cooking time: 15 minutes **Servings:** 4
Ingredients:

- Olive Oil (1 teaspoon)
- Kale (2 cups, Chopped)
- Buffalo Sauce (½ cup)
- Seitan (1 cup, Chopped)
- Whole Wheat Wraps
- Tomatoes (1 cup, Diced)
- Cashews (1 cup)
- Salt (to taste)
- Dried Dill (1/2 teaspoon)
- Pepper (to Taste)
- Dried Parsley (1/2 teaspoon)
- Almond Milk (8 tablespoons)
- Apple Cider Vinegar (1 ½ tablespoons)

Directions:
This recipe is the perfect way to get a buffalo chicken wrap without the chicken! You will want to start by making your ranch dressing. You can accomplish this by taking out your blender and mixing the almond milk, apple cider vinegar, cashews, pepper, salt, parsley, and dill. Once this is done, set your sauce to the side. Next, you will need to get out a saucepan and place it over medium heat. Once warm, add in some olive oil and begin cooking your seitan pieces. Normally, this will take you eight minutes.

When the seitan is cooked through, add in the buffalo sauce and cook for another minute. With these steps done, you will want to now take a moment to take the kale and mix it in a bowl with olive oil and seasoning. Finally, it is time to assemble your wrap! You can do this by taking out your wrap and spreading your ranch dressing across the surface.

Once this is in place, begin building your wrap by layering the kale, tomato, and seitan pieces. For a final touch, add some more buffalo sauce over the top, and then wrap it up!

Per serving: Calories: 250Kcal; Fat: 15g; Carbs: 25g; Protein: 20g

509. Colorful Veggie Wrap

Preparation time: 10 minutes
Cooking time: 0 minutes **Servings:** 4
Ingredients:

- Large Lettuce Leaves
- Soy Sauce (1 tablespoon)
- Olive Oil (1 tablespoon)
- Seed Butter (½ cup)
- Garlic Powder (1 tablespoon)
- Lime Juice (2 tablespoons)
- Red Cabbage (1 cup, Shredded)
- Cucumber (1 cup, Chopped)
- Red Pepper (1 cup, Chopped)
- Carrot (1 cup, Chopped)
- Ground Ginger (1/4 teaspoon)

Directions:
This wrap looks pretty at and full of flavor! You can start this recipe off by making the sauce.

For the sauce, take out a petite bowl and combine the oil, garlic, soy sauce, juice of the lime, ground ginger, pepper flakes, and seed butter. Once everything is mixed together well, place it to the side. Next, it is time to build your wrap! Go ahead and lay the lettuce leaves out flat before spreading sauce across the surface. Once this is in place, you will want to layer the other vegetables before rolling the leaf up and enjoying your veggie-packed wrap!

Per serving: Calories: 250Kcal; Fat: 20g; Carbs: 15g; Protein: 10g

510. BBQ Chickpea Wrap

Preparation time: 10 minutes
Cooking time: 0 minutes **Servings:** 4
Ingredients:

- Whole-wheat Tortillas

- Coleslaw (2 cups)
- BBQ Sauce (½ cup)
- Chickpeas (2 cups)

Directions:
Are you in a rush for lunch? You can slap this wrap together in a snap! Start by taking out a blending bowl and combine the BBQ with the chickpeas.
Next, you will want to lay out your tortillas and place the coleslaw and chickpeas in the center.
For a nice touch, wrap your tortilla up and pop it into the microwave for a few seconds to heat it before enjoying it!
Per serving: Calories: 450Kcal; Fat: 5g; Carbs: 50g; Protein: 10g

511. Chickpea and Mango Wraps

Preparation time: 15 minutes
Cooking time: 0 minutes **Servings:** 3
Ingredients:
- 3 tablespoons tahini
- 1 tablespoon curry powder
- ¼ teaspoon sea salt (optional)
- Zest and juice of 1 lime
- 3 to 4 tablespoons water
- 1½ cups cooked chickpeas
- 1 cup diced mango
- ½ cup fresh cilantro, chopped
- 1 red bell pepper, deseeded and diced
- 3 large whole-wheat wraps
- 1½ cups shredded lettuce

Directions:
In a large bowl, stir together the tahini, curry powder, lime zest, lime juice, and sea salt (if desired) until smooth and creamy. Whisk in 3 to 4 tablespoons water to help thin the mixture. Add the cooked chickpeas, mango, cilantro, and bell pepper to the bowl. Toss until well coated. On a clean work surface, lay the wraps. Divide the chickpea and mango mixture among the wraps. Spread the shredded lettuce on top and roll up tightly. Serve immediately.
Per serving: Calories: 436Kcal; Fat: 17.9g; Carbs: 8.9g; Protein: 15.2g

512. Tofu and Pineapple in Lettuce

Preparation time: 2 hours
Cooking time: 15 minutes **Servings:** 4
Ingredients:
- ¼ cup low-sodium soy sauce
- 1 garlic clove, minced
- 2 tablespoons sesame oil (optional)
- 1 tablespoons coconut sugar (optional)
- 1 (14-oz. / 397-g) package extra firm tofu, drained, cut into ½-inch cubes
- 1 small white onion, diced
- ½ pineapple, peeled, cored, cut into cubes
- Salt and ground black pepper, to taste (optional)
- 4 large lettuce leaves
- 1 tablespoon roasted sesame seeds

Directions:
Combine the soy sauce, garlic, sesame oil (if desired), and coconut sugar in a bowl. Stir to mix well. Add the tofu cubes to the bowl of the soy sauce mixture, then press to coat well. Wrap the bowl in plastic and refrigerate to marinate for at least 2 hours. Pour the marinated tofu and marinade in a skillet and heat over medium heat. Add the onion and pineapple cubes to the skillet and stir to mix well. Sprinkle with salt (if desired) and pepper and sauté for 15 minutes or until the onions are lightly browned and the pineapple cubes are tender. Divide the lettuce leaves among 4 plates, then top the leaves with the tofu and pineapple mixture. Sprinkle with sesame seeds and serve immediately.
Per serving: Calories: 259Kcal; Fat: 15.4g; Carbs: 20.5g; Protein: 12.1g

513. Quinoa and Black Bean Lettuce Wraps

Preparation time: 30 minutes
Cooking time: 15 minutes **Servings:** 6
Ingredients:
- 2 tablespoons avocado oil (optional)
- ¼ cup deseeded and chopped bell pepper
- ½ onion, chopped
- 2 tablespoons minced garlic
- 1 teaspoon salt (optional)
- 1 teaspoon pepper (optional)
- ½ cup cooked quinoa
- 1 cup cooked black beans
- ½ cup almond flour
- ½ teaspoon paprika
- ½ teaspoon red pepper flakes
- 6 large lettuce leaves

Directions:
Heat 1 tablespoon of avocado oil (if desired) in a skillet over medium-high heat. Add the bell peppers, onions, garlic, salt (if desired), and pepper. Sauté for 5 minutes or until the bell peppers are tender. Turn off the heat and cool for 10 minutes, then pour the vegetables into a food processor. Add the quinoa, beans, flour. Sprinkle with paprika and red pepper flakes. Pulse until thick and well combined. Line a baking pan with parchment paper, then shape the mixture into 6 patties with your hands and place on the baking pan. Put the pan in the freezer for 5 minutes to make the patties firm. Heat the remaining avocado oil (if desired) in the skillet over high heat. Add the patties and cook for 6 minutes or until well browned on both sides. Flip the patties halfway through. Arrange the patties in the lettuce leaves and serve immediately.
Per serving: Calories: 200Kcal; Fat: 10.6g; Carbs: 40.5g; Protein: 9.5g

514. Maple Bagel Spread

Preparation time: 10 minutes
Cooking time: 10 minutes **Servings:** 1
Ingredients:
- Cream cheese
- Maple syrup

- Cinnamon
- Walnuts

Directions:
Beat the cinnamon, syrup, and cream cheese in a big bowl until it becomes smooth, then mix in walnuts.
Let it chill until ready to serve. Serve it with bagels.
Per serving: Calories: 586Kcal; Fat: 7g; Carbs: 23g; Protein: 4g

515. Peanut and Ginger Tofu Wrap

Preparation time: 30 minutes
Cooking time: 10 minutes **Servings:** 4 wraps
Ingredients:
Crispy Tofu
- 2 tablespoons of avocado/peanut oil
- 1 piece of 14-ounce extra-firm tofu, pressed for 30 minutes, cut into 16 spear-shaped pieces

Peanut Ginger Spread
- 2 tablespoons of lime juice
- 1 tablespoon of water
- 6 tablespoons of creamy peanut butter
- 1 tablespoon of tamari
- 1 tablespoon of ginger juice
- 2-3 tablespoons of coconut sugar or light brown sugar

Wrap
- ¼ cup of cilantro leaves
- 4 large whole-grain tortillas or sandwich wraps
- ¼ cup of sliced green onions
- 1 freshly peeled and shredded carrot
- Lime wedges
- Sriracha/sweet chili sauce
- 1 small red bell pepper, cored and cut into thin strips

Directions:
Put a large skillet on medium-high heat. Heat some oil and add the tofu, cooking it for 5 minutes. The tofu will be crisp and brown on both sides. Shift the tofu to a paper-lined dish so that the excess oil is absorbed. Whisk all the ingredients to make the peanut spread. If you want a less thick consistency, you can add a few drops of water to the mix.
Start assembling the tofu, pepper strips, carrot cilantro, and green onions on top of the peanut spread on the wraps. Add a dash of lime juice followed by the sauce of your choice.
Your healthy wrap is ready to be eaten!
Per serving: Calories: 557Kcal; Fat: 22.7g; Carbs: 34.1g; Protein: 22.4g

516. Quick-Fix Veggie Wrap

Preparation time: 15 minutes
Cooking time: 15 minutes **Servings:** 8
Ingredients:
- 1 finely diced medium red onion
- ½ freshly diced large green bell pepper
- 4 freshly minced garlic cloves
- ½ freshly diced large red bell pepper
- 1 teaspoon of curry powder
- 4 cups of shredded butter lettuce
- 4 cups of chopped veggies: cauliflower, steamed potatoes, zucchini, broccoli, carrots, and green beans
- 3 tablespoons of vegan feta
- 8 flour tortillas
- ½ cup of hummus

Directions:
In a large pan, sauté the curry powder, green and red bell peppers, onion, and garlic in a little water for about 5 minutes. To these sautéed ingredients, add the shredded lettuce and chopped veggies. Cover everything, reduce the heat, and steam for another 10 minutes. On a non-stick skillet, warm the tortillas. You can also warm them in a microwave by wrapping them in a wet towel. Spoon ½ cup of veggies in the middle of the tortilla and put 2 tablespoons of hummus on one side of the tortilla.
Fold the other side and then make a roll. If you are hungry and need a quick fix, this healthy veggie wrap will never disappoint.
Per serving: Calories: 202Kcal; Fat: 5.5g; Carbs: 32.6g; Protein: 7.2g

517. Delicious Collard Wraps

Preparation time: 15 minutes
Cooking time: 0 minutes **Servings:** 4
Ingredients:
- 4 large collard leaves
- ½ lime
- 1 teaspoon of extra virgin olive oil
- 1 red bell pepper
- 2-3 ounces of alfalfa sprouts
- 1 avocado
- ½ teaspoon of minced garlic
- 1 cup of raw pecans
- ½ teaspoon of grated ginger
- 1 tablespoon of tamari

Directions:
Wash the collard leaves thoroughly and cut off the white stem. Put them in warm water with a dash of lemon juice. Allow the leaves to soak for about 10 minutes. Dry the leaves with a paper towel and, with a sharp knife, cut off the central root. Slice the pepper and avocado. In a blender, combine the pecan, cumin, tamari, and olive oil. Pulse everything until you have a clumpy mix. Spread a collard leaf and spoon the pecan mixture onto it. Top it with the red bell pepper and avocado slices. Add some lime juice. Lastly, add the alfalfa sprouts. Fold the bottom and top and then wrap on both sides. Slice the wrap in half and serve it to your guests!
Per serving: Calories: 279Kcal; Fat: 26g; Carbs: 11g; Protein: 4g

518. Falafel Wrap

Preparation time: 30 minutes
Cooking time: 30 minutes **Servings:** 6
Ingredients:
For the falafel patties
- 1 (14-ounce) can chickpeas, drained and rinsed, or 1½ cups cooked
- 1 zucchini, grated

- 2 scallions, minced
- ¼ cup fresh parsley, chopped
- 2 tablespoons black olives, pitted and chopped (optional)
- 1 tablespoon tahini, or almond, cashew, or sunflower seed butter
- 1 tablespoon lemon juice or apple cider vinegar
- ½ teaspoon ground cumin
- ¼ teaspoon paprika - ¼ teaspoon sea salt
- 1 teaspoon olive oil (optional, if frying)

For the wrap
- 1 whole-grain wrap or pita
- ¼ cup classic hummus
- ½ cup fresh greens
- 1 baked falafel patty
- ¼ cup cherry tomatoes, halved
- ¼ cup diced cucumber
- ¼ cup chopped avocado, or guacamole
- ¼ cup cooked quinoa, or tabbouleh salad (optional)

Directions:
To make the falafel
Use a food processor to pulse the chickpeas, zucchini, scallions, parsley, and olives (if using) until roughly chopped. Just pulse—don't purée. Or use a potato masher to mash the chickpeas in a large bowl and stir in the grated and chopped veggies. In a small bowl, whisk together the tahini and lemon juice, and stir in the cumin, paprika, and salt. Pour this into the chickpea mixture, and stir well (or pulse the food processor) to combine. Taste and add more salt, if needed. Using your hands, form the mix into 6 patties. You can either panfry or bake the patties. To panfry, heat a large skillet to medium, add 1 teaspoon of olive oil, and cook the patties for about 10 minutes on the first side. Flip and cook for another 5 to 7 minutes. To bake them, put them on a baking sheet lined with parchment paper and bake at 350°f for 30 to 40 minutes.

To make the wrap
Lay the wrap on a plate and spread the hummus down the center. Then lay on the greens and crumble the falafel patty on top. Add the tomatoes, cucumber, avocado, and quinoa.
Fold in both ends, and wrap up as tightly as you can. If you have a sandwich press, you can press the wraps for about 5 minutes. This will travel best in a reusable lunch box or reusable plastic lunch wrap.

Per serving (1 wrap): Calories: 546Kcal; Fat: 19g; Carbs: 81g; Fiber: 14g; Protein: 18g

519. Curried Mango Chickpea Wrap
Preparation time: 15 minutes
Cooking time: 0 minutes **Servings:** 3
Ingredients:
- 3 tablespoons tahini
- Zest and juice of 1 lime
- 1 tablespoon curry powder
- ¼ teaspoon sea salt
- 3 to 4 tablespoons water
- 1 (14-ounce) can chickpeas, rinsed and drained, or 1½ cups cooked
- 1 cup diced mango
- 1 red bell pepper, seeded and diced small
- ½ cup fresh cilantro, chopped
- 3 large whole-grain wraps
- 1 to 2 cups shredded green leaf lettuce

Directions:
In a medium bowl, whisk together the tahini, lime zest and juice, curry powder, and salt until the mixture is creamy and thick. Add 3 to 4 tablespoons of water to thin it out a bit. Or you can process this all in a blender. The taste should be strong and salty to flavor the whole salad. Toss the chickpeas, mango, bell pepper, and cilantro with the tahini dressing. Spoon the salad down the center of the wraps, top with shredded lettuce, and then roll up and enjoy.

Per serving (1 wrap): Calories: 437Kcal; Fat: 8g; Carbs: 79g; Fiber: 12g; Protein: 15g

520. Paprika Olives Spread
Preparation time: 10 minutes
Cooking time: 0 minutes **Servings:** 4
Ingredients:
- 1 cup kalamata olives, pitted and halved
- 1 cup black olives, pitted, and halved
- 1 avocado, peeled, pitted, and cubed
- 2 scallions, chopped
- 2 teaspoons sweet paprika
- 1 tablespoon olive oil
- 1 tablespoon lime juice
- Salt and black pepper to the taste
- ½ cup coconut cream

Directions:
In a blender, combine the olives with the avocado, scallions, and the other ingredients, pulse well, divide into bowls and serve for breakfast.

Per serving: Calories: 287Kcal; Fat: 27.8g; Carbs: 12.2g; Fiber: 6.8g; Protein: 2.5g

521. Korean Barbecue Tempeh Wraps
Preparation time: 15 minutes
Cooking time: 25 minutes **Servings:** 4
Ingredients:
For the Korean barbecue sauce:
- ¾ cup water
- 1/3 cup soy sauce
- ¼ cup maple syrup
- ¼ cup tomato paste
- 2 tablespoons gochujang
- 2 garlic cloves, minced
- 2 teaspoons ginger, grated
- 1 teaspoon sesame oil

For the Tempeh filling:
- 2 tablespoons vegetable oil
- 2-8 oz. packages tempeh, cubed
- 1 red bell pepper, thinly sliced
- 1 onion, thinly sliced
- 2 scallions, chopped
- 2 teaspoons sesame seeds
- For the wraps:

- 4 large flour tortillas
- 4 large lettuce leaves
- 1 large avocado sliced

Directions:
Combine the Korean sauce ingredients in a bowl.
Place a large skillet over medium heat, add sauce and bring it to a simmer, lower the heat and let it simmer for 10 minutes. Place another skillet over medium heat and add oil. Add and cook tempeh for about 5 minutes. Increase the heat, add bell pepper, onion and cook for 2 minutes, then lower the heat, add sauce and cook for 3 minutes. Once done, remove them from heat and set them aside. Put the tortilla on a working surface, place lettuce leaves, avocado slices, and tempeh mixture on top. Wrap like a burrito to enclose the fillings inside Do this for all tortillas before serving.
Per serving: Calories: 48Kcal; Fat: 11g; Carbs: 10g; Protein: 4g

522. Black Bean Wrap with Hummus

Preparation time: 5 minutes
Cooking time: 30 minutes **Servings:** 2 Wraps
Ingredients:
- 1 Poblano Pepper, roasted
- ½ packet Spinach
- 1 Onion, chopped
- 2 Whole Grain Wraps
- ½ can Black Beans
- 1 Bell Pepper, seeded & chopped
- 4 oz. Mushrooms, sliced
- ½ cup Corn
- 8 oz. Red Bell Pepper Hummus, roasted

Directions:
First, preheat the oven to 450°F. Next, spoon in oil to a heated skillet and stir in the onion. Cook them for 2 to 3 minutes or until softened. After that, stir in the bell pepper and sauté for another 3 minutes. Then, add mushrooms and corn to the skillet. Sauté for 2 minutes. In the meantime, spread the hummus over the wraps. Now, place the sautéed vegetables, spinach, Poblano strips, and beans. Roll them in a burrito and place them on a baking sheet with the seam side down. Finally, bake them for 9 to 10 minutes. Serve them warm.
Per serving: Calories: 293Kcal; Fat: 8.8g; Carbs: 42.8g; Protein: 13.7g

523. Sprout Wraps

Preparation time: 15 minutes
Cooking time: 15 minutes **Servings:** 2
Ingredients:
- Tortillas, whole-wheat, 2 large
- Parsley, 1/2 cup chopped
- Onion, green, 2 stalks
- Black pepper, 1 teaspoon
- Cucumber, 1 sliced thin
- Bean sprouts, 1 cup
- Salt, 1/2 teaspoon
- Lemon juice, 1 tablespoon
- Olive oil, 1 tablespoon

Directions:
Lay out each of the tortilla wraps on a plate. Divide all of the ingredients between the two tortillas evenly, leaving about two inches on either side for rolling the tortilla up. When you have added all of the ingredients to the tortilla, then fold in the sides and roll the tortilla up into a cylinder shape.
Per serving: Calories: 226Kcal; Fat: 3g; Carbs: 12g; Protein: 10g

524. Collard Wraps

Preparation time: 20 minutes
Cooking time: 30 minutes **Servings:** 4
Ingredients:
Wrap
- Cherry tomatoes, four cut in half
- Black olives, sliced, 1/4 cup
- Purple onion, 1/2 cup diced fine
- Red bell pepper, 1/2 of 1 cut in julienne strips
- Cucumber, 1 medium-sized cut in julienne strips
- Green collard leaves, 4 large

Sauce
- Black pepper, 1 teaspoon
- Salt, 1/2 teaspoon
- Dill, fresh, minced, 2 tablespoons
- Cucumber, seeded and grated, 1/4 cup
- Olive oil, 2 tablespoons
- White vinegar, 1 tablespoon
- Garlic powder, 1 teaspoon

Directions:
Place all of the ingredients on the list for the sauce in a mixing bowl and mix well. Store the dressing in the refrigerator. Wash off the collard leaves and dry them, and then cut off the stem from each leaf. Cover each leaf with two tablespoons of the sauce you just made. In the middle of the collard leaf layer, all of the other ingredients. Fold the leaf up like a burrito by first folding the ends and then rolling the leaf until it is all rolled. Cut into slices and serve with more dressing for dipping.
Per serving (1 wrap): Calories: 165Kcal; Fat: 11.25g; Carbs: 7.36g; Protein: 6.98g

525. Lite Tuna Melt Wrap

Preparation time: 20 minutes
Cooking time: 20 minutes **Servings:** 2
Ingredients:
Creamy tuna
- 1 (5-ounce) can chunk light tuna in water, drained - 1/4 teaspoon black pepper
- 1/4 cup plain low-fat Greek yogurt or clean mayo - 1/4 teaspoon kosher or sea salt

To Assemble
- 4 large leaves butter or iceberg lettuce
- 4 pickle slices or jalapeño slices, optional
- 1 large whole wheat wrap
- 1/2 cup shredded reduced-fat cheddar cheese

Directions:
Mix all ingredients for creamy tuna. Spread in a broiler-safe baking dish/pan and sprinkle cheese on top. Place under broiler for one to two minutes, just until cheese melts. Lay

wrap flat and line with lettuce leaves. Scoop tuna with melted cheese over wrap. Top with pickles or pickled jalapeño slices, if using. Tuck under one end and roll wrap. Cut in half and serve. **Per serving:** Calories: 329Kcal; Fat: 15g; Carbs: 18g; Fiber: 1g; Protein: 30g

526. Curry Wraps
Preparation time: 5 minutes
Cooking time: 22 minutes **Servings:** 5
Ingredients:
- Chapatis (8)
- Sliced garlic cloves
- Sliced onions
- Olive oil (2 Tablespoon.)
- Tandoori curry paste (2 Tablespoon.) Cubed tofu (600g)
- Mint sauce (3 Tbs.)
- Yogurt (4 Tablespoon.)
- Shredded red cabbage head Quartered lime

Directions:
We can start this out by taking out a bowl and mix the yogurt, cabbage, and mint sauce, then set it to the side. Toss the tofu and the tandoori paste into a frying pan with some of the oil. Then cook this for a bit on each side to make it all golden brown. Take out of the heat when you are done with this. Next, we can add the garlic and onions into the same pan and cook those for a bit. After ten minutes, add the tofu back in and cook a bit longer. Heat the chapatis using the directions on the package and then fill them up with the tandoori tofu and the sauce you made. Serve with the lime quarters.
Per serving: Calories: 211Kcal; Fat: 7g; Carbs: 22g; Protein: 19g

527. Leeks Spread
Preparation time: 5 minutes
Cooking time: 10 minutes **Servings:** 4
Ingredients:
- 3 leeks, sliced
- 2 scallions, chopped
- 1 tablespoon avocado oil
- ¼ cup coconut cream
- Salt and black pepper to the taste
- ¼ teaspoon garlic powder
- ½ teaspoon thyme, dried
- 1 tablespoon cilantro, chopped

Directions:
Heat a pan with the oil over medium heat, add the scallions and the leeks and sauté for 5 minutes.
Add the rest of the ingredients, cook everything for 5 minutes more, blend using an immersion blender, divide into bowls and serve for breakfast.
Per serving: Calories: 83Kcal; Fat: 4.2g; Carbs: 11.3g; Fiber: 2g; Protein: 1.6g

528. Eggplant Spread
Preparation time: 10 minutes
Cooking time: 25 minutes **Servings:** 4
Ingredients:
- 1-pound eggplants
- 2 tablespoons olive oil
- 4 spring onions, chopped
- ½ teaspoon chili powder
- 1 tablespoon lime juice
- Salt and black pepper to the taste

Directions:
Arrange the eggplants in a roasting pan and bake them at 400 degrees F for 25 minutes. Peel the eggplants, put them in a blender, add the rest of the ingredients, pulse well, divide into bowls and serve for breakfast.
Per serving: Calories: 97Kcal; Fat: 7.3g; Carbs: 8.9g; Fiber: 4.6g; Protein: 1.5g

529. Vegan Mediterranean Wraps
Preparation time: 20-25 minutes
Cooking time: 30-60 minutes **Servings:** 2
Ingredients:
- 1 small cucumber, grate half and dice half
- 1 small tomato, diced
- 1/8 green bell pepper, diced
- 1/8 red onion, diced
- ½ jar (from a 19 ounces jar) chickpeas, drained
- 1 tablespoon chopped fresh dill
- ½ tablespoon lemon juice
- 1 cup chopped lettuce - Salt to taste
- 2 tablespoons chopped kalamata olives
- 7 ounces soy yogurt or any other vegan yogurt
- 2 small cloves garlic, peeled, minced
- Pepper to taste
- 2 large tortillas

Directions:
Sprinkle a large pinch of salt over the grated cucumber and place it in a strainer. Place the strainer on top of a bowl. Let it drain for 15 minutes. Squeeze off the excess moisture.
To make tzatziki sauce: Add grated cucumber, dill, salt, pepper, lemon juice, garlic, and yogurt into a bowl and stir. Add chickpeas into a bowl and mash with a fork. Mix diced cucumber, tomato, olives, and lettuce into a bowl and toss. Spread the tortillas on your countertop. Divide the vegetable mixture and chickpeas among the tortillas. Spoon some tzatziki sauce over the chickpeas. Wrap and place with its seam side facing down. Heat the wrap in a pan if desired. Serve with some more tzatziki sauce if desired.
Per serving (1 wrap): Calories: 347Kcal; Fat: 8g; Carbs: 55g; Fiber: 8g; Protein: 12g

530. Jackfruit Wrap
Preparation time: 20-25 minutes
Cooking time: 30-60 minutes **Servings:** 2
Ingredients:
- ½ can (from a 20 ounces can) green jackfruit, drained, rinsed
- ¼ teaspoon garlic powder
- ½ teaspoon onion powder
- ¼ cup BBQ sauce
- ¼ cup vegetable broth
- Salt to taste

- 1 cup shredded Romaine lettuce
- 1 small red onion, sliced
- 1 small tomato, sliced
- Few avocado slices
- 2 large gluten-free tortillas

For garlic aioli sauce:
- 2 tablespoons vegan mayonnaise
- 1 small clove garlic, crushed
- ¼ teaspoon lemon juice or to taste
- Salt to taste

Directions:
Add jackfruit into a bowl. Sprinkle onion powder and garlic powder and toss well. Place a skillet over medium heat. Add broth, jackfruit, and BBQ sauce and mix well. Cover and cook until jackfruit is tender. Remove the jackfruit and place it on your cutting board. Shred the jackfruit with a pair of forks. Meanwhile, make the garlic aioli by mixing all the ingredients for aioli in a bowl. Warm the tortillas and place them on your countertop. Spread garlic aioli sauce on the tortillas. Divide the lettuce, tomato, avocado, and onion slices among the tortillas. Divide the jackfruit among the tortillas. Wrap like a burrito.

Cut into 2 halves and serve.

Tip: You can use any other sauce of your choice instead of garlic aioli. I keep trying a new sauce each time.

Per serving (1 wrap): Calories: 370Kcal; Fat: 14g; Carbs: 50g; Protein: 4g

CHAPTER 25:
Snacks & Appetizers

531. Nori Snack Rolls
Preparation time: 5 minutes
Cooking time: 10 minutes
Servings: 4 Rolls
Ingredients:
- 2 tablespoons almond, cashew, peanut, or another nut butter
- 2 tablespoons tamari or soy sauce
- 4 standard nori sheets - 1 mushroom, sliced
- 1 tablespoon pickled ginger
- ½ cup grated carrots

Directions:
Preheat the oven to 350°F. Mix the nut butter and tamari until smooth and very thick. Lay out a nori sheet, rough side up, the long way. Spread a thin line of the tamari mixture on the far end of the nori sheet, from side to side. Lay the mushroom slices, ginger, and carrots in a line at the other end (the end closest to you). Fold the vegetables inside the nori, rolling toward the tahini mixture, which will seal the roll. Repeat to make 4 rolls. Finish and Serve Put on a baking sheet and bake for 8-10 minutes, or until the rolls are slightly browned and crispy at the ends. Let the rolls cool for a few minutes, then slice each roll into 3 smaller pieces.
Per serving (1 roll): Calories: 79Kcal; Fat: 5g; Carbs: 6g; Fiber: 2g; Protein: 4g

532. Risotto Bites
Preparation time: 15 minutes
Cooking time: 20 minutes **Servings:** 12 Bites
Ingredients:
- ½ cup panko bread crumbs - 1 teaspoon paprika
- 1 teaspoon chipotle powder or ground cayenne pepper - 1½ cups cold Green Pea Risotto
- Nonstick cooking spray

Directions:
Preparing the ingredients.
Preheat the oven to 425°F. Line a baking sheet with parchment paper. On a large plate, combine the panko, paprika, and chipotle powder. Set aside.
Roll 2 tablespoons of the risotto into a ball. Gently roll in the bread crumbs and place them on the prepared baking sheet. Repeat to make a total of 12 balls.
Bake
Spritz the tops of the risotto bites with nonstick cooking spray and bake for 15-20 minutes until they begin to brown.
Finish and Serve
Cool completely before storing in a large airtight container in a single layer (add a piece of parchment paper for a second layer) or in a plastic freezer bag.
Per serving (6 bites): Calories: 100Kcal; Fat: 2g; Carbs: 17g; Fiber: 5g; Protein: 6g

533. Garden Patch Sandwiches On Multigrain Bread
Preparation time: 15 minutes **Cooking time:** 0 minutes
Servings: 4 Sandwiches
Ingredients:
- 1 pound extra-firm tofu, drained and patted dry
- 1 medium red bell pepper, finely chopped
- 1 celery rib, finely chopped - 3 green onions, minced
- ¼ cup shelled sunflower seeds
- ½ cup vegan mayonnaise, homemade or store-bought
- ½ teaspoon salt - ½ teaspoon celery salt
- ¼ teaspoon freshly ground black pepper
- 8 slices whole-grain bread
- 4 (¼-inch) slices ripe tomato
- 4 lettuce leaves

Directions:
Crumble the tofu and place it in a large bowl. Add bell pepper, celery, green onions, and sunflower seeds. Stir in the mayonnaise, salt, celery salt, and pepper and mix until well combined. Finish and Serve Toast the bread, if desired. Spread the mixture evenly onto 4 slices of the bread. Top each with a tomato slice, lettuce leaf, and the remaining bread. Cut the sandwiches diagonally in half and serve.
Per serving (6 bites): Calories: 479Kcal; Fat: 24.21g; Carbs: 42.87g; Fiber: 8.4g; Protein: 26.3g

534. Black Sesame Wonton Chips
Preparation time: 5 minutes
Cooking time: 5 minutes **Servings:** 24 Chips
Ingredients:
- 12 Vegan Wonton Wrappers
- Toasted sesame oil
- 1/3 cup black sesame seeds
- Salt

Directions:
Preparing the ingredients.
Preheat the oven to 450°F. Lightly oil a baking sheet and set it aside. Cut the wonton wrappers in half crosswise, brush them with sesame oil, and arrange them in a single layer on the prepared baking sheet.
Sprinkle wonton wrappers with sesame seeds and salt.
Bake
Bake until crisp and golden brown.
Finish and Serve
Cool completely before serving. These are best eaten on the day they are made but once cooled, they can be covered and stored at room temperature for 1-2 days.
Per serving (6 bites): Calories: 60Kcal; Fat: 1.5; Carbs: 9.51g; Fiber: 0.5g; Protein: 1.99g

535. Tamari Toasted Almonds

Preparation time: 2 minutes
Cooking time: 8 minutes **Servings:** ½ Cup
Ingredients:

- ½ cup raw almonds or sunflower seeds
- 2 tablespoons tamari or soy sauce
- 1 teaspoon toasted sesame oil

Directions:
Heat a dry skillet to medium-high heat, then add the almonds, stirring frequently to keep them from burning. Once the almonds are toasted—7-8 minutes for almonds, or 34 minutes for sunflower seeds—pour the tamari and sesame oil into the hot skillet and stir to coat. You can turn off the heat, and as the almonds cool, the tamari mixture will stick and dry on the nuts. **Per serving (1 tablespoon):** Calories: 89Kcal; Fat: 8g; Carbs: 3g; Fiber: 2g; Protein: 4g

536. Avocado And Tempeh Bacon Wraps

Preparation time: 10 minutes
Cooking time: 8 minutes **Servings:** 4 Wraps
Ingredients:

- 2 tablespoons extra-virgin olive oil
- 8 ounces tempeh bacon, homemade or store-bought
- 4 (10-inch) soft flour tortillas or lavash flat bread
- ¼ cup vegan mayonnaise, homemade or store-bought
- 4 large lettuce leaves
- 2 ripe Hass avocados, pitted, peeled, and cut into ¼-inch slices
- 1 large ripe tomato, cut into ¼-inch slices

Directions:
Preparing the ingredients.
In a large skillet, heat the oil over medium heat. Add the tempeh bacon and cook until browned on both sides, about 8 minutes. Remove from the heat and set aside. Place 1 tortilla on a work surface. Spread with some of the mayonnaise and one-fourth of the lettuce and tomatoes.
Finish and Serve
Pit, peel, and thinly slice the avocado and place the slices on top of the tomato. Add the reserved tempeh bacon and roll up tightly. Repeat with remaining **Ingredients:** and serve.
Per serving: Calories: 590Kcal; Fat: 32.45g; Carbs: 60.98g; Fiber: 17.2g; Protein: 24g

537. Tempeh-Pimiento Cheeze Ball

Preparation time: 5 minutes
Cooking time: 30 minutes **Servings:** 8
Ingredients:

- 8 ounces tempeh, cut into ½-inch pieces
- 1 (2-ounce) jar chopped pimientos, drained
- ¼ cup nutritional yeast
- ¼ cup vegan mayonnaise, homemade or store-bought
- 2 tablespoons soy sauce
- ¾ cup chopped pecans

Directions:
Preparing the ingredients.
In a medium saucepan of simmering water, cook the tempeh for 30 minutes. Set aside to cool. In a food processor, combine the cooled tempeh, pimientos, nutritional yeast, mayo, and soy sauce. Process until smooth. Transfer the tempeh mixture to a bowl and refrigerate until firm and chilled for at least 2 hours or overnight.
Finish and Serve
In a dry skillet, toast the pecans over medium heat until lightly toasted. Set aside to cool.
Shape the tempeh mixture into a ball, and roll it in the pecans, pressing the nuts slightly into the tempeh mixture so that they stick. Refrigerate for at least 1 hour before serving. If not using right away, cover and keep refrigerated until needed. Properly stored, it will keep for 2-3 days.
Per serving: Calories: 171Kcal; Fat: 12.93g; Carbs: 7.06g; Fiber: 1.7g; Protein: 9g

538. Peppers and Hummus

Preparation time: 15 minutes
Cooking time: 0 minutes **Servings:** 4
Ingredients:

- 1 15-ounce can chickpeas, drained and rinsed
- juice of 1 lemon, or 1 tablespoon prepared lemon juice - ¼ cup tahini
- 3 tablespoons extra-virgin olive oil
- ½ teaspoon ground cumin
- 1 tablespoon water - ¼ teaspoon paprika
- 1 red bell pepper, sliced
- 1 green bell pepper, sliced
- 1 orange bell pepper, sliced

Directions:
Preparing the ingredients.
In a food processor, combine chickpeas, lemon juice, tahini, 2 tablespoons of olive oil, cumin, and water.
Finish and Serve
Process on high speed until blended for about 30 seconds. Scoop the hummus into a bowl and drizzle with the remaining tablespoon of olive oil. Sprinkle with paprika and serve with sliced bell peppers.
Per serving: Calories: 294Kcal; Fat: 15.37g; Carbs: 31.72g; Fiber: 8.7g; Protein: 10.86g

539. Savory Roasted Chickpeas

Preparation time: 5 minutes
Cooking time: 25 minutes **Servings:** 1 Cup
Ingredients:

- 1 (14-ounce) can chickpeas, rinsed and drained, or 1½ cups cooked
- 2 tablespoons tamari or soy sauce
- 1 tablespoon nutritional yeast
- 1 teaspoon smoked paprika or regular paprika - 1 teaspoon onion powder
- ½ teaspoon garlic powder

Directions:
Preparing the ingredients.
Preheat the oven to 400°F. Toss the chickpeas with all the other ingredients, and spread them out on a baking sheet.

Bake
Bake for 20-25 minutes, tossing halfway through.
Bake these at a lower temperature until fully dried and crispy if you want to keep them longer. You can easily double the batch, and if you dry them out, they will keep about a week in an airtight container.
Per serving (¼ cup): Calories: 121Kcal; Fat: 2g; Carbs: 20g; Fiber: 6g; Protein: 8g

540. Savory Seed Crackers

Preparation time: 5 minutes
Cooking time: 50 minutes
Servings: 20 Crackers
Ingredients:
- ¾ cup pumpkin seeds (pepitas)
- ½ cup sunflower seeds
- ½ cup sesame seeds - ¼ cup chia seeds
- 1 teaspoon minced garlic (about 1 clove)
- 1 teaspoon tamari or soy sauce
- 1 teaspoon vegan Worcestershire sauce
- ½ teaspoon ground cayenne pepper
- ½ teaspoon dried oregano - ½ cup water

Directions:
Preparing the ingredients.
Preheat the oven to 325°F.
Line a rimmed baking sheet with parchment paper.
In a large bowl, combine the pumpkin seeds, sunflower seeds, sesame seeds, chia seeds, garlic, tamari, Worcestershire sauce, cayenne, oregano, and water.
Bake
Transfer to the prepared baking sheet and spread it out to all sides. Bake for 25 minutes. Remove the pan from the oven, and flip the seed "dough" over so the wet side is up. Bake for another 20-25 minutes until the sides are browned.
Finish and Serve
Cool completely before breaking up into 20 pieces. Divide evenly among 4 glass jars and close tightly with lids.
Per serving (5 crackers): Calories: 339Kcal; Fat: 29g; Carbs: 17g; Fiber: 8g; Protein: 14g

541. Tomato and Basil Bruschetta

Preparation time: 10 minutes
Cooking time: 6 minutes
Servings: 12 Bruschetta
Ingredients:
- 3 tomatoes, chopped
- ¼ cup chopped fresh basil
- 1 tablespoon extra-virgin olive oil
- pinch of sea salt
- 1 baguette, cut into 12 slices
- 1 garlic clove, sliced in half

Directions:
Preparing the ingredients.
In a small bowl, combine the tomatoes, basil, olive oil, and salt and stir to mix. Set aside. Preheat the oven to 425°F. Place the baguette slices in a single layer on a baking sheet and toast in the oven until brown for about 6 minutes. **Finish and Serve**
Flip the bread slices over once during cooking.
Remove from the oven and rub the bread on both sides with the sliced clove of garlic. Top with the tomato-basil mixture and serve immediately.
Per serving: Calories: 11Kcal; Fat: 0.57g; Carbs: 1.29g; Fiber: 0.4g; Protein: 0.39g

542. Refried Bean And Salsa Quesadillas

Preparation time: 5 minutes **Cooking time:** 6 minutes
Servings: 4 Quesadillas
Ingredients:
- 1 tablespoon canola oil, plus more for frying
- 1½ cups cooked or 1 (15.5-ounce) can pinto beans, drained and mashed
- 1 teaspoon chili powder
- 4 (10-inch) whole-wheat flour tortillas
- 1 cup tomato salsa, homemade or store-bought - ½ cup minced red onion (optional)

Directions:
In a medium saucepan, heat the oil over medium heat. Add the mashed beans and chili powder and cook, stirring, until hot, about 5 minutes. Set aside.
To assemble, place 1 tortilla on a work surface and spoon about ¼ cup of the beans across the bottom half. Top the beans with salsa and onion, if using. Fold the top half of the tortilla over the filling and press slightly. In a large skillet, heat a thin layer of oil over medium heat. Place folded quesadillas, 1 or 2 at a time, into the hot skillet and heat until hot, turning once, about 1 minute per side. Cut quesadillas into 3 or 4 wedges and arrange on plates. Serve immediately. **Per serving:** Calories: 264Kcal; Fat: 8.1g; Carbs: 38.76g; Fiber: 10.7g; Protein: 10.36g

543. Jicama and Guacamole

Preparation time: 15 minutes
Cooking time: 0 minutes **Servings:** 4
Ingredients:
- juice of 1 lime, or 1 tablespoon prepared lime juice
- 2 has avocados, peeled, pits removed, and cut into cubes - ½ teaspoon sea salt
- ½ red onion, minced
- 1 garlic clove, minced
- ¼ cup chopped cilantro (optional)
- 1 jicama bulb, peeled and cut into matchsticks

Directions:
Preparing the ingredients.
In a medium bowl, squeeze the lime juice over the top of the avocado and sprinkle with salt. Lightly mash the avocado with a fork. Stir in the onion, garlic, and cilantro, if using.
Finish and Serve
Serve with slices of jicama to dip in guacamole. To store, place plastic wrap over the bowl of guacamole and refrigerate. The guacamole will keep for about 2 days.
Per serving: Calories: 189Kcal; Fat: 14.88g; Carbs: 15.34g; Fiber: 8.9g; Protein: 3g

544. Tempeh Tantrum Burgers

Preparation time: 15 minutes **Cooking time:** 14 minutes
Servings: 4 Burgers
Ingredients:
- 8 ounces tempeh, cut into ½-inch dice
- ¾ cup chopped onion
- 2 garlic cloves, chopped
- ¾ cup chopped walnuts
- ½ cup old-fashioned or quick-cooking oats
- 1 tablespoon minced fresh parsley
- ½ teaspoon dried oregano
- ½ teaspoon dried thyme - ½ teaspoon salt
- ¼ teaspoon freshly ground black pepper
- 3 tablespoons extra-virgin olive oil
- Dijon mustard - 4 whole grain burger rolls
- Sliced red onion, tomato, lettuce, and avocado

Directions:
Preparing the ingredients.
In a medium saucepan of simmering water, cook the tempeh for 30 minutes. Drain and set aside to cool.
In a food processor, combine the onion and garlic, then process until minced. Add the cooled tempeh, walnuts, oats, parsley, oregano, thyme, salt, and pepper. Process until well blended. Shape the mixture into 4 equal patties. In a large skillet, heat the oil over medium heat.
Add the burgers and cook until cooked thoroughly and browned on both sides for about 7 minutes per side.
Finish and Serve
Spread the desired amount of mustard onto each half of the rolls and layer each roll with lettuce, tomato, red onion, and avocado as desired. Serve immediately.
Per serving: Calories: 281Kcal; Fat: 20.9g; Carbs: 13.78g; Fiber: 2g; Protein: 13.98g

545. Sesame-Wonton Crisps

Preparation time: 10 minutes
Cooking time: 10 minutes **Servings:** 12 Crisps
Ingredients:
- 12 Vegan Wonton Wrappers
- 2 tablespoons toasted sesame oil
- 12 shiitake mushrooms, lightly rinsed, patted dry, stemmed, and cut into 1/4-inch slices
- 4 snow peas, trimmed and cut crosswise into thin slivers - 1 teaspoon soy sauce
- 1 tablespoon fresh lime juice
- ½ teaspoon brown sugar
- 1 medium carrot, shredded
- Toasted sesame seeds or black sesame seeds, if available

Directions:
Preparing the ingredients.
Preheat the oven to 350°F. Lightly oil a baking sheet and set it aside. Brush the wonton wrappers with 1 tablespoon of the sesame oil and arrange them on the baking sheet. Bake until golden brown and crisp for about 5 minutes. Set aside to cool. (Alternately, you can tuck the wonton wrappers into mini-muffin tins to create cups for the filling. Brush with sesame oil and bake them until crisp.) In a large skillet, heat the extra olive oil over medium heat. Add the mushrooms and cook until softened. Stir in the snow peas and the soy sauce and cook for 30 seconds. Set aside to cool. In a large bowl, combine the lime juice, sugar, and remaining 1 tablespoon sesame oil. Stir in the carrot and cooled shiitake mixture.
Finish and Serve
Top each wonton crisp with a spoonful of the shiitake mixture. Sprinkle with sesame seeds and arrange on a platter to serve.
Per serving: Calories: 128Kcal; Fat: 2.88g; Carbs: 22.09g; Fiber: 1.1g; Protein: 3.53g

546. Macadamia-Cashew Patties

Preparation time: 10 minutes
Cooking time: 10 minutes **Servings:** 4 Patties
Ingredients:
- ¾ cup chopped macadamia nuts
- ¾ cup chopped cashews
- 1 medium carrot, grated
- 1 small onion, chopped
- 1 garlic clove, minced
- 1 jalapeño or other green chile, seeded and minced
- ¾ cup old-fashioned oats
- ¾ cup dry unseasoned bread crumbs
- 2 tablespoons minced fresh cilantro
- ½ teaspoon ground coriander
- Salt and freshly ground black pepper
- 2 teaspoons fresh lime juice
- Canola or grapeseed oil, for frying
- 4 sandwich rolls
- Lettuce leaves and condiment of choice

Directions:
Preparing the ingredients.
In a food processor, combine the macadamia nuts, cashews, carrot, onion, garlic, chile, oats, bread crumbs, cilantro, coriander, and salt and pepper. Process until well mixed. Add the lime juice and process until well blended. Taste, adjusting the seasonings if necessary. Shape the mixture into 4 equal patties. In a large skillet, heat a thin layer of oil over medium heat. Add the patties and cook until golden brown on both sides, turning once, for about 10 minutes in total.
Finish and Serve
Serve on sandwich rolls with lettuce and condiments of choice.
Per serving: Calories: 258Kcal; Fat: 14.74g; Carbs: 24.5g; Fiber: 2.5g; Protein: 9.96g

547. Lemon Coconut Cilantro Rolls

Preparation time: 30 minutes
Cooking time: 30 minutes **Servings:** 16 Pieces
Ingredients:
- ½ cup fresh cilantro, chopped
- 1 cup sprouts (clover, alfalfa)
- 1 garlic clove, pressed
- 2 tablespoons ground Brazil nuts or almonds
- 2 tablespoons flaked coconut
- 1 tablespoon coconut oil
- Pinch cayenne pepper - Pinch sea salt

- Pinch freshly ground black pepper
- Zest and juice of 1 lemon
- 2 tablespoons ground flaxseed
- 1 to 2 tablespoons water
- 2 whole-wheat wraps, or corn wraps

Directions:
Preparing the ingredients.
Put everything but the wraps in a food processor and pulse to combine. Or combine the ingredients in a large bowl. Add the water, if needed, to help the mix come together.
Spread the mixture out over each wrap, roll it up, and place it in the fridge for 30 minutes to set.
Finish and Serve
Remove the rolls from the fridge and slice each into 8 pieces to serve as appetizers or sides with a soup or stew. Get the best flavor by buying whole raw Brazil nuts or almonds, toasting them lightly in a dry skillet or toaster oven, then grinding them in a coffee grinder.
Per serving (1 piece): Calories: 66Kcal; Fat: 4g; Carbs: 6g; Fiber: 1g; Protein: 2g

548. Seeded Crackers

Preparation time: 1 hour
Cooking time: 10 minutes **Servings:** 36 crackers
Ingredients:
- ½ cup pumpkin seeds
- ½ cup sunflower seeds
- ¼ cup sesame seeds
- ¼ cup chia seeds - ¾ cup water
- ¾ teaspoon salt
- 1 teaspoon rosemary
- 1 teaspoon onion powder

Directions:
Preheat oven to 350°F. Set aside two large pieces of parchment paper. Combine all ingredients in a large bowl. Set aside to rest for 15 minutes. Oil one side of each of the two sheets of parchment paper to avoid sticking in the next step. Place the dough between the two pieces of parchment paper. Roll out the dough thin using a rolling pin (roll to approximately 10 x 14-inch rectangle). Slide the rolled-out dough onto a baker's half sheet. Bake for 20 minutes.
Remove from oven and cut into large pieces. Flip each piece over when finished.
Bake for an additional 14 minutes.
Let cool and store in an airtight container.
Per serving: Calories: 26Kcal; Fat: 2g; Carbs: 2g; Fiber: 1g; Protein: 1g

549. Banana Bites

Preparation time: 15 minutes
Cooking time: 15 minutes
Servings: 4
Ingredients:
- 2 bananas - ½ cup vegan chocolate, melted
- 1 cup roasted pistachios, in pieces or finely crushed

Directions:
Set aside a parchment-lined baking sheet. Peel the bananas and stick a toothpick on both ends to make the next step easier. Dip and fully coat the bananas in the melted chocolate.
Set onto the parchment paper. If using whole pistachios, place the nuts into a food processor and pulse until fine. Leave some pistachios intact. Sprinkle the pistachios on top of the banana. Freeze the bananas to set the chocolate and pistachios for 5 minutes. Remove the bananas and cut them into bites. Return to the freezer in a glass container. When ready to consume, remove bananas from the freezer and thaw for 10 minutes to soften.
Per serving: Calories: 273Kcal; Fat: 14g; Carbs: 37g; Fiber: 5g; Protein: 6g

550. Sweet Potato Toast

Preparation time: 5 minutes
Cooking time: 10 minutes **Servings:** 1
Ingredients:
- ½ of 1 Avocado, ripe
- 2 tbsp. Sun-dried Tomatoes
- 1 Sweet Potato, sliced into ¼-inch thick slices
- ½ cup Chickpeas
- Salt & Pepper, as needed
- 1 tsp. Lemon Juice
- Pinch of Red Pepper
- 2 tbsp. Vegan Cheese

Directions:
Start by slicing the sweet potato into five ¼ inch wide slices. Next, toast the sweet potato in the toaster for 9 to 11 minutes. Then, place the chickpeas in a medium-sized bowl and mash with the avocado. Stir in the crushed red pepper, lemon juice, pepper, and salt. Stir until everything comes together. Finally, place the mixture on the top of the sweet potato toast. Top with cheese and sun-dried tomatoes.
Per serving: Calories: 452Kcal; Fat: 11g; Carbs: 77g; Protein: 19g

551. Hummus Toast

Preparation time: 5 minutes
Cooking time: 5 minutes **Servings:** 1
Ingredients:
- 1 tbsp. Hemp Seeds
- 1 tbsp. Sunflower Seeds, roasted & unsalted
- 2 Vegan Bread Slices
- ¼ cup Hummus

For the hummus:
- 15 oz. Chickpeas
- ¾ tsp. Salt
- 2 tbsp. Lime Juice, fresh
- 2 tbsp. Extra Virgin Olive Oil
- 2 Garlic cloves
- ½ cup Tahini

Directions:
To begin with, toast the bread for 1 to 1 ½ minutes or until lightly toasted. Meanwhile, to make the hummus, place the undrained chickpeas and garlic cloves in a medium bowl. Microwave for 2 to 3 minutes on high heat. After that, put the lime juice, tahini, and salt along with the cooked chickpeas into a food processor. Blend for 2 to 3 minutes or until smooth. While blending, spoon in the olive oil gradually. Combine. Taste the mixture for seasoning. If needed, add

more salt and pepper. Next, top the toast with hummus, hemp, and sunflower seeds. Serve and enjoy.
Per serving: Calories: 316Kcal; Fat: 16g; Carbs: 24g; Protein: 19g

552. Tacos
Preparation time: 10 minutes
Cooking time: 30 minutes **Servings:** 4
Ingredients:
- 6 Taco Shells
- For the slaw:
- 1 cup Red Cabbage, shredded
- 3 Scallions, chopped
- 1 cup Green Cabbage, shredded
- 1 cup Carrots, sliced

For the dressing:
- 1 tbsp. Sriracha
- ¼ cup Apple Cider Vinegar
- ¼ tsp. Salt - 2 tbsp. Sesame Oil
- 1 tbsp. Dijon Mustard
- 1 tbsp. Lime Juice - ½ tbsp. Tamari
- 1 tbsp. Maple Syrup
- ¼ tsp. Salt

Directions:
To start with, make the dressing, whisk all the ingredients in a small bowl until mixed well.
Next, combine the slaw ingredients in another bowl and toss well. Finally, take a taco shell and place the slaw in it. Serve and enjoy.
Per serving: Calories: 216Kcal; Fat: 13g; Carbs: 15g; Protein: 10g

553. Kale Chips
Preparation time: 10 minutes
Cooking time: 1 Hour 30 minutes **Servings:** 10
Ingredients:
- ½ tsp. Smoked Paprika
- 2 bunches of Curly Kale
- 1 tsp. Garlic Powder
- ½ cup Nutritional Yeast
- 2 cups Cashew, soaked for 2 hours
- 1 tsp. Salt
- ½ cup Nutritional Yeast

Directions:
To make these tasty, healthy chips place the kale in a large mixing bowl. Now, combine all the remaining ingredients in the high-speed blender and blend for 1 minute or until smooth. Next, pour this dressing over the kale chips and mix well with your hands.
Then, preheat your oven to 225 °F or 107 °C.
Once heated, arrange the kale leaves on a large baking sheet leaving ample space between them.
Bake the leaves for 80 to 90 minutes, flipping them once in between. Finally, allow them to cool completely and then store them in an air-tight container.
Per serving: Calories: 191Kcal; Fat: 12g; Carbs: 16g; Protein: 9g

554. Spicy Roasted Chickpeas
Preparation time: 10 minutes
Cooking time: 25 minutes **Servings:** 6
Ingredients:
- ½ tsp. Cumin
- 2 × 15 oz. Chickpeas
- ¼ tsp. Cayenne Pepper
- ¼ cup Olive Oil
- ½ tsp. Onion Powder
- 1 tsp. Sea Salt
- ¾ tsp. Garlic Powder
- ½ tsp. Chili Powder
- ¾ tsp. Paprika
- Sea Salt, as needed

Directions:
Preheat the oven to 425 °F.
After that, put the chickpeas in a strainer lined with a paper towel and allow to dry for 10 to 15 minutes.
Then, transfer the chickpeas onto a baking paper-lined baking sheet and then spoon some olive oil over it. Coat the chickpeas with the oil. Sprinkle a dash of salt over it. Now, put the baking sheet in the oven and bake for 23 to 25 minutes, tossing them every 5 minutes or until they are golden brown. Once they have become crispy, remove the sheet from the oven. Next, mix all the remaining seasoning ingredients in another bowl until combined well. Finally, stir the chickpeas into this mixture and toss well. Serve immediately.
Per serving: Calories: 212Kcal; Fat: 7.4g; Carbs: 28.9g; Protein: 9.3g

555. Nuts Trail Mix
Preparation time: 10 minutes
Cooking time: 10 minutes **Servings:** 2
Ingredients:
- 1 cup Walnuts, raw
- 2 cups Tart Cherries, dried
- 1 cup Pumpkin Seeds, raw
- 1 cup Almonds, raw
- 1 cup Cashew

Directions:
First, mix all the ingredients needed to make the trail mix in a large mixing bowl until combined well.
Store in an air-tight container.
Per serving: Calories: 596Kcal; Fat: 39.5g; Carbs: 46.1g; Protein: 17.5g

556. Crispy Cauliflower
Preparation time: 10 minutes
Cooking time: 30 minutes **Servings:** 6
Ingredients:
- 1 head cauliflower, cut into florets
- 2 tbsp potato starch - 1/2 tsp salt
- 1/4 tsp black pepper - 1/2 tsp turmeric
- 1 tbsp nutritional yeast, optional
- 1/2 tsp chili powder or paprika
- 1 tbsp avocado oil

Directions:
Start by preheating the oven to 450 degrees F. Grease a baking sheet with a tablespoon of oil. Add cauliflower to the baking sheet and toss in oil and the rest of the ingredients. Mix well, then bake for 30 minutes. Serve.
Per serving: Calories: 172Kcal; Fat: 11.8g; Carbs: 45.8g; Fiber: 0.6g; Protein: 4g

557. Spinach Mushroom Pockets

Preparation time: 10 minutes
Cooking time: 23 minutes **Servings:** 4
Ingredients:
- 1 package puff pastry
- 16 oz mushrooms, sliced
- 2 bags spinach
- 1 1/2 tbsp garlic, minced - 1 pinch salt
- 1 block extra-firm tofu, pressed
- 1 tsp onion powder
- 1 tsp basil - 1 tsp oregano
- Black pepper, to taste
- 1/4 tsp salt
- 2 1/2 tbsp nutritional yeast
- 2 tbsp lemon juice
- 1 tsp mustard - 1 tbsp milk

Directions:
Place mushrooms in a large pot and heat them until they release their liquid. Stir in 1.5 teaspoons garlic and spinach, then cover with a lid. Cook for 3 minutes until spinach wilts. Toss the rest of the ingredients into a bowl and set it aside. Spread the pastry into a thin sheet and cut circles out of it. Divide the filling in the circles and fold the circle, then pinch the edges closed. Bake them for 20 minutes approximately in the oven at 375 degrees.
Serve.
Per serving: Calories: 246Kcal; Fat: 7.4g; Carbs: 29.4g; Fiber: 2.7g; Protein: 7.2g

558. Breaded Tofu

Preparation time: 10 minutes
Cooking time: 10 minutes **Servings:** 4
Ingredients:
- 1 (14-oz) package extra-firm tofu
- ½ cup cornstarch - ½ cup breadcrumbs
- ¼ cup of water - ¼ cup of vegetable oil
- 2 tbsp soy sauce - 1 tbsp nutritional yeast
- 1 pinch salt
- ½ cup BBQ sauce

Directions:
Drain the tofu, then slice it into finger-length strips. Whisk water, soy sauce, and cornstarch in a small bowl. Mix breadcrumbs with salt and yeast in a shallow bowl. Pour vegetable oil into a large pan and heat over medium-high heat. First, dip the tofu in the cornstarch mixture, then coat them with breadcrumbs mixture. Shallow fry the tofu for 3 minutes per side. Serve.
Per serving: Calories: 293Kcal; Fat: 16g; Carbs: 25.2g; Fiber: 1.9g; Protein: 4.2g

559. Raisin Protein Balls

Preparation time: 10 minutes
Cooking time: 30 minutes
Servings: 6
Ingredients:
- 1 cup dry oats
- ½ cup creamy peanut butter
- ¼ cup raisins

Directions:
Start by thoroughly mixing all the ingredients in a bowl. Make golf ball-sized fat bombs out of it.
Place them on a baking sheet and freeze for 30 minutes. Serve.
Per serving: Calories: 169Kcal; Fat: 10.6g; Carbs: 31.4g; Fiber: 0.2g; Protein: 4.6g

560. Cheese Cucumber Bites

Preparation time: 10 minutes
Cooking time: 0 minutes **Servings:** 8
Ingredients:
- 4 large cucumbers - 1 cup raw sunflower seeds
- 1/2 tsp salt
- 2 tbsp raw red onion, chopped
- 1 handful fresh chives, chopped
- 1 clove fresh garlic, chopped
- 2 tbsp nutritional yeast
- 2 tbsp fresh lemon juice
- 1/2 cup water

Directions:
Start by blending sunflower seeds with salt in a food processor for 20 seconds. Toss in remaining ingredients, except for the cucumber and chives, and process until smooth. Slice the cucumber into 1.5-inch thick rounds. Top each slice with the sunflower mixture. Garnish with sumac and chives.
Serve.
Per serving: Calories: 211Kcal; Fat: 25.5g; Carbs: 32.4g; Fiber: 0.7g; Protein: 1.4g

561. Hummus without Oil

Preparation time: 5 minutes
Cooking time: 5 minutes **Servings:** 6
Ingredients:
- 2 tablespoons of lemon juice
- 1 15-ounce can of chickpeas
- 2 tablespoons of tahini
- 1-2 freshly chopped/minced garlic cloves
- Red pepper hummus
- 2 tablespoons of almond milk pepper

Directions:
Rinse the chickpeas and put them in a high-speed blender with garlic. Blend them until they break into fine pieces. Add the other ingredients and blend everything until you have a smooth paste. Add some water if you want a less thick consistency.
Your homemade hummus dip is ready to be served with eatables!
Per serving: Calories: 202Kcal; Fat: 3g; Carbs: 35g; Protein: 11g

562. Tempting Quinoa Tabbouleh

Preparation time: 10 minutes
Cooking time: 10 minutes **Servings:** 6
Ingredients:

- 1 cup of well-rinsed quinoa
- 1 finely minced garlic clove
- ½ teaspoon of kosher salt
- ½ cup of extra virgin olive oil
- 2 tablespoons of fresh lemon juice
- Freshly ground black pepper
- 2 Persian cucumbers, cut into ¼-inch pieces
- 2 thinly sliced scallions
- 1 pint of halved cherry tomatoes
- ½ cup of chopped fresh mint
- 2/3 cup of chopped parsley

Directions:
Put a medium saucepan on high heat and boil the quinoa mixed with salt in 1 ¼ cups of water. Decrease the heat to medium-low, cover the pot, and simmer everything until the quinoa is tender. The entire process will take 10 minutes. Remove the quinoa from heat and allow it to stand for 5 minutes. Fluff it with a fork. In a small bowl, whisk the garlic with the lemon juice. Add the olive oil gradually. Mix the salt and pepper to taste. On a baking sheet, spread the quinoa and allow it to cool. Shift it to a large bowl and mix ¼ of the dressing. Add the tomatoes, scallions, herbs, and cucumber. Give them a good toss and season everything with pepper and salt. Add the remaining dressing.
Per serving: Calories: 292Kcal; Fat: 20g; Carbs: 25g; Protein: 5g

563. Quick Peanut Butter Bars

Preparation time: 10 minutes
Cooking time: 15 minutes
Servings: 10
Ingredients:

- 20 soft-pitted Medjool dates
- 1 cup of raw almonds
- 1 ¼ cup of crushed pretzels
- 1/3 cup of natural peanut butter

Directions:
Put the almonds in a food processor and mix them until they are broken. Add the peanut butter and the dates. Blend them until you have a thick dough Crush the pretzels and put them in the processor. Pulse enough to mix them with the rest of the ingredients. You can also give them a good stir with a spoon.
Take a small, square pan and line it with parchment paper. Press the dough onto the pan, flattening it with your hands or a spoon. Put it in the freezer for about 2 hours or in the fridge for about 4 hours.
Once it is fully set, cut it into bars. Store them and enjoy them when you are hungry. Just remember to store them in a sealed container.
Per serving: Calories: 343Kcal; Fat: 23g; Carbs: 33g; Protein: 5g

564. Hummus Made with Sweet Potato

Preparation time: 15 minutes
Cooking time: 55 minutes **Servings:** 3-4 cups
Ingredients:

- 2 cups of cooked chickpeas
- 2 medium sweet potatoes
- 3 tablespoons of tahini
- 3 tablespoons of olive oil
- 3 freshly peeled garlic gloves
- Freshly squeezed lemon juice
- Ground sea salt
- ¼ teaspoon of cumin
- Zest from half a lemon
- ½ teaspoon of smoked paprika
- 1 ½ teaspoon of cayenne pepper

Directions:
Preheat the oven to 400°F. Put the sweet potatoes on the middle rack of the oven and bake them for about 45 minutes. You can also bake the potatoes in a baking dish. You will know that they are ready when they become soft and squishy. Allow the sweet potatoes to cool down. Blend all the other ingredients in a food processor. After the sweet potatoes have sufficiently cooled down, use a knife to peel off the skin. Add the sweet potatoes to a blender and blend well with the rest of the ingredients.
Once you have a potato mash, sprinkle some sesame seeds and cayenne pepper and serve it!
Per serving: Calories: 33.6Kcal; Fat: 0.9g; Carbs: 5.6g; Protein: 1g

565. Crisp Balls Made with Peanut Butter

Preparation time: 29 minutes
Cooking time: 20 minutes **Servings:** 16 balls
Ingredients:

- ¼ cup of wheat germ
- ½ cup of natural peanut butter
- 1/3 cup of rolled oats
- ¼ cup of unsweetened flaked coconut
- ¼ cup of whole quick oats
- ½ teaspoon of ground cinnamon
- ¼ cup of brown rice crisp cereal
- 1 tablespoon of maple syrup
- ¼ cup of apple cider vinegar

Directions:
In a bowl, mix all the ingredients apart from the rice cereal. Combine everything properly. Create 16 balls out of the mixture. Each ball should be 1 inch in diameter. In a shallow dish, add the rice cereal and roll each ball on the crispiest. See that the balls are properly coated. Enjoy your no-bake crisp balls.
Store them in a refrigerator for later use.
Per serving: Calories: 79Kcal; Fat: 4.8g; Carbs: 6.3g; Protein 3.5g

566. Healthy Protein Bars

Preparation time: 19 minutes **Cooking time:** 15 minutes
Servings: 12 balls
Ingredients:
- 1 large banana
- 1 cup of rolled oats
- 1 serving of vegan vanilla protein powder

Directions:
In a food processor, blend the protein powder and rolled oats. Blend them for 1 minute until you have a semi-coarse mixture. The oats should be slightly chopped, but not powdered. Add the banana and form a pliable and coarse dough. Shape into either balls or small bars and store them in a container.
Eat one and store the rest in an airtight container in the refrigerator!
Per serving: Calories: 47Kcal; Fat: 0.7g; Carbs: 8g; Protein: 2.7g

567. Tofu Saag

Preparation time: 25 minutes **Cooking time:** 20 minutes
Servings: 6
Ingredients:
- 21 Ounces Water Packed Tofu, Fir & Cubed into 1 Inch Pieces - 10 Ounces Baby Spinach, Torn
- 2 Tablespoons Canola Oil, Divided
- 10 Ounces Baby Kale, Stemmed
- 1 Teaspoon Cumin - 1 Teaspoon Fennel
- 8 Green Cardamom Pods
- 6 Whole Cloves - 3 Red Chilies, Red
- 2 Tablespoon Ginger, Fresh & Minced
- Sea Salt to Taste - 1 Teaspoon Water
- 1/8 Teaspoon Red Pepper

Directions:
Cook your tofu in two batches, making sure to drain it on paper towels. Your tofu should be golden. Get out a Dutch oven and then bring two inches of water to a boil, adding your kale and spinach. Cover and cook until wilted. This should take four minutes, and then stir occasionally. Drain well, and reserve the cooking liquid. Place your spinach and kale into a blender, and blend until smooth. Use your cooking liquid as needed to blend. Combine a tablespoon of oil, a teaspoon of cumin seeds, fennel, and red chilies to a skillet. Cook for two minutes until golden brown and fragrant. Make sure to stir frequently. Stir in your ginger, and cook for thirty seconds. Remove your cardamom and cloves, and then discard them. Stir in your spinach, and then add a quarter cup of cooking liquid into a blender, making a puree. Scrape it down, and then put it in the pan. Stir in your salt, and then cook for five more minutes. Put your tofu on top of your spinach mix, and then cover. Cook for another five more minutes. Combine your ghee, cumin, fennel, and remaining red chilies. Cook for two minutes, and then add in your ground red pepper. Add in a teaspoon of water, and then stir to mix before serving.
Per serving: Calories: 210Kcal; Fat: 13.7g; Carbs: 13g; Protein: 12g

568. Mango Sticky Rice

Preparation time: 15 minutes
Cooking time: 20 minutes **Servings:** 3
Ingredients:
- ½ Cup Sugar - 1 Mango, Sliced
- 14 Ounces Coconut Milk, Canned
- ½ Cup Basmati Rice

Directions:
Cook your rice per package instructions, and add half of your sugar. When cooking your rice, substitute half of your water for half of your coconut milk.
Boil your remaining coconut milk in a saucepan with your remaining sugar.
Boil on high heat until it's thick, and then add in your mango slices.
Per serving: Calories: 571Kcal; Fat: 29.6g; Carbs: 77.6g; Protein: 6g

569. Oatmeal Sponge Cookies

Preparation time: 25 minutes
Cooking time: 15 minutes
Servings: 12
Ingredients:
- ¼ Cup Applesauce
- ½ Teaspoon Cinnamon
- 1/3 Cup Raisins
- ½ Teaspoon Vanilla Extract, Pure
- 1 Cup Ripe Banana, Mashed
- 2 Cups Oatmeal

Directions:
Start by heating your oven to 350F. Mix everything. It should be gooey. Drop it onto an ungreased baking sheet by the tablespoon, and then flatten. Bake for fifteen minutes.
Per serving: Calories: 79.1Kcal; Fat: 1g; Carbs: 16.4g; Protein: 2g

Amanda Kale

CHAPTER 26:
Desserts

570. Zesty Orange-Cranberry Energy Bites

Preparation time: 10 minutes
Cooking time: 0 minutes **Servings:** 12 bites
Ingredients:
- 2 tablespoons almond butter, or cashew or sunflower seed butter
- 2 tablespoons maple syrup or brown rice syrup 3/4 cup cooked quinoa
- 1/4 cup sesame seeds, toasted
- 1 tablespoon chia seeds
- ½ teaspoon almond extract, or vanilla extract
- Zest of 1 orange
- 1 tablespoon dried cranberries
- ¼ cup ground almonds

Directions:
In a medium bowl, mix the nut or seed butter and syrup until smooth and creamy. Stir in the rest of the ingredients, and mix to make sure the consistency is holding together in a ball. Form the mix into 12 balls.
Place them on a baking sheet lined with parchment or waxed paper and put them in the fridge to set for about 15 minutes.
If your balls aren't holding together, it's likely because of the moisture content of your cooked quinoa. Add more nut or seed butter mixed with syrup until it all sticks together.
Per serving (1 bite): Calories: 109Kcal; Fat: 7g; Carbs: 11g; Fiber: 3g; Protein: 3g

571. Chocolate and Walnut Farfalle

Preparation time: 10 minutes
Cooking time: 0 minutes
Servings: 4
Ingredients:
- 1/2 cup chopped toasted walnuts
- 1/4 cup vegan semisweet chocolate pieces
- 8 ounces farfalle
- 3 tablespoons vegan margarine
- 1/4 cup light brown sugar

Directions:
In a food processor or blender, grind the walnuts and chocolate pieces until crumbly. Do not over-process. Set aside.
In a pot of boiling salted water, cook the farfalle, stirring occasionally, until al dente, about 8 minutes. Drain well and return to the pot.
Add the margarine and sugar and toss to combine and melt the margarine.
Transfer the noodle mixture to a serving
Per serving: Calories: 81Kcal; Fat: 37.64g; Carbs: 42.38g; Fiber: 4.8 g; Protein: 8.68g

572. Almond-Date Energy Bites

Preparation time: 5 minutes **Servings:** 24 bites
Ingredients:
- 1 cup dates, pitted
- 1 cup unsweetened shredded coconut
- ¼ cup chia seeds
- ¾ cup ground almonds
- ¼ cup cocoa nibs, or non-dairy chocolate chips

Directions:
Purée everything in a food processor until crumbly and sticking together, pushing down the sides whenever necessary to keep it blending. If you don't have a food processor, you can mash soft medjool dates. But if you're using harder baking dates, you'll have to soak them and then try to purée them in a blender.
Form the mix into 24 balls and place them on a baking sheet lined with parchment or waxed paper. Put in the fridge to set for about 15 minutes. Use the softest dates you can find. Medjool dates are the best for this purpose. The hard dates you see in the baking aisle of your supermarket are going to take a long time to blend up. If you use those, try soaking them in water for at least an hour before you start and then draining.
Per serving (1 bite): Calories: 152Kcal; Fat: 11g; Carbs: 13g; Fiber: 5g; Protein: 3g

573. Pumpkin Pie Cups (Pressure Cooker)

Preparation time: 5 minutes
Cooking time: 6 minutes **Servings:** 4-6
Ingredients:
- 1 cup canned pumpkin purée
- 1 cup nondairy milk
- 6 tablespoons unrefined sugar or pure maple syrup (less if using sweetened milk), plus more for sprinkling
- ¼ cup spelt flour or all-purpose flour
- ½ teaspoon pumpkin pie spice
- Pinch salt

Directions:
Preparing the ingredients. In a medium bowl, stir together the pumpkin, milk, sugar, flour, pumpkin pie spice, and salt. Pour the mixture into 4 heat-proof ramekins. Sprinkle a bit more sugar on the top of each, if you like. Put a trivet in the bottom of your electric pressure cooker's cooking pot and pour in a cup or two of water. Place the ramekins onto the trivet, stacking them if needed (3 on the bottom, 1 on top).
High pressure for 6 minutes. Close and lock the lid and ensure the pressure valve is sealed, then select high pressure and set the time for 6 minutes.

Pressure release. Once the cooking time is complete, quick release the pressure, being careful not to get your fingers or face near the steam release. Once all the pressure has been released, carefully unlock and remove the lid. Let cool for a few minutes before carefully lifting out the ramekins with oven mitts or tongs. Let cool for at least 10 minutes before serving.

Per serving: Calories: 129Kcal; Fat: 1g; Carbs: 28g; Fiber: 3g; Protein: 3g

574. Granola-Stuffed Baked Apples

Preparation time: 10 minutes
Cooking time: 60 minutes
Servings: 4
Ingredients:
- 1/2 cup vegan granola, homemade or store-bought
- 2 tablespoons creamy peanut butter or almond butter
- 1 tablespoon vegan margarine
- 1 tablespoon pure maple syrup
- 1/2 teaspoon ground cinnamon
- 4 granny smith or other firm baking apples
- 1 cup apple juice

Directions:
Preheat the oven to 350°f. Grease a 9 x 13-inch baking pan and set it aside. In a medium bowl, combine the granola, peanut butter, margarine, maple syrup, and cinnamon and mix well.
Core the apples and stuff the granola mixture into the centers of the apples, packing tightly.
Place the apples upright in the prepared pan. Pour the apple juice over the apples and bake until tender, about 1 hour. Serve warm.

Per serving: Calories: 361Kcal; Fat: 13.65g; Carbs: 60.8g; Fiber: 8.4g; Protein: 7.65g

575. Better Pecan Bars

Preparation time: 5 minutes
Cooking time: 20 minutes
Servings: 12 bars
Ingredients:
- 1 cup whole-grain flour
- 1 cup light brown sugar, divided
- 1/2 cup plus 1/4 cup vegan margarine, softened
- 1 cup pecan pieces
- 1/4 cup pure maple syrup
- 1/3 cup vegan semisweet chocolate chips

Directions:
Preheat the oven to 350°f. Lightly oil an 8-inch square baking pan and set it aside. In a food processor, combine the flour, 1/2 cup of sugar, and 1/2 cup of margarine. Process to mix well.
Transfer the mixture to the prepared baking pan and press it firmly into the bottom. Bake for 12 minutes. Remove from the oven and set aside.
In a saucepan, combine the remaining 1/2 cup of sugar and the remaining 1/4 cup margarine. Cook over medium heat, stirring constantly until the mixture boils. Add the pecans and maple syrup and boil for about 30 seconds, stirring constantly. Pour the mixture evenly over the crust.
Bake until the caramel layer is bubbly and the crust is lightly browned, about 7 minutes. Remove from oven and sprinkle with chocolate chips. Allow chips to melt slightly, then drag a fork through them to swirl into the top. Cool slightly, then refrigerate to set the topping before cutting into bars. Store in an airtight container.

Per serving: Calories: 373Kcal; Fat: 26.12g; Carbs: 46.5g; Fiber: 2.7g; Protein: 2.96g

576. Chocolate-Almond Bars

Preparation time: 5 minutes
Cooking time: 30 minutes
Servings: 12 bars
Ingredients:
- 2/3 cup vegan margarine, melted
- 1/2 cup almond butter
- 1 teaspoon pure vanilla extract
- 1/2 teaspoon salt - 1 cup light brown sugar
- 2 cups whole-grain flour
- 1 cup vegan semisweet chocolate chips
- 3/4 cup slivered almonds

Directions:
Preheat the oven to 375°f. Lightly grease an 8-inch square baking pan and set it aside. In a large bowl, combine the margarine, almond butter, vanilla, and salt. Add the sugar and stir until well blended. Add the flour and stir until well blended. Fold in the chocolate chips and half of the almonds. Press the dough into the prepared pan. Sprinkle the remaining almonds over the top and press them into the dough. Bake until browned, 25 to 30 minutes. Cool completely before cutting into bars. Store in an airtight container.

Per serving: Calories: 546Kcal; Fat: 47.2g; Carbs: 45.9g; Fiber: 5.1g; Protein: 7.94g

577. Coconut and Almond Truffles

Preparation time: 15 minutes
Cooking time: 0 minutes **Servings:** 8 truffles
Ingredients:
- 1 cup pitted dates - 1 cup almonds
- ½ cup sweetened cocoa powder, plus extra for coating
- ½ cup unsweetened shredded coconut
- ¼ cup pure maple syrup
- 1 teaspoon vanilla extract
- 1 teaspoon almond extract - ¼ teaspoon sea salt

Directions:
In the bowl of a food processor, combine all the ingredients and process until smooth. Chill the mixture for about 1 hour. Roll the mixture into balls and then roll the balls in cocoa powder to coat. Serve immediately or keep chilled until ready to serve.

Per serving: Calories: 95Kcal; Fat: 0.96g; Carbs: 18.1g; Fiber 3.3g; Protein: 1.6g

578. Pecan and Date-Stuffed Roasted Pears

Preparation time: 10 minutes **Cooking time:** 30 minutes
Servings: 4
Ingredients:
- 4 firm ripe pears, cored
- 1 tablespoon fresh lemon juice
- 1/2 cup finely chopped pecans
- 4 dates, pitted and chopped
- 1 tablespoon vegan margarine
- 1 tablespoon pure maple syrup
- 1/4 teaspoon ground cinnamon
- 1/8 teaspoon ground ginger
- 1/2 cup pear, white grape, or apple juice

Directions:
Preheat the oven to 350°f. Grease a shallow baking dish and set it aside. Halve the pears lengthwise and use a melon baller to scoop out the cores. Rub the exposed part of the pears with lemon juice to avoid discoloration. In a medium bowl, combine the pecans, dates, margarine, maple syrup, cinnamon, and ginger and mix well. Stuff the mixture into the centers of the pear halves and arrange them in the prepared baking pan. Pour the juice over the pears. Bake until tender, 30 to 40 minutes. Serve warm.
Per serving: Calories: 283Kcal; Fat: 20.81g; Carbs: 31.8g; Fiber: 4.4g; Protein: 2.67g

579. Lime-Macerated Mangos

Preparation time: 10 minutes
Cooking time: 0 minutes **Servings:** 4 to 6
Ingredients:
- 3 ripe mangos - 1/3 cup light brown sugar
- 2 tablespoons fresh lime juice
- 1/2 cup dry white wine
- Fresh mint sprigs

Directions:
Peel, pit, and cut the mangos into 1/2-inch dice. Layer the diced mango in a large bowl, sprinkling each layer with about 1 tablespoon of the sugar. Cover with plastic wrap and refrigerate for 2 hours. Pour in the lime juice and wine, mixing gently to combine with the mango. Cover and refrigerate for 4 hours. About 30 minutes before serving time, bring the fruit to room temperature. To serve, spoon the mango and the liquid into serving glasses and garnish with mint.
Per serving: Calories: 103Kcal; Fat: 5.62g; Carbs: 10.9g; Fiber: 0.2g; Protein: 4.55g

580. Fudgy Brownies (Pressure Cooker)

Preparation time: 10 minutes
Cooking time: 11 minutes **Servings:** 4-6
Ingredients:
- 3 ounces dairy-free dark chocolate
- 1 tablespoon coconut oil or vegan margarine
- ½ cup applesauce
- 2 tablespoons unrefined sugar
- 1/3 cup all-purpose flour
- ½ teaspoon baking powder
- Pinch salt

Directions:
Preparing the ingredients. Put a trivet in your electric pressure cooker's cooking pot and pour in a cup or two of water. Select sauté or simmer. In a large heat-proof glass or ceramic bowl, combine the chocolate and coconut oil. Place the bowl over the top of your pressure cooker, as you would a double boiler. Stir occasionally until the chocolate is melted, then turn off the pressure cooker. Stir the applesauce and sugar into the chocolate mixture. Add the flour, baking powder, and salt and stir just until combined. Pour the batter into 3 heat-proof ramekins. Put them in a heat-proof dish and cover them with aluminum foil.

Using a foil sling or silicone helper handles, lower the dish onto the trivet. (alternately, cover each ramekin with foil and place them directly on the trivet, without the dish.) High pressure for 6 minutes. Close and lock the lid and ensure the pressure valve is sealed, then select high pressure and set the time for 5 minutes. Pressure release. Once the cooking time is complete, quick release the pressure, being careful not to get your fingers or face near the steam release. Once all the pressure has been released, carefully unlock and remove the lid.

Let cool for a few minutes before carefully lifting out the dish, or ramekins, with oven mitts or tongs. Let cool for a few minutes more before serving.

Top with fresh raspberries and an extra drizzle of melted chocolate.
Per serving: Calories: 316Kcal; Fat: 14g; Carbs: 49.3g; Fiber: 5g; Protein: 5g

581. Chocolate-Banana Fudge

Preparation time: 10 minutes **Cooking time:** 0 minutes
Servings: about 36 pieces
Ingredients:
- 1 ripe banana
- ¾ cup vegan semisweet chocolate chips
- 4 cups confectioners' sugar
- 1 teaspoon pure vanilla extract

Directions:
Line an 8-inch square baking pan with enough waxed paper or aluminum foil so that the ends hang over the edge of the pan. (this will help you get the fudge out of the pan later.) Set aside. Place the banana in a food processor and blend until smooth. 9melt the chocolate chips in a double boiler or microwave, then add to the pureed banana along with the sugar and vanilla and process until smooth. Scrape the mixture into the prepared pan. Smooth the top and refrigerate until firm, at least 2 hours.

Once chilled, grip the waxed paper, lift the fudge from the pan, and transfer it to a cutting board. Remove and discard the waxed paper. Cut the fudge into small pieces and serve. Cover and refrigerate any leftovers.
Per serving: Calories: 65Kcal; Fat: 1.24g; Carbs:13.8 g; Fiber: 0.3g; Protein: 0.18g

582. Chocolate–Almond Butter Truffles

Preparation time: 15 minutes
Cooking time: 0 minutes
Servings: about 24 truffles
Ingredients:
- 1 cup vegan semisweet chocolate chips
- 1/2 cup almond butter
- 2 tablespoons plain or vanilla soy milk
- 1 tablespoon pure vanilla extract
- 1 cup confectioners' sugar
- 2 tablespoons unsweetened cocoa powder
- 1/2 cup finely chopped toasted almonds

Directions:
Melt the chocolate in a double boiler or microwave.
In a food processor, combine the almond butter, soy milk, and vanilla and blend until smooth. Add the sugar, cocoa, and the melted chocolate and blend until smooth and creamy. Transfer the mixture to a bowl and refrigerate until chilled, at least 45 minutes.
Roll the chilled mixture into 1-inch balls and place them on an ungreased baking sheet. Place the ground almonds in a shallow bowl and roll the balls in them, turning to coat. Place the truffles on a serving platter, refrigerate for 30 minutes, and serve.
Per serving: Calories: 118Kcal; Fat: 8.03g; Carbs: 12.9g; Fiber: 1.6g; Protein: 2.58g

583. Chocolate Macaroons

Preparation time: 10 minutes
Cooking time: 15 minutes **Servings:** 8 macaroons
Ingredients:
- 1 cup unsweetened shredded coconut
- 2 tablespoons cocoa powder
- 2/3 cup coconut milk
- ¼ cup agave
- Pinch of sea salt

Directions:
Preheat the oven to 350°f. Line a baking sheet with parchment paper. In a medium saucepan, cook all the ingredients over -medium-high heat until a firm dough is formed. Scoop the dough into balls and place on the baking sheet.
Bake for 15 minutes, remove from the oven and let cool on the baking sheet. Serve cooled macaroons or store in a tightly sealed container
Per serving: Calories: 55Kcal; Fat: 5.03g; Carbs: 3.9g; Fiber: 1.2g; Protein: 0.92g

584. Chocolate Pudding

Preparation time: 5 minutes
Cooking time: 0 minutes
Servings: 1
Ingredients:
- 1 banana
- 2 to 4 tablespoons nondairy milk
- 2 tablespoons unsweetened cocoa powder
- 2 tablespoons sugar (optional)
- ½ ripe avocado or 1 cup silken tofu (optional)

Directions:
In a small blender, combine the banana, milk, cocoa powder, sugar (if using), and avocado (if using). Purée until smooth. Alternatively, in a small bowl, mash the banana very well, and stir in the remaining ingredients.
Per serving: Calories: 244Kcal; Fat: 3g; Carbs:59g; Fiber: 8g; Protein: 4g

585. Avocado Pudding

Preparation time: 10 minutes
Cooking time: 0 minutes **Servings:** 8
Ingredients:
- 2 ripe avocados, peeled, pitted, and cut into pieces
- 1 tbsp fresh lime juice
- 14 oz can coconut milk
- 80 drops of liquid stevia
- 2 tsp vanilla extract

Directions:
Add all ingredients into the blender and blend until smooth. Serve and enjoy.
Per serving: Calories: 317Kcal; Fat: 30.1g; Carbs: 9.3g; Protein: 3.4g

586. Almond Butter Brownies

Preparation time: 30 minutes
Cooking time: 0 minutes **Servings:** 4
Ingredients:
- 1 scoop protein powder
- 2 tbsp cocoa powder
- 1/2 cup almond butter, melted
- 1 cup bananas, overripe

Directions:
preheat the oven to 350 f/ 176 c.
spray brownie tray with cooking spray.
add all ingredients into the blender and blend until smooth. pour batter into the prepared dish and bake in preheated oven for 20 minutes. serve and enjoy.
Per serving: Calories: 82Kcal; Fat: 2.1g; Carbs: 11.4g; Protein: 6.9g

587. Raspberry Chia Pudding

Preparation time: 3 hours 10 minutes
Cooking time: 0 minutes **Servings:** 2
Ingredients:
- 4 tbsp chia seeds
- 1 cup coconut milk
- 1/2 cup raspberries

Directions:
Add raspberry and coconut milk in a blender and blend until smooth. Pour the mixture into the mason jar. Add chia seeds in a jar and stir well. Close the jar tightly with the lid and shake well. Place in refrigerator for 3 hours. Serve chilled and enjoy.
Per serving: Calories: 361Kcal; Fat: 33.4g; Carbs: 13.3g; Protein: 6.2g

588. Chocolate Fudge

Preparation time: 10 minutes
Cooking time: 0 minutes **Servings:** 12
Ingredients:

- 4 oz unsweetened dark chocolate
- 3/4 cup coconut butter
- 15 drops liquid stevia
- 1 tsp vanilla extract

Directions:
Melt coconut butter and dark chocolate.
Add ingredients to the large bowl and combine well.
Pour the mixture into a silicone loaf pan and place in the refrigerator until set. Cut into pieces and serve.
Per serving: Calories: 157Kcal; Fat: 14.1g; Carbs: 6.1g; Protein: 2.3 g

589. Quick Chocó Brownie

Preparation time: 10 minutes
Cooking time: 0 minutes **Servings:** 1
Ingredients:

- 1/4 cup almond milk
- 1 tbsp cocoa powder
- 1 scoop chocolate protein powder
- 1/2 tsp baking powder

Directions:
In a microwave-safe mug, blend baking powder, protein powder, and cocoa. Add almond milk in a mug and stir well. Place mug in microwave and microwave for 30 seconds. Serve and enjoy.
Per serving: Calories: 207Kcal; Fat: 15.8g; Carbs: 9.5g; Protein: 12.4g

590. Cinnamon Coconut Chips

Preparation time: 7 minutes
Cooking time: 25 minutes **Servings:** 2
Ingredients:

- ¼ cup coconut chips, unsweetened
- ¼ teaspoon of sea salt - ¼ cup cinnamon

Directions:
Add cinnamon and salt to a mixing bowl and set aside. Heat a pan over medium heat for 2 minutes.
Place the coconut chips in the hot pan and stir until coconut chips crisp and lightly brown. Toss toasted coconut chips with cinnamon and salt. Serve and enjoy!
Per serving: Calories: 228Kcal; Fat: 21g; Carbs: 7.8g; Protein: 1.9g

591. Peach Cobbler

Preparation time: 20 minutes
Cooking time: 4 hours **Servings:** 4
Ingredients:

- 4 cups peaches, peeled and sliced
- ¼ cup of coconut sugar
- ½ teaspoon cinnamon powder
- 1 ½ cups vegan sweet crackers, crushed
- ¼ cup stevia
- ¼ teaspoon nutmeg, ground
- ½ cup almond milk
- 1 teaspoon vanilla extract
- Cooking spray

Directions:
In a bowl, mix peaches with coconut sugar and cinnamon and stir. In a separate bowl, mix crackers with stevia, nutmeg, almond milk, and vanilla extract and stir. Shower your slow cooker with cooking spray and spread peaches on the bottom. Add crackers mix, spread, cover, and cook on Low for 4 hours. Divide cobbler between plates and serve. Enjoy!
Per serving: Calories: 212Kcal; Fat: 4g; Carbs: 7g; Protein: 3g

592. Chocolate Brownies

Preparation time: 10 minutes
Cooking time: 20 minutes **Servings:** 4
Ingredients:

- Two tablespoons cocoa powder
- One scoop protein powder
- 1 cup bananas, over-ripe
- ½ cup almond butter, melted

Directions:
Preheat the oven to 350 F.
Spray the brownie pan with cooking spray.
Add the real ingredients to your blender and blend until smooth. Pour the batter into the prepared pan.
Put in the oven for 20 minutes. Serve and enjoy!
Per serving: Calories: 82Kcal; Fat: 2.1g; Carbs: 11.4g; Protein: 6.9g

593. The Keto Lovers "Magical" Grain-Free Granola

Preparation time: 30 minutes
Cooking time: 1 Hour and 15 minutes
Servings:
Ingredients:

- ½ cup of raw sunflower seeds
- ½ cup of raw hemp hearts
- ½ cup of flaxseeds - ¼ cup of chia seeds
- 2 tablespoons of Psyllium Husk powder
- 1 tablespoon of cinnamon - Stevia
- ½ teaspoon of baking powder
- ½ teaspoon of salt - 1 cup of water

Directions:
Preheat your oven to 300 F. Make sure to line a baking page with a parchment piece. Take your food processor and grind all the seeds. Add the dry ingredients and mix well. Stir in water until fully incorporated. Let the mixture sit for a while. Wait until it thickens up. Spread the mixture evenly-giving a thickness of about ¼ inch. Bake for 45 minutes. Break apart the granola and keep baking for another 30 minutes until the pieces are crunchy. Remove and allow them to cool. Enjoy!
Per serving: Calories: 292Kcal; Fat: 25g; Carbs: 12g; Protein: 8g

594. Keto Ice Cream

Preparation time: 10 minutes **Cooking time:** 3-4 Hours to Freeze **Servings:** 4-5
Ingredients:

- 1 ½ teaspoon of natural vanilla extract

- 1/8 teaspoon of salt
- 1/3 cup of erythritol
- 2 cups of artificial coconut milk, full fat

Directions:
Stir together the vanilla extract, salt, sweetener, and milk. If you do not come up with an ice cream machine, freeze the mixture in ice cube trays, then use a high-speed blender to blend the frozen cubes or thaw them enough to meld in a regular blender or food processor. If you have an ice cream machine, just blend according to the manufacturer's directions.
Eat as it is or freeze for a firmer texture.
Per serving: Calories: 184Kcal; Fat: 19.1g; Carbs: 4.4g; Protein: 1.8 g

595. Apple Mix
Preparation time: 10 minutes
Cooking time: 4 Hours **Servings:** 6
Ingredients:
- 6 apples, cored, peeled, and sliced
- 1½ cups almond flour - Cooking spray
- 1 cup of coconut sugar
- 1 tablespoon cinnamon powder
- ¾ cup cashew butter, melted

Directions:
Add apple slices to your slow cooker after you have greased it with cooking spray. Add flour, sugar, cinnamon, and coconut butter, stir gently, cover, cook on High for 4 hours, divide into bowls and serve cold. Enjoy!
Per serving: Calories: 200Kcal; Fat: 5g; Carbs: 8g; Protein: 4g

596. Almond Butter Fudge
Preparation time: 17 minutes
Cooking time: 2-3 Hours to Freeze **Servings:** 8
Ingredients:
- 2 ½ tablespoons coconut oil
- 2 ½ tablespoons honey
- ½ cup almond butter

Directions:
In a saucepan, pour almond butter, then add coconut oil warm for 2 minutes or until melted. Add honey and stir. Pour the mixture into a candy container and store it in the fridge until set. Serve and enjoy!
Per serving: Calories: 63Kcal; Fat: 4.8g; Carbs: 5.6g; Protein: 0.2g

597. The Vegan Pumpkin Spicy Fat Bombs
Preparation time: 20 minutes
Cooking time: 1 Hour and 20 minutes
Servings: 12
Ingredients:
- ¾ cup of pumpkin puree
- ¼ cup of hemp seeds
- ½ cup of coconut oil
- 2 teaspoons of pumpkin pie spice
- 1 teaspoon of vanilla extract
- Liquid Stevia

Directions:
Take a blender and add together all the ingredients. Blend them well and portion the mixture out into silicon molds.
Allow them to chill and enjoy!
Per serving: Calories: 103Kcal; Fat: 10g; Carbs: 2g; Protein: 1g

598. Orange Cake
Preparation time: 25 minutes
Cooking time: 5 Hours and 10 minutes
Servings: 4
Ingredients:
- Cooking spray
- 1 teaspoon baking powder
- 1 cup almond flour
- 1 cup of coconut sugar
- ½ teaspoon cinnamon powder
- 3 tablespoons coconut oil, melted
- ½ cup almond milk
- ½ cup pecans, chopped
- ¾ cup of water
- ½ cup raisins
- ½ cup orange peel, grated
- ¾ cup of orange juice

Directions:
In a bowl, mix flour with half of the sugar, baking powder, cinnamon, two tablespoons oil, milk, pecans, and raisins, stir and pour this in your slow cooker after you have sprayed it with cooking spray.
Warm a small pan over medium heat. Add water, orange juice, orange peel, the rest of the oil, and the remainder of the sugar, stir, bring to a boil, pour over the blend in the slow cooker, cover, and cook on Low for 5 hours.
Divide into dessert bowls and serve cold.
Enjoy!
Per serving: Calories: 182Kcal; Fat: 3g; Carbs: 4g; Protein: 3g

599. Chia Raspberry Pudding
Preparation time: 10 minutes
Cooking time: 3 Hours **Servings:** 2
Ingredients:
- 4 tablespoons chia seeds
- ½ cup raspberries
- 1 cup of coconut milk

Directions:
Add the raspberry and coconut milk into your blender and blend until smooth. Pour the mixture into a mason jar. Add chia seeds and stir. Cap jar and shake. Set in the fridge for 3 hours. Serve and enjoy!
Per serving: Calories: 408Kcal; Fat: 38.8g; Carbs: 22.3g; Protein: 9.1g

600. Pumpkin Cake
Preparation time: 20 minutes
Cooking time: 2 Hours and 10 minutes **Servings:** 10
Ingredients:
- 1 ½ teaspoons baking powder

- Cooking spray
- 1 cup pumpkin puree
- 2 cups almond flour
- ½ teaspoon baking soda
- 1 ½ teaspoons cinnamon, ground
- ¼ teaspoon ginger, ground
- One tablespoon coconut oil, melted
- One tablespoon flaxseed mixed with two tablespoons water
- One tablespoon vanilla extract
- 1/3 cup maple syrup
- One teaspoon lemon juice

Directions:
In a bowl, flour with baking powder, baking soda, cinnamon, and ginger, then stir. Add flaxseed, coconut oil, and vanilla, pumpkin puree, and maple syrup, and lemon juice, stir and pour in your slow cooker after spraying it with cooking spray parchment paper. Cover pot and cook on Low for 2 hours and 20 minutes. Leave the cake to cool down, slice, and serve. Enjoy!
Per serving: Calories: 182Kcal; Fat: 3g; Carbs: 3g; Protein: 1g

601. Banana Bread
Preparation time: 10 minutes
Cooking time: 50 minutes **Servings:** 6 to 8
Ingredients:
- 1½ cups flour
- One teaspoon baking soda
- One teaspoon baking powder
- ¼ cup brown sugar
- ½ teaspoon salt
- ½ cup rolled oats
- Three large ripe bananas
- Two tablespoons ground flaxseed
- 1/3 Cup unsweetened soy milk
- 1/3 Cup vegetable oil
- Two tablespoon maple syrup
- One tablespoon vanilla extract
- 1 cup mini dairy-free chocolate chips, divided

Directions:
Preheat the oven to 350°F. Fat a loaf pan or line with parchment paper covering all four sides. In a large bowl, combine the flour, baking soda, baking powder, brown sugar, salt, and rolled oats. Set aside.
Mash the bananas until almost no chunks remain. Add the flaxseed, milk, oil, maple syrup, and vanilla extract. Stir to combine. Steadily pour down the wet ingredients into the dry materials and stir until just combined. Stir in 1/2 cup of the mini chocolate chips. Drench the cake batter into the greased or lined pan and spread it out evenly. Sprinkle the remaining chocolate chips on top in an even layer—Bake for 50 minutes. You may also wait until a toothpick incorporated in the center of the cake comes out clean. Cool it for 10 minutes.
Move it to a wire rack to continue cooling.
Per serving: Calories: 420Kcal; Fat: 19g; Carbs: 57g; Fiber: 5g; Protein: 7g

602. Apple Crisp
Preparation time: 10 minutes
Cooking time: 40 minutes **Servings:** 6
Ingredients:
- ½ cup vegan butter
- Six large apples, diced large
- 1 cup dried cranberries
- Two tablespoons granulated sugar
- Two teaspoons ground cinnamon, divided
- ¼ teaspoon ground nutmeg
- ¼ teaspoon ground ginger
- Two teaspoons lemon juice
- 1 cup all-purpose flour
- 1 cup rolled oats
- 1 cup brown sugar
- 1/4 teaspoon salt

Directions:
Preheat the oven to 350°F. Gently grease an 8-inch square baking dish with butter or cooking spray.
Make the filling. In a large bowl, combine the apples, cranberries, granulated sugar, one teaspoon of cinnamon, the nutmeg, ginger, and lemon juice. Toss to coat. Move the apple mixture to the prepared baking dish. Make the topping. In the same large bowl, now empty, combine the all-purpose flour, oats, brown sugar, and salt. Stir to combine. Add Up the butter and, using a pastry cutter (or two knives moving in a crisscross pattern), cut back the butter into the flour and oat mixture until the butter is small. Spread the topping over the apples evenly, patting down slightly—Bake for 35 minutes or until golden and bubbly.
Per serving: Calories: 488Kcal; Fat: 9g; Carbs: 101g; Fiber: 10g; Protein: 5g

603. Secret Ingredient Chocolate Brownies
Preparation time: 10 minutes
Cooking time: 35 minutes **Servings:** 6 to 8
Ingredients:
- ¾ cup flour
- ¼ teaspoon baking soda
- ¼ teaspoon salt
- 1/3 Cup vegan butter
- ¾ cup of sugar
- Two tablespoon water
- 1¼ cups semi-sweet or dark dairy-free chocolate chips
- Six tablespoons aquafaba, divided
- One Teaspoon Vanilla Extract

Directions:
Preheat the oven to 325°F. Line Up a 9-inch square baking pan with parchment or grease well.
In a large bowl, combine the flour, baking soda, and salt. Set aside. In a medium saucepan, mix up the butter, sugar, and water. Bring to a boil, stirring occasionally. Reduce from heat and stir in the chocolate chips. Whisk in 3 tablespoons of aquafaba until thoroughly combined. Add the vanilla extract and the remaining three tablespoons of aquafaba, and whisk

until mixed. Add the chocolate mixture into the flour mixture and stir until mixed. Pour down in an even layer into the prepared pan. Bake for 35 minutes until the top is set, but the brownie jiggles when slightly shaken. Allow cooling completely, 45 minutes to 1 hour, before removing and serving.
Per serving: Calories: 369Kcal; Fat: 19g; Carbs: 48g; Fiber: 1g; Protein: 4g

604. Chocolate Chip Pecan Cookies
Preparation time: 10 minutes
Cooking time: 16 minutes
Servings: 30 Small Cookies
Ingredients:
- ¾ cup pecan halves, toasted
- 1 cup vegan butter
- ½ teaspoon salt
- ½ cup powdered sugar
- Two teaspoons vanilla extract
- 2 cups all-purpose flour
- 1 cup mini dairy-free chocolate chips

Directions:
Preheat the oven to 350°F. Line a large rimmed baking page with parchment paper. In a small skillet over medium heat, toast the pecans until warm and fragrant, about 2 minutes. Remove from the pan. Once these are cool, chop them into small pieces. Make use of an electric hand mixer or a stand mixer fitted with a paddle attachment, combine the butter, salt, and powdered sugar, and cream together at high speed for 3 to 4 minutes, until light and fluffy. Add the vanilla extract and beat for 1 minute. Turn the mixer on low and slowly add the flour, ½ cup at a time, until a dough form. Combine the chocolate chips and pecans and mix until just incorporated. Using your hands, a large spoon, or a 1-inch ice cream scoop, drop 1-inch balls of dough on the baking sheet, spread out 1 inch apart. Gently press down on the cookies to flatten them slightly. Bake for 10 to 15 minutes. Wait until just yellow around the edges. Let it cool for 5 minutes. Transfer them to a wire rack. Serve or store in an airtight container.
Per serving: Calories: 152Kcal; Fat: 11g; Carbs: 13g; Fiber: 1g; Protein: 2g

605. No-Bake Chocolate Coconut Energy Balls
Preparation time: 15 minutes
Cooking time: 3 to 4 Hours for Chilling
Servings: 9 Energy Balls
Ingredients:
- ¼ cup dry roasted or raw pumpkin seeds
- ¼ cup dry roasted or raw sunflower seeds
- ½ cup unsweetened shredded coconut
- Two tablespoons chia seeds
- ¼ teaspoon salt
- 1½ tablespoons Dutch-process cocoa powder
- ¼ cup rolled oats
- Two tablespoons coconut oil, melted
- Six pitted dates
- Two tablespoons all-natural almond butter

Directions:
Mix the pumpkin seeds, sunflower seeds, coconut, chia seeds, salt, cocoa powder, and oats in a food processor. Pulse until the mix is coarsely crumbled. Add the coconut oil, dates, and almond butter. Pulse until the mixture is fused and sticks together when squeezed between your fingers. Scoop out two tablespoons of the mix at a time and roll them into 1½-inch balls with your hands. Place them spaced apart on a freezer-safe plate and freeze for 15 minutes. Remove from the freezer and keep refrigerated in an airtight container for up to 4 days.
Per serving: Calories: 230Kcal; Fat: 12g; Carbs: 27g; Fiber: 5g; Protein: 5g

606. Blueberry Hand Pies
Preparation time: 6 to 8 minutes
Cooking time: 20 minutes plus Chill Time
Servings: 6 to 8
Ingredients:
- 3 cups all-purpose flour, plus extra for sifting work surface
- ½ teaspoon salt
- ¼ cup, plus two tablespoons granulated sugar, divided
- 1 cup vegan butter
- ½ cup of cold water
- 1 cup fresh blueberries
- Two teaspoons lemon zest
- Two teaspoons lemon juice
- ¼ teaspoon ground cinnamon
- One teaspoon cornstarch
- ¼ cup unsweetened soy milk
- Coarse sugar, for sprinkling

Directions:
Preheat the oven to 375°F. Set aside.
In a large bowl, merge the flour, salt, two tablespoons of granulated sugar, and vegan butter. Using a pastry cutter or two knives moving in a crisscross pattern, cut the butter into the other ingredients until the butter is small peas.
Add the cold water and knead to form a dough. Tear the dough in half and wrap the halves separately in plastic wrap. Refrigerate for 15 minutes.
Make the blueberry filling. In a medium bowl, mix the blueberries, lemon zest, lemon juice, cinnamon, cornstarch, and the remaining ¼ cup of sugar.
Remove one half of the dough. On a floured side, roll out the dough to ¼- to ½-inch thickness. Turn a 5-inch bowl upside down and, using it as a guide, cut the dough into circles to make mini pie crusts. Reroll scrap dough to cut out more circles. Repeat with the second half of the dough. You should come to an end up with 8 to 10 circles. Place the circles on the prepared sheet pan. Spoon 1½ tablespoons of blueberry filling onto each circle, leaving a ¼-inch border and folding the circles in half to cover the filling, forming a half-moon shape. Use a fork to press the edges of the dough to seal the pies. When all the pies are assembled, use a paring knife to score the pies by cutting three lines through the top crusts. Brush each pie with soy milk and sprinkle with coarse sugar.

Bake for 20 minutes or until the filling is bubbly and the tops are golden. Let cool before serving.
Per serving: Calories: 416Kcal; Fat: 23g; Carbs: 46g; Fiber: 5g; Protein: 6g

607. Date Squares
Preparation time: 20 minutes
Cooking time: 25 minutes **Servings:** 12
Ingredients:
- Cooking spray, for greasing
- 1½ cups rolled oats
- 1½ cups all-purpose flour
- ¾ cup, plus 1/3 cup brown sugar, divided
- ½ teaspoon ground cinnamon
- ¼ teaspoon ground nutmeg
- One teaspoon baking soda
- ¼ teaspoon salt - ¾ cup vegan butter
- 18 pitted dates
- One teaspoon lemon zest
- One teaspoon lemon juice
- 1 cup of water

Directions:
Preheat the oven to 350°F. Lightly grease or shower an 8-inch square baking plate. Set aside. Make the base and topping mixture. In a large bowl, blend the rolled oats, flour, and ¾ cup of brown sugar, cinnamon, nutmeg, baking soda, and salt. Combine the butter and, using a pastry cutter or two knives working in a crisscross motion, cut the butter into the blend to form a crumbly dough. Press half of the dough into the prepared baking dish and set the remaining half aside. To make a date filling, place a small saucepan over medium heat. Add the dates, the remaining 1/3 cup of sugar, the lemon zest, lemon juice, and water. Bring to a boil and cook for 7 to 10 minutes, until thickened. When cooked, pour the date mixture over the dough base in the baking dish and top with the remaining crumb dough. Gently press down and spread evenly to cover all the filling. Bake for 25 minutes until lightly golden on top. Cool before serving. Store in an airtight container.
Per serving: Calories: 443Kcal; Fat: 12g; Carbs: 81g; Fiber: 7g; Protein: 5g

608. Homemade Chocolates with Coconut and Raisins
Preparation time: 10 minutes
Cooking time: Chilling time **Servings:** 20
Ingredients:
- 1/2 cup cacao butter, melted
- 1/3 cup peanut butter
- 1/4 cup agave syrup
- A pinch of grated nutmeg
- A pinch of coarse salt
- 1/2 teaspoon vanilla extract
- 1 cup dried coconut, shredded
- 6 ounces dark chocolate, chopped
- 3 ounces raisins

Directions:
Carefully combine all the ingredients, not including the chocolate, in a mixing bowl. Spoon the mixture into molds. Leave to sit in a cool place. Melt the dark chocolate in your microwave. Pour in the melted chocolate until the fillings are covered. Leave to sit in a cool place. Enjoy!
Per serving: Calories: 130Kcal; Fat: 9.1g; Carbs: 12.1g; Protein: 1.3g

609. Easy Mocha Fudge
Preparation time: 10 minutes
Cooking time: 60 minutes
Servings: 20
Ingredients:
- 1 cup cookies, crushed
- 1/2 cup almond butter
- 1/4 cup agave nectar
- 6 ounces dark chocolate, broken into chunks
- One teaspoon instant coffee
- A pinch of grated nutmeg
- A pinch of salt

Directions:
Line a large baking layer with parchment paper. Melt the chocolate in your microwave and add in the remaining ingredients; stir to combine well. Scrape the batter into a parchment-lined baking sheet. Put it in your freezer for a minimum of 1 hour to set. Cut into squares and serve. Bon appétit!
Per serving: Calories: 105Kcal; Fat: 5.6g; Carbs: 12.9g; Protein: 1.1g

610. Key Lime Pie
Preparation time: 3 hours and 15 minutes
Cooking time: 0 minutes **Servings:** 12
Ingredients:
For the Crust:
- ¾ cup coconut flakes, unsweetened
- 1 cup dates, soaked in warm water for 10 minutes in water, drained
- For the Filling:
- ¾ cup of coconut meat
- 1 ½ avocado, peeled, pitted
- 2 tablespoons key lime juice
- ¼ cup agave

Directions:
Prepare the crust, and for this, place all its ingredients in a food processor and pulse for 3 to 5 minutes until the thick paste comes together. Take an 8-inch pie pan, grease it with oil, pour crust mixture in it and spread and press the mixture evenly in the bottom and along the sides, and freeze until required. Prepare the filling and for this, place all its ingredients in a food processor, and pulse for 2 minutes until smooth. Pour the filling into the prepared pan, smooth the top, and freeze for 3 hours until set.
Cut pie into slices and then serve.
Per serving: Calories: 213Kcal; Fat: 10g; Carbs: 29g; Fiber: 6g; Protein: 12g

611. Chocolate Mint Grasshopper Pie

Preparation time: 4 hours and 15 minutes
Cooking time: 0 minutes **Servings:** 4
Ingredients:
For the Crust:
- 1 cup dates, soaked in warm water for 10 minutes in water, drained
- 1/8 teaspoons salt
- 1/2 cup pecans
- 1 teaspoons cinnamon
- 1/2 cup walnuts

For the Filling:
- ½ cup mint leaves
- 2 cups of cashews, soaked in warm water for 10 minutes in water, drained
- 2 tablespoons coconut oil
- 1/4 cup and 2 tablespoons of agave
- 1/4 teaspoons spirulina
- 1/4 cup water

Directions:
Prepare the crust, and for this, place all its ingredients in a food processor and pulse for 3 to 5 minutes until the thick paste comes together. Take a 6-inch springform pan, grease it with oil, place crust mixture in it and spread and press the mixture evenly in the bottom and along the sides, and freeze until required.
Prepare the filling and for this, place all its ingredients in a food processor, and pulse for 2 minutes until smooth. Pour the filling into the prepared pan, smooth the top, and freeze for 4 hours until set. Cut pie into slices and then serve.
Per serving: Calories: 223.7Kcal; Fat: 7.5g; Carbs: 36g; Fiber: 1g; Protein: 2.5g

612. Peanut Butter Energy Bars

Preparation time: 5 hours and 15 minutes
Cooking time: 5 minutes **Servings:** 16
Ingredients:
- 1/2 cup cranberries
- 12 Medjool dates, pitted
- 1 cup roasted almond
- 1 tablespoon chia seeds
- 1 1/2 cups oats
- 1/8 teaspoon salt
- 1/4 cup and 1 tablespoon agave nectar
- 1/2 teaspoon vanilla extract, unsweetened
- 1/3 cup and 1 tablespoon peanut butter, unsalted
- 2 tablespoons water

Directions:
Place an almond in a food processor, pulse until chopped, and then transfer into a large bowl. Add dates into the food processor along with oats, pour in water, and pulse for dates are chopped. Add dates mixture into the almond mixture, add chia seeds and berries and stir until mixed. Take a saucepan, place it over medium heat, add remaining butter and remaining ingredients, stir, and **Cooking time:** for 5 minutes until mixture reaches a liquid consistency.
Pour the butter mixture over the date mixture, and then stir until well combined.

Take an 8 by 8 inches baking tray, line it with a parchment sheet, add date mixture in it, spread and press it evenly and refrigerate for 5 hours. Cut it into sixteen bars and serve.
Per serving: Calories: 187Kcal; Fat: 7.5g; Carbs: 27.2g; Fiber 4.7g; Protein: 2g

613. Black Bean Brownie Pops

Preparation time: 45 minutes
Cooking time: 2 minutes **Servings:** 12
Ingredients:
- 3/4 cup chocolate chips
- 15-ounce cooked black beans
- 1 tablespoon maple syrup
- 5 tablespoons cacao powder
- 1/8 teaspoon sea salt
- 2 tablespoons sunflower seed butter

Directions:
Place black beans in a food processor, add remaining ingredients, except for chocolate, and pulse for 2 minutes until combined and the dough starts to come together. Shape the dough into twelve balls, arrange them on a baking sheet lined with parchment paper, then insert a toothpick into each ball and refrigerate for 20 minutes. Then meat chocolate in the microwave for 2 minutes, and dip brownie pops in it until covered. Return the pops into the refrigerator for 10 minute until set and then serve.
Per serving: Calories: 130Kcal; Fat: 6g; Carbs: 17g; Fiber: 1g Protein: 4g

614. Lemon Cashew Tart

Preparation time: 3 hours and 15 minutes
Cooking time: 0 minutes **Servings:** 12
Ingredients:
For the Crust:
- 1 cup almonds
- 4 dates, pitted, soaked in warm water for 10 minutes in water, drained
- 1/8 teaspoon crystal salt
- 1 teaspoon vanilla extract, unsweetened

For the Cream:
- 1 cup cashews, soaked in warm water for 10 minutes in water, drained
- 1/4 cup water
- 1/4 cup coconut nectar
- 1 teaspoon coconut oil
- 1 teaspoon vanilla extract, unsweetened
- 1 lemon, Juiced
- 1/8 teaspoon crystal salt

For the Topping:
- Shredded coconut as needed

Directions:
Prepare the cream and for this, place all its ingredients in food processor, pulse for 2 minutes until smooth, and then refrigerate for 1 hour.
Then prepare the crust, and for this, place all its ingredients in a food processor and pulse for 3 to 5 minutes until the thic paste comes together.

Take a tart pan, grease it with oil, place crust mixture in it and spread and press the mixture evenly in the bottom and along the sides, and freeze until required.
Pour the filling into the prepared tart, smooth the top, and refrigerate for 2 hours until set.
Cut tart into slices and then serve.
Per serving: Calories: 166Kcal; Fat: 10g; Carbs: 15g; Fiber: 1g; Protein: 5g

615. Peppermint Oreos
Preparation time: 2 hours
Cooking time: 0 minutes **Servings:** 12
Ingredients:
For the Cookies:
- 1 cup dates
- 2/3 cup brazil nuts
- 3 tablespoons carob powder
- 2/3 cup almonds
- 1/8 teaspoon sea salt
- 3 tablespoons water

For the Crème:
- 2 tablespoons almond butter
- 1 cup coconut chips
- 2 tablespoons melted coconut oil
- 1 cup coconut shreds
- 3 drops of peppermint oil
- 1/2 teaspoon vanilla powder

For the Dark Chocolate:
- 3/4 cup cacao powder
- 1/2 cup date paste
- 1/3 cup coconut oil, melted

Directions:
Prepare the cookies, and for this, place all its ingredients in a food processor and pulse for 3 to 5 minutes until the dough comes together. Then place the dough between two parchment sheets, roll the dough, then cut out twenty-four cookies of the desired shape and freeze until solid.
Prepare the crème, and for this, place all its ingredients in a food processor and pulse for 2 minutes until smooth.
When cookies have hardened, sandwich crème between the cookies by placing dollops on top of a cookie and then pressing it with another cookie.
Freeze the cookies for 30 minutes and in the meantime, prepare chocolate and for this, place all its ingredients in a bowl and whisk until combined.
Dip frouncesen cookie sandwich into chocolate, at least two times, and then freeze for another 30 minutes until chocolate has hardened.
Serve straight away.
Per serving: Calories: 470Kcal; Fat: 32g; Carbs: 51 g; Fiber: 12g; Protein: 7g

616. Snickers Pie
Preparation time: 4 hours
Cooking time: 0 minutes **Servings:** 16
Ingredients:
For the Crust:
- 12 Medjool dates, pitted
- 1 cup dried coconut, unsweetened
- 5 tablespoons cocoa powder
- 1/2 teaspoon sea salt
- 1 teaspoon vanilla extract, unsweetened
- 1 cup almonds

For the Caramel Layer:
- 10 Medjool dates, pitted, soaked for 10 minutes in warm water, drained
- 2 teaspoons vanilla extract, unsweetened
- 3 teaspoons coconut oil
- 3 tablespoons almond butter, unsalted

For the Peanut Butter Mousse:
- 3/4 cup peanut butter
- 2 tablespoons maple syrup
- 1/2 teaspoon vanilla extract, unsweetened
- 1/8 teaspoon sea salt
- 28 ounces coconut milk, chilled

Directions:
Prepare the crust, and for this, place all its ingredients in a food processor and pulse for 3 to 5 minutes until the thick paste comes together. Take a baking pan, line it with parchment paper, place crust mixture in it and spread and press the mixture evenly in the bottom, and freeze until required. Prepare the caramel layer, and for this, place all its ingredients in a food processor and pulse for 2 minutes until smooth. Pour the caramel on top of the prepared crust, smooth the top and freeze for 30 minutes until set. Prepare the mousse and for this, separate coconut milk and its solid, then add solid from coconut milk into a food processor, add remaining ingredients and then pulse for 1 minute until smooth.
Top prepared mousse over caramel layer, and then freeze for 3 hours until set. Serve straight away.
Per serving: Calories: 456Kcal; Fat: 33g; Carbs: 37g; Fiber: 5g; Protein: 8.3g

617. Double Chocolate Orange Cheesecake
Preparation time: 4 hours
Cooking time: 0 minutes **Servings:** 12
Ingredients:
For the Base:
- 9 Medjool dates, pitted
- 1/3 cup Brazil nuts
- 2 tablespoons maple syrup
- 1/3 cup walnuts
- 2 tablespoons water
- 3 tablespoons cacao powder

For the Chocolate Cheesecake:
- 1/2 cup cacao powder
- 1 1/2 cups cashews, soaked for 10 minutes in warm water, drained
- 1/3 cup liquid coconut oil
- 1 teaspoon vanilla extract, unsweetened
- 1/3 cup maple syrup
- 1/3 cup water

For the Orange Cheesecake:
- 2 oranges, juiced
- 1/4 cup maple syrup
- 1 cup cashews, soaked for 10 minutes in warm water, drained
- 1 teaspoon vanilla extract, unsweetened
- 2 tablespoons coconut butter
- 1/2 cup liquid coconut oil
- 2 oranges, zested
- 4 drops of orange essential oil

For the Chocolate Topping:
- 3 tablespoons cacao powder
- 3 drops of orange essential oil
- 2 tablespoons liquid coconut oil
- 3 tablespoons maple syrup

Directions:
Prepare the base, and for this, place all its ingredients in a food processor and pulse for 3 to 5 minutes until the thick paste comes together. Take a cake tin, place crust mixture in it and spread and press the mixture evenly in the bottom, and freeze until required. Prepare the chocolate cheesecake, and for this, place all its ingredients in a food processor and pulse for 2 minutes until smooth. Pour the chocolate cheesecake mixture on top of the prepared base, smooth the top and freeze for 20 minutes until set. Then prepare the orange cheesecake and for this, place all its ingredients in a food processor, and pulse for 2 minutes until smooth Top orange cheesecake mixture over chocolate cheesecake, and then freeze for 3 hours until hardened. Then prepare the chocolate topping and for this, take a bowl, add all the ingredients in it and stir until well combined. Spread chocolate topping over the top, freeze the cake for 10 minutes until the topping has hardened, and then slice to serve.

Per serving: Calories: 508Kcal; Fat: 34.4g; Carbs:44g; Fiber: 3g; Protein: 8g

618. Coconut Ice Cream Cheesecake

Preparation time: 3 hours
Cooking time: 0 minutes **Servings:** 4
Ingredients:
For the First Layer:
- 1 cup mixed nuts
- 3/4 cup dates, soaked for 10 minutes in warm water
- 2 tablespoons almond milk

For the Second Layer:
- 1 medium avocado, diced
- 1 cup cashew nuts, soaked for 10 minutes in warm water
- 3 cups strawberries, sliced
- 1 tablespoon chia seeds, soaked in 3 tablespoons soy milk
- 1/2 cup agave
- 1 cup melted coconut oil
- 1/2 cup shredded coconut
- 1 lime, juiced

Directions:
Prepare the first layer, and for this, place all its ingredients in a food processor and pulse for 3 to 5 minutes until the thick paste comes together. Take a springform pan, place crust mixture in it and spread and press the mixture evenly in the bottom, and freeze until required. Prepare the second layer, and for this, place all its ingredients in a food processor and pulse for 2 minutes until smooth. Pour the second layer on top of the first layer, smooth the top, and freeze for 4 hours until hard. Serve straight away.

Per serving: Calories: 411.3Kcal; Fat: 30.8g; Carbs: 28.7g; Fiber: 1.3g; Protein: 4.7g

619. Matcha Coconut Cream Pie

Preparation time: 5 minutes
Cooking time: 0 minutes **Servings:** 4
Ingredients:
For the Crust:
- 1/2 cup ground flaxseed
- 3/4 cup shredded dried coconut
- 1 cup Medjool dates, pitted
- 3/4 cup dehydrated buckwheat groats
- 1/4 teaspoons sea salt

For the Filling:
- 1 cup dried coconut flakes
- 4 cups of coconut meat
- 1/4 cup and 2 Tablespoons coconut nectar
- 1/2 Tablespoons vanilla extract, unsweetened
- 1/4 teaspoons sea salt
- 2/3 cup and 2 Tablespoons coconut butter
- 1 Tablespoon matcha powder
- 1/2 cup coconut water

Directions:
Prepare the crust, and for this, place all its ingredients in a food processor and pulse for 3 to 5 minutes until the thick paste comes together. Take a 6-inch springform pan, grease it with oil, place crust mixture in it and spread and press the mixture evenly in the bottom and along the sides, and freeze until required.
Prepare the filling and for this, place all its ingredients in a food processor, and pulse for 2 minutes until smooth. Pour the filling into the prepared pan, smooth the top, and freeze for 4 hours until set. Cut pie into slices and then serve.

Per serving: Calories: 209Kcal; Fat: 18g; Carbs: 10g; Fiber: 2g; Protein: 1g

620. Chocolate Peanut Butter Cake

Preparation time: 5 minutes
Cooking time: 0 minutes **Servings:** 8
Ingredients:
For the Base:
- 1 tablespoon ground flaxseeds
- 1/8 cup millet
- 3/4 cup peanuts
- 1/4 cup and 2 tablespoons shredded coconut unsweetened
- 1 teaspoon hemp oil
- 1/2 cup flake oats

For the Date Layer:
- 1 tablespoon ground flaxseed
- 1 cup dates

- 1 tablespoon hemp hearts
- 2 tablespoons coconut
- 3 tablespoons cacao

For the Chocolate Layer:
- 3/4 cup coconut flour
- 2 tablespoons and 2 teaspoons cacao
- 1 tablespoon maple syrup
- 8 tablespoons warm water
- 2 tablespoons coconut oil
- 1/2 cup coconut milk
- 2 tablespoons ground flaxseed

For the Chocolate Topping:
- 7 ounces coconut cream
- 2 1/2 tablespoons cacao
- 1 teaspoon agave

For Assembly:
- 1/2 cup almond butter

Directions:
Prepare the crust, and for this, place all its ingredients in a food processor and pulse for 3 to 5 minutes until the thick paste comes together. Take a loaf tin, grease it with oil, place crust mixture in it and spread and press the mixture evenly in the bottom and along the sides, and freeze until required. Prepare the date layer, and for this, place all its ingredients in a food processor and pulse for 2 minutes until smooth. Prepare the chocolate layer, and for this, place flour and flax in a bowl and stir until combined. Take a saucepan, add remaining ingredients, stir until mixed and **Cooking time:** for 5 minutes until melted and smooth. Add it into the flour mixture, stir until dough comes together, and set aside. Prepare the chocolate topping, place all its ingredients in a food processor and pulse for 3 to 5 minutes until smooth.
Press date layer into the base layer, refrigerate for 1 hour, then press chocolate layer on its top, finish with chocolate topping, refrigerate for 3 hours and serve.
Per serving: Calories: 390Kcal; Fat: 24.3g; Carbs: 35g; Fiber: 2g; Protein: 10.3g

621. Chocolate Raspberry Brownies

Preparation time: 4 hours
Cooking time: 0 minutes **Servings:** 4
Ingredients:
For the Chocolate Brownie Base:
- 12 Medjool Dates, pitted
- 3/4 cup oat flour
- 3/4 cup almond meal
- 3 tablespoons cacao
- 1 teaspoon vanilla extract, unsweetened
- 1/8 teaspoon sea salt
- 3 tablespoons water
- 1/2 cup pecans, chopped

For the Raspberry Cheesecake:
- 3/4 cup cashews, soaked, drained
- 6 tablespoons agave nectar
- 1/2 cup raspberries
- 1 teaspoon vanilla extract, unsweetened
- 1 lemon, juiced

- 6 tablespoons liquid coconut oil

For the Chocolate Coating:
- 2 1/2 tablespoons cacao powder
- 3 3/4 tablespoons coconut Oil
- 2 tablespoons maple syrup
- 1/8 teaspoon sea salt

Directions:
Prepare the crust, and for this, place all its ingredients in a food processor and pulse for 3 to 5 minutes until the thick paste comes together. Take a 6-inch springform pan, grease it with oil, place crust mixture in it and spread and press the mixture evenly in the bottom and along the sides, and freeze until required. Prepare the cheesecake topping, and for this, place all its ingredients in a food processor and pulse for 2 minutes until smooth. Pour the filling into the prepared pan, smooth the top, and freeze for 8 hours until solid. Prepare the chocolate coating and for this, whisk together all its ingredients until smooth, drizzle on top of the cake and then serve.
Per serving: Calories: 371Kcal; Fat: 42.4g; Carbs: 42g; Fiber: 2g; Protein: 5.5g

622. Brownie Batter

Preparation time: 5 minutes
Cooking time: 0 minutes **Servings:** 4
Ingredients:
- 4 Medjool dates, pitted, soaked in warm water
- 1.5 ounces chocolate, unsweetened, melted
- 2 tablespoons maple syrup - 4 tablespoons tahini
- ½ teaspoon vanilla extract, unsweetened
- 1 tablespoon cocoa powder, unsweetened
- 1/8 teaspoon sea salt
- 1/8 teaspoon espresso powder
- 2 to 4 tablespoons almond milk, unsweetened

Directions:
Place all the ingredients in a food processor and process for 2 minutes until combined. Set aside until required. **Per serving:** Calories: 44Kcal; Fat: 1g; Carbs: 6g; Fiber: 0 g; Protein: 2g

623. Strawberry Mousse

Preparation time: 5 minutes
Cooking time: 15 minutes **Servings:** 4
Ingredients:
- 8 ounces coconut milk, unsweetened
- 2 tablespoons honey - 5 strawberries

Directions:
Place berries in a blender and pulse until the smooth mixture comes together. Place milk in a bowl, whisk until whipped, and then add remaining ingredients and stir until combined. Refrigerate the mousse for 10 minutes and then serve.
Per serving: Calories: 145Kcal; Fat: 23g; Carbs: 15g; Fiber: 1g; Protein: 5g

624. Blueberry Mousse

Preparation time: 20 minutes
Cooking time: 0 minutes **Servings:** 2
Ingredients:
- 1 cup wild blueberries

- 1 cup cashews, soaked for 10 minutes, drained
- 1/2 teaspoon berry powder
- 2 tablespoons coconut oil, melted
- 1 tablespoon lemon juice
- 1 teaspoon vanilla extract, unsweetened
- 1/4 cup hot water

Directions:
Place all the ingredients in a food processor and process for 2 minutes until smooth. Set aside until required.
Per serving: Calories: 433Kcal; Fat: 32.3g; Carbs: 44g; Fiber: 0g; Protein: 5.1g

625. Black Bean Balls
Preparation time: 10-20 minutes
Cooking time: 20 minutes **Servings:** 12 balls, 3 per serving
Ingredients:
- 420g can black beans, rinsed
- 80g raw cacao powder
- 30g almond butter
- 15ml maple syrup

Directions:
In a food processor, combine 420g black beans, 60g cacao powder, almond butter, and maple syrup.
Process until the mixture is well combined.
Shape the mixture into 12 balls. Roll the balls through the remaining cacao powder. Place the balls in a refrigerator for 10 minutes. Serve.
Per serving: Calories: 245Kcal; Fat: 3g; Carbs: 41.4g; Fiber: 17.1g; Protein: 13.1g

626. Chia Soy Pudding
Preparation time: 10-20 minutes
Cooking time: 5 minutes **Servings:** 2
Ingredients:
- 45g almond butter
- 15ml maple syrup
- ¼ teaspoon vanilla paste
- 235ml soy milk
- 45g chia seeds
- 1 small banana, sliced
- 10g crushed almonds

Directions:
Combine almond butter, maple syrup, vanilla, and soy milk in a jar. Stir in chia seeds. Cover and refrigerate for 3 hours. After 3 hours, open the jar.
Top the chia pudding with banana and crushed almonds. Serve.
Per serving: Calories: 298Kcal; Fat: 13.8g; Carbs: 37.2g; Fiber: 10.8g; Protein: 10.1g

627. Blueberry Ice Cream
Preparation time: 10-20 minutes
Cooking time: 10 minutes **Servings:** 4
Ingredients:
- 140g raw cashews, soaked overnight
- 125g silken tofu
- 230g fresh blueberries
- 5g lemon zest
- 100ml maple syrup
- 100ml coconut oil
- 15g almond butter

Directions:
Rinse and drain cashews.
Place the cashews, blueberries, pale syrup, coconut oil, and almond butter in a food processor. Process until smooth. Transfer the mixture into the freezer-friendly container. Cover with plastic foil and freeze for 4 hours.
Remove the ice cream from the fridge 15 minutes before serving. Scoop the ice creams and transfer them into a bowl. Serve.
Per serving: Calories: 544Kcal; Fat: 40.7g; Carbs: 43.4g; Fiber: 2.6g; Protein: 8.1g

628. Chickpea Choco Slices
Preparation time: 10-20 minutes **Cooking time:** 50 minutes
Servings: 12 slices, 2 per serving
Ingredients:
- 400g can chickpeas, rinsed, drained
- 250g almond butter
- 70ml maple syrup
- 15ml vanilla paste
- 1 pinch salt
- 2g baking powder
- 2g baking soda
- 40g vegan chocolate chips

Directions:
Preheat oven to 180C/350F. Grease a large baking pan with coconut oil. Combine chickpeas, almond butter, maple syrup, vanilla, salt, baking powder, and baking soda in a food blender. Blend until smooth. Stir in half the chocolate chips. Spread the batter into the prepared baking pan. Sprinkle with reserved chocolate chips. Bake for 45-50 minutes or until an inserted toothpick comes out clean. Cool on a wire rack for 20 minutes, slice, and serve.
Per serving: Calories: 426Kcal; Fat: 27.2g; Carbs: 39.2g; Fiber: 4.9g; Protein: 10g

629. Chocolate Orange Mousse
Preparation time: 10-20 minutes
Cooking time: 10 minutes **Servings:** 4
Ingredients:
- 450g can black beans, rinsed, drained
- 55g dates, pitted, soaked in water for 15 minutes
- 30ml coconut oil
- 110ml maple syrup
- 60ml soy milk
- 1 orange, zested

Directions:
Place the black bean in a food processor. Add drained dates and process until smooth. Add coconut oil, maple syrup, and soy milk. Process for 1 minute.
Finally, stir in lemon zest. Spoon the mixture into four dessert bowls. Chill for 1 hour before serving.
Per serving: Calories: 375Kcal; Fat: 12.1g; Carbs: 68.5g; Fiber: 12.1g; Protein: 11.3g

CHAPTER 27:
30 Min Recipes

630. Strawberry Shake
Preparation time: 10 minutes
Cooking time: 0 minutes **Servings:** 2
Ingredients:
- 1½ cups fresh strawberries, hulled
- 1 large frozen banana, peeled
- 2 scoops unsweetened vegan vanilla protein powder
- 2 tablespoons hemp seeds
- 2 cups unsweetened hemp milk

Directions:
In a high-speed blender, place all the ingredients and pulse until creamy. Pour into two glasses and serve immediately. **Per serving:** Calories: 325Kcal; Fat: 13g; Carbs: 23.3g; Fiber: 3.9g; Protein: 31.2g

631. Chocolatey Banana Shake
Preparation time: 10 minutes
Cooking time: 0 minutes **Servings:** 2
Ingredients:
2 medium frozen bananas, peeled
- 4 dates, pitted
- 4 tablespoons peanut butter
- 4 tablespoons rolled oats
- 2 tablespoons cacao powder
- 2 tablespoons chia seeds
- 2 cups unsweetened soymilk

Directions:
Place all the ingredients in a high-speed blender and pulse until creamy. Pour into two glasses and serve immediately.
Per serving: Calories: 583Kcal; Fat: 25.2g; Carbs: 75g; Fiber: 15.3g; Protein: 23.1g

632. Fruity Tofu Smoothie
Preparation time: 10 minutes
Cooking time: 0 minutes
Servings: 2
Ingredients:
- 12 ounces silken tofu, pressed and drained
- 2 medium bananas, peeled
- 1½ cups fresh blueberries
- 1 tablespoon maple syrup
- 1½ cups unsweetened soymilk
- ¼ cup ice cubes

Directions:
Place all the ingredients in a high-speed blender and pulse until creamy. Pour into two glasses and serve immediately. **Per serving:** Calories: 398Kcal; Fat: 8.6g; Carbs: 65g; Fiber: 7g; Protein: 19.9g

633. Green Fruity Smoothie
Preparation time: 10 minutes
Cooking time: 0 minutes **Servings:** 2
Ingredients:
- 1 cup frozen mango, peeled, pitted, and chopped
- 1 large frozen banana, peeled
- 2 cups fresh baby spinach
- 1 scoop unsweetened vegan vanilla protein powder -
- ¼ cup pumpkin seeds
- 2 tablespoons hemp hearts
- 1½ cups unsweetened almond milk

Directions:
In a high-speed blender, place all the ingredients and pulse until creamy. Pour into two glasses and serve immediately.
Per serving: Calories: 355Kcal; Fat: 16.1g; Carbs: 34.6g; Fiber: 6.2g; Protein: 23.4g

634. Protein Latte
Preparation time: 10 minutes
Cooking time: 10 minutes **Servings:** 2
Ingredients:
- 2 cups hot brewed coffee
- 1¼ cups coconut milk
- 2 teaspoons coconut oil
- 2 scoops unsweetened vegan vanilla protein powder

Directions:
Place all the ingredients in a high-speed blender and pulse until creamy. Pour into two serving mugs and serve immediately. **Per serving:** Calories: 503Kcal; Fat: 41.4g; Carbs: 8.3g; Fiber: 3.3g; Protein: 29.1g

635. Chocolatey Bean Mousse
Preparation time: 10 minutes
Cooking time: 0 minutes **Servings:** 3
Ingredients:
- ½ cup unsweetened almond milk
- 1 cup cooked black beans
- 4 Medjool dates, pitted and chopped
- ½ cup walnuts, chopped
- 2 tablespoons cacao powder
- 1 teaspoon vanilla extract
- 3 tablespoons fresh blueberries
- 1 teaspoon fresh mint leaves

Directions:
In a food processor, add all ingredients and pulse until smooth and creamy. Transfer the mousse into serving bowls and refrigerate to chill before serving. Garnish with blueberries and mint leaves and serve.
Per serving: Calories: 465Kcal; Fat: 14.5g; Carbs: 69.9g; Fiber: 15g; Protein: 21.1g

636. Tofu & Strawberry Mousse

Preparation time: 10 minutes
Cooking time: 10 minutes
Servings: 4
Ingredients:
- 2 cups fresh strawberries, hulled and sliced
- 2 cups firm tofu, pressed and drained
- 3 tablespoons maple syrup
- 4 tablespoons walnuts, chopped

Directions:
In a blender, add the strawberries and pulse until just pureed. Add the tofu and maple syrup and pulse until smooth. Transfer the mousse into serving bowls and refrigerate to chill before serving. Garnish with walnuts and serve.
Per serving: Calories: 199Kcal; Fat: 10.1g; Carbs: 18.5g; Fiber: 3.1g; Protein: 12.7g

637. Tofu & Chia Seed Pudding

Preparation time: 15 minutes
Cooking time: 0 minutes **Servings:** 4
Ingredients:
- 1-pound silken tofu, pressed and drained
- ¼ cup banana, peeled
- 3 tablespoons cacao powder
- 1 teaspoon vanilla extract
- 3 tablespoons chia seeds
- ¼ cup walnuts, chopped - ¼ cup black raisins

Directions:
In a food processor, add tofu, banana, cocoa powder, and vanilla, and pulse till smooth and creamy.
Transfer into a large serving bowl and stir in chia seeds till well mixed.
Now, place the pudding in serving bowls evenly.
With plastic wraps, cover the bowls. Refrigerate to chill before serving. Garnish with raspberries and serve.
Per serving: Calories: 188Kcal; Fat: 10.4g; Carbs: 17.1g; Fiber: 4.2g; Protein: 12g

638. Banana Brownies

Preparation time: 15 minutes
Cooking time: 20 minutes **Servings:** 8
Ingredients:
- 6 bananas
- 2 scoops unsweetened vegan vanilla protein powder
- 1 cup creamy peanut butter
- ½ cup cacao powder

Directions:
Preheat the oven the 350ºF. Line a square baking dish with greased parchment paper. In a food processor, add all the ingredients and pulse until smooth. Transfer the mixture into the prepared baking dish evenly and with the back of a spatula, smooth the top surface. Bake for about 18–20 minutes. Remove from oven and place onto a wire rack to cool completely. With a sharp knife, cut into equal-sized brownies and serve.
Per serving: Calories: 310Kcal; Fat: 17.8g; Carbs: 29.1g; Fiber: 5.7g; Protein: 16.4g

639. Cherry Smoothie with Oat Milk

Preparation time: 10 minutes
Cooking time: 0 minutes **Servings:** 3
Ingredients:
- 1 cup of cherries (frozen or fresh)
- ½ cup of blueberries (frozen or fresh)
- 1 banana
- 1 cup of oat milk
- 1/2 cup of orange juice
- 2 teaspoons of honey
- ½ cup of almond milk
- dark chocolate

Directions:
Blend the cherries, blueberries, and banana using a blender. Add the orange juice and honey.
Pour the oat milk and almond milk.
Mix well using a mixer. Grate the dark chocolate on top - and your smoothie is ready!
Per serving: Calories: 129Kcal; Fat: 7g; Carbs: 13g; Protein: 2g

640. Chocolate Mousse with Almonds

Preparation time: 10 minutes
Cooking time: 20 minutes
Servings: 2
Ingredients:
- 1 ¼ cups of dark chocolate
- ¼ cup of almonds, ground
- 1 cup cream
- 2 tbsp. erythritol
- 15 drops of liquid stevia
- 1 teaspoon vanilla

Directions:
Melt the dark chocolate on low heat and allow the chocolate to cool down. Whisk the cream with a mixer until the foam and add erythritol and stevia, and then blend. Add the vanilla and almonds.
Gradually, whisking, bring the cooled chocolate mass into the cream. Put the chocolate mousse in the crockery, small bowls or cups. Grate some chocolate on top. Before serving, put the chocolate mousse into the refrigerator for an hour. Bon Appetite!
Per serving: Calories: 290Kcal; Fat: 7g; Carbs: 9g; Protein: 5g

641. Banana and Orange Mousse

Preparation time: 15 minutes
Cooking time: 0 minutes **Servings:** 2
Ingredients:
1 banana
- 2 oranges - 2 kiwi's - 1 tbsp. ground cinnamon
- 15 drops of liquid stevia
- 2 tbsp. liquid honey
- few mint leaves - dark chocolate

Directions:
Squeeze the orange juice.
Peel the fruits and mix them using a blender. Add the orange juice, honey, stevia, cinnamon, mint leaves and mix using a

blender. Before serving, put the mousse into the refrigerator for two hours. Grate cinnamon and dark chocolate on top. Bon Appetite!

Per serving: Calories: 76Kcal; Fat: 2.8g; Carbs: 15; Protein: 1.5g

642. Golden Milk Smoothie

Preparation time: 10 minutes
Cooking time: 0 minutes **Servings:** 1
Ingredients:
- 1 cup frozen banana, ripe & sliced
- 1 cup light coconut milk
- 1/2 tsp ground turmeric
- 1 tbsp fresh ginger
- 1 dash ground cinnamon
- 1 dash black pepper
- 1 dash ground nutmeg
- 1 dash ground clove and cardamom
- 1/4 cup fresh carrot juice

For Serving:
- 1 tbsp hemp seeds

Directions:
Prepare the smoothie by throwing all the ingredients into a blender jug. Press the pulse button and blend until well incorporated. Serve chilled.

Per serving: Calories: 155Kcal; Fat: 13g; Carbs: 16g; Fiber: 2g; Protein: 2g

643. Zucchini Blueberry Smoothie

Preparation time: 10 minutes **Cooking time:** 0 minutes **Servings:** 2
Ingredients:
- 1 large ripe frozen banana, peeled & sliced
- 1 cup wild blueberries
- 1 large stem celery
- 2/3 cup zucchini, sliced
- 1 handful greens - 1 tbsp hemp seeds
- 1/4 tsp ground cinnamon
- 1 cup light coconut milk
- 1/2 tsp maca powder

Directions:
Prepare the smoothie by throwing all the ingredients into a blender jug. Press the pulse button and blend until well incorporated. Serve chilled.

Per serving: Calories: 125Kcal; Fat: 11g; Carbs: 15g; Fiber: 2g; Protein: 0.6g

644. Avocado Banana Green Smoothie

Preparation time: 10 minutes
Cooking time: 0 minutes **Servings:** 2
Ingredients:
- 1 large frozen banana, peeled & sliced
- 1/2 medium ripe avocado
- 1 scoop plain protein powder
- 1 large handful greens 3/4 unsweetened almond milk

Optional add-ins
- 1 tbsp seed of choice
- 1/2 tsp maca

- 1/2 cup frozen cucumber

Directions:
Prepare the smoothie by throwing all the ingredients into a blender jug. Press the pulse button and blend until well incorporated. Serve chilled.

Per serving: Calories: 131Kcal; Fat: 13g; Carbs: 9.7g; Fiber: 3.1g; Protein: 2g

645. Gingery Mango Smoothie

Preparation time: 10 minutes
Cooking time: 0 minutes **Servings:** 2
Ingredients:
- 2 1/4 cups frozen mango, chopped
- 1 1/4 cups frozen raspberries
- 1 cup light coconut milk
- 1 medium lime, juiced
- 2 tbsp fresh ginger
- 1 tbsp unsweetened shredded coconut
- 1/8 tsp cayenne pepper
- 1-2 tbsp hemp seeds

For Serving: (Optional)
- Coconut Yogurt - Berries
- Shredded coconut - Hemp seeds

Directions:
Prepare the smoothie by throwing all the ingredients into a blender jug. Press the pulse button and blend until well incorporated. Serve chilled with optional garnishes. **Per serving:** Calories: 141Kcal; Fat: 9g; Carbs: 16g; Fiber: 4g; Protein: 3.1g

646. Green Spirulina Smoothie

Preparation time: 10 minutes
Cooking time: 0 minutes **Servings:** 1
Ingredients:
- 1 medium ripe banana
- 1/2 cup cucumber, sliced
- 1 cup light coconut milk
- 1 cup spinach
- 1 tsp spirulina powder
- 1 tbsp hemp seed

For Serving:
- 1/4 cup frozen or fresh blueberries
- 1/4 cup granola

Directions:
Prepare the smoothie by throwing all the ingredients into a blender jug. Press the pulse button and blend until well incorporated. Serve chilled with berries and granola on top.

Per serving: Calories: 142Kcal; Fat: 2g; Carbs: 5g; Fiber: 3.2g; Protein: 1.1g

647. Ginger Kale Smoothie

Preparation time: 10 minutes
Cooking time: 0 minutes **Servings:** 2
Ingredients:
- 1 cup ice
- 2 cups packed kale
- 1 cup ripe frozen mango cubes

- 1 cup ripe frozen peaches
- 1 tbsp minced fresh ginger
- 2 lemons or limes, juiced
- 2 cups of water
- 1 tbsp maple syrup

Directions:
Prepare the smoothie by throwing all the ingredients into a blender jug. Press the pulse button and blend until well incorporated. Serve chilled.

Per serving: Calories: 135Kcal; Fat: 2g; Carbs: 33g; Fiber: 1g; Protein: 2g

648. Mushroom Scramble

Preparation time: 10 minutes
Cooking time: 19 minutes **Servings:** 6
Ingredients:

- 1 red onion, peeled and diced
- 1 red bell pepper, seeded and diced
- 1 green bell pepper, seeded and diced
- 2 cups mushrooms, sliced
- 1 large head cauliflower, florets
- Sea salt, to taste
- ½ tsp freshly ground black pepper
- 1½ tsp turmeric
- ¼ tsp cayenne pepper
- 3 cloves garlic, peeled and minced
- 2 tbsp soy sauce
- ¼ cup nutritional yeast

Directions:
First, take a medium skillet and place it over medium heat. Toss in mushrooms and the green and red peppers along with the onion.
Stir cook for 8 minutes, then add 2 tablespoons of water.
Toss in cauliflower and continue cooking for 6 minutes.
Stir in the turmeric, pepper, salt, cayenne, soy sauce, yeast, and garlic. Cook for another 5 minutes, then serve.

Per serving: Calories: 284Kcal; Fat: 7.9g; Carbs: 46g; Fiber: 3.6g; Protein: 7.9g

649. Apple-Lemon Bowl

Preparation time: 10 minutes
Cooking time: 0 minutes
Servings: 2
Ingredients:

- 5 medium apples, any variety
- 6 dates, pitted
- 1 lemon, juiced
- 2 tbsp walnuts
- ¼ tsp ground cinnamon

Directions:
First, core the apples and dice them into large pieces.
Add dates, walnuts, lemon juice, cinnamon, and ¾ apple to a food processor. Blend the apple mixture, then top with the remaining apples. Serve.

Per serving: Calories: 134Kcal; Fat: 0.6g; Carbs: 54.1g; Fiber: 7g; Protein: 6.2g

650. Portabella Eggs Florentine

Preparation time: 5 minutes
Cooking time: 25 minutes **Servings:** 2
Ingredients:

- 2 large portabella mushroom caps
- 2 tablespoons balsamic vinegar
- 1 tablespoon olive oil
- ½ teaspoon kosher salt, divided
- ½ teaspoon freshly ground black pepper, divided
- 1 tablespoon unsalted butter
- 1 teaspoon garlic paste
- ½ teaspoon Dijon mustard
- 3 tablespoons heavy (whipping) cream
- 1 (5-ounce) bag baby spinach
- 2 large eggs

Directions:
Preheat the oven to 400°F.
Remove the stems from the portabellas and scrape out the gills with a spoon. In a medium-size bowl, whisk together the vinegar, olive oil, and ¼ teaspoon each of salt and pepper. Add the portabellas and coat them with the marinade. Place the mushrooms in an oven-safe skillet, gill-side up, and roast for 15 minutes. While the portabellas are roasting, melt the butter in a medium skillet over medium heat. Stir in the garlic paste, mustard, and remaining ¼ teaspoon each of salt and pepper. Cook for about 1 minute. Whisk in the cream and cook until thickened, about 1 minute. Fold in the spinach and gently toss until completely coated and wilted, 2 to 3 minutes. Once the portabellas have roasted for 15 minutes, spoon the creamed spinach into their cavities. Form a nest within the creamed spinach using a large spoon. Break an egg into each nest. It's fine if the white of the egg runs over a bit as long as the yolk remains inside the mushroom cap. Roast for another 10 to 12 minutes, or until the egg white is completely set, but the yolk remains runny.

Per serving: Calories: 306Kcal; Fat: 27g; Carbs: 9g; Fiber: 3g; Protein: 11g

651. Quinoa And Nectarine Slaw

Preparation time: 10 minutes
Cooking time: 6 minutes **Servings:** 2
Ingredients:

- 1 cup cooked quinoa, at room temperature
- 2 nectarines, cut into ½-inch wedges
- ½ cup shredded white cabbage
- ½ cup chopped curly kale
- 1/3 cup thinly sliced scallions
- 1/3 cup Roasted Pumpkin Seeds
- 3 tablespoons Lemon Vinaigrette
- ½ cup feta cheese (optional)

Directions:
In a large bowl, combine the quinoa, nectarines, cabbage, kale, scallions, and pumpkin seeds. Toss with the vinaigrette. Serve topped with the feta cheese (if using).

Per serving: Calories: 396Kcal; Fat: 18g; Carbs: 52g; Fiber: 7g; Protein: 11g

652. Zucchini Fritters

Preparation time: 15 minutes
Cooking time: 15 minutes
Servings: 10 Fritters
Ingredients:
- 1 Yukon Gold potato
- ½ cup cooked quinoa
- 1 large zucchini, grated using the large holes on a box grater
- 1 cup freshly crumbled feta cheese
- ½ cup thinly sliced leek, white and light green parts only
- ¼ cup panko breadcrumbs
- 1 egg, beaten
- 1 teaspoon freshly squeezed lemon juice
- 1 teaspoon kosher salt
- ½ teaspoon freshly ground black pepper
- 2 tablespoons olive oil

Directions:
Poke a few holes in the potato. Microwave on high until tender, about 5 minutes. When cool enough to handle, peel and coarsely grate into a large bowl. You should end up with about 1 cup of grated potato.
Place the potato, quinoa, zucchini, cheese, leek, breadcrumbs, egg, lemon juice, salt, and pepper in a large bowl. Toss a few times to thoroughly mix.
Scoop out ¼ cup of the zucchini batter and form it into a patty. Repeat with the remaining batter.
Heat the olive oil in a large skillet over medium heat. Add the zucchini patties and cook for about 4 minutes, or until browned and slightly crisp. Carefully flip the fritters over and continue cooking for another 3 to 4 minutes.
Serve warm with a salad.
MAKE IT AHEAD: The fritters can be made ahead through step 4, then wrapped in plastic and refrigerated for a couple of days before being cooked.
Per serving (2 fritters): Calories: 235Kcal; Fat: 14g; Carbs: 20g; Fiber: 3g; Protein: 9g

653. Loaded Sweet Potato Nacho Fries

Preparation time: 15 minutes
Cooking time: 15 minutes **Servings:** 2
Ingredients:
2 tablespoons olive oil
- ½ (19-ounce) bag frozen sweet potato fries - ¼ teaspoon kosher salt, plus 1/8 teaspoon
- ¼ teaspoon ground cumin
- 1 (15-ounce) can black beans, drained and rinsed
- 1 cup halved cherry tomatoes
- 1 cup fresh or frozen corn kernels
- 2 scallions, thinly sliced
- ½ cup grated Mexican cheeses or Cheddar cheese
- ½ cup Mexican crema or sour cream
- ¼ cup plain Greek yogurt
- 1 whole chipotle chile in adobo sauce, minced into a paste
- 1 tablespoon freshly squeezed lime juice
- 1 avocado, chopped

Directions:
Heat the oil in a cast-iron skillet or another heavy skillet over medium-high heat. Add the sweet potato fries, and season with ¼ teaspoon of salt and cumin. Sauté for about 10 minutes, stirring occasionally to prevent over-browning. If there's a lot of splattering from ice crystals, reduce the heat and cover with a lid. When the fries are tender, toss one final time, then top with the beans, tomatoes, corn, scallions, and cheese. Cover with a lid and cook for 2 to 3 minutes, or until the cheese is melted. In a small bowl, make a chipotle crema by combining the Mexican crema, yogurt, chipotle chile paste, lime juice, and remaining 1/8 teaspoon of salt. Serve the nachos topped with avocado chunks and drizzled with the chipotle crema.
FLEXITARIAN TIP: Fry ½ pound chorizo in a separate pan. Drain and add to the sweet potato fries with the black beans in step 2.
SUBSTITUTION TIP: Use ranch dressing as a quick and easy substitution for the chipotle crema.
Per serving: Calories: 724Kcal; Fat: 45g; Carbs: 66g; Fiber: 24g; Protein: 26g

654. Smashed Chickpea Avocado Toasts

Preparation time: 15 minutes
Cooking time: 0 minutes **Servings:** 4
Ingredients:
Gluten-free: Serve in a lettuce wrap
Vegan: Use vegan mayonnaise
- 1 (15-ounce) can chickpeas, drained and rinsed
- ½ cup finely diced celery
- ¼ cup thinly sliced scallions, white parts, and most of the green stalk
- 2 tablespoons mayonnaise
- 1½ tablespoons minced garlic or garlic paste - 1 tablespoon chopped fresh dill
- 2 teaspoons freshly squeezed lemon juice
- ½ teaspoon kosher salt
- 4 slices whole-wheat bread
- 2 avocados, sliced lengthwise
- 4 tablespoons extra-virgin olive oil
- Seasoned salt, to taste

Directions:
Place the chickpeas in a shallow bowl and coarsely mash them with a fork or potato masher. They shouldn't be completely smooth or completely whole. Stir in the celery, scallions, mayonnaise, garlic, dill, lemon juice, and salt to create a spread. Toast the bread. Spread 3 to 4 tablespoons of the chickpea mixture on top of each piece of toast. Arrange a couple of slices of avocado on the chickpea spread, and finish with a drizzle of olive oil and a shower of seasoned salt.
Per serving: Calories: 565Kcal; Fat: 39g; Carbs: 46g; Fiber: 15g; Protein: 13g

655. Broccoli And White Beans On Toast

Preparation time: 10 minutes
Cooking time: 20 minutes **Servings:** 6 Toasts
Ingredients:
- 2 pounds broccoli, stalks, and florets, trimmed, peeled, and chopped into ½-inch pieces
- 3 tablespoons olive oil, divided
- 1 teaspoon kosher salt, divided
- 2 teaspoons garlic paste or minced garlic
- 2 teaspoons minced fresh rosemary or ½ to ¾ teaspoon dried rosemary
- ¼ teaspoon freshly ground black pepper
- 2 (15-ounce) cans cannellini beans, drained and rinsed
- 6 slices crusty bread, such as ciabatta
- ½ cup Balsamic Roasted Tomatoes

Directions:
Preheat the oven to 425°F. Line a rimmed baking sheet with parchment paper. Toss the broccoli with 2 tablespoons of olive oil and ½ teaspoon of salt. Arrange on the baking sheet in a single layer and roast until crisp-tender, 15 to 20 minutes. While the broccoli is roasting, heat the remaining 1 tablespoon of olive oil in a medium skillet over medium heat. Add the garlic, rosemary, and pepper and sauté until fragrant, about 1 minute. Add the beans and cook, tossing occasionally, for 10 minutes. The beans should be very soft. Transfer the bean mixture to a large bowl. Smash with a fork until you have a chunky spread. Toast the bread.
Spread the mashed beans on the toasts and top with the roasted broccoli and tomatoes. Serve the toasts warm and eat with a knife and fork.
SUBSTITUTION TIP: If you don't have the Balsamic Roasted Tomatoes on hand, halve cherry tomatoes, toss in olive oil, and arrange, cut-side up, on another part of the baking sheet with the broccoli in step 1. Roast them with the broccoli, but take them out of the oven after 10 minutes, then drizzle with 1 teaspoon of balsamic vinegar.
Per serving: Calories: 268Kcal; Fat: 9g; Carbs: 39g; Fiber: 10g; Protein: 13g

656. Asparagus, Leek, And Ricotta Flatbreads

Preparation time: 10 minutes
Cooking time: 10 minutes **Servings:** 2
Ingredients:
- 2 large eggs
- 2 slices naan or other thick flatbread, such as pizza crust
- 2 tablespoons olive oil, divided
- 1 teaspoon kosher salt, divided
- ½ teaspoon freshly ground black pepper, divided
- 2 medium leeks, white and light green parts only, thinly sliced crosswise
- 1 bundle asparagus, about ½ pound when trimmed, cut into ½-inch pieces
- 1 teaspoon dried thyme or 2½ teaspoons chopped fresh thyme
- 4 tablespoons Lemon Vinaigrette, divided
- 1/3 cup part-skim ricotta cheese
- 4 teaspoons Parmesan cheese

Directions:
Preheat the oven to 400°F.
In a small pot, cover the eggs with 2 inches of cold water. Bring to a simmer and cook for 12 minutes. Drain. When the eggs are cool enough to handle, peel and coarsely chop. Set aside. Baste the naan with 1 tablespoon of olive oil and sprinkle with ¼ teaspoon each of salt and pepper. Place on a rimmed baking sheet and lightly toast in the oven for 8 to 10 minutes. While the naan is toasting, heat the remaining 1 tablespoon of olive oil in a medium skillet over medium heat. Add the leeks and asparagus, and sauté until softened, 8 to 10 minutes. Stir in the thyme and season with the remaining ¾ teaspoon of salt and ¼ teaspoon of pepper. Transfer to a medium bowl and toss with 3 tablespoons of vinaigrette. Spread the ricotta across the naan, and top with the dressed leeks and asparagus and the chopped eggs. Serve with a final drizzle of the remaining 1 tablespoon of vinaigrette, a few sprinkles of freshly ground pepper, and the Parmesan cheese.
SUBSTITUTION TIP: Use 1½ cups thinly sliced scallions instead of the leeks.
Per serving: Calories: 620Kcal; Fat: 38g; Carbs: 32g; Fiber: 4g; Protein: 19g

657. Middle Eastern Cauliflower Steaks

Preparation time: 5 minutes
Cooking time: 25 minutes **Servings:** 4
Ingredients:
- 1 large head cauliflower
- 1 tablespoon olive oil
- ½ teaspoon kosher salt
- ¼ teaspoon freshly ground black pepper
- ¼ cup Smooth and Creamy Hummus or store-bought
- 2 tablespoons Lemony Moroccan Chermoula Sauce -
- ½ cup coarsely crushed peanuts

Directions:
Preheat the oven to 425°F.
Cut off the cauliflower stems and remove all leaves at the base. Place the head cut-side down and slice it in half down the middle. Starting from that cut, begin to slice each half into ¾-inch-thick steaks—any thinner will make it difficult for them to hold together as steaks. As you reach the rounded edge, you'll have loose florets. Arrange the cauliflower steaks on a baking sheet in a single layer and place the loose florets around them. Drizzle with olive oil and sprinkle with salt and pepper. Bake until golden brown, 20 to 25 minutes. They'll be lightly browned and tender when pierced with a knife. Take them out before they become completely limp.
If you don't have the hummus or chermoula on hand, make them now. This will increase the prep time on the recipe but not the overall time, since you can prep them while the cauliflower roasts.Spread the hummus on each steak, using about 2 teaspoons for the largest steaks. Drizzle with the chermoula and top with the peanuts. The loose roasted florets can be added on top with the peanuts.
Per serving: Calories: 167Kcal; Fat: 13g; Carbs: 10g; Fiber: 4g; Protein: 6g

658. Warm Sweet Potato Noodle Salad

Preparation time: 20 minutes
Cooking time: 7 minutes **Servings:** 4
Ingredients:

- 4 tablespoons Miso Butter
- 2 tablespoons ginger paste or finely grated fresh ginger
- 1 teaspoon garlic paste or minced garlic
- 2 tablespoons olive oil
- 2 cups spiralized sweet potato noodles (from about 2 large sweet potatoes)
- 2 (5-ounce) bags baby spinach
- 1½ cups Crispy Spicy Chickpeas
- 1 bunch scallions, thinly sliced
- 1 avocado, cut into chunks
- 1 to 2 teaspoons tamari or low-sodium soy sauce

Directions:
Combine the miso butter, ginger, and garlic in a small bowl. Set aside. Heat the olive oil and 2 tablespoons of the miso butter mixture in a well-seasoned cast-iron pan or a nonstick skillet over medium heat. Add the sweet potato noodles. Use tongs to gently toss the noodles and coat them in the butter. Cook for 5 to 7 minutes, occasionally tossing the noodles. They'll start to collapse into the skillet after about 3 minutes, but should retain their shape and height. The finished noodles should be tender with a little crunch. If the skillet dries out, add another tablespoon of the miso butter mixture.
While the noodles are cooking, combine the spinach, chickpeas, scallions, and avocado in a large bowl. When the sweet potato noodles are ready, add them to the bowl along with 1 tablespoon of the miso butter mixture, if needed, and the tamari. Using your hands, toss the salad to coat the spinach with the miso butter and soy sauce. Taste and season with additional miso butter or tamari, if needed. Serve warm.
FLEXITARIAN TIP: Either grill or broil flank steak that has been well-seasoned with salt and pepper. Thinly slice across the grain and place on top of the warm salad.
Per serving: Calories: 426Kcal; Fat: 24g; Carbs: 45g; Fiber: 3g; Protein: 11g

659. Chopped Kale Salad With Apples And Pumpkin Seeds

Preparation time: 10 minutes
Cooking time: 5 minutes
Servings: 4
Ingredients:

- 2 cups green beans, halved
- 8 cups thinly sliced curly kale leaves
- 2 cups store-bought shredded broccoli slaw
- ½ cup dried cranberries
- ½ cup Roasted Pumpkin Seeds
- 2 Granny Smith apples, cored and chopped
- ¼ cup ranch dressing
- Freshly ground black pepper
- 2 tablespoons grated Parmesan cheese

Directions:
Fill a medium pot with 2 inches of water and insert a steamer basket. Put the beans in the basket, cover, and bring the water to a boil. Reduce the heat to a simmer and steam the beans until tender, about 5 minutes. Transfer the beans to a colander and immediately douse them with cold water until cool.
In a large bowl, combine the kale with the broccoli slaw, cranberries, pumpkin seeds, apples, and cooked beans. Drizzle with the dressing and toss to coat, adding more to taste. Season the salad with black pepper and serve topped with Parmesan cheese.
SUBSTITUTION TIP: For a lighter dressing, use the Lemon Vinaigrette, or do an Asian twist with the Tahini Miso Dressing.
Per serving: Calories: 291Kcal; Fat: 10g; Carbs: 46g; Fiber: 8g; Protein: 9g

660. Fresh And Hearty Quinoa Salad

Preparation time: 10 minutes
Cooking time: 5 minutes **Servings:** 2
Ingredients:

- 1 tablespoon olive oil - ¾ cup thinly sliced scallions - ½ cup cooked quinoa
- 1 (15-ounce) can black beans, drained and rinsed
- 1 teaspoon garlic paste or minced garlic
- 1 teaspoon ground cumin
- ½ cup halved red grapes
- 1 tablespoon freshly squeezed lime juice or rice vinegar
- 1 avocado, diced
- ¼ teaspoon kosher salt
- ¼ teaspoon freshly ground black pepper
- 1 tablespoon nutritional yeast

Directions:
Heat the olive oil in a medium skillet over medium heat. Add the scallions, quinoa, beans, garlic, cumin, and grapes. Cook until fragrant, about 5 minutes. Remove the skillet from the heat. Place the quinoa mixture in a serving bowl and toss with the lime juice, avocado, salt, pepper, and nutritional yeast.
Per serving: Calories: 647Kcal; Fat: 30g; Carbs: 78g; Fiber: 27g; Protein: 25g

661. Summer Tomato And Burrata Panzanella Salad

Preparation time: 15 minutes
Cooking time: 15 minutes
Servings: 2
Ingredients:

- 2 tablespoons balsamic vinegar
- 1¼ teaspoons kosher salt, divided
- ½ teaspoon freshly ground black pepper, plus 1/8 teaspoon
- 6 tablespoons olive oil, divided
- 4 cups chopped tomatoes
- 1 (15-ounce) can chickpeas, drained and rinsed
- ½ sweet onion, thinly sliced
- 2 tablespoons thinly sliced fresh basil
- 3 (1-inch-thick) slices crusty bread, such as ciabatta

- 1 teaspoon garlic paste or minced garlic
- 2 balls burrata mozzarella cheese, torn into 4 to 6 pieces

Directions:
Preheat the oven to 400°F. Line a rimmed baking sheet with parchment paper. In a large bowl, whisk together the vinegar, 1 teaspoon of salt, ½ teaspoon of black pepper, and 3 tablespoons of olive oil. Add the tomatoes, chickpeas, onion, and basil, and toss to evenly coat. Set aside. Tear or cut the bread into large pieces, about 2 inches across. Add the remaining 3 tablespoons of olive oil to a large bowl and stir in the garlic.

Toss the bread with garlic and olive oil and arrange it in a single layer on the baking sheet. Season the bread with the remaining ¼ teaspoon of salt and the remaining 1/8 teaspoon of pepper. Bake for 10 minutes. Turn the bread pieces over and bake for another 5 minutes.

To serve, place the pieces of burrata on a serving plate. Toss the toasted bread with the tomato salad and pour everything over the burrata, including any residual dressing.

Per serving: Calories: 935Kcal; Fat: 55g; Carbs: 88g; Fiber: 18g; Protein: 29g

662. Lebanese Lentil Salad

Preparation time: 15 minutes
Cooking time: 15 minutes
Servings: 4
Ingredients:

- 3 cups vegetable broth or water
- 1 cup French green lentils
- 1 teaspoon kosher salt, divided
- 3 tablespoons sherry vinegar
- 1 teaspoon Dijon mustard
- 2 tablespoons olive oil
- 3 scallions, thinly sliced
- 2 cups peeled and diced cucumber
- 1½ cups halved cherry tomatoes
- ½ cup crumbled feta cheese
- ¼ cup fresh mint leaves, thinly sliced
- ¼ teaspoon freshly ground black pepper

Directions:
Bring the broth to a boil in a medium pot. Add the lentils and ½ teaspoon of salt. Reduce the heat to a simmer, cover, and simmer for 15 to 20 minutes, or until the lentils are tender and the liquid is absorbed. If there is any liquid remaining, drain it. In a large bowl, whisk together the sherry vinegar and Dijon mustard. Whisk in the olive oil until emulsified. Add the cooked lentils, scallions, cucumber, tomatoes, feta cheese, and mint, and toss to coat. Season to taste with the remaining ½ teaspoon of salt and pepper. Serve at room temperature. FLEXITARIAN TIP: This salad is great with lamb chops. Season the chops on both sides with salt and pepper, and sauté in a little olive oil over medium-high heat. Cook for about 3 minutes on each side for medium-rare, depending on the thickness of the chops.

Per serving: Calories: 337Kcal; Fat: 13g; Carbs: 36g; Fiber: 17g; Protein: 20g

663. Chickpea Niçoise Salad

Preparation time: 10 minutes
Cooking time: 17 minutes **Servings:** 4
Ingredients:

- ½ cup Lemony Moroccan Chermoula Sauce
- 3 large eggs
- 1 tablespoon kosher salt
- 1 pound small red or fingerling potatoes
- ½ pound green beans, trimmed
- 1 head Bibb lettuce
- 2 (15-ounce) cans chickpeas, drained and rinsed
- 1 (6-ounce) jar marinated artichokes, drained
- ½ cup halved cherry tomatoes
- ½ cup Niçoise or Kalamata olives

Directions:
Put the chermoula sauce in a large bowl and set it aside. Put the eggs in a small pot and cover them with at least 1 inch of water. Bring to a low boil over medium-high heat. Reduce the heat to medium to maintain a simmer. Simmer the eggs for 1 minutes, then remove them from the pot. When the eggs are cool enough to handle, peel them. While the eggs are cooking, fill a medium pot with 2 inches of water and salt. Insert steamer basket in the pot, and put the potatoes in the basket. Bring to a boil over medium-high heat. Cover with a lid and reduce the heat to medium-low to maintain a steady low boil. Cook until the potatoes are tender, 10 to 12 minutes, depending on the size of the potatoes. Using tongs, transfer the potatoes to the bowl of chermoula, leaving the steamer basket and water in the pot. Toss the warm potatoes to coat in the sauce. Add the beans to the steamer basket. Cover and simmer until tender, about 5 minutes. Transfer the beans to the bowl with the potatoes and sauce, and toss to coat. Spread the lettuce leaves on a serving plate. Arrange the chickpeas, artichokes, cherry tomatoes, and olives on the lettuce, leaving enough room for the eggs, potatoes, and beans. Slice the eggs in half lengthwise and place on the lettuce. Remove the potatoes and beans from the chermoula, arrange on the lettuce, and drizzle the remaining chermoula over the entire salad. Serve at room temperature.

INGREDIENT TIP: If you have extra time, add crispy baked tofu to the recipe. Just follow the instructions here.

FLEXITARIAN TIP: For my nonvegetarian guests, I add canned albacore tuna drizzled with olive oil and lemon juice and serve it all with small toasted slices of French bread for crostini. Sliced cheeses, crackers, and fancy spreads complete the table.

SUBSTITUTION TIP: In place of the chermoula, you can substitute a store-bought aioli or vinaigrette or make the Easy Roasted Red Pepper Aioli.

Per serving: Calories: 572Kcal; Fat: 31g; Carbs: 63g; Fiber: 18g; Protein: 21g

664. Grilled Mediterranean Salad With Quinoa

Preparation time: 15 minutes
Cooking time: 12 minutes **Servings:** 4
Ingredients:

- 1 small eggplant, peeled and sliced into ½-inch rounds

- 3 tablespoons olive oil, divided
- 1 medium zucchini, sliced into long strips
- 2 yellow summer squash, sliced into long strips
- 2 bell peppers, any color, sliced into thick strips
- 4 scallions
- 1½ teaspoons kosher salt, divided
- 1 teaspoon freshly ground black pepper, divided
- 2 cups cooked quinoa
- ¼ cup Lemon Vinaigrette
- ¼ cup thinly sliced basil

Directions:
Preheat the grill.
Baste both sides of the eggplant slices with a little olive oil, and toss the strips of zucchini, summer squash, bell peppers, and scallions with the remaining oil. Season with salt and pepper. Arrange the vegetables on a vegetable grill pan designed for a gas grill, with the eggplant and bell peppers on one side of the pan and the zucchini, summer squash, and scallions on the other. Adjust the flame to medium heat. Grill for 4 minutes, then turn over the faster-cooking squash and scallions. Grill for another 2 minutes, then flip over the eggplant and bell peppers. Continue to grill the vegetables until they're tender and slightly charred. This might take another 2 or 3 minutes for the zucchini, squash, and scallions and 4 to 6 minutes for the eggplant and peppers. Transfer to a cutting board. Slice the eggplant, zucchini, summer squash, bell peppers, and scallions into bite-size chunks and place in a large bowl. Add the quinoa, drizzle with the vinaigrette, and toss to coat.
Serve topped with basil.
INGREDIENT TIP: If you make a dip or sauce with eggplant, soak the eggplant slices in milk for 30 minutes before preparing the recipe. This not only tempers the bitterness; it also makes the end result beautifully creamy.
FLEXITARIAN TIP: Season flank steak with salt and pepper, and grill alongside the vegetables. Thinly slice across the grain and serve with the salad.
COOKING TIP: If you don't have a grill, this salad can be made on the stove top using a grill pan, griddle, or large skillet. Depending on the size of your pan, you may need to sauté each ingredient separately in batches. The other option is to roast the veggies using two sheet pans. One sheet pan holds the zucchini, squash, and scallions, and the other one holds the eggplant and peppers. Roast at 400°F until tender, about 15 minutes for the zucchini, squash, and scallions, and 30 minutes for the eggplant and peppers. **Per serving:** Calories: 395Kcal; Fat: 19g; Carbs: 50g; Fiber: 10g; Protein: 10g

665. Tortilla Soup

Preparation time: 10 minutes
Cooking time: 15 minutes **Servings:** 4
Ingredients:

- 1 tablespoon olive oil
- 1 tablespoon garlic paste or minced garlic
- 1 teaspoon chili powder
- 2 (15-ounce) cans black beans, drained and rinsed
- 2 cups vegetable broth or Better Than Bouillon No Chicken Base
- 1 cup fresh or frozen corn kernels

Plant based cookbook for beginners

- 1 (15-ounce) jar salsa
- Kosher salt (optional)
- Freshly ground black pepper (optional)
- ½ cup shredded mix of Mexican cheeses, for garnish
- ½ cup thinly sliced scallions, for garnish
- ½ avocado, diced, for garnish
- 1 cup crumbled tortilla chips, for garnish
- Lime wedges, for serving

Directions:
In a large, heavy-bottomed pot, warm the olive oil over medium heat. Add the garlic and chili powder and cook until very fragrant, about 1 minute. Stir in the black beans, broth, corn, and salsa. Bring to a simmer and cook for 10 minutes. Season to taste with salt and pepper (if using). Serve garnished with cheese, scallions, avocado, and tortilla chips, with lime wedges on the side.
FLEXITARIAN TIP: Purchase a pre-roasted chicken and dice the breast meat. Stir into the soup in step 2. **Per serving:** Calories: 369Kcal; Fat: 14g; Carbs: 48g; Fiber: 15g; Protein: 20g

666. Cheesy Broccoli Soup

Preparation time: 15 minutes
Cooking time: 15 minutes **Servings:** 4
Ingredients:

- 2 tablespoons olive oil - 1 yellow onion, diced
- 1-pound broccoli, cut into 1-inch florets and stems thinly sliced
- 2 large apples, peeled, cored, and coarsely chopped
- 1 teaspoon kosher salt
- ½ teaspoon freshly ground black pepper
- 3 cups vegetable broth
- ½ cup shredded Cheddar cheese, plus more for serving
- Apple cider vinegar or freshly squeezed lemon juice (optional, to taste)

Directions:
Heat the olive oil in a large, heavy-bottomed pot over medium-high heat. Add the onion and sauté until softened, about 5 minutes. Add the broccoli, apples, salt, pepper, and broth. Bring to a rapid boil, cover, reduce the heat to low, and simmer for 10 to 15 minutes, or until the broccoli is tender. Use an immersion blender to purée the soup. Alternatively, transfer the soup to a blender (in batches, if necessary) and purée, then return the soup to the pot.
Stir in the cheese and season to taste with additional salt and pepper, if needed. Add a little apple cider vinegar to sharpen the flavors (if desired). Serve hot with additional cheese for the cheese lovers in your family and crusty bread if gluten isn't something you're avoiding. **Per serving:** Calories: 238Kcal; Fat: 13g; Carbs: 28g; Fiber: 7g; Protein: 7g

667. Butternut Squash Soup With Apple Cider

Preparation time: 10 minutes
Cooking time: 20 minutes **Servings:** 6
Ingredients:

- 2 tablespoons olive oil

- 2 cups diced yellow onion
- 10 cups (1-inch) cubed butternut squash
- 4 cups vegetable broth
- 1 cup apple cider
- 1 teaspoon kosher salt

Optional Toppings
- ¼ cup crème fraîche
- 2 tablespoons sliced almonds
- 1 tablespoon salted sunflower seeds
- 1 tablespoon chopped fresh parsley
- 2 tablespoons Crispy Spicy Chickpeas

Directions:
In a large, heavy-bottomed pot, heat the oil over medium-high heat. Add the onion and sauté until it begins to soften, about 5 minutes. Add the squash, broth, cider, and salt. Bring to a simmer and cook until the squash becomes tender, about 15 minutes.
Use an immersion blender to purée into a smooth, silky soup. Alternatively, pour the soup into a blender (in batches, if necessary) and purée it. Serve in bowls with a dollop of crème fraîche, if using.
Garnish with a sprinkling of one or more of the optional toppings, if desired.
Per serving: Calories: 151Kcal; Fat: 5g; Carbs: 27g; Fiber: 5g; Protein: 2g

668. Black Bean And Quinoa Wrap

Preparation time: 10 minutes **Cooking time:** 15 minutes
Servings: 4
Ingredients:
- ⅔ cup cooked quinoa
- 1 (15-ounce) can black beans, drained and rinsed - 1 teaspoon garlic powder
- 2/3 cup quartered cherry tomatoes
- 2 tablespoons freshly squeezed lime juice
- ½ teaspoon kosher salt
- ¼ cup Smooth and Creamy Hummus or store-bought - 4 (8-inch) flour tortillas
- ½ cup baby spinach leaves

Directions:
In a medium pot, combine the cooked quinoa with the beans and garlic powder and warm through over medium-low heat. Remove the pot from the heat and stir in the tomatoes, lime juice, and salt. Spread the hummus evenly on each tortilla, lightly cover with spinach leaves, and spoon about 1/3 cup of the quinoa mixture in a heaped row, slightly off center, across the tortilla. Fold one side of the tortilla over the quinoa and roll up fairly tightly. Use a toothpick to hold it closed or wrap it in aluminum foil.
Per serving: Calories: 342Kcal; Fat: 6g; Carbs: 58g; Fiber: 11g; Protein: 15g

669. Spicy Chickpea Gyros

Preparation time: 15 minutes **Cooking time:** 0 minutes
Servings: 4
Ingredients:
- 2 slices naan bread, halved, or whole pita rounds - 1 cup Tzatziki
- 1½ cups Crispy Spicy Chickpeas
- 4 Bibb lettuce leaves- 1 large tomato, chopped
- ¼ red onion, thinly sliced

Directions:
Lay the halved naan slices on a flat workspace and divide the tzatziki among them, spreading it across the surface. Layer the chickpeas, lettuce, tomato, and red onion on top of each naan half. Fold the naan in half around the filling, and serve with extra tzatziki.
FLEXITARIAN TIP: Sauté a few lamb loin chops in a medium skillet and slice off the meat to add to the gyro with, or instead of, the chickpeas. Depending on the thickness of the chops, cooking for 3 minutes on each side over medium-high heat will result in medium-rare meat. Other cuts of lamb are equally suitable but take longer to cook. **Per serving:** Calories: 120Kcal; Fat: 5g; Carbs: 16g; Fiber: 3g; Protein: 5g

CHAPTER 28:
Easiest Recipes

670. Blueberry and Banana Smoothie
Preparation time: 10 minutes
Cooking time: 0 minutes **Servings:** 4
Ingredients:
- 1 cup of blueberries, frozen
- 1 whole banana - ½ a cup of almond milk
- 1 tablespoon of almond butter
- Water as needed

Directions:
Add the listed ingredients to your blender and blend well until you have a smoothie-like texture Chill and serve Enjoy!
Per serving: Calories: 321; Fat: 11g; Carbs: 55g; Protein: 5g

671. Lemon and Rosemary Iced Tea
Preparation time: 1 minute
Cooking time: 5 minutes **Servings:** 4
Ingredients:
- 4 cups of water - 4 earl grey tea bags
- ¼ cup of sugar - 2 lemons
- 1 sprig rosemary

Directions:
Peel two lemons and keep them on the side Take a medium-sized saucepan and place it over medium heat, add water, sugar, and lemon peels Bring the mix to a boil Remove from heat and add rosemary and tea into the mix Cover saucepan and steep for 5 minutes Add the juice of peeled lemons to the mixture Strain and chill Enjoy!
Per serving: Calories: 88; Fat: 2g; Carbs: 14g; Protein: 2g

672. Lavender and Mint Ice Tea
Preparation time: 1 minute
Cooking time: 5 minutes **Servings:** 4
Ingredients:
- 8 cups of water - ¼ cup dried lavender buds
- ¼ cup mint

Directions:
Add mint and lavender to the pot, keep it on the side
Add in 8 cups of boiling water to the pot, sweeten as needed
Cover and let it steep for 10 minutes
Strain and chill

Serve and enjoy!
Per serving: Calories: 120; Fat: 0g; Carbs: 8g; Protein: 1g

673. Thai Iced Tea
Preparation time: 1 minute
Cooking time: 5 minutes **Servings:** 4
Ingredients:
- 4 cups of water
- 1 can of light coconut milk
- ¼ cup maple syrup
- ¼ cup muscovado sugar
- 1 teaspoon vanilla sugar
- 1 teaspoon vanilla extract

Directions:
Take a large-sized saucepan and place it over medium heat, bring water to a boil Remove heat and add tea, let it steep for 5 minutes Strain the tea into a bowl and add maple syrup and vanilla extract, whisk well
Set it in the fridge and let it chill Serve as needed with a topping of coconut milk Enjoy!
Per serving: Calories: 100; Fat: 3g; Carbs: 14g; Protein: 3g

674. Healthy Coffee Smoothie
Preparation time: 10 minutes
Cooking time: 0 minutes **Servings:** 1
Ingredients:
- 1 tablespoon chia seeds
- 2 cups strongly brewed coffee, chilled
- 1-ounce Macadamia Nuts
- 1-2 packets Stevia, optional
- 1 tablespoon MCT oil

Directions:
Add all the listed ingredients to a blender. Blend on high until smooth and creamy. Enjoy your smoothie.
Per serving: Calories: 395; Fat: 39g; Carbs: 11g; Protein: 5.2g

675. Berry and Strawberry Smoothie
Preparation time: 10 minutes
Cooking time: 0 minutes **Servings:** 3
Ingredients:
- 1 cup crushed ice
- ½ cup unsweetened almond milk
- ½ cup frozen raspberries
- ½ cup strawberries
- 1 tablespoon coconut oil
- ½ teaspoon fresh vanilla bean extract

Directions:
Add the listed ingredients to a blender
Blend on low until everything is incorporated well
Increase to high speed and blend until smooth
Add a few drops of liquid stevia for extra taste
Divide into 3 servings and enjoy!
Per serving: Calories: 232; Fat: 22g; Carbs: 16g; Protein: 3g

676. Mint Flavored Pear Smoothie
Preparation time: 5 minutes
Cooking time: 0 minutes **Servings:** 2
Ingredients:
- ¼ honeydew - 2 green pears, ripe

Amanda Kale

- ½ an apple, juiced - 1 cup of ice cubes
- ½ cup fresh mint leaves

Directions:
Add the listed ingredients to your blender and blend until smooth Serve chilled!
Per serving: Calories: 200; Fat: 10g; Carbs: 14g; Protein: 2g

677. Epic Pineapple Juice
Preparation time: 10 minutes
Cooking time: 0 minutes **Servings:** 4
Ingredients:
- 4 cups of fresh pineapple, chopped
- 1 pinch of salt
- 1 and a ½ cups of water

Directions:
Add the listed ingredients to your blender and blend well until you have a smoothie-like texture Chill and serve Enjoy!
Per serving: Calories: 82; Fat: 0.2g; Carbs: 21g; Protein: 21g

678. Chilled Watermelon Smoothie
Preparation time: 5 minutes
Cooking time: 0 minutes **Servings:** 2
Ingredients:
- 1 cup watermelon chunks
- ½ cup of coconut water
- 1 and ½ teaspoons of lime juice
- 4 mint leaves - 4 ice cubes

Directions:
Add the listed ingredients to your blender and blend until smooth Serve chilled!
Per serving: Calories: 200; Fat: 10g; Carbs: 14g; Protein: 2g

679. The Mocha Shake
Preparation time: 10 minutes
Cooking time: 0 minutes
Servings: 1
Ingredients:
- 1 cup whole almond milk
- 2 tablespoons cocoa powder
- 2 pack stevia
- 1 cup brewed coffee, chilled
- 1 tablespoon coconut oil

Directions:
Add listed ingredients to a blender
Blend until you have a smooth and creamy texture
Serve chilled and enjoy!
Per serving: Calories: 293; Fat: 23g; Carbs: 19g; Protein: 10g

680. Cinnamon Chiller
Preparation time: 10 minutes
Cooking time: 0 minutes
Servings: 1
Ingredients:
- 1 cup unsweetened almond milk
- 2 tablespoons vanilla protein powder
- ½ teaspoon cinnamon
- ¼ teaspoon vanilla extract
- 1 tablespoon chia seeds
- 1 cup ice cubes

Directions:
Add listed ingredients to a blender
Blend until you have a smooth and creamy texture
Serve chilled and enjoy!
Per serving: Calories: 145; Fat: 4g; Carbs: 1.6g; Protein: 0.6g

681. Sensational Strawberry Medley
Preparation time: 5 minutes
Cooking time: 0 minutes **Servings:** 2
Ingredients:
- 1-2 handful baby greens
- 3 medium kale leaves
- 5-8 mint leaves
- 1-inch piece ginger, peeled
- 1 avocado
- 1 cup strawberries
- 6-8 ounces coconut water + 6-8 ounces filtered water
- Fresh juice of one lime
- 1-2 teaspoon olive oil

Directions:
Add all the listed ingredients to your blender Blend until smooth Add a few ice cubes and serve the smoothie Enjoy!
Per serving: Calories: 200; Fat: 10g; Carbs: 14g; Protein: 2g

682. Alkaline Strawberry Smoothie
Preparation time: 5 minutes
Cooking time: 0 minutes **Servings:** 2
Ingredients:
- ½ cup of organic strawberries/blueberries
- Half a banana
- 2 cups of coconut water
- ½ inch ginger
- Juice of 2 grapefruits

Directions:
Add all the listed ingredients to your blender
Blend until smooth Add a few ice cubes and serve the smoothie Enjoy! **Per serving:** Calories: 200; Fat: 10g; Carbs: 14g; Protein: 2g

683. Awesome Orange Smoothie
Preparation time: 5 minutes
Cooking time: 0 minutes **Servings:** 2
Ingredients:
- 1 orange, peeled - ¼ cup fat-free yogurt
- 2 tablespoons frozen orange juice concentrate
- ¼ teaspoon vanilla extract - 4 ice cubes

Directions:
Add the listed ingredients to your blender and blend until smooth Serve chilled! **Per serving:** Calories: 200; Fat: 10g; Carbs: 14g; Protein: 2g

684. Pineapple and Coconut Milk Smoothie

Preparation time: 5 minutes **Cooking time:** 0 minutes
Servings: 2
Ingredients:
- ¼ cup pineapple, frozen
- ¾ cup of coconut milk

Directions:
Add the listed ingredients to a blender and blend well on high
Once the mixture is smooth, pour the smoothie into a tall glass and serve Chill and enjoy it!
Per serving: Calories: 200; Fat: 10g; Carbs: 14g; Protein: 2g

685. Sweet Potato and Almond Smoothie

Preparation time: 5 minutes
Cooking time: 0 minutes **Servings:** 2
Ingredients:
- 1 cup sweet potato, chopped
- 1 cup almond milk - ¼ teaspoon nutmeg
- ¼ teaspoon ground cinnamon
- 1 teaspoon flaxseed - 1 small avocado, cubed
- Few spinach leaves, torn

Toppings
- A handful of crushed almonds
- A handful of crushed cashews
- 3 tablespoons orange juice

Directions:
Blend all the ingredients until smooth
Add a few ice cubes to make it chilled
Add your desired toppings Enjoy!
Per serving: Calories: 200; Fat: 10g; Carbs: 14g; Protein: 2g

686. The Sunshine Offering

Preparation time: 5 minutes
Cooking time: 0 minutes **Servings:** 2
Ingredients:
- 2 cups of fresh spinach
- 1 and ½ cups of almond milk
- ½ cup of coconut water
- 3 cups of fresh pineapple
- 2 tablespoons of coconut unsweetened flakes

Directions:
Add all the listed ingredients to your blender
Blend until smooth Add a few ice cubes and serve the smoothie Enjoy!
Per serving: Calories: 200; Fat: 10g; Carbs: 14g; Protein: 2g

687. Strawberry and Rhubarb Smoothie

Preparation time: 5 minutes
Cooking time: 3 minutes **Servings:** 1
Ingredients:
- 1 rhubarb stalk, chopped
- 1 cup fresh strawberries, sliced
- ½ cup plain Greek yogurt
- Pinch of ground cinnamon
- 3 ice cubes

Directions:
Take a small saucepan and fill it with water over high heat Bring to boil and add rhubarb, boil for 3 minutes Drain and transfer to a blender Add strawberries, honey, yogurt, and cinnamon and pulse mixture until smooth Add ice cubes and blend until thick and has no lumps Pour into a glass and enjoy chilled
Per serving: Calories: 295; Fat: 8g; Carbs: 56g; Protein: 6g

688. Vanilla Hemp Drink

Preparation time: 10 minutes
Cooking time: 0 minutes **Servings:** 1
Ingredients:
- 1 cup of water
- 1 cup unsweetened hemp almond milk, vanilla
- 1 and ½ tablespoons coconut oil, unrefined
- ½ cup frozen blueberries, mixed
- 4 cup leafy greens, kale, and spinach
- 1 tablespoon flaxseed
- 1 tablespoon almond butter

Directions:
Add listed ingredients to a blender
Blend until you have a smooth and creamy texture
Serve chilled and enjoy! **Per serving:** Calories: 250; Fat: 20g; Carbs: 10g; Protein: 7g

689. Minty Cherry Smoothie

Preparation time: 5 minutes
Cooking time: 0 minutes **Servings:** 2
Ingredients:
- ¾ cup cherries
- 1 teaspoon mint
- ½ cup almond milk - ½ cup kale
- ½ teaspoon fresh vanilla

Directions:
Wash and cut cherries Take the pits out
Add cherries to the blender Pour almond milk
Wash the mint and put two sprigs in blender
Separate the leaves of kale from stems Put kale in a blender
Press vanilla bean and cut lengthwise with a knife
Scoop out your desired amount of vanilla and add to the blender Blend until smooth 1Serve chilled and enjoy!
Per serving: Calories: 200; Fat: 10g; Carbs: 14g; Protein: 2g

690. Hot Pink Smoothie

Preparation time: 5 minutes
Cooking time: 0 minutes - **Servings:** 1
Ingredients:
- 1 clementine, peeled, segmented
- 1/2 frozen banana
- 1 small beet, peeled, chopped
- 1/8 teaspoon sea salt
- 1/2 cup raspberries
- 1 tablespoon chia seeds
- 1/4 teaspoon vanilla extract, unsweetened
- 2 tablespoons almond butter

- 1 cup almond milk, unsweetened

Directions:
Place all the ingredients in the order in a food processor or blender and then pulse for 2 to 3 minutes at high speed until smooth.
Pour the smoothie into a glass and then serve.
Per serving: Calories: 278; Fat: 5.6g; Carbs: 37.2g; Fiber: 13.2g; Protein: 6.2g

691. Maca Caramel Frap

Preparation time: 5 minutes
Cooking time: 0 minutes **Servings:** 4
Ingredients:
- 1/2 of frozen banana, sliced
- 1/4 cup cashews, soaked for 4 hours
- 2 Medjool dates, pitted
- 1 teaspoon maca powder
- 1/8 teaspoon sea salt
- 1/2 teaspoon vanilla extract, unsweetened
- 1/4 cup almond milk, unsweetened
- 1/4 cup cold coffee, brewed

Directions:
Place all the ingredients in the order in a food processor or blender and then pulse for 2 to 3 minutes at high speed until smooth.
Pour the smoothie into a glass and then serve.
Per serving: Calories: 450; Fat: 170g; Carbs: 64g; Fiber: 7g; Protein: 0g

692. Peanut Butter Vanilla Green Shake

Preparation time: 5 minutes
Cooking time: 0 minutes **Servings:** 1
Ingredients:
- 1 teaspoon flax seeds
- 1 frozen banana
- 1 cup baby spinach
- 1/8 teaspoon sea salt
- 1/2 teaspoon ground cinnamon
- 1/4 teaspoon vanilla extract, unsweetened
- 2 tablespoons peanut butter, unsweetened
- 1/4 cup ice
- 1 cup coconut milk, unsweetened

Directions:
Place all the ingredients in the order in a food processor or blender and then pulse for 2 to 3 minutes at high speed until smooth. Pour the smoothie into a glass and then serve.
Per serving: Calories: 298; Fat: 11g; Carbs: 32g; Fiber: 8g; Protein: 24g

693. Green Colada

Preparation time: 5 minutes
Cooking time: 0 minutes **Servings:** 1
Ingredients:
- 1/2 cup frozen pineapple chunks
- 1/2 banana
- 1/2 teaspoon spirulina powder
- 1/4 teaspoon vanilla extract, unsweetened
- 1 cup of coconut milk

Directions:
Place all the ingredients in the order in a food processor or blender and then pulse for 2 to 3 minutes at high speed until smooth. Pour the smoothie into a glass and then serve.
Per serving: Calories: 127; Fat: 3g; Carbs: 25g; Fiber: 4g; Protein: 3g

694. Chocolate Oat Smoothie

Preparation time: 5 minutes
Cooking time: 0 minutes **Servings:** 1
Ingredients:
- ¼ cup rolled oats
- 1 ½ tablespoon cocoa powder, unsweetened
- 1 teaspoon flax seeds - 1 large frozen banana
- 1/8 teaspoon sea salt
- 1/8 teaspoon cinnamon
- ¼ teaspoon vanilla extract, unsweetened
- 2 tablespoons almond butter
- 1 cup coconut milk, unsweetened

Directions:
Place all the ingredients in the order in a food processor or blender and then pulse for 2 to 3 minutes at high speed until smooth. Pour the smoothie into a glass and then serve.
Per serving: Calories: 262; Fat: 7.3g; Carbs: 50.4g; Fiber: 9.6g; Protein: 8.1g

695. Peach Crumble Shake

Preparation time: 5 minutes
Cooking time: 0 minutes
Servings: 1
Ingredients:
- 1 tablespoon chia seeds
- ¼ cup rolled oats
- 2 peaches, pitted, sliced
- ¾ teaspoon ground cinnamon
- 1 Medjool date, pitted
- ½ teaspoon vanilla extract, unsweetened
- 2 tablespoons lemon juice - ½ cup of water
- 1 tablespoon coconut butter
- 1 cup coconut milk, unsweetened

Directions:
Place all the ingredients in the order in a food processor or blender and then pulse for 2 to 3 minutes at high speed until smooth. Pour the smoothie into a glass and then serve.
Per serving: Calories: 270; Fat: 4g; Carbs: 28g; Fiber: 3g; Protein: 25g

696. Wild Ginger Green Smoothie

Preparation time: 5 minutes
Cooking time: 0 minutes
Servings: 1
Ingredients:
- 1/2 cup pineapple chunks, frozen
- 1/2 cup chopped kale
- 1/2 frozen banana
- 1 tablespoon lime juice

- 2 inches ginger, peeled, chopped
- 1/2 cup coconut milk, unsweetened
- 1/2 cup coconut water

Directions:
Place all the ingredients in the order in a food processor or blender and then pulse for 2 to 3 minutes at high speed until smooth. Pour the smoothie into a glass and then serve.
Per serving: Calories: 331; Fat: 14g; Carbs: 40g; Fiber: 9g; Protein: 16g

697. Berry Beet Velvet Smoothie

Preparation time: 5 minutes
Cooking time: 0 minutes **Servings:** 1
Ingredients:
- 1/2 of frozen banana
- 1 cup mixed red berries
- 1 Medjool date, pitted
- 1 small beet, peeled, chopped
- 1 tablespoon cacao powder
- 1 teaspoon chia seeds
- 1/4 teaspoon vanilla extract, unsweetened
- 1/2 teaspoon lemon juice
- 2 teaspoons coconut butter
- 1 cup coconut milk, unsweetened

Directions:
Place all the ingredients in the order in a food processor or blender and then pulse for 2 to 3 minutes at high speed until smooth. Pour the smoothie into a glass and then serve.
Per serving: Calories: 234; Fat: 5g; Carbs: 42g; Fiber: 7g; Protein: 11g

698. Spiced Strawberry Smoothie

Preparation time: 5 minutes
Cooking time: 0 minutes **Servings:** 1
Ingredients:
- 1 tablespoon goji berries, soaked
- 1 cup strawberries
- 1/8 teaspoon sea salt
- 1 frozen banana
- 1 Medjool date, pitted
- 1 scoop vanilla-flavored whey protein
- 2 tablespoons lemon juice
- ¼ teaspoon ground ginger
- ½ teaspoon ground cinnamon
- 1 tablespoon almond butter
- 1 cup almond milk, unsweetened

Directions:
Place all the ingredients in the order in a food processor or blender and then pulse for 2 to 3 minutes at high speed until smooth. Pour the smoothie into a glass and then serve.
Per serving: Calories: 182; Fat: 1.3g; Carbs: 34g; Fiber: 0.7g; Protein: 6.4g

699. Banana Bread Shake With Walnut Milk

Preparation time: 5 minutes
Cooking time: 0 minutes **Servings:** 2
Ingredients:
- 2 cups sliced frozen bananas
- 3 cups walnut milk
- 1/8 teaspoon grated nutmeg
- 1 tablespoon maple syrup
- 1 teaspoon ground cinnamon
- 1/2 teaspoon vanilla extract, unsweetened
- 2 tablespoons cacao nibs

Directions:
Place all the ingredients in the order in a food processor or blender and then pulse for 2 to 3 minutes at high speed until smooth.
Pour the smoothie into two glasses and then serve.
Per serving: Calories: 339.8; Fat: 19g; Carbs: 39g; Fiber: 1g; Protein: 4.3g

700. Double Chocolate Hazelnut Espresso Shake

Preparation time: 5 minutes
Cooking time: 0 minutes
Servings: 1
Ingredients:
- 1 frozen banana, sliced
- 1/4 cup roasted hazelnuts
- 4 Medjool dates, pitted, soaked
- 2 tablespoons cacao nibs, unsweetened
- 1 1/2 tablespoons cacao powder, unsweetened
- 1/8 teaspoon sea salt
- 1 teaspoon vanilla extract, unsweetened
- 1 cup almond milk, unsweetened
- 1/2 cup ice
- 4 ounces espresso, chilled

Directions:
Place all the ingredients in the order in a food processor or blender and then pulse for 2 to 3 minutes at high speed until smooth.
Pour the smoothie into a glass and then serve.
Per serving: Calories: 210; Fat: 5g; Carbs: 27g; Fiber: 0.2g; Protein: 16.8g

701. Strawberry, Banana, and Coconut Shake

Preparation time: 5 minutes
Cooking time: 0 minutes **Servings:** 1
Ingredients:
- 1 tablespoon coconut flakes
- 1 1/2 cups frozen banana slices
- 8 strawberries, sliced
- 1/2 cup coconut milk, unsweetened
- 1/4 cup strawberries for topping

Directions:
Place all the ingredients in the order in a food processor or blender, except for topping, and then pulse for 2 to 3 minutes at high speed until smooth.
Pour the smoothie into a glass and then serve.
Per serving: Calories: 335; Fat: 5g; Carbs: 75g; Fiber: 9g; Protein: 4g

702. Tropical Vibes Green Smoothie
Preparation time: 5 minutes
Cooking time: 0 minutes **Servings:** 1
Ingredients:
- 2 stalks of kale, ripped
- 1 frozen banana
- 1 mango, peeled, pitted, chopped
- 1/8 teaspoon sea salt
- ¼ cup of coconut yogurt
- ½ teaspoon vanilla extract, unsweetened
- 1 tablespoon ginger juice
- ½ cup of orange juice
- ½ cup of coconut water

Directions:
Place all the ingredients in the order in a food processor or blender and then pulse for 2 to 3 minutes at high speed until smooth.
Pour the smoothie into a glass and then serve.
Per serving: Calories: 197.5; Fat: 1.3g; Carbs: 30g; Fiber: 4.8g; Protein: 16.3g

703. Peanut Butter and Mocha Smoothie
Preparation time: 5 minutes
Cooking time: 0 minutes **Servings:** 1
Ingredients:
- 1 frozen banana, chopped
- 1 scoop of chocolate protein powder
- 2 tablespoons rolled oats
- 1/8 teaspoon sea salt
- ¼ teaspoon vanilla extract, unsweetened
- 1 teaspoon cocoa powder, unsweetened
- 2 tablespoons peanut butter
- 1 shot of espresso
- ½ cup almond milk, unsweetened

Directions:
Place all the ingredients in the order in a food processor or blender and then pulse for 2 to 3 minutes at high speed until smooth. Pour the smoothie into a glass and then serve.
Per serving: Calories: 380; Fat: 14g; Carbs: 29g; Fiber: 4g; Protein: 38g

704. Tahini Shake with Cinnamon and Lime
Preparation time: 5 minutes
Cooking time: 0 minutes
Servings: 1
Ingredients:
- 1 frozen banana
- 2 tablespoons tahini
- 1/8 teaspoon sea salt
- ¾ teaspoon ground cinnamon
- ¼ teaspoon vanilla extract, unsweetened
- 2 teaspoons lime juice
- 1 cup almond milk, unsweetened

Directions:
Place all the ingredients in the order in a food processor or blender and then pulse for 2 to 3 minutes at high speed until smooth.
Pour the smoothie into a glass and then serve.
Per serving: Calories: 225; Fat: 15g; Carbs: 22g; Fiber: 8g; Protein: 6g

705. Fig Oatmeal Bake
Preparation time: 5 minutes
Cooking time: 15 minutes
Servings: 4
Ingredients:
- 2 fresh figs, sliced
- 5 dried figs, chopped
- 4 tablespoons chopped walnuts
- 1 ½ cups oats
- 1 teaspoon cinnamon
- 2 tablespoons agave syrup
- 1 teaspoon baking powder
- 2 tablespoons unsalted butter, melted
- 3 tablespoons flaxseed egg
- ¾ cup of coconut milk

Directions:
Switch on the oven, then set it to 350 degrees F and let it preheat.
Meanwhile, take a bowl, place all the ingredients in it, except for fresh figs, and stir until combined.
Take an 8-inch square pan, line it with a parchment sheet, spoon in the prepared mixture, top with fig slices, and bake for 30 minutes until cooked and set.
Serve straight away
Per serving: Calories: 372.8; Fat: 9.2g; Carbs: 65.6g; Fiber: 11.1g; Protein: 11.6g

706. Vegan Breakfast Sandwich
Preparation time: 15 minutes
Cooking time: 8 minutes
Servings: 3
Ingredients:
- 1 cup of spinach
- 6 slices of pickle
- 14 oz tofu, extra-firm, pressed
- 2 medium tomatoes, sliced
- 1/2 teaspoon garlic powder
- ¼ teaspoon ground black pepper
- 1/2 teaspoon black salt
- 1 teaspoon turmeric
- 1 tablespoon coconut oil
- 2 tablespoons vegan mayo
- 3 slices of vegan cheese

- 6 slices of gluten-free bread, toasted

Directions:
Cut tofu into six slices, and then season its one side with garlic, black pepper, salt, and turmeric. Take a skillet pan, place it over medium heat, add oil and when hot, add seasoned tofu slices in it, season side down, and cooking time for 3 minutes until crispy and light brown. Then flip the tofu slices and continue cooking for 3 minutes until browned and crispy. When done, transfer tofu slices on a baking sheet, in the form of a set of two slices side by side, then top each set with a cheese slice and broil for 3 minutes until cheese has melted. Spread mayonnaise on both sides of slices, top with two slices of tofu, cheese on the side, top with spinach, tomatoes, pickles, and then close the sandwich.
Cut the sandwich into half and then serve.
Per serving: Calories: 364; Fat: 12g; Carbs: 51g; Fiber: 3g; Protein: 16g

707. Vegan Fried Egg

Preparation time: 5 minutes
Cooking time: 8 minutes **Servings:** 4
Ingredients:
- 1 block of firm tofu, firm, pressed, drained
- ½ teaspoon ground black pepper
- ½ teaspoon salt
- 1 tablespoon vegan butter
- 1 cup vegan toast dipping sauce

Directions:
Cut tofu into four slices, and then shape them into a rough circle using a cookie cutter. Take a frying pan, place it over medium heat, add butter and when it melts, add prepared tofu slices in a single layer and cooking time for 3 minutes per side until light brown.
Transfer tofu to serving dishes, make a small hole in the middle of tofu by using a small cookie cutter, and fill the hole with dipping sauce.
Garnish eggs with black pepper and sauce and then serve.
Per serving: Calories: 86; Fat: 9g; Carbs: 0.5g; Fiber: 0g; Protein: 2g

708. Sweet Crepes

Preparation time: 5 minutes
Cooking time: 8 minutes **Servings:** 5
Ingredients:
- 1 cup of water
- 1 banana
- 1/2 cup oat flour
- 1/2 cup brown rice flour
- 1 teaspoon baking powder
- 1 tablespoon coconut sugar
- 1/8 teaspoon salt

Directions:
Take a blender, place all the ingredients in it except for sugar and salt, and pulse for 1 minute until smooth.
Take a skillet pan, place it over medium-high heat, grease it with oil, and when hot, pour in ¼ cup of batter, spread it as thin as possible, and cooking time for 2 to 3 minutes per side until golden brown.
Cook the remaining crepes in the same manner, then sprinkle with sugar and salt and serve.
Per serving: Calories: 160; Fat: 4.3g; Carbs: 22g; Fiber: 0.6g; Protein: 8.3g

709. Tofu Scramble

Preparation time: 5 minutes
Cooking time: 18 minutes **Servings:** 4
Ingredients:
For The Spice Mix:
- 1 teaspoon black salt
- 1/4 teaspoon garlic powder
- 1 teaspoon red chili powder
- 1 teaspoon ground cumin
- 3/4 teaspoons turmeric
- 2 tablespoons nutritional yeast

For The Tofu Scramble:
- 2 cups cooked black beans
- 16 ounces tofu, firm, pressed, drained
- 1 chopped red pepper
- 1 1/2 cups sliced button mushrooms
- 1/2 of white onion, chopped
- 1 teaspoon minced garlic
- 1 tablespoon olive oil

Directions:
Take a skillet pan, place it over medium-high heat, add oil, and when hot, add onion, pepper, mushrooms, and garlic and cooking time for 8 minutes until golden. Meanwhile, prepare the spice mix and for this, place all its ingredients in a bowl and stir until combined.
When vegetables have cooked, add tofu in it, crumble it, then add black beans, sprinkle with prepared spice mix, stir, and cooking time for 8 minutes until hot.
Serve straight away
Per serving: Calories: 175; Fat: 9g; Carbs: 10g; Fiber: 3g; Protein: 14g

Amanda Kale

CHAPTER 29:
Whole Food Recipes

710. Spicy Curry Lentil Burgers
Preparation time: 30 minutes
Cooking time: 1 Hour 20 minutes **Servings:** 12
Ingredients:
- 1 cup of lentils - 3 cups of water
- 3 grated carrots
- 1 small diced onion
- ¾ cups of whole-grain flour
- 2 teaspoons of curry powder
- ½ a teaspoon of sea salt
- A pinch of black pepper
- 12 whole wheat burger buns
- 12 pieces of Romaine lettuce
- 12 slices of tomatoes
- Vegan mayonnaise

Directions:
Boil the lentils in a medium-sized saucepan for approximately 30 minutes until they become soft.
Place the onion and the carrots in a large bowl, add the salt, pepper, curry powder, and flour and toss to combine. Drain the excess water from the lentil and add them to the bowl with the vegetables. Use a potato masher to combine the ingredients, if you need to add more flour, do so. Use your hands to form 12 patties. You can either bake or pan fry the burgers. To bake the burgers, preheat the oven to 350 degrees F. Lay parchment paper on a baking tray and arrange the patties on it. Bake the patties for 40 minutes. Once cooked, remove the patties from the oven. 1Toast the burger buns and arrange them on plates. 1Layer with lettuce and tomatoes. 1Arrange the burgers over the top. 1Add some mayonnaise, top with the remaining burger bun, and serve.
Per serving: Calories: 114Kcal; Fat: 1g; Carbs: 22g; Protein: 6g

711. Loaded Pizza With Black Beans
Preparation time: 20 minutes
Cooking time: 30 minutes **Servings:** 2
Ingredients:
- 2 prebaked pizza crusts
- ½ a cup of spicy black bean dip
- 1 thinly sliced tomato
- A pinch of black pepper
- 1 grated carrot - A pinch of sea salt
- 1 thinly sliced red onion
- 1 sliced avocado

Directions:
Preheat the oven to 400 degrees F. Arrange the pizza crusts on a large baking tray.
Spread each pizza crust with half of the black bean dip. Arrange the tomato slices over the top and sprinkle with salt.
In a small bowl, sprinkle the grated carrot with sea salt and use your hands to massage the salt into the carrots. Arrange the carrots over the tomatoes. Spread the onions over the top.
Bake the pizza for 20 minutes. Top the pizza with avocado, sprinkle with pepper, slice, and serve.
Per serving: Calories: 379Kcal; Fat: 13g; Carbs: 59g; Protein: 13g

712. Thai Pad Bowl
Preparation time: 10 minutes
Cooking time: 20 minutes **Servings:** 2
Ingredients:
- 7 ounces of brown rice noodles
- 1 teaspoon of olive oil
- 2 carrots, julienned and peeled
- 1 cup of red cabbage thinly sliced
- 2 finely chopped scallions
- 2 tablespoons of finely chopped fresh mint
- 1 cup of bean sprouts - ¼ cup of peanut sauce
- ¼ cup of finely chopped cilantro
- 2 tablespoons of chopped roasted peanuts
- Fresh lime wedges

Directions:
Cook the rice noodles according to the instructions. Once cooked, drain, rinse and set them to one side to cool down. Heat the oil in a large frying pan and sauté the bell pepper, cabbage, and carrots for 7 to 8 minutes. Add the bean sprouts, mint, and scallions and cook for a further two minutes and take the saucepan off the stove. Combine the vegetables and the noodles and add the peanut sauce. Divide into bowls and sprinkle with peanuts and cilantro. Squeeze the lime wedge over the top and serve.
Per serving: Calories: 660Kcal; Fat: 19g; Carbs: 110g; Protein: 15g

713. Sushi Bowl
Preparation time: 1 hour
Cooking time: 20 minutes
Servings: 1
Ingredients:
- ½ a cup of fresh edamame beans
- ¼ cup of water
- ¾ cup of cooked brown rice
- ½ a cup of chopped spinach
- ¼ cup of sliced avocado
- ¼ cup of sliced bell pepper
- ¼ cup of chopped fresh cilantro
- 1 chopped scallion
- ¼ nori sheet
- 2 tablespoons of soy sauce

- 1 tablespoon of sesame seeds

Directions:
Put the edamame beans into a saucepan and steam them with a ¼ cup of water for 15 minutes. Combine the scallions, bell pepper, avocado, spinach, rice, and edamame in a bowl and stir to combine. Use scissors to cut the nori into small pieces and sprinkle it over the top of the vegetables and rice.
Drizzle soy sauce over the top and serve.
Per serving: Calories: 467Kcal; Fat: 20g; Carbs: 56g; Protein: 22g

714. Sweet Potato Patties

Preparation time: 30 minutes
Cooking time: 15 minutes
Servings: 6
Ingredients:
- 1 cup of cooked brown rice, short grain, fully cooled
- 1 cup of grated sweet potato
- ½ a cup of chopped onions
- A pinch of sea salt
- ¼ cup of finely chopped fresh parsley
- 1 tablespoon of fresh, chopped dill
- 2 tablespoons of nutritional yeast (optional)
- ½ a cup of whole-grain breadcrumbs
- 1 tablespoon of olive oil
- Coconut flour

Directions:
In a large bowl, combine the onion, sweet potato, rice, and salt and stir to combine. Leave the mixture to sit for a couple of minutes to allow the salt to draw out the moisture from the onion and potato. Add the nutritional yeast (if using), dill, parsley, and enough flour to make the batter sticky. If you need to add a couple of spoonsful of water.
Use your hands to form the mixture into balls, and then flatten them slightly to make patties.
Heat the oil in a frying pan and cook the patties for 5 minutes on each side.
Remove the patties from the frying pan and serve.
Per serving: Calories: 146Kcal; Fat: 2g; Carbs: 29g; Protein: 6g

715. Summer Vietnamese Rolls

Preparation time: 15 minutes
Cooking time: 50 minutes **Servings:** 10
Ingredients:
- 10 wraps, made from rice roll
- ¼ cup of fresh basil leaves
- 10 Romaine lettuce leaves
- 2 grated carrots
- ½ a julienned cucumber
- 1 mango, peeled and cut into thin, long pieces
- 3 scallions cut into quarters and sliced lengthwise
- 1 cup of bean sprouts
- ½ a cup of peanut sauce

Directions:
Pour room temperature water into a deep plate.
Put one rice roll wrap into the water for a couple of minutes to soften it. Remove it from the water and leave it to drip for a couple of seconds and then place it on a plate. Arrange two fresh basil leaves down the middle of the wrap. Top with a lettuce leaf. Top with bean sprouts, scallions, mango, cucumber, and carrots. Fold the bottom and the top of the wrap, fold one side over the filling and push the end under the filling. Use your hand to squeeze the roll slightly and then roll it to the other end. Leave the wraps to sit for a while so that they can stick together. Slice the wraps in half, and serve with peanut sauce for dipping.
Per serving: Calories: 77Kcal; Fat: 5g; Carbs: 8g; Protein: 3g

716. Sesame Stir Fry

Preparation time: 20 minutes
Cooking time: 30 minutes **Servings:** 4
Ingredients:
- 1 cup of quinoa
- 2 cups of water
- A pinch of sea salt
- 1 head of broccoli
- 2 teaspoons of olive oil
- 1 cup of snow peas
- 1 cup of frozen peas
- 2 cups of chopped Swiss chard
- 2 chopped scallions
- 2 tablespoons of water
- 1 teaspoon of toasted sesame oil
- 1 tablespoon of soy sauce
- 2 tablespoons of sesame seeds

Directions:
In a medium saucepan, add the quinoa, water, and sea salt and boil for one minute. Reduce the temperature, put a lid on the saucepan, and leave it to simmer for 20 minutes. While the quinoa is cooking, don't stir it. Chop the broccoli up into florets and chop the stem into bite-sized pieces. Heat the sesame oil in a frying pan and sauté the broccoli with a pinch of sea salt. Push the broccoli around the pan with a spoon so that it doesn't burn. Add the snow peas and keep stirring, add the scallions and Swiss chard and toss to combine. Add two tablespoons of water to steam the vegetables. Drizzle some sesame oil and soy sauce over the top, toss to combine, and remove from the heat. Divide the quinoa into plates, top with the stir fry, sprinkle with sesame seeds and some more soy sauce, and serve.
Per serving: Calories: 334Kcal; Fat: 13g; Carbs: 42g; Protein: 17g

717. Lime-Mint Creamy Spaghetti Squash

Preparation time: 15 minutes
Cooking time: 40 minutes
Servings: 3
Ingredients:
For the Dressing
- 3 tablespoons of tahini
- The juice and zest of 1 small lime
- 2 tablespoons of chopped fresh mint
- 1 pressed small clove of garlic
- 1 tablespoon of nutritional yeast

- A pinch of sea salt

For The Spaghetti Squash
- 1 spaghetti squash
- A pinch of sea salt
- 1 cup of chopped cherry tomatoes
- 1 cup of bell pepper, chopped
- Ground black pepper

Directions:
To Make the Dressing
Combine all the ingredients in a food processor and blend until smooth. Set the dressing to one side.
To Make the Spaghetti Squash
Boil a large pot of water.
Slice the squash in half and used a spoon to scrape the seeds out.
Add salt to the boiling water and boil the squash halves for 30 minutes.
Take the squash out of the pot and leave it to cool down before handling it.
Scoop the squash out and then break apart the strands.
When the squash is boiling, it absorbs water and so put the squash noodles into a strainer and leave them to drain for 10 minutes.
Place the spaghetti squash into a bowl and add the dressing.
Top with the bell pepper and cherry tomatoes, sprinkle with black pepper and nutritional yeast (if you are using it), and serve.
Per serving: Calories: 199Kcal; Fat: 10g; Carbs: 27g; Protein: 7g

718. Pesto And Sun-Dried Tomato Quinoa

Preparation time: 20 minutes
Cooking time: 15 minutes **Servings:** 1
Ingredients:
- 1 teaspoon of olive oil
- 1 cup of onion, chopped
- 1 clove of garlic, minced
- 1 cup of zucchini, chopped
- A pinch of sea salt - 1 chopped tomato
- 2 tablespoons of chopped sun-dried tomatoes
- 3 tablespoons of basil pesto
- 1 cup of chopped spinach
- 2 cups of cooked quinoa
- 1 tablespoon of cheesy sprinkle (optional)

Directions:
In a large frying pan over a medium temperature, heat the oil. Sauté the onions for 5 minutes. Add the garlic, zucchini, and salt and cook for a further 5 minutes. Remove the frying pan from the stove and add the sun-dried and fresh tomatoes and the pesto and toss to combine. Arrange the spinach and quinoa on a plate and top with the zucchini mixture. Top with the cheesy sprinkle (if using).
Per serving: Calories: 535Kcal; Fat: 23g; Carbs: 69g; Protein: 20g

719. White Bean and Olive Pasta

Preparation time: 15 minutes
Cooking time: 10 minutes **Servings:** 1
Ingredients:
- ½ a cup of whole-grain pasta
- A pinch of sea salt
- 1 teaspoon of olive oil
- ¼ red bell pepper, thinly sliced
- ¼ cup of zucchini, thinly sliced
- ½ cup of cooked cannellini beans
- ½ a cup of spinach
- 1 tablespoon of balsamic vinegar
- 3 black olives, chopped and pitted
- 1 tablespoon of nutritional yeast

Directions:
Cook the pasta according to the instructions on the packet. Once cooked, drain and rinse and set to one side. Heat the oil in a large saucepan and sauté the zucchini and the bell pepper. Add the beans and cook for 2 minutes. Add the spinach and leave it to wilt. Drizzle the vinegar over the top.
Arrange the pasta onto plates, top with the bean mixture, sprinkle the nutritional yeast and the olives over the top and serve.
Per serving: Calories: 387Kcal; Fat: 17g; Carbs: 42g; Protein: 18g

720. Buckwheat And Spaghetti Meatballs

Preparation time: 15 minutes
Cooking time: 1 Hour 5 minutes
Servings: 2
Ingredients:
For the Meatballs
- ½ a cup of toasted buckwheat
- 2 ¼ cups of water
- A pinch of sea salt
- 2 tablespoons of ground flaxseeds
- 2 tablespoons of tomato paste
- 1 tablespoon of stone ground mustard
- 2 tablespoons of soy sauce
- 1 tablespoon of mixed dried herbs
- 1 teaspoon of onion powder
- 1 teaspoon of garlic powder
- ½ a teaspoon of ground cumin
- ½ a teaspoon of smoked paprika

For The Spaghetti
- 7 ounces of whole-grain spaghetti
- 2 cups of marinara sauce
- 3 tablespoons of cheesy sprinkle

Directions:
Prepare the oven by preheating it to 350 degrees F.
Grease a baking sheet with olive oil. Add the buckwheat and two cups of water into a small pot, add a pinch of salt and boil it. Reduce the heat, put a lid on the saucepan, and leave it to simmer for 5 minutes. Combine the ground flaxseed with ¼ cup of water, stir and set it to one side. In a large bowl, combine the paprika, cumin, garlic powder, onion powder,

herbs, soy sauce, mustard, and tomato paste and stir to combine. Add the soaked flaxseed and buckwheat and stir to combine. Form the mixture into 2- to 24 small meatballs. Arrange the meatballs onto the baking sheet, and bake for 30 minutes. Cook the spaghetti according to the instructions on the packet; once cooked, drain and rinse it. Remove the meatballs from the oven once they are cooked.

Arrange the spaghetti onto plates, top with marinara, meatballs, and the cheesy sprinkles, and serve.

Per serving: Calories: 651Kcal; Fat: 15g; Carbs: 115g; Protein: 26g

721. Black-Eyed Pea Burritos

Preparation time: 10 minutes
Cooking time: 50 minutes **Servings:** 6
Ingredients:

- 1 tablespoon of olive oil - 1 diced red onion
- 2 cloves of minced garlic
- 1 chopped zucchini
- 1 diced and seeded bell pepper
- 1 diced tomato
- 2 tablespoons of chili powder
- A pinch of sea salt
- 1 can of black-eyed peas drained and rinsed
- 6 whole-wheat tortillas

Directions:
Prepare the oven by preheating it to 350 degrees F.
Heat the olive oil in a large frying pan over medium temperature. Sauté the onions for approximately 5 minutes. Add the garlic and continue to sauté for a couple of minutes. Add the zucchini and sauté for five minutes. Add the bell pepper and the tomato and cook for another two minutes. Add the black-eyed peas, salt and chili powder and stir to combine. Lay a tortilla onto a plate and spoon out some of the black-eyed pea mixture into the center. Fold the ends in and roll into a burrito. Repeat for all six burritos.

Arrange the burritos seam side down into a baking dish and pour the vegetable juice from the pan over the top.

Bake the burritos for 30 minutes. Once cooked, remove from the oven and serve.

Per serving: Calories: 334Kcal; Fat: 6g; Carbs: 58g; Protein: 12g

722. Chickpea Curry

Preparation time: 60 minutes
Cooking time: 15 minutes
Servings: 2
Ingredients:

- Ground black pepper
- The juice of ½ a lemon
- 1 can of drained and rinsed chickpeas
- 1 tablespoon of maple syrup
- 1/3 cup of tomato paste
- 1 cup of water
- 1 teaspoon of turmeric
- 2 teaspoons of garam masala
- 2 teaspoons of ground cumin
- 2 teaspoons of ground coriander
- 1 tablespoon of chili powder
- 1 tablespoon of fresh minced ginger
- Salt
- 1 chopped onion
- 1 tablespoon of olive oil
- 2 cups of brown rice

Directions:
Cook the brown rice according to the instructions on the packet and set it to one side. In a medium-sized frying pan, heat the oil over medium heat. Add the onions and a pinch of salt, stir until the onions become soft. Add the ginger and garlic and cook for another 1 minute. Add the garam masala, cumin, coriander, and chili powder, stir to combine, and cook for another 1 minute. Add the chickpeas, maple syrup, tomato paste, water, and some salt, stir to combine, place a lid over the pan, reduce the temperature to low and leave the ingredients to simmer for 10 minutes. Add the lemon juice and black pepper and stir to combine. Spoon the brown rice out onto dishes, top with the curry, and serve.

Per serving: Calories: 274Kcal; Fat: 5g; Carbs: 49g; Fiber: 9g; Protein: 10g

723. Sweet Potato Shephard's Pie

Preparation time: 60 minutes
Cooking time: 1 Hour 10 minutes **Servings:** 6
Ingredients:

- Coarsely chopped parsley
- 1 teaspoon of smoked paprika
- 2 tablespoons of tamari
- 3 tablespoons of tomato paste
- 1 teaspoon of garlic powder
- ¼ cup of unsweetened almond milk
- 2 medium-sized sweet potatoes
- 2 ½ cups of vegetable broth
- 1 cup of brown lentils
- 3 cloves of minced garlic
- Salt
- 2 stalks of finely chopped celery
- 1 finely chopped carrot
- 1 finely chopped onion
- 1 tablespoon of coconut oil

Directions:
Heat the oil in a medium-sized saucepan and add the celery, carrot, onion, and a pinch of salt. Stir to combine and cook for about 1 minute. Add the garlic and cook for a further 1 minute. Add the vegetable broth and the lentils and bring to a boil. Let the ingredients simmer for 30 minutes. Steam the potatoes for 10 minutes in a steamer basket. Once they are soft, transfer the potatoes into a medium-sized bowl. Add the garlic powder and the milk and a pinch of salt. Use a potato masher to mash the potatoes and combine the mixture. Once the tomatoes are cooked, add the smoked paprika, Tamari, and tomato paste and stir to combine. Pour the lentils into a baking dish, top with a layer of the sweet mashed potatoes, and bake for 15 minutes until the top becomes crisp. Remove the dish from the oven, garnish with fresh parsley and serve.

Per serving: Calories: 189Kcal; Fat: 3g; Carbs: 32g; Fiber: 9g; Protein: 9g

724. Stovetop Maple Beans

Preparation time: 10 minutes
Cooking time: 20 minutes **Servings:** 6
Ingredients:
- Ground black pepper
- 1 teaspoon of smoked paprika
- 1 teaspoon of Dijon mustard
- 2 teaspoons of apple cider vinegar
- 1 tablespoon of tamari
- 2 tablespoons of fancy molasses
- 3 tablespoons of maple syrup
- 1 can of diced tomatoes
- 7 cups of white navy beans
- 3 cloves of minced garlic
- Salt
- 1 stalk of finely chopped celery
- 1 finely chopped carrot
- 1 finely chopped onion
- 1 tablespoon of olive oil
- Rosemary parsley protein

Directions:
In a large stockpot, heat the oil over a medium temperature. Add the celery, carrots and onions and sauté until the onions become translucent. Add the garlic and cook for a further one minute. Add the paprika, mustard, apple cider vinegar, aminos, molasses, syrup, tomatoes and beans and stir to combine. Serve the beans with rosemary parsley protein bread.
Per serving: Calories: 364Kcal; Fat: 3g; Carbs: 67g; Fiber: 19g; Protein: 19g

725. Cabbage Roll Stew

Preparation time: 1 hour 30 minutes
Cooking time: 50 minutes **Servings:** 6
Ingredients:
- 2 cups of brown rice
- Chopped parsley for garnish
- 2 tablespoons of apple cider vinegar
- 1 coarsely chopped cabbage
- 1 can of diced tomatoes
- 3 cups of vegetable broth
- 2 teaspoons of dried thyme
- 1 cup of dried brown lentils
- 2 cups of chopped brown mushrooms
- 2 cloves of minced garlic
- Salt
- 1 chopped onion
- 1 tablespoon of olive oil

Directions:
Cook the brown rice according to the directions on the packet and set it to one side. Heat the oil in a large stockpot over medium heat. Add the onions and a pinch of salt and cook until the onions become translucent. Add the mushrooms and garlic and cook for a further 5 minutes. Add the broth, thyme, and lentils and let the ingredients boil. Turn the heat down to low, put a lid on the stockpot and leave it to simmer for 25 minutes. Add the vinegar, cabbage, tomatoes, and some salt and cook for a further five minutes. Divide the rice onto plates, spoon the cabbage stew over the top, garnish with parsley and serve.
Per serving: Calories: 211Kcal; Fat: 3g; Carbs: 36g; Fiber: 7g; Protein: 10g

726. Walnut, Coconut, and Oat Granola

Preparation time: 15 minutes
Cooking time: 1 hour 40 minutes
Servings: 4¼ cups
Ingredients:
- 1 cup chopped walnuts
- 1 cup unsweetened, shredded coconut
- 2 cups rolled oats
- 1 teaspoon ground cinnamon
- 2 tablespoons hemp seeds
- 2 tablespoons ground flaxseeds
- 2 tablespoons chia seeds
- ¾ teaspoon salt, optional
- ¼ cup maple syrup
- ¼ cup water
- 1 teaspoon vanilla extract
- ½ cup dried cranberries

Directions:
Preheat the oven to 250ºF (120ºC). Line a baking sheet with parchment paper. Mix the walnuts, coconut, rolled oats, cinnamon, hemp seeds, flaxseeds, chia seeds, and salt (if desired) in a bowl.
Combine the maple syrup and water in a saucepan. Bring to a boil over medium heat, then pour in the bowl of walnut mixture. Add the vanilla extract to the bowl of the mixture. Stir to mix well. Pour the mixture into the baking sheet, then level with a spatula so that the mixture coats the bottom evenly.
Place the baking sheet in the preheated oven and bake for 90 minutes or until browned and crispy. Stir the mixture every 15 minutes. Remove the baking sheet from the oven. Allow to cool for 10 minutes, then serve with dried cranberries on top.
TIP: Store the granola in an airtight container in the refrigerator for over 2 weeks or in the freezer for up to 3 months.
Per serving: Calories: 440Kcal; Fat: 27g; Carbs: 56g; Fiber: 16g; Protein: 14g

727. Ritzy Fava Bean Ratatouille

Preparation time: 15 minutes
Cooking time: 40 minutes
Servings: 4
Ingredients:
- 1 medium red onion, peeled and thinly sliced
- 2 tablespoons low-sodium vegetable broth
- 1 large eggplant, stemmed and cut into ½-inch dice
- 1 red bell pepper, seeded and diced
- 2 cups cooked fava beans
- 2 Roma tomatoes, chopped
- 1 medium zucchini, diced
- 2 cloves garlic, peeled and finely chopped

- ¼ cup finely chopped basil
- Salt, to taste (optional)
- Ground black pepper, to taste

Directions:
Add the onion to a saucepan and sauté for 7 minutes or until caramelized. Add the vegetable broth, eggplant and red bell pepper to the pan and sauté for 10 more minutes. Add the fava beans, tomatoes, zucchini, and garlic to the pan and sauté for an additional 5 minutes. Reduce the heat to medium-low. Put the pan lid on and cook for 15 minutes or until the vegetables are soft. Stir the vegetables halfway through. Transfer them onto a large serving plate. Sprinkle with basil, salt (if desired), and black pepper before serving.
TIP: To make this a complete meal, you can serve it with lentil mushroom soup.
Per serving: Calories: 114Kcal; Fat: 1g; Carbs: 24.2g; Fiber: 10.3g; Protein: 7.4g

728. Peppers and Black Peans with Brown Rice

Preparation time: 15 minutes
Cooking time: 20 minutes **Servings:** 4
Ingredients:
- 2 jalapeño peppers, diced
- 1 red bell pepper, seeded and diced
- 1 medium yellow onion, peeled and diced
- 2 tablespoons low-sodium vegetable broth
- 1 teaspoon toasted and ground cumin seeds
- 1½ teaspoons toasted oregano
- 5 cloves garlic, peeled and minced
- 4 cups cooked black beans
- Salt, to taste (optional)
- Ground black pepper, to taste
- 3 cups cooked brown rice
- 1 lime, quartered
- 1 cup chopped cilantro

Directions:
Add the jalapeño peppers, bell pepper, and onion to a saucepan and sauté for 7 minutes or until the onion is well browned and caramelized.
Add vegetable broth, cumin, oregano, and garlic to the pan and sauté for 3 minutes or until fragrant.
Add the black beans and sauté for 10 minutes or until the vegetables are tender. Sprinkle with salt (if desired) and black pepper halfway through.
Arrange the brown rice on a platter, then top with the cooked vegetables. Garnish with lime wedges and cilantro before serving.
TIP: HOW TO COOK BROWN RICE: Pour the rinsed and drained brown rice in a pot of water. Bring to a boil over medium heat.
Reduce the heat to low. Simmer for 45 minutes or until the water is almost absorbed. Allow to cool for 10 to 15 minutes before using.
Per serving: Calories: 426Kcal; Fat: 2.6g; Carbs: 82.4g; Fiber: 19.5g; Protein: 20.2g

729. Black-Eyed Pea, Beet, and Carrot Stew

Preparation time: 15 minutes
Cooking time: 40 minutes **Servings:** 2
Ingredients:
- ½ cup black-eyed peas, soaked in water overnight - cups water
- 1 large beet, peeled and cut into ½-inch piece (about ¾ cup)
- 1 large carrot, peeled and cut into ½-inch piece (about ¾ cup)
- ¼ teaspoon turmeric
- ¼ teaspoon toasted and ground cumin seeds
- 1/8 teaspoon asafetida
- ¼ cup finely chopped parsley
- ¼ teaspoon cayenne pepper
- ¼ teaspoon salt, optional
- ½ teaspoon fresh lime juice

Directions:
Pour the black-eyed peas and water into a pot, then cook over medium heat for 25 minutes. Add the beet and carrot to the pot and cook for 10 more minutes. Add more water necessary. Add the turmeric, cumin, asafetida, parsley, an cayenne pepper to the pot and cook for an additional minutes or until the vegetables are soft. Stir the mixtur periodically. Sprinkle with salt, if desired. Drizzle the lim juice on top before serving in a large bowl. TIP: Soak th black-eyed peas in water overnight can make the cooking tim of the peas shorter.
Per serving: Calories: 84Kcal; Fat: 0.7g; Carbs: 16.6g; Fibe 4.5g; Protein: 4.1g

730. Koshari

Preparation time: 15 minutes
Cooking time: 2 hours 10 minutes **Servings:** 6
Ingredients:
- 1 cup green lentils, rinsed
- 3 cups water - Salt, to taste (optional)
- 1 large onion, peeled and minced
- 2 tablespoons low-sodium vegetable broth
- 4 cloves garlic, peeled and minced
- ½ teaspoon ground allspice
- 1 teaspoon ground coriander
- 1 teaspoon ground cumin
- 2 tablespoons tomato paste
- ½ teaspoon crushed red pepper flakes
- 3 large tomatoes, diced
- 1 cup cooked medium-grain brown rice
- 1 cup whole-grain elbow macaroni, cooked, draine and kept warm
- 1 tablespoon brown rice vinegar

Directions:
Put the lentils and water in a saucepan, and sprinkle with sal if desired. Bring to a boil over high heat. Reduce the heat t medium, then put the pan lid on and cook for 45 minutes o until the water is mostly absorbed. Pour the cooked lenti into the bowl and set aside. Add the onion to a nonstic

skillet, then sauté over medium heat for 15 minutes or until caramelized. Add vegetable broth and garlic to the skillet and sauté for 3 minutes or until fragrant. Add the allspice, coriander, cumin, tomato paste, and red pepper flakes to the skillet and sauté for an additional 3 minutes until aromatic. Add the tomatoes to the skillet and sauté for 15 minutes or until the tomatoes are wilted. Sprinkle with salt, if desired. Arrange the cooked brown rice on the bottom of a large platter, then top the rice with macaroni, and then spread the lentils over. Pour the tomato mixture and brown rice vinegar over before serving.
TIP: HOW TO COOK BROWN RICE: Pour the rinsed and drained brown rice in a pot of water. Bring to a boil over medium heat. Reduce the heat to low. Simmer for 45 minutes or until the water is almost absorbed. Allow to cool for 10 to 15 minutes before using. **Per serving:** Calories: 201Kcal; Fat: 1.6g; Carbs: 41.8g; Fiber: 3.6g; Protein: 6.5g

731. Roasted Cauliflower With Navy Bean Purée and Quinoa Risotto

Preparation time: 15 minutes
Cooking time: 45 minutes **Servings:** 4
Ingredients:
- 5 to 6 cups cauliflower, cut into 1- to 1½-inch florets
- Salt, to taste (optional)
- Ground black or white pepper, to taste
- 2 cups cooked navy beans
- 2 1/3 cups low-sodium vegetable broth, divided
- 1 tablespoon fresh lemon juice
- Pinch of nutritional yeast
- 4 to 5 shallots, finely diced
- 2 teaspoons minced fresh thyme leaves (about 4 sprigs) - 1 cup quinoa
- 1/2 cup chopped fresh flat-leaf parsley

Directions:
Preheat the oven to 400ºF (205ºC). Line a baking sheet with parchment paper. Arrange the cauliflower florets on the baking sheet. Sprinkle with salt (if desired) and pepper. Toss to coat well. Roast in the preheated oven for 25 minutes or until golden brown. Flip the florets every 5 minutes to roast evenly. Meanwhile, put the navy beans, 1/3 cup of the vegetable broth, lemon juice, and nutritional yeast in a food processor. Pulse to purée until creamy and smooth. Set aside. Heat a saucepan over medium heat. Add the shallots and sauté for 4 minutes or until lightly browned. Add the thyme to the pan and sauté for 1 minute or until aromatic. Make the risotto: Add the quinoa and remaining vegetable broth to the pan. Stir to combine well. Bring to a boil, then reduce the heat to medium-low and simmer for 14 minutes or until the liquid is mostly absorbed. Mix in the navy bean purée. Sprinkle with salt (if desired) and pepper. Spread the parsley and roasted cauliflower florets over the risotto. Serve warm.
Tip: How To Cook Navy Beans: Put the navy beans in a pot, then pour in the water to cover the beans by about 1 inch. Bring to a boil over medium heat. Reduce the heat to low and simmer for 40 minutes or until the water is absorbed. Allow to cool before using.
Per serving: Calories: 456Kcal; Fat: 5.1g; Carbs: 84.9g; Fiber: 20.8g; Protein: 21.7g

732. Butternut Squash with Quinoa and Almonds

Preparation time: 20 minutes
Cooking time: 25 to 30 minutes **Servings:** 4
Ingredients:
Squash:
- 1 medium (1½-pound/680-g) butternut squash, deseeded and cut into 1-inch cubes
- ¼ teaspoon dried chili flakes
- 1 teaspoon smoked paprika
- 1 clove garlic, thinly sliced
- 1 teaspoon fresh thyme leaves (about 2 sprigs)
- Salt, to taste (optional)
- Ground black or white pepper, to taste
- 12 green olives
- 4 lemon slices

Almond Quinoa:
- 3/4 cup cooked quinoa
- 1/3 cup chopped arugula
- 1/3 cup chopped fresh flat-leaf parsley
- 1 teaspoon fresh lemon juice
- Salt, to taste (optional)
- Ground black or white pepper, to taste
- ¼ cup toasted and chopped almonds

Directions:
Preheat the oven to 400ºF (205ºC). Line a baking sheet with parchment paper. Combine the butternut squash with chili flakes, paprika, garlic, thyme, salt (if desired), and pepper in a large bowl. Toss to coat well. Pour the butternut squash mixture into the baking sheet, then top them with olives and lemon slices. Bake in the preheated oven for 25 to 30 minutes or until the butternut squash cubes are soft. Shake the baking sheet every 5 or 10 minutes so that the cubes are cooked evenly. Meanwhile, combine the cooked quinoa with arugula, parsley, lemon juice, salt (if desired), and pepper on a large serving plate. Toss to combine well. Top the quinoa with cooked butternut squash and almond before serving.
TIP: HOW TO COOK QUINOA: Put the quinoa in a saucepan, then pour the water in the pan to cover the quinoa. Bring to a boil over medium-high heat. Reduce the heat to medium, then simmer for 15 minutes or until the water is absorbed. Allow to cool before using.
Per serving: Calories: 172Kcal; Fat: 5.1g; Carbs: 30.2g; Fiber: 6g; Protein: 5.2g

733. Harissa Lentils with Riced Cauliflower

Preparation time: 50 minutes **Cooking time:** 6 to 10 minutes
Servings: 4
Ingredients:
Harissa:
- 3 tablespoons cumin seeds
- 3 tablespoons caraway seeds
- 3 tablespoons coriander seeds
- 2 tablespoons tomato paste

- 1/3 cup fresh lemon juice
- 1 tablespoon lemon zest
- 2 cloves garlic, chopped
- 3 to 4 small red chili peppers, seeded and chopped
- Salt, to taste (optional)
- Ground black or white pepper, to taste
- 2 tablespoons low-sodium vegetable broth
- 1 cup cooked French or black beluga lentils

Cauliflower Rice:
- 5 cups chopped cauliflower florets
- 1 tablespoon low-sodium vegetable broth
- Salt, to taste (optional)
- Ground black or white pepper, to taste
- ¼ cup chopped fresh mint leaves
- ¼ cup chopped fresh flat-leaf parsley
- 2 teaspoons fresh lemon juice
- 2 green onions, thinly sliced

Directions:
Heat a skillet over medium heat, then add and sauté the seeds to toast for 2 minutes or until lightly browned. Make the harissa: Pour the toasted seeds in a food processor, then add the tomato paste, lemon juice and zest, garlic, chili peppers, salt (if desired), and pepper. Process until the mixture is creamy and smooth. Pour the harissa in a bowl and set aside until ready to use. Heat the vegetable broth in a saucepan over medium heat. Add the cooked lentils and ¾ cup of harissa to the pan and simmer for 5 to 10 minutes until the mixture is glossy and smooth and has a thick consistency. Keep stirring during the simmering.

Put the cauliflower florets in a food processor, then process to rice the cauliflower. Heat the vegetable broth in a nonstick skillet over medium heat. Add the riced cauliflower, then sprinkle with salt (if desired) and pepper. Sauté for 1 minute or until lightly softened. Transfer the cooked cauliflower rice to a large bowl, then add the mint, parsley, lemon juice, and green onions. Toss to combine well. Serve the riced cauliflower with harissa lentils on top.

TIP: HOW TO COOK LENTILS: Bring a saucepan of water to a boil over medium-high heat. Pour the lentils and a touch of salt (if desired) into the pan. Simmer over low heat for 35 minutes or until the water is absorbed. Allow to cool before using.

Per serving: Calories: 176Kcal; Fat: 3.4g; Carbs: 32.2g; Fiber: 12.4g; Protein: 11.2g

734. Lemony Farro and Pine Nut Chard Rolls with Marinara Sauce

Preparation time: 40 minutes
Cooking time: 30 minutes **Servings:** 4
Ingredients:
- 1 cup semi-pearled farro
- ¼ cup toasted and chopped pine nuts
- 1 teaspoon nutritional yeast
- 1 tablespoon fresh lemon juice
- 1 teaspoon lemon zest
- Salt, to taste (optional)
- Ground black or white pepper, to taste
- 8 chard leaves
- 2 cups low-sodium marinara sauce
- ½ cup water

Directions:
Preheat the oven to 350ºF (180ºC). Combine the cooked farro, pine nuts, nutritional yeast, lemon juice and zest, salt (if desired), and pepper in a mixing bowl. Set aside. Remove the stems of the chard leaves so you have 16 chard leaf halves, then blanch the leaves in a bowl of boiling water for 5 minutes or until wilted. Pour ½ cup of marinara sauce on a baking dish. Take a chard half, then spoon 2 tablespoons of farro mixture in the middle of the leaf half. Fold the leaf over the filling, then tuck the leaf and roll up to wrap the filling. Repeat with the remaining chard and farro mixture. Arrange the chard rolls on the baking dish over the marinara sauce, seam side down, then top them with remaining marinara sauce and water. Cover the baking dish with aluminum foil and bake in the preheated oven for 30 minutes or until the sauce bubbles. Remove the chard rolls from the oven and serve immediately.

TIP: HOW TO COOK FARRO: Put the farro in a saucepan, then pour in the water to cover the farro by about 1 inch. Bring to a boil over medium-high heat. Reduce the heat to medium-low, then simmer for 28 minutes or until the water is absorbed. Allow to cool before using.

Per serving: Calories: 254Kcal; Fat: 9g; Carbs: 39g; Fiber: 6.5g; Protein: 7.7g

735. Easy Rice Blend with Almond, Parsley, and Cranberries

Preparation time: 10 minutes
Cooking time: 40 minutes
Servings: 2
Ingredients:
- 1 cup wild and brown rice blend, rinsed
- ¼ teaspoon ground sumac
- ¼ cup chopped almonds, for garnish
- ¼ cup chopped fresh flat-leaf parsley
- ¼ cup unsweetened dried cranberries
- ½ teaspoon ground coriander
- 1 teaspoon apple cider vinegar
- 2 green onions, thinly sliced
- Salt, to taste (optional)
- Ground black or white pepper, to taste

Directions:
Pour the rice blend into a saucepan, then pour in the water to cover the rice by about 1 inch. Bring to a boil over medium-high heat. Reduce the heat to low. Put the pan lid on and simmer for 40 minutes or until the water is absorbed. Transfer the rice to a bowl and allow to cool for 5 minutes. Add the remaining ingredient to the bowl and toss to combine well. Serve immediately.

TIP: Replace the ground sumac with lemon zest, lemon pepper seasoning, or vinegar to add the acidic flavor to this recipe.

Per serving: Calories: 105Kcal; Fat: 0.9g; Carbs: 21.1g; Fiber: 3g; Protein: 3.1g

736. Crispy Buckwheat

Preparation time: 15 minutes
Cooking time: 50 minutes **Servings:** 5 Cups
Ingredients:

- 1 cup raw buckwheat groats, soaked in water for at least 1 hour, well rinsed
- ½ cup raw sunflower seeds
- 1 cup sliced almonds
- 1 cup large-flake coconut
- 2 tablespoons chia seeds
- ¼ teaspoon ground ginger
- ¼ teaspoon ground nutmeg
- 1½ teaspoons ground cinnamon
- 3 tablespoons maple sugar
- ¼ teaspoon sea salt, optional
- ¼ cup maple syrup
- 1 teaspoon vanilla extract

Directions:
Preheat the oven to 325°F (163°C). Line a baking sheet with parchment paper. Combine the buckwheat groats with the remaining ingredients in a large bowl. Toss to coat well. Spread the mixture on the baking sheet to coat the bottom evenly. Bake in the preheated oven for 50 minutes or until lightly browned and crispy. Flip them halfway through the cooking time. Remove the crispy buckwheat from the oven and allow it to cool before serving. TIP: HOW TO RINSE BUCKWHEAT GROATS: Rinse the buckwheat groats in a mesh strainer. Remove the slimy liquid as much as possible. Scrap the rinsed buckwheat groats with a kitchen towel or paper towels. Per serving (1cup): Calories: 369Kcal; Fat: 23.8g; Carbs: 34.7g; Fiber: 8.3g; Protein: 9.5g

737. Simple Maple Navy Bean Bake

Preparation time: 50 minutes
Cooking time: 2 hours **Servings:** 8 to 10
Ingredients:

- 1 pound (454 g) dried navy beans, soaked overnight and drained, cooked
- 1 medium sweet onion, chopped (about 1 cup)
- 1 tablespoon grainy mustard
- 2 teaspoons smoked paprika
- ¼ cup tomato paste
- ¼ cup apple cider vinegar
- ¼ cup unsulfured molasses
- ½ cup maple syrup
- 6 Medjool dates, pitted and chopped
- 2 cups low-sodium vegetables broth, plus more if necessary
- Salt, to taste (optional)
- Ground black or white pepper, to taste

Directions:
Preheat the oven to 325°F (163°C). Combine all the ingredients in an oven-safe pot. Stir to mix well. Put the pot lid on and cook in the preheated oven for 2 hours or until the mixture is lightly saucy. Stir the mixture and add more vegetable broth if necessary, every half an hour. Remove the pot from the oven and serve the beans warm.

TIP: HOW TO COOK NAVY BEANS: Put the navy beans in a pot, then pour in the water to cover the beans by about 1 inch. Bring to a boil over medium heat. Reduce the heat to low and simmer for 40 minutes or until the water is absorbed. Allow to cool before using.
Per serving: Calories: 241Kcal; Fat: 1.3g; Carbs: 55.9g; Fiber: 4g; Protein: 6.6g

738. Nasi Goreng

Preparation time: 20 minutes
Cooking time: 20 minutes
Servings: 4
Ingredients:

- 2 shallots, finely sliced
- Sea salt, to taste (optional)
- 1 cup peas
- 5 baby courgettes, sliced at an angle
- Handful of fine green beans, chopped
- 1 cup tofu cubes
- 1 red bell pepper, finely sliced
- 1 red onion, finely sliced
- 2 tablespoons low-sodium vegetable broth
- 2 cups basmati, soaked in water for 1 hour, cooked
- Handful of toasted cashew nuts
- 3 tablespoons kecap manis

Sambal

- 3 red chilies
- 1 tablespoon tomato purée
- 1 tablespoon lemongrass paste
- 3 garlic cloves
- Juice and zest of 1 lime
- 1 teaspoon sea salt, optional

Directions:
Heat a nonstick skillet over high heat, then add the shallot and sprinkle with salt, if desired. Sauté for 5 minutes or until caramelized. Transfer the shallots to a bowl and set aside until ready to serve.
Put the ingredients for the sambal in a blender, then process until smooth.
Pour the sambal in the cleaned skillet, then sauté over high heat for 1 minute.
Add the peas, baby courgettes, green beans, tofu cubes, bell peppers, red onion, and vegetable broth to the skillet and sauté for 6 minutes or until tender.
Add the cooked basmati to the skillet and sauté with the vegetables for 4 minutes until well mixed. Add the cashew nuts and kecap manis halfway through the cooking time.
Transfer the basmati and vegetables onto a large plate, and serve with caramelized shallots on top.
TIP: HOW TO COOK BASMATI: Put the basmati in a pot, then pour in the water to cover the basmati by about 1 inch. Bring to a boil over medium heat. Reduce the heat to low and simmer for 40 minutes. Allow to cool before using.
Per serving: Calories: 658Kcal; Fat: 19.1g; Carbs: 100.3g; Fiber: 7.1g; Protein: 25.7g

739. Chickpea and Black Bean Stew with Pearl Parley

Preparation time: 40 minutes
Cooking time: 35 minutes
Servings: 4
Ingredients:
- 1 red onion, finely chopped
- 1 fresh chili, finely chopped
- 3 garlic cloves, minced
- 2 teaspoons sea salt, optional
- 2 teaspoons dried thyme
- 2 teaspoons dried oregano
- 2 teaspoons ground cumin
- ½ teaspoon ground cinnamon
- 1 teaspoon ground coriander
- 14 ounces (397 g) cooked chickpeas
- 14 ounces (397 g) cooked black beans
- 2 tablespoons chipotle paste
- 2 tablespoons tomato purée
- Juice of 1 lime
- 2 tablespoons soy sauce
- 2 cups water
- Handful of chopped cilantros
- 1 tablespoon chopped dark chocolate
- Handful of cherry tomatoes, halved
- Vegan yogurt, for serving

Pearl Barley:
- 1½ cups cooked pearl barley
- Zest and juice of 1 lime
- Salt, to taste (optional)
- Ground black or white pepper, to taste

Directions:
Heat a saucepan over medium heat, then add the onion and sauté for 5 minutes or until lightly browned. Add the chili, garlic, and salt (if desired) to the pan and sauté for 1 to 2 minutes or until fragrant.
Add the thyme, oregano, cumin, cinnamon, and coriander to the pan and sauté for 4 minutes or until aromatic. Add the chickpeas, black beans, chipotle paste, tomato purée, lime juice, soy sauce, and water to the pan. Stir to combine well. Put the pan lid on and simmer for 20 minutes or until the mixture has a thick consistency. Meanwhile, combine the pearl barley with lime juice and zest, salt (if desired), and pepper in a large bowl. Mix the chopped cilantro and chocolate in the chickpea and black bean stew. Transfer the stew to a large plate. Top with cherry tomatoes and vegan yogurt, then serve with pearl barley.
TIP: HOW TO COOK PEARL BARLEY: Put the pearl barley in a pot, then pour in the water to cover by about 1 inch. Bring to a boil over high heat. Reduce the heat to low and simmer for 25 minutes. Allow to cool before using.
Per serving: Calories: 469Kcal; Fat: 6.5g; Carbs: 85.7g; Fiber: 22.6g; Protein: 22.3g

740. Mexican Rice Bowl with Pinto Beans

Preparation time: 60 to 90 minutes
Cooking time: 35 minutes **Servings:** 2 to 4
Ingredients:
- ½ cup diced red onion (about ½ medium onion)
- 1 teaspoon minced garlic (about 2 small cloves)
- 1 cup medium-grain white rice
- ¼ cup frozen peas
- ¼ cup chopped carrots
- 3 tablespoons low-sodium vegetable broth
- ½ cup tomato sauce
- ½ teaspoon ground cumin
- ½ to 1 teaspoon salt, optional
- 2 cups water

Toppings:
- 15 ounces (425 g) pinto beans, soaked in water overnight, cooked
- ¼ cup corn kernels - 1 avocado, sliced
- 1 cup chopped lettuce
- Handful chopped coriander
- Handful chopped cherry tomato
- Ground black or white pepper, to taste

Directions:
Heat a saucepan over medium-high heat, then add the onion and sauté for 5 minutes or until lightly browned. Add the garlic and sauté for 1 to 2 minutes or until fragrant. Add the white rice, peas, carrots, and vegetable broth and cook for 3 minutes or until the rice is golden brown. If desired, add the tomato sauce and sprinkle with cumin and salt, then pour the water over. Stir to mix well. Bring to a boil, then reduce the heat to low and put the pan lid on. Simmer for 20 minutes or until the mixture is thickened. Transfer all of them to a large serving bowl, then spread all the topping ingredients over and stir to combine well before serving.
TIP: HOW TO COOK PINTO BEANS: Put the soaked pinto beans in a saucepan, then pour in the water to cover by about 1 inch. Sprinkle with salt, if desired. Bring to a boil over medium-high heat. Reduce the heat to low and simmer for 60 to 90 minutes or until tender. Allow to cool before using.
Per serving: Calories: 324Kcal; Fat: 8.7g; Carbs: 56.7g; Fiber: 8g; Protein: 7.3g

741. Bibimbap

Preparation time: 1 hour 30 minutes
Cooking time: 20 minutes **Servings:** 1 Bowl
Ingredients:
- 2 tablespoons tamari, divided
- ½ cup chickpeas, soaked in water overnight, cooked - ¾ cup cooked quinoa
- 3 tablespoons low-sodium vegetable broth, divided
- 1 carrot, scrubbed or peeled, and julienned
- 2 garlic cloves, minced, divided
- ½ cup asparagus, cut into 2-inch pieces
- ½ cup chopped spinach - ½ cup bean sprouts
- 3 tablespoons gochujang
- 1 scallion, chopped

- 1 tablespoon toasted sesame seeds

Directions:
Add 1 tablespoon of tamari in a small bowl, then dunk the chickpeas in the tamari and set aside to marinade until ready to use. Put the cooked quinoa in a large serving bowl. Heat 1 tablespoon of vegetable broth in a nonstick skillet over medium heat. Add the carrot and 1 garlic clove and sauté for 5 minutes or until tender. Transfer the cooked carrots and garlic to the serving bowl and place over the quinoa. Add the asparagus and 1 tablespoon of vegetable broth and sauté for 5 minutes or until soft. Transfer the asparagus to the serving bowl and place it beside the carrot. Add spinach, the other garlic clove, and 1 tablespoon of vegetable broth to the skillet, then sauté for 5 minutes or until wilted. Drizzle with remaining tamari and transfer the spinach to the serving bowl and place beside the asparagus. Add the bean sprouts and sauté for 1 minute, then transfer to the serving bowl and place beside the spinach. Put the marinated chickpeas in the serving bowl and place them beside the bean sprouts. Top them with gochujang, chopped scallion, and sesame seeds. Stir to mix them well and enjoy.
TIP: HOW TO COOK CHICKPEAS: Put the soaked chickpeas in a saucepan, then pour in the water to cover by about 1 inch. Bring to a boil over medium-high heat. Reduce the heat to low and simmer for 60 minutes or until soft. Allow to cool before using.
Per serving: Calories: 665Kcal; Fat: 33g; Carbs: 32g; Fiber: 16g; Protein: 22g

742. Lentil, Bulgur, and Mushroom Burgers

Preparation time: 40 minutes
Cooking time: 50 minutes **Servings:** 12
Ingredients:
- 4 tablespoons low-sodium vegetable broth, divided, plus more if needed
- 1-pound (454 g) cremini mushrooms, trimmed and sliced - 1 celery rib, minced
- 1 small leek, white and light green parts only, chopped and washed thoroughly 2 onions, chopped
- 2 garlic cloves, minced
- ¾ cup medium-grind bulgur, rinsed
- 2 cups water - Salt, to taste (optional)
- 1 cup raw cashews
- ¾ cup rinsed and cooked brown lentils
- 1/3 cup aquafaba
- 2 cups panko bread crumbs - 12 burger buns

Directions:
Heat 2 tablespoons of vegetable broth in a nonstick skillet over medium heat. Add the mushrooms to the skillet and sauté for 12 minutes or until tender.
Add the celery, leek, onions, and garlic to the skillet and sauté for 10 minutes or until fragrant, and the celery and leek are wilted. Turn off the heat and allow it to cool for 30 minutes. Put the bulgur, water, and salt (if desired) in a large bowl, then microwave, covered, for 5 minutes or until soft. Drain the bulgur in a strainer. Put the cashews in a food processor and pulse for 25 times to grind. Combine the lentils, vegetables, bulgur, cashews, and aquafaba in a bowl. Stir to mix well. Pour the mixture into the food processor and pulse for about 15 times to grind the mixture. Then pour the ground mixture back to the bowl and fold in the panko and 1 teaspoon of salt (if desired). Divide the mixture into 12 portions, then shape them into 4-inch patties. Heat 2 tablespoons of vegetable broth in the skillet over medium heat.
Arrange the patties in the skillet and cook for 8 minutes or until the patties are crispy and golden brown. Flip the patties halfway through the cooking time. You may need to work in batches to avoid overcrowding. Allow the patties to cool, then assemble the patties with buns to make burgers and serve.
TIP: HOW TO COOK BROWN LENTILS: Put the brown lentils, 3 cups of water, and 1 teaspoon of salt (if desired) in a saucepan. Bring to a boil over high heat. Reduce the heat to medium-low and simmer for 25 minutes or until the lentils are soft. Allow to cool and pat dry before using. **Per serving:** Calories: 438Kcal; Fat: 18.7g; Carbs: 58.5g; Fiber: 4.6g; Protein: 9.8g

743. Easy Chickpea Salad Sandwiches

Preparation time: 15 minutes
Cooking time: 0 minutes **Servings:** 6
Ingredients:
- 15 ounces (425 g) cooked chickpeas
- 1 tablespoon lemon juice
- ½ cup vegan mayonnaise
- Salt, to taste (optional) - ¼ cup water
- 1/3 cup finely chopped dill pickles
- 2 celery ribs, finely chopped
- 2 tablespoons minced fresh parsley
- 2 scallions, sliced thin
- Ground black or white pepper, to taste
- 12 slices hearty multigrain bread, toasted

Directions:
Add the chickpeas, lemon juice, mayo, salt (if desired), and water to a food processor. Pulse until creamy and smooth. Pour the mixture into a bowl and set aside. Add the pickles, celery, parsley, and scallions to the bowl of chickpea mixture. Sprinkle with salt (if desired) and pepper, then stir to combine well. Assemble the chickpea mixture with bread slices to make 6 sandwiches and serve immediately.
TIP: HOW TO COOK CHICKPEAS: Put the soaked chickpeas in a saucepan, then pour in the water to cover by about 1 inch. Bring to a boil over medium-high heat. Reduce the heat to low and simmer for 60 minutes or until soft. Allow to cool before using.
Per serving: Calories: 344Kcal; Fat: 10.2g; Carbs: 50.1g; Fiber: 8.7g; Protein: 14.1g

744. Falafel With Tahini-Milk Sauce

Preparation time: 20 minutes
Cooking time: 12 minutes **Servings:** 6 to 8
Ingredients:
Falafel:
- 12 ounces (340 g) dried chickpeas (about 2 cups), soaked in water overnight
- 1 cup fresh parsley leaves
- 1 cup fresh cilantro leaves
- 10 scallions, chopped coarsely

- 1/8 teaspoon ground cinnamon
- ½ teaspoon ground cumin
- 6 garlic cloves, minced
- ½ cup low-sodium vegetable broth
- Salt, to taste (optional)
- Ground black or white pepper, to taste

Sauce:
- 1/3 cup tahini
- 3 tablespoons lemon juice
- 1 garlic clove, minced
- 1/3 cup unsweetened coconut milk
- Salt, to taste (optional)
- Ground black or white pepper, to taste

Directions:
Preheat the oven to 375ºF (190ºC). Line baking sheet with parchment paper. Add the soaked chickpeas, parsley, cilantro, scallions, cinnamon, cumin, garlic, vegetables broth, salt (if desired), and pepper to a food processor. Pulse until smooth and creamy.
Make the falafel: Drop 2 tablespoons of chickpea mixture on the baking sheet, then flatten with a spatula to make a ½-inch thick and 1-inch wide disk. Repeat with the remaining chickpea mixture.
Slide the baking sheet in the preheated oven and bake for 4 to 6 minutes or until crispy and well browned. Flip the falafel halfway through.
Meanwhile, make the sauce: Combine all the ingredients for the sauce in a bowl. Stir to mix well.
Serve the falafel immediately with the sauce.
TIP: You can replace coconut milk with almond milk or soy milk.
Per serving: Calories: 264Kcal; Fat: 9.9g; Carbs: 35.3g; Fiber: 7.8g; Protein: 11.8g

745. Brown Rice with Spiced Vegetables
Preparation time: 10 minutes
Cooking time: 16 to 18 minutes **Servings:** 6
Ingredients:
- 2 teaspoons grated fresh ginger
- 2 cloves garlic, crushed - ½ cup water
- ¼ pound (113 g) green beans, trimmed and cut into 1-inch pieces
- 1 carrot, scrubbed and sliced
- ½ pound (227 g) mushrooms, sliced
- 2 zucchinis, cut in half lengthwise and sliced
- 1 bunch scallions, cut into 1-inch pieces
- 4 cups cooked brown rice
- 3 tablespoons soy sauce

Directions:
Place the ginger and garlic in a large pot with the water. Add the green beans and carrot and sauté for 3 minutes. Add the mushrooms and sauté for another 2 minutes. Stir in the zucchini and scallions. Reduce the heat. Cover and cook for 6 to 8 minutes, or until the vegetables are tender-crisp, stirring frequently.
Stir in the rice and soy sauce. Cook over low heat for 5 minutes or until heated through.
Serve warm.
Per serving: Calories: 205Kcal; Fat: 3g; Carbs: 38g; Fiber: 6.4g; Protein: 4.4g

746. Spiced Tomato Brown Rice
Preparation time: 10 minutes
Cooking time: 15 minutes **Servings:** 4 to 6
Ingredients:
- 1 onion, diced
- 1 green bell pepper, diced
- 3 cloves garlic, minced
- ¼ cup water
- 15 to 16 ounces (425 to 454g) tomatoes, chopped - 1 tablespoon chili powder
- 2 teaspoons ground cumin
- 1 teaspoon dried basil
- ½ teaspoon Parsley Patch seasoning, general blend
- ¼ teaspoon cayenne
- 2 cups cooked brown rice

Directions:
Combine the onion, green pepper, garlic and water in a saucepan over medium heat. Cook for about 5 minutes, stirring constantly, or until softened.
Add the tomatoes and seasonings. Cook for another 5 minutes. Stir in the cooked rice. Cook for another 5 minutes to allow the flavors to blend.
Serve immediately.
Per serving: Calories: 107Kcal; Fat: 1.1g; Carbs: 21.1g; Fiber: 2.9g; Protein: 3.2g

747. Noodle and Rice Pilaf
Preparation time: 5 minutes
Cooking time: 33 to 44 minutes - **Servings:** 6 to 8
Ingredients:
- 1 cup whole-wheat noodles, broken into 1/8-inch pieces
- 2 cups long-grain brown rice
- 6 1/2 cups low-sodium vegetable broth
- 1 teaspoon ground cumin
- ½ teaspoon dried oregano

Directions:
Combine the noodles and rice in a saucepan over medium heat and cook for 3 to 4 minutes, or until they begin to smell toasted. Stir in the vegetable broth, cumin and oregano. Bring to a boil. Reduce the heat to medium-low. Cover and cook for 30 to 40 minutes, or until all water is absorbed.
Per serving: Calories: 287Kcal; Fat: 2.5g; Carbs: 58.1g; Fiber: 5g; Protein: 7.9g

748. Easy Millet Loaf
Preparation time: 5 minutes
Cooking time: 1 hour 15 minutes **Servings:** 4
Ingredients:
- 1¼ cups millet
- 4 cups unsweetened tomato juice
- 1 medium onion, chopped
- 1 to 2 cloves garlic
- ½ teaspoon dried sage

- ½ teaspoon dried basil
- ½ teaspoon poultry seasoning

Directions:

Preheat the oven to 350ºF (180ºC).
Place the millet in a large bowl. Place the remaining ingredients in a blender and pulse until smooth. Add to the bowl with the millet and mix well. Pour the mixture into a shallow casserole dish. Cover and bake in the oven for 1¼ hours or until set. Serve warm.

Per serving: Calories: 315Kcal; Fat: 3.4g; Carbs: 61.6g; Fiber: 6g; Protein: 10.2g

49. Spaghetti with Spinach, Tomatoes, and Beans

Preparation time: 10 minutes
Cooking time: 35 minutes
Servings: 4 to 6

Ingredients:

- 1 cup low-sodium vegetable broth
- 3 garlic cloves, minced
- Salt, to taste (optional)
- 1 onion, chopped fine
- 1¼ pounds (567 g) curly-leaf spinach, stemmed and cut into 1-inch pieces
- ½ teaspoon red pepper flakes
- 2 tablespoons nutritional yeast
- 2 tablespoons white miso
- 14½ ounces (411 g) fresh tomatoes, diced
- ¾ cup pitted kalamata olives, chopped coarsely
- 15 ounces (425 g) cooked cannellini beans
- 4 quarts water
- 1 pound (454 g) whole-wheat spaghetti
- Ground black or white pepper, to taste

Directions:

Heat 2 tablespoons of vegetable broth in a nonstick skillet over medium heat. Add the garlic and sauté for 3 minutes or until fragrant. Transfer the garlic to a plate and sprinkle with salt (if desired).
Add another 2 tablespoons of vegetable broth to the skillet, then add the onion and sauté for 6 minutes or until translucent.
Add half of the spinach and red pepper flakes to the skillet. Sauté for 2 minutes or until the vegetables are wilted.
Mix in ¾ cup of the vegetable broth, nutritional yeast, and miso, then add the remaining spinach, tomatoes, and ¾ teaspoon of salt (if desired).
Bring them to a simmer, then put the skillet lid on and cook for 10 minutes or until the vegetables are soft. During the cooking, open the lid once and give them a stir.
Add the olives and beans to the skillet. Remove the skillet from the heat, put the lid on to keep warm and set aside.
In a large pot, bring the water to a boil, then add the spaghetti to the water, and sprinkle with salt, if desired. Cook for 8 minutes. Keep stirring during the cooking.
Reserve ½ cup of the cooking water and set aside. Add the cooked vegetables to the pot and cook over medium heat for 2 minutes or until the spaghetti is al dente and it absorbs most of the liquid.
Turn off the heat and pour the reserved cooking water and the remaining 1 tablespoon of vegetable broth over. Sprinkle with salt (if desired) and ground black pepper. Serve warm.
TIP: To make this a complete meal, you can serve it with asparagus and green bean salad.

Per serving: Calories: 264Kcal; Fat: 4.4g; Carbs: 48.4g; Fiber: 10.1g; Protein: 16g

CHAPTER 30:
Tasty Recipes

750. Zucchini Zoodles Soup
Preparation time: 20 minutes
Cooking time: 25 minutes
Servings: 2
Ingredients:
- 3 cups vegetable broth
- 1 large zucchini, spiralized
- 1/2 cup carrots, sliced
- 1 cup kale, cut
- ¼ cup green onions, sliced
- 2 garlic gloves, minced
- 4 tbsp sunflower seeds
- 4 tbsp pepitas
- ½ tsp kosher salt
- 2 tbsp sesame oil
- Ground black pepper

Directions:
Divide all ingredients between the jars.
Before serving, pour half of the vegetable broth over the veggies and let it stand for 5 minutes.
Sprinkle with pepitas, sunflower seeds and ground black pepper.
Eat immediately.
Per serving: Calories: 300Kcal; Fat: 23g; Carbs: 20g; Protein: 12g

751. Broccoli Slaw Wrap
Preparation time: 10 minutes
Cooking time: 5 minutes
Servings: 1
Ingredients:
- 1 tortilla
- 3 tbsp Spicy Hummus
- 3 leaves of romaine lettuce
- ½ cup broccoli slaw
- ¼ apple, sliced
- 2 tsp dairy-free plain yogurt, unsweetened
- ½ tsp fresh lemon juice
- Salt & pepper (to taste)

Directions:
Mix the yogurt, broccoli slaw, and lemon juice. Add salt and pepper to taste, mix well and set aside. Lay your tortilla flat and spread the spicy hummus all over. Next, lay down the lettuce, cover with broccoli slaw and top with the apple slices.
Fold up the sides, starting with the end that holds the apples and slaw. Roll tightly, cut in half and enjoy!
Per serving: Calories: 120Kcal; Fat: 2g; Carbs: 25g; Protein: 4g

752. Avocado Salad Sandwiches
Preparation time: 5 minutes
Cooking time: 5 minutes **Servings:** 4 sandwiches
Ingredients:
- 1 baguette, cut into 4 equal slices and halved lengthwise
- 2 tsp olive oil, plus more for the baguettes
- ¼ tsp garlic powder
- 1/3 cup parsley, chopped
- 2 avocados, peeled, pitted, and chopped
- 1 cup cherry tomatoes, diced
- Salt to taste

Directions:
Preheat oven to 350°F. Lightly brush olive oil onto the inside of the baguette pieces. Toast for 4 minutes in the oven until lightly browned. In a large mixing bowl, add the olive oil, parsley, and garlic powder. Mix well. Next, gently toss in and combine the tomato and avocado, ensuring you don't completely smash the avocado. Season with salt. Scoop the avocado and place inside the baguettes and enjoy.
Per serving: Calories: 392Kcal; Fat: 17g; Carbs: 30g; Protein: 12g

753. Rainbow Taco Boats
Preparation time: 10 minutes
Cooking time: 5 minutes **Servings:** 12 Taco boats
Ingredients:
- 1 large romaine lettuce head, stem removed and separated into individual leaves

For the Filling
- ½ cup beet hummus, raw
- 1 cup cherry tomatoes, halved
- ½ cup alfalfa sprouts
- 1 cup carrots, finely shredded
- ¾ cup red cabbage, thinly sliced
- 1 avocado, medium ripe and cubed

For the Sauce
- 1/3 cup tahini, untoasted
- 2 tbsp lemon juice - 1 tbsp maple syrup
- 1 pinch sea salt (optional) - Water for thinning

Directions:
Start preparing the sauce by combining tahini, maple syrup, lemon juice, and salt in a small mixing bowl. Next, add a tablespoon of water until you have pourable dressing. Set aside. Place a large serving platter on a table and arrange the lettuce boats on top. Fill with hummus and top with tomatoes, cabbage, avocado, sprouts, and carrots. Drizzle the tahini sauce on top. Enjoy!
Per serving: Calories: 320Kcal; Fat: 24.6g; Carbs: 23g; Protein: 9g

754. Tofu Egg Salad

Preparation time: 10 minutes
Cooking time: 10 minutes **Servings:** 4
Ingredients:
- 1 block firm tofu, crumbled
- ½ cup vegan mayo
- 1 tbsp brown mustard, spicy
- 1 tsp hot sauce
- 1/3 cup parsley, chopped
- 2 spring onions, chopped
- ½ cup carrot, minced
- ¼ cup nutritional yeast
- 2 tsp turmeric
- 2 tsp Italian seasoning
- ¾ tsp garlic powder
- ½ tsp onion powder
- ½ tsp sea salt
- 8 whole wheat bread slices

Directions:
In a medium-sized bowl, combine and mix all the ingredients. Spread the tofu mixture onto the bread.
Place the sandwiches in a preheated to 350F oven.
Bake for 7 minutes until they start to brown. Enjoy.
Per serving: Calories: 330Kcal; Fat: 17g; Carbs: 26.8g; Protein: 12g

755. Delicious Chana Masala

Preparation time: 10 minutes
Cooking time: 23 minutes **Servings:** 4
Ingredients:
- 3 tbsp canola oil
- 1 onion, chopped
- 2 tbsp red chili flakes
- 2 tbsp cumin, ground
- 2 tbsp coriander, ground
- ½ tsp turmeric, ground
- 2 bay leaves
- 2 cardamon pods
- 4 garlic cloves, minced
- 2 tbsp fresh ginger, minced
- 2 small cans chickpeas, drained and rinsed
- 2 cups vegetable broth, clear
- 1 small can tomato, crushed
- 1 ½ tsp salt
- 1 small lemon, juiced
- Handful of fresh cilantro, roughly chopped
- 1 tsp Garam Masala

To serve (optional)
Steamed rice Onion slices, Roughly chopped cilantro, julienne ginger pieces, and lemon juice

Directions:
In a large cooking pot, add oil and onions and sauté over medium heat for 8 minutes. Once ready, sprinkle in the cumin, coriander, turmeric, chili flakes, bay leaves, and cardamom. Continue cooking for 3 minutes. Add in the ginger and minced garlic sauté for another 3 minutes or until fragrant. Next, pour in the chickpeas, crushed tomatoes, vegetable broth, and salt. Stir well. Raise the heat and bring to a boil and then reduce to simmer. Cook for 10 more minutes, stirring. Mix in cilantro, Garam Masala, and lemon juice. Add the seasoning as needed and serve with steamed basmati rice, onion slices, cilantro, and julienne ginger.
Per serving: Calories: 268Kcal; Fat: 17.3g; Carbs: 29g; Protein: 16g

756. Easy Gazpacho Soup

Preparation time: 10 minutes
Cooking time: 30 minutes
Servings: 4
Ingredients:
- 1 cup red onion, diced
- 1 cucumber, peeled, seeded, and diced
- 6 tomatoes, peeled and seeded
- 1 red bell pepper, seeded and diced
- 2 garlic cloves, minced
- 2 cups tomato juice
- 5 drops Tabasco sauce
- 3 tsp balsamic vinegar
- 2 tsp Worcestershire sauce
- ¼ cup extra virgin olive oil
- Salt and Pepper to taste

Directions:
Set aside ¼ of the cucumber, onion, and pepper.
Place all other ingredients in a high-powered blender and puree until smooth. Add salt and pepper to taste.
Refrigerate for 30 minutes. Serve cold and garnish with the diced veggies.
Per serving: Calories: 215Kcal; Fat: 15g; Carbs: 22g; Protein: 3g

757. Greek Quinoa Salad

Preparation time: 10 minutes
Cooking time: 17 minutes **Servings:** 2
Ingredients:
- 2 cups quinoa, rinsed
- 4 cups water
- 1 cup cherry tomatoes, halved
- ½ cup feta cheese, crumbled
- ½ cup fresh parsley, chopped
- 1 red bell pepper, diced
- 1 cucumber, chopped
- 1 tbsp fresh lemon juice
- 2 tbsp olive oil - ¾ tsp salt or to taste

Directions:
Add the water to a cooking pot and add quinoa. Bring to a boil and reduce the heat to simmer for 15 minutes. Fluff the mixture using a fork, and leave it to cool to room temperature. In a large mixing bowl, combine quinoa, feta, cucumber, tomatoes, parsley, and pepper. Drizzle with olive oil, lemon juice, and salt. Mix and enjoy.
Per serving: Calories: 230Kcal; Fat: 9g; Carbs: 29g; Protein: 9g

758. Roasted Butternut Squash Salad

Preparation time: 5 minutes
Cooking time: 30 minutes
Servings: 3
Ingredients:
- 1 cup butternut squash, cubed
- 2 cups mixed lettuce
- 10 olives
- 6 tomatoes, sun-dried and chopped
- 2 tbsp Parmesan cheese, shaved
- 2 tbsp olive oil
- 1 tbsp balsamic vinegar
- 1 tsp oregano, dried
- 1 tsp rosemary, dried
- ¼ tsp cumin
- 1 tsp garlic powder
- 1 pinch sea salt and black pepper
- 1 lemon (juice only)

Directions:
Preheat your oven to 350°F. Slice the butternut squash into small 2 cm cubes. Transfer the cubes into a mixing bowl and combine with 1 tbsp oil, spices, herbs, and salt and pepper. Put on a baking tray, and bake for 30 minutes. In the meantime, place the salad leaves in a medium bowl and dress with the remaining oil, vinegar, and lemon juice. Place into a serving bowl and top with the roasted squash, tomatoes, olives, and cheese.
Per serving: Calories: 300Kcal; Fat: 17g; Carbs: 26g; Protein: 10g

759. Pasta Salad with Yogurt Dressing

Preparation time: 10 minutes
Cooking time: 35 minutes **Servings:** 4
Ingredients:
Pasta salad:
- ½ cup pasta
- 1 onion, thinly sliced
- 1 green pepper, thinly sliced
- 1 carrot, thinly sliced
- A handful of cherry tomatoes, halved
- A handful of olives, thinly sliced
- 1/4 cup feta cheese, cubed
- 2 tbsp extra virgin olive oil
- Salt and pepper to taste

Mint yogurt dressing
- ½ cup, dairy free yogurt
- 1/2 cup mint leaves, loosely packed
- ½ green chili
- ¼ cup, walnuts
- 2 garlic cloves, roasted
- 1 tbsp lemon juice
- Himalayan pink salt

Directions:
Cook the pasta as indicated on the package. Drain, cool and add a tablespoon of oil. Mix well. Add in the sliced veggies, olives, and feta cheese cubes. Next, add all the yogurt dressing ingredients to a blender Blend all ingredients for the yogurt dressing in a blender for 1 minute. Once ready, pour the puree into a medium bowl and refrigerate for 30 minutes. Serve your salad and drizzle the dressing on top.
Per serving: Calories: 304Kcal; Fat: 20g; Carbs: 15g; Protein: 12g

760. Vegan Cauliflower Steaks

Preparation time: 10 minutes
Cooking time: 20 minutes **Servings:** 4
Ingredients:
- 2 cauliflowers, heads
- 4 tbsp olive oil
- ½ tsp kosher salt
- ½ tsp garlic powder
- ½ tsp black pepper
- ½ tsp paprika
- ½ tbsp fresh parsley, chopped

Directions:
Preheat your oven to 350°F.
Cut the cauliflower head in two halves. From each half, cut the steaks 1,5 sm thick. It depends on the size of the head. If it is possible to make more steaks from the half, try carefully. Repeat the process with the second head. Cover the large baking sheet with parchment paper and place the steaks closely to each other. Sprinkle both steak sides with olive oil.
In a small bowl, combine salt, pepper, paprika and garlic powder. Top the cauliflower with seasoning mixture, cover with foil and bake for 7 min.
Remove the foil and bake for 13 minutes until golden brown, flipping 2 times. Serve immediately and garnish with the chopped parsley.
Per serving: Calories: 150Kcal; Fat: 12g; Carbs: 9g; Protein: 4g

761. Tomato Cucumber Salad

Preparation time: 10 minutes
Cooking time: 4 minutes **Servings:** 4
Ingredients:
- 1 cucumber, sliced into rounds
- ¼ cup red onion, thinly sliced
- 2 tomatoes, chopped
- 1 tbsp red wine vinegar - 2 tbsp olive oil
- ¼ tsp coarse sea salt
- Black pepper to taste

Directions:
Toss all the veggies into a large mixing bowl and coat with vinegar and olive oil. Sprinkle salt and pepper on top and serve.
Per serving: Calories: 130Kcal; Fat: 14g; Carbs: 5.1g; Protein: 2g

762. Healthy Apple Chickpea Salad

Preparation time: 10 minutes
Cooking time: 5 minutes
Servings: 3
Ingredients:
Apple Chickpea Salad:
- 2 tbsp extra virgin olive oil

- 1 cup chickpea, cooked
- 1 tbsp paprika
- ½ medium lemon, juice only
- A handful of fresh parsley
- 4 medium apples
- 2 celery stalks
- Avocado Peanut Butter Dressing:
- 2 tbsp peanut butter
- 1 tbsp extra virgin olive oil
- 1 small ripe avocado
- ½ lemon, juiced
- 1 tbsp soy sauce, optional
- ½ cup water

Directions:
In a medium skillet pan, heat the oil. Add chickpeas and continue roasting for 5 minutes, stirring. Add paprika and continue stirring until the chickpeas are completely coated. Roast for 5 more minutes and turn off the heat. Combine with lemon juice and chopped parsley. Season with salt and a pinch of pepper. Throw the apples and celery into a serving bowl alongside the roasted chickpea.

For the dressing:
Combine all the dressing ingredients in a food processor and blend until smooth. Drape on top of the bowl or serve on the side. Enjoy!

Per serving: Calories: 390Kcal; Fat: 20g; Carbs: 33g; Protein: 14g

763. Sweet Potato Chickpea Bowl

Preparation time: 10 minutes
Cooking time: 35 minutes **Servings:** 4
Ingredients:
Veggies:
- 3 tbsp olive oil
- ½ red onion, sliced
- 2 sweet potatoes, halved
- 1 bundle broccoli stems removed and chopped
- 2 handfuls kale, stems removed
- ¼ tsp salt
- ¼ tsp black pepper

Chickpeas:
- 15-ounce chickpeas, drained, rinsed, and patted dry
- 1 tsp cumin
- ¾ tsp chili powder
- ¾ tsp garlic powder
- ¼ tsp salt
- ¼ tsp pepper
- ½ tsp oregano, optional
- ¼ tsp turmeric, optional

Directions:
Preheat your oven to 400 degrees F.
Place the sweet potatoes and onions on a baking sheet. Next, drizzle with one tablespoon of oil, making sure that everything is properly coated. Flip the sweet potatoes skin side facing down and bake for 10 minutes. Once ready, remove from the oven and add broccoli. Drizzle with 1 teaspoon of oil and season with salt and pepper. Return to the oven and bake for 10 more minutes and then remove. Add kale and drizzle with a touch of oil. Bake for another 5 minutes, then set aside. Next, heat a skillet over medium heat and start mixing the chickpeas with seasonings. Once the skillet starts smoking, add 1 tbsp of oil and toss in the chickpeas. Sauté for 10 minutes until brown, ensuring you stir frequently.
Slice the sweet potatoes into bite-size pieces and serve with the chickpeas on top.
Per serving: Calories: 488Kcal; Fat: 24g; Carbs: 50g; Protein: 14g

764. Skinny Pasta Primavera

Preparation time: 10 minutes
Cooking time: 15 minutes **Servings:** 3
Ingredients:
- 4 ounces spaghetti noodles, broken in half
- 1 leek, sliced
- ¼ lb asparagus
- ¼ lb broccoli florets
- ½ cup brown mushrooms, stemmed and sliced
- 2 garlic cloves, peeled and minced
- 1 ½ cups almond milk, unsweetened
- ¼ cup vegetable broth
- ¼ tsp red pepper flakes - 1 tsp kosher salt
- 3 fresh thyme sprigs, stems removed
- 1 tbsp olive oil
- 6 kale sprouts, ends trimmed and leaves separated
- ¼ cup English peas
- ¼ lemon, juiced and zested
- ½ cup parmesan cheese, grated and more for garnishing
- ¼ cup dill leaves, roughly chopped

Directions:
On a Dutch oven, pour the almond milk, vegetable broth, broken spaghetti noodles, asparagus, leek, broccoli, garlic, mushrooms, red pepper flakes, salt, and thyme leaves. Bring to a boil on high heat and then reduce the heat to simmer for 8 minutes, stirring to prevent the pasta from sticking together. Once the time elapse, add the kale sprouts and peas and continue to cook for another 3 minutes. Add in the lemon juice, cheese, and dill, and remove from the stove. Allow to cool and serve, not forgetting to garnish with dill leaves.
Per serving: Calories: 240Kcal; Fat: 9g; Carbs: 27g; Protein: 12g

765. Grilled Vegetable Sandwich

Preparation time: 10 minutes
Cooking time: 25 minutes **Servings:** 2
Ingredients:
- 1 cup vegan cashew ricotta cheese
- 1 tbsp parsley, basil, and chives, chopped
- 1 garlic clove, minced
- 1 tbsp extra virgin olive oil, plus more for drizzling
- Kosher salt and freshly ground black pepper to taste
- 1 large Portobello mushroom
- 1 zucchini, sliced lengthwise
- 1 yellow squash, sliced lengthwise

- ½ eggplant, sliced
- ½ red onion, sliced into rounds
- ½ red bell pepper, seeded and sliced in quarters
- 2 tsp oregano, dried
- 1 loaf ciabatta bread, sliced into 6-inch sections
- ½ cup arugula leaves
- Balsamic glaze

Directions:
In a small mixing bowl, mix the ricotta, garlic clove, fresh herbs, 1 tbsp olive oil, salt, and black pepper until smooth. Set aside.

Oil your grill grates with olive oil and preheat the grill for 15 minutes on high. Drizzle the veggies with extra virgin olive oil and season with salt, pepper, and dried oregano. Next, grease the cut side of the ciabatta with some olive oil. Place your vegetables on the grill and cook for 6 minutes. Once they start to soften, gently flip them using a spatula and cook the underside for another 5 minutes. Toast the two sides of ciabatta and transfer them along with the vegetables to a platter. Apply the herbed ricotta mixture on the toasted ciabatta bread and lay the grilled vegetables and arugula sides on top. Drizzle with the balsamic glaze and serve warm.

Per serving: Calories: 196Kcal; Fat: 12g; Carbs: 27g; Protein: 9g

766. Vegetarian Pancit Bihon

Preparation time: 10 minutes
Cooking time: 20 minutes **Servings:** 4
Ingredients:
- 2 cups vegetable stock
- 4 oz Bihon noodles - 2 tbsp canola oil
- 1 medium onion, finely diced
- 3 cloves garlic, crushed
- ½ lb mushrooms, sliced into small pieces
- 3 oz firm tofu drained, dried, and sliced (optional)
- 2 tbsp soy sauce
- Ground pepper to taste
- ½ cabbage, sliced - 1 carrot, cut
- 2 celery stalks, sliced - ½ cup snow peas
- Cilantro and lemon wedges for garnish

Directions:
Add the vegetable to a large pot and bring to boil. Toss in your noodles and cook for 4 minutes. Drain and set both the stock and noodles aside. In a large wok, add the oil and heat over medium-low heat for 3 minutes. Next, add the onions and garlic and sauté for 8 minutes until transparent. Add tofu, mushrooms, soy sauce, salt, and pepper. Cook for 5 minutes and add the vegetables, stirring. To prevent your food from sticking, add a little oil or some of the reserved stock. Once the vegetables are crisp, pour in the noodles and the stock. Stir well until well incorporated and sprinkle with cilantro and lemon wedges. Serve immediately.

Per serving: Calories: 200Kcal; Fat: 3g; Carbs: 30g; Protein: 7g

767. Easy Vegetable Lasagna

Preparation time: 20 minutes
Cooking time: 1 hr 20 minutes
Servings: 4
Ingredients:
- 7 lasagna noodles, plus 2 more for filling in the holes
- 1 medium zucchini, sliced into ½-inch pieces
- 1 medium yellow squash, sliced into ½-inch pieces
- 6 ounces red peppers, roasted and cut into ½-inch pieces
- ½ can tomatoes, crushed
- A generous handful of basil leaves, freshly chopped
- 6 ounces vegan cashew ricotta cheese
- 1 tbsp extra-virgin olive oil
- ½ cup onion, chopped
- ½ tbsp garlic, minced
- 1/8 tsp red pepper flakes, crushed
- Salt and fresh ground black pepper, to taste

Directions:
For the Noodles:
Add water and salt to a medium cooking pot and bring to boil. Cook your lasagna noodles according to directions indicated on the packaging. Once ready, drain and lay on a flat aluminum foil sheet.

For the Vegetable Sauce:
Start by preheating your oven to 350 F degrees.
Lightly oil a 13x 9-inch baking dish.
Next, heat the olive oil in a large skillet pans over medium heat and add the onion. Cook for 8 minutes until translucent and add the zucchini, squash, garlic, red pepper flakes, and a pinch of salt. Continue cooking for 8 minutes until softened, stirring. Add in the roasted peppers and crushed tomatoes. Lower the heat and simmer for 5 minutes until the liquid has thickened. Sprinkle the basil on top and adjust the seasoning with additional salt and pepper.

For the Cheese Filling:
vegan cashew ricotta cheese
Assembling the Lasagna:
Spoon enough vegetable mixture into your baking dish and arrange four noodles lengthwise and side by side, ensuring that the bottom is covered.
Spread half of your ricotta cheese on top of the noodles. Finish it off with a third of the vegetable mixture.
Repeat the process until all your ingredients are done and loosely cover the baking dish with aluminum foil. Bake for 20 minutes, remove the cover and continue baking for 15 minutes. Once ready, remove from the oven and let cool for 20 minutes.
Slice and serve.

Per serving (1/8 Lasagna): Calories: 450Kcal; Fat: 20g; Carbs: 36g; Protein: 27g

768. Curry Lentil Soup with Butternut Squash

Preparation time: 10 minutes
Cooking time: 55 minutes **Servings:** 4
Ingredients:
- ½ tbsp olive oil

- 1 cup red onion, chopped
- 1 tsp kosher salt, divided
- 4 cloves garlic, minced
- 1 tbsp ginger, freshly grated
- ½ tbsp curry powder
- ½ tsp garam masala
- ¼ tsp cinnamon, ground
- 2 cups vegetable broth
- 2 cups water
- 1 cup green lentils
- 2 cups butternut squash, diced
- ½ 15-ounce can garbanzo beans, drained
- ½ tbsp fresh lemon juice

Directions:
Heat a large Dutch oven over medium heat. Add oil, onion, and 1 teaspoon of kosher salt, and cook for 5 minutes until softened, stirring often. Add in the garlic, ginger, garam masala, ground cinnamon, curry powder and cook 3 minutes until fragrant. Pour in the water and vegetable broth and bring to a boil. Toss in the lentils, cover, and lower the heat. Simmer for 40 minutes, stirring often. Add the squash, garbanzo beans, and seasoning with the remaining kosher salt. Cook for 10 more minutes until the squash is tender. Add the leafy greens and stir in the lemon juice. Serve immediately.
Per serving: Calories: 202Kcal; Fat: 3g; Carbs: 28g; Protein: 9g

769. Glazed Avocado

Preparation time: 10 minutes
Cooking time: 12 minutes **Servings:** 4
Ingredients:
- 1 tablespoon stevia - 1 teaspoon olive oil
- 1 teaspoon water
- 1 teaspoon lemon juice
- ½ teaspoon rosemary, dried
- ½ teaspoon ground black pepper
- 2 avocados, peeled, pitted, and cut into large pieces

Directions:
Heat a pan with the oil over medium heat, add the avocados, stevia, and the other ingredients, toss, cook for 12 minutes, divide into bowls and serve.
Per serving: Calories: 262Kcal; Fat: 7.9g; Carbs: 6.5g; Protein: 7.9g

770. Mango and Leeks Meatballs

Preparation time: 20 minutes
Cooking time: 10 minutes **Servings:** 4
Ingredients:
- 1 tablespoon mango puree
- 1 cup leeks, chopped
- ½ cup tofu, crumbled
- 1 teaspoon dried oregano
- 1 tablespoon almond flour
- 1 teaspoon olive oil
- 1 tablespoon flax meal
- ½ teaspoon chili flakes

Directions:
In the mixing bowl, mix up mango puree with leeks, tofu, and the other ingredients, except for the oil, and stir well. Make the small meatballs. After this, pour the olive oil into the skillet and heat it. Add the meatballs to the skillet and cook them for 4 minutes from each side.
Per serving: Calories: 147Kcal; Fat: 8.6g; Carbs: 5.6g; Protein: 5.3g

771. Spicy Carrots and Olives

Preparation time: 15 minutes
Cooking time: 10 minutes **Servings:** 4
Ingredients:
- ½ teaspoon hot paprika
- 1 red chili pepper, minced
- ¼ teaspoon ground cumin
- ¼ teaspoon dried oregano
- ¼ teaspoon dried basil
- ½ teaspoon salt
- 1 tablespoon olive oil
- 1-pound baby carrots, peeled
- 1 cup kalamata olives, pitted and halved
- juice of 1 lime

Directions:
Heat a pan with the oil over medium heat, add the carrots, olives, and the other ingredients, toss, cook for 10 minutes, divide between plates and serve.
Per serving: Calories: 141Kcal; Fat: 5.8g; Carbs: 7.5g; Protein: 9.6g

772. Harissa Mushrooms

Preparation time: 15 minutes
Cooking time: 30 minutes **Servings:** 4
Ingredients:
- 1-pound mushroom caps - 1 teaspoon harissa
- 1 teaspoon rosemary, dried
- 2 spring onions, chopped
- 1 leek, sliced - 1 teaspoon thyme, dried
- 1 cup crushed tomatoes
- 1 teaspoon sweet paprika
- A pinch of salt and black pepper
- 1 tablespoon olive oil
- ½ teaspoon lemon juice

Directions:
In a roasting pan, mix the mushrooms with the harissa, rosemary, and the other ingredients and toss.
Preheat the oven to 360F and put the pan inside.
Cook the mix for 30 minutes, divide between plates and serve.
Per serving: Calories: 250Kcal; Fat: 12.1g; Carbs: 14.5g; Protein: 12.9g

773. Leeks and Artichokes Mix

Preparation time: 10 minutes
Cooking time: 30 minutes **Servings:** 4
Ingredients:
- 2 cups canned artichoke hearts, drained and quartered

- 3 leeks, sliced
- 1 cup cherry tomatoes, halved
- ¼ cup coconut cream
- 1 tablespoon almond flakes
- 1 teaspoon olive oil
- 1 teaspoon oregano, dried
- 1 teaspoon salt
- 1 teaspoon ground black pepper
- ¼ cup of chives, chopped

Directions:
Heat a pan with the oil over medium heat, add the leeks, oregano, salt and pepper, stir and cook for 10 minutes. Add artichokes and the other ingredients, toss, cook for 20 minutes, divide into bowls and serve. **Per serving:** Calories: 234Kcal; Fat: 9.7g; Carbs: 9.6g; Protein: 12.3g

774. Coconut Avocado

Preparation time: 10 minutes
Cooking time: 0 minutes **Servings:** 2
Ingredients:

- 2 avocados, halved, pitted, and roughly cubed
- 1 teaspoon dried thyme
- 2 tablespoons coconut cream
- 1 cup spring onions, chopped
- 1 teaspoon turmeric powder
- Salt and black pepper to the taste
- ¼ teaspoon cayenne pepper
- ½ teaspoon onion powder
- ½ teaspoon garlic powder
- 1 teaspoon paprika
- Salt and black pepper to the taste
- 2 tablespoons lemon juice

Directions:
In a bowl, mix the avocados with the thyme, coconut cream and the other ingredients, toss, divide between plates and serve. **Per serving:** Calories: 160Kcal; Fat: 6.9g; Carbs: 12g; Protein: 7g

775. Avocado Cream

Preparation time: 10 minutes
Cooking time: 0 minutes **Servings:** 4
Ingredients:

- 2 avocados, pitted, peeled and chopped
- 3 cups veggie stock
- 1 teaspoon curry powder
- 1 teaspoon cumin, ground
- 1 teaspoon basil, dried
- 2 scallions, chopped
- Salt and black pepper to the taste
- 2 tablespoons coconut oil
- 2/3 cup coconut cream, unsweetened

Directions:
In a blender, mix the avocados with the stock, curry powder, and the other ingredients, blend and serve.
Per serving: Calories: 212Kcal; Fat: 8g; Carbs: 6.1g; Protein: 1g

776. Tamarind Avocado Bowls

Preparation time: 10 minutes
Cooking time: 0 minutes **Servings:** 2
Ingredients:

- 1 teaspoon cumin seeds
- 1 tablespoon olive oil
- ½ teaspoon garam masala
- 1 teaspoon ground ginger
- 2 avocados, peeled, pitted and roughly cubed
- 1 mango, peeled and cubed
- 1 cup cherry tomatoes, halved
- ½ teaspoon cayenne pepper
- 1 teaspoon turmeric powder
- 3 tablespoons tamarind paste

Directions:
In a bowl, mix the avocados with the mango and the other ingredients, toss and serve.
Per serving: Calories: 170Kcal; Fat: 4.5g; Carbs: 5g; Protein: 6g

777. Onion and Tomato Bowls

Preparation time: 10 minutes
Cooking time: 0 minutes **Servings:** 4
Ingredients:

- 1 tablespoon olive oil
- 2 red bell peppers, cut into thin strips
- 2 red onions, cut into thin strips
- Salt and black pepper to the taste
- 1 teaspoon dried basil
- 1-pound tomatoes, cut into wedges
- 1 teaspoon balsamic vinegar
- 1 teaspoon sweet paprika

Directions:
In a bowl, mix the peppers with the onions and the other ingredients, toss and serve.
Per serving: Calories: 107Kcal; Fat: 4.5g; Carbs: 7.1g; Protein: 6g

778. Avocado and Leeks Mix

Preparation time: 10 minutes
Cooking time: 0 minutes **Servings:** 4
Ingredients:

- 1 small red onion, chopped
- 2 avocados, pitted, peeled and chopped
- 1 teaspoon chili powder
- 2 leeks, sliced - 1 cup cucumber, cubed
- 1 cup cherry tomatoes, halved
- Salt and black pepper to the taste
- 2 tablespoons cumin powder
- 2 tablespoons lime juice
- 1 tablespoon parsley, chopped

Directions:
In a bowl, mix the onion with the avocados, chili powder, and the other ingredients, toss and serve.
Per serving: Calories: 120Kcal; Fat: 2g; Carbs: 7g; Protein: 4g

779. Lemon Lentils and Carrots

Preparation time: 10 minutes
Cooking time: 20 minutes **Servings:** 6
Ingredients:

- 1 cup brown lentils, soaked overnight and drained
- 1 cup carrots, shredded
- 1 cup spring onions, chopped
- 1 teaspoon curry powder
- 1 teaspoon turmeric powder
- 1 teaspoon garam masala
- 2 tablespoons lemon juice
- ¼ cup parsley, chopped
- 2 garlic cloves, minced
- A pinch of salt and black pepper
- ½ teaspoon thyme, dried
- 2 tablespoons olive oil

Directions:
Heat a pan with the oil over medium heat, add the garlic, carrots, and spring onions and cook for 5 minutes. Add the lentils and the other ingredients, toss and simmer over medium heat for 15 minutes.
Divide between plates and serve.
Per serving: Calories: 240Kcal; Fat: 7g; Carbs: 12g; Protein: 6g

780. Cabbage Bowls

Preparation time: 10 minutes
Cooking time: 10 minutes **Servings:** 4
Ingredients:

- 1 green cabbage head, shredded
- 1 red cabbage head, shredded
- 1 teaspoon garam masala
- 1 teaspoon basil, dried
- 1 teaspoon coriander, ground
- 1 teaspoon mustard seeds
- 1 tablespoon balsamic vinegar
- ¼ cup tomatoes, crushed
- A pinch of salt and black pepper
- 3 carrots, shredded
- 1 yellow bell pepper, chopped
- 1 orange bell pepper, chopped
- 1 red bell pepper, chopped
- 2 tablespoons dill, chopped
- 2 tablespoons olive oil

Directions:
Heat a pan with the oil over medium heat, add the peppers and carrots and cook for 2 minutes.
Add the cabbage and the other ingredients, toss, cook for 10 minutes, divide between plates and serve.
Per serving: Calories: 150Kcal; Fat: 9g; Carbs: 3.3g; Protein: 4.4g

781. Pomegranate and Pears Salad

Preparation time: 10 minutes
Cooking time: 0 minutes **Servings:** 3
Ingredients:

- 3 big pears, cored and cut with a spiralizer
- ¾ cup pomegranate seeds
- 2 cups baby spinach
- ½ cup black olives, pitted and cubed
- ¾ cup walnuts, chopped1 tablespoon olive oil
- 1 tablespoon coconut sugar
- 1 teaspoon white sesame seeds
- 2 tablespoons chives, chopped
- 1 tablespoon balsamic vinegar
- 1 garlic clove, minced
- A pinch of sea salt and black pepper

Directions:
In a bowl, mix the pears with the pomegranate seeds, spinach, and the other ingredients, toss and serve.
Per serving: Calories: 200Kcal; Fat: 3.9g; Carbs: 6g; Protein: 3.3g

782. Bulgur and Tomato Mix

Preparation time: 15 minutes
Cooking time: 0 minutes **Servings:** 4
Ingredients:

- 1 ½ cups hot water
- 1 cup bulgur
- Juice of 1 lime
- 1 cup cherry tomatoes, halved
- 4 tablespoons cilantro, chopped
- ½ cup cranberries, dried
- juice of ½ lemon
- 1 teaspoon oregano, dried
- 1/3 cup almonds, sliced
- ¼ cup green onions, chopped
- ½ cup red bell peppers, chopped
- ½ cup carrots, grated
- 1 tablespoon avocado oil
- A pinch of sea salt and black pepper

Directions:
Place bulgur into a bowl, add boiling water to it, stir, cover, and set aside for 15 minutes. Fluff bulgur with a fork and transfer to a bowl. Add the rest of the ingredients, toss and serve.
Per serving: Calories: 260Kcal; Fat: 4.4g; Carbs: 7g; Protein: 10g

783. Beans Mix

Preparation time: 10 minutes
Cooking time: 15 minutes **Servings:** 4
Ingredients:

- 1 ½ cups cooked black beans
- 1 cup cooked red kidney beans
- ½ teaspoon garlic powder
- ½ teaspoon smoked paprika
- 2 teaspoons chili powder
- 1 tablespoon olive oil
- 1 ½ cups chickpeas, cooked
- 1 teaspoon garam masala
- 1 red bell pepper, chopped
- 2 tomatoes, chopped

- 1 cup cashews, chopped - ½ cup veggie stock
- 1 tablespoon balsamic vinegar
- 1 tablespoon oregano, chopped
- 1 tablespoon dill, chopped
- 1 cup corn kernels, chopped

Directions:
Heat a pan with the oil over medium heat, add the beans, garlic powder, chili powder, and the other ingredients, toss and cook for 15 minutes. Divide between plates and serve.
Per serving: Calories: 300Kcal; Fat: 8.3g; Carbs: 6g; Protein: 13g

784. Smoked Green Beans
Preparation time: 10 minutes
Cooking time: 10 minutes **Servings:** 4
Ingredients:
- 3 tablespoons balsamic vinegar
- 2 tablespoons olive oil
- 1/3 cup kalamata olives, pitted and minced
- 1 garlic clove, minced
- 1-pound green beans, trimmed and halved
- ½ teaspoon lemon zest, grated
- ½ red onion, sliced
- 2 cups baby arugula
- 1 teaspoon smoked paprika
- 1 tablespoon cilantro, chopped

Directions:
Heat a pan with the oil over medium heat, add the garlic, onion, and paprika and cook for 5 minutes.
Add the green beans, vinegar, and the other ingredients, stir and cook for 5 more minutes.
Divide between plates and serve.
Per serving: Calories: 212Kcal; Fat: 3g; Carbs: 6g; Protein: 4g

785. Lentil and Sunflower Seeds Salad
Preparation time: 10 minutes
Cooking time: 0 minutes
Servings: 2
Ingredients:
- 1 cup canned and cooked green lentils, drained
- 1 carrot, grated
- 4 cups arugula
- 2 spring onions, chopped
- 1 cucumber, sliced
- ¼ cup black olives, pitted and sliced
- 1 radish, sliced
- 1 tablespoon sunflower oil
- 1 tablespoon balsamic vinegar
- 2 tablespoons sunflower seeds

Directions:
In a bowl, mix the lentils with the arugula, carrot, and the other ingredients, toss, divide between plates and serve.
Per serving: Calories: 179Kcal; Fat: 3g; Carbs: 6g; Protein: 7.1g

786. Chives Chickpeas Mix
Preparation time: 10 minutes
Cooking time: 0 minutes
Servings: 2
Ingredients:
- 16 ounces canned chickpeas, drained
- 1 tablespoon capers, drained
- 1 handful baby arugula
- ½ tablespoon lemon juice
- 4 tablespoons olive oil
- 1 teaspoon cumin, ground
- 1 teaspoon oregano, dried
- 1 teaspoon basil, dried
- 1 tablespoon chives, chopped
- A pinch of sea salt and black pepper
- ½ teaspoon chili flakes

Directions:
In a bowl, mix the chickpeas with the capers, arugula, and the other ingredients, toss and serve.
Per serving: Calories: 200Kcal; Fat: 3.6g; Carbs: 12g; Protein: 5.4g

787. Balsamic Olives Salad
Preparation time: 10 minutes
Cooking time: 0 minutes
Servings: 4
Ingredients:
- 1 handful kalamata olives, pitted and sliced
- 1 handful black olives, pitted and sliced
- 1 handful, green olives, pitted and sliced
- 2 tablespoons basil, chopped
- 1 tablespoon mint, chopped
- 2 tablespoons balsamic vinegar
- 1 garlic cloves, minced
- A pinch of salt and black pepper
- 2 tablespoons olive oil
- 1 punnet cherry tomatoes, halved
- 2 cucumbers, sliced
- 1 red onion, chopped

Directions:
In a bowl, mix the olives with the basil, mint, and the other ingredients, toss and serve.
Per serving: Calories: 200Kcal; Fat: 5.5g; Carbs: 6g; Protein: 5.5g

788. Chickpeas and Spinach Mix
Preparation time: 10 minutes
Cooking time: 0 minutes **Servings:** 4
Ingredients:
- 15 ounces canned chickpeas, drained
- 2 tablespoons avocado oil
- 1 teaspoon turmeric powder
- 1 teaspoon sweet paprika
- ½ cup spinach, chopped
- ½ cup cucumber, sliced
- 1 tablespoon basil, chopped

- 1 tablespoon parsley, chopped
- A pinch of sea salt
- 2 tablespoon vinegar

Directions:
In a bowl, mix chickpeas with spinach, cucumber, and the rest of the ingredients, toss and serve.

Per serving: Calories: 140Kcal; Fat: 5g; Carbs: 9g; Protein: 9.1g

789. Brussels Sprout Skewers

Preparation time: 10 minutes
Cooking time: 20 minutes
Servings: 4
Ingredients:
- ½ of a medium red onion, peeled, sliced into 1-inch squares
- 1-pound Brussels sprouts, halved
- ¼ teaspoon of sea salt
- 1 tablespoon maple syrup
- 3 tablespoons balsamic vinegar
- 1 tablespoon Dijon mustard
- 3 tablespoons olive oil

Directions:
Take a large pot half full with water, place it over medium-high heat and then bring it to a boil.
Add Brussel sprouts, cook for 1 minute until tender, remove them from the pot, rinse well until cold water and then pat dry with paper towels. Transfer Brussel sprouts in a large bowl, add onion and remaining ingredients, and then toss until coated. Take a griddle pan, place it over medium-high heat, grease it with oil and then let it heat until hot. Thread Brussel sprouts and onions on skewers, four sprouts per skewer, and then brush with remaining marinade.
Arrange the prepared skewers onto the grill pan and then cook for 7 to 10 minutes per side until vegetables turn nicely brown.
Serve straight away.

Per serving: Calories: 159.3Kcal; Fat: 10.5g; Carbs: 13.2g; Protein: 3.9g

790. Thai Peanut Butter Cauliflower Wings

Preparation time: 15 minutes
Cooking time: 30 minutes **Servings:** 4
Ingredients:
- ½ of large head cauliflower, cut into florets
- 1 tablespoon minced Thai chili
- ½ teaspoon ginger powder
- 1 cup panko breadcrumbs
- 2 tablespoons lime juice
- 2 teaspoons soy sauce
- ½ cup peanut butter
- ¼ cup of water

Directions:
Switch on the oven, then set it to 400 degrees F and let it preheat. Meanwhile, take a medium bowl, add ginger, minced chili, peanut butter, water, lime juice, and soy sauce and then whisk until smooth.
Take a shallow dish and then spread panko breadcrumbs in it. Working on cauliflower florets at a time, dip into the peanut butter mixture, coat in breadcrumbs, and then place on a baking sheet lined with a parchment sheet.
Spray oil over the cauliflower florets and then bake for 30 minutes until florets turn crisp, turning halfway.
Serve straight away.

Per serving: Calories: 130Kcal; Fat: 4g; Carbs: 19g; Protein: 4g

791. Potato SaladErrore. Il segnalibro non è definito.

Preparation time: 45 minutes
Cooking time: 45 minutes
Servings: 6
Ingredients:
- 2.8-pound potatoes
- 1 cup chopped dill pickles
- 23 ounces cooked peas
- 3 tablespoons chopped dill
- ¾ teaspoon salt
- 1 tablespoon coconut sugar
- ½ teaspoon ground black pepper
- 2 ¼ cup mayonnaise, plant-based

Directions:
Rinse the potatoes, place them in a large pot, and then pour in enough water until potatoes are covered by 1-inch. Place the pot over medium-high heat and then cook for 20 to 30 minutes until tender.
When done, drain the potatoes and let them cool for 15 minutes. Meanwhile, take a large bowl, place mayonnaise in it, add sugar, salt, and black pepper and then whisk until combined. Peel the cooled potatoes, cut them into small pieces, add to the mayonnaise mixture along with peas, pickles, and dill and then mix until thoroughly coated.
Let the salad in the refrigerator for 30 minutes until chilled and then serve.

Per serving: Calories: 178.9Kcal; Fat: 5.1g; Carbs: 31.4g; Protein: 4.2g

792. Carrot Patties

Preparation time: 10 minutes
Cooking time: 15 minutes
Servings: 15 patties
Ingredients:
- 14 ounces cooked white beans
- 2 cups grated carrots
- 1 medium white onion, peeled, chopped
- ½ cup white whole-wheat flour
- ½ teaspoon curry powder
- ¾ teaspoon dried rosemary
- 1 teaspoon salt
- ¾ teaspoon dried thyme
- ½ teaspoon cumin powder
- 2 tablespoons olive oil

Directions:
Take a large bowl, place beans in it, and then mash with a fork. Add remaining ingredients, except for the oil, stir until

well combined, and then shape the mixture into fifteen patties. Take a large skillet pan, place it over medium-high heat, add oil and let it heat. Arrange the prepared patties in the pan and then cook for 2 to 3 minutes per side until golden brown and thoroughly cooked. Serve straight away.
Per serving: Calories: 96Kcal; Fat: 5g; Carbs: 12.2g; Protein: 2.6g

793. Eggplant and Potatoes in Tomato Sauce

Preparation time: 5 minutes
Cooking time: 15 minutes **Servings:** 4
Ingredients:
- 3 large potatoes, boiled, cut into cubes
- 14 ounces crushed tomatoes
- 1 medium eggplant, destemmed, cut into cubes
- 2 tablespoons minced garlic
- 1 teaspoon salt
- 1 tablespoon curry powder
- 1 tablespoon soy sauce
- 3 tablespoons olive oil

Directions:
Take a large skillet pan, place it over medium heat, add oil, and let it heat. Add eggplant pieces, stir until coated, and then cook for 5 minutes until golden brown. Add garlic, season with salt and curry powder, cook for 1 minute and then stir in tomatoes. Cover the skillet pan with its lid and then simmer the vegetables for 7 minutes until thoroughly cooked. Add potato cubes, drizzle with soy sauce, stir until well combined, and then cook for 1 to 2 minutes until thoroughly hot. Serve straight away.
Per serving: Calories: 76Kcal; Fat: 0.5g; Carbs: 18.3g; Protein: 2.5g

794. Grilled Mushrooms with Garlic Sauce

Preparation time: 10 minutes **Cooking time:** 30 minutes
Servings: 2
Ingredients:
- 2 large Portobello mushrooms

For the Marinade:
- 1 tablespoon minced garlic
- 1/3 teaspoon salt
- ¾ teaspoon smoked paprika
- 1/3 teaspoon ground black pepper
- 2 tablespoons balsamic vinegar
- 2 teaspoons lemon juice
- 2 teaspoons soy sauce
- 1 teaspoon white wine vinegar
- 1 teaspoon olive oil

For the Garlic Sauce:
- ¼ cup cashews
- 1 medium white onion, peeled, chopped
- 4 teaspoons minced garlic
- ½ teaspoon salt
- 1 tablespoon arrowroot powder
- 1 tablespoon nutritional yeast
- 1 tablespoon lemon juice
- 2 tablespoons white wine
- 1 teaspoon and 1 tablespoon olive oil
- 1 ½ cup water

Directions:
Switch on the oven, then set it to 400 degrees F and let it preheat. Meanwhile, prepare the marinade and for this, take a shallow dish, place all the ingredients in it and then stir until well combined. Add mushrooms into the marinade dish, toss until well coated, and then let them marinate for 15 minutes.
Arrange the mushrooms on a baking sheet lined with foil and then bake for 30 minutes until tender.
Meanwhile, prepare the garlic sauce and for this, take a medium skillet pan, place it over medium heat, add 1 teaspoon oil and let it heat until hot.
Add onion and garlic, cook for 5 minutes until tender, and then transfer half of this mixture into a food processor or blender.
Add remaining ingredients for the sauce in it, cover with the lid, and then pulse for 1 minute or more until well combined.
Spoon the mixture into the skillet pan, stir until mixed with the remaining onion mixture and then cook for 4 to 6 minutes until thickened to the desired level. When the mushrooms have baked, divide them evenly among plates, drizzle with the garlic sauce and then serve.
Per serving: Calories: 198Kcal; Fat: 12g; Carbs: 17.8g; Protein: 5g

795. Sesame Tofu and Veggies Noodles

Preparation time: 10 minutes
Cooking time: 30 minutes **Servings:** 3
Ingredients:
For the Noodles:
- 6 ounces brown rice noodles
- 1 teaspoon lemon juice
- ½ teaspoon sesame oil
- ¼ teaspoon red pepper flakes

For the Sesame Tofu:
- 14 ounces tofu, extra-firm, pressed, drained, cut into cubes
- 1 cup of mixed vegetables
- ½ of large red bell pepper, cored, sliced
- 1 hot green chile, chopped
- 1 large green bell pepper, cored, sliced
- ½ cup sliced carrots
- 2 tablespoons chopped garlic
- 1 tablespoon grated ginger
- 1 tablespoon cornstarch
- 1 teaspoon olive oil
- 2 teaspoons sesame oil
- ½ cup of water
- 1 teaspoon sesame seeds

For the Sauce:
- ¼ teaspoon salt
- 1/8 teaspoon ground black pepper
- ¼ cup maple syrup

- 1/3 cup soy sauce
- 3 teaspoons Sriracha sauce
- 3 tablespoons apple cider vinegar
- 1 tablespoon orange juice

Directions:
Prepare the noodles by following the instructions on its package, rinse them under cold water, drain well, and then place them in a large bowl.

Add remaining ingredients for the noodles in it, toss until combined, divide evenly among three bowls, and then set aside until required.

Prepare the tofu and for this, take a large skillet pan, place it over medium heat, add olive oil and then let it heat until hot. Add tofu, cook for 2 to 3 minutes per side until golden brown and then transfer to a shallow dish. Add sesame oil into the pan, add green chile, bell pepper, and vegetables, toss until coated in oil, and then cook for 4 minutes until tender-crisp.

Stir in ginger and garlic, cook for 3 minutes, add all the ingredients for the sauce, stir until mixed and cook for 1 minute. Return tofu pieces into the pan, toss until coated, bring the sauce to a rolling boil and cook for 3 minutes. Whisk together cornstarch and water, add to the sauce, stir until mixed, and then cook for 3 to 4 minutes until the sauce has thickened to the desired level. Spoon tofu and sauce over the noodles, sprinkle with sesame seeds, and then serve.

Per serving: Calories: 488Kcal; Fat: 9g; Carbs: 84g; Protein: 14.1g

796. Bombay Potatoes and Peas

Preparation time: 10 minutes
Cooking time: 35 minutes **Servings:** 3
Ingredients:
- 3 medium potatoes, 1/2-inch cubed
- 1 small red onion, peeled, chopped
- 1 large tomato
- 1 cup cooked peas
- 2 tablespoons minced garlic
- 1-inch piece of ginger, grated
- ¾ teaspoon salt
- ½ teaspoon red chili powder
- ½ teaspoon cumin seeds
- 1 teaspoon ground coriander
- ½ teaspoon turmeric powder
- 1 teaspoon mustard seeds
- ½ teaspoon ground cumin
- ½ teaspoon garam masala
- 2 teaspoons olive oil
- 1 cup of water
- ¼ cup chopped cilantro

Directions:
Take a large skillet pan, place it over medium heat, add oil and let it heat until hot. Add mustard and cumin seeds, cook for 1 to 2 minutes until golden brown and fragrant, then stir in onion and cook for 5 minutes. Meanwhile, cut tomatoes into pieces, add them into a blender, add ginger and garlic and then pulse until pureed. Pour the tomato mixture into the pan, add all the spices, stir until mixed, and then cook for 5 minutes until the tomato mixture has thickened to the desired level.

Add potatoes, season with salt, pour in water, stir until mixed, cover the pan with its lid, and then cook for 10 minutes. Stir peas into the potato mixture, taste to adjust seasoning, switch heat to medium-low level and then continue simmering the vegetables for 10 to 12 minutes until potatoes turn tender. When done, garnish potatoes and peas with cilantro and then serve.

Per serving: Calories: 232.3Kcal; Fat: 3.9g; Carbs: 42.4g; Protein: 9.8g

797. BBQ Tofu Pizza

Preparation time: 25 minutes
Cooking time: 15 minutes
Servings: 2
Ingredients:
For the Crust:
- ¾ cup spelt flour
- 2 teaspoons active yeast
- 1 tablespoon cornstarch
- 1/3 teaspoon salt - 2 teaspoons olive oil
- 1 teaspoon maple syrup
- ¼ cup and 2 tablespoons hot water

For the Tofu:
- 1 cup tofu cubes, pressed, drained
- ½ teaspoon garlic powder
- 3 teaspoons Sriracha sauce
- 2 tablespoons BBQ sauce

For the Toppings:
- 1 medium red bell pepper, cored, sliced
- 1 medium red onion, peeled, sliced
- 2/3 cup marinara sauce
- 1 ½ cup shredded cashew cheese

Directions:
Prepare the tofu and for this, take a large bowl, place tofu pieces in it, add remaining ingredients, toss until well coated, and then let the tofu rest until required. Prepare the crust and for this, take a small bowl, place maple syrup in it, add yeast, pour in the water, whisk until combined, and then let the mixture rest for 5 minutes until frothy. Take a large bowl, place flour in it, add yeast, cornstarch, and salt and then stir until combined. Add the yeast mixture into the flour mixture, add oil, stir until well combined, and then knead the mixture for 2 minutes until a smooth dough comes together. Transfer the dough onto the clean working surface dusted with flour, roll it into 12-inch wide round crust and then let it rest at a warm place for a minimum of 10 minutes. Meanwhile, switch on the oven, then set it to 450 degrees F and let it preheat. After 10 minutes, transfer the crust to a baking sheet, spread marinara sauce on it, and then scatter with red bell pepper pieces and onion slices. Sprinkle salt and black pepper over the vegetables, scatter tofu pieces on the crust, sprinkle cheese on top, and then bake for 12 to 15 minutes until thoroughly cooked. When done, let the pizza rest for 15 minutes, cut into slices, and then serve.

Per serving: Calories: 394Kcal; Fat: 11g; Carbs: 55g; Protein: 15g

798. Quinoa Tacos

Preparation time: 10 minutes
Cooking time: 35 minutes **Servings:** 10 tacos
Ingredients:
- ½ of medium red bell pepper, cored, sliced
- 1 cup quinoa
- ½ of medium orange bell pepper, cored, sliced
- 2 green onions
- 4 cups mixed greens
- 1 teaspoon onion powder
- 1 teaspoon garlic powder
- ½ teaspoon salt, divided
- 1 tablespoon cumin powder
- 1 teaspoon dried oregano
- 1 tablespoon paprika
- 3 tablespoons coconut oil
- 2 cups vegetable broth
- 2 tablespoons lime juice
- 12 tablespoons cashew cream
- 12 tablespoons salsa
- 12 corn tortillas

Directions:
Cook the quinoa, and for this, take a medium saucepan, place it over medium heat and let it heat until hot. Add quinoa, cook for 3 to 4 minutes until toasted, transfer quinoa to a strainer, and then rinse it well. Return quinoa into the saucepan, pour in the vegetable broth, stir in ¼ teaspoon salt and then bring quinoa to boil. Switch heat to the low level, cover the pan with its lid and then simmer quinoa for 15 to 20 minutes until the quinoa has absorbed all the liquid. Meanwhile, take a medium bowl, place red bell pepper slices in it, drizzle with 1 tablespoon of lime juice, toss until coated, and then set aside until required. When done, remove the saucepan from heat, let the quinoa rest for 5 minutes, uncover the pan and then fluff with a fork. Take a large skillet pan, place it over medium heat, add oil and let it heat until melted. Add quinoa, stir until combined, stir in remaining salt, onion powder, garlic powder, cumin, and paprika and then cook for 5 minutes until bottom begins to turn crisp, don't stir. Remove pan from heat, add green onions and remaining lime juice, and stir until mixed. Assemble the tacos and for this, warm the tortillas until hot and slightly blacken and then fill evenly with mixed greens.
Stuff the tortillas with quinoa mixture, red bell peppers, salsa, and cashew cream, and then serve.
Per serving: Calories: 150.5Kcal; Fat: 5.2g; Carbs: 23.3g; Protein: 4g

799. Teriyaki Noodle Stir-Fry

Preparation time: 15 minutes
Cooking time: 15 minutes **Servings:** 3
Ingredients:
- 2 cups shredded cabbage
- 1 large red bell pepper, cored, sliced
- 2 medium carrots, julienned
- 4 button mushrooms, sliced
- 1 cup snow peas
- 1 teaspoon minced garlic
- 1 tablespoon olive oil
- 8 ounces of rice noodles
- 4 green onions, chopped

For the Sauce:
- ¼ cup of soy sauce
- 1 tablespoon coconut sugar
- 1 teaspoon apple cider vinegar
- ½ teaspoon sesame oil
- 1/8 teaspoon ground black pepper

Directions:
Prepare the noodles and for this, take a large bowl, place noodles in it, cover with hot water and then let it rest for 10 minutes until tender. Meanwhile, prepare the sauce and for this, take a small bowl, place all of its ingredients in it, stir until well mixed, and then set aside until required. Then drain the noodles, rinse under cold water, and set aside until required. Take a large skillet pan, place it over medium-high heat, add oil and let it heat until hot.
Add mushrooms, carrots, cabbage, and bell pepper, stir in garlic and then cook for 2 to 3 minutes until tender-crisp. Add green onions and snow peas, continue cooking for 1 minute, and then add noodles. Drizzle half of the prepared sauce over the noodles, toss until coated, switch heat to a high level, and then cook for 2 minutes until thoroughly hot.
Add more sauce if needed, toss until coated, and then serve.
Per serving: Calories: 302Kcal; Fat: 16.6g; Carbs: 27.8g; Protein: 4.1g

800. Garlicky Tofu

Preparation time: 5 minutes
Cooking time: 15 minutes **Servings:** 2
Ingredients:
- 2 tablespoons cornstarch
- 14 ounces tofu, extra-firm, pressed, drained
- 1 tablespoon sesame oil
- 1 teaspoon sesame seeds

For The Sauce:
- 2 teaspoons cornstarch
- 2 teaspoons maple syrup
- ½ teaspoon apple cider vinegar
- ¼ cup of soy sauce
- 1 ½ teaspoon chili garlic sauce
- 2 tablespoons water

Directions:
Take a large bowl, place tofu pieces in it, sprinkle with cornstarch, and then toss until coated. Prepare the sauce and for this, take a medium bowl, place all of its ingredients in it and then whisk until combined.
Take a large skillet pan, place it over medium-high heat, add oil in it, and then let it heat until hot.
Add tofu pieces, and then cook for 2 to 3 minutes per side until golden brown. Pour in the prepared sauce, toss until coated, and then cook for 3 to 4 minutes until the sauce has thickened to the desired level. Garnish the tofu with sesame seeds, and then serve.
Per serving: Calories: 313Kcal; Fat: 16g; Carbs: 17g; Protein: 19g

801. Mac and Cheese

Preparation time: 5 minutes
Cooking time: 10 minutes **Servings:** 2
Ingredients:
- 1 cup pasta, uncooked
- 4 tablespoons nutritional yeast
- ½ teaspoon onion powder
- 1 teaspoon turmeric powder
- 1 teaspoon Dijon mustard
- 4 tablespoons ketchup
- 1 cup of water - ½ cup carrot puree

Directions:
Take a large heatproof bowl, place pasta in it, pour in water, and then stir until combined.
Place the bowl into the microwave, cook it for 2 minutes, stir the pasta and then continue cooking it for 2 minutes or more until the pasta has absorbed all the liquid.
Add remaining ingredients, except for the ketchup, stir until combined, and then continue microwaving for 3 minutes until hot.
Top the pasta with ketchup and then serve.
Per serving: Calories: 270Kcal; Fat: 2g; Carbs: 52g; Protein: 11.6g

802. Peanut Butter and Pumpkin Soup

Preparation time: 5 minutes
Cooking time: 12 minutes **Servings:** 4
Ingredients:
- 1 tablespoon Thai red curry paste
- 1 tablespoon agave syrup
- 2 tablespoons peanut butter
- 1 tablespoon soy sauce
- 1 tablespoon Sriracha sauce
- 2 cups vegetable broth
- ¼ cup coconut milk, unsweetened
- 1 2/3 cup pumpkin puree

Directions:
Take a large pot, place it over medium-high heat and then let it heat until hot. Add curry paste into the pot, cook for 1 minute until fragrant, add remaining ingredients, and then whisk until combined. Cook the soup for 5 to 10 minutes until thoroughly hot and then serve.
Per serving: Calories: 132Kcal; Fat: 10g; Carbs: 8g; Protein: 3g

803. Sweet Korean Lentils

Preparation time: 5 minutes
Cooking time: 10 minutes **Servings:** 2
Ingredients:
For the Lentils:
- 1 cup red lentils
- ½ of a medium white onion, peeled, chopped
- 2 green onions, chopped
- 1 tablespoon peanut oil
- 1 tablespoon sesame seeds

For the Sauce:
- 1 teaspoon minced garlic
- 3 tablespoons coconut sugar
- 1-inch piece of ginger, grated
- ½ teaspoon crushed red pepper flakes
- 1 teaspoon sesame oil
- ¼ cup of soy sauce - 2 cups of water

Directions:
Prepare the sauce and for this, take a medium bowl, place all of its ingredients in it and then whisk until combined. Take a large skillet pan, place it over medium heat, add oil and then let it heat until hot. Add onion, cook for 5 minutes until beginning to brown, add lentils, pour in the sauce, and then stir until mixed. Cover the pan with its lid, bring the lentils to simmer, and then cook for 8 to 10 minutes until lentils have turned tender and have absorbed most of the cooking liquid. When done, garnish lentils with green onions and sesame seeds and then serve.
Per serving: Calories: 253Kcal; Fat: 6g; Carbs: 36g; Protein: 13g

804. Pasta Puttanesca

Preparation time: 10 minutes
Cooking time: 40 minutes
Servings: 4
Ingredients:
- 28 ounces diced tomatoes
- ½ cup olives
- 2 teaspoons coconut sugar
- ¼ teaspoon salt
- ½ teaspoon red pepper flakes
- 2 teaspoons minced garlic
- 8 ounces pasta
- 1 tablespoon capers
- 1 tablespoon olive oil

Directions:
Prepare the pasta, and for this, cook it according to the instructions on its package and then set aside until required. Take a large skillet pan, place it over medium-high heat, add oil and then let it heat until hot. Add olives, capers, and garlic, stir until mixed, and then cook for 2 minutes until garlic turns golden brown. Add tomatoes, stir in salt, red pepper flakes, and sugar, and then simmer the mixture for 25 to 30 minutes until thoroughly cooked. Add cooked pasta, toss until coated, and then cook for 2 to 3 minutes until hot. Serve straight away.
Per serving: Calories: 290Kcal; Fat: 7.5g; Carbs: 46.5g; Protein: 9.5g

805. Walnut Meat Tacos

Preparation time: 10 minutes
Cooking time: 20 minutes
Servings: 8 tacos
Ingredients:
For the Meat:
- ½ cup walnuts
- 6 sun-dried tomatoes
- 1 cup almonds
- ¼ teaspoon onion powder
- ¼ teaspoon garlic powder
- 1/3 teaspoon salt

- ¼ teaspoon ground black pepper
- ½ teaspoon paprika
- ¼ teaspoon cayenne pepper

For Serving:
- 8 taco shells
- 8 tablespoons salsa
- 8 tablespoons shredded cashew cheese

Directions:
Switch on the oven, then set it to 350 degrees F and let it preheat. Take a medium bowl, place walnuts in it, cover with hot water, and then let it soak for 20 minutes. Take a separate medium bowl, place tomatoes in it, cover with hot water, and then let it soak for 20 minutes. After 20 minutes, drain the walnuts and tomatoes, and then place them in a food processor. Add remaining ingredients for the meat and then pulse until the crumbly mixture comes together. Spread the meat into a baking dish and then bake for 20 minutes until cooked, stirring halfway.

When done, spoon the meat evenly among taco shells, top each shell with 1 tablespoon of salsa and cashew cheese and then serve. **Per serving:** Calories: 240Kcal; Fat: 23.7g; Carbs: 5.6g; Protein: 5.7g

806. Couscous with Olives

Preparation time: 5 minutes
Cooking time: 30 minutes **Servings:** 4
Ingredients:
- ½ cup sliced black olives
- 1 medium shallot, peeled, minced
- 1/3 cup chopped sun-dried tomatoes
- 2 teaspoons minced garlic
- 5 tablespoons olive oil, divided
- 1 cup vegetable broth
- ½ cup pine nuts
- ¼ cup chopped parsley

For the Couscous:
- 2 cups couscous - 1/8 teaspoon salt
- 1/8 teaspoon ground black pepper
- 1 1/4 cups vegetable broth
- 1 1/4 cups water

Directions:
Prepare the couscous and for this, take a medium saucepan, place it over medium-high heat, add vegetable broth and water and then bring it to a boil.

Add couscous, stir in salt and black pepper, switch heat to the low level, and then simmer the couscous for 8 minutes until it has absorbed all of its cooking liquid. When done, remove the pan from heat, let couscous rest for 5 minutes, fluff it with a fork and then let it rest until required. Take a large skillet pan, place it over medium-high heat, add 3 tablespoons of oil and then let it heat until hot. Add peanuts, stir until coated, and then cook for 1 minute until nuts turn golden brown, set aside until required. Take a separate saucepan, place it over medium heat, add the remaining oil, and then let it heat. Add shallot and garlic, cook for 2 minutes until shallot begins to turn tender, add tomatoes and olives, and then continue cooking for 3 minutes. Pour in the vegetable broth, bring the sauce to boil, then switch heat to a low level, and then simmer the sauce for 8 to 10 minutes until reduced by half. Take a large bowl, place couscous in it, add cooked sauce and stir until well combined. Top the couscous with parsley and pine nuts, and then serve.

Per serving: Calories: 527.7Kcal; Fat: 29.3g; Carbs: 55.5g; Protein: 13g

807. Black Bean and Corn Salad

Preparation time: 5 minutes
Cooking time: 0 minutes **Servings:** 6
Ingredients:
- 30 ounces black beans
- 1 large avocado, peeled, pitted, diced
- 1 1/2 cups frozen corn kernels
- 1 large red bell pepper, cored, chopped
- 6 green onions, thinly sliced
- 2 large tomatoes, chopped
- ½ cup chopped cilantro

For the Salad Dressing:
- 1/3 cup lime juice - ½ cup olive oil
- ½ teaspoon minced garlic
- 1 teaspoon salt
- 1/8 teaspoon ground cayenne pepper

Directions:
Prepare the salad dressing, and for this, take a small jar, place all of its ingredients in it. Cover the jar with its lid, and then shake it well until mixed. Take a large salad bowl, place all the ingredients for the salad in it, and then pour the prepared salad dressing over it.

Stir until well coated, and then serve the salad.
Per serving: Calories: 391Kcal; Fat: 24.5g; Carbs: 35.1g; Protein: 10.5g

808. Chickpea Salad Sandwich

Preparation time: 10 minutes
Cooking time: 0 minutes **Servings:** 2
Ingredients:
- 1 1/2 cups cooked chickpeas
- 1 rib celery, sliced
- 1 cup mixed greens
- 3 green onions, sliced
- ½ teaspoon salt
- ½ teaspoon ground black pepper
- 1 teaspoon celery seed
- 1 tablespoon lemon juice
- 2 tablespoons cashew cream
- 4 slices of whole-wheat bread

Directions:
Take a large bowl, place chickpeas in it, and then mash with a fork. Add remaining ingredients, except for the bread and then stir until well combined.

Spread the salad evenly on top of two bread slices, cover the top with remaining bread slices, and then serve.
Per serving: Calories: 384Kcal; Fat: 12.2g; Carbs: 54.3g; Protein: 11.4g

Conclusion

The plant-based diet has been around for a long time and is not a recently invented diet. It has sustained many people for thousands of years and is not something modern. People who follow it do so by their own choice; none are forced to do so.

There are many reasons people turn to this diet, such as personal health, religious reasons, but also morality and environmental concerns are some examples. People believe that "good food" makes you feel good, or at least feel less bad than eating meat. It is good for your body and also good for the planet on which we live. The environment cares for us; we should care for it by making small changes in our eating habits.

The diet is simple. People don't need to learn too many new things, but they need to eat a lot more vegetables and fruits and a lot less meat, poultry, fish, dairy products, and eggs. You may be worried at first if you eat meat; however, to start, it is possible to do so while eating the same amount or even more vegetables and fruits.

You can keep track of your eating by using an app or writing down what you eat in a logbook. There are many guides for this purpose. Most important is that you cut down on consuming meat and increase the intake of vegetables and fruits. This is because the plant-based diet contains a lot of fiber which is good for your digestive system.

If you want to go further and follow a vegan or vegetarian diet, that is good too. But for most people, it is enough to remove meat from your diet.

The plant-based diet is not a diet of short duration; generally, diets that are very restrictive last for just a few weeks. For those who want to lose weight, it is an excellent way to do so. The book "Body for Life" was written in the 1960s by Professor Clifford Hardin and is still being used today for losing weight. The plan requires you to eat large quantities of vegetables, fruits, and whole grains.

There is no need to worry about the general nutrition for those who are following the diet for health purposes. You can eat a lot of vegetables and fruits and not be hungry. Vegetables are rich in proteins and fiber, which are important for good health.

The benefits of this type of diet go beyond weight loss. Many other things that improve our lives: it helps prevent cardiovascular diseases, strengthens the immune system, prevents cancer, among others, have been discovered by scientists who follow it or by people who ate it before any study was conducted on it.

The plant-based diet has been around for a long time, but it is not new. Therefore you can try it without worrying that it is some fad that will lose its popularity.

So if you want to get started on this diet and don't know how, start by adding more fruits and vegetables to your meals. Everything else will be easy to learn.

Amanda Kale

Recipe Index

A

Acorn Squash, Sweet Potatoes, And Apples	134
African Peanut Lentil Soup	141
African Pineapple Peanut Stew	145
Alfredo with Peas	102
Alkaline Strawberry Smoothie	213
Almond Butter Brownies	191
Almond Butter Fudge	193
Almond Parmesan Crumbles	44
Almond-Date Energy Bites	188
Amazing Chickpea and Noodle Soup	84
Apple Crisp	194
Apple Mix	193
Apple-Lemon Bowl	205
Applesauce Crumble Muffins	52
Aromatic Millet Bowl	93
Artichoke White Bean Sandwich Spread	119
Arugula Beans Salad	65
Arugula Salad	114
Asparagus & Green Peas Soup	78
Asparagus, Leek, And Ricotta Flatbreads	207
Authentic African Mielie-Meal	92
Avocado & Radish Salad	71
Avocado & White Bean Salad	66
Avocado and Leeks Mix	240
Avocado And Tempeh Bacon Wraps	179
Avocado and Watermelon Salad	62
Avocado Banana Green Smoothie	204
Avocado Cream	240
Avocado Dill Dressing	161
Avocado Mint Soup	114
Avocado Pudding	191
Avocado Salad Sandwiches	234
Awesome Orange Smoothie	213

B

Baby Bok Choy	153
Baked Banana French Toast with Raspberry Syrup	53
Baked Brussels Sprouts	109
Baked Cheesy Broccoli With Quinoa	136
Baked Cheesy Eggplant with Marinara	131
Baked Eggplant Parmesan	137
Baked Tofu	112
Balsamic Lentil Stew	143
Balsamic Olives Salad	242
Banana and Orange Mousse	203
Banana Bites	182
Banana Bread	194
Banana Bread Shake With Walnut Milk	216
Banana Brownies	203
Banana Nut Smoothie	51
Barbecue Chickpea Burgers with Slaw	170
Barbeque Sauce	41
Barley Lentil Stew	147
Basic Baked Potatoes	109
Basil Tomato and Cabbage Bowls	61
BBQ Chickpea Wrap	171
BBQ Tofu Pizza	245
Bean and Carrot Spirals	123
Bean and Mushroom Chili	142
Bean and Rice Burritos	124
Beans & Greens Bowl	120
Beans And Lentils Soup	127
Beans Mayonnaise	160
Beans Mix	241

Bell Pepper and Spinach Stew	146
Berry and Strawberry Smoothie	212
Berry Beet Velvet Smoothie	216
Better Pecan Bars	189
Bibimbap	229
Black Bean & Corn Salad with Avocado	70
Black Bean and Corn Salad	248
Black Bean and Quinoa Stew	142
Black Bean And Quinoa Wrap	211
Black Bean Balls	201
Black Bean Brownie Pops	197
Black Bean Burgers	122
Black Bean Lentil Salad	64
Black Bean Meatball Salad	92
Black Bean Wrap with Hummus	175
Black Beans & Brown Rice	120
Black Beans Stew	79
Black Sesame Wonton Chips	178
Black-Eyed Pea Burritos	223
Black-Eyed Pea, Beet, and Carrot Stew	225
Black-Eyed Peas with Herns	121
Blueberry and Banana Smoothie	212
Blueberry Hand Pies	195
Blueberry Ice Cream	201
Blueberry Mousse	200
Blueberry Muffins	57
Bombay Potatoes and Peas	245
Bread Pudding with Raisins	87
Breaded Tofu	184
Breakfast French Toast	58
Breakfast Taquitos Casserole	135
Broccoli and Tomatoes Air Fried Stew	156
Broccoli And White Beans On Toast	207
Broccoli Mix	156
Broccoli Slaw Wrap	234
Brown Rice & Red Beans & Coconut Milk	121
Brown Rice with Spiced Vegetables	231
Brown Rice with Vegetables and Tofu	86
Brownie Batter	200
Brussel Sprouts Stew	150
Brussels Sprout Skewers	243
Brussels Sprouts and Tomatoes Mix	156
Brussels Sprouts Salad	66
Buckwheat And Spaghetti Meatballs	222
Buffalo Chickpea Wraps	168
Bulgur and Tomato Mix	241
Bulgur Pancakes with a Twist	92
Bulgur Wheat Salad	87
Bursting Black Bean Soup	80
Butter Bean Hummus	121
Butternut Squash Black Rice Bean Salad	65
Butternut Squash Soup	79
Butternut Squash Soup With Apple Cider	210
Butternut Squash with Quinoa and Almonds	226

C

Cabbage Bowls	241
Cabbage Roll Stew	224
Cabbage Salad with Seitan	64
Cabbage Stew	149
Caesar Dressing	164
Cajun Sweet Potatoes	108
Cannellini Pesto Spaghetti	96
Caramelized Onion Mac 'N' Cheese	103
Carrot Patties	243
Carrot-Pineapple Casserole	116
Cashew Cheese Sauce	16
Cashew Cream	16
Cashew Cream Cheese	4
Cashew Mayonnaise	4
Cashew Mustard Dressing	16
Cauliflower & Apple Salad	7
Cauliflower Hash	6
Cauliflower Popcorn	4
Cauliflower Stew	14

Cesar Style Dressing	162
Chai Chia Smoothie	50
Chard Wraps With Millet	90
Cheddar, Squash, And Zucchini Casserole	132
Cheese Cucumber Bites	184
Cheese Sauce	40
Cheesy Broccoli Soup	210
Cheesy Garlic Pasta with Ciabatta	103
Cheesy Hash Browns Egg Bake	135
Cheesy Macaroni with Broccoli	111
Chef Salad	67
Cherry Smoothie with Oat Milk	203
Cherry Tomato Couscous Salad	68
Chia and Coconut Pudding	62
Chia Flaxseed Waffles	60
Chia Raspberry Pudding	193
Chia Soy Pudding	201
Chickpea and Black Bean Stew with Pearl Parley	229
Chickpea and Mango Wraps	172
Chickpea Avocado Sandwich	120
Chickpea Choco Slices	201
Chickpea Curry	223
Chickpea Niçoise Salad	209
Chickpea Noodle Soup	74
Chickpea Salad Sandwich	248
Chickpea Scramble	54
Chickpea Scramble Breakfast Basin	59
Chickpeas and Spinach Mix	242
Chickpeas Avocado Salad	64
Chickpeas On Toast	56
Chili Spinach and Zucchini Pan	61
Chilled Watermelon Smoothie	213
Chinese Bowls	156
Chinese Cauliflower Rice	156
Chinese Long Beans Mix	157
Chipotle Cilantro Rice	93
Chipotle Seitan Taquitos	169
Chives Avocado Mix	60
Chives Chickpeas Mix	242
Chocolate and Walnut Farfalle	188
Chocolate Brownies	192
Chocolate Chip Pecan Cookies	195
Chocolate Fudge	192
Chocolate Icing	166
Chocolate Macaroons	191
Chocolate Mint Grasshopper Pie	197
Chocolate Mousse with Almonds	203
Chocolate Oat Smoothie	215
Chocolate Orange Mousse	201
Chocolate PB Smoothie	51
Chocolate Peanut Butter Cake	199
Chocolate Pudding	191
Chocolate Quinoa Breakfast Bowl	54
Chocolate Raspberry Brownies	200
Chocolate Rye Porridge	92
Chocolate-Almond Bars	189
Chocolate–Almond Butter Truffles	191
Chocolate-Banana Fudge	190
Chocolatey Banana Shake	202
Chocolatey Bean Mousse	202
Chopped Kale Salad With Apples And Pumpkin Seeds	208
Chunky Black Lentil Veggie Soup	82
Chunky Potato Soup	81
Cilantro Chili Dressing	161
Cilantro-Lime Dressing	163
Cinnamon Apple Chips with Dip	47
Cinnamon Apple Toast	53
Cinnamon Chiller	213
Cinnamon Coconut Chips	192
Classic Garlicky Rice	86
Classic Vegetable Soup	74
Coconut and Almond Truffles	189
Coconut Avocado	240
Coconut Curry Lentils	90
Coconut Curry Noodle	109
Coconut Curry Sauce	164

Coconut Ice Cream Cheesecake 199
Coconut Quinoa Pudding 94
Coconut Sorghum Porridge 88
Coconut Veggie Wraps 168
Cold Peanut Noodle Salad 64
Collard Green Pasta 110
Collard Wraps 175
Color Pasta 103
Colorful Veggie Wrap 171
Comfort Soup 83
Cool Tofu Mix 157
Coriander Endives 157
Corn & Black Bean Salad 70
Corn and Bean Salad 68
Cornmeal Porridge with Maple Syrup 89
Country Cornbread with Spinach 86
Couscous with Olives 248
Cranberry and Orange Sauce 42
Cranberry Dressing 162
Cream of Miso Mushroom Stew 74
Creamed Kimchi Pasta 96
Creamy Avocado and Nuts Bowls 62
Creamy Spinach Quiche 131
Creamy Tahini Dressing 163
Cremini Mushroom Risotto 94
Crisp Balls Made with Peanut Butter 185
Crispy Buckwheat 228
Crispy Cauliflower 183
Crunchy Asparagus Spears 47
Cucumber Edamame Salad 114
Cucumber Tomato Chopped Salad 113
Curried Cauliflower Tetrazzini 137
Curried Mango Chickpea Wrap 174
Curry Lentil Soup 121
Curry Lentil Soup with Butternut Squash 238
Curry Wraps 176

D

Dad's Aromatic Rice 88
Dairy-Free Pumpkin Pancakes 59
Date Purée 43
Date Squares 196
Decadent Bread Pudding with Apricots 93
Delicious Chana Masala 235
Delicious Collard Wraps 173
Double Chocolate Hazelnut Espresso Shake 216
Double Chocolate Orange Cheesecake 198

E

Easy Chickpea Salad Sandwiches 230
Easy Gazpacho Soup 235
Easy Millet Loaf 231
Easy Mocha Fudge 196
Easy Rice Blend with Almond, Parsley, and Cranberries 227
Easy Sweet Maize Meal Porridge 88
Easy Vegetable Lasagna 238
Edamame Hummus 160
Edamame Salad 71
Egg Avocado Salad 114
Eggplant and Broccoli Casserole 62
Eggplant and Potatoes in Tomato Sauce 244
Eggplant Parmesan Pasta 102
Eggplant Salad 69
Eggplant Spread 176
Eggplant Vegan Pasta 102
Eggplant, Onion and Tomato Stew 150
Egyptian Stew 144
Epic Pineapple Juice 213
Ethiopian Cabbage, Carrot, and Potato Stew 143
Everyday Savory Grits 88

F

Falafel With Tahini-Milk Sauce 230

Falafel Wrap	173
Fennel and Chickpeas Provençal	140
Fig Oatmeal Bake	217
Five-Bean Chili	142
Flavorful Refried Beans	123
Flax Almond Muffins	60
Freekeh Bowl with Dried Figs	89
Fresh And Hearty Quinoa Salad	208
Fresh Tomato Basil Tart	132
Fruit Salad with Zesty Citrus Couscous	54
Fruits Stew	147
Fruity Granola	54
Fruity Kale Salad	71
Fruity Tofu Smoothie	202

G

Garden Patch Sandwiches On Multigrain Bread	178
Garden Salad Wraps	115
Garlic & White Wine Pasta	101
Garlic and Herb Noodles	109
Garlic and White Bean Soup	90
Garlic Butter	165
Garlic Cilantro Dressing	162
Garlic Eggplants	157
Garlic Grilled Vegetables	155
Garlicky Tofu	246
General Tso Sauce	166
Ginger Brown Rice	89
Ginger Kale Smoothie	204
Gingery Mango Smoothie	204
Glazed Avocado	239
Glazed Curried Carrots	116
Golden Milk Smoothie	204
Granola-Stuffed Baked Apples	189
Greek Grilled Eggplant Steaks	154
Greek Quinoa Salad	235
Greek-Inspired Macaroni and Cheese	106

Greek-Style Barley Salad	88
Greek-Style Gigante Beans	121
Green Beans Gremolata	115
Green Beans with vegan Bacon	120
Green Chili Mac 'N' Cheese	103
Green Colada	215
Green Fruity Smoothie	202
Green Spirulina Smoothie	204
Greens And Grains Soup	75
Grilled Broccoli	154
Grilled Chopped Veggies	155
Grilled Mediterranean Salad With Quinoa	209
Grilled Mushrooms with Garlic Sauce	244
Grilled Vegetable Sandwich	237
Grilled Vegetables	155

H

Harissa Bulgur Bowl	94
Harissa Lentils with Riced Cauliflower	226
Harissa Mushrooms	239
Harissa Sauce	41
Health is Wealth Salad: Dash of Chickpea and Tomato	69
Healthy Apple Chickpea Salad	236
Healthy Cabbage Soup	81
Healthy Coffee Smoothie	212
Healthy Protein Bars	186
Hearty Black Lentil Curry	122
Hearty Vegetable Stew	147
Hearty Vegetarian Lasagna Soup	81
Hemp Falafel With Tahini Sauce	42
Herb Avocado Salad Dressing	162
Herbed Croutons	164
Herby Split Pea Soup	75
High Protein Salad	113
Homemade Chocolates with Coconut and Raisins	196
Homemade Trail Mix	47
Honey Buckwheat Coconut Porridge	58

Hot Cabbage Mix	157
Hot Pink Smoothie	214
Hot-And-Sour Tofu Soup	77
Hummus and Quinoa Wrap	170
Hummus Made with Sweet Potato	185
Hummus Toast	182
Hummus without Oil	184
Hydration Station	50

I

Incredible Tomato Basil Soup	82
Indian Potatoes	158
Indonesia Green Noodle Salad	97
Instant Savory Gigante Beans	128
Instant Turmeric Risotto	128

J

Jackfruit Wrap	176
Jalapeno Rice Noodles	110
Jicama and Guacamole	180

K

Kale and Broccoli Pan	63
Kale Chips	183
Keto Ice Cream	192
Key Lime Pie	196
Kidney Bean and Pomegranate Salad	68
Kimchi Stew	150
Kofta-Style Chickpea "Meatball" Pitas	133
Korean Barbecue Tempeh Wraps	174
Koshari	225
Kung Pao Lentils	125

L

Lasagna Noodles in a Creamy Mushroom Sauce	107
Lavender and Mint Ice Tea	212
Lebanese Lentil Salad	209
Leeks and Artichokes Mix	239
Leeks Medley	158
Leeks Spread	176
Lemon & Strawberry Soup	79
Lemon and Rosemary Iced Tea	212
Lemon Bow Tie Pasta	99
Lemon Cashew Tart	197
Lemon Coconut Cilantro Rolls	181
Lemon Lentils and Carrots	241
Lemon Tahini	160
Lemony Broccoli Penne	98
Lemony Farro and Pine Nut Chard Rolls with Marinara Sauce	227
Lemony Pasta with Broccoli and Chickpeas	105
Lentil and Sunflower Seeds Salad	242
Lentil and Turnip Soup	125
Lentil and Wild Rice Soup	91
Lentil Brown Rice Soup	126
Lentil Potato Salad	70
Lentil Sandwich Spread	119
Lentil Soup the Vegan Way	83
Lentil Stroganoff	125
Lentil Tacos	124
Lentil with Spinach	127
Lentil, Bulgur, and Mushroom Burgers	230
Lime-Macerated Mangos	190
Lime-Mint Creamy Spaghetti Squash	22
Linguine With Pea-Basil Pesto	105
Linguine with Wine Sauce	11
Lite Tuna Melt Wrap	17
Loaded Pizza With Black Beans	22
Loaded Sweet Potato Nacho Fries	20
Louisiana Hot Sauce	4
Lovely Parsnip & Split Pea Soup	8

M

Mac and Cheese	247
Maca Caramel Frap	215
Macadamia Mozzarella	45
Macadamia-Cashew Patties	181
Mango Achar From India	40
Mango and Leeks Meatballs	239
Mango Madness	50
Mango Sticky Rice	186
Maple Bagel Spread	172
Maple Dijon Dressing	161
Maple Roasted Brussels sprouts	152
Marinated Mushroom Wraps	115
Matcha Coconut Cream Pie	199
Max Power Smoothie	50
Mediterranean Chickpea Wraps	169
Mediterranean Chickpeas	158
Mediterranean Hummus Pizza	108
Mediterranean Vegan Stew	145
Mediterranean Veggie Wrap	170
Mexican Casserole	137
Mexican Lentil Soup	121
Mexican Peppers Mix	158
Mexican Rice Bowl with Pinto Beans	229
Middle Eastern Cauliflower Steaks	207
Millet Porridge with Sultanas	87
Minestrone in Minutes	76
Mint Coriander Nutty Salad	67
Mint Flavored Pear Smoothie	212
Minted Peas	116
Minty Cherry Smoothie	214
Minty Lime Dressing	166
Miso Spaghetti Squash	109
Mix Grain Salad	67
Mixed Vegetable Platter	155
Mom's Millet Muffins	89
Moroccan Eggplant Stew	75

Moroccan Stew	144
Muesli and Berries Bowl	53
Mushroom & Wild Rice Stew	143
Mushroom And Quinoa "Gumbo"	78
Mushroom Scramble	205
Mushroom Stew	146
Mushroom, Lentil, and Barley Stew	148

N

Nasi Goreng	228
Nettle Soup with Rice	128
New England Corn Chowder	78
No-Bake Chocolate Coconut Energy Balls	195
Noodle and Rice Pilaf	231
Noodle Salad with Spinach	101
Noodles with Red Lentil Curry	97
Nori Snack Rolls	178
Nut Butter Maple Dip	47
Nut Milk	44
Nuts Trail Mix	183

O

Oat Porridge with Almonds	93
Oatmeal Breakfast Cookies	52
Oil-Free Rainbow Roasted Vegetables	133
Okra with Grated Tomatoes (Slow Cooker)	128
Olive & Fennel Salad	71
One-Skillet Veggie Hash	154
Onion and Tomato Bowls	240
Orange Cake	193
Orange Mango Dressing	161
Oven Baked Sesame Fries	48
Oven-baked Smoked Lentil 'Burgers'	129
Overnight Oats On the Go	51
Oyster (Mushroom) Stew	77

P

Paprika Broccoli	158
Paprika Olives Spread	174
Parm Sprinkle	165
Parsley Salad	72
Pasta Puttanesca	247
Pasta Salad with Yogurt Dressing	236
Pasta with Sun-Dried Tomato Sauce	104
Pastry Dough	45
Peach Cobbler	192
Peach Crumble Shake	215
Peanut and Ginger Tofu Wrap	173
Peanut and Lentil Soup	126
Peanut Butter and Mocha Smoothie	217
Peanut Butter Energy Bars	197
Peanut Butter Vanilla Green Shake	215
Peanut Sauce	163
Peas And Carrot Stew	145
Pecan and Date-Stuffed Roasted Pears	190
Penne with Indian-Style Tomato Sauce and Mushrooms	105
Penne with Swiss Chard and Olives	97
Peppered Pinto Beans	124
Peppermint Oreos	198
Peppers and Black Peans with Brown Rice	225
Peppers and Hummus	179
Peppers Casserole	61
Pesto And Sun-Dried Tomato Quinoa	222
Pesto and White Bean Pasta	124
Pineapple and Coconut Milk Smoothie	214
Pineapple Fried Rice	91
Pink Panther Smoothie	51
Piri Sauce	41
Pizza Dough	46
Plantain Chips	152
Plant-Based Buffalo Wrap	171
Plant-Based Keto Lo Mein	112
Pomegranate and Pears Salad	241
Pomegranate and Walnut Stew	140
Ponzu Pea Rice Noodle Salad	98
Popcorn Tofu	153
Portabella Eggs Florentine	205
Potato and Chickpeas Stew	146
Potato Carrot Salad	112
Potato Gratin	136
Potato Salad	243
Powerful Spinach and Mustard Leaves Puree	129
Protein Blueberry Bars	59
Protein Latte	202
Pumpkin Cake	193
Pumpkin Muffins	55
Pumpkin Orange Spice Hummus	48
Pumpkin Pie Cups (Pressure Cooker)	188
Pumpkin Tasty Seeds	159

Q

Quick Chocó Brownie	192
Quick English Muffin Mexican Pizzas	48
Quick Ketchup	43
Quick Lentil Wrap	170
Quick Peanut Butter Bars	185
Quick-Fix Veggie Wrap	173
Quinoa and Black Bean Chili	148
Quinoa and Black Bean Lettuce Wraps	172
Quinoa and Chickpea Salad	68
Quinoa And Nectarine Slaw	205
Quinoa and Rice Stuffed Peppers (Oven-Baked)	129
Quinoa Avocado Salad	119
Quinoa Meatballs	91
Quinoa Porridge with Dried Figs	87
Quinoa Soup with a Dash of Kale	84
Quinoa Stuffed Bell Peppers	132
Quinoa Tacos	246
Quinoa Trail Mix Cups	48
Quinoa, Oats, Hazelnut and Blueberry Salad	59

R

Radish Avocado Salad	67
Rainbow Soba Noodles	110
Rainbow Taco Boats	234
Raisin Protein Balls	184
Ranch Dressing	166
Raspberry Chia Pudding	191
Raspberry Vinaigrette	163
Raw Nut Cheese	118
Red Applesauce and Beet	42
Red Lentil and Chickpea Bowl	124
Red Pepper & Broccoli Salad	70
Red Potatoes and Green Beans	159
Refried Bean And Salsa Quesadillas	180
Refried Beans	164
Rice and Bean Burritos	119
Rice and Tofu Salad	68
Rice and Veggie Bowl	113
Rice and Veggies	159
Rice Pudding with Currants	87
Rice Stuffed Jalapeños	91
Risotto Bites	178
Ritzy Fava Bean Ratatouille	224
Roasted Butternut Squash Salad	236
Roasted Butternut Squash with Mushrooms and Cranberries	152
Roasted Cauliflower With Navy Bean Purée and Quinoa Risotto	226
Roasted Corn	152
Roasted Garlic	152
Roasted Garlic Grilled Vegetables	154
Roasted Green Beans	153
Roasted Ragu with Whole Wheat Linguine	96
Roasted Veg with Creamy Avocado Dip	55
Roasted Vegetable Hummus Plate	133
Roasted Vegetable Kebabs	154
Roasted Veggies In Lemon Sauce	42
Root Vegetable Stew	142

Rye Porridge with Blueberry Topping	88

S

Sambal Sauce	40
Sautéed Cabbage	114
Savory Roasted Chickpeas	179
Savory Seed Crackers	180
Scotch Bonnet Pepper Sauce	40
Scrambled Tofu Breakfast Burrito	57
Secret Ingredient Chocolate Brownies	194
Seeded Crackers	182
Seitan	46
Seitan Shawarma	169
Sensational Strawberry Medley	213
Sesame Soba Noodles with Vegetables	99
Sesame Stir Fry	221
Sesame Tofu and Veggies Noodles	244
Sesame-Wonton Crisps	181
Shiitake and Bean Sprout Ramen	100
Shishito Peppers	153
Silk Tofu Penne with Spinach	129
Simple Barbecue Sauce	165
Simple Maple Navy Bean Bake	228
Simple Syrup	165
Simple Vegan Breakfast Hash	56
Singapore Rice Noodles	98
Skinny Pasta Primavera	237
Slow-Cooked Butter Beans, Okra and Potatoes Stew	130
Smashed Chickpea Avocado Toasts	206
Smoked Green Beans	242
Smoky Coleslaw	108
Smoky Red Beans and Rice	123
Snickers Pie	198
Sniffle Soup	79
Soba Noodles with Tofu	112
Sour Cream	165
Soya Minced Stuffed Eggplants	130

Spaghetti with Spinach, Tomatoes, and Beans	232
Spanish Chickpea and Sweet Potato Stew	140
Spanish Paella	134
Spiced Strawberry Smoothie	216
Spiced Tomato Brown Rice	231
Spiced Zucchini and Eggplant Bowls	63
Spicy Bean Stew	150
Spicy Black-Eyed Peas	123
Spicy Cajun Boiled Peanuts	82
Spicy Carrots and Olives	239
Spicy Chickpea Gyros	211
Spicy Chickpeas	120
Spicy Curry Lentil Burgers	220
Spicy Eggplant Penne	96
Spicy Hummus and Apple Wrap	168
Spicy Mac and Ricotta Cheese with Spinach	106
Spicy Nut-Butter Noodles	125
Spicy Pad Thai Pasta	111
Spicy Refried Bean Stew	77
Spicy Roasted Chickpeas	183
Spicy Sweet Potato Enchiladas	118
Spicy Watermelon Tomato Salad	69
Spinach & Orange Salad	70
Spinach and Avocado Dressing	161
Spinach and Berries Salad	63
Spinach and Cannellini Bean Stew	149
Spinach and Green Beans Casserole	63
Spinach and Zucchini Hash	61
Spinach Artichoke Quiche	55
Spinach Mushroom Pockets	184
Spinach Pesto	164
Spinach Pesto Pasta	106
Spinach Rotelle Provençale	100
Spring Salad	65
Sprout Wraps	175
Squash and Beans Stew	147
Steamed Cauliflower	108
Steamed Tomatoes	112

Stir-fry Vegetables	154
Stovetop Maple Beans	224
Strawberry and Rhubarb Smoothie	214
Strawberry Mousse	200
Strawberry Peach Vinaigrette	163
Strawberry Shake	202
Strawberry, Banana, and Coconut Shake	216
Stuffed Baked Potato	133
Stuffed Mushrooms	132
Stuffed Peppers	133
Stuffed Roasted Sweet Potatoes	135
Stuffed Tomatoes with Bread Crumbs and Cheese	133
Summer Chickpea Salad	71
Summer Tomato And Burrata Panzanella Salad	208
Summer Vietnamese Rolls	221
Sumptuous Shiitake Udon Noodles	100
Sun-Dried Tomato Spread	168
Sunshine Muffins	52
Sushi Bowl	220
Sweet and Spicy Brussels Sprout Hash	116
Sweet Crepes	218
Sweet Korean Lentils	247
Sweet Oatmeal "Grits"	89
Sweet Potato Chickpea Bowl	237
Sweet Potato Chili with Quinoa	118
Sweet Potato Patties	221
Sweet Potato Sandwich Spread	169
Sweet Potato Shephard's Pie	221
Sweet Potato Stew	77
Sweet Potato Toast	182
Sweet Potato, Kale and Peanut Stew	141
Swiss Chard And Orzo Gratin	136

T

Tacos	18
Tahini Shake with Cinnamon and Lime	21
Tamari Toasted Almonds	17

Tamarind Avocado Bowls	240
Tangy Chickpea Soup with a Hint of Lemon	83
Tangy Corn Chowder	80
Tangy Tomato Soup	74
Tartar Sauce	40
Teff Porridge with Dried Figs	93
Tempeh and Potato	58
Tempeh Tantrum Burgers	181
Tempeh-Pimiento Cheeze Ball	179
Tempting Quinoa Tabbouleh	185
Teriyaki Mushrooms and Cashews with Rice Noodles	105
Teriyaki Noodle Stir-Fry	246
Tex-Mex Tofu & Beans	122
Thai Iced Tea	212
Thai Pad Bowl	220
Thai Peanut Butter Cauliflower Wings	243
Thai Peanut Dressing	162
Thai Peanut Sauce	43
Thai Roasted Broccoli	109
Thai Tofu Noodles	98
Thai Vegetable and Tofu Wrap	171
The Keto Lovers "Magical" Grain-Free Granola	192
The Mocha Shake	213
The Sunshine Offering	214
The Vegan Pumpkin Spicy Fat Bombs	193
Thick Mushroom Sauce	43
Three-Bean Chili	76
Tofu & Chia Seed Pudding	203
Tofu & Strawberry Mousse	203
Tofu and Pineapple in Lettuce	172
Tofu and Veggies Stew	146
Tofu Egg Salad	235
Tofu Feta	45
Tofu Island Dressing	43
Tofu Ranch Dressing	44
Tofu Saag	186
Tofu Scramble	218
Tofu Sour Cream	44
Tomatillo Green Sauce	42
Tomato and Artichoke Rigatoni	101
Tomato and Asparagus Quiche	56
Tomato and Basil Bruschetta	180
Tomato and Black Bean Rotini	97
Tomato and Chickpea Curry	125
Tomato and Cucumber Salad	62
Tomato and Zucchini Fritters	61
Tomato Cucumber Salad	236
Tomato Lentil Salad	65
Tomato Pesto Pasta	102
Tomato Red Lentil Pasta	104
Tomato Soup with Kale & White Beans	80
Tomato Spaghetti	101
Tomato, Kale, and White Bean Skillet	90
Tortilla Soup	210
Tricolore Salad	69
Triple Beans and Corn Salad	130
Tropical Vibes Green Smoothie	217
Tropi-Kale Breeze	50

U

Ultimate Breakfast Sandwich	57

V

Vanilla Hemp Drink	214
Vanilla Icing	166
Vegan "Beef" Stew	144
Vegan Breakfast Sandwich	217
Vegan Cauliflower Steaks	236
Vegan Fried Egg	218
Vegan Mediterranean Wraps	176
Vegan Raw Pistachio Flaxseed 'Burgers'	130
Vegan Red Bean 'Fricassee'	131
Vegan Thousand Island	163
Vegan Tzatziki	43
Vegan Wrap with Apples and Spicy Hummus	113

Vegetable Medley	116
Vegetarian Gumbo	141
Vegetarian Irish Stew	148
Vegetarian Pancit Bihon	238
Veggie And Chickpea Fajitas	134
Veggie Hash	154
Vinegary Maple Syrup Dressing	161

W

Waffles with Fruits	57
Walnut Meat Tacos	247
Walnut, Coconut, and Oat Granola	224
Walnuts and Olives Bowls	62
Warm Sweet Potato Noodle Salad	208
Watercress & Blood Orange Salad	72
Wedge Salad	66
White Bean & Tomato Salad	66
White Bean and Cabbage Stew	149
White Bean and Olive Pasta	222
White Bean Stew	141
White Beans Dip	160
White Chili	76
White Mushrooms Mix	159
Whole Wheat Pizza with Summer Produce	60

Wild Ginger Green Smoothie	215
Winter Stew	144
Winter Vegetarian Frittata	132

Y

Yam Mix	159
Yellow Potato Soup	75
Yogurt Soup with Rice	81
Yucatan Bean & Pumpkin Seed Appetizer	120
Yummy Lentil Rice Soup	80

Z

Zesty Green Pea and Jalapeño Pesto Pasta	104
Zesty Orange-Cranberry Energy Bites	188
Zucchini & Lemon Salad	72
Zucchini Blueberry Smoothie	204
Zucchini Fritters	206
Zucchini Pan	60
Zucchini Pasta Salad	114
Zucchini Soup	81
Zucchini Zoodles Soup	234

Made in the USA
Las Vegas, NV
09 June 2021